CONTEMPORARY FEMINIST THEORY

A Text/Reader

Mary F. Rogers
The University of West Florida

Boston   Burr Ridge, IL   Dubuque, IA   Madison, WI   New York   San Francisco   St. Louis
Bangkok   Bogotá   Caracas   Lisbon   London   Madrid
Mexico City   Milan   New Delhi   Seoul   Singapore   Sydney   Taipei   Toronto

McGraw-Hill

A Division of The **McGraw·Hill** *Companies*

CONTEMPORARY FEMINIST THEORY: A TEXT/READER

Copyright © 1998 by The McGraw-Hill Companies, Inc. Printed in the United States of America. Except as permitted under the United States Copyright Act of 1976, no part of this publication may be reproduced or distributed in any form or by any means, or stored in a data base or retrieval system, without the prior written permission of the publisher.

This book is printed on acid-free paper.

1 2 3 4 5 6 7 8 9 0 DOC/DOC 9 0 9 8 7

ISBN 0-07-054002-0

Publisher: *Phillip A. Butcher*
Sponsoring editor: *Jill Gordon*
Developmental editor: *Katherine Blake*
Marketing manager: *Sally Constable*
Project manager: *Amy Hill*
Production supervisor: *Michael R. McCormick*
Senior designer: *Laurie J. Entringer*
Compositor: *Shepherd, Incorporated*
Typeface: *10/12 Times Roman*
Printer: *R. R. Donnelley & Sons Company*

Library of Congress Cataloging-in-Publication Data

Contemporary feminist theory : a text/reader / [edited and with
  introductory essays by] Mary F. Rogers.
     p. cm.
  Includes bibliographical references.
  ISBN 0-07-054002-0 (alk. paper)
   1. Feminist theory.   2. Feminism.   3. Women in politics.   4. Power
(Social sciences)   5. Sex role.   6. Women—Sociological aspects.
 I. Rogers, Mary F. (Mary Frances), 1944-   .
HQ1190.C668   1998
305.42'01—dc21   97-40213

http://www.mhhe.com

for Christy

CONTENTS

PART FOUR

Transformation, Border Crossing, and Feminist Theory

ACKNOWLEDGMENTS

Needing to thank as many people as I do is a sign of great fortune. Such interpersonal privilege escapes the net of words, leaving the impression of an individual at work where really there is a far-flung community. I begin, then, with awareness of the fiction "I" throughout these pages. I begin, too, with expressions of appreciation that can only be feeble in the face of unutterable blessings.

Christy Garrett went far beyond what love and friendship mandate—an ear always ready, a mind always alert and informed, and a heart always open and welcoming; a feminist consciousness shedding brilliant light into the corners of these pages; cybertechnical encouragement and assistance; collards and tomatoes fresh from her garden, newspaper clippings, compact discs, caladium bulbs, freshly tilled earth, and much else to soothe and nourish the senses; above all, safe harbor for who I am and who I aspire to become. I dedicate these pages to her.

Phil Lott worked as permissions editor for this volume, but characteristically his efforts extended well beyond that sphere of responsibility. Always collegial and helpful, responsive and kindhearted, Phil energized this project in myriad ways with his wit, courage, and fortitude. D. J. Webb chased citations, electronically as well as across campus, and was generous with unsolicited but welcome favors, small and big. Gen Rogers boosted me in all the ways good moms do, but she also proofread and queried and debated at times.

At the John C. Pace Library of The University of West Florida, I at times overwhelmed the interlibrary loan office with more work than it could handle. Never, though, did that circumstance defeat the commitment to getting me everything I needed as speedily as possible. For their prodigious efforts and high spirits, I thank Ann Ivey, Debbie Marshall, and Juanita Reynolds.

Among the reviewers of *Contempory Feminist Theory* were five individuals whose insights and suggestions proved crucial. George Ritzer wrote a review that encouraged without being uncritical. As consulting editor, he was consistently accessible and responsive when I needed theoretical counsel or collegiality. Joan Alway read with the theoretical acumen anyone acquainted with her work would expect. Acquainted not only with her work but also with her, I take pleasure in thanking her for the care she took with this manuscript.

With Susan Chase, I am more than acquainted. Over the past 10 or so years we have become fast friends as well as close colleagues. Stunned that she agreed to review this work amidst all her other commitments, I gained from the gift of her review renewed appreciation for her lively intelligence, feminist dedication, and theoretical grace. Her suggestions smoothed several jagged edges and raised my consciousness, too.

Judith Barker, a long-distance colleague whom I have never met, wrote a most impressive review. Its enthusiastic support and insightful suggestions, coupled with descriptions of her feminist theory courses, made me want to enroll in one of her courses. Marjorie Pryse wrote a review like what I myself would hope to have written. She inspired a number of refinements of the manuscript and alerted me to resources that had escaped my attention. The generosity and rigor of her review renewed my flagging energies. Hers are also courses I would like to take.

At McGraw-Hill, Kathy Blake helped me thrive in more ways than I can count. Her dispatches always encouraged me, and the care and dedication that stamp her work fed my own. Kathy's good cheer made an enormous difference. So did Jill Gordon's confidence in me. Her willingness to give me great leeway as the manuscript was in its formative stages made my work a lot more pleasurable. Jill's expertise kept me on track without assigning me a routine, let alone rigid, route.

Don Eisman's passion for routines, on the other hand, staved off chaos as I focused sharply on the task at hand. His willingness to handle the nuts and bolts so that I could live with these ideas was a great gift.

Finally, I thank Gloria Mattingly for her steadfast interest, intellectual company, and wonderful friendship. A student in the very first women's studies course I taught, Gloria has taught me a great deal about feminism within and way beyond the classroom.

Mary F. Rogers
Pensacola, Florida

INTRODUCTION

Feminist theory takes shape around the dialectic between its partnered terms. "Feminist" connotes activism and shaking things up, while "theory" connotes dispassionate scholarship and abstract ideas. Feminist theory defeats that divergence by making theory and practice collateral projects.[1] It shows how ideas and actions work together as close companions.

At this point I am tempted to line up definitions of "feminist theory" like academic ducks in a neat row awaiting footnotes. We will gain stronger insights, though, by moving quickly to substantive matters and those texts that pass as feminist theory. We will also learn more by rejecting labels for the theorists we meet and the works they have crafted. Instead of grouping theorists using names like "standpoint theorist" or "materialist feminist" or "womanist theorist," then, I have organized our work around substantive topics like identity, community, and economy.

The topics on our horizon concern experiences and circumstances ensuring some commonality among women. Even though we cannot experience our gender apart from our social class, age, sexual orientation, race, ethnicity, and other dimensions of our situations, women do face some odds that put us in the same big boat (if not on the same deck, let alone in the same cabin).

The odds are, for instance, that we grew up with some negative notions about our female bodies—menstruation is dirty and disgusting; gray hair is unappealing; the curves of our bodies often get way out of hand; visible muscularity is unfeminine; nappy hair and thick lips are unattractive; most of our body parts are too big, too small, or sadly misshapen. The odds are too that we have often been interrupted during conversation; been repeatedly dismissed or silenced for being "just a girl" or "just a woman"; been heckled on the streets or pawed on the bus; been treated like a guidance counselor or mother confessor at work, at church or synagogue, or at school.

The odds are that we have gone to a physician of the other sex,[2] taken multiple courses with professors of the other sex, listened to a rabbi or minister or priest of the other sex while worshipping, or on graduating, shaken the hand of the male high school principal or college president. The odds are also that those of us who are heterosexual and partnered earn less than our partners and, especially if the state has recognized our bond, that we do more than our fair share of the housework. Irrespective of our sexual orientation, the odds are that we have moved or been willing to move to satisfy the career ambitions of our partner and that we have listened, at least sporadically, to the biological clock said to be ticking as our wombs age.

If we have adopted or given birth, we are likely to have spent untold hours (often at the most inopportune times) nurturing our children physically, emotionally, and spiritually. If we have opted for full-time work in the home, the odds are that we have sometimes felt "out of it," even demeaned by those who have made other commitments. If we are trying to figure out how to combine committed parenthood with a satisfying career, perplexity may pervade our figuring. If we have retired, we are unlikely to have an enviable pension; if we are anticipating retirement, we are likely to worry at least a little about how we will make ends meet. The odds are that rape leaps to mind whenever we feel physically isolated and vulnerable, even if we have never been sexually assaulted. The odds are, too, that breast cancer has crossed our minds and will touch our lives (if it hasn't already) by invading our own bodies or those of our mothers, grandmothers, sisters, friends, lovers, aunts, co-workers, and neighbors.

Feminist theorists have devoted a lot of attention to these and other aspects of women's lives. By and large, I focus on their theorizing about North American women, even though the experiences and prospects of women on this continent are inexorably linked with those of women around the planet—women trying to immigrate to North America, women whose exploited labor puts fruits and vegetables on our tables and toys in our children's rooms, women whose human-rights struggles must inform our own feminist commitments. The sheer diversity of North American women makes adequate coverage a challenge even in a volume this size. So does the sheer prolificacy of some groups of feminist theorists, such as feminist film and literary critics, whose work I have little more than acknowledged here. (Besides, in women's studies programs feminist literary criticism and literary theory, like feminist aesthetics, are usually offered as courses complementing those feminist theory courses focused more on society, culture, and social change.)

As you may already have noticed, each chapter includes only two or three readings. I make no claims, then, to comprehensive coverage. Instead, I want to show you the range and promise of contemporary feminist theory while drawing from diverse theoretical approaches so as to ensure some balance. I also want to stimulate your appetite for feminist theory more than feed you some version of its standard menu. In the process I work as a theorist, making connections among and drawing inferences from the riches at hand.

Put differently, this volume is a text/reader, which is a fairly new genre among instructional resources. Neither a textbook nor an anthology, a text/reader aims to combine the benefits of both. It does so by launching each chapter with an essay that surveys key concepts and principles in a broad topic area, such as women's work. Then come several readings complementing and extending that survey. Thus, each chapter of this book consists of an essay I have written, together with several readings illustrating other feminist theorists' work on the general topic at hand. You and your instructor may decide to further supplement some or all of the chapters with additional journal articles or book-length works that address your specific interests. A text/reader generally leaves ample room for such local initiatives.

In any case, you will soon see that the theorists at hand offer differing interpretations and recommendations. Yet feminist theory is not a free-for-all where just anyone can chime in with a distinctive spin on women's situations. A women-centered approach *is* necessary for feminist theorizing, but it is insufficient. Coupled with it are some beliefs and values that people engaged in feminist struggle share, by and large. Let's look at a few of these commonalities to position ourselves for saying in preliminary terms what "feminist" involves. Then we will look at "theory" to develop a preliminary conception of it before moving to the first two readings.

For me, the word "feminism" is beautiful, powerful, and proud; it is also active, insistent, and visionary. Feminism is the driving force behind efforts to make things fair between women and men. As such, it comprises beliefs and values that bring together diverse individuals. Feminists believe that women and men are equally entitled to all the good things a society makes available to its members—all the opportunities, rewards, respect and status, power and responsibilities. Feminists thus believe that gender should not be a distributive mechanism in society, a basis for social hierarchy, or a means whereby some parts of people get stunted and other parts get overdeveloped. Feminism serves, then, as an "intervention in the ideology of gender."[3]

Yet not all feminists simply seek parity with relatively privileged men. Many are challenging what gender itself illustrates: namely, hierarchy. Although feminists' thoughts about hierarchy are diverse, common themes do emerge. First, feminists commonly question the standards used to justify why some people get to the top and other people get trapped at the bottom of various hierarchies. Patricia J. Williams (the author of Reading 13) argues, for instance, that standards boil down to preferences that get widely institutionalized.[4] Second, feminists are inclined to question hierarchical approaches to a group's problem solving or projects. In theory and in practice, they often turn to alternative approaches such as collaborative decision making, agreement by consensus, and cooperative modes of dividing labor and rewards. Thus, feminists often believe that hierarchy has been overdone in societies like ours and seek fairer ways of getting jobs done.

Besides such core beliefs are some values joining most feminists. Social justice is the paramount one, even though that phrase is not itself much used. Whether it is called distributive justice, equality, fairness, or equal rights, social justice entails seeing that each person's dignity gets honored, each person's needs get recognized and addressed, and any person's or group's claims to extras are anchored in merits or needs widely agreed upon and open to debate among members. Alongside social justice stands feminists' emphasis on the democratic process. As a value, democracy requires that each person's voice be heard or at least effectively represented and that no one buy or bully her or his way into other people's lives. Hand in hand with democracy, feminists commonly value individuals and expressions of individuality, even while they often decry rugged individualism. A fourth value commonplace among contemporary feminists is little noticed, especially in the mass media. As a group, feminists favor extending responsibility beyond oneself and one's circle of loved ones, especially to those who depend heavily on the rest of us for sustenance and nurturance.

A fifth value feminists tend to share is inclusionary thinking. Through hard and painful lessons learned as lesbian feminists challenged heterosexism and homophobia and women of color challenged racism among feminists, contemporary feminists learned the practical limits of their "sisterhood." We have a long way to go before women's precious diversity gets taken into full account in feminist classrooms, marches, meetings, cultural events, and elsewhere.

Yet some developments have moved us toward inclusionary stances and interactions. One is feminist theorizing itself, reaching back to at least 1970 when Robin Morgan's celebrated *Sisterhood Is Powerful* appeared. That anthology included papers not only on professional women but also on the "secretarial proletariat," female factory workers, and women on welfare; on women's aging and on high school women; on black and Chicana and white and Chinese women; on birth control, prostitution, orgasms, housework, and radical lesbianism. It looked at "poetry as protest" and reprinted documents from diverse feminist groups like NOW (National Organization for Women) and SCUM (Society for Cutting Up Men). It provided reading lists and abortion counseling information and titles of consciousness-raising films.[5] It offered, in short, something for nearly every literate woman.

Another inclusionary development has been movement away from dualistic, binary, either/or thinking—the very thinking that pits male *against* female as superior against inferior, strong against weak, and rational against emotional. By and large, contemporary feminist theorists—those theorizing after the watershed of activism in the 1960s—have made it their business to overcome "what Gloria Steinem has aptly called 'prefeminist, either/or, polarized thinking.'"[6] Feminist theorists commonly recognize that we women are both old and young, monosexual and bisexual, low income and middle income. Yet "both" is problematic. It implies a pair of realities where usually there are multiple ones, such as red, yellow, brown, black, and white or inner city, urban, suburban, rural, and frontier.

Today, then, feminist theorists often build up inclusionary perspectives that go beyond nondualistic usages. Yet we lapse often—and sometimes woefully. In the feminist journal *Gender & Society,* for instance, I came across "Wives' and Husbands' Perceptions of Why Wives Work."[7] All the study's participants were white. Thus, the paper's title should have referred to *white* spouses' attitudes. In our white-dominated society the title would surely have referred to *black* spouses' attitudes had all the participants been black.

Such instances parallel those that erase or marginalize women or girls and thus occasion feminist theorizing in the first place. Recently, for example, the sociological journal *Social Forces* published "Self-Determination as a Source of Self-Esteem in Adolescence." The paper's abstract opens, "This research examines the effects of the sense of self-determination in three spheres of *male* adolescents' lives. . . ."[8] Thus, boys' experiences were taken as universal—that is, capable of supporting generalizations about girls as well as boys. Had the researchers looked only at adolescent girls' experiences, again we have every reason to believe the paper's title would have reflected that focus.

Feminist theorists try to circumvent such lapses. When writing about motherhood, for instance, they try to make clear whose activities and experiences they are meaning to theorize: birth mothers, custodial mothers, lesbian mothers, othermothers or *comadres* (in the African American and Latina traditions, respectively), surrogate mothers, single mothers, teenage mothers, white mothers, nonemployed mothers, or some combination of these. In this case, good feminism makes for good theory. As postmodernist theorists (among others) emphasize, virtually no social categories approach uniformity. Instead, they mask diversity unless we theorists take care to articulate all the differences gathered together under terms like Women, Mothers, Lesbians, Chicanas, or Widows. Yet good theory, like good feminism, is no easy accomplishment. Trinh T. Minh-ha asks,

> How do you inscribe difference without bursting into a series of euphoric narcissistic accounts of yourself and your own kind? Without indulging in a marketable romanticism or in a naive whining about your condition? . . . Between the twin chasms of navel-gazing and navel-erasing, the ground is narrow and slippery.[9]

The inclusionary intentions of contemporary feminist theory link it with multiculturalism, which mandates curricular attention to the experiences, historical and contemporary, of women and men of color, lesbians and gay men of all races and ethnicities, and women with diverse sexual, racial, and ethnic identities. To the extent that its inclusionary intentions succeed, contemporary feminist theory both feeds into and draws on multiculturalism. That connection makes for rich but problematic theorizing insofar as "many of the factors which divide women also unite some women with men."[10] As Joan Wallach Scott observes, feminism is "a site where differences conflict and coalesce, where common interests are articulated and contested, where identities achieve temporary stability—where politics and history are made."[11]

A final value central to feminist theorizing is freedom and its close allies, liberation and self-actualization. In the long run and across diverse domains, feminists aim to enhance women's freedom to choose the circumstances and purposes of their lives. For a variety of reasons, rooted in their experiences of androcentric (male-centered) institutions, feminists mostly abhor doctrine, orthodoxy, and anything else that decontextualizes people's choice making. Disinclined to prescribe or proscribe anything specific for women, feminists commonly lean toward nonjudgmental stances about women's actual choices, even those they themselves may not favor. Feminism is *not* about "enlightened" women who, having raised their consciousness, then tell other women how they should live. Yet feminist theory *is* normative. How might we reconcile these two stances, at least in principle?

Sandra Lee Bartky (the author of Reading 3) says feminism involves both critique and resistance.[12] Characteristically, feminists challenge whatever demeans, hurts, impedes, or otherwise treats unfairly large numbers of women. Thus, most feminist writing includes critique among its defining features. At the same time, most such writing delineates how women resist and can further resist such unfair circumstances. All these normative concerns are macro level. That is, they address a society's or community's social structure, its culture (values, norms, beliefs), and diverse female groupings' opportunities and outcomes. While normative, these concerns are large scale and impersonal; they have to do with *systemic* patterns and *aggregated* human activities.

At the micro level, the personal and interpersonal spheres where selfhood and relationships are embodied, feminists turn away from normative thinking. Like many other contemporary theorists, they recognize that each person makes choices within a biographical situation that no one else can fully apprehend; that she chooses by drawing on the resources available to her while being hemmed in by the givens of her situation; that all of us make misbegotten choices, some revocable and others less so. Thus, one might hear a feminist decry the objectification of women but never hear her criticize a real-life person who works as a fashion model.

Feminists recognize, then, that women lead "lives of multiple commitments and multiple beginnings."[13]

Reading 1 focuses on such beliefs and values, specifically those of the Combahee River Collective. Written 20 years ago, their statement captures the spirit and substance of much contemporary feminist theory. It also raises the matter of differences among women, which demands recurrent attention in the pages ahead. For starters, Drucilla Cornell's formulation is helpful: "My brand of feminism operates within the space kept open for rearticulation by the impossibility of a full account of Woman."[14]

Among other theorists articulating feminist beliefs and values, one person who holds great sway with me is bell hooks. Her ideas show how to theorize in liberatory ways as well as how to grapple with the perplexities of daily life, the indignities and pains of oppression, and the rough-and-tumble politics of social change and cultural transformation. In *Teaching to Transgress* (1994), hooks devotes a chapter to "Theory as Liberatory Practice." Here I explore its main points so as to lay preliminary grounds for theorizing "theory." Thereafter I join hands with hooks, whose voice resounds throughout these pages as that of a companion theorist keeping me honest and inspired.[15]

Hooks has no patience with theory divorced from our daily lives. Nor does she think theory can be apolitical, as if unwedded to the structures of domination that further some people's interests while ignoring other people's needs. Hooks treats theory as a challenge to the status quo. (p. 60) Moreover, one theorizes in order to transform what is within as well as beyond oneself; good theory links the "within" of the person with the "beyond" of social structure and culture. Along those lines, hooks connects the interventionist enterprise of theorizing with the advancement of self and group: "When our lived experience of theorizing is fundamentally linked to processes of self-recovery, of collective liberation, no gap exists between theory and practice." (p. 61)

Hooks concedes, "Theory is not inherently healing, liberatory, or revolutionary. . . ." She insists, though, that it can be all those things when we demand that it be. (p. 61) Barbara Smith makes the point this way:

> Feminism is the political theory and practice that struggles to free *all* women: women of color, working-class women, poor women, disabled women, lesbians, old women—as well as white, economically privileged, heterosexual women. Anything less than this vision of total freedom is not feminism, but merely female self-aggrandizement.[16]

Such thinking as hooks's and Smith's points to criteria we might apply to the feminist theorizing in the pages ahead. Is the theory healing? Does it, for instance, restore or advance our sense of wholeness? Does it challenge rifts among women or build bridges among us? Is the theory liberatory? Does it release our imaginations? Does it inspire action on behalf of self and community? Does it en-courage? Finally, is the theory revolutionary? Does it spark attention and raise eyebrows? Does it raise difficult questions, imply better alternatives, hold powerful people accountable, and empower those hungry for change?

Historically, asking such questions about theory led to charges of promoting ideology or confusing scholarship with social movements. Thanks to the sociology of knowledge, exemplified by Peter L. Berger and Thomas Luckmann's *Social Construction of Reality,* and to recent feminist theorizing, illustrated by the work of Dorothy E. Smith, we now understand that all knowledge is socially constructed and variously linked to what Smith calls the "relations of ruling" in society,[17] which we consider in Chapter 1. Theory is a product of the real world, not a leap into the stratosphere of "pure" ideas. Zillah R. Eisenstein says that and more: "Theory must grow out of reality, but it must be able to pose another vision of reality as well."[18]

Such theory emanates from people's lived experiences. As individuals make sense in their everyday lives, they make theory in nascent but assuredly real forms. Such theorizing often shows up in ordinary conversations, mundane storytelling, or everyday banter, where people not only draw on but also constitute cultural resources such as argot and truisms. Hooks herself implies that when we look for theory, we must cast our net widely enough to reach well beyond the university or think tank. As she puts it,

> Our search leads us back to where it all began, to that moment when an individual woman or child, who may have thought she was all alone, began a feminist uprising, began to name her practice, indeed began to formulate theory from lived experience. (pp. 74–5)

Sad to say, much theorizing rides roughshod over that point of origin. Often in academic contexts, hooks says, theory is unduly abstract and jargon-ridden; it is hard to read. The very term "theoretical" makes many students shudder and many practitioners roll their eyes. Yet as Trinh observes, theory "can upset rooted ideologies by exposing the mechanics of their workings" and can "shake established canons and question every norm validated as 'natural' or 'human.'"[19] In large measure, feminist theory takes up such tasks. Its "various successes" lie in "naming, analyzing, and contesting illicit power" used against women, while its various "failures lie with inadequate analyses of power and also with our complicity with illicit power."[20]

Theory is thus meant to serve human ends beyond career mobility and scholarly reputations. It is meant to illuminate. Theory gives us a vocabulary for naming or renaming those of our experiences that were once painfully hard to articulate; it provides propositions that can further our insights into the similarities and differences within and between social groupings, like lesbian sadomasochists and female heterosexual sadomasochists; it offers the wherewithal for connecting experiences such as sexual harassment with female employees' nonfeminist stances;[21] it lays grounds for explaining how social realities and people's lived experiences take the shapes they do and how they might be changed for the better. Theory thus empowers. It gives us a big, firm place to stand when trying to understand our own and others' experiences and how the social world got to be the way it is.

For the most part, I have avoided highly abstract, jargonistic work here, favoring instead more accessible works that may be difficult at times but are generally rewarding the first time we read them. Put differently, I join hooks in eschewing theory that seems "useless" as well as "politically nonprogressive, a kind of narcissistic, self-indulgent practice that most seeks to create a gap between theory and practice so as to perpetuate class elitism," among other things. (p. 64) Hooks is quick to concede that such theorizing "may also contain important ideas, thoughts, visions, that could, if used differently, serve a healing, liberatory function." (p. 65) Thereby she encourages us to approach theory imaginatively enough to grasp what might be worthwhile there. So, if you do come across readings in this volume that strike you as leaning toward the extremes hooks decries, try to tease out what might be helpful there without denying your frustration. I have tried, though, to spare you such experiences.

WHAT LIES AHEAD

Before we turn to the first two readings, let me sketch you a map showing the main roads through the theoretical terrain ahead. The next three chapters introduce and then illustrate two pivotal concepts at work in this book, Patricia Hill Collins's *matrix of domination* and Dorothy E. Smith's *relations of ruling.* Chapter 1, where both concepts get defined, focuses on the phenomenology and social psychology of these realities. It shows how they take shape in women's lived experiences and daily interactions—that is, how hierarchy, domination, and oppression infiltrate our everyday lives.

Chapters 2 and 3 look at some potent cultural resources commonly put to use against women. Chapter 2 focuses on the culture of science, which scorns subjectivity while mystifying objectivity. This culture finds expression not only in the natural and social sciences but also in the arts and humanities. Although the chapter centers on the institution of science and the values central to its culture, its reach extends to academic knowledge in general, whether anchored in a field like marketing or one like film studies. Chapter 3 turns our attention to popular culture, especially its self-help genres, as a purveyor of values that similarly sustain the matrix of domination and relations of ruling whereby women get diffusely inferiorized.

The next four chapters look at the major institutional sites of girls' and women's subordination. Chapter 4 focuses on the institution of education; Chapter 5 on government; Chapter 6 on the economy and work; and Chapter 7 on the institutions of heterosexuality, marriage, and family.

These institutions bear down on women in diverse ways, denying them equality, begrudging them acceptance and respect, or robbing them of alternative ways to make lives for themselves. These chapters thus deal with *social structure,* the overarching, entrenched routines massively (though not monolithically) built up as a society's members seek survival, togetherness, stability, and pleasure for themselves.

The next three chapters revolve around prospects for girls' and women's empowerment. Although the idea of empowerment informs these chapters mostly in implicit ways, it nonetheless threads them together. Chapter 8 considers caring and community as projects capable of giving women power enough to demand more for themselves in the way of attention and support as well as rights and responsibilities. Chapter 9 looks at identity and selfhood as performative and thus amenable to affirmative, empowering approaches. Chapter 10 returns us to the notion of consciousness first examined in Chapter 1. This return emphasizes its embodiment. The chapter implicitly tackles the question of how our awareness of our bodies might hold some prospect of empowerment. Given our widespread discontent with the weight and shape and features of our bodies and our resistance to the signs of their aging, this chapter serves as a bridge to the last section of the book. It invites us to transform our body loathing into whatever measure of self-acceptance we can muster.

The last two chapters concern transformation, border crossing, and feminist theory.[22] Chapter 11 looks at the challenges of changing social structure and transforming culture through social movements such as various women's movements. The last chapter reviews the course of our travels, in part by rejecting the borders commonly thought to divide feminist theorists. Together, chapters 11 and 12 imply that transformations of individuals, social structures, and cultures require multiple, meaningful border crossings.

Reading 1 now stands on the horizon. It serves as a welcome to feminist theory as well as an introduction to a specific group of feminists theorizing their feminism. After it comes sociologist Judith Lorber's reading on getting beyond dualistic categories of thinking to lay hold of the multiplicity such categories mask. Lorber's exploration includes a few technical terms you may have come across while studying literary criticism, sociology, philosophy, political science, or women's studies. If you have, the next few paragraphs may serve as review; if not, they offer a swift introduction to some key terms in contemporary social theory, whether feminist or not.

The most important phrase Lorber introduces is "social construction," which appears in her opening paragraph. *Social construction* refers to how people create and sustain their shared realities through interactions largely shaped by tradition, habit, language, and social norms. When we say a given reality such as gender is socially constructed, we mean that it derives from people's interactions with one another, not from genes, hormones, divine ordination, or natural law. Saying that a reality is socially constructed does imply that it is fundamentally arbitrary as well as historically and culturally specific. It does not imply, however, that that reality can be readily changed. Socially constructed realities often exhibit great staying power.

In her second paragraph Lorber refers to postmodern feminists and queer theorists, two groupings with much in common. Both—the one centered on women and the other on people who transgress heterosexual codes—favor outlooks emphasizing the fluid, decentered, unstable, and localized character of social realities such as identity and gender. Where modernists see content, postmodernists see process; where modernists impute stable features, postmodernists impute flux and multiplicity; where modernists say "something," postmodernists say "whatever."

In her third paragraph Lorber refers to "deconstructing," an endeavor masterminded by the contemporary French thinker Jacques Derrida. Without oversimplifying, one can think of *deconstruction* as an effort to disassemble a text or other reality not only by untangling its features such as metaphors, pronominal usages (first- versus third-person pronouns, for instance), and parenthetical diversions but also by taking serious note of its gaps, vacancies, and absences. The focus of deconstruction is not the human agent(s) responsible for producing the reality at hand but the reality itself as a multilayered, dense tangle of meanings produced through acts of interpretation.

The last two sections of Lorber's essay raise issues central to Chapter 2. Focusing primarily on sociological research, Lorber thus builds a bridge we will later cross by exploring whose knowledge prevails in today's world and how it might be transformed toward lesser bias and greater inclusiveness.

NOTES

1. Pamela Moore and Devoney Looser describe the stereotypes of theory and feminism: Theory is masculine and resides in "ivory towers"; feminism is "identified with woman-friendly practices and real-life practices"; see their "Theoretical Feminisms: Subjectivity, Struggle, and the 'Conspiracy' of Poststructuralism," *Style* 27, no. 4 (Winter 1993), p. 530. For a look at how diverse feminists join theory and practice, see the special issue on "Feminist Theory and Practice" in *Signs: Journal of Women in Culture and Society* 21, no. 4 (Summer 1996).

2. See Alexandra Dundas Todd, *Intimate Adversaries: Cultural Conflict between Doctors and Women Patients* (Philadelphia: University of Pennsylvania Press, 1989), for a brief survey of this situation, specifically with reference to contraception.

3. Judith Grant, *Fundamental Feminism: Contesting the Core Concepts of Feminist Theory* (New York: Routledge, 1993), p. 179.

4. Patricia J. Williams, *The Alchemy of Race and Rights* (Cambridge, MA: Harvard University Press, 1991), p. 103.

5. Robin Morgan, *Sisterhood Is Powerful: An Anthology of Writings from the Women's Liberation Movement* (New York: Vintage Books, 1970). On the ideological dimension of Morgan's anthology, see Judith Roof, "How to Satisfy a

Woman 'Every Time'. . ." in Diane Elam and Robin Wiegman (eds.), *Feminism beside Itself* (New York: Routledge, 1995), pp. 56–69.

6. Ginette Castro, *American Feminism: A Contemporary History* (New York: New York University Press, 1990), p. 169, trans. Elizabeth Loverde-Bagwell (orig. 1984).

7. Joan V. Spade, "Wives' and Husbands' Perceptions of Why Wives Work," *Gender & Society* 8, no. 2 (June 1994), pp. 170–88.

8. Timothy J. Owens, Heylan T. Mortimer, and Michael D. Finch, "Self-Determination as a Source of Self-Esteem in Adolescence," *Social Forces* 74, no. 4 (June 1996), p. 1377; emphasis added.

9. Trinh T. Minh-ha, *Woman, Native, Other: Writing Postcoloniality and Feminism* (Bloomington: Indiana University Press, 1989), p. 28.

10. Nancy Hartsock, "Foucault on Power: A Theory for Women?" in Linda J. Nicholson (ed.), *Feminism/Postmodernism* (New York: Routledge, 1990), p. 158.

11. Joan Wallach Scott, "Introduction" in Joan Wallach Scott (ed.), *Feminism & History* (New York: Oxford University Press, 1996), p. 13.

12. Sandra Lee Bartky, "Reply to Commentators on *Femininity and Domination*," *Hypatia: A Journal of Feminist Philosophy* 8 (Winter 1993), p. 193.

13. Mary Catherine Bateson, *Composing a Life* (New York: Penguin Books, 1990), p. 17.

14. Drucilla Cornell, *Transformations: Recollective Imagination and Sexual Difference* (New York: Routledge, 1993), p. 11.

15. One reviewer of *Contemporary Feminist Theory* interpreted this theoretical move as "invoking a race credential" (hooks is African American; I am not). That reading of my motives merits response. Together with three other people, hooks happens to be among my favorite theorists. Were the two white theorists or the other African American theorist as prolific and far-ranging as hooks, I could just as readily have chosen one of them as a companion theorist.

16. Barbara Smith, "Racism and Women's Studies" in Gloria T. Hull, Patricia Bell Scott, and Barbara Smith (eds.), *All the Women Are White, All the Blacks Are Men, But Some of Us Are Brave: Black Women's Studies* (New York: The Feminist Press, 1982), p. 49.

17. See Peter L. Berger and Thomas Luckmann, *The Social Construction of Reality: A Treatise in the Sociology of Knowledge* (New York: Anchor Books, 1967); Dorothy E. Smith, *The Conceptual Practices of Power: A Feminist Sociology of Knowledge* (Boston: Northeastern University Press, 1990).

18. Zillah R. Eisenstein, "Introduction" in Zillah R. Eisenstein (ed.), *Capitalist Patriarchy and the Case for Socialist Feminism* (New York and London: Monthly Review Press, 1979), p. 3.

19. Trinh, *Women, Native, Other,* p. 42.

20. Christine Di Stefano, "Who the Heck Are We? Theoretical Turns against Gender," *Frontiers* XII, no. 2 (1991), p. 87.

21. See Janet Rosenberg, Harry Perlstadt, and William R. F. Phillips, "Now That We Are Here: Discrimination, Disparagement, and Harassment at Work and the Experience of Women Lawyers," *Gender & Society* 7 (September 1993), pp. 415–33.

22. I thank Marjorie Pryse not only for suggesting that I undertake the discussion at hand but also for helping me rethink the title for this last section of *Contemporary Feminist Theory*.

A Black Feminist Statement

The Combahee River Collective

We are a collective of black feminists who have been meeting together since 1974.[1] During that time we have been involved in the process of defining and clarifying our politics, while at the same time doing political work within our own group and in coalition with other progressive organizations and movements. The most general statement of our politics at the present time would be that we are actively committed to struggling against racial, sexual, heterosexual, and class oppression and see as our particular task the development of integrated analysis and practice based upon the fact that the major systems of oppression are interlocking. The synthesis of these oppressions creates the conditions of our lives. As black women we see black feminism as the logical political movement to combat the manifold and simultaneous oppressions that all women of color face.

. . .

WHAT WE BELIEVE

Above all else, our politics initially sprang from the shared belief that black women are inherently valuable, that our liberation is a necessity not as an adjunct to somebody else's but because of our need as human persons for autonomy. This may seem so obvious as to sound simplistic, but it is apparent that no other ostensibly progressive movement has ever considered our specific oppression a priority or worked seriously for the ending of that oppression. Merely naming the pejorative stereotypes attributed to black women (e.g., mammy, matriarch,

Sapphire, whore, bulldagger), let alone cataloguing the cruel, often murderous, treatment we receive, indicates how little value has been placed upon our lives during four centuries of bondage in the Western hemisphere. We realize that the only people who care enough about us to work consistently for our liberation is us. Our politics evolve from a healthy love for ourselves, our sisters, and our community which allows us to continue our struggle and work.

This focusing upon our own oppression is embodied in the concept of identity politics. We believe that the most profound and potentially the most radical politics come directly out of our own identity, as opposed to working to end somebody else's oppression. In the case of black women this is a particularly repugnant, dangerous, threatening, and therefore revolutionary concept because it is obvious from looking at all the political movements that have preceded us that anyone is more worthy of liberation than ourselves. We reject pedestals, queenhood, and walking ten paces behind. To be recognized as human, levelly human, is enough.

We believe that sexual politics under patriarchy is as pervasive in black women's lives as are the politics of class and race. We also often find it difficult to separate race from class from sex oppression because in our lives they are most often experienced simultaneously. We know that there is such a thing as racial–sexual oppression which is neither solely racial nor solely sexual, e.g., the history of rape of black women by white men as a weapon of political repression.

Although we are feminists and lesbians, we feel solidarity with progressive black men and do not advocate the fractionalization that white women who are separatists demand. Our situation as black people necessitates that we have solidarity around the fact of race, which white women of course do not need to have with white men, unless it is their negative solidarity as racial oppressors. We struggle together with black men against racism, while we also struggle with black men about sexism.

We realize that the liberation of all oppressed peoples necessitates the destruction of the political–economic systems of capitalism and imperialism as well as patriarchy. We are socialists because we believe the work must be organized for the collective benefit of those who do the work and create the products and not for the profit of the bosses. Material resources must be equally distributed among those who create these resources. We are not convinced, however, that a socialist revolution that is not also a feminist and antiracist revolution will guarantee our liberation. We have arrived at the necessity for developing an understanding of class relationships that takes into account the specific class position of black women who are generally marginal in the labor force, while at this particular time some of us are temporarily viewed as doubly desirable tokens at white-collar and professional levels. We need to articulate the real class situation of persons who are not merely raceless, sexless workers, but for whom racial and sexual oppression are significant determinants in their working/economic lives. Although we are in essential agreement with Marx's theory as it applied to the very specific economic relationships he analyzed, we know that this analysis must be extended further in order for us to understand our specific economic situation as black women.

A political contribution which we feel we have already made is the expansion of the feminist's principle that the personal is political. In our consciousness-raising sessions, for example, we have in many ways gone beyond white women's revelations because we are dealing with the implications of race and class as well as sex. Even our black women's style of talking/testifying in black language about what we have experienced has a resonance that is both cultural and political. We have spent a great deal of energy delving into the cultural and experiential nature of our oppression out of necessity because none of these matters have ever been looked at before. No one before has ever examined the multilayered texture of black women's lives.

As we have already stated, we reject the stance of lesbian separatism because it is not a viable political analysis or strategy for us. It leaves out far too much and far too many people, particularly black men, women, and children. We have a great deal of criticism and loathing for what men have been socialized to be in this society: what they support, how they act, and how they oppress. But we do not have the misguided notion that it is their maleness, per se—i.e., their biological maleness—that makes them what they are. As black women we find any type of biological determinism a particularly dangerous and reactionary basis upon which to build a politic. We must also question whether lesbian separatism is an adequate and progressive political analysis and strategy, even for those who practice it, since it so completely denies any but the sexual sources of women's oppression, negating the facts of class and race.

. . .

BLACK FEMINIST ISSUES AND PRACTICE

During our time together we have identified and worked on many issues of particular relevance to black women. The inclusiveness of our politics makes us concerned with any situation that impinges upon the lives of women, Third World, and working people. We are of course particularly committed to working on those struggles in which race, sex, and class are simultaneous factors in oppression. We might, for example, become involved in workplace organizing at a factory that employs Third World women or picket a hospital that is cutting back on already inadequate health care to a Third World community, or set up a rape crisis center in a black neighborhood. Organizing around welfare or daycare concerns might also be a focus. The work to be done and the countless issues that this work represents merely reflect the pervasiveness of our oppression.

Issues and projects that collective members have actually worked on are sterilization abuse, abortion rights, battered women, rape, and health care. We have also done many workshops and educationals on black feminism on college campuses, at women's conferences, and most recently for high school women.

One issue that is of major concern to us and that we have begun to publicly address is racism in the white women's movement. As black feminists we are made constantly and painfully aware of how little effort white women have made to understand and combat their racism, which requires among other things that they have a more than superficial comprehension of race, color, and black history and culture. Eliminating racism in the white women's movement is by definition work for white women to do, but we will continue to speak to and demand accountability on this issue.

In the practice of our politics we do not believe that the end always justifies the means. Many reactionary and destructive acts have been done in the name of achieving "correct" political goals. As feminists we do not want to mess over people in the name of politics. We believe in collective process and a nonhierarchical distribution of power within our own group and in our vision of a revolutionary society. We are committed to a continual examination of our politics as they develop through criticism and self-criticism as an essential aspect of our practice. As black feminists and lesbians we know that we have a very definite revolutionary task to perform and we are ready for the lifetime of work and struggle before us.

NOTES

1. This statement is dated April 1977.

READING 2

Beyond the Binaries: Depolarizing the Categories of Sex, Sexuality, and Gender

Judith Lorber

. . . Most research designs in sociology assume that each person has one sex, one sexuality, and one gender, which are congruent with each other and fixed for life. Sex and gender are used interchangeably, and sex sometimes means sexuality, sometimes physiology or biology, and sometimes social status. The social construction of bodies is examined only when the focus is medicine, sports, or procreation (Butler 1993). Variations in gender displays are ignored: A woman is assumed to be a feminine female; a man a masculine male. Heterosexuality is the uninterrogated norm against which variations are deviance (Ingraham 1994). These research variables—"sex" polarized as "females" and "males," "sexuality" polarized as "homosexuals" and "heterosexuals," and "gender" polarized as "women" and "men"—reflect unnuanced series that conventionalize bodies, sexuality, and social location (Young 1994). Such designs cannot include the experiences of hermaphrodites, pseudohermaphrodites, transsexuals, transvestites, bisexuals, third genders, and gender rebels as lovers, friends, parents, workers, and sports participants. Even if the research sample is restricted to putative "normals," the use of unexamined categories of sex, sexuality, and gender will miss complex combinations of status and identity, as well as differently gendered sexual continuities and discontinuities (Chodorow 1994, 1995).

Postmodern feminists and queer theorists have been interrogating bodies, desires, and genders, but sociologists have not, despite the availability of concepts from labeling theory and symbolic interaction: "The idea that sexuality is socially constructed was promoted by interpretive sociologists and feminist theorists at least two decades before queer theory emerged on the intellectual scene" (Stein and Plummer 1994, p. 183).[1] Current debates over the global assumptions of only two gender categories have led to the insistence that they must be nuanced to include race and class, but they have not gone much beyond that (Collins 1990; Spelman 1988; Staples 1982). Similarly, the addition of sexual orientation has expanded gendered sexual statuses only to four: heterosexual women and men, gays, and lesbians.

Deconstructing sex, sexuality, and gender reveals many possible categories embedded in social experiences and social practices, as does the deconstruction of race and class. As queer theorists have found, multiple categories disturb the neat polarity of familiar opposites that assume one dominant and one subordinate group, one normal and one deviant identity, one hegemonic status and one "other" (Martin 1994; Namaste 1994). But in sociology, as Barrie Thorne (1993) comments in her work on children,

> The literature moves in a circle, carting in cultural assumptions about the nature of masculinity (bonded, hierarchical, competitive, "tough"), then highlighting behavior that fits those parameters and obscuring the varied styles and range of interactions among boys as a whole. (p. 100)

Behavior that is gender-appropriate is considered normal; anything else (girls insulting, threatening, and physically fighting boys and other girls) is considered "gender deviance" (Thorne 1993, pp. 101–3). The juxtaposition both assumes and reproduces seemingly clear and stable contrasts. Deconstructing those contrasts reveals that the "normal" and the "deviant" are both the product of deliberate social practices and cultural discourses. Of all the so-

cial sciences, sociology is in the best position to analyze those practices and discourses, rather than taking their outcome for granted.

But as long as sociological research uses only the conventional dichotomies of females and males, homosexuals and heterosexuals, women and men, it will take the "normal" for granted by masking the extent of subversive characteristics and behavior. Treating deviant cases as markers of the boundaries of the "normal" implies that the "normal" (e.g., heterosexuality) does not have to be explained as equally the result of processes of socialization and social control (Ingraham 1994). Such research colludes in the muffling and suppressing of behavior that may be widespread, such as heterosexual men who frequently cross-dress, which, if not bracketed off as "deviant," could subvert conventional discourses on gender and sexuality (Stein and Plummer 1994).

Our commonsense knowledge of the real world tells us that behavior is situational and that sexual and gender statuses combined with race and social class produce many identities in one individual (West and Fenstermaker 1995). This individual heterogeneity is nonetheless overridden by the major constructs (race, class, gender) that order and stratify informal groups, formal organizations, social institutions, and social interaction. By accepting these constructs as given, by not unpacking them, sociologists collude in the relations of ruling (Smith 1990a, 1990b).

As researchers, as theorists, and as activists, sociologists have to go beyond paying lip service to the diversity of bodies, sexualities, genders, and racial–ethnic and class positions. We have to think not only about how these characteristics variously intermingle in individuals and therefore in groups but what the extent of variation is *within these categories.* For example, using conventional categories, where would we place the competitive runner in woman's competitions who has XY chromosomes and normal female genitalia (Grady 1992)? Or the lesbian transsexual (Bolin 1988)? Or the woman or man who has long-term relationships with both women and men (Weinberg, Williams, and Pryor 1994)? Or the wealthy female husband in an African society and her wife (Amadiume 1987)? These are not odd cases that can be bracketed off in a footnote (Terry 1991). As did the concept of conflicting latent statuses (e.g., black woman surgeon), they call our attention to the rich data about social processes and their outcomes that lie beneath neat comparisons of male and female, heterosexual and homosexual, men and women.

DECONSTRUCTING SEX, SEXUALITY, AND GENDER

In rethinking gender categories, it is important to split what is usually conflated as sex/gender or sex/sexuality/gender into three conceptually distinct categories: sex (or biology, physiology), sexuality (desire, sexual preference, sexual orientation), and gender (a social status, sometimes with sexual identity). Each is socially constructed but in different ways. Gender is an overarching category—a major social status that organizes almost all areas of social life. Therefore bodies and sexuality are gendered; biology, physiology, and sexuality, in contrast, do not add up to gender, which is a social institution that establishes patterns of expectations for individuals, orders the social processes of everyday life, is built into the major social organizations of society, such as the economy, ideology, the family, and politics, and is also an entity in and of itself (Lorber 1994).

For an individual, the components of gender are the sex category assigned at birth on the basis of the appearance of the genitalia; gender identity; gendered sexual orientation; marital and procreative status; a gendered personality structure; gender beliefs and attitudes; gender displays; and work and family roles. All these social components are supposed to be consistent and congruent with perceived physiology. The actual combination of genes and genitalia; prenatal, adolescent, and adult hormonal input; and procreative capacity may or may not be congruous with each other and with the components of gender and sexuality, and the components may also not line up neatly on only one side of the binary divide.

Deconstructing Sex

Anne Fausto-Sterling (1993) says that "no classification scheme could more than suggest the variety of sexual anatomy encountered in clinical practice" (p. 22), or seen on a nudists' beach. Male and female genitalia develop from the same fetal tissue, and so, because of various genetic and hormonal inputs, at least 1 in 1,000 infants is born with ambiguous genitalia, and perhaps more (Fausto-Sterling 1993). The "mix" varies; there are

> the so-called true hermaphrodites . . . , who possess one testis and one ovary . . . ; the male pseudohermaphrodites . . . , who have testes and some aspects of the female genitalia but no ovaries; and the female pseudohermaphrodites . . . , who have ovaries and some aspects of the male genitalia but lack testes. Each of these categories is in itself complex; the percentage of male and female characteristics . . . can vary enormously among members of the same subgroup. (Fausto-Sterling 1993, p. 21)

Because of the need for official categorization in bureaucratically organized societies, these infants must legally be labeled "boy" or "girl" soon after birth, yet they are subject to rather arbitrary sex assignment (Epstein 1990). Suzanne Kessler (1990) interviewed six medical specialists in pediatric intersexuality and found that whether an infant with XY chromosomes and anomalous genitalia was categorized as a boy or a girl depended on the size of the penis. If the penis was very small, the child was categorized as a girl, and sex-change surgery was used to make an artificial vagina.

An anomaly common enough to be found in several feminine-looking women at every major international sports competition is the existence of XY chromosomes that have not produced male anatomy or physiology because of other genetic input (Grady 1992). Now that hormones have proved unreliable, sports authorities nonetheless continue to find ways of separating "women" from "men." From the point of view of the sociological researcher, the interesting questions are why certain sports competitions are gender-neutral and others are not, how different kinds of sports construct different kinds of women's and men's bodies, and how varieties of masculinities and femininities are constructed through sports competitions (Hargreaves 1986; Messner 1992; Messner and Sabo 1994).

As for hormones, recent research suggests that testosterone and other androgens are as important to normal development in females as in males, and that in both, testosterone is converted to estrogen in the brain.[2] Paradoxically, maximum androgen levels seem to coincide with high estrogen levels and ovulation, leading one researcher to comment: "The borders between classic maleness and femaleness are much grayer than people realized. . . . We're mixed bags, all of us" (quoted in Angier 1994).

From a societal point of view, the variety of combinations of genes, genitalia, and hormonal input can be rendered invisible by the surgical and hormonal construction of maleness and femaleness (Epstein 1990). But this variety, this continuum of physiological sex cannot be ignored. Sociologists may not want to explore the varieties of biological and physiological sexes or the psychology of the hermaphrodite, pseudohermaphrodite, or transsexual, but the rationales given for the categorization of the ambiguous as either female or male shed a great deal of light on the practices that maintain the illusion of clear-cut sex differences. Without such critical exploration, sex differences are easily invoked as the "natural causes" of what is actually socially constructed.

Deconstructing Sexuality

Categories of sexuality—conventionally, homosexual and heterosexual—also mask diversity that can be crucial for generating accurate data. Sexuality is physically sexed because female and male anatomies and orgasmic experiences

differ. It is gendered because sexual scripts differ for women and for men whether they are heterosexual, homosexual, bisexual, transsexual, or transvestite. Linking the experience of physical sex and gendered social prescriptions for sexual feelings, fantasies, and actions are individual bodies, desires, and patterns of sexual behavior, which coalesce into gendered sexual identities. These identities, however various and individualized, are categorized and socially patterned into gendered sexual statuses. There are certainly more than two gendered sexual statuses: "If one uses the criteria of linguistic markers alone, it suggests that people in most English-speaking countries . . . recognize four genders: woman, lesbian (or gay female), man and gay male" (Jacobs and Roberts 1989, p. 439). But there is not the variety we might find if we looked at what is actually out there.[3]

Studies of bisexuality have shown that the conventional sexual categories are hard to document empirically. At what point does sexual desire become sexual preference, and what turns sexual preference into a sexual identity or social status? What sexual behavior identifies a "pure" heterosexual or a "pure" homosexual? Additionally, a sexual preference involves desired and actual sexual attraction, emotions, and fantasies, not just behavior. A sexual identity involves self-identification, a lifestyle, and social recognition of the status (Klein, Sepekoff, and Wolf 1985).

Sexual identities (heterosexual, homosexual, bisexual) are responses not just to psychic constructs but also to social and cultural strictures and pressures from family and friends. Because Western culture constructs sexuality dichotomously, many people whose sexual experiences are bisexual are forced to choose between a heterosexual and homosexual identity as their "real" identity (Blumstein and Schwartz 1976a, 1976b; Garber 1995; Rust 1992, 1993, forthcoming; Valverde 1985, pp. 109–20). Rust's research on bisexual and lesbian sexual identity found that 90 percent of the 323 self-identified lesbians who answered her questionnaire had

had heterosexual experiences, 43 percent after coming out as lesbians (1992, 1993). They discounted these experiences, however; what counted for these lesbians was their current relationships. The forty-two women who identified themselves as bisexual, in contrast, put more emphasis on their sexual attraction to both women and men. Assuming that all self-identified homosexual men and lesbians have exclusively same-sex partners not only renders invisible the complexities of sexuality but can also have disastrous health outcomes, as has been found in the spread of HIV and AIDS among women (Goldstein 1995).

The interplay of gender and sexuality needs to be explored as well. One study found that heterosexual men labeled sexual provocativeness toward them by gay men sexual harassment, but heterosexual women did not feel the same about lesbians' coming on to them (Giuffre and Williams 1994). The straight men felt their masculinity was threatened by the gay men's overtures; the straight women did not feel that a lesbian's interest in them impugned their heterosexuality.

Weinberg, Williams, and Pryor (1994) found five types of bisexuals among the 49 men, 44 women, and 11 transsexuals they interviewed in 1983 (pp. 46–8). In their research, gender was as salient a factor as sexuality. On the basis of sexual feelings, sexual behaviors, and romantic feelings, they estimated that only 2 percent of the self-identified bisexual men in their research and 17 percent of the self-identified bisexual women were equally sexually and romantically attracted to and involved with women and men, but about a third of both genders were around the midpoint of their scale. About 45 percent of the men and 20 percent of the women leaned toward heterosexuality, and 15 percent of each gender leaned toward homosexuality. About 10 percent of each were varied in their feelings and behavior.

Weinberg, Williams, and Pryor (1994) found that although gender was irrelevant to choice of partner among bisexuals, sexual scripting was not only gendered, but quite conventional, with both women and men saying that women partners were more emotionally attuned and men partners were more physically sexual (pp. 49–58). Paradoxically, they say,

> In a group that often sets itself against societal norms, we were surprised to discover that bisexual respondents organized their sexual preferences along the lines of traditional gender stereotypes. As with heterosexuals and homosexuals, gender is the building material from which they put together their sexuality. Unlike these groups, however, the edifice built is not restricted to one gender. (p. 57)

The meaning of gender and sexuality to self-identified homosexuals cannot be taken for granted by researchers. Eve Kosofsky Sedgwick notes that some homosexuals want to cross into the other gender's social space (e.g., gay drag queens and butch lesbians), whereas for others (e.g., macho gay men and lesbian separatists) ". . . it is instead the most natural thing in the world that people of the same gender, people grouped under the single most determinative diacritical mark of social organization, people whose economic, institutional, emotional, physical needs and knowledges may have so much in common, should bond together also on the axis of sexual desire" (1990, p. 87).

Paula Rust (forthcoming), in her research on varieties of sexuality, found that her respondents spoke of being attracted to another person because of particular personality characteristics, ways of behaving, interests, intellect, looks, style. What heterosexuals do—choose among many possible members of the opposite sex—is true of gays and lesbians for same-sex partners, and bisexuals for either sex. The physical sex, sexual orientation, masculinity, femininity, and gender markers are just the beginning set of parameters, and they might differ for a quick sexual encounter, a romantic liaison, a long-term relationship. Rather than compare on categories of gender or sexuality, researchers might want to compare on types of relationships.

Deconstructing Gender

Gendered behavior is constantly normalized by processes that minimize or counteract contradictions to the expected. Competitive women bodybuilders downplay their size, use makeup, wear their hair long and blond, and emphasize femininity in posing by using "dance, grace and creativity"; otherwise, they don't win competitions (Mansfield and McGinn, 1993):

> There are a wide variety of styles of dress and personal presentation available to Western women of the late twentieth century to the extent that the notion of female-to-male cross-dressing has become almost meaningless. However, in the same way as it is necessary for the extreme gender markers of the hyper-feminine to be adopted by the male cross-dressers in order to make it clear that they wish to be recognized as "women," so too is it necessary for women bodybuilders. . . . It seems that the female muscled body is so dangerous that the proclamation of gender must be made very loudly indeed. (p. 64)

Iris Marion Young (1994) argues that gender, race, and class are *series*—comparatively passive social collectives grouped by their similar tasks, ends, or social conditioning. These locations in social structures may or may not become sources of self-identification, significant action by others, or political action. When and how they do is an area for research. For example, U.S. lesbians first identified with homosexual men in their resistance to sexual discrimination, but after experiencing the same gender discrimination as did women in the civil rights and draft-resistance movements, they turned to the feminist movement, where, unhappily, they experienced hostility to their sexuality from many heterosexual women. Subsequently, some lesbian feminists have created an oppositional, woman-identified, separatist movement that identifies heterosexuality as the main source of the oppression of women (Taylor and Rupp 1993).

David Collinson and Jeff Hearn (1994) argue that men in management exhibit multiple masculinities: aggressive authoritarianism, benevolent paternalism, competitive entrepreneurialism, buddy-buddy informalism, and individualist careerism. These multiple masculinities among men managers have different effects on relationships with men colleagues, women colleagues, as well as on sponsor–protégé interactions. Collinson and Hearn call for a simultaneous emphasis on unities and differences among men. Cynthia Cockburn similarly says about women, "We can be both the same as you *and* different from you, at various times and in various ways" (1991, p. 10).

Igor Kopytoff (1990), raising the question of why it seems to be easier for women in traditional societies than in Westernized societies to claim positions of political power and rule as heads of state, uses a concept of core or existential gender identities. He argues that in Africa and many other traditional societies the core of womanhood (or immanent or existential being as a woman) is childbearing—but all the rest is praxis and negotiable, transferable. Because women do not have to bring up their children to be women in traditional societies, just birth them, he argues that they are free to take on other time-consuming roles. In the West, in contrast, since the nineteenth century, being a "real" woman means one must be married with children, and must bring them up personally, while also keeping an impeccable house and attractive appearance, and looking after a husband's sexual and emotional needs. "Once existentially complete, she can then turn to other occupations," but will rarely have the time to assume a position of leadership (p. 93).

> The crucial question . . . is this: granted that most and perhaps all societies posit that being a woman is an existential identity with a set of features immanent in it, how many such immanent features are there and what are they? Or, to put it most simply, the problem of women's roles is not whether a society recognizes women as being different from men (they invariably do) but how it organizes other things around the difference. (p. 91)

USEFUL METHODOLOGIES

The sociologists' task should be to deconstruct the conventional categories of sex, sexuality, and gender and build new complex, cross-cutting constructs into research designs. There are several ways to rethink the conventional "manageable units" that laypeople construct (Rodkin 1993, p. 635). We can deconstruct the commonly used categories to tease out components; we can add categories; we can also reconstruct categories entirely. That is, we can take a critical stance toward the conventional categories without abandoning them entirely, examining the social construction and meanings of sex, sexuality, and gender, as has already been done for race, ethnicity, and social class. We can adapt categories to particular research questions, cross-cutting sex, sexuality, and gender the way race, ethnicity, and social class have been used as cross-cutting categories. Or, we can do research that predicts behavior from processes and social location without the overlay of status categories, examining what people do to and with whom and how these processes construct, maintain, or subvert statuses, identities, and institutional rules and social structures. None of these new approaches discards familiar sociological tools, but all of them demand thoughtful examination of the familiar binaries.

Sociology has several methodologies that do not rely on polarized categories. Among them are analysis of positions in a social network (Knoke and Kuklinski 1982), examination of the clustering of attitudinal perspectives through Q-sorting (Stephenson 1953), letting patterns emerge from the data as recommended by grounded theory (Glaser, 1992; Straus and Corbin, 1990), and the critical deconstruction of social texts (Reinharz 1992, pp. 145–63). The familiar categories can be used in the next level of analysis to see whether the emergent network positions, attitude clusters, typical behavior, and subtexts are characteristic of those of different genders, races, ethnic groups, and classes, and they can be taken to a third level describing how they relate to power and resource

control. Or they can be dropped entirely in favor of category names more descriptive of empirical content. Using grounded theory to analyze the varieties of behavior of male cross-dressers, Richard Ekins (1993) distinguished patterns related to sex ("body femaling"), sexuality ("erotic femaling"), and role behavior ("gender femaling").

Letting patterns emerge from the data, the methodology long recommended by ethnomethodologists and other qualitative researchers, permits the analysis of processes within structures (West and Fenstermaker 1995; West and Zimmerman 1987). As Marilyn Frye notes, "Pattern discovery and invention requires encounters with difference, with variety. . . . Discovering patterns requires novel acts of attention" (1990, p. 180). These patterns can also be used for quantitative comparisons, as Mary Clare Lennon and Sarah Rosenfeld (1994) did in their statistical analysis built on Arlie Hochschild's (1989) interview data on the extent of housework done by husbands and wives where the woman was the greater earner. Organizing data without reliance on the conventional dichotomous categories does not confine researchers to single-case analysis or a limited number of in-depth interviews; quantitative methods will still be applicable.

The common practice of comparing females and males, women and men, or homosexuals and heterosexuals frequently produces data that are so mixed that it takes another level of analysis to sort out meaningful categories for comparison. It would be better to start with categories derived from data analysis of all subjects and see the extent to which they attach to the conventional global categories of sex, sexuality, and gender, or better yet, to one or more of the components. However, in order to do this second level of analysis, the sample groups have to be heterogenous on the conventional categories in the first place. Thus, the familiar categories do not have to be dispensed with entirely, but their use in analysis can be bracketed until after other differentiating variables are revealed.

These differentiating variables are likely to break up and recombine the familiar categories in new ways that go beyond the conventional dichotomies but do not remove the category from our lexicon. As Linda Nicholson (1994) says in "Interpreting *Gender*,"

> Thus I am advocating that we think about the meaning of *woman* as illustrating a map of intersecting similarities and differences. Within such a map the body does not disappear but rather becomes a historically specific variable whose meaning and import are recognized as potentially different in different historical contexts. Such a suggestion . . . [assumes] that meaning is found rather than presupposed. (pp. 101–2)

CHALLENGE CATEGORIES, CHALLENGE POWER

. . . The goal of sociological research should similarly be multiple levels of analysis that include the heterogeneity of people's lives, the varied dimensions of status categories, and the power relations between and among them. As Dorothy Smith (1990a) says,

> The social scientist must work with the constraint of actuality and is not privileged to draw relations between observables arbitrarily. A theoretical account is not fixed at the outset, but evolves in the course of inquiry dialectically as the social scientist seeks to explicate the properties of organization discovered in the way people order their activities. Hence the structure of a theoretical account is constrained by the relations generated in people's practical activities. (p. 48)

Research using a variety of gendered sexual statuses has already challenged long-accepted theories. Lesbian and homosexual parenting, as well as single-parent households, call into question ideas about parenting and gendered personality development based on heterogendered nuclear families. In psychoanalytic theory, having a woman as a primary parent allows girls to maintain their close bonding and identification with women, but forces boys to differentiate and separate in order to establish their masculinity. The personality structure of adult women remains more open than that of men, whose ego boundaries make them less emotional. Women in heterosexual relationships want children to bond with as substitutes for their lack of intense emotional intimacy with their men partners. But there are lesbians who have deep and intense relationships with women who also want children, as do some homosexual men (Lewin 1993). Furthermore, not all full-time mothering is emotionally intense, nor is all intensive mothering done by women. Barbara Risman (1987), in her study of fifty-five men who became single fathers because of their wives' death, desertion, or giving up custody, found that their relationships with their children were as intimate as those of single mothers and mothers in traditional marriages. And Karen Hansen's studies (1992) of nineteenth-century heterosexual men's friendships reveal a world of feeling similar to that described by Carroll Smith-Rosenberg (1975) for women.

In work organizations, position in the hierarchy does and does not override a worker's gender. The behavior of men and women doctors sometimes reflects their professional status and sometimes their gender, and it is important to look at both aspects to understand their relationships with patients (Lorber 1985). The men workers in women's occupations and the women workers in men's occupations cannot be lumped in a minority category. The women come up against the glass ceiling that blocks their upward mobility, whereas the men are on what Christine Williams has called a "glass escalator": They are encouraged to compete for managerial and administrative positions (Williams 1989, 1992).

Joey Sprague (1991) found that because material interests reflect positions in the social relations of production and reproduction, as well as more immediate community contexts, political attitudes hew more closely to class, gender role, and affiliation with social movements than to a simple division of men versus women (also see Henderson-King and Stewart 1994).

There are revolutionary possibilities inherent in rethinking the categories of gender, sexuality, and physiological sex. Sociological data that challenge conventional knowledge by reframing the questions could provide legitimacy for new ways of thinking. When one term or category is defined only by its opposite, resistance reaffirms the polarity (Fuss 1991). The margin and the center, the insider and the outsider, the conformist and the deviant are two sides of the same concept. Introducing even one more term, such as bisexuality, forces a rethinking of the oppositeness of heterosexuality and homosexuality. "A critical sexual politics, in other words, struggles to move beyond the confines of an inside/outside model" (Namaste 1994, p. 230). The politics of identity are challenged, but such political stances are already split racially and by social class. Data that undermine the supposed natural dichotomies on which the social orders of most modern societies are still based could radically alter political discourses that valorize biological causes, essential heterosexuality, and traditional gender roles in families and workplaces.

NOTES

1. For widely cited postmodern feminist and queer theorists, see Butler (1990), Flax (1990), Frye (1992), Nicholson (1990), and Sedgwick (1990). The symposium on queer theory and sociology in the July 1994 issue of *Sociological Theory* addresses some of the questions raised in this article.
2. For summaries of recent research on estrogen and testosterone, see Angier (1994, 1995).
3. Grimm (1987, Tables 1–3, pp. 74–6) comes up with 45 different types of erotic and nonerotic, complementary and similar relationships.

REFERENCES

Amadiume, Ifi. *Male Daughters, Female Husbands: Gender and Sex in an African Society.* London: Zed Books, 1987.

Angier, Natalie. "Does Testosterone Equal Aggression? Maybe Not." *New York Times,* June 20, 1995.

_____. "Male Hormone Molds Women, Too, in Mind and Body." *New York Times,* May 3, 1994.

Blumstein, Philip W., and Pepper Schwartz. "Bisexuality in Women." *Archives of Sexual Behavior* 5 (1976a), pp. 171–81.

_____. "Bisexuality in Men." *Urban Life* 5 (1976b), pp. 339–58.

Bolin, Anne. *In Search of Eve: Transsexual Rites of Passage.* South Hadley, MA: Bergin & Garvey, 1988.

Butler, Judith. *Bodies that Matter: On the Discursive Limits of "Sex."* New York and London: Routledge, 1993.

_____. *Gender Trouble: Feminism and the Subversion of Identity.* New York and London: Routledge, 1990.

Chodorow, Nancy. "Gender as Personal and Cultural." *Signs: Journal of Women in Culture and Society* 20 (1995), pp. 516–44.

_____. *Femininities, Masculinities, Sexualities: Freud and Beyond.* Lexington: University Press of Kentucky, 1994.

Cockburn, Cynthia. *In the Way of Women: Men's Resistance to Sex Equality in Organizations.* Ithaca, NY: ILR, 1991.

Collins, Patricia Hill. *Black Feminist Thought: Knowledge, Consciousness, and the Politics of Empowerment.* Boston: Unwin Hyman, 1990.

Collinson, David, and Jeff Hearn. "Naming Men as Men: Implication for Work, Organization and Management." *Gender, Work and Organization* 1 (1994), pp. 2–22.

Ekins, Richard. "On Male Femaling: A Grounded Theory Approach to Cross-dressing and Sex-changing." *Sociological Review* 41 (1993), pp. 1–29.

Epstein, Julia. "Either/Or—Neither/Both: Sexual Ambiguity and the Ideology of Gender." *Genders* 7 (1990), pp. 100–42.

Fausto-Sterling, Anne. "The Five Sexes: Why Male and Female Are Not Enough." *The Sciences,* March/April 1993, pp. 20–5.

Flax, Jane. *Thinking Fragments: Psychoanalysis, Feminism, and Postmodernism in the Contemporary West.* Berkeley: University of California Press, 1990.

Frye, Marilyn. *Willful Virgin: Essays in Feminism.* Freedom, CA: The Crossing Press, 1992.

_____. "The Possibility of Feminist Theory." In *Theoretical Perspectives on Sexual Difference,* ed. Deborah L. Rhode. New Haven, CT: Yale University Press, 1990.

Fuss, Diana (ed.). *Inside/Out: Lesbian Theories, Gay Theories.* New York and London: Routledge, 1991.

Garber, Marjorie. *Vice Versa: Bisexuality and the Eroticism of Everyday Life.* New York: Simon and Schuster, 1995.

Giuffre, Patti A., and Christine L. Williams. "Boundary Lines: Labelling Sexual Harassment in Restaurants." *Gender and Society* 8 (1994), pp. 378–401.

Glaser, Barney G. *Basics of Grounded Theory Analysis.* Mill Valley, CA: Sociology Press, 1992.

Goldstein, Nancy. "Lesbians and the Medical Profession: HIV/AIDS and the Pursuit of Visibility." *Women's Studies: An Interdisciplinary Journal* 24, 1995, pp. 531–52.

Grady, Denise. "Sex Text of Champions: Olympic Officials Struggle to Define What Should Be Obvious: Just Who Is a Female Athlete." *Discover* 13 (June 1992), pp. 78–82.

Grimm, David E. "Toward a Theory of Gender Transsexualism, Gender, Sexuality, and Relationships." *American Behavioral Scientist* 31 (1987), pp. 66–85.

Hansen, Karen V. " 'Our Eyes Behold Each Other': Masculinity and Intimate Friendship in Antebellum New England." In *Men's Friendships,* ed. Peter M. Nardi. Newbury Park, CA: Sage, 1992.

Hargreaves, Jennifer A. "Where's the Virtue? Where's the Grace? A Discussion of the Social Production of Gender Relations in and through Sport." *Theory, Culture, and Society* 3 (1986), pp. 109–21.

Henderson-King, Donna H., and Abigail J. Stewart. "Women or Feminists? Assessing Women's Group Consciousness." *Sex Roles* 31 (1994), pp. 505–16.

Hochschild, Arlie, with Anne Machung. *The Second Shift: Working Parents and the Revolution at Home.* New York: Viking, 1989.

Ingraham, Chrys. "The Heterosexual Imaginary: Feminist Sociology and Theories of Gender." *Sociological Theory* 12 (1994), pp. 202–19.

Jacobs, Sue-Ellen, and Christine Roberts. "Sex, Sexuality, Gender, and Gender Variance." In *Gender and Anthropology,* ed. Sandra Morgen. Washington, DC: American Anthropological Association, 1989.

Kessler, Suzanne J. "The Medical Construction of Gender: Case Management of Intersexed Infants." *Signs* 16 (1990), pp. 3–26.

Klein, Fritz, Barry Sepekoff, and Timothy J. Wolf. "Sexual Orientation: A Multi-Variable Dynamic Process." *Journal of Homosexuality* 11, no. 1/2 (1985), pp. 35–49.

Knoke, David, and James H. Kuklinski. *Network Analysis.* Newbury Park, CA: Sage, 1982.

Kopytoff, Igor. "Women's Roles and Existential Identities." In *Beyond the Second Sex: New Directions in the Anthropology of Gender,* ed. Peggy Reeves Sanday and Ruth Gallagher Goodenough, Philadelphia: University of Pennsylvania Press, 1990.

Lennon, Mary Clare, and Sarah Rosenfeld. "Relative Fairness and the Division of Housework: The Importance of Options." *American Journal of Sociology* 100 (1994), pp. 506–31.

Lewin, Ellen. *Lesbian Mothers: Accounts of Gender in American Culture.* Ithaca, NY: Cornell University Press, 1993.

Lorber, Judith. *Paradoxes of Gender.* New Haven, CT: Yale University Press, 1994.

_____. "More Women Physicians: Will It Mean More Humane Health Care?" *Social Policy* 16 (Summer 1985), pp. 50–4.

Mansfield, Alan, and Barbara McGinn. "Pumping Irony: The Muscular and the Feminine." In *Body Matters: Essays on the Sociology of the Body,* ed. Sue Scott and David Morgan. London: Falmer, 1993.

Martin, Jane Roland. "Methodological Essentialism, False Difference, and Other Dangerous Traps." *Signs* 19 (1994), pp. 630–57.

Messner, Michael A. *Power at Play: Sports and the Problem of Masculinity.* Boston: Beacon, 1992.

Messner, Michael A., and Donald F. Sabo. *Sex, Violence, and Power in Sports: Rethinking Masculinity.* Freedom, CA: The Crossing Press, 1994.

Namaste, Ki. "The Politics of Inside/Out: Queer Theory, Poststructuralism, and a Sociological Approach to Sexuality." *Sociological Theory* 12 (1994), pp. 220–31.

Nicholson, Linda J. "Interpreting *Gender.*" *Signs* 20 (1994), pp. 79–105.

_____ (ed). *Feminism/Postmodernism.* New York: Routledge, 1990.

Reinharz, Shulamit. *Feminist Methods in Social Research.* New York: Oxford University Press, 1992.

Risman, Barbara J. "Intimate Relationships from a Microstructural Perspective: Men Who Mother." *Gender & Society* 1 (1987), pp. 6–32.

Rodkin, Philip C. "The Psychological Reality of Social Constructions." *Ethnic and Racial Studies* 16 (1993), pp. 633–56.

Rust, Paula C. *The Challenge of Bisexuality to Lesbian Politics: Sex, Loyalty, and Revolution.* New York: New York University Press. Forthcoming.

_____. " 'Coming Out' in the Age of Social Constructionism: Sexual Identity Formation among Lesbian and Bisexual Women." *Gender & Society* 7 (1993), pp. 50–77.

_____. "The Politics of Sexual Identity: Attraction and Behavior among Lesbian and Bisexual Women." *Social Problems* 39 (1992), pp. 366–86.

Sedgwick, Eve Kosofsky. *Epistemology of the Closet.* Berkeley: University of California Press, 1990.

Smith, Dorothy E. *The Conceptual Practices of Power: A Feminist Sociology of Knowledge.* Toronto: University of Toronto Press, 1990a.

_____. *Texts, Facts, and Femininity: Exploring the Relations of Ruling.* New York and London: Routledge, 1990b.

Smith-Rosenberg, Carroll. "The Female World of Love and Ritual: Relations between Women in Nineteenth-Century America." *Signs* 1 (1975), pp. 1–29.

Spelman, Elizabeth. *Inessential Woman: Problems of Exclusion in Feminist Thought.* Boston: Beacon, 1988.

Sprague, Joey. "Gender, Class and Political Thinking." In *Research in Political Sociology* 5, ed. Philo Wasburn. Greenwich, CT: JAI, 1991.

Staples, Robert. *Black Masculinity: The Black Male's Roles in American Society.* San Francisco, CA: Scholar Press, 1982.

Stein, Arlene, and Ken Plummer. " 'I Can't Even Think Straight.' 'Queer' Theory and the Missing Sexual Revolution in Sociology." *Sociological Theory* 12 (1994), pp. 178–87.

Stephenson, William. *The Study of Behavior: Q-Technique and Its Methodology.* Chicago: University of Chicago Press, 1953.

Straus, Anselm L., and Juliet Corbin. *Basics of Qualitative Research: Grounded Theory Procedures and Techniques.* Newbury Park, CA: Sage, 1990.

Taylor, Verta, and Leila Rupp. "Women's Culture and Lesbian Feminist Activism: A Reconsideration of Cultural Feminism." *Signs* 19 (1993), pp. 32–61.

Terry, Jennifer. "Theorizing Deviant Histography." *Differences: A Journal of Feminist Cultural Studies* 3, no. 2 (1991), pp. 55–74.

Thorne, Barrie. *Gender Play: Boys and Girls in School.* New Brunswick, NJ: Rutgers University Press, 1993.

Valverde, Mariana. *Sex, Power and Pleasure.* Toronto: Women's Press, 1985.

Weinberg, Martin S., Colin J. Williams, and Douglas W. Pryor. *Dual Attraction: Understanding Bisexuality.* New York: Oxford University Press, 1994.

West, Candace, and Sarah Fenstermaker. "Doing Difference." *Gender & Society* 9 (1995), pp. 8–37.

West, Candace, and Don Zimmerman. "Doing Gender." *Gender & Society* 1 (1987), pp. 125–51.

Williams, Christine L. "The Glass Escalator: Hidden Advantages for Men in the 'Female' Professions." *Social Problems* 39 (1992), pp. 253–67.

_____. *Gender Differences at Work: Women and Men in Nontraditional Occupations.* Berkeley: University of California Press, 1989.

Young, Iris Marion. "Gender as Seriality: Thinking about Women as a Social Collective." *Signs* 19 (1994), pp. 713–38.

PART ONE

THE MATRIX OF DOMINATION AND RELATIONS OF RULING

CHAPTER 1

Hierarchy, Domination, and Oppression

This chapter focuses on three intertwined realities shaping women's lives. *Hierarchy* is a structural phenomenon having to do with layering people or groups so that some have more and others have less in the way of opportunities and rewards. Generically, social scientists call such systems of inequality "social stratification." *Domination* is a relational reality having to do with some individuals' or groups' socially constructed and routinely exercised right to regulate other people's actions, opportunities, and outcomes. Social scientists often talk about such relationships, whether interpersonal and small scale or intergroup and large scale, in terms of exploitation, social injustice, and social problems. *Oppression* is an experiential notion concerning how people in the lower reaches of social hierarchies—those more dominated than dominating—react over time by way of their identities and emotions. Oppression thus measures the toll that social hierarchies and systems of domination take on those whom they hold back with various degrees of cruelty.

What Gayle Rubin calls the *sex/gender system*[1] revolves around a hierarchy that advantages men over women by giving them higher status, wider opportunities, and greater, more consistent material and psychic rewards. The sex/gender system also comprises a system of domination that entitles men to regulate women's lives, in both large-scale structures such as the economy and small-scale ones such as the family. The sex/gender system is also oppressive, costing women a great deal in terms of the security and reach of their identities and their emotional well-being throughout their life cycle. Because the male/female hierarchy and the system of male domination function in connection with other such hierarchies and systems, however, various groupings of girls and women pay their gender tolls in differing amounts and forms. Femininity is neither uniformly nor equally oppressive for girls and women, then. Its oppressiveness varies with the other circumstances of our lives.

As a midlife woman, for instance, I am much less oppressed by culturally mandated styles of feminine flesh than women 20 or 30 years younger. Already desexualized from a mainstream, heterosexist viewpoint, I am less harshly penalized for excess pounds and a bare face. Yet I have reached neither an age nor a stage of life where people have *no* gendered expectations about my body. I am not supposed, for example, to be premenopausal *and* gray. Indeed, in the middle-class world I largely inhabit, women are not supposed to be gray-haired until their 70s and maybe not even then. I can count on one hand the number of female colleagues and close acquaintances roughly my age whose gray, white, and silver strands are evident. Thus, my hair signals people to ask whether I am retired or have set my retirement date yet. At 53, then, I find myself sometimes treated as 10 or more years older. It's as if my hair color is taking my 50s away from me. That experience is not painfully oppressive, but it is disheartening. In any case, such fleeting experiences point to the variegated impact of cultural mandates about femininity.

Patricia Hill Collins's notion of a *matrix of domination* emphasizes how various systems of domination, such as those based on age and gender, intersect and interplay while remaining distinct from one another.[2] Such systems build up not only around gender and age but also around racial, class, sexual, and ethnic hierarchies as well as the one letting able-bodied people presume that "handicapped" parking solves problems of access. All these hierarchies profoundly shape people's experiences.

Thus, we know what gender means only as individuals of a given social class with a given racial/ethnic identity and sexual orientation, of a certain age, and more or less able-bodied. No dimension of our identity transcends the dense circumstances of our social lives enough to assign us a fate narrowly in common with others whose identity also has that dimension. "Women" thus comprises dramatic diversity as well as substantial commonality. It exacts a toll, to be sure, but the tolls women pay are incurred on different but intersecting roadways, are governed by different fee structures, and entail different methods of payment.

Throughout *Contemporary Feminist Theory,* the matrix of domination will demand attention, if only as a reminder about the hazards of generalizing too swiftly or widely about women. The stubborn, unfair realities of the matrix of domination thus serve as an antidote to unadulterated *essentialism,* whereby women (or members of any other diverse, subordinated grouping) are widely assumed to share some core characteristics independently of history, culture, and social structure. Not surprisingly, those characteristics (a maternal instinct or a strong other-orientation, for instance) are widely treated as traits definitive of the group's "difference" from the dominant group and widely seen as reasonable grounds for treating its members differently.

The attributions associated with crude essentialism thus serve to justify discrimination against subordinated groups while erasing the rich diversity of group members' circumstances and identifications. Keeping the matrix of domination at the theoretical forefront combats such tugs toward overgeneralizing by implying various femininities and, more generally, laying hold of the embodied, situated character of our multifaceted identities.

Also throughout the chapters ahead, Dorothy E. Smith's notion *relations of ruling* will crop up again and again. With that phrase Smith

> designates the complex of extra-local relations that provide . . . a specialization of organization, control, and initiative. They are those forms that we know as bureaucracy, administration, management, professional organization, and media. They include also the complex of discourses, scientific, technical, and cultural, that intersect, interpenetrate, and coordinate the multiple sites of ruling.[3]

Relations of ruling are the regulatory structures of society and culture—the organizational and discursive means whereby some people get authorized to get their way more often than not and others learn that their preferences don't much matter. Relations of ruling extend way beyond formal organizations and dominant *discourses,* or networks of meaning that serve widely as interpretive resources. They find expression in patterns of interrupting, agenda setting, space grabbing, touching, smiling, making eye contact, initiating contact, handshaking, and so forth. Relations of ruling also show up in our vocabularies, our taken-for-granted beliefs, our double standards, and our sense of entitlement, which generally entails some other group's disentitlement. Thus, relations of ruling concern the very presuppositions of orderly social life. No theorist better fleshes out these broad ideas than bell hooks, whose treatment of "voice," a concept central to contemporary feminist theory, completes this chapter's foundation.

Most of hooks's theorizing ultimately revolves around oppressed people's struggle to establish their voices—to be heard, to be taken into account. Hooks's *Feminist Theory,* for example, is subtitled *From Center to Margins,* which implies multiple meanings. One is that feminism itself has involved a white center marginalizing women of color as specific *types* of women whose credibility extends only to those issues deemed pertinent to their respective groupings, such as African American women, Latinas, or Asian American women. In a white-supremacist society, then, white women can speak for "women," while other women can speak only for their racialized niche among female human beings. The same is true for women who are not heterosexual, middle-class, or able-bodied. Women departing from the norms of our heterosexist, racist class structure are seen as deviations from or variations on full-fledged women. Thus, they get heard as working-class women, lesbians, visually impaired women, or American Indian women except within their social class, sexual or racial grouping, and other groupings that anchor their identities. For certain women, then, voice is a challenge made all the more profound by their location in the larger matrix of domination, where some women fare worse than others.

Reading 4 addresses these issues and more. Chéla Sandoval describes the experiences of Third World feminists heard, if at all, as "specialists" among feminists. Sandoval thus looks at voice in a particularly painful context where some women expect to find safe, supportive grounds for their feminist consciousness but instead find their credibility undermined and their feminism somehow suspect. Their voices stifled, these women find themselves relegated to the margins of feminism.

The margins where such women's voices reverberate imply "centers" comprising people whose social positioning marks them as "normal," respectable, and worthy. Centers bring together heterosexual women and men, white women and men, able-bodied women and men, elite women and men, female and male adults not yet retired or otherwise "old," and of course men. Hooks recognizes these multiple centers in her insistence that "gender is not the sole factor determining constructions of femaleness," and she explores them by continually returning to issues of voice—that is, issues of who gets listened to and who gets dismissed when preferences get registered and decisions get made.

In that connection, hooks observes that "intimacy and care can coexist with domination."[4] As life in gender hierarchies makes poignantly clear, brothers and husbands and fathers and uncles can care about their sisters, wives, daughters, and nieces yet dominate them in clear-cut, consistent fashion. Without coercing, without demanding, without ridiculing or belittling, the men we live with or call kin can hold us back even while loving us. "Love" is, in other words, a gendered activity entitling men to more than their fair share of household services, attention, support, and accommodation. Their love for the women providing those necessities and niceties routinely occludes exploitation and injustice. Such love allows for "not getting it" when women make a "big deal" over who stays home with a sick child, whose paid work takes priority, or who *really* listens to whom. It even allows for women who themselves see no "big deal" in their daily subordination.

Put differently, each of us can participate in our own oppression. Thus, hooks observes that our first point of resistance must be the "oppressor within." Further, she says that not only heterosexual women know how caring and domination can intertwine. So do women of color who have worked in white people's homes, often *under* the direct supervision of white women who felt affection for them.[5] In Reading 4 Sandoval implies that such caring is braided with domination in feminist groupings, too.

What hooks pinpoints is crucial. Much of the clout packed into social hierarchies and systems of domination derives from the benign character higher-ups seem to have. Not only are they commonly deemed superior—in control of themselves, objective, goal oriented—but they are also seen as fundamentally decent people, innocent of exploitation or malice. Because sexism, like racism and heterosexism and classism, is rooted in the very organization of work and schooling and worshipping and family making, its beneficiaries can escape judgment as they continue hogging power, enjoying undue privilege, and exploiting those below them on the hierarchy.

Put differently, victimization and privilege are built into social structure. Those more victimized than privileged within the matrix of domination express themselves in modulated, respectful, tentative voices, while those more privileged within that matrix often mince no words. Voice is thus a key to understanding the lived realities of hierarchy, domination, and oppression. It is also a key to resisting their nasty intrusions into our lives while chastening their effects throughout society.

VOICE AND ANGER

In the face of being put down or held back because of one's gender or other socially constructed positionings, anger would seem as likely as frustration. Yet neither emotion necessarily flows from the daily realities of subordination. Because it gets institutionalized and thus normalized, people can come to accept (indeed, are pervasively trained to accept) their own subordination. As Sandra Lee Bartky points out in Reading 3, they commonly develop what Marx called *false consciousness*. Such consciousness is distortional. It takes the lived facts of a situation—doing more work than one's privileged counterparts, getting paid less for doing the same work they do, being put down as silly or subjective, being taken for granted as an emotional mainstay, and so forth—and fits them into some scheme where they make more or less sense.

Such schemes are widely available among those discourses central to the relations of ruling. Religious discourses, for example, often promote notions about the divine ordination of male dominance and the natural law of male superiority. Such discourses get flesh-and-blood support in the commonplace restrictions of the priesthood, ministry, or rabbinate to males alongside the liturgical marginalization of girls and women.

False consciousness is an accommodating consciousness—a way of getting by, a kind of cognitive treading water. False consciousness is the voice of the oppressor within; it echoes the voice of the oppressor without. That voice reflects what people have learned not only as worshippers but also as daughters and sons, students, workers, voters, athletes, volunteers, and consumers. Discursively and interactionally, we learn the terms of our inferiority, the reasons for our subordination, and the wherewithal of negotiating our daily way in an unfair world. We come to see those who dominate as agents who are self-sufficient, whole human beings. In their mirror we see ourselves as objects (or partial subjects) whose agency is continually deflated by radical contingency. We also learn that the more we fulfill commonplace stereotypes, the more "support and/or affirmation" we get in the short run.[6] Mainstream femininity thus becomes seductive. It holds out *secondary gains,* minor but not unimportant rewards for seeming to accept our subordination, that is, for "willingly" being cheated of the primary rewards such as equal pay, equal consideration, and fully reciprocated support and nurturance.

Thus, people can learn accommodation rather than resistance. We can learn to seek assimilation into the sex/gender system rather than transformation of it. In college classrooms we learn to keep our mouths shut in passive response to misogynist remarks or to laugh at instructors' ethnic "jokes"; until we get tenure as educators, we learn to go along with gender- and race-biased curricula replete with erasures of lesbigay people; until someone pledges us undying love, we learn to feign interest in his or her pastimes and projects; and so on until life becomes a series of small and large identifications with the status quo and the people most benefiting from it.

The primary alternative is to get angry and get a voice. Yet as many feminist scholars have shown, getting angry is no simple option among oppressed individuals. For starters, such individuals incline toward *victim consciousness,* a timid self-awareness shaped by inchoate but sharp senses of inferiority built up from recurrent maltreatment. Victims doubt themselves and wonder what they did to deserve nasty reactions or swift dismissal; they hold back; they make excuses for their partners, supervisors, instructors, or coaches; they compromise with their oppressors by giving life to the oppressor within. Commonly taught "to be passive and nonassertive, to take responsibility for others' feelings, to feel uncomfortable and unfeminine when exerting themselves physically, and to feel embarrassed or guilty about being victimized," women get taught to participate in their own subordination. Thus, they "frequently hesitate to 'make a scene' and are often unable to yell even in attack situations. . . ."[7]

By now, feminists commonly forswear the *v* word. Recognizing how "victim" disempowers people who identify themselves that way, feminists focus on women's agency and resistance alongside whatever constraints they variously face in their daily lives. As hooks notes, "victim" seldom appears in the vocabulary of the civil rights era. She implies the eminent good sense expressed by that absence:

> The image of blacks as victims had an accepted place in the consciousness of every white person; it was the image of black folks as equals, as self-determining that had no place—that could evoke no sympathetic response.[8]

Parallels exist with other people of color, lower-class people, and less able-bodied people as well as with white women. Routinely, members of subordinated groups get seen as victims unable to make their own choices and manage their own lives. Culturally, victims are people in need of special surveillance, guidelines, control, or "protection." They are not whole, let alone autonomous, individuals. Victims are objects buffeted about by their sexual appetites, premenstrual syndromes, or menopausal symptoms; they are creatures of nature whose bodies are unruly. Overall, the victim "is a disappearing subject, the subject who does not assert herself, who is absent in her own actions. . . ."[9] Such a woman finds the straightforward, effective expression of anger a practical challenge.

Naomi Scheman sketches further reasons for that state of affairs. She first observes how myths about emotions, particularly women's, stress their irrational character. That portrayal renders emotions suspect as guides to action, even as reactions to experience. Already widely seen as irrational, women face emotional double binds. If we are emotionally expressive, we may gain acceptance as feminine people but diminish our credibility as competent adults; if we are emotionally inexpressive, we may gain some credibility as competent adults but diminish our acceptance as feminine people.

In any case anger is fundamentally judgmental, and that circumstance also blocks women's expressions of anger on many occasions. Scheman says anger is a "feeling that someone (or some group) has acted badly. In order to be straightforwardly angry, one . . . has to trust one's own reactions and take oneself to be in a position to judge."[10] Women are less likely than men to feel entitled to such judgments. As Carol Gilligan and others have suggested (see Chapter 8), sizable numbers of women may incline toward forms of moral reasoning that take into account the particulars of people's situations, resulting in densely contextualized assessments. Anger is less circumspect and thus less straightforwardly available to many women.

Scheman says that a third circumstance making anger difficult for women to experience and express is its "object-hungry" nature. By that, she means that anger requires a target. If one senses "there is no one and nothing to be angry at, it will be harder to see oneself as really angry." If one's husband does more than most husbands or one's boss is less intolerant of family emergencies than most bosses, for instance, a sort of gratitude may infiltrate one's chronic frustrations as a wife or employee. Instead of unadulterated anger toward her husband or boss, such a woman may feel a diffuse, nameless rage at the systems making her home and work lives hard to combine in the Monday-to-Friday cycle of activities.

Finally, Scheman notes that other people, including "experts," often see fit to interpret women's emotions for them.[11] Time and again, women express anger only to have it translated into something else. "Honey, you're just tired" or "I see that time of the month has rolled around again" dismisses women's anger by renaming it. Recurrent responses of that type, particularly when they cut across various situations such as home and work, may introduce ambiguity where emotional clarity would otherwise prevail.

Such ambiguity implies a voice awaiting development and expression. Anger recognized as such can occasion such development. As Audre Lorde puts it,

> Every woman has a well-stocked arsenal of anger potentially useful against those oppressions, personal and institutional, which brought that anger into being. Focused with precision it can become a powerful source of energy serving progress and change.

Lorde goes on to emphasize that when we express and take action against the circumstances angering us, anger becomes "a liberating and strengthening act of clarification. . . ." She understands, though, that women often fear anger:

> we were taught that our lives depended upon the good will of patriarchal power. The anger of others was to be avoided at all costs because there was nothing to be learned from it but pain, a judgment that we had been bad girls, come up lacking, not done what we were supposed to do.

Lorde is angrily aware of how some women have been browbeaten or battered into hiding their anger for fear of another scene of humiliation and pain. Nevertheless she believes other women can arrive at a place where they, too, declare that "Anger is what I do best. It is easier to be furious than to be yearning."[12]

Anger can thus strengthen our voices over time. It can move us more and more past that style of talk that "identifies us as uncommitted, as lacking in critical consciousness, which signifies a condition of oppression and exploitation. . . ."[13] Anger helps us to stop talking the way victims talk, pandering to the people who benefit from our subordination and sounding as if we have not the common sense to see who is winning what at our expense. Anger can get us *talking back,* that is, speaking as an equal with those positioned above us in one or another social hierarchy or system of domination.[14]

The typical struggle, then, is not to move from silence to speech but from speech to voice—to a dialogic style of talk that "compels listeners" and thus "is heard." Such a style bespeaks resistance. It "challenges politics of domination that would render us nameless and voiceless," and it "demand[s] that listeners even alter ways of hearing and being."[15] Voice thus expresses agency; it announces a capable subject; it signals an individual who is not interchangeable with every other woman; it affirms one's dignity. Contrary to some usages, one does not "find" her voice. One *makes* her voice one occasion at a time by matching her priorities and intentions with the words they demand rather than the words expected of feminine people.

At the individual level, voice achieves what "oppositional communities" establish at the group level. It criticizes, at least implicitly, "existing oppressive institutions and conceptual frameworks and provide[s] a central place to challenge racist, sexist, classist, heterosexist, speciesist, and other biases."[16] Whenever women and members of other subordinated groups say what they think and insist on being heard and resist being interrupted, their very actions imply a critique of the matrix of domination that assigns them lowly positions. Making one's voice thus means crafting one's own critique of and challenge to the status quo. It need not, however, mean disconnecting from the targets of one's anger. As Alice Walker puts it, "No matter in what anger I have written about the black man, I have never once let go of his hand."[17]

FEMINIST CONSCIOUSNESS

Making one's voice also means raising one's feminist consciousness. Such consciousness lies at one end of a continuum whose other end is victim consciousness or something like false consciousness, as we have seen. Feminist consciousness is more like common sense: a tried and true, resourceful consciousness capable of seeing the individual through her round of activities with her dignity intact, her selfhood expressed, and her projects advanced.

Awareness of gender subordination is a necessary but not a sufficient condition for the emergence of feminist consciousness. Such consciousness is an awareness that one's own subordination, while biographically unique, emanates from systems whereby other people like oneself are also subordinated and suffering. Also commonly informing feminist consciousness is awareness of other groupings disadvantaged by and exploited within the matrix of domination. During the early 1970s one theorist articulating such awareness was Sheila Rowbotham, who insisted that all subordinated people need to see themselves "as pitted against a total oppressive system rather than simply against the indignity . . . done to them through the subordination of their own kind. . . ." More recently, Linda Alcoff and Elizabeth Potter put it this way: "Each lives at a different node in the web of oppressions. Thus, to refer to a liberatory project as 'feminist' cannot mean that it is only for or about women, but that it is informed by or consistent with feminism." From a Marxist–feminist perspective, Teresa L. Ebert makes the same point:

> a truncated feminist theory (a theory only of women, by women, for women), no matter how reassuring and supportive it may seem, is in the long run complicit with the very economic and social forces of patriarchal capitalism that revolutionary feminists are struggling to overthrow.[18]

Feminist consciousness is thus an embracing consciousness. Its reach is such that feminists such as Patricia Ireland, president of the National Organization for Women, were prominent among those protesting so-called welfare reform during 1996, when the U.S. Congress passed three consecutive bills aimed at making social-assistance programs harsher. Organizations like NOW registered disgust not only because women and children are disproportionately hurt by such cutbacks but also because feminists often struggle against oppression in all its interlocked forms, including impoverishment. Feminist consciousness does, though, center on issues of gender, not because "patriarchal domination . . . is the foundation of all other oppressive structures but because it is that form of domination we are most likely to encounter in an ongoing way in everyday life." It is, moreover, that form of domination infiltrating family life and other intimate relationships, thus seizing hold of the personal.[19]

Feminist consciousness is also ultimately self-affirming. It struggles against senses of inferiority, pangs of self-doubt, and capitulations to self-loathing—inroads the sex/gender system makes into consciousness. As hooks notes, "A culture of domination demands of all its citizens self-negation."[20]

The self-negation demanded of women commonly revolves around caregiving. Ann Ferguson observes that "in all societies where male dominance is a part of the dominant culture, women are expected to perform the function of serving and caring for men and children. . . ."[21] Feminist consciousness overrides such mandatory caring. It insists on each woman's right to commit or not commit herself to caring for a partner, one or more children, or other individuals.

Such consciousness also looks toward fair exchanges on the social–emotional terrain where caring takes shape. It intervenes in the gender subordination that goes home with most women. As Bartky, the author of Reading 3, points out in the closing chapter of her book *Femininity and Domination,* feminist consciousness attunes us to how oppressive our daily acts of caring are when they get taken for granted as a husband's birthright, are left unreciprocated by a boyfriend whose masculinity precludes generosity of spirit, or get token recognition on designated days such as anniversaries or Valentine's Day. Feminist consciousness thus grows out of personal pain. It knows domination not as a concept but as an experience; it knows loneliness not as isolation but as neglect within a relationship; it knows hunger that gnaws at one's spirit, if not one's belly; it knows that language turns feeble in the face of oppression.

One example of such consciousness is Taslima Nasreen, the Bangladeshi feminist whose poetry, novels, and essays exude resistance as well as creativity. In 1994, she accepted Sweden's offer of protection after Islamic fundamentalists and the Bangladeshi government forced her out of Bangladesh in fear of her life. Indefatigable, Nasreen says that

> Compared to my feminist sisters in the West, I have written little about patriarchy, religion, man–woman relations and the rights of women. Nevertheless, I have been marked out as an enemy of Islam and of my own society. I do not mind being hunted by mullahs and their frenzied followers. I am happy that I have penetrated a bastion of patriarchy guarded by frantic religious orthodoxies. . . . I use the refined vocabulary of men and throw questions into their faces as a free human being.[22]

Feminist consciousness also comprises awareness of covert, not just overt, ways of keeping women down. Paramount among the covert forms are those unofficially regulating women's bodies. Feminist consciousness thus promotes an awareness that

> All the oppressed—the obviously exploited and others—share in the minds of the privileged a defining connection to the body, whether it is seen primarily as the laboring body, the sexual body, the body insufficiently under the control of the rational will, or some combination of these. The privileged are precisely those who are defined not by the meanings and uses of their bodies for others but by their ability either to control their bodies for their own ends or to seem to exist virtually bodilessly. They are those who have conquered the sexual, dependent, mortal, and messy parts of themselves—in part by projecting all those qualities onto others, whom they thereby earn the right to dominate and, if the occasion arises, exploit.[23]

Feminist consciousness grows out of and reacts against such exploitation. All the while, it sees women's bodies regulated not only in dramatic forms such as the female genital mutilation practiced in more than 25 countries[24] or the wife battering that occurs in every country but also in the daily routines exploiting women's labor.

Feminist consciousness also recognizes how women get pushed to the sidelines of social life. Feminist theorists call the social sidelines the *margins* of formal organizations, social situations, and societal institutions. As Scheman points out, feminists contrast marginality with privilege; the margin starkly lacks privilege.[25] Yet the margin can hold promise, even power. Hooks, for example, distinguishes "between that marginality which is imposed by oppressive structures and that marginality one chooses as site of resistance—as location of radical openness and possibility."[26] Hers is a feminist consciousness pointing toward the value of marginality as a potential source of critical consciousness. Bartky's stance resonates with hooks's.[27]

Following Frantz Fanon, Bartky emphasizes in Reading 3 that psychological oppression amounts to "'psychic alienation'—the estrangement or separating of a person from some of the essential attributes of personhood." She ties such alienation to the alienation of labor and in turn links both to the matrix of domination. Hers is a feminist consciousness wide in its angle of vision and guarded in its hopes for a better world. In *Femininity and Domination,* Bartky does argue that despite "its disturbing aspects" feminist consciousness

> is an immeasurable advance over that false consciousness which it replaces. The scales fall from our eyes. We are no longer required to struggle against unreal enemies, to put others' interests ahead of our own, or to hate ourselves. We begin to understand why so many of us are lacking any genuine conviction of personal worth. Understanding, even beginning to understand this, makes it possible to *change.* Coming to see things differently, we are able to make out possibilities for liberating collective action and for unprecedented personal growth, possibilities which a deceptive sexist social reality had heretofore concealed.[28]

Like Bartky, Sandoval emphasizes that feminist consciousness is oppositional. In Reading 4 she draws from U.S. feminists of color to delineate five varieties of oppositional consciousness. Her delineation builds up around a contrast between (white) hegemonic feminism and (U.S. Third World) marginalized feminisms. As you acquaint yourself with Sandoval's theorizing, bear in mind that "hegemonic" does not mean monolithic. Rather, hegemony has to do with which ideas hold sway—that is, garner greater credibility and legitimacy—in a given cultural and political context. Sandoval is thus arguing not that white feminists all think alike but that what gets seen as "real" feminism comes from white women. Much in line with the theorizing discussed in Chapter 9, Sandoval is also arguing that that oppositional consciousness she calls "differential" is *performative* (or continuously enacted and constructed). Such consciousness is associated with a flexible identity and a border-crossing outlook.

Besides its attention to marginality as a site of opposition, feminist consciousness carries in its wake a burgeoning awareness that "Pleasure is the opposite of oppression. . . ."[29] The person developing feminist consciousness is on the brink of experiencing the pleasures of sustainable freedom achieved not by inverting oppressive notions but by "vacating" them, thereby making them "null and void."[30] An example is the sexual objectification Bartky describes in Reading 3. One promotes freedom not by inverting the idea so that men become its objects but by emptying the idea of lived content. Another illustrative construct is "full-time mother," which implies that some mothers are part-time or temporary mothers. One advances freedom not by constructing "full-time father" but by abandoning the idea of full-time versus other-time parents. Parenthood is responsible or not, a notion that gets buried beneath notions such as full-time mother.

The opposite of oppression, then, is the abiding pleasure that comes with liberation. This pleasure entails "humor or lightheartedness—the humor that comes from seeing all categories, all explanations, all identities as provisional. Such a sense is rooted in the appreciation of ambiguity. . . ."[31] Feminist consciousness thus finds in ambiguity not grounds for being overwhelmed but occasions for being tantalized. It opens us to the pleasures of self-nurturance and self-affirmation as well as the pleasures of collective action and female solidarity, no matter how trying at times. Feminist consciousness is a pathway "to the strength and power that emerge from sustained resistance"; it attests to how liberatory struggle "can be healing, can protect us from dehumanization and despair."[32]

In the margins of social life, then, lie pathways to hard-won pleasures. Women of all colors, of all religious and spiritual persuasions, with all sorts of bodies, of all ages, lesbian and bisexual and heterosexual, Arab American and Korean American and Italian American, working- and middle-class, southern and midwestern can all find in their consciousness the space where feminism can take root, where struggle can begin and pleasure can loom larger and larger on the horizon. In *The Female Eunuch* (1970), Germaine Greer said that such pleasure

does not mean riotous glee, but it does mean the purposive employment of energy in a self-chosen enterprise. It does mean pride and confidence. It does mean communication and cooperation with others based on delight in their company and your own. To be emancipated from helplessness and need and walk freely upon the earth that is your birthright. To refuse hobbles and deformity and take possession of your body and glory in its power, accepting its own laws of loveliness. To have something to desire, something to make, something to achieve, and at last something genuine to give. To be free from guilt and shame and the tireless self-discipline of women.[33]

In feminist consciousness lies great promise. Although the hopes it inculcates take shape from the specific hardships of a woman's subordination, feminist consciousness promises all women a better life through social change and cultural transformation (see Chapter 11). Feminism invigorates consciousness. In the process it undercuts hierarchy, challenges domination, and tempers oppression.

NOTES

1. Gayle Rubin, "The Traffic in Women: Notes on the 'Political Economy' of Sex" in Rayna Reiter (ed.), *Toward an Anthropology of Women* (New York: Monthly Review Press, 1974), pp. 157–210. Rubin has since repudiated this notion, as Kathleen Martindale (among others) has pointed out. Broadly, Rubin's later work emphasizes sexuality more than gender, thus tilting it more toward lesbian and gay studies than women's studies as such; see Kathleen Martindale, *Un/Popular Culture: Lesbian Writing after the Sex Wars* (Albany: State University of New York Press, 1997), pp. 8–10.
2. Patricia Hill Collins, *Black Feminist Thought: Knowledge, Consciousness, and the Politics of Empowerment* (New York: Routledge, 1991).
3. Dorothy E. Smith, *Texts, Facts, and Femininity: Exploring the Relations of Ruling* (New York: Routledge, 1990), p. 6.
4. bell hooks, *Teaching to Transgress: Education as the Practice of Freedom* (New York: Routledge, 1994), pp. 63, 98. Mary Romero has done some of the best studies of this situation; see her "Life as the Maid's Daughter: An Exploration of the Everyday Boundaries of Race, Class, and Gender" in Donna Stanton and Abigail Stewart (eds.), *Feminisms in the Academy* (Ann Arbor: University of Michigan Press, 1995).
5. bell hooks, *Talking Back: Thinking Feminist, Thinking Black* (Boston: South End Press, 1989), p. 21; hooks, *Teaching to Transgress,* pp. 98–100.
6. bell hooks, *Black Looks: Race and Representation* (Boston: South End Press, 1992), p. 18. Hooks writes specifically about black people enacting racist stereotypes.
7. Patricia Searles and Ronald J. Berger, "The Feminist Self-Defense Movement: A Case Study," *Gender & Society* 1, no. 1 (March 1987), p. 65.
8. bell hooks, *Killing Rage: Ending Racism* (New York: Henry Holt and Co., 1995), pp. 53, 54.
9. Smith, *Texts, Facts, and Femininity,* p. 191. For a superb alternative to "victim" among women, see Martha T. McCluskey, "Transforming Victimization," TIKKUN 9, no. 2 (March/April 1994), pp. 54–6.
10. Naomi Scheman, *Engenderings: Constructions of Knowledge, Authority, and Privilege* (New York: Routledge, 1993), pp. 25–6.
11. *Ibid.,* pp. 26, 28.

12. Audre Lorde, *Sister Outsider: Essays and Speeches* (Freedom, CA: The Crossing Press, 1984), pp. 127, 131, 153.
13. hooks, *Talking Back,* p. 18.
14. Cf. *ibid.,* p. 5.
15. *Ibid.,* pp. 6, 7, 8, 16.
16. Lori Gruen, "Toward an Ecofeminist Moral Epistemology" in Karen J. Warren (ed.), *Ecological Feminism* (London and New York: Routledge, 1994), p. 128. The phrase "oppositional community" comes from an unpublished paper by Ann Ferguson; the term "speciesist" refers to someone who regards life on the planet as a hierarchy of species with human beings at the top.
17. Alice Walker, *Living by the Word: Selected Writings 1973–1987* (New York: Harcourt Brace Jovanovich, 1988), p. 95.
18. Sheila Rowbotham, *Women, Resistance and Revolution: A History of Women and Revolution in the Modern World* (New York: Vintage Books, 1974), p. 109; Linda Alcoff and Elizabeth Potter, "Introduction: When Feminisms Intersect Epistemology" in Linda Alcoff and Elizabeth Potter (eds.), *Feminist Epistemologies* (New York: Routledge, 1993), p. 4; Teresa L. Ebert, *Ludic Feminism and After: Postmodernism, Desire, and Labor in Late Capitalism* (Ann Arbor: University of Michigan Press, 1996), p. xiii.
19. *Ibid.,* pp. 21, 22.
20. bell hooks, *Black Looks,* p. 18.
21. Ann Ferguson, *Sexual Democracy: Women, Oppression, and Revolution* (Boulder, CO: Westview Press, 1991), p. 116.
22. Taslima Nasreen, "The Oppressor and the Oppressed," *Women: A Cultural Review* 6, no. 1 (Summer 1995), p. 117.
23. Scheman, *Engenderings,* p. 88.
24. Ann Louise Bardach, "Tearing Off the Veil," *Vanity Fair* 56 (August 1993), p. 126.
25. Scheman, *Engenderings,* p. 235.
26. bell hooks, *Yearning: Race, Gender, and Cultural Politics* (Boston: South End Press, 1990), p. 153.
27. Bat-Ami Bar On, "Reading Bartky: Identity, Identification, and Critical Self-Reflection," *Hypatia: A Journal of Feminist Philosophy* 8 (Winter 1993), p. 161.
28. Sandra Lee Bartky, *Femininity and Domination: Studies in the Phenomenology of Oppression* (New York: Routledge, 1990), p. 21.
29. Graciela Hierro, "Gender and Power," *Hypatia* 9 (Winter 1994), p. 182.
30. Jeffner Allen, "Motherhood: The Annihilation of Women" in Joyce Trebilcot (ed.), *Mothering: Essays in Feminist Theory* (Totowa, NJ: Rowman & Allanheld, 1984), p. 315.
31. Shane Phelan, *Identity Politics: Lesbian Politics and the Limits of Community* (Philadelphia: Temple University Press, 1989), pp. 156–7.
32. hooks, *Talking Back,* p. 8.
33. Germaine Greer, *The Female Eunuch* (New York: Bantam Books, 1970; reprint, 1972), p. 351 (page citations are to the reprint edition).

On Psychological Oppression

Sandra Lee Bartky

In *Black Skin, White Masks,* Frantz Fanon offers an anguished and eloquent description of the psychological effects of colonialism on the colonized, a "clinical study" of what he calls the "psychic alienation of the black man." "Those who recognize themselves in it," he says, "will have made a step forward,"[1] Fanon's black American readers saw at once that he had captured the corrosive effects not only of classic colonial oppression but of domestic racism too, and that his study fitted well the picture of black America as an internal colony. Without wanting in any way to diminish the oppressive and stifling realities of black experience that Fanon reveals, let me say that I, a white woman, recognize myself in this book too, not only in my "shameful livery of white incomprehension,"[2] but as myself the victim of a "psychic alienation" similar to the one Fanon has described. In this paper I shall try to explore that moment of recognition, to reveal the ways in which the psychological effects of sexist oppression resemble those of racism and colonialism.

To oppress, says Webster, is "to lie heavy on, to weigh down, to exercise harsh dominion over." When we describe a people as oppressed, what we have in mind most often is an oppression that is economic and political in character. But recent liberation movements, the black liberation movement and the women's movement in particular, have brought to light forms of oppression that are not immediately economic or political. It is possible to be oppressed in ways that need involve neither physical deprivation, legal inequality, not economic exploitation;[3] one can be oppressed psychologically—the "psychic alienation" of which Fanon speaks. To be psychologically oppressed is to be weighed down in your mind; it is to have a harsh dominion exercised over your self-esteem. The psychologically oppressed become their own oppressors; they come to exercise harsh dominion over their own self-esteem. Differently put, psychological oppression can be regarded as the "internalization of intimations of inferiority."[4]

Like economic oppression, psychological oppression is institutionalized and systematic; it serves to make the work of domination easier by breaking the spirit of the dominated and by rendering them incapable of understanding the nature of those agencies responsible for their subjugation. This allows those who benefit from the established order of things to maintain their ascendancy with more appearance of legitimacy and with less recourse to overt acts of violence than they might otherwise require. Now, poverty and powerlessness can destroy a person's self-esteem, and the fact that one occupies an inferior position in society is all too often racked up to one's being an inferior sort of person. Clearly, then, economic and political oppression are themselves psychologically oppressive. But there are unique modes of psychological oppression that can be distinguished from the usual forms of economic and political domination. Fanon offers a series of what are essentially phenomenological descriptions of psychic alienation.[5] In spite of considerable overlapping, the experiences of oppression he describes fall into three categories: stereotyping, cultural domination, and sexual objectification. These, I shall contend, are some of the ways in which the terrible messages of inferiority can be delivered even to those who may enjoy certain material benefits; they are special modes of psychic alienation. In what follows, I shall examine some of the ways in which American women—white women and women of color—are stereotyped, culturally dominated, and sexually objectified. In the course of the discussion, I shall argue that our ordinary concept of oppression needs to be altered and expanded, for it is too restricted to encompass what an analysis of psychological oppression reveals about the nature of oppression in general. Finally, I shall be concerned throughout to show how both fragmentation and mystification are present in each mode of psychological oppression, although in varying degrees: fragmentation, the splitting of the whole person into parts of a person which, in stereotyping, may take the form of a war between a "true" and "false" self—or, in sexual objectification, the form of an often coerced and degrading identification of a person with her body; mystification, the systematic obscuring of both the reality and agencies of psychological oppression so that its intended effect, the depreciated self, is lived out as destiny, guilt, or neurosis.

The stereotypes that sustain sexism are similar in many ways to those that sustain racism. Like white women, black and brown persons of both sexes have been regarded as childlike, happiest when they are occupying their "place"; more intuitive than rational, more spontaneous than deliberate, closer to nature, and less capable of substantial cultural accomplishment. Black men and women of all races have been victims of sexual stereotyping: the black man and the black women, like the "Latin spitfire," are lustful and hotblooded; they are thought to lack the capacities for instinctual control that distinguish people from animals. What is seen as an excess in persons of color appears as a deficiency in the white woman; comparatively frigid, she has been, nonetheless, defined by sexuality as well, here her reproductive role or function. In regard to capability and competence, black women have, again, an excess of what in white women is a deficiency. White women have been seen as incapable and incompetent: no matter, for these are traits of the truly feminine woman. Black women, on the other

hand, have been seen as overly capable, hence, as unfeminine bitches who threaten, through their very competence, to castrate their men.

Stereotyping is morally reprehensible as well as psychologically oppressive on two counts, at least. First, it can hardly be expected that those who hold a set of stereotyped beliefs about the sort of person I am will understand my needs or even respect my rights. Second, suppose that I, the object of some stereotype, believe in it myself—for why should I not believe what everyone else believes? I may then find it difficult to achieve what existentialists call an authentic choice of self, or what some psychologists have regarded as a state of self-actualization. Moral philosophers have quite correctly placed a high value, sometimes the highest value, on the development of autonomy and moral agency. Clearly, the economic and political domination of women—our concrete powerlessness—is what threatens our autonomy most. But stereotyping, in its own way, threatens our self-determination too. Even when economic and political obstacles on the path to autonomy are removed, a depreciated alter ego still blocks the way. It is hard enough for me to determine what sort of person I am or ought to try to become without being shadowed by an alternate self, a truncated and inferior self that I have, in some sense, been doomed to be all the time. For many, the prefabricated self triumphs over a more authentic self which, with work and encouragement, might sometime have emerged. For the talented few, retreat into the *imago* is raised to the status of art of comedy. Muhammad Ali has made himself what he could scarcely escape being made into—personification of Primitive Man; while Zsa Zsa Gabor is not so much a woman as the parody of a woman.

Female stereotypes threaten the autonomy of women not only by virtue of their existence but also by virtue of their content.[6] In the conventional portrait women deny their femininity when they undertake action that is too self-regarding or independent. As we have seen, black women are condemned (often by black men) for supposedly having done this already; white women stand under an injunction not to follow their example. Many women in many places lacked (and many still lack) the elementary right to choose our own mates; but for some women even in our own society today, this is virtually the only major decision we are thought capable of making without putting our womanly nature in danger; what follows ever after is or ought to be a properly feminine submission to the decisions of men. We cannot be autonomous, as men are thought to be autonomous, without in some sense ceasing to be women. When one considers how interwoven are traditional female stereotypes with traditional female roles—and these, in turn, with the ways in which we are socialized—all this is seen in an even more sinister light: White women, at least, are psychologically conditioned not to pursue the kind of autonomous development that is held by the culture to be a constitutive feature of masculinity.

The truncated self I am to be is not something manufactured out there by an anonymous Other which I encounter only in the pages of *Playboy* or the *Ladies' Home Journal;* it is inside of me, a part of myself. I may become infatuated with my feminine persona and waste my powers in the more or less hopeless pursuit of a *Vogue* figure, the look of an *Essence* model, or a home that "expresses my personality." Or I may find the parts of myself fragmented and the fragments at war with one another. Women are only now learning to identify and struggle against the forces that have laid these psychic burdens upon us. More often than not, we live out this struggle, which is really a struggle against oppression, in a mystified way: What we are enduring we believe to be entirely intrapsychic in character, the result of immaturity, maladjustment, or even neurosis.

Tyler, the great classical anthropologist, defined culture as all the items in the general life of a people. To claim that women are victims of cultural domination is to claim that all the items in the general life of our people—our language,

our institutions, our art and literature, our popular culture—are sexist; that all, to a greater or lesser degree, manifest male supremacy. There is some exaggeration in this claim, but not much. Unlike the black colonial whom Fanon describes with such pathos, women qua women are not now in possession of an alternate culture, a "native" culture which, even if regarded by everyone, including ourselves, as decidedly inferior to the dominant culture, we could at least recognize as our own. However degraded or distorted an image of ourselves we see reflected in the patriarchal culture, the culture of our men is still our culture. Certainly in some respects, the condition of women is like the condition of a colonized people. But we are not a colonized people; we have never been more than half a people.[7]

This lack of cultural autonomy has several important consequences for an understanding of the condition of women. A culture has a global character; hence, the limits of my culture are the limits of my world. The subordination of women, then, because it is so pervasive a feature of my culture, will (if uncontested) appear to be natural—and because it is natural, unalterable. Unlike a colonized people, women have no memory of a "time before": a time before the masters came, a time before we were subjugated and ruled. Further, since one function of cultural identity is to allow me to distinguish those who are like me from those who are not, I may feel more kinship with those who share my culture, even though they oppress me, than with the women of another culture, whose whole experience of life may well be closer to my own than to any man's.

Our true situation in regard to male supremacist culture is one of domination and exclusion. But this manifests itself in an extremely deceptive way; mystification once more holds sway. Our relative absence from the "higher" culture is taken as proof that we are unable to participate in it ("Why are there no great women artists?"). Theories of the female nature must then be brought forward to try to account for this.[8] The splitting or fragmenting of women's consciousness which takes place in the cultural sphere is also apparent. While remaining myself, I must at the same time transform myself into that abstract and "universal" subject for whom cultural artifacts are made and whose values and experience they express. This subject is not universal at all, however, but *male.* Thus, I must approve the taming of the shrew, laugh at the mother-in-law or the dumb blonde, and somehow identify with all those heroes of fiction from Faust to the personae of Norman Mailer and Henry Miller, whose *Bildungsgeschichten* involve the sexual exploitation of women. Women of color have, of course, a special problem: The dominant cultural subject is not only male, but *white,* so their cultural alienation is doubled; they are expected to assimilate cultural motifs that are not only masculinist but racist.[9]

Women of all races and ethnicities, like Fanon's "black man," are subject not only to stereotyping and cultural depreciation but to sexual objectification as well. Even though much has been written about sexual objectification in the literature of the women's movement, the notion itself is complex, obscure, and much in need of philosophical clarification. I offer the following preliminary characterization of sexual objectification: A person is sexually objectified when her sexual parts or sexual functions are separated out from the rest of her personality and reduced to the status of mere instruments or else regarded as if they were capable of representing her. On this definition, then, the prostitute would be a victim of sexual objectification, as would the *Playboy* bunny, the female breeder, and the bathing beauty.

To say that the sexual part of a person is regarded as if it could represent her is to imply that it cannot, that the part and the whole are incommensurable. But surely there are times, in the sexual embrace perhaps, when a woman might want to be regarded as nothing but a sexually intoxicating body and when attention paid to some other aspect of her person—say,

to her mathematical ability—would be absurdly out of place. If sexual relations involve some sexual objectification, then it becomes necessary to distinguish situations in which sexual objectification is oppressive from the sorts of situations in which it is not.[10] The identification of a person with her sexuality becomes oppressive, one might venture, when such an identification becomes habitually extended into every area of her experience. To be routinely perceived by others in a sexual light on occasions when such a perception is inappropriate is to have one's very being subjected to that compulsive sexualization that has been the traditional lot of both white women and black men and women of color generally. "For the majority of white men," says Fanon, "the Negro is the incarnation of a genital potency beyond all moralities and prohibitions."[11] Later in *Black Skin, White Masks,* he writes that "the Negro is the genital."[12]

One way to be sexually objectified, then, is to be the object of a kind of perception, unwelcome and inappropriate, that takes the part for the whole. An example may make this clearer. A young woman was recently interviewed for a teaching job in philosophy by the academic chairman of a large department. During most of the interview, so she reported, the man stared fixedly at her breasts. In this situation, the woman is a bosom, not a job candidate. Was this department chairman guilty only of a confusion between business and pleasure? Scarcely. He stares at her breasts for his sake, not hers. Her wants and needs not only play no role in the encounter but, because of the direction of his attention, she is discomfited, feels humiliated, and performs badly. Not surprisingly, she fails to get the job. Much of the time, sexual objectification occurs independently of what women want; it is something done to us against our will. It is clear from this example that the objectifying perception that splits a person into parts serves to elevate one interest above another. Now it stands revealed not only as a way of perceiving, but as a way of maintaining dominance as well. It is not clear to me that the sexual and nonsexual spheres of experience can or ought to be kept separate forever (Marcuse, for one, has envisioned the eroticization of all areas of human life); but as things stand now, sexualization is one way of fixing disadvantaged persons in their disadvantage, to their clear detriment and within a narrow and repressive eros.

Consider now a second example of the way in which that fragmenting perception, which is so large an ingredient in the sexual objectification of women, serves to maintain the dominance of men. It is a fine spring day, and with an utter lack of self-consciousness, I am bouncing down the street. Suddenly I hear men's voices. Catcalls and whistles fill the air. These noises are clearly sexual in intent and they are meant for me; they come from across the street. I freeze. As Sartre would say, I have been petrified by the gaze of the Other. My face flushes and my motions become stiff and self-conscious. The body which only a moment before I inhabited with such ease now floods my consciousness. I have been made into an object. While it is true that for these men I am nothing but, let us say, a "nice piece of ass," there is more involved in this encounter than their mere fragmented perception of me. They could, after all, have enjoyed me in silence. Blissfully unaware, breasts bouncing, eyes on the birds in the trees, I could have passed by without having been turned to stone. But I must be *made* to know that I am a "nice piece of ass": I must be made to see myself as they see me. There is an element of compulsion in this encounter, in this being-made-to-be-aware of one's own flesh; like being made to apologize, it is humiliating. It is unclear what role is played by sexual arousal or even sexual connoisseurship in encounters like these. What I describe seems less the spontaneous expression of a healthy eroticism than a ritual of subjugation.

Sexual objectification as I have characterized it involves two persons: the one who objectifies and the one who is objectified. But the observer and the one observed can be the same person. I can, of course, take pleasure in my own body as

another might take pleasure in it and it would be naive not to notice that there are delights of a narcissistic kind that go along with the status "sex object." But the extent to which the identification of women with their bodies feeds an essentially infantile narcissism—an attitude of mind in keeping with our forced infantilization in other areas of life—is, at least for me, an open question. Subject to the evaluating eye of the male connoisseur, women learn to evaluate themselves first and best. Our identities can no more be kept separate from the appearance of our bodies than they can be kept separate from the shadow-selves of the female stereotype. "Much of a young woman's identity is already defined in her kind of attractiveness and in the selectivity of her search for the man (or men) by whom she wishes to be sought."[13] There is something obsessional in the preoccupation of many women with their bodies, although the magnitude of the obsession will vary somewhat with the presence or absence in a woman's life of other sources of self-esteem and with her capacity to gain a living independent of her looks. Surrounded on all sides by images of perfect female beauty—for, in modern advertising, the needs of capitalism and the traditional values of patriarchy are happily married—of course we fall short. The narcissism encouraged by our identification with the body is shattered by these images. Whose nose is not the wrong shape, whose hips are not too wide or too narrow? Anyone who believes that such concerns are too trivial to weigh very heavily with most women has failed to grasp the realities of the feminine condition.

The idea that women ought always to make themselves as pleasing to the eye as possible is very widespread indeed. It was dismaying to come across this passage in a paper written by eminent Marxist humanist in defense of the contemporary women's movement:

There is no reason why a woman's liberation activist should not try to look pretty and attractive. One of the universal human aspirations of all times was to raise reality to the level of art, to make the world more beautiful, to be more beautiful within given limits. Beauty is a value in itself; it will always be respected and will attract—to be sure various forms of beauty but not to the exclusion of physical beauty. A woman does not become a sex object in herself, or only because of her pretty appearance. She becomes a sexual object in relationship, when she allows a man to treat her in a certain depersonalizing, degrading way; and vice versa, a woman does not become a sexual subject by neglecting her appearance.[14]

It is not for the sake of mere men that we women—not just we women, but we women's liberation activists—ought to look "pretty and attractive," but for the sake of something much more exalted: for the sake of beauty. This preoccupation with the way we look and the fear that women might stop trying to make themselves pretty and attractive (so as to "raise reality to the level of art") would be a species of objectification anywhere; but it is absurdly out of place in a paper on women's emancipation. It is as if an essay on the black liberation movement were to end by admonishing blacks not to forget their natural rhythm, or as if Marx had warned the workers of the world not to neglect their appearance while throwing off their chains.

Markovic's concern with women's appearance merely reflects a larger cultural preoccupation. It is a fact that women in our society are regarded as having a virtual duty "to make the most of what we have." But the imperative not to neglect our appearance suggests that we can neglect it, that it is within our power to make ourselves look better—not just neater and cleaner, but prettier and more attractive. What is presupposed by this is that we don't look good enough already, that attention to the ordinary standards of hygiene would be insufficient, that there is something wrong with us as we are. Here, the "intimations of inferiority" are clear: Not only must we continue to produce ourselves as beautiful bodies, but the bodies we have to work with are deficient to begin with. Even within an already inferiorized identity (i.e., the identity of one who is principally and most im-

portantly a body), I turn out once more to be inferior, for the body I am to be, never sufficient unto itself, stands forever in need of plucking or painting, of slimming down or fattening up, of firming or flattening.

The foregoing examination of three modes of psychological oppression, so it appears, points up the need for an alteration in our ordinary concept of oppression. Oppression, I believe, is ordinarily conceived in too limited a fashion. This has placed undue restrictions both on our understanding of what oppression itself is and on the categories of persons we might want to classify as oppressed. Consider, for example, the following paradigmatic case of oppression:

> And the Egyptians made the children of Israel to serve with rigor; and they made their lives bitter with hard bondage, in mortar and in brick, and in all manner of service in the field; all their service wherein they made them serve, was with rigor.[15]

Here the Egyptians, one group of persons, exercise harsh dominion over the Israelites, another group of persons. It is not suggested that the Israelites, however great their sufferings, have lost their integrity and wholeness *qua* persons. But psychological oppression is dehumanizing and depersonalizing; it attacks the person in her personhood. I mean by this that the nature of psychological oppression is such that the oppressor and oppressed alike come to doubt that the oppressed have the capacity to do the sorts of things that only persons can do, to be what persons, in the fullest sense of the term, can be. The possession of autonomy, for example, is widely thought to distinguish persons from nonpersons; but some female stereotypes, as we have seen, threaten the autonomy of women. Oppressed people might or might not be in a position to exercise their autonomy, but the psychologically oppressed may come to believe that they lack the capacity to be autonomous whatever their position.

Similarly, the creation of culture is a distinctly human function, perhaps the most human function. In its cultural life, a group is able to affirm its values and to grasp its identity in acts of self-reflection. Frequently, oppressed persons, cut off from the cultural apparatus, are denied the exercise of this function entirely. To the extent that we are able to catch sight of ourselves in the dominant culture at all, the images we see are distorted or demeaning. Finally, sexual objectification leads to the identification of those who undergo it with what is both human and not quite human—the body. Thus, psychological oppression is just what Fanon said it was—"psychic alienation"—the estrangement or separating of a person from some of the essential attributes of personhood.

Mystification surrounds these processes of human estrangement. The special modes of psychological oppression can be regarded as some of the many ways in which messages of inferiority are delivered to those who are to occupy an inferior position in society. But it is important to remember that messages of this sort are neither sent nor received in an unambiguous way. We are taught that white women and (among others) black men and women are deficient in those capacities that distinguish persons from nonpersons, but at the same time we are assured that we are persons after all. *Of course* women are persons; *of course* blacks are human beings. Who but the lunatic fringe would deny it? The Antillean Negro, Fanon is fond of repeating, is a *Frenchman.* The official ideology announces with conviction that "all men are created equal"; and in spite of the suspect way in which this otherwise noble assertion is phrased, we women learn that they mean to include us after all.

It is itself psychologically oppressive both to believe and at the same time not to believe that one is inferior—in other words, to believe a contradiction. Lacking an analysis of the larger system of social relations which produced it, one can only make sense of this contradiction in two ways. First, while accepting in some quite formal sense the proposition that "all men are created equal," I can believe, inconsistently, what my oppressors have always believed: that some types of persons are less equal than others. I may then live

out my membership in my sex or race in *shame;* I am "only a woman" or "just a nigger." Or, somewhat more consistently, I may reject entirely the belief that my disadvantage is generic; but having still to account for it somehow, I may locate the cause squarely within myself, a bad destiny of an entirely private sort—a character flaw, an "inferiority complex," or a neurosis.

Many oppressed persons come to regard themselves as uniquely unable to satisfy normal criteria of psychological health or moral adequacy. To believe that my inferiority is a function of the kind of person I am may make me ashamed of being one of *this* kind. On the other hand, a lack I share with many others just because of an accident of birth would be unfortunate indeed, but at least I would not have to regard myself as having failed uniquely to measure up to standards that people like myself are expected to meet. It should be pointed out, however, that both of these "resolutions"—the ascription of one's inferiority to idiosyncratic or else to generic causes—produces a "poor self-image," a bloodless term of the behavioral sciences that refers to a very wide variety of possible ways to suffer.[16]

To take one's oppression to be an inherent flaw of birth, or of psychology, is to have what Marxists have characterized as "false consciousness." systematically deceived as we are about the nature and origin of our unhappiness, our struggles are directed inward toward the self, or toward other similar selves in whom we may see our deficiencies mirrored, not outward upon those social forces responsible for our predicament. Like the psychologically disturbed, the psychologically oppressed often lack a viable identity. Frequently we are unable to make sense of our own impulses or feelings, not only because our drama of fragmentation gets played out on an inner psychic stage, but because we are forced to find our way about in a world which presents itself to us in a masked and deceptive fashion. Regarded as persons, yet depersonalized, we are treated by our society the way the parents of some schizophrenics are said by

R. D. Laing to treat their children—professing love at the very moment they shrink from their children's touch.

In sum, then, to be psychologically oppressed is to be caught in the double bind of a society which both affirms my human status and at the same time bars me from the exercise of many of those typically human functions that bestow this status. To be denied an autonomous choice of self, forbidden cultural expression, and condemned to the immanence of mere bodily being is to be cut off from the sorts of activities that define what is to be human. A person whose being has been subjected to these cleavages may be described as "alienated." Alienation in any form causes a rupture within the human person, an estrangement from self, a "splintering of human nature into a number of misbegotten parts."[17] Any adequate theory of the nature and varieties of human alienation, then, must encompass psychological oppression—or, to use Fanon's term once more, "psychic alienation."

Much has been written about alienation, but it is Marx's theory of alienation that speaks most compellingly to the concerns of feminist political theory. Alienation for Marx is primarily the alienation of labor. What distinguishes human beings from animals is "labor"—for Marx, the free, conscious, and creative transformation of nature in accordance with human needs. But under capitalism, workers are alienated in production, estranged from the products of their labor, from their own productive activity, and from their fellow workers.

Human productive activity, according to Marx, is "objectified" in its products. What this means is that we are able to grasp ourselves reflectively primarily in the things we have produced; human needs and powers become concrete "in their products as the amount and type of change which their exercise has brought about."[18] But in capitalist production, the capitalist has a right to appropriate what workers have produced. Thus, the product goes to augment capital, where it becomes part of an alien force exercising power over those who produced

it. An "objectification" or extension of the worker's self, the product is split off from this self and turned against it. But workers are alienated not only from the products they produce but from their own laboring activity as well, for labor under capitalism is not, as labor should be, an occasion for human self-realization but mere drudgery which "mortifies the body and ruins the mind."[19] The worker's labor "is therefore not voluntary, but coerced; it is forced labor. It is therefore not the satisfaction of a need; it is merely a means to satisfy needs external to it."[20] When the free and creative productive activity that should define human functioning is reduced to a mere means to sustain life, to "forced labor," workers suffer fragmentation and loss of self. Since labor is the most characteristic human life activity, to be alienated from one's own labor is to be estranged from oneself.

In many ways, psychic alienation and the alienation of labor are profoundly alike. Both involve a splitting off of human functions from the human person, a forbidding of activities thought to be essential to a fully human existence. Both subject the individual to fragmentation and impoverishment. Alienation is not a condition into which someone might stumble by accident; it has come both to the victim of psychological oppression and to the alienated worker from without, as a usurpation by someone else of what is, by rights, *not his to usurp*.[21] Alienation occurs in each case when activities which not only belong to the domain of the self but define, in large measure, the proper functioning of this self, fall under the control of others. To be a victim of alienation is to have a part of one's being stolen by another. Both psychic alienation and the alienation of labor might be regarded as varieties of alienated productivity. From this perspective, cultural domination would be the estrangement or alienation of production in the cultural sphere; while the subjective effects of stereotyping as well as the self-objectification that regularly accompanies sexual objectification could be interpreted as an alienation in the production of one's own person.

All the modes of oppression—psychological, political, and economic—and the kinds of alienation they generate serve to maintain a vast system of privilege—privilege of race, of sex, and of class. Every mode of oppression within the system has its own part to play, but each serves to support and to maintain the others. Thus, for example, the assault on the self-esteem of white women and of black persons of both sexes prepares us for the historic role that a disproportionate number of us are destined to play within the process of production: that of a cheap or reserve labor supply. Class oppression, in turn, encourages those who are somewhat higher in the hierarchies of race or gender to cling to a false sense of superiority—a poor compensation indeed. Because of the interlocking character of the modes of oppression, I think it highly unlikely that any form of oppression will disappear entirely until the system of oppression as a whole is overthrown.

NOTES

1. Frantz Fanon, *Black Skins, White Masks* (New York: Grove Press, 1967), p. 12.
2. *Ibid.*
3. For an excellent comparison of the concepts of exploitation and oppression, see Judith Farr Tormey, "Exploitation, Oppression and Self-Sacrifice," in *Women and Philosophy,* ed. Carol C. Gould and Marx W. Wartofsky (New York: G. P. Putnam's Sons, 1976), pp. 206–21.
4. Joyce Mitchell Cook, paper delivered at Philosophy and the Black Liberation Struggle Conference, University of Illinois, Chicago Circle, November 19–20, 1970.
5. Fanon's phenomenology of oppression, however, is almost entirely a phenomenology of the oppression of colonized *men.* He seems unaware of the ways in which the oppression of women by their men in the societies he examines is itself similar to the colonization of natives by Europeans. Sometimes, as in *A Dying Colonialism* (New York: Grove Press, 1968), he goes so far

as to defend the clinging to oppressive practices, such as the sequestration of women in Moslem countries, as an authentic resistance by indigenous people to Western cultural intrusion. For a penetrating critique of Fanon's attitude toward women, see Barbara Burris, "Fourth World Manifesto," in *Radical Feminism,* ed. A. Koedt, E. Levine, and A. Rapone (New York: Quadrangle, 1973), pp. 322–57.
6. I have in mind Abraham Maslow's concept of autonomy, a notion which has the advantage of being neutral as regards the controversy between free will and determinism. For Maslow, the sources of behavior of autonomous or "psychologically free" individuals are more internal than reactive: "Such people become far more self-sufficient and self-contained. The determinants which govern them are now primarily inner ones. . . . They are the laws of their own inner nature, their potentialities and capacities, their talents, their latent resources, their creative impulses, their needs to know themselves and to become more and more integrated and unified, more and more aware of what they really are, of what they really want, of what their call or vocation or fate is to be." *Toward a Psychology of Being,* 2d ed. (New York: D. Van Nostrand Co., 1968), p. 35). It would be absurd to suggest that most men are autonomous in this sense of the term. Nevertheless, insofar as there are individuals who resemble this portrait, I think it likelier that they will be men than women—at least white women. I think it likely that more white men than white women *believe* themselves to be autonomous; this belief, even if false, is widely held, and this in itself has implications that are important to consider. Whatever the facts may be in regard to men's lives, the point to remember is this: women have been thought to have neither the capacity nor the right to aspire to an ideal of autonomy, an ideal to which there accrues, whatever its relation to mental health, an enormous social prestige.
7. Many feminists would object vigorously to my claim that there has been no female culture (see, e.g., Burris, "Fourth World Manifesto"). I am not claiming that women have had no enclaves within the dominant culture, that we have never made valuable contributions to the larger culture, or even that we have never dominated any avenue of

cultural expression—one would have to think only of the way in which women have dominated certain forms of folk art (e.g., quilting). What I am claiming is that none of this adds up to a "culture," in the sense in which we speak of Jewish culture, Arapesh culture, or Afro-American culture. Further, the fact that many women are today engaged in the self-conscious attempt to create a female culture testifies, I think, to the situation regarding culture being essentially as I describe it.

8. The best-known modern theory of this type is, of course, Freud's. He maintains that the relative absence of women from the higher culture is the consequence of a lesser ability to sublimate libidinal drives. See "Femininity" in *New Introductory Lectures in Psychoanalysis* (New York: W. W. Norton, 1933).

9. I take it that something like this forms the backdrop to the enjoyment of the average movie. It is daunting to consider the magnitude of the task of neutralization or transformation of hostile cultural messages that must fall constantly to the average female, nonwhite or even working-class white male TV watcher or moviegoer. The pleasure we continue to take in cultural products that may disparage us remains, at least to me, something of a mystery.

10. There might be some objection to regarding ordinary sexual relations as involving sexual objectification, since this use of the term seems not to jibe with its use in more ordinary contexts. For Hegel, Marx, and Sartre, "objectification" is an important moment in the dialectic of consciousness. My decision to treat ordinary sexual relations or even sexual desire alone as involving some objectification is based on a desire to remain within this tradition. Further, Sartre's phenomenology of sexual desire in *Being and Nothingness* (New York: Philosophical Library, 1966) draws heavily on a concept of objectification in an unusually compelling description of the experienced character of that state: "The caress by realizing the Other's incarnation reveals to me my own incarnation; that is, I make myself flesh in order to impel the Other to realize for-herself and for-me her own flesh, and my caresses cause my flesh to be born for me in so far as it is for the Other

flesh causing her to be born as flesh. I make her enjoy my flesh through her flesh in order to compel her to feel herself flesh. And so possession truly appears as a double reciprocal incarnation." (p. 508) What I call "objectification," Sartre here calls "incarnation," a refinement not necessary for my purposes. What he calls "sadism" is incarnation without reciprocity. Most of my examples of sexual objectification would fall into the latter category.

11. Fanon, *Black Skin, White Masks,* p. 177. Eldridge Cleaver sounds a similar theme in *Soul on Ice* (New York: Dell, 1968). The archetypal white man in American society, for Cleaver, is the "Omnipotent Administrator," the archetypal black man the "Super-Masculine Menial."

12. *Ibid.,* p. 180.

13. Erik Erikson, "Inner and Outer Space: Reflections on Womanhood," *Daedalus* 93 (1961), pp. 582–606.

14. Mihailo Markovic, "Women's Liberation and Human Emancipation," in *Women and Philosophy,* pp. 165–6. In spite of this lapse and some questionable opinions concerning the nature of female sexuality, Markovic's paper is a most compelling defense of the claim that the emancipation of women cannot come about under capitalism.

15. Exod. 1:13–14.

16. The available clinical literature on the psychological effects of social inferiority supports this claim. See William H. Grier and Price M. Cobbs, *Black Rage* (New York: Grosset & Dunlap, 1969); Pauline Bart, "Depression in Middle-Aged Women." in *Women in Sexist Society,* ed. Vivian Gornick and Barbara Moran (New York: New American Library, 1971), pp. 163–86; also Phyllis Chesler, *Women and Madness* (New York: Doubleday, 1972).

17. Bertell Ollman, *Alienation: Marx's Conception of Man in Capitalist Society* (London and New York: Cambridge University Press, 1971), p. 135.

18. *Ibid,* p. 143.

19. Karl Marx, *The Economic and Philosophical Manuscripts of 1844,* ed. Dirk J. Struik (New York: International Publishers, 1964), p. 111.

20. *Ibid.*

21. The use of the masculine possessive pronoun is deliberate.

Feminist Forms of Agency and Oppositional Consciousness: U.S. Third World Feminist Criticism

Chéla Sandoval

The enigma that is U.S. third world feminist criticism has yet to be confronted fully by analysts of social change. For these late twentieth-century cultural theorists it has remained inconceivable that U.S. third world feminism represents a form of historical consciousness whose very structure lies outside the conditions of possibility that have regulated the oppositional expressions of dominant feminism. In enacting this new form of historical consciousness, U.S. third world feminism provides access to a different way of conceptualizing not only U.S. feminist consciousness but also oppositional activity in general. Indeed, U.S. third world feminism comprises a methodology for theory and action that is capable of aligning U.S. movements for social justice with worldwide movements of decolonization.

Both in spite of and because they represent varying internally colonized communities, U.S. third world feminists generated a common speech, a theoretical structure that remained just outside the purview of the dominant feminist theory emerging during the 1970s. Even though this unimaginable presence arose to reinvigorate and refocus the politics and priorities of dominant feminist theory during the eighties, what remains is an uneasy alliance between what appears on the surface to be two different understandings of domination, subordination, and the nature of effective resistance—a shotgun arrangement at best between what literary critic

Gayatri Spivak characterizes as a "hegemonic feminist theory," on the one side, and what I call "U.S. third world feminist theory," on the other.[1] I do not mean to suggest here, however, that the perplexing situation that exists between U.S. third world and hegemonic feminisms should be understood merely in binary terms. On the contrary, what this investigation reveals is the way in which the theory of oppositional consciousness and social movement considered here and enacted under U.S. third world feminism was made deeply invisible, by the manner of its appropriation, in the terms of what became during the 1970s a hegemonic feminist theory and practice.

U.S. third world feminism rose out of the matrix of the very discourses denying, permitting, and producing difference. Out of the imperatives born of necessity came a mobility of identity that generated the activities of a new citizen-subject, a new sense of being and action that insists upon another model for the self-conscious production of political opposition and social movement. In this essay I lay out U.S. third world feminism as the design for oppositional political activity and consciousness in the United States. In mapping this new design, the model reveals a way for social activists to chart the points through which contending liberation ideologies and practices might meet, in spite of their varying trajectories. This knowledge becomes important when one begins to wonder how organized oppositional activity and consciousness can be made possible under the coopting nature of first world "postmodern" cultural conditions.[2]

A BRIEF HISTORY

From the beginning of what has been known as the second wave of the women's movement, U.S. third world feminists have claimed feminisms at odds with those being developed by U.S. white women. Already in 1970 with the publication of *Sisterhood Is Powerful,* black feminist Francis Beal was naming the second wave of U.S. feminism as a "*white* women's movement" because it insisted on organizing along the binary gender division male/female alone.[3] U.S. third world feminists, however, have long understood that especially one's race, but also culture, sexuality, or class often deny comfortable or easy access to either gender category, that the interactions between social categories produce other genders within the social hierarchy. As far back as the middle of the last century, Sojourner Truth found it necessary to remind a convention of white suffragists of her female gender with the rhetorical question, "Ar'n't I a woman?"[4] American Indian Paula Gunn Allen has written of Native women that "the place we live now is an idea, because whiteman took all the rest."[5] In 1971, Toni Morrison wrote of U.S. third world women that "there is something inside us that makes us different from other people. It is not like men and it is not like white women."[6] That same year Chicana Velia Hancock concluded: "Unfortunately, many white women focus on the maleness of our present social system as though, by implication, a female-dominated white America would have taken a more reasonable course" for people of color of either sex.[7]

These signs of a lived experience of difference from white female experience in the United States repeatedly appear throughout U.S. third world feminist writings. Such expressions imply the existence of at least one other category of gender, reflected in the very titles of books written by U.S. feminists of color, such as *All the Women Are White, All the Blacks Are Men, But Some of Us Are Brave* or *This Bridge Called My Back,* titles that imply that women of color somehow exist in the interstices between the legitimized categories of the social order.[8] Moreover, in the title of bell hooks's 1981 book, the question "Ain't I a Woman" is transformed into a defiant statement, while Amy Ling's feminist analysis of Asian-American writings, *Between Worlds,* or the title of the journal for U.S. third world feminist writings, *The Third Woman,* also call for the recognition of a new category for social identity.[9] This in-between space, this

third gender category, is also recognized in the early writings of such well-known authors as Maxine Hong Kingston, Gloria Anzaldúa, Audre Lorde, Alice Walker, and Cherrie Moraga, all of whom argue that U.S. third world feminists represent a different kind of "human"—new "mestizas," "Woman Warriors" who live and are gendered "between and among" the lines, "Sister Outsiders" who inhabit a new psychic terrain that Anzaldúa calls "the Borderlands," or "la nueva Frontera," and which is available only through a "la conciencia de la mestiza." In 1980, Audre Lorde summarized the U.S. white women's movement by saying that "today, there is a pretense to a homogeneity of experience covered by the word SISTERHOOD in the white women's movement. When white feminists call for 'unity,' they are misnaming a deeper and real need for homogeneity." We began the 1980s, she says, with "white women" agreeing "to focus upon their oppression as women" while continuing "to ignore difference." Chicana sociologist Maxine Baca Zinn rearticulated this position in 1986, saying that "there now exists in women's studies an increased awareness of the variability of womanhood," yet for U.S. feminists of color "such work is often tacked on, its significance for feminist knowledge" and for political practice "still unrecognized and unregarded."[10]

How did 1980s hegemonic feminism respond to this other kind of feminist theoretical activity? The publication of *This Bridge Called My Back* in 1981 made the presence of U.S. third world feminism impossible to ignore, but soon the writings and theoretical challenges of U.S. third world feminists were marginalized into the category of mere "description" and their essays deferred to "the special force of poetry."[11] Meanwhile the shift in paradigm I refer to as "differential consciousness," represented in the praxis of U.S. third world feminism, was bypassed and ignored. If, during the 1980s, U.S. third world feminism had become a theoretical problem, an inescapable mystery to be solved for hegemonic feminism then perhaps a theory of difference—but imported from Europe—could subsume if not solve it. I would like to provide an example of how this systematic repression of the theoretical implications of U.S. third world feminism occurs.

FEMINISM'S GREAT HEGEMONIC MODEL

During the eighties, hegemonic feminist scholars produced histories of feminist praxis that have fast become the official stories by which the white women's movement understands itself and its interventions in history. I analyze these narratives as systematic accounts that, once typologized, make clear the structure of a hegemonic feminism. It is U.S. third world feminism, recognized and utilized as a theoretical and methodological apparatus, that enables us to view each category in its relationship to the others as a separate though linked social system of constraints, required repressions, and permissible sublimations. Here, each category is considered a different though connected ideology, a strategy not only of feminist resistance but also of domination and subordination.

Though the overall rationale of this dominant typology of resistance furthers certain feminist political aims, it also denies and makes invisible the expression of another form of feminism, a form capable of transforming the very grounds upon which feminism as an oppositional movement understood itself, the nature of consciousness in resistance, and the possibilities of enacting or "performing" politics. What emerges from this analysis is U.S. third world feminism as theory and method, as the "other" form of consciousness in opposition capable of clarifying the accepted taxonomy of feminist forms and their meanings, while extending their possibilities into a realm of new and more effective oppositional activity under contemporary first world cultural conditions.

In a longer essay I traced the structure of this hegemonic typology, this shared code, through the works of feminist scholars Gayle Greene,

Coppélia Kahn, Julia Kristeva, Toril Moi, Gerda Lerner, Cora Kaplan, Alice Jardine, and Judith Kegan Gardiner.[12] For the purposes of this shorter essay, I follow its expression through several key texts of the 1980s: the influential 1985 essay by literary critic and feminist theorist Elaine Showalter, "Toward a Feminist Poetics"; through the introduction to the now-classic set of essays on the "future of difference" in the women's movement published in 1985 and edited by feminist critics Hester Eisenstein and Alice Jardine; and through political scientist Alison Jaggar's massive dictionary of all the possible genera of feminist consciousness and politics, published in 1983.

Elaine Showalter developed what she identifies as a three-phase "taxonomy, if not a poetics, of feminist criticism." What is interesting is that a similar three-stage structure continually emerges across the 1980s text of hegemonic feminist theory and criticism, and this structure is always conceptualized by feminist thinkers as proceeding temporally. For example, in Showalter's version of a first-stage feminism, "Women wrote in an effort to equal the intellectual achievements of the male culture." Meanwhile, feminist thinker Hester Eisenstein apparently agrees, arguing in her book that in a first-phase women's movement, women wanted to "demonstrate that differences between women and men were exaggerated, and that they could be reduced" to a common denominator of sameness. In another place, Alison Jaggar emphasizes that a first stage of what might be considered a feminist history of consciousness, this effort, that is, to find sameness, can be paradigmatically understood as a "liberal" form of feminism.[13]

The second phase of what became a shared feminist typology of the 1980s Showalter describes by saying that women came to "reject the accommodating postures" of the first "feminine" phase, and instead came to "use literature to dramatize wronged womanhood." Eisenstein's typology puts it this way: a second "assumption about difference evolved," she writes, "specifically that women's lives *were* different from men's, and that it was precisely this difference that required illumination." Jaggar's argument is that it was during a second-phase feminism that, historically speaking, women turned to Marxism as a way to undermine first-phase liberalism. Their desire was to restructure the old society so that it becomes incapable of subordinating the differences that the class of women represent.[14]

In the third, "female" and final phase for Showalter, "women reject" both earlier stages as forms of dependency on men and their culture and "turn instead to female experience as the source of an autonomous art." Eisenstein's similar third phase identified "female differences originally seen as a source of oppression" as "a source of enrichment." This is a "woman-centered" phase, she argues, wherein maleness, not femaleness, is the difference that matters— now men, not women, become "the Other"; Jaggar names her similarly conceptualized third phase as either radical or cultural feminist.[15]

Throughout this developing feminist history of consciousness, however, according to Lydia Sargent, "Racism, while part of the discussion, was never successfully integrated into feminist theory and practice."[16] In attempting to remedy this situation, a fourth and utopian category was often added to the previous three. This fourth category always represents the unachieved category of *possibility* wherein differences represented by race and class can be (simply) accounted for; Jaggar names this fourth effort "socialist feminism." In Eisenstein's typology, since it is above all a chronology, the differences represented by U.S. feminists of color become visible only at this last stage. In the eighties, she argues, as the women's movement "grew more diverse," it "became *forced* to confront and debate issues of difference, most notably those of race and class."[17] However, this confrontation with difference (which might have generated a fourth "socialist feminist" category

in Eisenstein's typology) disappears from her book, ironically titled *The Future of Difference,* where, she admits, "the very issues of race and ethnicity in relation to feminism" are only superficially "broached."[18] Indeed, the most well-meaning socialist feminist scholars are unable to make socialist feminism account for the differences represented by the political activities of U.S. feminists of color. Alison Jaggar, a leading proponent of socialist feminism, succinctly sums up the situation in 1983. She writes that "a fully adequate theory of women's liberation cannot ignore the experience of any group of women and to the extent that socialist feminism fails to theorize the experience of women of color, it cannot be accepted as complete." Jaggar nevertheless excuses her own book's determined celebration of a fourth-phase socialist feminism by making the following argument: the theoretical contributions of feminists of color (such as Paula Gunn Allen, Audre Lorde, Nellie Wong, Gloria Anzaldúa, Cherríe Moraga, Toni Morrison, Mitsuye Yamada, bell hooks, the third world contributors to *Sisterhood Is Powerful* or *This Bridge,* to name only a few U.S. third world feminist authors published by 1983), operate, she argues, "mainly at the level of description." Those writings that have been theoretical, she continues, have yet to contribute to any "unique or distinctive and comprehensive theory of women's liberation."[19] For this reason, Jaggar explains, it is not that she has "omitted" U.S. third world feminism from her book, but she has rather simply "assimilated" its expressions into one of the "four genera" of hegemonic feminism we have just examined. This unfortunate move limits one's capacities to think or act outside the boundaries of what became for the 1980s women's movement a hegemonic four-phase structure.

This typology of feminist consciousness can be understood as follows: that women are the same as men, that women are a class different from men, that women are superior to men, and that women are a class that is also divided by race was challenged at every level by U.S. third world feminists. Indeed, this kind of conceptual model, this typology for organizing history, identity, criticism, and theory, must be understood as useful for oppositional actors only insofar as it is understood as a mental map of a given time, place, and cultural condition. This symbolic container has its own political aims, both hoped for and achieved, but we must also understand how it has functioned to make the specific presence of U.S. third world feminism, considered as a specific form of political practice, all but invisible.

PERFORMING POLITICS: THE DIFFERENTIAL FORM OF OPPOSITIONAL CONSCIOUSNESS AND SOCIAL MOVEMENT

Let me propose an alternative typology, this one generated from the insights born of oppositional activity beyond the inclusive scope of the 1980s hegemonic women's movement. It is important to remember that the form of U.S. third world feminism it represents and enacts has been influenced not only by struggles against gender domination, but also by the struggles against race, class, cultural, and sexual hierarchies that mark the 20th century in the United States. It is a mapping of consciousness in opposition to the dominant social order that charts the white and hegemonic feminist histories of consciousness we have just surveyed, while also making visible the different ground from which a specific U.S. third world feminist praxis occurs. It is important to understand that this new typology is not necessarily "feminist" in nature but is rather a history of oppositional consciousness. Let me explain what I mean by this.

Any social order that is hierarchically organized into relations of domination and subordination creates particular subject positions within which the subordinated can legitimately function. These subject positions, once self-consciously recognized by their inhabitants, can become transformed into more effective

sites of resistance to the current ordering of power relations. From the perspective of the form of U.S. third world feminism identified here, the histories of consciousness produced by U.S. white feminists are, above all, only further examples of subordinated consciousness in opposition: they are not viewed as particularly *feminist* in nature. In order to make the specific nature of U.S. third world feminist criticism visible within U.S. feminist theory and within the field of cultural studies in general, I suggest in place of the preceding typology a *topography,* a mapping of the ideological spaces wherein oppositional activity in the U.S. takes place (a cognitive mapping, if you will), a mapping that identifies the modes the subordinated of the United States (of any sex, gender, race, or class) enact as political stances in resistance to domination. Unlike the preceding hegemonic feminist version, the topography that follows is not historically organized; no enactment is privileged over any other; and the recognition that each oppositional site is as potentially effective in opposition as any other makes visible another mode of resistance—enacted by feminists of color over the past thirty years—that is particularly effective under late capitalist and postmodern cultural conditions in the United States. The following topography compasses the parameters of an emerging theory and practice of consciousness-in-opposition that gathers up the modes of ideology–praxis represented within previous liberation movements into a fifth, differential, and postmodern paradigm. This paradigm can, among other things, make clear the vital connections, the alliances, that exist between feminist theories in general and other modes of theory and practice also concerned with issues of social hierarchy, race, marginality, and, above all, resistance. U.S. third world feminist criticism, then, considered as an enabling theory and method of differential social movement, brings the following oppositional ideological practices into view as enactments, or performances of politics, of consciousness, and of identity itself:

1. Within the first, what I call "equal rights" enactment of consciousness in opposition, the members of the subordinated group argue that their differences—for which they have been assigned inferior status—lie only in appearance, not reality. Behind what they argue are only *exterior* physical differences from the most legitimated form of the human-in-society, they maintain, is a content, an essence that is the same as the essence of the human-in-power. These oppositional actors thus argue for civil rights based on the philosophy that all humans are created as equal. Practitioners of this particular ideological tactic will demand that their own humanity be legitimated, recognized as the same under the law, and assimilated into the most favored form of the human-in-power. The expression of this mode of social movement and identity politics can be traced throughout the writings generated from within U.S. liberation movements of the post-World War II era, in all civil rights politics, from the League of United Latin American Citizens (LULAC) to the National Organization for Women (NOW).

2. Under the second and "revolutionary" ideological tactic, members of the subordinated group claim their differences in both form *and* content from those in power, in both physical difference *and* internal being. Practitioners of this mode of resistance thus call for a kind of social transformation that will accommodate and legitimate those differences, by force if necessary. Unlike the previous "equal rights" tactic that insists on the internal similarities between social, racial, sexual, and gender classes across their physical differences, "revolutionary" practitioners have no belief that assimilation is possible within the present categories by which the social order is organized. The enactment of revolutionary ideology seeks instead to affirm subordinated differences through radical societal reformation that will ultimately produce a new culture capable of operating beyond present domination/subordination power axes. Examples of this mode include the Brown Berets, the Black Panthers, and Marxist and socialist feminisms.

3. Under "supremacism," the third form of oppositional consciousness and practice, not only do the oppressed claim their differences, but they also assert that those very differences have provided them access to an evolutionary level superior to that of those in power. Whether one sees one's differences as resulting from biological or social causes is of little final import; what matters is the consequence of those differences: that the group has evolved to a higher stage of cultural and psychological existence than those currently holding power. Moreover, these differences now comprise the essence of what is good in human existence. The mission of these practitioners is to provide the social order with a higher ethical and moral vision and consequently with more effective leadership. We see this in the politics of La Raza Cosmica, cultural feminism, and ethnic nationalisms, for example.

4. "Separatism" is the final tactic of resistance of these most commonly mobilized under previous modes of capitalism. As in the previous three forms, practitioners of this form of resistance also recognize that their differences have been branded as inferior with respect to the category of the most human. Under this mode of agency, however, the subordinated do not desire an "equal rights" type of integration with the dominant order, nor do they seek its "revolutionary" transformation or leadership. Rather, this form of political resistance is organized to protect and nurture the differences that define it through complete separation from the dominant social order.

As we saw under the previous hegemonic typology, the maturation of a resistance movement means that these four ideological positions will emerge in response to dominating powers and that these positions will become more and more clearly articulated. Unfortunately, however, as we witnessed in the late 1970s hegemonic women's movement, such ideological positions eventually divide the movement of resistance from within, for each of these sites tends to generate sets of tactics, strategies, and identity politics that historically have appeared to be mutually exclusive. What remains all the more profound, however, is that the differential practice of U.S. Third World feminism undermines this appearance of the mutual exclusivity of oppositional practices of consciousness and social movement; moreover, it is U.S. third world feminist praxis that allows their recognition on new terms. U.S. feminists of color, insofar as they involved themselves with the 1970s white women's liberation movement, were also enacting one or more of the ideological positionings just outlined, but rarely for long and rarely adopting the kind of fervid belief systems and identity politics that tend to accompany the construction of these ideological positionings under hegemonic understandings. This unusual affiliation with the movement was variously interpreted as disloyalty, betrayal, absence, or lack: "When they *were* there, they were rarely there for long," went the usual complaint, or, "they seemed to shift from one type of women's group to another." They were the mobile (yet ever present in their "absence") members of this particular liberation movement. It is precisely the significance of this mobility that most inventories of oppositional ideology and agency have not been able to register.

Yet it is in the activity of what Anzaldúa calls weaving "between and among" oppositional ideologies that another and fifth mode of oppositional consciousness and activity can be found.[20] I have named this activity of consciousness "differential" insofar as it enables movement "between and among" ideological positionings (the equal rights, revolutionary, supremacist, and separatist modes of opposi-

tional consciousness) considered as variables, in order to disclose the distinctions among them. In this sense the differential mode of consciousness operates like the clutch of an automobile, the mechanism that permits the driver to select, engage, and disengage gears in a system for the transmission of power. This differential represents the variant; emerges out of correlation, intensities, junctures, crises. A differential positioning is thus performative; it is the form of agency self-consciously constructed to mobilize and enact power. For analytic purposes I place this mode of differential consciousness in the fifth position, even though it functions as the medium through which the "equal rights," "revolutionary," "supremacist," and "separatist" modes of oppositional consciousness became effectively transformed, lifted out of their earlier hegemonic activity. Together, when enacted differentially, they become ideological and, above all, *tactical* weaponry for confronting the shifting currents of power.

The differences between this processual and differential five-location topography of consciousness in opposition and the previous typology of hegemonic feminism have been made available for analysis through the recognition of U.S. third world feminism considered as a theory and method for understanding and enacting oppositional political consciousness and activity. U.S. third world feminism thus represents a central locus of possibility, an insurgent movement that works to shatter the construction of any one of the collective ideologies as the single most correct site where truth can be represented. Without making this move beyond the hegemonic typological understanding of resistance outlined earlier, any "liberation" or social movement is destined to repeat the same oppressive authoritarianism from which it is attempting to free itself and become trapped inside a drive for truth that can only end in producing its own brand of dominations. What U.S. third world feminism demands is a new subjectivity, a political revision that denies any one ideology as the final answer, while instead positing a *tactical,* indeed a performative, subjectivity with the capacity to de- and recenter depending upon the kinds of oppression to be confronted, depending upon the history of the moment. This is what is required in the shift from enacting a hegemonic oppositional theory and practice to engaging in differential social movement, as performed, however unrecognized, over the last thirty years under U.S. third world feminist praxis.

Chicana theorist Aida Hurtado defines U.S. third world feminism as a differential and performative mode of social movement and consciousness in the following manner: "by the time women of color reach adulthood, we have developed informal political skills to deal with State intervention. The political skills required by women of color are neither the political skills of the White power structure that White liberal feminists have adopted nor the free spirited experimentation followed by the radical feminists." Rather, she insists, "women of color are more like urban guerillas trained through everyday battle with the state apparatus." As such, "women of color's fighting capabilities are often neither understood by white middle-class feminists" nor leftist activists in general, and up until now, she asserts, these fighting capabilities have "not been codified anywhere for them to learn."[21] Cherríe Moraga continues by claiming U.S. third world feminist "guerilla warfare" as a way of life: "Our strategy," she writes, "is how we cope" on an everyday basis, "how we measure and weigh what is to be said and when, what is to be done and how, and to whom . . . daily deciding/risking who it is we can call an ally, call a friend (whatever that person's skin, sex, or sexuality)." Feminists of color are "women without a line. We are women who contradict each other."[22]

In 1981, Anzaldúa identified the growing coalition between U.S. feminists of color as one of women who do not have the same culture, language, race, sexual orientation, or ideology; "nor do we derive similar solutions," she insists, to the problems of oppression. For a U.S. third

world feminism enacted as a differential theory and method of oppositional consciousness, however, she writes, such "differences do not become opposed to each other."[23] Instead, as Lorde continued the argument in 1979, all ideological differences, all tactical social positionings, must be understood as "a fund of necessary polarities between which our creativities spark like a dialectic. Only within that interdependency," each ideological position "acknowledged and equal, can the power to seek new ways of being in the world generate, as well as the courage and sustenance to act where there are no charters."[24] Such *movement,* however, must be linked to a concurrent desire for ideological location; both are necessary, together, in enacting a differential praxis. Differential social movement creates a space where, in the words of third world feminist philosopher Maria Lugones, "cross-cultural and cross-racial loving" takes place, through the requisite that the self shift its perimeters and identities, to "morph," to multiply its agency in a performative activity self-consciously grounded in the demands of history but organized for the sake of egalitarian social relations, a differential form of social being Lugones calls "world-traveling."[25]

Perhaps we can now better understand the utopian content underlying definitions of U.S. third world feminism written by feminists of color throughout the 1970s and 1980s, as in this statement made in 1985 by African-American literary critic Barbara Christian, writing to other U.S. feminists of color: "The struggle is not won. Our vision is still seen, even by many progressives, as secondary, our words trivialized as minority issues," our oppositional stances "characterized by others as divisive. But there is a deep philosophical recording that is occurring" among us "that is already having its effects on so many of us whose lives and expressions are an increasing revelation of the *intimate* face of universal struggle."[26] This "philosophical reordering," referred to by Christian, the "different strategy, a different foundation" called for by hooks, must be recognized as, in the words of Audre Lorde, part of "a whole other structure of opposition that touches every aspect of our existence at the same time that we are resisting." According to Barbara Smith, the recognition of U.S. third world feminism as a fundamentally different paradigm will "alter life as we know it" for those who act in resistance to dominant social hierarchy.[27] In 1981, Merle Woo insisted that U.S. third world feminism represents a "new framework." This framework will not "support repression, hatred, exploitation and isolation, but will be a human and beautiful framework, created in a community, bonded not by color, sex or class, but by love and the common goal for the liberation of mind, heart, and spirit."[28] The praxis of a differential form of oppositional consciousness has continually called up utopian visions such as these throughout the 1960s, 1970s, and 1980s within the writings of U.S. feminists of color, and across their boundaries of race, culture, ethnicity, class, and sexual differences.

U.S. third world feminism must be recognized as that "different strategy," that "new framework." Indeed, it comprises a theory, method, and practice of oppositional consciousness in the postmodern world. This theory and method can be understood as apprehending and organizing consciousness, identity, agency, aesthetics, and politics around the following five points of resistance to social hierarchy: 1) the integrationist, 2) the revolutionary, 3) the supremacist or nationalist, 4) the separatist, and 5) the differential forms of U.S. third world feminism. It is the differential mode that allows the previous four to be understood and utilized as *tactics* for changing social relations. Under the differential theory and method of U.S. third world feminist criticism, these five modes of resistance, ideology, and political practice are seen and deployed as *technologies of power*. When enacted differentially, U.S. third world feminism demands of its practitioners a commitment to the process of metamorphosis itself: the activity of the trickster who practices subjectivity-as-masquerade. This "morphing" is accomplished not simply for survival's sake, as in earlier times. Rather, it is a kind of conversion that allows movement through and over dominant systems of resistance, identity, race, gender, sex, and national meanings.

A differential oppositional consciousness views the five technologies of power as consensual illusions, transformable social narratives designed to intervene in reality for the sake of social justice. This sleight-of-consciousness creates a new space, a cyberspace where the transcultural, transnational leaps necessary to the generation of new forms of oppositional praxis are made possible. To identify a work as U.S. third world feminist is to find a work born of disruptions and of taking place, of immigrations and crossing borders, of traveling style, politics, poetics, and procedures, of tactics, strategies, and movement, all produced with the aim of, as Merle Woo puts it in *This Bridge,* equalizing power on behalf of the third world, the colonized, the class, race, gender, or sexually subordinated. Ironically, given the history of U.S. third world feminism, the so-called flexibility of identity demanded for living under colonial and subordinated conditions is currently demanded of every first world citizen affected by transforming global economies. This condition creates new grounds for coalition across borders in U.S. third world feminist praxis, that is, in an understanding of resistance that focuses on the differential deployment of consciousness in opposition.

In this chapter I have identified the hegemonic structure that has trapped not only U.S. feminist theory and practice but which has also determined and constricted the politics and forms-of-being possible within all U.S. social movements of the 1950s, 1960s, 1970s, and 1980s. This hegemonic structure of consciousness and agency stands out in relief against the praxis of U.S. third world feminism, which has evolved to center the differences of U.S. third world feminists across their varying languages, cultures, ethnicities, races, classes, sexualities, and genders. I have suggested that the "philosophical reordering" referred to by Christian is imaginable only through U.S. third world feminism, recognized as a specific and new condition of possibility, another kind of gender, race, sex, and class consciousness that allows us to define the "differential" as a specific form of resistance, agency, and politics. The differential form of oppositional consciousness was utilized by U.S. feminists of color within the 1970s white women's movement, yet it is also a form of consciousness in resistance well utilized among subordinated classes under various conditions of domination and subordination. The recognition and acknowledgment of this consciousness and praxis, this thought and action, carves out the space wherein hegemonic feminisms have the possibility of becoming aligned with other spheres of theoretical and daily practice that are also concerned with issues of marginality.

The form of U.S. third world feminism represented by the differential form of oppositional consciousness is threaded throughout the experience of social marginality. As such it is being woven into the fabric of experience belonging to more and more citizens caught in the crisis of late capitalism and expressed in the cultural angst most often referred to as the postmodern dilemma. The juncture I am proposing, therefore, is extreme. It is a location wherein the praxis of U.S. third world feminism links with the aims of white feminism; with studies of race, ethnicity, sexuality, and marginality; and with postmodern theories of culture, as they crosscut and join together in new relationships through what is becoming a shared comprehension of the dynamics of oppositional consciousness in the postmodern world.

NOTES

1. Gayatri Spivak, "The Rani of Sirmur" in Barker (ed.), *Europe and its Others,* vol. 1 (Essex: University of Essex, 1985), p. 147. Here, "U.S. Third World Feminism" represents the political alliance made during the 1960s and 1970s among a generation of U.S. feminists of color who were separated by culture, race, class, sexuality, or gender identification but united through their similar responses to the experience of race oppression.

The most recent theorization of "U.S. Third World feminism" can be found in (eds.) Lourdes Torres and Chandra Mohanty, *Third World Women and the Politics of Feminism* (Bloomington: Indiana University Press, 1991). See also Gloria Anzaldúa, ed., *Making Face, Making Soul—Haciendo Caras: Creative and Critical Perspectives by Women of Color* (San Francisco: Aunt Lute Press, 1990). Earlier definitions can be found in Cherrie Moraga's "Between the Lines: On Culture, Class and Homophobia," in (eds.) Cherrie Moraga and Gloria Anzaldúa, *This Bridge Called My Back: A Collection of Writings by Radical Women of Color* (Watertown, MA: Persephone Press, 1981), p. 106. Also see Sandoval, "The Struggle Within: A Report on the 1981 NWSA Conference" (Oakland, CA: Center for Third World Organizing, 1982), reprinted by Anzaldúa in *Making Face, Making Soul—Haciendo Caras,* p. 55–71; id. "Comment on Krieger's *The Mirror Dance,* a U.S. Third World Feminist Perspective," *Signs: Journal of Women in Culture and Society* 9, no. 4 (Summer 1984), p. 725; id, "U.S. Third World Feminism," forthcoming in *Oxford Companion to Women's Writing in the U.S.* (New York: Oxford University Press, 1994).

2. See Fredric Jameson's "Postmodernism, or the Cultural Logic of Late Capitalism," *New Left Review* 146 (July/Aug 1984), pp. 53–92.

Interesting to certain third world scholars is the coalescing relationship between theories of postmodernism (especially those that celebrate the fragmentations of consciousness that postmodernism demands) and the form of differential oppositional consciousness that has been most clearly articulated by the marginalized and which I outline in this text. The juncture I am analyzing here is that which connects the disoriented first world subject who, like Jameson, is either repulsed by the "depoliticized" aesthetics of postmodernism or longs for the postmodern cultural aesthetic as a key to a new sense of identity and redemption, and the form of differential oppositional consciousness developed by subordinated and marginalized Western or colonized subjects, who have been forced to experience the aesthetics of what is called "postmodernism" as a requisite for survival. It is the members of this constituency who are most familiar with what citizenship in this realm requires and makes possible.

The juncture between all of these interests is comprised of the differential form of oppositional consciousness that postmodern cultural conditions are making available to all of its citizenry in an historically unique democratization of oppression that crosses class, race, sex, and gender identifications. Its practice contains the possibility for the emergence of a new historical moment—a new citizen—and a new arena for unity between peoples.

3. Francis Beal, "Double Jeopardy: To Be Black and Female," in *Sisterhood Is Powerful: An Anthology of Writings from the Women's Liberation Movement,* ed. Robin Morgan (New York: Random House, 1970), p. 136. Emphasis mine.

4. Sojourner Truth, "Ain't I a Woman?" in *The Norton Anthology of Literature by Women* (New York: Norton, 1985), p. 252.

5. Paula Gunn Allen, "Some Like Indians Endure," in Will Roscoe (ed.), *Living the Spirit* (New York: St. Martin's, 1987), p. 9.

6. Toni Morrison, quoted by Bettye J. Parker, "Complexity: Toni Morrison's Women—an Interview Essay," in Roseanne Bell, Bettye Parker, and Beverly Guy-Sheftall (eds.), *Sturdy Black Bridges: Visions of Black Women in Literature* (New York: Anchor/Doubleday, 1979), p. 63.

7. Velia Hancock, "La Chicana, Chicano Movement and Women's Liberation," *Chicano Studies Newsletter,* University of California, Berkeley, Feb/Mar 1971. The intuition that people of color occupy an "in-between/outsider" status is a frequent theme among third world liberationist writers both within and outside the borders of the United States. See, for example, Desmond Tutu as reported by Richard N. Osting, "Searching for New Worlds," *Time,* October 29, 1984; Rosa Maria Villafane-Sisolak, from a 1983 journal entry cited in Gloria Anzaldúa (ed.), *Making Face, Making Soul—Haciendo Caras;* Alice Walker, "In the Closet of the Soul: A Letter to an African-American Friend," *Ms.,* November 1986, pp. 32–5; Gloria Anzaldúa, "La Prieta," in Moraga and Anzaldúa (eds), *This Bridge Called My Back,* pp. 198–209.

8. See Gloria Hull, Patricia Bell Scott, Barbara Smith, *All Women Are White, All the Blacks Are Men, But Some of Us Are Brave: Black Women's Studies* (New York: Feminist Press, 1982); Moraga and Anzaldúa (eds.), *This Bridge Called My Back.*

9. bell hooks, *Ain't I a Woman: Black Women and Feminism* (Boston: South End Press, 1981); Amy Ling, *Between Worlds* (New York: Pergamon Press, 1990); Norma Alarcon (ed), *The Third Woman* (Bloomington, IN: Third Woman Press, 1981).

10. See Alice Walker, "Letter to an African-American Friend," *Ms.,* November 1986. See also Gloria Anzaldúa, *Borderlands, La Frontera: The New Mestiza* (San Francisco: Spinsters/Aunt Lute, 1987); Maxine Hong Kingston, *The Woman Warrior* (New York: Vintage Books, 1977); Moraga and Anzaldúa (eds.), *This Bridge Called My Back*; Audre Lorde, *Sister Outsider* (New York: Crossing Press, 1984); Maxine Baca Zinn, Lynn Weber Cannon, Elizabeth Higginbotham, and Bonnie Thornton Dill, "The Costs of Exclusionary Practices in Women's Studies," *Signs* 11, no. 2 (Winter 1986), p. 296.

11. Alison Jaggar, *Feminist Politics and Human Nature* (New York: Rowman and Allenheld, 1983), p. 11; Hester Eisenstein and Alice Jardine, *The Future of Difference* (New Brunswick, NJ: Rutgers University Press, 1985), p. xxi.

12. See Sandoval, "U.S. Third World Feminism: The Theory and Method of Oppositional Consciousness in the Postmodern World," *Genders* 10 "Consciousness in the Postmodern World."

13. Elaine Showalter, "Toward a Feminist Poetics," in *The New Feminist Criticism: Essays on Women, Literature and Theory* (New York: Pantheon, 1985), pp. 128, 137; Eisenstein, "Difference," in Eisenstein and Jardine, *The Future of Difference,* p. xvi; Jaggar, *Feminist Politics,* p. 27.

14. Showalter, "Feminist Poetics," p. 138; Eisenstein, "Difference," p. xviii; Jaggar, *Feminist Politics,* p. 51.

15. Showalter, "Feminist Poetics," p. 139; Eisenstein, "Difference," p. xix; Jaggar, *Feminist Politics,* p. 83.

16. Lydia Sargent, *Women and Revolution: A Discussion of the Unhappy Marriage of Marxism and Feminism* (Boston: South End Press, 1981), p. xx.

17. Eisenstein, "Difference," p. xix (emphasis mine).

18. Ibid., p. xxiii.

19. See Sandoval, "U.S. Third World Feminism," for varying responses by feminist theorists of color to Jaggar's claim.

20. Gloria Anzaldúa writes that she lives "between and among" cultures, in "La Prieta," in Moraga and Anzaldúa (eds.), *This Bridge Called My Back*, p. 209.

21. Aida Hurtado, "Reflections on White Feminism: A Perspective from a Woman of Color," unpublished manuscript (1985). Another version of this quotation appears in Hurtado's essay "Relating to Privilege: Seduction and Rejection in the Subordination of White Women and Women of Color," *Signs* (Summer 1989), pp. 833–55.

22. Moraga and Anzaldúa (eds.), *This Bridge Called My Back*, p. xix.

23. Anzaldúa, "La Prieta," in Moraga and Anzaldúa, (eds.), *This Bridge Called My Back*, p. 209.

24. Audre Lorde, "Comments at 'The Personal and the Political Panel,'" Second Sex Conference, New York, September 1979. Published in Moraga and Anzaldúa (eds.), *This Bridge Called My Back*, p. 98. Also see Lorde, "The Uses of the Erotic," in *Sister Outsider,* pp. 58–63, which calls for challenging and undoing authority in order to enter a utopian realm accessible only through a processual form of consciousness that she names the "erotic."

25. Differential consciousness is comprised of seeming contradictions and difference, which then serve as tactical interventions in the other mobility that is power. Entrance into the realm "between and amongst" the others demands a mode of consciousness once relegated to the province of intuition and psychic phenomena, but which now must be recognized as a specific practice. I define differential consciousness as a kind of anarchic activity (but with method), a form of ideological guerilla warfare, and a new kind of ethical activity that is being privileged here as the way in which opposition to oppressive authorities is achieved in a highly technologized and disciplinzed society. Inside this realm reside the only possible grounds of unity across differences. Entrance into this new order requires an emotional commitment within which one experiences the violent shattering of the unitary sense of self, as the skill that allows a mobile identity to form takes hold. As Bernice Reagon has written, "most of the time you feel threatened to the core, and if you don't, you're not really doing no coalescing" ("Coalition Politics: Turning the Century," in Barbara Smith (ed.), *Home Girls: A Black Feminist Anthology,* [New York: Kitchen Table, Women of Color Press, 1983], pp. 356–68). Citizenship in this political realm is comprised of strategy and risk. Within the realm of differential consciousness there are no ultimate answers, no terminal utopia (though the imagination of utopias can motivate its tactics), no predictable final outcomes. Its practice is not biologically determined, restricted to any class or group, nor must it become static. The fact that it is a process capable of freezing into a repressive order—or of disintegrating into relativism—should not shadow its radical activity.

    To name the theory and method made possible by the recognition of differential consciousness, "oppositional" refers only to the ideological effects its activity can have under present cultural conditions. It is a naming that signifies a realm with constantly shifting boundaries which serve to delimit, for differential consciousness participates in its own dissolution even as it is in action. Differential consciousness under postmodern conditions is not possible without the creation of another ethics, a new morality, which will bring about a new subject of history. Movement into this realm is heralded by the claims of U.S. third world feminists, a movement that makes manifest the possibility of ideological warfare in the form of a theory and method, a praxis of oppositional consciousness. But to think of the activities of U.S. third world feminism in this way is only a metaphorical avenue that allows one conceptual access to the threshold of this other realm, a realm accessible to all people. See Maria Lugones, "Playfulness, World-Traveling, and Loving Perception," from *Hypatia: A Journal of Feminist Philosophy* 2, no. 2 (1987), pp. 84–98.

26. Barbara Christian, "Creating A Universal Literature: Afro-American Women Writers," *KPFA Folio,* Special African History Month Edition, February 1983, p. 1. Reissued in Barbara Christian, *Black Feminist Criticism: Perspectives on Black Women Writers* (New York: Pergamon Press, 1985), p. 163.

27. bell hooks, *Feminist Theory: From Margin to Center* (Boston: South End Press, 1994), p. 87; Audre Lorde, "An Interview: Audre Lorde and Adrienne Rich," *Signs* 6, no. 4 (Summer 1981), pp. 168–75; and Smith (ed.), *Home Girls,* p. xxv.

28. Merle Woo, "Letter to Ma," in Moraga and Anzaldúa (eds.), *This Bridge Called My Back.*

CHAPTER 2

The Politics of Knowledge

Social hierarchies and systems of domination are maintained by our daily choices and routine interactions. Yet their efficient perpetuation also presupposes the institutions and discourses that make up the relations of ruling. In societies like ours, those discourses are fundamentally secular and significantly specialized. They are the cultural property of experts; they are technically inaccessible to most of us; they mystify. Science, institutionalized as objective and surefooted, exemplifies such discourse. Discursive systems making scientific claims or peddling scientific pretensions hold sway in mainstream American culture. Technological discourses such as those associated with cybernetics and biotechnology are illustrative, as is medical discourse.

The arts also demand attention inasmuch as they are often pitted against "popular culture," "crafts," or "folk arts." What gets defined as "artistic" can reinforce the matrix of domination. In college curricula, for example, women's literature is ghettoized in separate courses rather than treated as the real thing in courses on Renaissance poetry or the Victorian novel. Courses in art history commonly ignore or demean quiltmaking, pottery, or weaving as unworthy enterprises while giving female artists less attention or treating them as exceptions to the rule of female inferiority. As Amy Mullin emphasizes, feminist art theory rejects the premise of "art, politics, and knowledge as three separate domains."[1]

What counts as knowledge thus comes down to who counts as a person. Since the people who count occupy the upper reaches of social hierarchies, what counts as knowledge commonly reflects a privileged outlook. The structure of knowledge parallels the structure of social relations, then. The one resonates with and reinforces the other, while commonsense knowledge goes unrecognized or gets put down as naive, subjective, and provincial. Not surprisingly, experts characterize common sense the same way that oppressors characterize the oppressed. Privileged people *know*; disprivileged people intuit, guess, or merely believe.

FEMINIST CRITIQUES OF THE SCIENCES

Between 1957 and 1977 Evelyn Reed, a feminist theorist trained in anthropology, published five papers in the *International Socialist Review* criticizing commonplace stances among scientists. Reed thus stands among the first feminist theorists to challenge the *institution of science*—that is, the discourses and practices firmly entrenched and widely accepted as providing objective knowledge about material, social, cultural, and psychic realities.

Reed was an early critic of E. O. Wilson's first book (1975) on sociobiology. She says that even though *sociobiology* "implies the fusion of two sciences—sociology (or anthropology) and biology. . . ," Wilson's perspective is "predominantly biological." Reed concludes that he offers nothing new: "Biologism" and "crude biologizers" have been around for a long while.[2] Reed also criticizes anthropologist Lionel Tiger, whose *Men in Groups* (1969) argues "that only males have the capacity to form attachments to one another, a trait. . . . built into the 'biological infrastructure' of the male sex. . . ." (p. 73) Similarly, she chases down scientific wannabes popular during the 1960s such as Robert Ardrey, Konrad Lorenz, and Desmond Morris, who insist on the "biological aggressiveness of human nature" and humankind's "animal nature." Overall, Reed shows that science is "subject to all the biases current in the established social system. . . ." (p. 7)

Reed helped to launch one of the most influential areas of feminist theorizing. She forecasted the "wave of biological determinism" that mobilized other feminist critics of science; she opened the floodgates that let us see how sexism and racism as well as "slavery, colonialism, laissez-faire capitalism, communism, [and] patriarchy . . . have all been supported, at one time or other, by the work of scientists."[3] By the 1970s feminists had delineated in detail how various disciplines had taken shape around "the historic exclusion (or misrepresentation) of the lives and experiences of women."[4] Virtually all academic disciplines now bear the stamp of such studies.[5]

By 1987, when Riane Eisler was publishing her widely read *The Chalice and the Blade,* she could write that her work would have been impossible

without the work of scholars such as Simone de Beauvoir, Jessie Bernard, Ester Boserup, Gita Sen, Mary Daly, Dale Spender, Florence Howe, Nancy Chodorow, Adrienne Rich, Kate Millett, Barbara Gelpi, Alice Schlegel, Annette Kuhn, Charlotte Bunch, Carol Christ, Judith Plaskow, Catharine Stimpson, Rosemary Radford Ruether, Charlene Spretnak, Catherine MacKinnon,

Wilma Scott Heide, Jean Baker Miller, and Carol Gilligan, to name but a few. Dating from the time of Aphra Behn in the 17th century and even earlier, but only coming into its own during the past two decades, the emerging body of data and insight provided by feminist scholars is, like "chaos" theory, opening new frontiers for science.[6]

Yet as recently as 1996, Susan Bordo delineated how feminist scholars continue being seen as Others in the academic world.[7]

Over time, "feminist theorists have moved from the 'reactive' stance" expressed in critiques of science to "feminist knowledge" itself.[8] In principle, such knowledge counteracts "canonized" or institutionally endorsed knowledge, which is socially constructed along lines reinforcing the matrix of domination and relations of ruling. Integrating the diverse feminist scholarship on science and knowledge are concerns with language, methodology, and topics of inquiry.

LANGUAGE

Science has its roots in what phenomenologists call the *lebenswelt* or life-world, the arena of commonsense action and taken-for-granted routines where people go about their everyday lives. Science draws many resources from that arena, but its biggest steal is language. From humble articles like "the," as in "*the* world," to profound nouns like "family" and "community," as in "family of man" or "community of scholars," scientists lift words from their mundane context where they are used prereflectively and put them to work in an academic context where reflective uses of language are supposed to prevail.

Science and other formal systems of knowledge revolve around *concepts,* words scrutinized carefully and defined explicitly to optimize their usefulness as typifying or categorizing instruments. When scholars import commonsense terms into their discourse with little concern about their cultural and political ramifications, scholarship suffers and so do women. Consider the importation of "head of household," which presupposes a domestic hierarchy. Less obviously problematic are terms like "community," which get used as spatial or sociopolitical concepts that erase the social–emotional fabric woven from women's work as nurturers. Similarly, "domestic violence" masks the strong statistical skewing toward *male* violence in the home.

As Michele Barrett and Anne Phillips emphasize, "The concepts and categories through which we appropriate and construct the world have a history within which we are ourselves implicated."[9] When we uncritically adopt the vocabulary institutionalized within academic disciplines, "we yield power to those who developed them . . ."[10] and bolster the relations of ruling, if only by perpetuating whatever ideology gains its force from that terminology. *Ideology* is, to be sure, a slippery concept in the Marxian repertoire, but it consistently implies biased knowledge serving the interests of the powerful and impeding the mobilization of the less powerful in society. By now, thanks in part to feminist scholars, we know that "there is no place in science, technology, medicine or other forms of expertise where you cannot find ideology operating as a constitutive determinant."

Its most fundamental site is the concepts promoting "the naturalization of value systems" in this or that discipline.[11] As terms like "head of household" get taken for granted among experts and their audiences, domestic hierarchies come to seem all the more like givens—just the way things "naturally" are. Thus does ideology infiltrate scholarship, and thus does scholarship augment the relations of ruling. "Ready-made concepts" are, therefore, suspect among feminist scholars.[12] Feminist literary critics question, for example, why male-authored romances were called "novels" while females' parallel works were called "romances."

All this hullabaloo about scholarly terminology points to the profound power of naming. To name persuasively is to shape people's perceptions. Consider *mammal*. Taken for granted as a useful way to distinguish some animate creatures (including human beings) from others, the term reflects the male/female dualism. Introduced as "mammalia" by Carolus Linnaeus in 1758, it means "of the breast." Linnaeus, the influential taxonomer of the day, also introduced *Homo sapiens* ("man of wisdom") to distinguish humans from other primates. Thus, "a female characteristic (the lactating mamma) ties humans to brutes, while a traditionally male characteristic (reason) marks our separateness" from other animals. Similarly, the "romance" of the egg and the sperm reflects stereotypes about active males and passive females.[13]

As they import the language of the life-world, scientists use figurative language without much recognizing their flights from literalism. Their metaphors say a lot about their stances and purposes. Attention to scientists' metaphors goes back to at least the early 20th century, when a debate ensued between those defending and those denigrating metaphors in scientific discourse. By the 1960s Mary Hesse was showing that useful metaphors "must draw on widely understood social meanings," just as "mammal" does. Since metaphors also "express value judgments,"[14] the most useful ones resonate with those values supporting the relations of ruling, including the sex/gender system.

Perhaps, nowhere is that better seen than in the rise of modern science. Evelyn Fox Keller has shown that to understand its emergence requires "attending to the role played by metaphors of gender in the formation of the particular set of values, aims, and goals embodied in the scientific enterprise." Focusing on the "sexual dialectic" in Francis Bacon's scientific writings, the gender imagery in debates among 17th-century natural philosophers, and the sexualized imagery in their more pointed debate over witchcraft, Keller concludes that out of such intellectual furor came a

modern science [that] opted for an ever greater polarization of mind and nature, reason and feeling, objective and subjective; in parallel with the gradual
desexualization of women, it offered a deanimated, desanctified, and increasingly mechanized conception of nature.[15]

Such science has yet to be demodernized or postmodernized in the
wake of feminist challenges. Even if it were, figurative language would
persist, since wholly literal discourse is unattainable. The best we can do
is to be vividly aware of our metaphors and their ideological bent. Had
19th- as well as 20th-century scholars been so, they might have seen that
the analogy "linking race to gender . . . occupied a strategic place in scientific theorizing about human variation. . . ." They might also have
seen how such analogies "neglect or even suppress information about
human experience of the world that does not fit the similarity implied by
the metaphor." They might even have seen that scientists eschew their
metaphors because of the "intellectually privileged status that science has
traditionally enjoyed as the repository of nonmetaphorical, empirical, politically neutral, universal knowledge."[16]

We must do better. Elizabeth E. Wheatley, for one, proposes the "*productive* and *mobilizing* metaphor of *dance*" as a guiding image for feminist scholarship.[17] More generally, Emily Martin displaces the idea of
"dead" metaphors with that of sleeping ones that we must continuously
awaken.[18] Such a stance is central to whatever *methodologies,* or logics of
inquiry, feminists forge for themselves.

METHODOLOGY

Writing about their own discipline of psychology, Michelle Fine and
Susan Merle Gordon observe that

> Feminists can fit into psychology all too easily. We can do it by pretending
> that psychology is an apolitical discipline; by representing ourselves uncriti-
> cally as objective researchers; by misrepresenting gender, within frames of sex
> roles, sex differences, or gender-neutral analyses without discussing power,
> social context, and meanings; and by constructing the rich and contradictory
> consciousness of girls and women into narrow factors and scales.[19]

Fine and Gordon thus identify four dimensions of feminist methodology:
awareness of the political dimensions of one's research, critical stances
toward objectivity, commitment to exposing the power-laden, contextual
nature of gender and its meanings, and attunement to the dense realities of
girls' and women's consciousness.

Awareness of the politics of research entails seeing how power figures
into it. Such awareness is important enough that some feminist researchers value "sensitivity to, and responsibility for, power relations, representation, [and] dissemination" over "issues of which method to use."[20]
Aware of the power of the expert and the imperialist posturing built into
human-subject research, feminists incline toward power-sharing methods

of gathering data. Indeed, they find the notion of "gathering" data problematic, since it implies that data are simply "there" awaiting the researcher's attention. Because of their attunement to power, including the power of naming, feminist researchers commonly know that they themselves are constituting their data. Thus, the social-constructionist stance common among them shapes their methodology.

Not surprisingly, feminist researchers largely abjure the arrogance researchers are culturally licensed to exhibit in our society. Yet as Sofia Villenas later shows in Reading 11, such a commitment is tricky to execute. Nevertheless, many feminist researchers incline toward empathetic or connective stances.[21] Rejecting conceptions of science that emphasize narrowly circumscribed goals and standards of success,[22] they theorize their cultural and political responsibilities as key parts of their methodologies.

As Renate Klein has suggested, feminist researchers "cannot speak for others but . . . can, and must, speak *out* for others."[23] Like all "good enough" research, feminist research must "account for the conditions of its own production," "interrogate how researchers create our texts," and "traverse the frameworks it uses so it can . . . look towards new ways of thinking, doing and knowing."[24] It must, in other terms, combat the dualisms still informing the sciences and humanities that at least implicitly denigrate girls and women—dualisms such as analysis/empathy, thought/pleasure, and body/mind.[25]

Among the most pernicious dualisms is objectivity/subjectivity. Undergirding it are convenient but simplistic assumptions about the interchangeability of knowers[26] and the possibility of universal principles. Also at work is the assumption that investigators can occupy a cognitive nonplace where "the specifics of one's real place [are] irrelevant. It used to be God's place; now it is the scientist's." Naomi Scheman goes on,

> The person who speaks from this privileged nonplace has no race (i.e., is white), no gender (male), no cultural identity (Western European), no class (bourgeois), no sexual identity (heterosexual), and so on. The rest of us see the world from narrow, specific, distorting perceptions: we perceive in adjective-laden ways.

Yet, Scheman concludes, "No one really is generic. . . ."[27] Thus, feminist research commonly takes shape around "conscious subjectivity" rather than unattainable objectivity. Characteristically, it also entertains ideas like those of Donna Haraway, who "insist[s] metaphorically on the particularity and embodiment of all vision [, which] allows us to construct a usable, but not an innocent, doctrine of objectivity."[28]

In one way or other, such research serves as an interrogation of, if not intervention in, gender. Cynthia Fuchs Epstein emphasizes "the continuous work that must be done in society to differentiate the sexes and to perpetuate inequality between them." She concludes that "*Not* thinking according to sex-defined boundaries . . . may be one of the most important contributions scientific objectivity can offer."[29] Thinking *beyond gender*—or, more realistically, *trying* to think beyond it—is one application of a methodological axiom common among feminist investigators, namely, "Dichotomy, duality, linearity, fixity . . . are not the properties of nature nor of human life and experiencing."[30] That axiom steers researchers toward the ambiguities and contradictions of girls' and women's *lived* experiences.

Feminist research also entails looking for oneself in one's work.[31] It means looking for one's uncertain self, who might find some meaningful interpretations of her data threatening; it means looking for one's careerist self, who might be tempted to put an intellectually popular spin on data that cry out for less timid interpretations; it means looking for one's white or heterosexual or middle-aged or able-bodied self, who assumes that everyone enjoys such privileged statuses; it means looking for one's bold, imaginative self, who will do the utmost justice to data that might make this gender-unjust world less so.

I follow Haraway, then, in favoring "politics and epistemologies of location, positioning, and situating, where partiality and not universality is the condition of being heard to make rational knowledge claims." Haraway concludes that feminists favor "the sciences and politics of interpretation, translation, stuttering, and the partly understood."[32]

It helps to sense at the outset of one's research what the foregoing ideas imply, namely that "the subject of feminist knowledge . . . must be multiple and even contradictory."[33] It helps, then, to launch one's work expecting no easy fix on the topic at hand and no simple interpretation of its ins and outs. It also helps to remind oneself continuously that women's careers, alcoholism, athletics, and comedy are just as fully instances of those realities as men's are.

As Elizabeth Kamarck Minnich stresses, tradition dictates that we not "teach particular kinds of art, literature, religious practices, cultures, and the rest as the *thing-itself, except in the case of those particular kinds that stand at the defining center of the fields.*" Just as curricula should not treat men's achievements as definitive of the "things themselves" (whether novels or equations) research should neither treat men's achievements that way nor treat women's achievements as "different" from the "real" thing.

The same principle applies on the sexual, racial, class, age, and ethnic fronts; thus, we need adjectives that specify just whose achievements or experiences are under consideration. Yet some adjectives—"heterosexual," "white," "Euro-American," "male"—go against the grain of hegemonic discourse because they "are not used there to mark *kinds* of people or works."[34] Feminist methodologies presuppose resistance to hegemonic discourse and thus invite researchers to name their social locations so as to make clear whose stances shape and limit their work.

Recognizing that one's positioning as a heterosexual or an upper-middle-class professional affects one's outlook need not mean, however, conceding that we can never understand the experiences of people whose positioning is not the same as our own, as Uma Narayan points out in Reading 5. To be sure, some feminist researchers do emphasize the narrow limits of our capacity for such understanding. In the main, though, their work implies that people can dramatically enlarge their understanding of people positioned differently from themselves. Middle-class researchers can, for instance, effectively study low-income women. Valerie Polakow's *Lives on the Edge: Single Women and Their Children in the Other America*[35] exemplifies such work. By portraying poor mothers' experiences from their own standpoints, Polakow shows that

> We need to learn to particularize whatever and whomever we study, and then to contextualize, to historicize—to hold whatever abstractions we draw from the material of our study close to that material for as long as is necessary to keep us from thinking that apparently parallel terms but actually hierarchical categories are reversible.[36]

That methodological stance lets Polakow show that "single" and "married" moms are *not* parallel but hierarchical terms that cannot be readily reversed because of the historical weight and political dynamite they carry. Moreover, Polakow implies what Minnich pinpoints, namely, how

> faulty generalization leads to circular reasoning in which the *sources* of standards, justifications, interpretations, reappear as *examples* of that which is best, most easily justified, most richly interpreted by those standards.[37]

Just as white, married, middle-class mothers serve as the source of maternal standards in our society and then get cited as models of what they themselves were used to originate, men's achievements work the same way. Men's performances are used as the source of standards for athletics, mathematics, career paths, and so forth, and so women's performances come to be seen as "different" while men's are cited as examples of the "thing itself."

Even in the area of scholarly work,

> Performances such as seminars or writing styles or fieldwork establish certain kinds of masculinity as more or less acceptable; they enact particular masculinities. Moreover, women can and do participate in such performances, whether with commitment, or in parody, or with reluctance.[38]

Gillian Rose goes on to imply that feminist researchers intervene in the masculine performances of ethnography, experimentation, content analysis, and other modes of constructing data out of others' experiences. Often, then, they resist the "fitting in" Fine and Gordon describe. Moreover, they generally talk about the "Other" explicitly and grapple with the frustrations of trying to understand people whom they experience in "otherly" fashion.

One methodological propensity that positions feminist researchers for rich understanding rather than mere reporting is their experiential emphasis. While they do use diverse research methods,[39] they favor methods putting them in close touch with the hum and buzz of people's lives. Thus, those methods relying on people's own accounts hold particular appeal to feminist researchers. Yet feminists do not kid themselves about the hard work of tapping into people's experiences. As Joan W. Scott observes,

> Experience is not a word we can do without, although it is tempting, given its usage to essentialize identity and reify the subject, to abandon it altogether. But experience is so much a part of everyday language, so imbricated in our narratives that it seems futile to argue for its expulsion. . . . it seems more useful to work with it, to analyze its operations and to redefine its meaning. This entails focusing on processes of identity production, insisting on the discursive nature of "experience" and on the politics of its construction. Experience is at once always already an interpretation *and* in need of interpretation.[40]

That experience can never be "raw" or "uninterpreted" means that *standpoints* figure prominently in feminist research.

FEMINIST EPISTEMOLOGIES AND WOMEN'S STUDIES

Like most feminist theorists, Naomi Scheman makes much of the fact that

> modern epistemic authority has attached to those who did minimal physical labor, who neither bore nor reared their own children, grew or cooked or cleaned up after their own food, built or maintained their own homes, produced or cleaned their own clothing, nor nursed the illnesses or eased the deaths of those close to them.[41]

Until feminists began developing their own epistemologies, such cognitive skewing got little attention. What, in the end, did elite men know of life's most mundane, ordinary moments? Of love's daily tasks or the sweaty labor that makes a home welcoming and comfortable? Centuries passed with little skepticism expressed toward the epistemic authority of people ignorant of such realities. This century reversed that trend, though, as subordinated groups rose up in protests that eventually led to Chicana/o studies, African American studies, lesbigay studies, Native American studies, Asian American studies, and of course women's studies. As Narayan indicates in Reading 5, in such circles epistemic benefits were commonly thought to accrue to members of subordinated groups whose circumstances necessitated knowledge about their own group's culture as well as mainstream culture. Narayan points out the costs, including alienation, of such "double vision."

The first women's courses emerged around 1970, and the first annual meeting of the National Women's Studies Association was in 1979. Women's studies represents academic feminism. It centers attention on women with an eye toward enhancing their prospects and curtailing their oppression. Thus, women's studies involves not teaching and research *on* women as much as teaching and research *for* women,[42] as Chapter 4 implies. Women's studies challenges disciplinary borders, perhaps to the point of being transdisciplinary (*beyond* disciplines) rather than multi- or interdisciplinary.[43] Before the emergence of women's studies, women got substantial attention mostly in courses dealing with gender.

I began teaching what amounted to pre-women's studies courses in 1972 when I first taught sociology of sex roles (now sociology of gender), which I have been teaching ever since. I taught from a feminist perspective using works now considered feminist classics—Evelyn Reed's *Problems of Women's Liberation* and Shulamith Firestone's *The Dialectic of Sex,* for example. In a women's studies course today those books still hold at least historical interest, but in a sociology course on gender they would invite charges of male bashing and reverse prejudice.

Back then feminist approaches were less threatening because most people thought that the women's movement would amount to little or nothing. Back then colleges and universities had no policies or procedures for dealing with sexual harassment; much smaller percentages of undergraduates and graduate students were women; fewer women were professors; mothers with preschool children were likely to be working only in the home; feminists were often seen as a handful of left-thinking women incapable of involving other women in their issues. By now circumstances have shifted enough that women's studies has solid grounding as an academic field. Despite resistance from tradition-minded faculty and administrators, women's studies has soundly challenged the epistemic authority once reserved for elite men.

A lot of that challenge has come from feminist epistemologists, whose efforts Narayan surveys from a non-Western perspective in Reading 5. A complement to both Bartky's treatment of alienation and Sandoval's of oppositional consciousness, Narayan's theorizing shows how taking women's experiences into account dramatically changes the what, why, and how of knowledge construction. She emphasizes that feminist ideas derive their practical meaning and political potential in specific contexts, such as the non-Western and Western contexts, which make for distinctly different challenges and struggles. Also noteworthy is Narayan's discussion of nonpositivist perspectives that are at least as troublesome for feminism as positivism itself.

Among their many contributions, feminist epistemologists and other feminist theorists have developed *standpoint theory,* which assumes that "knowledge is always *relative to* (i.e., a perspective *on,* a standpoint *in*) specifiable circumstances." Standpoint theorists aim for "an account of the world which treats [women's] perspectives not as subjugated or disruptive knowledges but as primary and constitutive of a different world."[44] As formulated by Sandra Harding, the author of Reading 7, the idea is broadly that "men's dominating position in social life results in partial and perverse understandings, whereas women's subjugated position provides the possibility of more complete and less perverse understandings."[45]

One influential standpoint theorist driving home that idea is Dorothy E. Smith, the author of Reading 6, whose starting point is that "We can only know society as insiders. . . ." Coupled with that axiom is an equally central one in her framework, namely, "for any set of actual events, there is always more than one version that can be treated as what has happened, even within a simple cultural community." Given these two axioms, Smith urges continual attention to "how a given version is authorized as that version which can be treated by others as what has happened."[46] Thus, no one insider and no one account can ever prove adequate. Multiple insiders offering multiple accounts hold our only hope of understanding what happened. All the while, people's lived experiences remain central to such understanding.

For example, Bonnie Zimmerman observes,

> Most lesbians see the world as a heterosexual for some period of their lives and develop a multiple perspectivity—a form of cultural "bilingualism"—that can reinforce the connections . . . between lesbian and heterosexual feminist perspectives.

Zimmerman goes on to "suggest that lesbian-feminist readers resist 'heterotexts' by privately rewriting and thus appropriating them as lesbian texts," specifically by "picking up on hints and possibilities that the author, consciously or not, has strewn in the text."[47] Thus does Zimmerman show how valuable standpoint theory can be. By focusing on readers whose standpoints are usually ignored or distorted, we gain insights not only into the dynamics of coping with a heterosexist world but also into how readers generally appropriate and complete the texts they read. In parallel fashion, Joyce A. Joyce points to the applicability of standpoint theory to African American women's and men's literatures:

> The Euro-American literary establishment privileges the separation of art and social circumstances and judges literary works with overt moral values and didactic subjects inferior to those whose covert meanings are expressed in figurative and obscure language.[48]

Needless to say, standpoint theory is no panacea for what is distortional in and absent from extant knowledge. Indeed, it poses its own distinctive challenges, as those favoring "analytic feminism" tend to emphasize.[49] Yet feminist standpoint theory does represent a move away from false certainties, facile overgeneralizations, and narrowly skewed perspectives that leave women out or marginalize their viewpoints. Such movement can be unsettling, at least in the short run. As Alcoff and Potter point out, feminist epistemology involves "the uneasy alliance of feminism and philosophy, an alliance made uneasy by [a] contradictory pull between the concrete and the universal." Alongside that source of tension stands the diversity of standpoints among women. Thus, when theorists like Dale Spender "theorise about theorising," they conclude that "tolerat[ing] ambiguity and contradiction" is part and parcel of feminist theory. Similarly, Harding suggests that we use as our standard of adequate theorizing a fidelity to certain parameters of dissonance with and between the assumptions of these discourses. This approach to theorizing captures the feminist emphasis on contextual thinking and decision making . . . where we recognize that we cannot order reality into the forms we might desire. We need to be able to cherish certain kinds of intellectual, political, and psychic discomforts, to see as inappropriate and even dangerous certain kinds of clear solutions to the problems we have been posing.[50]

Theorizing does illuminate, but what it illuminates is often full of ambiguities and contradictions. When we theorize, then, we practice an art—the art of respecting language and understanding its profound powers for reinforcing or reconstructing the relations of ruling; the art of taking multiple standpoints into serious account and cultivating complex understandings; the art of appreciating the awesome riches of social life, the unutterable singularity of each individual, and the connections that keep people strong. Theorizing is no science, then. But science is no science either when stripped of the constructions that position it near the core of the relations of ruling. Instead, it is a complex quest and, like art, it demands imagination, stamina, and derring-do from those who aim to make a difference through their work.

In Reading 6, Smith illustrates these and other points by showing how the incorporation of women's experiences, including our "bifurcation of consciousness," or what Narayan calls our "double vision," turns a discipline like sociology inside out and upside down. "Knowing a society from within," knowing it from women's perspectives, moves us past the objectivity that mystifies power and privilege and props up authoritative accounts of social reality. Knowing from within challenges the relations of ruling; it forces us to accept other people's reality as an "unconditional datum."

In Reading 7, Harding makes resonant points by focusing a multicultural lens on the matrix of domination. Hers is an epistemological effort not only *from* but also *for* "rainbow coalition politics." Her theorizing resounds with some of the most crucial insights taking shape in contemporary feminist theory—insights about "difference," voice, multiplicity, subjectivity, feminist consciousness, struggle, and transformation. Harding's is thus an embracing vision replete not only with theoretical richness but also with practical ramifications.

NOTES

1. Amy Mullin, "Art, Politics and Knowledge: Feminism, Modernity, and the Separation of Spheres," *Metaphilosophy* 27, 1/2 (January/April 1996), p. 119.
2. Evelyn Reed, *Sexism & Science* (New York and Toronto: Pathfinder Press, 1978), pp. 34, 35, 43. The five published papers mentioned in the text, plus three others, appear together in this volume.

The Project of Feminist Epistemology: Perspectives from a Non-Western Feminist

Uma Narayan

A fundamental thesis of feminist epistemology is that our location in the world as women makes it possible for us to perceive and understand different aspects of both the world and human activities in ways that challenge the male bias of existing perspectives. Feminist epistemology is a particular manifestation of the general insight that the nature of women's experiences as individuals and as social beings, our contributions to work, culture, knowledge, and our history and political interests have been systematically ignored or misrepresented by mainstream discourses in different areas.

Women have been often excluded from prestigious areas of human activity (for example, politics or science) and this has often made these activities seem clearly "male." In areas where women were not excluded (for example, subsistence work), their contribution has been misrepresented as secondary and inferior to that of men. Feminist epistemology sees mainstream theories about various human enterprises, including mainstream theories about human knowledge, as one-dimensional and deeply flawed because of the exclusion and misrepresentation of women's contributions.

Feminist epistemology suggests that integrating women's contribution into the domain of science and knowledge will not constitute a mere adding of details; it will not merely widen the canvas but result in a shift of perspective en-abling us to see a very different picture. The inclusion of women's perspective will not merely amount to women participating in greater numbers in the existing practice of science and knowledge, but it will change the very nature of these activities and their self-understanding.

It would be misleading to suggest that feminist epistemology is a homogenous and cohesive enterprise. Its practitioners differ both philosophically and politically in a number of significant ways (Harding 1986). But an important theme on its agenda has been to undermine the abstract, rationalistic, and universal image of the scientific enterprise by using several different strategies. It has studied, for instance, how contingent historical factors have colored both scientific theories and practices and provided the (often sexist) metaphors in which scientists have conceptualized their activity (Bordo 1986; Keller 1985; Harding and O'Barr 1987). It has tried to reintegrate values and emotions into our account of our cognitive activities, arguing for both the inevitability of their presence and the importance of the contributions they are capable of making to our knowledge (Gilligan 1982; . . .). It has also attacked various sets of dualisms characteristic of western philosophical thinking—reason versus emotion, culture versus nature, universal versus particular—in which the first of each set is identified with science, rationality, and the masculine and the second is relegated to the nonscientific, the nonrational, and the feminine (Harding and Hintikka 1983; Lloyd 1984; . . .).

At the most general level, feminist epistemology resembles the efforts of many oppressed groups to reclaim for themselves the value of their own experience. The writing of novels that focused on working-class life in England or the lives of black people in the United States shares a motivation similar to that of feminist epistemology—to depict an experience different from the norm and to assert the value of this difference.

In a similar manner, feminist epistemology also resembles attempts by third-world writers and historians to document the wealth and complexity of local economic and social structures that existed prior to colonialism. These attempts are useful for their ability to restore to colonized peoples a sense of the richness of their own history and culture. These projects also mitigate the tendency of intellectuals in former colonies who are westernized through their education to think that anything western is necessarily better and more "progressive." In some cases, such studies help to preserve the knowledge of many local arts, crafts, lore, and techniques that were part of the former way of life before they are lost not only to practice but even to memory.

These enterprises are analogous to feminist epistemology's project of restoring to women a sense of the richness of their history, to mitigate our tendency to see the stereotypically "masculine" as better or more progressive, and to preserve for posterity the contents of "feminine" areas of knowledge and expertise—medical lore, knowledge associated with the practices of childbirth and child rearing, traditionally feminine crafts, and so on. Feminist epistemology, like these other enterprises, must attempt to balance the assertion of the value of a different culture or experience against the dangers of romanticizing it to the extent that the limitations and oppressions it confers on its subjects are ignored.

My essay will attempt to examine some dangers of approaching feminist theorizing and epistemological values in a noncontextual and nonpragmatic way, which could convert important feminist insights and theses into feminist epistemological dogmas. I will use my perspective as a nonwestern, Indian feminist to examine critically the predominantly Anglo-American project of feminist epistemology and to reflect on what such a project might signify for women in nonwestern cultures in general and for nonwestern feminists in particular. I will suggest that different cultural contexts and political agendas may cast a very different light on both the "idols" and the "enemies" of knowledge as they have characteristically been typed in western feminist epistemology.

In keeping with my respect for contexts, I would like to stress that I do not see nonwestern feminists as a homogenous group and that none of the concerns I express as a nonwestern feminist may be pertinent to or shared by *all* nonwestern feminists, although I do think they will make sense to many. . . .

NONWESTERN FEMINIST POLITICS AND FEMINIST EPISTEMOLOGY

Some themes of feminist epistemology may be problematic for nonwestern feminists in ways that they are not problematic for western feminists. Feminism has a much narrower base in most nonwestern countries. It is primarily of significance to some urban, educated, middle-class, and hence relatively westernized women, like myself. Although feminist groups in these countries do try to extend the scope of feminist concerns to other groups (for example, by fighting for child care, women's health issues, and equal wages issues through trade union structures), some major preoccupations of western feminism—its critique of marriage, the family, compulsory heterosexuality—presently engage the attention of mainly small groups of middle-class feminists.

These feminists must think and function within the context of a powerful tradition that, although it systematically oppresses women, also contains within itself a discourse that confers a high value on women's place in the general scheme of things. Not only are the roles of wife and mother highly praised, but women also are seen as the cornerstones of the spiritual well-being of their husbands and children, admired for their supposedly higher moral, religious, and spiritual qualities, and so on. In cultures that have a pervasive religious component, like the Hindu culture with which I am familiar, everything seems assigned a place and value as long as it keeps to its place. Confronted with a powerful traditional discourse that values woman's place as long as she keeps to the place prescribed, it may be politically counterproductive for nonwestern feminists to echo uncritically the themes of western feminist epistemology that seek to restore the value, cognitive and otherwise, of "women's experience."

The danger is that, even if the nonwestern feminist talks about the value of women's experience in terms totally different from those of traditional discourse, the difference is likely to be drowned out by the louder and more powerful voice of the traditional discourse, which will then claim that "what those feminists say" vindicates its view that the roles and experiences it assigns to women have value and that women should stick to those rules.

I do not intend to suggest that this is not a danger for western feminism or to imply that there is no tension for western feminists between being critical of the experiences that their societies have provided for women and finding things to value in them nevertheless. But I am suggesting that perhaps there is less at risk for western feminists in trying to strike this balance. I am inclined to think that in nonwestern countries feminists must still stress the negative sides of the female experience within that culture and that the time for a more sympathetic evaluation is not quite ripe.

But the issue is not simple and seems even less so when another point is considered. The imperative we experience as feminists to be critical of how our culture and traditions oppress women conflicts with our desire as members of once colonized cultures to affirm the value of the same culture and traditions.

There are seldom any easy resolutions to these sorts of tensions. As an Indian feminist currently living in the United States, I often find myself torn between the desire to communicate with honesty the miseries and oppressions that I think my own culture confers on its women and the fear that this communication is going to reinforce, however unconsciously, western prejudices about the "superiority" of western culture. I have often felt compelled to interrupt my communication, say on the problems of the Indian system of arranged marriages, to remind my western friends that the experiences of women under their system of "romantic love" seem no more enviable. Perhaps we should all attempt to cultivate the methodological habit of trying to understand the complexities of the oppression involved in different historical and cultural settings while eschewing, at least for now, the temptation to make comparisons across such settings, given the dangers of attempting to compare what may well be incommensurable in any neat terms.

THE NONPRIMACY OF POSITIVISM AS A PROBLEMATIC PERSPECTIVE

As a nonwestern feminist, I also have some reservations about the way in which feminist epistemology seems to have picked positivism as its main target of attack. The choice of positivism as the main target is reasonable because it has been a dominant and influential western position and it most clearly embodies some flaws that feminist epistemology seeks to remedy.

But this focus on positivism should not blind us to the facts that it is not our only enemy and that nonpositivist frameworks are not, by virtue of that bare qualification, any more worthy of our tolerance. Most traditional frameworks that nonwestern feminists regard as oppressive to women are not positivist, and it would be wrong to see feminist epistemology's critique of positivism given the same political importance for nonwestern feminists that it has for western feminists. Traditions like my own, where the influence of religion is pervasive, are suffused through and through with values. We must fight not frameworks that assert the separation of fact and value but frameworks that are pervaded by values to which we, as feminists, find ourselves opposed. Positivism in epistemology flourished at the same time as liberalism in western political theory. Positivism's view of values as individual and subjective related to liberalism's political emphasis on individual rights that were supposed to protect an individual's freedom to live according to the values she espoused.

Nonwestern feminists may find themselves in a curious bind when confronting the interrelations between positivism and political liberalism. As colonized people, we are well aware of the facts that many political concepts of liberalism are both suspicious and confused and that the practice of liberalism in the colonies was marked by brutalities unaccounted for by its theory. However, as feminists, we often find some of its concepts, such as individual rights, very useful in our attempts to fight problems rooted in our traditional cultures.

Nonwestern feminists will no doubt be sensitive to the fact that positivism is not our only enemy. Western feminists too must learn not to uncritically claim any nonpositivist framework as an ally; despite commonalities, there are apt to be many differences. A temperate look at positions we espouse as allies is necessary since "the enemy of my enemy is my friend" is a principle likely to be as misleading in epistemology as it is in the domain of Realpolitik.

. . .

THE POLITICAL USES OF "EPISTEMIC PRIVILEGE"

Important strands in feminist epistemology hold the view that our concrete embodiments as members of a specific class, race, and gender as well as our concrete historical situations necessarily play significant roles in our perspective on the world; moreover, no point of view is "neutral" because no one exists unembedded in the world. Knowledge is seen as gained not by solitary individuals but by socially constituted members of groups that emerge and change through history.

Feminists have also argued that groups living under various forms of oppression are more likely to have a critical perspective on their situation and that this critical view is both generated and partly constituted by critical emotional responses that subjects experience vis-à-vis their life situations. This perspective in feminist epistemology rejects the "Dumb View" of emotions and favors an intentional conception that emphasizes the cognitive aspect of emotions. It is critical of the traditional view of the emotions as wholly and always impediments to knowledge and argues that many emotions often help rather than hinder our understanding of a person or situation. . . .

Bringing together these views on the role of the emotions in knowledge, the possibility of critical insights being generated by oppression, and the contextual nature of knowledge may suggest some answers to serious and interesting political questions. I will consider what these epistemic positions entail regarding the possibility of understanding and political cooperation between oppressed groups and sympathetic members of a dominant group—say, between white people and people of color over issues of race or between men and women over issues of gender.

These considerations are also relevant to questions of understanding and cooperation between western and nonwestern feminists. Western feminists, despite their critical understanding of their own culture, often tend to be more a part of it than they realize. If they fail to see the contexts of their theories and assume that their perspective has universal validity for all feminists, they tend to participate in the dominance that western culture has exercised over nonwestern cultures.

Our position must explain and justify our dual need to criticize members of a dominant group (say men or white people or western feminists) for their lack of attention to or concern with problems that affect an oppressed group (say, women or people of color or nonwestern feminists, respectively), as well as for our frequent hostility toward those who express interest, even sympathetic interest, in issues that concern groups of which they are not a part.

Both attitudes are often warranted. On the one hand, one cannot but be angry at those who minimize, ignore, or dismiss the pain and conflict that racism and sexism inflict on their victims. On the other hand, living in a state of siege also necessarily makes us suspicious of expressions of concern and support from those who do not live these oppressions. We are suspicious of the motives of our sympathizers or the extent of their sincerity, and we worry, often with good reason, that they may claim that their interest provides a warrant for them to speak for us, as dominant groups throughout history have spoken for the dominated.

This is all the more threatening to groups aware of how recently they have acquired the power to articulate their own points of view. Nonwestern feminists are especially aware of this because they have a double struggle in trying to find their own voice: they have to learn to articulate their differences, not only from their own traditional contexts but also from western feminism.

Politically, we face interesting questions whose answers hinge on the nature and extent of the communication that we think possible between different groups. Should we try to share our perspectives and insights with those who have not lived our oppressions and accept that they may fully come to share them? Or should we seek only the affirmation of those like ourselves, who share common features of oppression, and rule out the possibility of those who have not lived these oppressions ever acquiring a genuine understanding of them?

I argue that it would be a mistake to move from the thesis that knowledge is constructed by human subjects who are socially constituted to the conclusion that those who are differently located socially can never attain *some* understanding of our experience or *some* sympathy with our cause. In that case, we would be committed to not just a perspectival view of knowledge but a relativistic one, Relativism, as I am using it, implies that a person could have knowledge of only the sorts of things she had experienced personally and that she would be totally unable to

communicate any of the contents of her knowledge to someone who did not have the same sorts of experiences. Not only does this seem clearly false and perhaps even absurd, but it is probably a good idea not to have any a priori views that would imply either that all our knowledge is always capable of being communicated to every other person or that would imply that some of our knowledge is necessarily incapable of being communicated to some class of persons.

"Nonanalytic" and "nonrational" forms of discourse, like fiction or poetry, may be better able than other forms to convey the complex life experiences of one group to members of another. One can also hope that being part of one oppressed group may enable an individual to have a more sympathetic understanding of issues relating to another kind of oppression—that, for instance, being a woman may sensitize one to issues of race and class even if one is a woman privileged in those respects.

Again, this should not be reduced to some kind of metaphysical presumption. Historical circumstances have sometimes conspired, say, to making working-class men more chauvinistic in some of their attitudes than other men. Sometimes one sort of suffering may simply harden individuals to other sorts or leave them without energy to take any interest in the problems of other groups. But we can at least try to foster such sensitivity by focusing on parallels, not identities, between different sorts of oppressions.

Our commitment to the contextual nature of knowledge does not require us to claim that those who do not inhabit these contexts can never have any knowledge of them. But this commitment does permit us to argue that it is *easier* and *more likely* for the oppressed to have critical insights into the conditions of their own oppression than it is for those who live outside these structures. Those who actually *live* the oppressions of class, race, or gender have faced the issues that such oppressions generate in a variety of different situations. The insights and emotional responses engendered by these situations are a legacy with which they confront any new issue or situation.

Those who display sympathy as outsiders often fail both to understand fully the emotional complexities of living as a member of an oppressed group and to carry what they have learned and understood about one situation to the way they perceive another. It is a commonplace that even sympathetic men will often fail to perceive subtle instances of sexist behavior or discourse.

Sympathetic individuals who are not members of an oppressed group should keep in mind the possibility of this sort of failure regarding their understanding of issues relating to an oppression they do not share. They should realize that nothing they may do, from participating in demonstrations to changing their lifestyles, can make them one of the oppressed. For instance, men who share household and child-rearing responsibilities with women are mistaken if they think that this act of choice, often buttressed by the gratitude and admiration of others, is anything like the woman's experience of being forcibly socialized into these tasks and of having others perceive this as her natural function in the scheme of things.

The view that we can understand much about the perspectives of those whose oppression we do not share allows us the space to criticize dominant groups for their blindness to the facts of oppression. The view that such an understanding, despite great effort and interest, is likely to be incomplete or limited, provides us with the ground for denying total parity to members of a dominant group in their ability to understand our situation.

Sympathetic members of a dominant group need not necessarily defer to our views on any particular issue because that may reduce itself to another subtle form of condescension, but at least they must keep in mind the very real difficulties and possibility of failure to fully understand our concerns. This and the very important need for dominated groups to control the means of discourse about their own situations are important reasons for taking seriously the claim that oppressed groups have an "epistemic advantage."

THE DARK SIDE OF "DOUBLE VISION"

I think that one of the most interesting insights of feminist epistemology is the view that oppressed groups, whether women, the poor, or racial minorities, may derive an "epistemic advantage" from having knowledge of the practices of both their own contexts and those of their oppressors. The practices of the dominant groups (for instance, men) govern a society; the dominated group (for instance, women) must acquire some fluency with these practices in order to survive in that society.

There is no similar pressure on members of the dominant group to acquire knowledge of the practices of the dominated groups. For instance, colonized people had to learn the language and culture of their colonizers. The colonizers seldom found it necessary to have more than a sketchy acquaintance with the language and culture of the "natives." Thus, the oppressed are seen as having an "epistemic advantage" because they can operate with two sets of practices and in two different contexts. This advantage is thought to lead to critical insights because each framework provides a critical perspective on the other.

I would like to balance this account with a few comments about the "dark side," the disadvantages, of being able to or of having to inhabit two mutually incompatible frameworks that provide differing perspectives on social reality. I suspect that nonwestern feminists, given the often complex and troublesome interrelationships between the contexts they must inhabit, are less likely to express unqualified enthusiasm about the benefits of straddling a multiplicity of contexts. Mere access to two different and incompatible contexts is not a guarantee that a critical stance on the part of an individual will result. There are many ways in which she may deal with the situation.

First, the person may be tempted to dichotomize her life and reserve the framework of a different context for each part. The middle class of nonwestern countries supplies numerous examples of people who are very westernized in public life but who return to a very traditional lifestyle in the realm of the family. Women may choose to live their public lives in a "male" mode, displaying characteristics of aggressiveness, competition, and so on, while continuing to play dependent and compliant roles in their private lives. The pressures of jumping between two different lifestyles may be mitigated by justifications of how each pattern of behavior is appropriate to its particular context and of how it enables them to "get the best of both worlds."

Second, the individual may try to reject the practices of her own context and try to be as much as possible like members of the dominant group. Westernized intellectuals in the nonwestern world often may almost lose knowledge of their own cultures and practices and be ashamed of the little that they do still know. Women may try both to acquire stereotypically male characteristics, like aggressiveness, and to expunge stereotypically female characteristics, like emotionality. Or the individual could try to reject entirely the framework of the dominant group and assert the virtues of her own despite the risks of being marginalized from the power structures of the society; consider, for example, women who seek a certain sort of security in traditionally defined roles.

The choice to inhabit two contexts critically is an alternative to these choices and, I would argue, a more useful one. But the presence of alternative contexts does not by itself guarantee that one of the other choices will not be made. Moreover, the decision to inhabit two contexts critically, although it may lead to an "epistemic advantage," is likely to exact a certain price. It may lead to a sense of totally lacking roots or any space where one is at home in a relaxed manner.

This sense of alienation may be minimized if the critical straddling of two contexts is part of an ongoing critical politics, due to the support of others and a deeper understanding of what is going on. When it is not so rooted, it may generate ambivalence, uncertainty, despair, and even madness, rather than more positive critical emotions and attitudes. However such a person determines her locus, there may be a sense of being an outsider in both contexts and a sense of clumsiness or lack of fluency in both sets of practices. Consider this simple linguistic example: most people who learn two different languages that are associated with two very different cultures seldom acquire both with equal fluency; they may find themselves devoid of vocabulary in one language for certain contexts of life or be unable to match real objects with terms they have acquired in their vocabulary. For instance, people from my sort of background would know words in Indian languages for some spices, fruits, and vegetables that they do not know in English. Similarly, they might be unable to discuss "technical" subjects like economics or biology in their own languages because they learned about these subjects and acquired their technical vocabularies only in English.

The relation between the two contexts the individual inhabits may not be simple or straightforward. The individual subject is seldom in a position to carry out a perfect "dialectical synthesis" that preserves all the advantages of both contexts and transcends all their problems. There may be a number of different "syntheses," each of which avoids a different subset of the problems and preserves a different subset of the benefits.

No solution may be perfect or even palatable to the agent confronted with a choice. For example, some Indian feminists may find some western modes of dress (say trousers) either more comfortable or more their "style" than some local modes of dress. However, they may find that wearing the local mode of dress is less socially troublesome, alienates them less from more traditional people they want to work with, and so on. Either choice is bound to leave them partly frustrated in their desires.

Feminists theory must be temperate in the use it makes of this doctrine of "double vision"—the claim that oppressed groups have an epistemic advantage and access to greater critical conceptual space. Certain types and contexts of oppression certainly may bear out the truth of this claim. Others certainly do not seem to do so; and even if they do provide space for critical insights, they may also rule out the possibility of actions subversive of the oppressive state of affairs.

Certain kinds of oppressive contexts, such as the contexts in which women of my grandmother's background lived, rendered their subjects entirely devoid of skills required to function as independent entities in the culture. Girls were married off barely past puberty, trained for nothing beyond household tasks and the rearing of children, and passed from economic dependency on their fathers to economic dependency on their husbands to economic dependency on their sons in old age. Their criticisms of their lot were articulated, if at all, in terms that precluded a desire or any radical change. They saw themselves sometimes as personally unfortunate, but they did not locate the causes of their misery in larger social arrangements.

I conclude by stressing that the important insight incorporated in the doctrine of "double vision" should not be reified into a metaphysics that serves as a substitute for concrete social analysis. Furthermore, the alternative to "buying" into an oppressive social system need not be a celebration of exclusion and the mechanisms of marginalization. The thesis that oppression may bestow an epistemic advantage should not tempt us in the direction of idealizing or romanticizing oppression and blind us to its real material and psychic deprivations.

REFERENCES

Bordo, S. "The Cartesian Masculinization of Thought." *Signs: Journal of Women in Culture and Society* 11 (1986), pp. 439–56.

Gilligan, C. *In a Different Voice: Psychological Theory and Women's Development.* Cambridge, MA: Harvard University Press, 1982.

Harding, S. *The Science Question in Feminism.* Ithaca, NY: Cornell University Press, 1986.

Harding, S., and M. Hintikka. *Discovering Reality: Feminist Perspectives on Epistemology, Metaphysics, Methodology, and Philosophy of Science.* Dordrecht: Reidel, 1983.

Harding, S., and J. O'Barr, eds. *Sex and Scientific Inquiry,* Chicago: University of Chicago Press, 1987.

Keller, E. F. *Reflections on Gender and Science.* New Haven, CT: Yale University Press, 1985.

Lloyd, G. *The Man of Reason.* Minneapolis: University of Minnesota Press, 1984.

READING 6

Women's Experience as a Radical Critique of Sociology

Dorothy E. Smith

RELATIONS OF RULING AND OBJECTIFIED KNOWLEDGE

When I speak . . . of governing or ruling I mean something more general than the notion of government as political organization. I refer rather to that total complex of activities, differentiated into many spheres, by which our kind of society is ruled, managed, and administered. It includes what the business world calls *management,* it includes the professions, it includes government and the activities of those who are selecting, training, and indoctrinating those who will be its governors. The last includes those who provide and elaborate the procedures by which it is governed and develop methods for accounting for how it is done—namely, the business schools, the sociologists, the economists. These are the institutions through which we are ruled and through which we, and I emphasize this *we,* participate in ruling.

Sociology, then, I conceive as much more than a gloss on the enterprise that justifies and rationalizes it, and at the same time as much less than "science." The governing of our kind of society is done in abstract concepts and symbols, and sociology helps create them by transposing the actualities of people's lives and experience into the conceptual currency with which they can be governed.

Thus the relevances of sociology are organized in terms of a perspective on the world, a view from the top that takes for granted the pragmatic procedures of governing as those that frame and identify its subject matter. Issues are formulated because they are administratively relevant, not because they are significant first in the experience of those who live them. The kinds of facts and events that matter to sociologists have already been shaped and given their character and substance by the methods and practice of governing. Mental illness, crimes, riots, violence, work satisfaction, neighbors and neighborhoods, motivation, and so on—these are the constructs of the practice of government. Many of these constructs, such as mental illness, crimes, or neighborhoods, are constituted as discrete phenomena in the institutional contexts of ruling; others arise as problems in relation to the actual practice of government or management (for example, concepts of violence, motivation, or work satisfaction).

The governing processes of our society are organized as social entities external to those persons who participate in and perform them. Sociologists study these entities under the heading of formal organization. They are objectified structures with goals, activities, obligations, and so on, separate from those of the persons who work for them. The academic professions are similarly constituted. Members of a discipline accumulate knowledge that is then appropriated by the discipline as its own. The work of members aims at contributing to that body of knowledge.

As graduate students learning to become sociologists, we learn to think sociology as it is thought and to practice it as it is practiced. We learn that some topics are relevant and others are not. We learn to discard our personal experience as a source of reliable information about the character of the world and to confine and focus our insights within the conceptual frameworks and relevances of the discipline. Should we think other kinds of thoughts or experience the world in a different way or with horizons that pass beyond the conceptual, we must discard them or find some way to sneak them in. We learn a way of thinking about the world that is recognizable to its practitioners as the sociological way of thinking.

We learn to practice the sociological subsumption of the actualities of ourselves and of other people. We find out how to treat the world as instances of a sociological body of knowledge. The procedure operates as a sort of conceptual imperialism. When we write a thesis or a paper, we learn that the first thing to do is to latch it on to the discipline at some point. This may be by showing how it is a problem within an existing theoretical and conceptual framework. The boundaries of inquiry are thus set within the framework of what is already established. Even when this becomes, as it happily often does, a ceremonial authorization of a project that has little to do with the theory used to authorize it, we still work within the vocabularies and within the conceptual boundaries of "the sociological perspective."

An important set of procedures that serve to separate the discipline's body of knowledge from its practitioners is known as *objectivity.* The ethic of objectivity and the methods used in its practice are concerned primarily with the separation of knowers from what they know and in particular with the separation of what is known from knowers' interests, "biases," and so forth, that are not authorized by the discipline. In the social sciences the pursuit of objectivity makes it possible for people to be paid to pursue a knowledge to which they are otherwise indifferent. What they feel and think about society can be kept out of what they are professionally or academically interested in. Correlatively, if they are interested in exploring a topic sociologically, they must find ways of converting their private interest into an objectified, unbiased form.

SOCIOLOGY PARTICIPATES IN THE EXTRALOCAL RELATIONS OF RULING

Sociologists, when they go to work, enter into the conceptually ordered society they are investigating. They observe, analyze, explain, and examine that world as if there were no problem in how it becomes observable to them. They move among the doings of organizations, governmental processes, and bureaucracies as people who are at home in that medium. The nature of that world itself, how it is known to them, the conditions of its existence, and their relation to it are not called into question. Their methods of observation and inquiry extend into it as procedures that are essentially of the same order as those that bring about the phenomena they are concerned with. Their perspectives and interests may differ, but the substance is the same. They work with facts and information that have been worked up from actualities and appear in the form of documents that are themselves the product of organizational processes, whether their own or those of some other agency. They fit that information back into a framework of entities and organizational processes which they take for granted as known, without asking how it is that they know them or by what social processes

the actual events—what people do or utter—are construed as the phenomena known.

Where a traditional gender division of labor prevails, men enter the conceptually organized world of governing without a sense of transition. The male sociologist in these circumstances passes beyond his particular and immediate setting (the office he writes in, the libraries he consults, the streets he travels, the home he returns to) without attending to the shift in consciousness. He works in the very medium he studies.

But, of course, like everyone else, he also exists in the body in the place in which it is. This is also then the place of his sensory organization of immediate experience; the place where his coordinates of here and now, before and after, are organized around himself as center; the place where he confronts people face to face in the physical mode in which he expresses himself to them and they to him as more and other than either can speak. This is the place where things smell, where the irrelevant birds fly away in front of the window, where he had indigestion, where he dies. Into this space must come as actual material events—whether as sounds of speech, scratchings on the surface of paper, which he constitutes as text, or directly—anything he knows of the world. It has to happen here somehow if he is to experience it at all.

Entering the governing mode of our kind of society lifts actors out of the immediate, local, and particular place in which we are in the body. What becomes present to us in the governing mode is a means of passing beyond the local into the conceptual order. This mode of governing creates, at least potentially, a bifurcation of consciousness. It establishes two modes of knowing and experiencing and doing, one located in the body and in the space it occupies and moves in, the other passing beyond it. Sociology is written in and aims at the latter mode of action. Robert Bierstedt writes, "Sociology can liberate the mind from time and space themselves and remove it to a new and transcendental realm where it no longer depends upon these

Aristotelian categories."[1] Even observational work aims at description in the categories and hence conceptual forms of the "transcendental realm." Yet the local and particular site of knowing that is the other side of the bifurcated consciousness has not been a site for the development of systematic knowledge.

WOMEN'S EXCLUSION FROM THE GOVERNING CONCEPTUAL MODE

The suppression of the local and particular as a site of knowledge has been and remains gender organized. The domestic sites of women's work, traditionally identified with women, are outside and subservient to this structure. Men have functioned as subjects in the mode of governing; women have been anchored in the local and particular phase of the bifurcated world. It has been a condition of a man's being able to enter and become absorbed in the conceptual mode, and to forget the dependence of his being in that mode upon his bodily existence, that he does not have to focus his activities and interests upon his bodily existence. Full participation in the abstract mode of action requires liberation from attending to needs in the concrete and particular. The organization of work in managerial and professional circles depends upon the alienation of subjects from their bodily and local existence. The structure of work and the structure of career take for granted that these matters have been provided for in such a way that they will not interfere with a man's action and participation in that world. Under the traditional gender regime, providing for a man's liberation from Bierstedt's Aristotelian categories is a woman who keeps house for him, bears and cares for his children, washes his clothes, looks after him when he is sick, and generally provides for the logistics of his bodily existence.

Women's work in and around professional and managerial settings performs analogous functions. Women's work mediates between the abstracted and conceptual and the material form in which it must travel to communicate. Women do the clerical work, the word processing, the interviewing for the survey; they take messages, handle the mail, make appointments, and care for patients. At almost every point women mediate for men at work the relationship between the conceptual mode of action and the actual concrete forms in which it is and must be realized, and the actual material conditions upon which it depends.

Marx's concept of alienation is applicable here in a modified form. The simplest formulation of alienation posits a relation between the work individuals do and an external order oppressing them in which their work contributes to the strength of the order that oppresses them. This is the situation of women in this relation. The more successful women are in mediating the world of concrete particulars so that men do not have to become engaged with (and therefore conscious of) that world as a condition to their abstract activities, the more complete men's absorption in it and the more effective its authority. The dichotomy between the two worlds organized on the basis of gender separates the dual forms of consciousness; the governing consciousness dominates the primary world of a locally situated consciousness but cannot cancel it; the latter is a subordinated, suppressed, absent, but absolutely essential ground of the governing consciousness. The gendered organization of subjectivity dichotomizes the two worlds, estranges them, and silences the locally situated consciousness by silencing women.

WOMEN SOCIOLOGISTS AND THE CONTRADICTION BETWEEN SOCIOLOGY AND EXPERIENCE

Bifurcation of consciousness is experienced as women move between these two modes with a working consciousness active in both. We are situated as sociologists across a contradiction in our discipline's relationship to our experience of the world. Traditional gender roles deny the existence of the contradiction; suppression makes it invisible, as it has made other contradictions between women and men invisible. Recognizing, exploring, and working within it means finding alternative ways of thinking and inquiry to those that would implicate us in the sociological practice of the relations of ruling.

The theories, concepts, and methods of our discipline claim to be capable of accounting for the world we experience directly. But they have been organized around and built up from a way of knowing the world that takes for granted and subsumes without examining the conditions of its own existence. It is not capable of analyzing its relation to its conditions because the sociological subject as an actual person in an actual concrete setting has been canceled in the procedures that objectify and separate her from her knowledge. Thus the linkage that points back to its conditions is obliterated.

For women those conditions are a direct practical problem to be somehow solved in doing sociological work and following a sociological career. How are we to manage career and children (including of course negotiating sharing that work with a man)? How is domestic work to get done? How is career time to be coordinated with family caring time? How is the remorseless structure of the children's school schedule to be coordinated with the equally exigent scheduling of professional and managerial work? Rarely are these problems solved by the full sharing of responsibilities between women and men. But for the most part these claims, these calls, these somehow unavoidable demands, are still ongoingly present and pressing for women, particularly, of course, for those with children. Thus the relation between ourselves as practicing sociologists and ourselves as working women is always there for us as a practical matter, an ordinary, unremarked, yet pervasive aspect of our experience of the world. The bifurcation of consciousness becomes for us a daily chasm to be crossed, on the one side of which is this special conceptual activity of thought, research, teaching, and administration, and on the other the world of local-

ized activities oriented toward particular others, keeping things clean, managing somehow the house and household and the children—a world in which the particularities of persons in their full organic immediacy (feeding, cleaning up the vomit, changing the diapers) are inescapable. Even if this isn't something that currently preoccupies us, as it no longer preoccupies me, our present is given shape by a past that was thus.

We have learned, as women in sociology, that the discipline has not been one that we could enter and occupy on the same terms as men. We do not fully appropriate its authority, that is, the right to author and authorize the acts of knowing and thinking that are the knowing and thinking of the discipline. Feminist theory in sociology is still *feminist* theory and not just plain sociological theory. The inner principles of our theoretical work remain lodged outside us. The frames of reference that order the terms upon which inquiry and discussion are conducted have originated with men. The subjects of sociological sentences (if they have a subject) are still male, even though protocol now calls for a degendering of pronouns. Even before we became conscious of our sex as the basis of an exclusion (they have not been talking about us), we nonetheless could not fully enter ourselves as the subjects of its statements. The problem remains; we must suspend our sex and suspend our knowledge of who we are as well as who it is that in fact is speaking and of whom. Even now, we do not fully participate in the declarations and formulations of its mode of consciousness. The externalization of sociology as a profession is for women an estrangement both in suppressing dimensions of our experience as women and in creating for our use systems of interpreting and understanding our society that enforce that suppression.

Women who move between these two worlds have access to an experience that displays for us the structure of the bifurcated consciousness. For those of us who are sociologists, it undermines our commitment to a sociology aimed at an externalized body of knowledge based on an organization of experience that excludes ours.

KNOWING A SOCIETY FROM WITHIN: A WOMAN'S PERSPECTIVE

An alternative sociological approach must somehow transcend this contradiction without reentering Bierstedt's "transcendental realm." Women's standpoint, as I am analyzing it here, discredits sociology's claim to constitute an objective knowledge independent of the sociologist's situation. Sociology's conceptual procedures, methods, and relevances organize its subject matter from a determinate position in society. This critical disclosure is the basis of an alternative way of thinking sociology. If sociology cannot avoid being situated, then it should take that as its beginning and build it into its methodological and theoretical strategies. As it is now, these strategies separate a sociologically constructed world from that of direct experience; it is precisely that separation that must be undone.

I am not proposing an immediate and radical transformation of the subject matter and methods of the discipline nor the junking of everything that has gone before. What I am suggesting is more in the nature of a reorganization of the relationship of sociologists to the object of our knowledge and of our problematic. This reorganization involves first placing sociologists where we are actually situated, namely, at the beginning of those acts by which we know or will come to know, and second, making our direct embodied experience of the everyday world the primary ground of our knowledge.

A sociology worked on in this way would not have as its objective a body of knowledge subsisting in and of itself; inquiry would not be justified by its contribution to the heaping up of such a body. We would reject a sociology aimed primarily at itself. We would not be interested in contributing to a body of knowledge whose uses are articulated to relations of ruling in which women participate only marginally, if at all. The professional sociologist is trained to think in the

objectified modes of sociological discourse, to think sociology as it has been and is thought; that training and practice have to be discarded. Rather, as sociologists we would be constrained by the actualities of how things come about in people's direct experience, including our own. A sociology for women would offer a knowledge of the social organization and determinations of the properties and events of our directly experienced world.[2] Its analyses would become part of our ordinary interpretations of the experienced world, just as our experience of the sun's sinking below the horizon is transformed by our knowledge that the world turns away from a sun that seems to sink.

The only way of knowing a socially constructed world is knowing it from within. We can never stand outside it. A relation in which sociological phenomena are objectified and presented as external to and independent of the observer is itself a special social practice also known from within. The relation of observer and object of observation, of sociologist to "subject," is a specialized social relationship. Even to be a stranger is to enter a world constituted from within as strange. The strangeness itself is the mode in which it is experienced.

. . .

To begin from direct experience and to return to it as a constraint or "test" of the adequacy of a systematic knowledge is to begin from where we are located bodily. The actualities of our everyday world are already socially organized. Settings, equipment, environment, schedules, occasions, and so forth, as well as our enterprises and routines, are socially produced and concretely and symbolically organized prior to the moment at which we enter and at which inquiry begins. By taking up a standpoint in our original and immediate knowledge of the world, sociologists can make their discipline's socially organized properties first observable and then problematic.

When I speak of *experience* I do not use the term as a synonym for *perspective*. Nor in proposing a sociology grounded in the sociologist's actual experience am I recommending the self-indulgence of inner exploration or any other enterprise with self as sole focus and object. Such subjectivist interpretations of *experience* are themselves an aspect of that organization of consciousness that suppresses the locally situated side of the bifurcated consciousness and transports us straight into mind country, stashing away the concrete conditions and practices upon which it depends. We can never escape the circles of our own heads if we accept that as our territory. Rather, sociologists' investigation of our directly experienced world as a problem is a mode of discovering or rediscovering the society from within. We begin from our own original but tacit knowledge and from within the acts by which we bring it into our grasp in making it observable and in understanding how it works. We aim not at a reiteration of what we already (tacitly) know, but at an exploration of what passes beyond that knowledge and is deeply implicated in how it is.

SOCIOLOGY AS STRUCTURING RELATIONS BETWEEN SUBJECT AND OBJECT

Our knowledge of the world is given to us in the modes by which we enter into relations with the object of knowledge. But in this case the object of our knowledge is or originates in the co-ordering of activities among "subjects." The constitution of an objective sociology as an authoritative version of how things are is done from a position in and as part of the practices of ruling in our kind of society. Our training as sociologists teaches us to ignore the uneasiness at the junctures where multiple and diverse experiences are transformed into objectified forms. That juncture shows in the ordinary problems respondents have of fitting their experience of the world to the questions in the interview schedule. The sociologist who is a woman finds it hard to preserve this exclusion, for she discovers, if she will, precisely that uneasiness in her relation to her discipline as a whole. The persistence of the privileged sociological version (or

versions) relies upon a substructure that has already discredited and deprived of authority to speak the voices of those who know the society differently. The objectivity of a sociological version depends upon a special relationship with others that makes it easy for sociologists to remain outside the other's experience and does not require them to recognize that experience as a valid contention.

Riding a train not long ago in Ontario I saw a family of Indians—woman, man, and three children—standing together on a spur above a river watching the train go by. I realized that I could tell this incident—the train, those five people seen on the other side of the glass—as it was, but that my description was built on my position and my interpretations. I have called them "Indians" and a family; I have said they were watching the train. My understanding has already subsumed theirs. Everything may have been quite different for them. My description is privileged to stand as what actually happened because theirs is not heard in the contexts in which I may speak. If we begin from the world as we actually experience it, it is at least possible to see that we are indeed located and that what we know of the other is conditional upon that location. There are and must be different experiences of the world and different bases of experience. We must not do away with them by taking advantage of our privileged speaking to construct a sociological version that we then impose upon them as their reality. We may not rewrite the other's world or impose upon it a conceptual framework that extracts from it what fits with ours. Their reality, their varieties of experience, must be an unconditional datum. It is the place from which inquiry begins.

A BIFURCATION OF CONSCIOUSNESS

My experience in the train epitomizes a sociological relation. I am already separated from the world as it is experienced by those I observe. That separation is fundamental to the character of that experience. Once I become aware of how my world is put together as a practical everyday matter and of how my relations are shaped by its concrete conditions (even in so simple a matter as that I am sitting in the train and it travels, but those people standing on the spur do not), I am led into the discovery that I cannot understand the nature of my experienced world by staying within its ordinary boundaries of assumption and knowledge. To account for that moment on the train and for the relation between the two experiences (or more) and the two positions from which those experiences begin I must posit a larger socioeconomic order in back of that moment. The coming together that makes the observation possible as well as how we were separated and drawn apart as well as how I now make use of that here—these properties are determined elsewhere than in that relation itself.

Furthermore, how our knowledge of the world is mediated to us becomes a problem of knowing how that world is organized for us prior to our participation in it. As intellectuals we ordinarily receive it as a media world, a world of texts, images, journals, books, talk, and other symbolic modes. We discard as an essential focus of our practice other ways of knowing. Accounting for that mode of knowing and the social organization that sets it up for us again leads us back into an analysis of the total socioeconomic order of which it is part. Inquiry remaining within the circumscriptions of the directly experienced cannot explore and explicate the relations organizing the everyday matrices of direct experience.

If we address the problem of the conditions as well as the perceived forms and organization of immediate experience, we should include in it the events as they actually happen and the ordinary material world we encounter as a matter of fact: the urban renewal project that uproots 400 families; how it is to live on welfare as an ordinary daily practice; cities as the actual physical structures in which we move; the organization of academic occasions such as that in which this chapter originated. When we examine them, we find that there are many aspects of how these things come about of which we, as sociologists, have little to say. We have a sense that the events entering our experience originate somewhere in a human intention, but we are unable to track back to find it and to find out how it got from there to here.

.   .   .

We might think of the appearances of our direct experience as a multiplicity of surfaces, the properties and relations among which are generated by social organizations not observable in their effects. The relations underlying and generating the characteristics of our own directly experienced world bring us into unseen relations with others. Their experience is necessarily different from ours. If we would begin from our experienced world and attempt to analyze and account for how it is, we must posit others whose experience is not the same as ours.

Women's situation in sociology discloses to us a typical bifurcate structure with the abstracted, conceptual practices on the one hand and the concrete realizations, the maintenance routines, and so forth on the other. Taking each for granted depends upon being fully situated in one or the other so that the other does not appear in contradiction to it. Women's direct experience places us a step back, where we can recognize the uneasiness that comes from sociology's claim to be about the world we live in, and, at the same time, its failure to account for or even describe the actual features we experience. Yet we cannot find the inner principle of our own activity through exploring what is directly experienced. We do not see how it is put together because it is determined elsewhere. The very organization of the world that has been assigned to us as the primary locus of our being, shaping other projects and desires, is determined by and subordinate to the relations of society founded in a capitalist mode of production. The aim of an alternative sociology would be to explore and unfold the relations beyond our direct experience that shape and determine it. An alternative sociology would be a means to anyone of understanding how the world comes about for us and how it is organized so that it happens to us as it does in our experience. An alternative sociology, from the standpoint of women, makes the everyday world its problematic.

THE STANDPOINT OF WOMEN AS A PLACE TO START

The standpoint of women situates the inquirer in the site of her bodily existence and in the local actualities of her working world. It is a standpoint that positions inquiry but has no specific content. Those who undertake inquiry from this standpoint begin always from women's experience as it is for women. We are the authoritative speakers of our experience. The standpoint of women situates the sociological subject prior to the entry into the abstracted conceptual mode, vested in texts, that is the order of the relations of ruling. From this standpoint, we know the everyday world through the particularities of our local practices and activities, in the actual places of our work and the actual time it takes. In making the everyday world problematic we also problematize the everyday localized practices of the objectified forms of knowledge organizing our everyday worlds.

A bifurcated consciousness is an effect of the actual social relations in which we participate as part of a daily work life. Entry as subject into the social relations of an objectified consciousness is itself an organization of actual everyday practices. The sociology that objectifies society and social relations and transforms the actualities of people's experience into the synthetic objects of its discourse is an organization of actual practices and activities. We know and use practices of thinking and inquiring sociologically that sever our knowledge of society from the society we know as we live and practice it. The conceptual practices of an alienated knowledge of society are also in and of the everyday world. In and through its conceptual practices and its

everyday practices of reading and writing, we enter a mode of consciousness outside the everyday site of our bodily existence and experiencing. The standpoint of women, or at least, *this* standpoint of women at work, in the traditional ways women have worked and continue to work, exposes the alienated knowledge of the relations of ruling as the everyday practices of actual individuals. Thus, though an alienated knowledge also alienates others who are not members of the dominant white male minority, the standpoint of women distinctly opens up for exploration the conceptual practices and activities of the extralocal, objectified relations of ruling as what actual people do.

NOTES

1. Bierstedt, Robert, "Sociology and General Education," in Charles H. Page (ed.), *Sociology and Contemporary Education* (New York: Random House, 1966).
2. Smith, Dorothy E., *The Everyday World as Problematic: A Feminist Sociology* (Boston: Northeastern University Press, 1987).

Subjectivity, Experience, and Knowledge: An Epistemology from/for Rainbow Coalition Politics

Sandra Harding

The issue of difference has come to play a complex role in the theory and politics of those new social movements that have as their goal increasing democracy.[1] Feminists criticized the idea of universal man and his transhistorical rationality; what has been claimed to be true for man and reason is in fact characteristic (at best) only of men in the dominant groups in the West and their preferred view of themselves and the world. Neo-Marxists and post-Marxists have continued the older critique of "rational economic man" and his distinctively bourgeois reason. Postcolonial critics have identified the Eurocentric character of Western assumptions. Criticisms of the "straight mind" have added compulsory heterosexuality to the coercive social structures that have generated partial and distorted accounts of nature and social life (Wittig 1980).

Each of these new social movements has come to recognize that the logic of its arguments also undermines the legitimacy of generalizations from a speaker's situation to *all* women, or economically disadvantaged people, or people of third world descent, or lesbians and gays, as the case may be. If there is no universal or even typical man and his transcendental reason, then neither can there be a universal or typical woman, poor person, person of third world descent, lesbian or gay person, or her or his uniquely legitimate view of the world. Consequently, there will necessarily be legitimately different versions of feminism, postcolonialism, and any other such theory and politics that are intended to advance democracy. For these movements, there can be no single true story of a world that is out there and ready-made for reflecting in our glassy-mirror minds. When we examine feminism, for example, we find many different feminisms that have been generated from the conditions of different women's lives.

In this sense, there are many different subjects (speakers, authors) of feminist thought and politics as, apparently, there must also be for the thought and politics of other new social movements. Since mainstream Western thought has assumed a single, unitary subject, we may feel as if we had dropped through Alice's rabbit hole when we try to grasp the consequences of multiple subjectivity for conventional philosophic issues and conventional understandings of progressive politics. Assumptions that appeared unremarkable suddenly become problematic. In this essay I want to explore some consequences of this emerging logic of multiple subjects for thinking about who can make liberatory knowledge and history, as well as discuss the relationship between experience and knowledge. I shall argue that the concern to articulate the experience of the marginalized in the liberatory accounts does not function to ground knowledge in any conventional sense. Instead, this process produces the kinds of subjects who can go on to create knowledge and history. The role of marginal experience has not always been clear either in the new social movements or to critics of their claims. First, I will review a necessary reconceptualization of gender, race, class, and sexuality and the basic arguments for multiple subjects.[2]

RECONCEPTUALIZING GENDER, RACE, CLASS, AND SEXUALITY

I begin with the observation that, in this society, each of us is located in a determinate place in gender, race, ethnicity, class, and sexuality relations.[3] That is, it is not just the marginalized who have a gender, or race, and so on. People of European descent, for example, do not escape a racial location just because they are not forced constantly to notice it or to qualify their speech by identifying the supposedly special interests, which others can see very well that it expresses. Thus, feminist analyses, for example, cannot simply be added to conventional analyses as if the latter would remain undisturbed by the addition, for the conventional analyses express special interests that are distorting: namely, the claim that a masculine perspective is identical to a gender-free and ideal human perspective.

Popular opinion, supported by the dominant tendencies in U.S. social science, conceptualizes gender, race, class, sexual orientation, and other such phenomena in ways that make it difficult to move past those misleading additive approaches to difference. In order to do so, it is helpful to keep in mind that these phenomena are fundamentally relations—structural ones—and are mutually constitutive. First, each of these phenomena should be thought of as a relation rather than as a thing or an inherent property of people. Race, gender, ethnicity, and sexuality do not designate any fixed set of qualities or properties of individuals, social or biological, such that if an individual possesses these and only these properties then he is a man, an African American, and so forth. Instead, masculinity is continuously defined and redefined as "not femininity," just as white means "not colored."

Second, these relations are deeply embedded in the structure of society. They are institutionalized relations that distribute economic, political, and social power. Contrary to popular opinion, such phenomena as racial and gender inequality have no biological causes.[4] Moreover, they are not *caused* by prejudice—by individual bad attitudes and false beliefs. The tendency to see prejudice as the cause of racial (or gender, class, or sexual) inequality tends to lodge responsibility for racism on already economically disadvantaged whites—the "Archie Bunkers" (in sociologist David Wellman's analysis)—who have not learned to avoid making overtly racist statements, as have middle-class people, and who are forced to bear a disproportionately large share of the burdens of affirmative action and equal opportunity programs. Racism is enacted in many different ways, and overt individual prejudice is just one of them. It is fundamentally a political relationship, a strategy that, in Wellman's words, "systematically provides economic, political, psychological, and social advantages for whites at the expense of Blacks and other people of color," and it is a dynamic relationship that is flexible enough to adapt to changing historical conditions (p. 37). Similarly, sexist prejudice is the effect, not the cause, of a dynamic and flexible male supremacist social structure.

Of course, individuals *should* be held responsible for their beliefs and behaviors: it is wrong to express or enact these kinds of prejudices and thereby increase the misery of the already disadvantaged. But to rest satisfied with this individualistic and idealist analysis and its recommended remedies is to fail to come to grips with the institutional race (or gender, class, or sexuality) supremacy that appears in the beliefs and behaviors of people who do not exhibit symptoms of prejudice. An individual can be well-informed about, and not at all hostile toward, people of color, women, the poor, or gays and lesbians—that is, he or she can have the proper *mental* characteristics that constitute lack of prejudice—and nevertheless continually and effectively support beliefs and practices that maintain economic, political, and social inequality.

These two points lead to a third. Systems of political hierarchy based on differences of gender, race, class, and sexual orientation are not parallel to each other, as the preceding analysis might suggest, but interlocked, mutually created, and mutually maintaining (Mies; hooks; Collins). A setback or advance in one reverberates through the whole matrix of hierarchy creating consequences far from where such change began. This point clarifies why the new social movements can and must try to center analyses from the perspective of lives that have been marginalized within each movement. For example, there are determinate causal relations between the lives of women of European and third world descent, economically privileged and poor women, heterosexual women and lesbians, ethnic and "nonethnic" women, as well as between the men and women who have been the primary focus of feminist concern.

From the perspective of this kind of understanding, it is odd that some critics of feminism (and some feminists) have believed that starting thought from a conceptual framework that centers differences between women will have the necessary consequence of abandoning gender as an analytic category. To the contrary, it is only what we might call essential, or transcendental, gender that would have been abandoned, and that is as mythical as the transcendental man feminists have criticized. If women and men can only be found in historically determinate races, classes, and sexualities, then a gender analysis—one from the perspective of women's lives—must scrutinize gender *as it exists* from the perspective of *all* women's lives. There is no other defensible choice. The point here is not just that to insist on transcendental woman distorts the lives of marginal women. It does so, but it also distorts the lives of those at the center. I, a white western woman, misunderstand my own life and the causes of my beliefs and actions if I cannot understand how they are shaped by institutional relations of race, class, and heterosexist supremacy as well as by male supremacy. Indeed, to understand the latter *is* to understand the former, and vice versa.

Of course racism, sexism, class exploitation, and heterosexism have their own distinctive histories, institutional forms, and dynamics; they are not identical in their histories or structures, as my account here might suggest. Nevertheless, they are widely recognized to be similar enough that they can be understood in the shared ways indicated here. Indeed, analogical reasoning from the theories and analytical strategies developed within one new social movement to the others has consistently provided important resources for grasping the logic of multiple subjects.

This brings us to the next challenge: if I must learn to understand my life from the standpoint of, say, third world women's lives, it is not so that I can speak *as* or *for* third world women. Men must learn to see themselves as they appear from the perspective of women's lives, but it is not that men can speak *as* or *for* women.

THE LOGIC OF MULTIPLE SUBJECTS

One main tendency in feminist epistemology has insisted that starting thought—theorizing—from women's lives decreases the partiality and distortion in our images of nature and social relations. It creates knowledge—not just opinion—that is socially situated. It is still partial in both senses of the word—interested and incomplete; but it is less distorting than thought originating in the agendas and perspectives of the lives of dominant group men. This is the feminist standpoint theory developed by Dorothy Smith, Nancy Hartsock, Hilary Rose, Alison Jaggar, myself, and others. This epistemology has been designed to account for the successes of feminist research in the social sciences and biology and to guide future research practices. Its argument is valuable in the humanities and in other natural sciences as well. Standpoint theories direct us to identify whose questions a knowledge project is asking and whose problems it has been designed to resolve. Is it asking questions that are of interest primarily to the dominant groups or to those whom the dominant groups marginalize? The disciplinary preoccupations of philosophy, sociology, biology, and literary criticism have been constructed to assist dominant institutions and individuals in their projects, not to address the concerns of the marginalized.

What does it mean to start thought from women's lives, to theorize from that location? Women lead lives different from each other; there is no typical "woman's life" from which feminists could start their thought. Moreover, in many cases women's lives are not just different from each other's but structurally opposed. In the United States, African American and Euroamerican women's lives are defined against each other by policy that is racist and sexist. African American and Euroamerican women often collude in this oppositional strategy by defining themselves as "not her"; Euroamerican women have vigorously participated in creating and maintaining racist institutions, practices, and beliefs. Nevertheless, all of these women's lives are in different respects valuable starting points for generating feminist knowledge projects. A variety of explanations for this can be gathered from mainstream social science theory.[5]

Women's lives are the ignored and devalued missing half of human lives from which scientific problems are supposed to be generated. In important ways women are "strangers" to their own societies; their lives are not the ones the society has been designed to enable or even to fit; nor have women been as well socialized into the dominant modes of thought. Starting thought from women's lives better reveals these features of societies. Women's lives reveal the "underside" of history, the part that the "winners" of history refuse to acknowledge or name (e.g., Harding 1991, chap. 5). Thought that begins with each of these different kinds of lives can generate new scientific problems, more critical questions, and thus less partial and distorted accounts of nature and social life. Women's lives provide grounds for feminist claims not in the sense of empirically and theoretically firmer *answers* but, most importantly, of more critical empirical and theoretical *questions*. Thus, as we explored above, there is not just one unitary and coherent "speech" that is feminist thought or knowledge; instead, we have multiple and frequently contradictory knowings.

Other liberatory movements have developed similar standpoint epistemology projects, whether or not they articulate them as such. While the intellectual history of standpoint theory traces its origins to Karl Marx, Friedrich Engels, Georg Lukács, and the "standpoint of the proletariat," a social history would note that when marginalized people begin to gain voice in the dominant circles from which they had been excluded, members of the dominant group invariably begin to hear about how, from the perspective of those marginal lives, dominant assumptions and claims are distorted.

The subject/agent of feminist (or other subjugated) knowledge is multiple and frequently contradictory in a second way that mirrors the situation for women as a class. It is the thinker whose consciousness is bifurcated (Smith), the outsider within (Collins), the marginal person now also located at the center (hooks), the person who is committed to two agendas that are themselves at least partially in conflict—the liberal feminist, socialist feminist, Nicaraguan feminist, Jewish feminist—who has generated feminist sciences and new knowledge. It is thinking from a contradictory social position that generates feminist knowledge. So the logic of the directive to "start thought from women's lives" requires that we start our thought from multiple lives that in many ways conflict with each other and have multiple and contradictory commitments. In contrast, the subject of knowledge for both the conventional liberal/empiricist philosophy and for Marxism was supposed to be unitary and coherent. The condition of one kind of idealized knower—the rational man and the male proletarian, respectively—were to be created and generalized for all who would know.

In an important if controversial sense, the subject of feminist knowledge must know what every other liberatory knowledge project knows. Since at least half of the poor, racially marginalized, and gay or "queer" people are women, all feminists will have to grasp how gender, race, class, and sexuality are used to construct each other. They will have to do so if feminism is to be liberatory for marginalized women but also if feminism is to avoid deluding dominant group women about their own situations. If this were not so, there would be no way to distinguish between feminism and the narrow self-interest of dominant group women—just as conventional androcentric thought permits no criterion for distinguishing between "best beliefs" and those that serve the self-interest of men as men (bourgeois thought permits no criterion for identifying specifically bourgeois self-interest, racist thought for identifying racist self-interest, etc.).

The subject of every other liberatory movement must also learn how gender, race, class, and sexuality are used to construct each other *in order to accomplish their goals*. For example, analyses of class relations must look also at their agendas from the perspective of women's lives, since women hold class positions. Moreover, as many critics have pointed out, leftist agendas need to deal with the fact that bosses regularly and all too successfully attempt to divide the working class against itself by manipulating gender hostilities. If women are forced to tolerate lower wages and double days of work, employers can increase their profit by firing men and hiring women. Antiracist movements must conceptualize their issues from the perspective of the lives of women as well as of men of color, and so forth. We must emphasize that it is not just the women in those other movements who must know the world from the perspective of women's lives. Everyone must do so if the movements are to succeed. This requires that women be active directors of the agendas of these movements. It also requires that men in those movements be able to generate original feminist knowledge by beginning their thought from feminist understanding of women's lives, as many would argue that John Stuart Mill, Marx and Engels, Frederick Douglass, and a host of contemporary male feminists have done.

If every other liberatory movement must generate feminist knowledge, women cannot claim to be the unique generators of feminist knowledge. Nor should men claim that they are unable to produce fully feminist analyses on the grounds that they are not women or do not have women's experiences. Men, too, can contribute distinctive forms of specifically feminist knowledge *as men*—that is, from their particular social situation. Shouldn't we want men's thought to use feminist theory to think from women's lives? Men's thought, too, would start there in order to come closer to maximally critical, objective theoretical frameworks for describing and explaining their own and women's lives. Starting their thought from women's lives is necessary if men are to produce more than the male supremacist "folk belief" about themselves and the world to which female feminists object. Male feminists, like female ones, are made, not born.

If experiencing women's lives—"being a woman"—is not a necessary condition for generating feminist knowledge, what is the relation between experience and knowledge for liberatory social movements such as feminism? Is there no significant *epistemological* difference between a female feminist and a male feminist? Can whites produce "African American knowledge"? (Whether they should *claim* to do so is quite another matter!) From the perspective of conventional thought about the relations between subjectivity, experience, and knowledge, an epistemological hornet's nest appears when we follow through the logic of multiple subjects and direct *everyone,* not just women, to start their thought from women's lives.

ACHIEVING SUBJECTIVITY AND GROUNDING KNOWLEDGE

Some feminists and also some of their critics have assumed that feminist research and scholarship must be grounded in women's *experiences* in the sense that those experiences provide traditional kinds of foundations—clear and certain ones—for feminist claims. This assumption has been made for several apparently good reasons. To repeat well-argued points, feminists have noted that only the experiences of men in the dominant groups have grounded Western knowledge and that the generation of knowledge agendas and problematics, concepts, and interpretations of data originating in women's experiences provide a needed corrective for the distortions of androcentric thought. The shared knowledge created through such practices as consciousness-rasing foregrounds women's experiences as the site where feminist knowledge processes begin. A standpoint is often assumed to be a view or perspective that is prior to the social, though standpoint theorists go to considerable effort to stress that they are talking about a location from which to generate feminist thought that is an achievement of feminist politics and theory. Women don't "naturally" have it; we have to struggle politically and conceptually to get to it. The critics are predisposed to interpret standpoint claims in this way, I wish to suggest, because mainstream empiricism assumes that the only alternative to its "objectivism" is the phenomenological approach that grounds its claims in the lived world—in "experiences."[6] Standpoint approaches are alternatives to empiricist *and* phenomenological ones and to absolutist and relativist epistemologies; but that is hard for empiricists to understand.

Standpoint approaches use the experiences of the marginalized to generate critical questions about the lives of marginalized people and of those in the dominant groups, as well as about the systematic structural and symbolic relations between them. However, I think that there is a second and crucial role that speaking one's experience plays in the generation of knowledge for marginalized people. In neither case does experience *ground* knowledge in any conventional sense. This relationship between experience and knowledge for the knowledge projects of the new social movements is troublesome precisely because the prevailing theories of experience and knowledge have been produced only from the standpoint of dominant group lives and have not recognized this second function that articulating experience plays in producing knowledge.

For women to name and describe their experiences in "their own terms" is a crucial scientific and epistemological act. Members of marginalized groups must *struggle* to name their own experiences *for* themselves in order to claim the subjectivity, the possibility of historical agency, that is given to members of dominant groups at birth (or at least, as psychoanalytic theorists report, in infancy). The Jamaican writer Michelle Cliff argues that "to write as a complete Caribbean woman, or man for that matter, demands of us retracing the African part of ourselves, reclaiming as our own, and as our subject, a history sunk under the sea, or scattered as potash in the canefields, or gone to bush, or trapped in a class system notable for its rigidity and absolute dependence on color strati-

fication" (p. 59). For marginalized people, to achieve subjectivity is to claim a subjugated history. Members of dominant groups are inserted into language, history, and culture as legitimate speakers and historical agents through no acts of their own, so to speak. They do not have to exert effort in order to see themselves in or as actively making history or to imagine themselves as authoritative speakers and actors. Their Dick and Jane readers, television programs, observable family and community social relations, and the structure of language itself already tell them that they are the "right stuff" to make community and history, as well as authoritative statements about reality. They simply *are* the subjectivities who *have* experiences that provide the raw material for creating dominant group conceptions of knowledge and history. For women and other marginalized groups, subjectivity and its possibility of legitimated "experience" must be achieved; subjectivity and experience are made, not born.[7] To be a recognizable subject of history and knowledge is to be permitted—indeed, expected—to have rage, anger, desire, a history, and speech, all of which are human features forbidden to marginalized people.

This denial of subjectivity is the product of material conditions. For example, it was illegal for slaves to read and write. Given formal and informal exclusionary policies, it has been difficult even for women in the dominant groups to gain access to Latin, mathematical, scientific, and other professional languages used to create and report knowledge, social theory, and public policy. It has been illegal for women to speak in public and difficult for them to publish their thoughts or travel without male chaperones. It is hard to teach philosophy without books, note several of the contributors to a special issue of the *Philosophical Forum* on apartheid (18, no. 2–3 [1987]).

But even this way of putting the point is not quite right. It is too tame. It too quickly integrates the difficult and often painful struggle of marginalized people to name their experience and so to gain a self-defined self. For marginalized people, naming their experience publicly is a cry for survival. As the African American literary critic Barbara Christian notes, "What I write and how I write is done in order to save my own life. And I mean that literally. For me literature is a way of knowing that I am not hallucinating, that whatever I feel/know *is*" (p. 343; see also Ellsworth; Lugones and Spelman). Henry Louis Gates, Jr., argues that Frederick Douglass, like other narrators of slave autobiographies, faced the difficult task of writing into subjectivity and history both himself and all of the other slaves whose lives would be represented by his story:

> The black slave's narrative came to be a communal utterance, a collective tale, rather than merely an individual's autobiography. Each slave author, in writing about his or her personal life's experiences, simultaneously wrote on behalf of the millions of silent slaves still held captive throughout the South. Each author, then, knew that *all* black slaves would be judged—on their character, integrity, intelligence, manners and morals, and their claims to warrant emancipation—on this published evidence provided by one of their number. (Gates, p. x)

For Douglass, his own survival and that of millions of others depended on his ability and that of other ex-slaves to fashion their self-understandings into narratives that voiced/ "created" the humanity of the silent slaves. Abdul JanMohamed notes that for Richard Wright, the choices were literally death or the recovery/creation of his own subjectivity. The Chicana writer Gloria Anzaldúa writes of birthing herself through her writing. For a marginalized person, articulating her or his experiences is an act of rebirthing.

Thus, marginalized people speaking their experiences is a crucial ontological and political act, the act that creates them as the kind of people who can make knowledge and history. Knowledge from the perspective of women's lives could not occur without this public act of women naming their experience in "their own terms." Subjects legitimate knowledge claims, but it takes difficult, painful, and frequently violent struggles to create such subjects. Self-created, marginal subjectivity is exactly what the dominant groups cannot permit.[8]

The naming and articulating of marginalized experience is not a task completed at a particular moment in history. It is a continuous process as long as oppression, exclusion, and silencing exist. Unless, for example, African Americans have the resources to name their experiences continuously in their terms—the literacy, university positions, government consultancies, policy directorates, and so on—all of us will lack the resources that *their* articulation of their experience could have brought.

Let me stress that this argument does not claim incorrigibility for expressions of marginalized experiences. As Uma Narayan has written, women's "epistemic privilege" does not include a privileged knowledge of the *causes* of their situation.[9] What women say is not held by feminist theorists, and certainly not by standpoint theorists, to be immune from revision by women or anyone else. All women have women's experiences but only at certain historical moments does anyone ever produce feminist knowledge. We could say that our experience often "lies to us" and that the experiences of the dominant gender, class, race, and sexuality produce more airtight, comprehensive, widely believed, and tenacious lies because these lies are used to create institutions and ways of thinking that subsequently structure everyone else's lives. For example, if women are excluded from education in philosophy and from participation in other institutional forms of philosophy—conference programs, publishing, honorary chairs, degrees, and so on—it will seem quite obvious to everyone that "women can't do philosophy," or at least "really good" philosophy. Thought starting from dominant group lives generates the "common sense" of the age. Marginalized people are forced to internalize and display what dominant groups believe of them. This is a somewhat simplistic account of how ideology works. My point is that all of us must live in social relations that naturalize, or seem to make necessary, social arrangements that are, in fact, optional at the cultural level; they have been created and made to appear natural by the power of the dominant groups.

TRANSFORMING SUBJECTIVITIES

If the subjectivities required to create knowledge can be *made* through social processes, then they can also be transformed by them. Members of the dominant groups, too, can learn how to see the world from the perspective of experiences and lives that are not theirs. After all, no woman was born with a feminist subjectivity. Women have had to learn to think from perspectives about women's lives that were not initially visible to them for "their" perspective on "their" life. Their lives and perspectives were structured by the patriarchal ideology of femininity, not by feminism. In order to transform feminine into feminist lives, they have had to listen to themselves and to other women telling about their lives, reflect on the gender (and class, race, and sexuality) aspects of their lives, undertake acts of resistance to male supremacy, reflect on the consequences of those acts, learn various feminist theories about gender relations that provide contexts into which they could insert their own experiences and perspectives . . . and so forth. They have had to *become* feminists. And, if they are, say, Euroamericans, they have had to start listening to women of color telling about their lives—and then themselves in contrast; they have had to reflect on the race aspects of their lives, undertake acts of resistance to race supremacy, reflect on the consequences of those acts, learn various theories produced by people of color about race relations and imperialism that provide contexts into which they could insert their own experiences and perspectives . . . and so forth. That is, they have had to learn how to become feminists who can function effectively as antiracists (that is, who *are* antiracist), rather than

feminists who, intentionally or not, perpetuate race supremacy. They have had to learn to take historical responsibility for their race, for the white skins from which they speak and act.

There is no place in this process where it would be appropriate to say that such a white person spoke *as* or *for* women of color. Only a women of color can speak *as* such; and women of color must be heard speaking *for* themselves. The reasons for this are many. Even though women of color's claims are not incorrigible, nor can they (anymore than anyone else) be expected to grasp the causes of their experiences, they do have a certain epistemic privilege about their own experiences. They can more easily detect the subtle forms of their marginalization and of discrimination against them. They often feel differently than do whites or the men in their own groups about what is and is not oppressive or exploitative. Furthermore, they must be heard as "equal voices" in order to *be,* to become, equal voices in discussions (Narayan). Feminists of third world descent have made such important contributions to feminist analyses in part because the necessity to theorize the connections between race, gender, class, and sexuality arises first in their lives on an everyday basis.

The logic of multiple subjects requires that all of our subjectivities be transformed in this manner, but it does not permit subjectivities to be interchangeable or, most importantly, permit members of dominant groups to speak as or for the dominated. Thus, I am not arguing that being other and "reinventing ourselves as other"—as disloyal to the dominant "civilization" and its conceptions of us—are epistemically equal social locations. They can never be so. But members of dominant groups—all of us who are Euroamerican, ethnically privileged, or masculine, economically privileged, or heterosexual—can learn to take historic responsibility for the social locations from which our speech and actions issue. This is a scientific and epistemological issue as well as a moral and political one.

CONCLUSION

The recognition and exploration of the existence of multiple subjects of knowledge in all of the democracy-advancing new social movements reveals that the relations between subjectivity, experience, and knowledge entrenched in conventional epistemology and political philosophy appear reasonable only from the perspective of dominant group lives. In the conventional accounts, there is an ambivalent relation to subjectivity. On the one hand, insofar as it bears the markers of its social location and, especially, of the social location of "others," it appears as something to be excluded or, at least, rigorously controlled in the production of knowledge. Socially situated subjectivity threatens to overwhelm or pollute "pure knowledge." Marginalized people are thought to be the most irretrievably mired in their social situation; women, "natives," the poor, and other others are the models for the irrationality, social passions, immersion in the bodily, and the subjective against which dispassionate reason, social justice, historical progress, "civilization," and the objective pursuit of knowledge have been defined. On the other hand, "rational man's" subjectivity is to be activated, nourished, and encouraged to range freely in the pursuit of truth, justice, and social progress.

Western science, for example, is supposedly the result of the active subjectivity of the great men of science: "In [Isaac] Newton's achievement we see how science advances by heroic exercises of the imagination rather than by patient collecting and sorting of myriads of individual facts. Who, after studying Newton's magnificent contribution to thought, could deny that pure science exemplifies the creative accomplishment on the human spirit at its pinnacle?" (Cohen, p. 190). This double standard arises from particular historical needs: to activate dominant group subjectivity but also to suppress any sign of autonomous subjectivity in marginalized groups.

Understanding nature and social relations requires not just knowing what we think of ourselves and the world but also what others think of us and our beliefs (Mura, p. 152). We must "reinvent ourselves as Other" in the sense of becoming "disloyal to civilization," in Adrienne Rich's memorable phrase, in order to develop the kinds of multiple subjectivities that are capable of understanding objectively their own social location, not just imagining that they understand the social locations of others.[10] This project requires the prior creations of authoritative subjectivities in the marginalized. For that, the public articulation of their different experience is a precondition. Thus the public articulation of marginalized experience is a necessary precondition for the creation of democracy-advancing knowledge, but it is not its grounds.

The new understandings of subjectivity, experience, and knowledge offer significant possibilities for coalition politics between groups who share, at a minimum, opposition to hegemonic politics and a renegade understanding of the crucial role that articulating "experience" plays in generating and legitimating just such sciences and politics—without ever needing conventionally to "ground" them.

NOTES

1. Both the feminist and antiracist/postcolonial epistemology discussions have been fast moving; a number of my claims here seem a lot less novel now than they did when I revised this essay in late 1990. . . .
2. I have made these arguments in other places, most recently in chapter 11, "Reinventing Ourselves as Other" (*Whose Science?* pp. 212–17, 284–8). Clarification of some of these epistemological concerns is explored in my "Rethinking Standpoint Epistemology."
3. In this chapter, the term "race" is always to be understood as in scare quotes to indicate that it is

a cultural construction, not a biological given. See many of the essays in my *"Racial" Economy of Science.*

4. Indeed, race is not a useful category of biological analysis, as biologists and physical anthropologists have pointed out for decades. It is a residue from the Linnean classificatory scheme; it conflicts with the evolutionary theory; and it is a social construct, as the essays in my book *"Racial" Economy* show.

5. These and other explanations are explored in chapter 5 of my *Whose Science?*

6. "Objectivism" is only "weak objectivity." Feminism and the other new social movements both demand and generate stronger standards for maximizing objectivity than objectivism's neutrality ideal permits. See chapter 6 of my *Whose Science?*, and my essay "After the Neutrality Ideal."

7. Mary Belenky and her colleagues point out that "It's my opinion" means "I have a right to my opinion" for men, but it means "It's just my opinion" for women. They also discuss the "women of silence" who do not yet "have" self, voice, or mind, whom some of their interviewees report having been.

8. Hence, I read the early feminist standpoint writings that give considerable attention to articulating the different human experiences that women have through their socially assigned activity in mothering, housework, emotional labor, and caring for others' bodies as making the following point: there is a different subjectivity from "the human" (i.e., ruling group men's), and it is created through interacting with the world in different ways than men are assigned. That is, women's experience functions in these accounts both as something to be explained and as a clue to the different social location from which much feminist research has emerged and from which everyone—not just the women who have some particular experiences or other—should start off thought. Women's experience does not function as the *grounds* for feminist claims on these standpoint accounts any more than "proletarian experience" provides the grounds for Marx's *Das Kapital.* In contrast, it does function as the grounds for knowledge in some feminist phenomenological sociology and in many radical feminist writings.

9. Narayan's illuminating arguments for the importance in the creation of knowledge of expressions of the emotions of the oppressed as they report their experiences may be read as providing additional arguments to those above for the important role that experiences play in the creation of knowledge from the standpoint of oppressed lives—and without claiming that experience *grounds* that knowledge.

10. V. Y. Mudimbe argues that African philosophers must reinvent the West as a bizarre and alien tradition from which they can learn important techniques but against which they can also ambiguously define their alterity. I am arguing that Westerners—and, more generally, members of dominant social groups—can also engage in this reclamation of self and historical agency against a hegemonic culture.

REFERENCES

Anzaldúa, Gloria. *Borderlands/La Frontera: The New Mestiza.* San Francisco: Spinsters/Aunt Lute, 1987.

Belensky, Mary Field, Blythe McVicker Clinchy, Nancy Rule Goldberger, and Jill Mattuck Tarule. *Women's Ways of Knowing: The Development of Self, Voice, and Mind.* New York: Basic Books, 1986.

Christian, Barbara. "The Race for Theory." In *Making Face, Making Soul/Haciendo Caras,* ed. Gloria Anzaldúa. San Francisco: Aunt Lute Foundation, 1990.

Cliff, Michelle. "A Journey into Speech." In *The Graywolf Annual Five: Multi-Cultural Literacy,* ed. Rick Simonson and Scott Walker. St. Paul, MN: Graywolf Press, 1988.

Cohen, I. Bernard. *The Birth of a New Physics.* New York: Doubleday, 1960.

Collins, Patricia Hill. *Black Feminist Thought: Knowledge, Consciousness, and the Politics of Empowerment.* Boston: Routledge, 1991.

Ellsworth, Elizabeth. "Why Doesn't This Feel Empowering? Working through the Repressive Myths of Critical Pedagogy." *Harvard Educational Review* 59, no. 3 (1989), pp. 297–324.

Gates, Henry Louis, Jr. "Introduction." In *The Classic Slave Narratives,* ed. Henry Louis Gates, Jr. New York: New American Library, 1987.

Harding, Sandra. "After the Neutrality Ideal: Politics, Science, and 'Strong Objectivity.'" *Social Research* 59, no. 3 (1992), pp. 567–87.

——. ed. *The "Racial" Economy of Science: Toward a Democratic Future.* Bloomington: Indiana University Press, 1993.

——. "Rethinking Standpoint Epistemology: What Is 'Strong Objectivity'?" In *Feminist Epistemologies,* ed. Linda Alcoff and Elizabeth Potter. New York: Routledge, 1993.

——. *The Science Question in Feminism.* Ithaca, NY: Cornell University Press, 1986.

——. *Whose Science? Whose Knowledge? Thinking from Women's Lives.* Ithaca, NY: Cornell University Press, 1991.

——. "Why Has the Sex–Gender System Become Visible Only Now?" In *Discovering Reality,* ed. Harding and Hintikka.

Harding, Sandra, and Merrill Hintikka, eds. *Discovering Reality: Feminist Perspectives on Epistemology, Metaphysics, Methodology, and Philosophy of Science.* Dordrecht, Holland: Reidel/Kluwer, 1983.

Hartsock, Nancy. "The Feminist Standpoint: Developing the Ground for a Specifically Feminist Historical Materialism." In *Discovering Reality,* ed. Harding and Hintikka.

hooks, bell. *Feminist Theory: From Margin to Center.* Boston: South End Press, 1983.

Jagger, Alison. *Feminist Politics and Human Nature.* Totowa, NJ: Rowman and Allenheld, 1983.

JanMohamed, Abdul. "Negating the Negation as a Form of Affirmation in Minority Discourse: The Construction of Richard Wright as Subject." *Cultural Critique* 7 (Fall 1987), pp. 245–66.

Lugones, Maria, and Elizabeth V. Spelman. "Have We Got a Theory for You! Feminist Theory, Cultural Imperialism, and the Demand for the Women's Voice." *Women's Studies International Forum* 6, no. 6 (1983), pp. 573–81.

Mies, Maria. *Patriarchy and Accumulation on a World Scale: Women in the International Division of Labor.* London: Zed Books, 1986.

Mudimbe, V. Y. *The Invention of Africa.* Bloomington: Indiana University Press, 1988.

Mura, David. "Strangers in the Village." In *The Graywolf Annual Five: Multi-Cultural Literacy,* ed. Rick Simonson and Scott Walker. St. Paul, MN: Graywolf Press, 1988.

Narayan, Uma. "Working Together across Difference: Some Considerations on Emotions and Political Practice." *Hypatia: A Journal of Feminist Philosophy* 3, no. 2 (1988), pp. 31–48.

Rose, Hilary. "Hand, Brain, and Heart: A Feminist Epistemology for the Natural Sciences." *Signs: Journal of Women in Culture and Society* 9 (1983), pp. 73–90.

Smith, Dorothy. *The Everyday World as Problematic: A Feminist Sociology.* Boston: Northeastern University Press, 1987.

Wellman, David. *Portraits of White Racism.* New York: Cambridge University Press, 1977.

Wittig, Monique. "The Straight Mind." *Feminist Issues* 1 (1980), pp. 103–11.

The first version of this essay appeared in *Multiple Subject: Feminist Perspectives on Postmodernism, Epistemology, and Science,* coauthored with Elvia Schieck and Ma Osietzki (Hamburg: Institute for Social Science, 1991) and in *Development and Change* 23, no. 3 (1992). That issue of *Development and Change* was subsequently reprinted as *Emancipations: Modern and Postmodern,* ed. Jan Nederveen Pieterse (London: Sage, 1992).

CHAPTER 3

Women and Popular Culture

From far-flung sources beyond the arts, sciences, and academe we pick up tips, advice, recipes, lore, and much else that helps us manage our daily lives. By now, popular culture shapes a great deal of such commonsense knowledge. Feminist cultural studies focus in part on that culture of the mass media. Broadly, feminist scholars look at "the tensions and contradictions between ideology and desire, or rather between the pleasures engendered by fantasies of autonomy and those afforded by more traditional images of femininity."[1] That focus first found powerful expression in Kate Millett's *Sexual Politics* (1970), which used a feminist standpoint to turn "the adventure of literary criticism" toward those "insights which literature affords into the life it describes, or interprets, or even distorts."[2] Dissecting works by D. H. Lawrence, Henry Miller, Norman Mailer, and Jean Genet, Millett showed how standpoint shapes an aesthetics.

The 1970s were a watershed in feminist cultural studies. In film studies, Laura Mulvey's "Visual Pleasure and Narrative Cinema" appeared in 1977. So did Elaine Showalter's *A Literature of Their Own.* Soon came Sandra Gilbert and Susan Gubar's *The Madwoman in the Attic* (1979), whose influence extended beyond literary criticism into feminist media studies.[3] Since that time feminist theorists have applied not only Marxian and neopsychoanalytic but also semiotic and postmodernist perspectives to the diverse products of popular culture.[4]

Theorizing remains, however, subordinated to empirical studies and hermeneutic analyses of specific cultural products and powerful icons, such as Madonna.[5] From the "consciousness-raising novels" of the 1970s to the plays of David Mamet and Eugene Ionesco, from Su Friedrich's films to "Northern Exposure," from the Baby-sitters Club books to the "carnal kitchen" as a pop-culture image,[6] feminist scholars have made rich, rigorous contributions. In the process they problematize and challenge the popular culture/high culture dualism institutionalized throughout the arts and humanities. As I myself (among others) have shown elsewhere, that dualism masks the similarities and overlap between what gets designated as popular fiction and what gets canonized as Literature. It even dims our awareness that many novelists esteemed in academic circles in fact write best-sellers.[7] In this chapter, then, we will be leaping across cultural boundaries deemed necessary and meaningful among nonfeminist (and some feminist) scholars, even though our primary focus will be the cultural fare offered through the mass media.

Particularly revelatory of feminist theorists' stances toward such popular fare are their analyses of women's humor, which generally "isn't seen as being about people—it's seen as being about women."[8] (Here we harken back to Elizabeth Minnich's insights.) Feminist scholars have shown otherwise by theorizing women's approaches to what is humorous.

Stereotypes have long portrayed women as lacking a sense of humor. As early as 1885 an anthology entitled *The Wit of Women* challenged that idea. Historian Nancy A. Walker links stereotypes about women's humorless nature to "the debate about [their] general intellectual capacity. . . ."[9] "She's got a terrific sense of humor" is "shorthand for 'physically unattractive'"[10] and thus perpetuates stereotypes of attractive women as unintelligent and bright women as unattractive. By exploring such stereotypes, Walker not only points to the cleverness associated with humor but also implies its potential for threatening commonplace beliefs about gender, hierarchy, authority, and what God or Mother Nature ordained. In this context, one quickly sees why feminists are often cast as humorless.[11]

Resistance to expressions of female "wittiness"[12] shows up a great deal in popular culture. One fictional portrayal of that resistance is William Dean Howells's *The Rise of Silas Lapham* (1885), published the same year as *The Wit of Women*. Throughout the novel the older Lapham daughter Penelope ("Pen"), is chastised for being "pert," that is, funny and irreverent. Not surprisingly, Pen is less attractive than her more conventional sister Irene and is also the only serious reader in the Lapham family. Paralleling Howells's characterization of her is his portrayal of Irene, who has no interest in ideas and is preoccupied with her looks and wardrobe.

Such portrayals tie in with long-held stereotypes of women—"the nag, the scold, the 'clinging vine' and the gold digger," for starters. These stereotypes appear not only in male-dominated popular culture but also in women's humor, which challenges them. The "dumb blonde" is illustrative. As the "20th-century version of the 'clinging vine,'" the dumb blonde largely derives from Anita Loos's *Gentlemen Prefer Blondes* (1925). Loos's protagonist, Lorelei Lee, is not allowed to be both gorgeous and smart. Lorelei *appears* to favor her appearance over her intelligence but in fact "uses her wits to turn the situation to her own—material if not emotional—advantage." Like Dorothy Parker in the short story "Big Blonde," Loos makes her character a "case study in social conditioning."[13] Much women's humor, it seems, revolves around this theme of gender socialization.

Other themes in women's humor include women's interest in power alongside "an exploration of powerlessness that constitutes a subversive protest against it."[14] Thus, women commonly make fun of "the powerful rather than the pitiful" with the blatant exception of "self-deprecating jokes," perhaps "the most 'traditional' form of women's humor."[15]

Women's humor can be defensive or aggressive. Judy Holliday running from a sexually harassing casting director illustrates the former. She "finally stopped running and removed the 'falsies' she had tucked into her bra. 'Here,' she told him, handing him two spheres of foam rubber, 'I believe it's these you're after.'" Tallulah Bankhead illustrates aggressive humor. Seeing a former lover enter a restaurant with a new date and ignore her, she shouted, "What's the matter, darling? Don't you recognize me with my clothes on?" Comedy is thus one way "women can be excessive and get away with it."[16] More pointedly, it is one way they can make a spectacle of themselves by facing the "danger . . . of an exposure."[17]

Humor also lets women and members of other subordinate groups turn the tables on members of dominant groups. For instance, when a male heckler yelled "Are you a lesbian?" to gay black activist Florynce Kennedy, she retorted, "Are you my alternative?"[18] Such a response is particularly characteristic of feminist humor, which has existed in American culture for more than a century. Like other feminist genres, it adopts women's perspectives while challenging the social injustices they face. Feminist humor often reconfigures gender, then. A contemporary example is Gloria Steinem's "If Men Could Menstruate," where she describes how men would brag about the volume of their flow, flaunt "being on the rag," and otherwise make honorific the monthly event widely loathed in American culture.

Other examples come from lesbian humorists who commonly reconfigure sexuality as well as gender. Kate Clinton and Lily Tomlin offer funny insights, as does Sharon McDonald, who

> recalls the process of deciding to make a public lifelong commitment to her female lover. The reaction in the feminist community, she says, "broke down into three categories: The Aghast, The Amused, and The Admiring. The Aghast, of course, were radical lesbian feminists. So were The Amused. So were The Admiring."[19]

Here heterosexuals, especially heterosexual feminists, are targeted, just as white people, especially white liberals, are sometimes the targets of black women's humor.

Whether it's Roseanne doing her stand-up routine with lines like "I will clean house when Sears comes out with a riding vacuum cleaner" or

Molly Ivins issuing barbs about politics as usual or Whoopi Goldberg enacting diverse female personae or Diane DiMassa sketching frames for
Hothead Paisan: Homicidal Lesbian Terrorist, women doing humor are
tapping into a cultural form that subverts established understandings and
raises consciousness while making for lighter moments. Feminists intensify these functions, as is evident from Gloria Kaufman's *Pulling Our
Own Strings* as well as DiMassa's hothead.

WOMEN'S CULTURE AND THE THERAPEUTIC CONTINUUM

Women's culture includes "all forms of media directed to an audience of
women or media utilized . . . primarily by women."[20] Two of its sectors
invite attention because they are extremely popular and well suited to illuminating women's complex cultural positioning. One is self-help products, ranging from advice columns to women's talk shows; the other is
mass-marketed romances. That both of these cultural forms—the self-help
work and the romance—are widely demeaned comes as no surprise. That
only feminist scholars have given them careful attention comes as no surprise either.

Self-help originated as a less gendered idea than it is today. Samuel
Smiles, who coined the phrase in a book by that title in 1854, wrote
about the early victims of industrialization and urbanization, who by his
reckoning should expect nothing from government or business and
everything from themselves. His cultural successors are today's authors
of self-help books, who also propound individualistic messages that deflect attention from social structure and culture and ignore the promise of
collective action.

In her study of women who read self-help books, Wendy Simonds concludes that

> Buying self-help, whatever form of media it takes, is about alienation *and* hope;
> about personal dissatisfaction *and* societal inadequacy; about wanting to con-
> form to achieve magical happiness *and* wanting to create new arrangements.[21]

Like most cultural forms, self-help works address diverse needs and thus
appeal to diverse audiences. They validate our individualism while feeding our dreams of community, for instance, and they let us hope for better
lives while distracting us from the project of making a better world.

Simonds traces "the current wave of self-help books" to Betty
Friedan's *The Feminine Mystique* (1963). Friedan's volume belongs in
that category inasmuch as self-help books let readers "feel a part of an invisible, and thus somewhat illusory, community of other women readers
who have the same concerns and problems"; they are "like the 'connected
knowers'" Mary Field Belenky and her coresearchers (see Chapter 8) describe. They "emphasiz[e] how comforting an activity their reading could
be"; during "bad times" they find "both nurturance and support" in self-

help volumes. (pp. 43, 47, 48) These readers do set aside books they dislike and disdain those they regard as "intrusively instructive." (p. 29) Simonds says that many of them "described self-help books as the cheaper end of a therapeutic continuum, where therapy was seen as the most desirable, but least attainable, end." (p. 58)

Considering self-help as a genre on a therapeutic continuum opens up theoretical space for thinking about other genres on that continuum. Simonds suggests that soap operas represent one such genre, and women's talk shows seem like another. Before we locate the mass-marketed romance there, the idea of such a continuum needs exploring. The "therapeutic by and large corresponds with the psychologistic as a problem-solving strategy and interpretive stance." Broadly, "therapy" addresses individuals' problems by focusing on how they themselves can ameliorate their situations. The therapeutic thus concerns individuals with problems, not individuals with problematic institutions or problem-ridden societies. Within the therapeutic worldview, individuals account for social and cultural outcomes, groups are reducible to their individual members, and social change means helping people clarify their values, find themselves, or get in touch with their feelings.

In many respects, then, what gets institutionalized as "therapeutic" opposes or undermines the political. It dodges issues of power and raises few questions about the common good; it tells individuals to use their own bootstraps or pull their own strings while demanding little from the community or society.

Yet as second-wave feminists insist, the personal is political. So too, then, is the therapeutic. Thus, feminist clinicians have developed their own forms of therapy, just as feminist philosophers and scientists have forged their own epistemologies and methodologies. Feminist therapies can raise awareness of the "oppressor within" (see Chapter 1) and thus promote critiques of the relations of ruling.[22]

The politics associated with the therapeutic continuum are class-bound as well as gendered. At one end of the continuum stand mass-marketed products for love junkies, compulsive eaters, chronic dieters, workaholics and codependents, among others; at the other end stand psychologists, psychiatrists, and counselors offering personal attention and specialized services. The one end is widely affordable and accessible; the other, fairly pricey and largely inaccessible to uninsured people who pose no apparent threat to themselves or others. More privileged women find favor toward the professionalized, costly end of the continuum, even though they don't have therapeutic equity due to gender-biased standards of mental health and gender-skewing among nonfeminist mental health workers (most psychiatrists are men and most counselors are women).

Across the entire continuum, however, a politics of representation is at work; such politics affect all women in varying degrees. That is, a contest of power ensues over whose images of women will prevail—broadly, mainstream inferiorizing ones or feminist empowering ones. Before looking at those politics, however, let us turn to some pop-culture products occupying the therapeutic continuum.

For women, as we have seen, three consequential cultural forms are soap operas, television talk shows, and romances.[23] All three illustrate what Simonds (pp. 213, 217) concludes: therapeutic culture is largely synonymous with self-help culture, which suffuses American women's (popular) culture. Yet soap operas, talk shows, and romances are far from interchangeable, and each form exhibits considerable variability. Moreover, what women make of and take from each varies dramatically. Joan Morgan reports, for instance, that she decided "to expose [herself] to the sexism of Dr. Dre, Ice Cube, Snoop Doggy Dogg, [and] the Notorious B.I.G." in order to find out why her "brothers are so angry at [her]."[24] The modern romance is a far cry from rap music, but it also holds both instructive and oppressive possibilities.

The modern romance belongs to a tradition of heroinism based in the late 18th and early 19th centuries. In the late 1970s Ellen Moers described the first "women romancers," including Aphra Behn, as "sexually experienced, highly literate, short of money, and indifferent to respectability."[25] Interestingly, contemporary readers of romances experience them as "chronicles of female triumph" much in line with the tradition they perpetuate. Moreover, readers commonly "project themselves into the story" and "become the heroine."[26] In her landmark study of their experiences, Janice A. Radway goes on to report that romances offer a "utopian vision" where women's caregiving coexists with female autonomy rather than deflating or defeating it. (p. 55) They also offer an optimistic outlook on communication as a corrective to misunderstandings between heterosexual lovers—a portrayal their readers like more than portrayals of sexuality. (p. 66)

According to Radway, the circumstances as well as the content of their reading appeal to women. First, their reading is something they themselves control. (p. 50) Second, it more or less fences them off from intrusions while letting them focus on their own "needs, desires, and pleasure." (pp. 59, 61) Their reading thus becomes an occasion for "self-indulgence." (p. 101) Third, by focusing on formulaic (and thus predictable) works, romance readers conserve their time and energy while guaranteeing their pleasure. (p. 196) Fourth, they value their reading for its capacity to lift their spirits. (p. 66) Finally, their reading connects them to other women with whom they regularly discuss the romances. (p. 96) Again, "connected knowers" in a wide-reaching sense looms as a meaningful notion.

As Christine Jarvis found, though, such readers may feel that what they read is "unsuitable" for serious consideration. Yet Jarvis found what Radway did, namely that such reading "was often part of a shared female culture."[27] Thus, reading sometimes constitutes "communities of women" not unlike the literary device used by novelists as different as Jane Austen and Louisa May Alcott.[28]

Such communities may also take symbolic shape among viewers of talk shows and soap operas. While most women who watch talk shows are not transgendered parents who have lost custody of their children or women partnered with people a generation younger than they are, they nevertheless can identify with the pain of social rejection, ridicule, and scorn. Above all, they can identify with the brute fact of experiencing problems as "personal" despite their anchorage in social structure and culture—problems one is considered solely responsible for originating and thus solely responsible for solving. As Susan Bordo theorizes, just about every talk show offers a "postmodern conversation" where "All sense of history and all ability (or inclination) to sustain cultural criticism . . . have disappeared."[29] Such shows may occasion identification with diverse women and face-to-face discussions of women's problems, but they themselves set aside society and its social constructions.

Like talk shows, soap operas promote self-help culture by presenting it "as an effective methodology for self-analysis." They "are reassuring both in the very reliability of their recurrent existence and in their reification of the therapeutic model of problem solving."[30] Perhaps, too, soaps are reassuring in their stubborn avoidance of how often women's problems derive from their relationships with men.[31] They also reassure by emphasizing sexual "equality" that does not necessitate major institutional or interpersonal changes.[32] Yet

> women in soap opera can never be simply happy with the positions they occupy. On the contrary, it is often these positions themselves that give rise to many problems and conflicts. This holds preeminently for the traditional positions . . . ascribed to women in contemporary society. So although motherhood is presented . . . as a feminine ideal, at the same time it is a source of constant care and worry. And marriage is not shown to be the blissful region of conjugal harmony but as subject to continual conflict. In a certain sense, then, a tense relationship is expressed in soap operas between the traditional destiny imposed on women by patriarchy and the nonviability of that destiny for women themselves. In other words, it would appear that some points made in feminist analysis of women's oppression are recognized in an intuitive way in soap operas.[33]

Nevertheless, like mass-marketed romances and talk shows, soap operas do treat the institution of heterosexuality as a *given,* not a massive set of entrenched and unfair social constructions.

Debbie Epstein and Deborah Lynn Steinberg illustrate this circumstance using Oprah Winfrey's show before its shift away from a self-help, confessional focus. These researchers like the show's interest in "empower[ing] . . . marginalized groups" as well as its progressive stances on diverse issues.[34] Yet they dislike its "presumption of heterosexuality and [its] use of therapy discourse." (p. 276)

Epstein and Steinberg point out that unlike black guests who appear as "'just guests' doing whatever other guests are doing," gay and lesbian guests are explicitly presented as such on lesbigay issues or—not being seen as such—they are presumed to be straight along with all the other guests. Thus, lesbian mothers are consistently presented as *lesbian* mothers, never simply as mothers alongside other mothers. (p. 277)

Further, even though the show considers women's problems in heterosexual relationships, heterosexuality itself goes unquestioned. Part of what sustains its taken-for-granted character on the show is therapeutic buzzwords like "dysfunctional family," "cycle of abuse," and "patterns we repeat." (pp. 278, 279) Although such phrases seem gender-neutral, in effect they let men off the hook. Problems with heterosexuality are presented as exceptional, not commonplace, and individual, not institutional. In this context, self-help and therapy often displace cultural critique and collective action.

Epstein and Steinberg do "see a radicalizing potential and radical elements" in Winfrey's show. They also see a forum for airing complaints about the typical forms heterosexuality takes, but that forum gets constructed so as to "reinvest in or recuperate" rather than critique those forms. (p. 279) What Epstein and Steinberg observe are ultimately the constraints of a popular cultural form—the sorts of constraints also exhibited by the domestic or situation comedy, the realistic novel, or the music video. Indeed, formal constraints also govern advice or self-help books, as Arlie Russell Hochschild implies in Reading 8. Treating such works as ventures in "emotional investment counseling," she looks at the "cultural cooling" they reflect and how they might in effect subvert feminism.

With respect to such books and a great deal more, however, women do "develop practices and strategies to get what they want out of life."[35] Women resist and rebel, deviate and dare, ply their resourcefulness and rely on their imaginations. Faced with pop-culture products and often relying on them as self-help aids, heterosexual women often do what lesbians do as consumers of popular culture. Lesbians make meaning from straight culture by

> picking up on hints and possibilities that the author, consciously or not, has strewn in the text. A text that manifests certain symbolic elements—perhaps the absence of men, of women's attention to men, or of marked femininity; perhaps the presence of female bonding or of strong and independent female characters—may trigger the act of lesbian reading.[36]

Valerie Traub illustrates with the 1987 film *Black Widow,* starring Debra Winger and Theresa Russell. Even though it appears to be a "mainstream, heterosexual 'woman's film,'" it does allow for a "homoerotic tension between the two female leads," thus "solicit[ing] a 'lesbian' gaze at the same time that it invite[s] male heterosexual enjoyment." Traub generalizes that lesbians' consumption of popular culture, like that of straight women, "does not exist outside of, but in complex relation to, the 'deployment of sexuality' dominating contemporary discourse."[37]

As reader-response theorists put it, readers complete their text. They fulfill its meanings not exclusively on their own terms but in interaction with the frameworks and content they find there. More generally, people turn on their televisions, pick up their magazines, and thumb through self-help paperbacks with purposes and needs ultimately their own. What they experience from those media significantly reflects what they need and want to find there. Thus, readers of mass-market romances focus on the restoration of clarity and mutuality between problem-plagued lovers, just as lesbian filmgoers may focus on the intense bonding between two apparently straight female characters.

Then, too, many women turn to specialized niches of women's culture. Many of us seek out feminist humor books or the "new feminist advice literature" such as Judith Martin's *Miss Manners' Guide to Excruciatingly Correct Behavior.*[38] Many of us look to Olivia Records for the women's music we enjoy and order from Ladyslipper, a mail-order business specializing in women's music of all types.[39] Many of us subscribe to *Lambda Book Report* or the *Women's Review of Books* or *Ms.* or *Sage* or *Lilith* for women's perspectives on matters that concern us. Publishers like the Naiad Press in Tallahassee and women's bookstores like Charis Books in Atlanta depend on our business, and the relative longevity of such second-wave feminist businesses (see Reading 20) suggests how profoundly they complement our efforts to make meaning of pop-culture fare. Such businesses build on the premise that important as it is, "Self-help is not enough."[40]

POPULAR CULTURE AND FEMINIST CHALLENGES

Bell hooks decries popular self-help books that purport an interest in women's health but offer no critique of patriarchy. Her own self-help volume *Sisters of the Yam: Black Women and Self-Recovery* links self-help and therapy to critical consciousness. Insisting that "end[ing] domination is fundamentally about a revolution in mental health," hooks moves past the either/or judgments usually associated with critiques of the self-help culture.[41] All the while, she remains vividly aware that popular culture pervades Americans' lives. Thus, a lot of her work focuses on pop-culture fare. In the aggregate, hooks's analyses show how these realities routinely exhibit internal tensions and contradictions, such as the radical and the conformist elements Epstein and Steinberg detect in Winfrey's show. Tania Modleski's pathbreaking work in feminist cultural studies underscores that point. Her analyses assume that popular culture

> not only contains contradictions, it also *functions* in a highly contradictory manner: while appearing to be merely escapist, [it] simultaneously challenges and reaffirms traditional values, behavior, and attitudes.[42]

Some women's sports are illustrative.

Among the most televised of women's sports, figure skating and gymnastics counteract stereotypes of weak, passive females. Yet these sports also reinforce inferiorizing notions about girls and women, in part by how the sports themselves are configured and in part by how the media present them. Judith Lorber (the author of Reading 2) reports, for example, how the 1992 Winter Olympics required male figure skaters to do three triple jumps in their compulsory program while limiting female skaters to no more than one. She also underscores that in effect we have *girls'* gymnastics and *men's* gymnastics.[43] Susan Gilbert puts it this way:

> Although girls and boys begin training between ages 5 and 7, girls have a limited time—usually from 12 until 19—to compete. While the sport rewards strength in male gymnasts, who compete well into their 20s, it prizes a small childlike body in female athletes.

Until 1972, though, female gymnasts in the Olympics were often in their 20s and sometimes their 30s. Today's "pixielike gymnasts" may yet make way for their return. The International Gymnastics Federation decided in 1996 to "require the athletes to be 16 before entering international competitions."[44]

Nonetheless, issues of femininity versus "musculinity" plague female athletes, who are routinely photographed so as to eroticize their bodies.[45] Then, too, shots of women in the stands are gendered. They "serve as comical targets or objects of sexual innuendo. . . . So popular is this practice that the term 'honey shot' was coined back in the 1970s to describe it. . . ." Finally, as Greta L. Cohen observes, "Intelligent, sophisticated commentary about female athletes is rare."[46]

Such patterns, the empirical beginnings of theorizing about female athletics, belong to the larger relations of ruling:

> The doctrines of the discourse of femininity are reproduced, revised, updated in popular philosophy, theology, and psychology, in magazines, in books, and as schemata governing the morality of soap operas, sitcoms, TV game shows, and so forth; their interpretive paradigms are commercially produced on television, in movies, in advertising in multiple settings, including packaging, and shop-window and counter displays. Forms of heterosexuality, the ordering of value, relations, agency, subjectivity, practices, are for women vested in appearances, *in what it is to be looked at [by men].*[47]

Thus, a great deal of feminist film criticism as well as critiques of popular culture revolve around the notion of the *male gaze,* a form of interpersonal power and cultural privilege that expresses men's widespread dominance. Alongside that notion is increasing attention to female spectatorship.[48]

Another key concept is *colonization,* whereby hegemonic notions about females get rooted in girls' and women's consciousness so that they themselves believe in their own inferiority. Recently, notions about "hyperreal" images have begun to take hold. As Susan Bordo illustrates in connection with body imagery, we all "know" that Cher and virtually every other female star over the age of 25 is the plastic product of numerous cosmetic surgeries on face and body. But, in the era of the "hyperreal" (as Baudrillard calls it), such "knowledge" is . . . unable to cast a shadow of doubt over the dazzling, compelling, authoritative images themselves. Like the knowledge of our own mortality when we are young and healthy, the knowledge that Cher's physical appearance is fabricated is an empty abstraction; it simply does not compute. It is the created image that has the hold on our most vibrant, immediate sense of what *is,* of what matters, of what we must pursue for ourselves.[49]

The sheer volume of such images, coupled with technologies for manipulating them persuasively, makes for fantastical images that beg to be experienced as attainable. When events like women's athletic competitions get pictorially rendered this way, the divide between the actual and the conceivable widens.

Throughout popular culture today, then, one sees virtual "representation wars" over the images of girls and women. Elayne Rapping sees "many large and small victories in winning hearts, minds, and air time for feminist views and concepts. . . ."[50] She is hard to argue with, especially in view of TV programs like "The Mary Tyler Moore Show" in its day or "Murphy Brown" these days. Yet such shows can take feminist themes only so far before they strain against the very structure of the sitcom or, more generally, the constraints of the cultural form.

Howells portrays Penelope Lapham as a quick-witted, congenial, assertive young woman, for instance. In the end, though, she gets married off to the relatively unimaginative (though financially secure) Tom Corey after a series of events deliver enough comeuppance to feminize her. Howells himself mentored the feminist Charlotte Perkins Gilman (see Chapter 6), best known for *The Yellow Wallpaper,* and considered himself a feminist.[51]

But the realistic novel does not allow for a fully feminist plot. Such a plot lands a text on that part of the cultural landscape designated as utopian, romantic, fantastic, or futuristic. To make female characters credible, realistic works must to some extent paint them in the soft colors of mainstream femininity. Think of Jane Austen's Emma Woodhouse in *Emma* or George Eliot's Dorothea Brookes in *Middlemarch.* Think, too, of the female exceptions who make the rule: Eliot's strong-willed Maggie Tulliver, whose fate in *The Mill on the Floss* is drowning, or Louisa May Alcott's androgynous Jo March, who ends up in *Little Women* a schoolmarm devoted, with her husband, to educating young boys. As Elizabeth G. Traube generalizes, "Unlimited ambition in women continue[s] to be constructed as a threat, requiring either their subordination to the appropriate men or their expulsion from the imagined community."[52]

As we near the 21st century, pop culture proliferates such messages. Yet as Rapping and others remind us, pop culture is far from monolithic and far from unaffected by second-wave feminism. Then, too, as Raymond and others show, consumers are neither passive nor unimaginative as they make meanings from mass-media fare. Bearing all that in mind, one is still hard pressed to exaggerate the narrowness of media images of women.

As hooks emphasizes, "There is a direct and abiding connection between the maintenance of white supremacist patriarchy in this society and the institutionalization via mass media of specific images. . . ."[53] She goes on to observe that "Within commodity culture, ethnicity becomes spice, seasoning that can liven up . . . mainstream white culture." (p. 21) Similarly, lesbians can serve as spice, just as working-class women or imprisoned women or military women can. Time and again recently I have come across references in the media to "lesbian chic." In mass advertising and popular programming, lesbians are supposedly showing up as fashionable, attractive people. The cover of a 1996 *Vanity Fair* that featured model Cindy Crawford and singer k. d. lang is but one example. As Diane Hamer and Belinda Budge point out, whatever "lesbian chic" means, it remains the case that "lesbian performers and audiences are struggling . . . to construct positions from which to speak that acknowledge both lesbian marginality *and* membership in the dominant culture."[54]

Their analysis points toward the realities Rosemary Hennessy explores in Reading 9. Hennessy focuses on commodity culture, where nearly everything can be commodified for the sake of increasing profits and expanding market niches. She calls "queer visibility" "a limited victory for gays, who are welcome to be visible as consumer subjects but not as social subjects." She goes on to note how commodity culture then mediates queer identities and politics. Hennessy thus raises crucial questions about how "progress" in popular culture is a mixed blessing for members of oppressed groups, whose dignity is far from secured in everyday life. Indeed, such "progress" represents yet one more web of contradictions in pop culture.

We cannot let popular culture be just about commercialism and corporate profits or escape and relaxation. In the end it must be about beauty that flies past the formulaic, the standardized, the stereotypical, and thus the uninspired. As Teresa de Lauretis expresses it, "feminist theory should now engage precisely in the redefinition of aesthetic and formal knowledges, much as women's cinema has been engaged in the transformation of vision."[55]

NOTES

1. Rita Felski, "Gazing at Gender: Recent Work in Feminist Media Studies," *American Literary History* 8, no. 2 (Summer 1996), p. 388.
2. Kate Millett, *Sexual Politics* (New York: Equinox Books, 1970; reprinted 1971), p. xii. Page number refers to reprint edition.
3. Laura Mulvey, "Visual Pleasure and Narrative Cinema" in Karyn Kay and Gerald Peary (eds), *Women and the Cinema* (New York: E. P. Dutton, 1977);

Sandra Gilbert and Susan Gubar, *The Madwoman in the Attic: The Woman Writer and the Nineteenth-Century Literary Imagination* (New Haven, CT: Yale University Press, 1979); Elaine Showalter, *A Literature of Their Own: British Women Novelists from Bronte to Lessing* (Princeton, NJ: Princeton University Press, 1977).

4. Particularly rich sources to examine are Teresa de Lauretis, *Alice Doesn't: Feminism, Semiotics, Cinema* (Bloomington: Indiana University Press, 1984); Laura Mulvey, *Fetishism and Curiosity* (Bloomington: Indiana University Press, 1996); and Liesbet Van Zoonen, *Feminist Media Studies* (Thousand Oaks, CA: Sage, 1994).

5. For starters, see bell hooks, "Madonna: Plantation Mistress or Soul Sister?" in *Black Looks: Race and Representation* (Boston: South End Press, 1992), pp. 157–64; Cathy Schwichtenberg (ed.), *The Madonna Connection: Representational Politics* (Boulder, CO: Westview Press, 1992); Susan Bordo, "Material Girl: The Effacements of Postmodern Culture" in *Unbearable Weight: Feminism, Western Culture, and the Body* (Berkeley: University of California Press, 1993), pp. 245–75; Pamela Robertson, "Does Feminist Camp Make a Difference? or, What We Talk about When We Talk about Madonna" in *Guilty Pleasures: Feminist Camp from Mae West to Madonna* (Durham, NC: Duke University Press, 1996), pp. 115–38.

6. See Lisa Maria Hogeland, "Sexuality in the Consciousness-Raising Novel of the 1970s," *Journal of the History of Sexuality* 5, no. 4 (April 1995), pp. 601–32; Verna Foster, "Sex, Power, and Pedagogy in Mamet's *Oleanna* and Ionesco's *The Lesson*," *American Drama* 5, no. 1 (Fall 1995), pp. 36–50; Chris Holmlund, "Fractured Fairytales and Experimental Identities: Looking for Lesbians in and around the Films of Su Friedrich," *Discourse* 17, no. 1 (Fall 1994), pp. 16–46; Leda M. Cooks and Roger C. Aden, "*Northern Exposure*'s Sense of Place: Constructing and Marginalizing the Matriarchal Community," *Women's Studies in Communication* 18, no. 1 (Spring 1995), pp. 1–17; Jill Laurie Goodman, "Reading toward Womanhood: The Babysitters Club Books and Our Daughters," *TIKKUN* 8, no. 6 (November/December 1993), pp. 7–10, 97; and Cindy J. Dorfman, "The Garden of Eating: The Carnal Kitchen in Contemporary American Culture," *Feminist Issues* 12, no. 1 (Spring 1992), pp. 21–38.

7. Mary F. Rogers, *Novels, Novelists, and Readers: Toward a Phenomenological Sociology of Literature* (Albany: State University of New York Press, 1991).

8. Regina Barreca, *They Used to Call Me Snow White . . . but I Drifted: Women's Strategic Use of Humor* (Harmondsworth, England: Penguin Books, 1992), p. 23.

9. Nancy A. Walker, *A Very Serious Thing: Women's Humor and American Culture* (Minneapolis: University of Minnesota Press, 1988), pp. 73, 80; see also Sevda Caliskan, "Is There Such a Thing as Women's Humor?" *American Studies International* XXXIII, no. 2 (October 1995), pp. 49–59; Annette Wheeler Cafarelli, "What Will Mrs. Grundy Say? Women and Comedy," *Criticism* XXXVIII, no. 1 (Winter 1996), pp. 69–83.

10. Barreca, *They Used to Call Me Snow White*, p. 28.

11. Mary Crawford, *Talking Difference: On Gender and Language* (Thousand Oaks, CA: Sage, 1995), p. 153.

12. Walker, *A Very Serious Thing*, p. 26.

13. *Ibid.*, pp. 92–4.

14. *Ibid.*, pp. 4, 10.

15. Barreca, *They Used to Call Me Snow White,* p. 13, 23.

16. *Ibid.*, pp. 93, 47.

17. Mary Russo, "Female Grotesques: Carnival and Theory" in Teresa de Lauretis (ed.), *Feminist Studies/Critical Studies* (Madison: University of Wisconsin Press, 1986), p. 213.

18. *Ibid.*, p. 96.

19. Walker, *A Very Serious Thing,* p. 162.

20. Wendy Simonds, *Women and Self-Help Culture: Reading between the Lines* (New Brunswick, NJ: Rutgers University Press, 1992), p. 2. A prime example of a medium directed at a female audience is the cable network Lifetime; see Jane Feuer, "Feminism on Lifetime: Yuppie TV for the Nineties," *camera obscura* 33–34 (1995), pp. 133–46; Pamela Wilson, "Upscale Feminist Angst: Molly Dodd, the Lifetime Cable Network and Gender Marketing," *camera obscura* 33–34 (1995), pp. 103–32.

21. Simonds, *Women and Self-Help Culture,* p. 226.

22. I thank Susan E. Chase for sharing this insight in response to an earlier formulation where I had failed to acknowlege the transformational—even subversive—potential of feminist therapies.

23. Tania Modleski helped to launch this sort of analysis; see her *Loving with a Vengeance: Mass-Produced Fantasies for Women* (Hamden, CT: Archon Books, 1982), where she focuses on Harlequin romances, gothic novels, and soap operas.

24. Joan Morgan, "Fly-Girls, Bitches, and Hoes: Notes of a Hip-Hop Feminist," *Social Text* 45 (Winter 1995), p. 153.

25. Ellen Moers, *Literary Women* (New York: Anchor Books, 1977), pp. 189, 219.

26. Janice A. Radway, *Reading the Romance: Women, Patriarchy, and Popular Literature* (Chapel Hill: University of North Carolina Press, 1984), pp. 54, 67.

27. Christine Jarvis, "Romancing the Curriculum: Empowerment through Popular Culture," *Convergence* XXVIII, no. 3 (1995), pp. 71, 72.

28. See Nina Auerbach, *Communities of Women: An Idea in Fiction* (Cambridge, MA: Harvard University Press, 1978).

29. Susan Bordo, *Unbearable Weight: Feminism, Western Culture, and the Body* (Berkeley: University of California Press, 1993), p. 258.

30. Simonds, *Women and Self-Help Culture,* p. 217.

31. Wendy Simonds, "Confessions of Loss: Maternal Grief in *True Story,* 1920–1985," *Gender & Society* 2, no. 2 (June 1988), p. 151.

32. Simonds, *Women and Self-Help Culture,* p. 48.

33. Ien Ang, *Watching Dallas: Soap Opera and the Melodramatic Imagination* (London and New York: Methuen, 1985), pp. 122–3, trans. Della Couling.

34. Debbie Epstein and Deborah Lynn Steinberg, "Twelve Steps to Heterosexuality? Common-Sensibilities on the Oprah Winfrey Show," *Feminism & Psychology* 5, no. 2 (1995), p. 276. For a similar critique, see Corinne Squire, "Empowering Women? The Oprah Winfrey Show," *Feminism & Psychology* 4, no. 1 (1994), pp. 63–79; see also Rosaria Champagne, "Oprah Winfrey's *Sacred Silent* and the Spectatorship of Incest," *Discourse* 17, no. 2 (Winter 1994–95), pp. 123–38.

35. Denise Farran, "Analysing a Photograph of Marilyn Monroe" in Liz Stanley (ed.), *Feminist Praxis: Research, Theory and Epistemology in Feminist Sociology* (London and New York: Routledge, 1990), p. 272.

36. Bonnie Zimmerman, "Seeing, Reading, Knowing: The Lesbian Appropriation of Literature" in Joan E. Hartman and Ellen Messer-Davidow (eds.), *(En)Gendering Knowledge: Feminists in Academe* (Knoxville: University of Tennessee Press, 1991), p. 94.

37. Valerie Traub, "The Ambiguities of 'Lesbian' Viewing Pleasure: The (Dis)articulations of *Black Widow*" in Julia Epstein and Kristina Straub (eds.), *Body Guards: The Cultural Politics of Gender Ambiguity* (New York: Routledge, 1991), pp. 307–8, 309.

38. Walker, *A Very Serious Thing,* p. 134.

39. On women and music, see Mavis Bayton, "Out on the Margins: Feminism and the Study of Popular Music," *Women* 3, no. 1 (Summer 1992), pp. 51–9; Lucy Green, "Music and Gender: Can Music Raise Our Awareness?" *Women* 5, no. 1 (Spring 1994), pp. 65–72; Rachel Musleah, "An Explosion of Jewish Women's Popular Music," *Lilith* 20, no. 4 (Winter 1995–96), pp. 18–29; and Avelardo Valdez and Jeffrey A. Halley, "Gender in the Culture of Mexican American Conjunto Music," *Gender & Society* 10, no. 2 (April 1996), pp. 148–67.

40. On Naiad Press and other lesbian publishing companies, see Karla Jay, "Is Lesbian Literature Going Mainstream?" *Ms.* IV (July/August 1993), pp. 70–74.

41. bell hooks, "Feminism: Crying for Our Souls," *Women & Therapy* 17, no. 1/2 (1995), pp. 265–72.

42. Modleski, *Loving with a Vengeance,* p. 112.

43. Judith Lorber, "Believing Is Seeing: Biology as Ideology," *Gender & Society* 7, no. 4 (December 1993), pp. 568–81. For an analysis of women's ice hockey, a sport with quite different cultural meanings, see Gai Ingham Berlage, "The Development of Intercollegiate Women's Ice Hockey in the United States," *Colby Quarterly* XXXII, no. 1 (March 1996), pp. 58–71.

44. Susan Gilbert, "The Smallest Olympians Pay the Biggest Price," *New York Times,* July 28, 1996, p. 4E.

45. Jennifer Hargreaves, *Sporting Females: Critical Issues in the History and Sociology of Women's Sports* (New York: Routledge, 1994), pp. 164, 173.

46. Greta L. Cohen, "Media Portrayal of the Female Athlete" in Greta L. Cohen (ed.), *Women in Sport: Issues and Controversies* (Newbury Park, CA: Sage, 1993), pp. 175, 173.

47. Dorothy E. Smith, *Texts, Facts, and Femininity: Exploring the Relations of Ruling* (New York: Routledge, 1990), p. 174.

48. See Jackie Stacey, *Star Gazing: Hollywood Cinema and Female Spectatorship* (London and New York: Routledge, 1994), especially chap. 2, "From the Male Gaze to the Female Spectator" (pp. 19–48).

49. Bordo, *Unbearable Weight,* p. 104.

50. Elayne Rapping, *Media-tions: Forays into the Culture and Gender Wars* (Boston: South End Press, 1994), pp. 13, 19.

51. See Joanne Karpinski, "When the Marriage of True Minds Admits Impediments: Charlotte Perkins Gilman and William Dean Howells" in Shirley Marchalonis (ed.), *Patrons and Protegees: Gender, Friendship, and Writing*

in Nineteenth-Century America (New Brunswick, NJ: Rutgers University Press, 1988), pp. 212–34.

52. Elizabeth G. Traube, "Transforming Heroes: Hollywood and the Demonization of Women," *Public Culture* 3, no. 2 (Spring 1991), p. 2.

53. bell hooks, *Black Looks: Race and Representation* (Boston: South End Press, 1992), p. 2.

54. Diane Hamer and Belinda Budge, "Introduction" in Diane Hamer and Belinda Budge (eds.), *The Good, the Bad, and the Gorgeous: Popular Culture's Romance with Lesbianism* (San Francisco: Pandora, 1994), pp. 1–14.

55. Teresa de Lauretis, *Technologies of Gender: Essays on Theory, Film, and Fiction* (Bloomington: Indiana University Press, 1987), p. 131.

READING 8

The Commercial Spirit of Intimate Life and the Abduction of Feminism: Signs from Women's Advice Books

Arlie Russell Hochschild

Praising and encouraging are very close to pushing, and when you do that you are trying again to take control of his life. Think about why you are lauding something he's done. Is it to help raise his self-esteem? That's manipulation. Is it so he will continue whatever behavior you're praising? That's manipulation. Is it so that he'll know how proud you are of him? That can be burden for him to carry. Let him develop his own pride from his own accomplishments.

—Robin Norwood, *Women Who Love Too Much*
(1985, p. 238)

Bestselling advice books for women published in the United States over the last two decades may offer a glimpse into a wider trend in popular culture. This trend is a curious, latter-day parallel to the very different cultural shift Max Weber describes in *The Protestant Ethic and the Spirit of Capitalism* (1958). The current cultural shift differs in the object of its ideas (love and not work), in the social sphere it most affects (the family and not the economy) and in the population most immediately influenced (women, not men). The cultural shift reflected in advice books concerns a more marginal ideology, feminism, and the commercial transmutation of it is a shift that is smaller, I hope, in scale. Like the earlier trend, this one represents the outcome of an ongoing cultural struggle, gives rise to counter-trends, and is uneven in its effect. But the parallel is there.

Just as Protestantism, according to Max Weber, "escaped from the cage" of the Church to be transposed into an inspirational "spirit of capitalism" that drove men to make money and build capitalism, so feminism may be "escaping from the cage" of a social movement to buttress a commercial spirit of intimate life that was originally separate from and indeed alien to it.[1] Just as market conditions ripened the soil for capitalism, so a weakened family prepares the soil for a commercialized spirit of domestic life (Fromm 1956; Weber 1958, p. 181). Magnified moments in advice books tell this story.

In exploring evidence of this shift, this parallel, I'm assuming that bestselling advice books for women published between 1970 and 1990 are a likely bellwether of trends in the popular ideas governing women's approach to intimate life. I also assume that advice books, like other commercial and professional conveyors of guidance, are becoming more important while traditional spheres of authority, families and to a degree churches, are becoming less so.[2] Thus, while the counsel of parents, grandparents, aunts and uncles, ministers, priests, and rabbis holds relatively less weight than it would have a century ago, that of professional therapists, television talk show hosts, radio commentators, video producers, magazine and advice book authors assumes relatively more weight (Lasch 1977). While people turn increasingly to anonymous authorities, the emotional problems they wish to resolve are probably more perplexing than ever (Giddens 1991).

Like other commercially-based advice-givers, the authors of advice books act as emotional investment counselors.[3] They do readings of broad social conditions and recommend to readers of various types, how, how much, and in whom to "invest" emotional attention. They recommend emotional practices—such as thinking of "praise" as "manipulation," so as to detach oneself from another person, as Robin Norwood recommends earlier. Writers also motivate their readers by hitching investment strategies to inspirational ideas and images. These ideas and images are buried in the "magnified moments" inside the parable-like stories that make up much of these books.

Neither author or reader, I imagine, is much aware that they are offering or receiving "emotional investment counseling." Rather, authors see themselves as giving, and readers see themselves as receiving, helpful advice. Sometimes it is. My basic point is that helping and being helped is a matter of such overwhelming importance that any cultural shift which "thins out" the process and empties the content of help should give us pause (Simonds 1992).

A CULTURAL COOLING: TRENDS AND COUNTER TRENDS

With these starting points, I propose that many bestselling advice books published between 1970 and 1990 have become "cooler" in their approach to intimate life. They reflect a "cultural cooling." This does not mean that individuals need one another less, only that they are invited to *manage their needs more.* The trend also reflects a paradox. Earlier advice books are far more patriarchal, less based on open and equal communication, but oddly, they often reflect more "warmth." More recent advice books call for more open and more equal communication, but they propose "cooler" emotional strategies with which to engage those equal bonds. From the vantage point of the early feminist movement, modern advice books reaffirm one ideal (equality) but undermine another (the development of emotionally rich social bonds).

Two literatures bear on this "cooling." One supports the observation of cooling but doesn't link it to advice books. The other analyzes advice books but doesn't focus on cooling. Christopher Lasch (1977), Ann Swidler (1986) and Francesca Cancian (1987), among others, argue that "commitment" plays a diminishing part in people's idea of love. Data from American national opinion pools document a decline over the last two decades in commitment to long-term love. In their study of daytime soap

opera heroes and heroines, Lee Harrington and Denise Bielby (1991) don't observe a shift away from the idea of lasting love, but they note a shift away from the practices that affirm it.

Analyses of the advice literature, on the other hand, say little about this cooling. Commentators have critiqued the authoritarianism, privatism, and ideology of victimhood implicit in many advice books. In *I'm Dysfunctional, You're Dysfunctional* (1992), Wendy Kaminer critiques advice books in the Recovery Movement (based on the 12-step program of Alcoholics Anonymous) for appealing to individual choice while taking it away. They give orders. In *Self-Help Culture: Reading Women's Readings* (1992) Wendy Simonds argues a second point, namely that self-oriented quick-fix books deflect attention away from problems in the public sphere that cause people to need private help in the first place. In "Beware the Incest-Survivor Machine" (1993) Carol Tavris critiques the cult of victimhood many "survivor" books seem to promote.

While there is much truth in all three critiques, I believe that something else is also going on—a shift in the cultural premises about human attachment.[4] To get it, we can draw an imaginary line through the emotional core of each advice book, by focusing on the best and worst "magnified moments" in it, the "top" and "bottom" of the personal experience the book portrays. This method works best with the therapeutic, interview, and autobiographical books.

Most books seem to have four parts. In one, the author establishes a tone of voice, a relationship to the reader, and connects the reader to a source of authority—the Bible, psychoanalysis, corporate expertise, Hollywood, or the school of hard knocks. In a second part, the author didactically describes moral or social reality. "This is how men are" or "that's what the job market's like," or "this is the rule" and how it bends under a variety of circumstances. In a third part, the book describes concrete practices; for example, "With your boyfriend, listen, with your girlfriend, you can talk" or "Wear blue to a 'power breakfast meeting' at work." In a fourth—and I believe most revealing—part of the advice book, the author tells stories. These stories are based on the lives of patients in an author's psychotherapeutic practice, interviewees, or the author's own life. Such stories tend to be either exemplary or cautionary. Exemplary stories tell one what to do and cautionary stories, what not to do.

Stories contain magnified moments, episodes of heightened importance, either epiphanies, moments of intense glee or unusual insight, or moments in which things go intensely but meaningfully wrong. In either case, the moment stands out; it is metaphorically rich, usually elaborate, and often echoes throughout the book.

One thing a magnified moment magnifies is the *feeling* a person holds up as ideal. It shows what a person, up until the experience began, *wanted* to feel. Thus, there is an ideal expressed in the moment and there is culture within the ideal. Magnified moments reflect a feeling ideal both when a person joyously lives up to it or, in some spectacular way, does not. More than the descriptions of the author's authority or beliefs, more than the long didactic passages in advice books about what is or isn't true or right, magnified moments show the experience we wish. About the experience, and the ideal against which it is measured, we may ask many questions.[5] Key among the questions are these. Does the advice support a general paradigm of trust or of caution? Does it center on expressing one's emotional needs, or marshaling strategic control over them? Is the book "warm" in the sense of legitimizing a high degree of care and social support, and offering scope for human needs? Or is it "cool" in the sense of presuming the individual should get by with relatively little support, and by presuming she or he has fewer needs?

DOORWAY DRAMA

Let us contrast two "magnified moments." The first is drawn from Marabel Morgan's (1973) *The Total Woman,* an arch-reactionary traditional-for-moderns which is curiously "warm." The second is taken from Colette Dowling's (1981) *The Cin-* *derella Complex,* a modern advice book which is curiously "cool."

From Marabel Morgan's *The Total Woman:*

If your husband comes home at 6:00, bathe at 5:00. In preparing for your six o'clock date, lie back and let go of the tensions of day. Think about that special man who's on his way home to you. . . . Rather than make your husband play hide-and-seek when he comes home tired, greet him at the door when he arrives. Make homecoming a happy time. Waltzing to the door in a cloud of powder and cologne is a great confidence builder. Not only can you respond to his advances, you will want to. . . . For an experiment, I put on pink baby-doll pajamas and white boots after my bubble bath. I must admit that I looked foolish and felt even more so. When I opened the door that night to greet Charlie, I was unprepared for his reaction. My quiet, reserved, non-excitable husband took one look, dropped his brief case on the doorstep, and chased me around the dining-room table. We were in stitches by the time he caught me, and breathless with that old feeling of romance. . . . Our little girls stood flat against the wall watching our escapade, giggling with delight. We all had a marvelous evening together, and Charlie forgot to mention the problems of the day. (Morgan 1973, pp. 114–5)

What did Marabel Morgan feel? First she felt delight and surprise at Charlie's response. Charlie was surprised, of course, but so was Marabel—at the very fact that her act succeeded.

In some ways, Morgan's peak moment is the same as other peak moments in advice books to women. She feels central, appreciated, in the middle of an experience she wants to have. But in other ways her moment is different. For one thing, her moment is "fun," and fun in a certain kind of way. It is sexually exciting within the context of the family. It is marital and family fun. She is breathless in her husband's arms—not in a lover's arms. And her two girls are nearby, "flat against the wall" and "giggling."

In addition to Morgan's husband and daughters, present in fantasy are a community of women who are also working on their marriages. After trying out a certain move at home, Morgan tells us, one "Total Woman" class member often calls another the next morning to see how it went. Spanning across families, like the women's movement, a community of Christian wives are "watching the show" in each others' homes.

Marabel Morgan's big moment doesn't occur naturally, as when one suddenly discovers a magnificent rainbow or sunset. It is not "spontaneous." Her moment is a well-planned, choreographed act. In addition to dressing in pink pajamas, she dresses as a pixie, a pirate, or comes to the door totally nude wrapped in cellophane. Her magnified moment is not an occasion for self-realization or revealing communication, not the "high" of sudden self-honesty or intimate communication. The act, the delighted response are a stylized, premodern form of communication in themselves. Marabel puts on her babydoll suit. Charlie sees she means to please him. He is pleased. She receives his pleasure. They have communicated. *That* is the high point. At the same time, Morgan's act paradoxically doubles as a shield against intimate communication. With doorway surprises, she advises her readers to "keep him off guard" (Morgan 1973, p. 123). Whether she is pleasing Charlie or getting her way with him by working female wiles, whether she draws inspiration from the Bible or Hollywood, Marabel Morgan is approaching her husband in an old-fashioned way.

At bottom, the pink pajamas and the "Total Woman" homework and tests are a Christian fundamentalist "solution" to disintegrating marriages—a trend quickly mounting through the 1960 and 1970s when Morgan wrote. Throughout the book, there is a drum-beat reminder of divorce. Speaking of a woman who could not adapt to her husband's desire to travel, Morgan cautions,

> Betty is now divorced. . . . Carl has since found someone else to enjoy his exciting new way of life with him. In your marriage it only makes sense for both of you to paddle in the same direction. Otherwise, you'll only go in circles,—or like Carl, he may pull out and go downstream. (Morgan 1973, p. 89)

In addition to friendly women in the same boat, then, are anonymous rivals who can replace the wife in a fading marriage. In spirit, these female rivals are present in the magnified moment of *The Total Woman* too.

I should add one social relationship on the scene—that between author and reader. The girl-to-girl back fence tone of voice, the open, conversational style with which Morgan tells her story is itself a message. Morgan talks to the reader, not as a priest or professional expert, but as a girl-friend. She does not offer the indisputable received wisdom of the ages concerning "the correct way" to conduct oneself in a given situation. Her advice is personal. Culturally, she seems to be saying, "you and I are on our own. This is what I did. Why don't you try?" Curiously, other American traditional-for-moderns eschew a voice of authority in favor of the voice of a "friend." How or whether you save your marriage is up to you, they seem to say, I wish you luck.

In contrast to her best moment, Morgan's worst moments virtually all focus on the discord that results when she challenges her husband's authority. Already criticized by her husband for being "uptight," her following bad moment occurs:

> I prepared a very nice dinner the next day and determined to be a sweet wife. However, the bottom fell out for me. Over the mashed potatoes, Charlie announced casually that we would be going out the next evening with some business associates. With no malice I blurted out, "Oh no, we can't." And then I began to tell him of the plans I had already made. A terrible stony look passed over my husband's face. I braced myself. In icy tones, with obvious control, he asked, "Why do you challenge me on every decision I make?" (Morgan 1973, pp. 11–12)

Elsewhere, she talks about confronting her husband "eye ball to eye ball" (Morgan 1973, p. 73). As this almost sexual image suggests, to Morgan patriarchy is what keeps a woman a woman; otherwise she'd be a man—and fight.

Like many traditional women, Morgan presumes men and women are adversaries. Patriarchy, for her, is the deal that ends the war with the following outcome: the man gets the power, the woman gets the stable home. These premises compose the cultural floorboard beneath magnified moments in *The Total Woman*.[6]

The magnified moment reflects an anxiety and what Morgan imagines as a solution to it. The anxiety is that of women who fear "getting fired" from their marriages and becoming the displaced homemakers of tomorrow. Morgan proposes to beat the 1960s disintegration of the family, complete with the pool of newly displaced women (the "other women" out there). And she does this on her own home turf. She incorporates the sexual revolution (including its ideal of sexual variety) into the monogamous, Christian marriage, and adds a little theater to a housewife's day.

While Morgan may seem to draw more from Hollywood than the Bible and feminine tradition, and she may seem more flamboyant than "warm," her magnified moments place her as both "traditional" and "warm." It is overwhelmingly clear that Morgan favors an authoritarian world in which men rule women, and men have greater human worth than women: in this she carries on patriarchy. But at the same time, her simple-minded tips are all about moving forward and in, not backward and out of relationships. However antiquated the ethic affirmed in her magnified moment, it is communal. As an emotional investment counselor, she recommends that women invest their emotion work in the family and community.

THE NO-NEEDS MODERN

At the other end of the spectrum, we find a moment from Colette Dowling's *The Cinderella Complex*:

> Powerful emotional experiences await those who are really living out their own scripts. A Chicago woman in her early 40s who still lives with and

loves her husband is also intensely involved with a man she works with. He too is married, so their time together is limited. They look forward to the business trips they manage to take together several times a year. On one of these, the woman decided after a few days that she wanted to go skiing. The man was not a skier and in any event had further work to do in Boston. "I decided that I should ski by myself," she told me [Dowling]. "I got on a bus in the middle of the afternoon and as we wound up into the Vermont mountains, it began to snow. I remember sitting by myself on this Greyhound bus, looking out the window and watching the lights come on in the little towns we passed through. I felt so good, so secure in the knowledge that I could be myself, do what I want—*and also be loved*—I started to cry." (Dowling 1981, p. 237)

Marabel Morgan is greeting Charlie in pink babydoll pajamas at dinnertime while her children watch. The "Chicago woman" leaves her husband for her lover, then leaves her lover, to ride a Greyhound bus up a mountain alone. One is in the thick of family life, the other pretty far outside it. One is acting; the other enjoying, perhaps, the release from acting. Morgan values "fun"; Dowling, aliveness and self-understanding.

Morgan is on stage, Dowling's Chicago woman is off stage. In their magnified moments, Morgan's husband is the audience, while Dowling's husband functions more as a stage. The drama in the Chicago woman's magnified moment doesn't take place between herself and her husband, but between her desire to be attached and her desire to be independent. Dowling's drama does not take place through the enactment of a social role but in an emotional space quite outside her regular life and beyond the labors of love. For even when she is off stage, away from her marriage, she's not working on her "intense affair." The focus moves to her feeling in the bus, the mountains, the snow, the anonymous context within which she feels attached but independent. She comes alive focusing inward—figuring out a troubled boundary between self and other (Chodorow 1978). Her feelings are in response to thinking about relationships, not in response to enacting them. If Morgan is inspired by her own success at breathing life into monogamous marriage, the Chicago woman is inspired, perhaps, by her daring to challenge it.

Who is on the scene in the Chicago woman's epiphany? She's honest. But who is she honest with? Her husband? Her lover? Her children? A close friend? A community of women? None of these; elsewhere we discover a somewhat people-less career, and the idea of exertion, excelling. Her exertion is private and internal, against her dependency on others.

For Dowling we're our best when we are by ourselves facing the elements alone, as in the myth of the cowboy, the Jack London trapper in a forest, Hemingway's man and the sea. Others of Dowling's positive moments are stories about women being sprung free into professional success, erotic freedom, and autonomy.[7] In her final chapter, she describes a scene from the life of Simone de Beauvoir, who broke her dependence on her life's partner, the philosopher Jean-Paul Sartre, through a series of fierce missions "climbing every peak, clambering down every gully . . . exploring every valley . . . around Marseille, through challenging solitary 10-hour hikes, 25 miles each day . . . Simone de Beauvoir's hikes became both the method and the metaphor of her rebirth as an individual," Dowling says. Quoting de Beauvoir she says, "Alone I walked the mists that hung over the summit of Sainte Victoire, and trod along the ridge of the Pilon de Roi, bracing myself against a violent wind which sent my beret spinning down into the valley below . . ." (Dowling 1981, p. 234). "When I was clambering over rocks and mountains or sliding down screes, I would work out shortcuts, so that each expedition was a work of art in itself" (Dowling 1981, p. 233). Once she charged up a steep gorge, unable to go back the way she came, but, having reached a fault in the rock, unable to jump across. Backtracking down the treacherous rocks, triumphantly she con-

cludes, *"I knew that I could now rely on myself"* (Dowling 1981, p. 234).

In her most dreadful moment, Dowling feels the opposite of this. She begins the book with this passage:

> I am lying alone on the third floor of our house with a bad bout of the flu, trying to keep my illness from the others. The room feels large and cold and as the hours pass, strangely inhospitable. I begin to remember myself as a little girl, small, vulnerable, helpless. By the time night falls I am utterly miserable, not so sick with flu as with anxiety. "What am I doing here, so solitary, so unattached, so . . . floating?" I ask myself. How strange to be so disturbed, cut off from family, from my busy, demanding life . . . disconnected . . .
>
> More than air and energy and life itself what I want is to be safe, warm, taken care of. (Dowling 1981, p. 1)

This desire to be "safe, warm, taken care of . . ." forms the basis of the dreaded "Cinderella Complex" which, Dowling goes on to generalize, is the "chief force holding women down today" (Dowling 1981, p. 21). Elsewhere in the book, Dowling points to the waste of brains when women don't have careers. She cites the Stanford Gifted Child Study of 600 California children with IQs above 135. She shows that most male geniuses had high level professional careers while most women geniuses didn't (Dowling 1981, p. 32). This isn't good for society, she says, nor fair to women; in this, Dowling's advice book is clearly modern.

The Total Woman and *The Cinderella Complex* are guided by different inspirations. Morgan tries to have fun, she likes to act and feel exuberantly playful in the confines of a unitary patriarchal world. The dangerous feelings for her are anger, assertiveness, strivings outside the home, feelings which do not fit a patriarchal world. Dowling, on the other hand, strives to be honest with herself, to control and tame her needs, in a sparsely populated and socially dispersed world. For her, the dangerous feeling is the desire to be "safe, warm, and taken care of." Indeed, her fear of being dependent on another person evokes the image of the American cowboy, alone, detached, roaming free with his horse. The American cowboy has long been a model for men struggling against the constraints of corporate capitalism. Now Dowling embraces this ideal for women. On the ashes of Cinderella, then, rises a postmodern cowgirl.

The two authors differ in their ideas about what is exciting: attaching yourself to a man or detaching yourself from him. They differ in their policies toward emotion management; one advises women to suppress any assertion of will in the service of binding them to men. The other advises women to suppress any feeling that would bind them to men too closely. They differ in the place they accord autonomy in the ideal feminine self and ultimately in their views about danger and safety in the world for women.

Although the books don't line up in the same rows on all dimensions, if we sort them according to their views on the role of women, roughly a third lean toward the "traditional" model. Examples are the humorous Erma Bombeck's *Motherhood: The Second Oldest Profession* (1983), her *The Grass Is Always Greener over the Septic Tank* (1976), or James Dobson's *Parenting Isn't for Cowards* (1987). Roughly two-thirds lean toward the modern model, of which *The Cinderella Complex* (1981) is an especially individualistic example. We find a lighter, more saucy version of it in Helen Gurley Brown's *Having It All* (1982). Equally searching but less focused on autonomy are Susan Forward and Joan Torres's *Men Who Hate Women and the Women Who Love Them* (1987), Robin Norwood's *Women Who Love Too Much* (1985), C. Cowan and M. Kinder's *Smart Women, Foolish Choices* (1985), and Barbara De Angelis's *Secrets about Men Every Woman Should Know* (1990).

Most of these modern books whisper to the reader, "let the emotional investor beware." If Morgan counsels women to accumulate domestic capital and invest at home, Dowling cautions women to invest them in the self as a solo enterprise. Most advice books of the 1970s and 1980s are spin-offs or mixtures of these two investment strategies. A handful of books are "warm moderns," emphasizing equality and social attachment, sharing and commitment. Examples are the Boston Women's Health Book Collective's *Ourselves and Our Children* (1978), and Harriet Lerner's *The Dance of Anger* (1985). But gaining the edge are the cool modern advice books. The postmodern cowgirl has sculpted herself to adjust to a paradigm of distrust. She devotes herself to the ascetic practices of emotional control, and expects to give and receive surprisingly little love from other human beings.

THE COOL MODERN AND THE COMMERCIAL SPIRIT OF INTIMATE LIFE

Cool modern advice books reveal a newly unfolding paradox that is reminiscent of an earlier paradox. In *The Protestant Ethic and the Spirit of Capitalism* (1958), Max Weber describes a set of beliefs held by a variety of Protestant sects—a belief in ascetic self-control, frugality, hard work, and devotion to a calling. He traces the way in which these *religious* ideas were adapted to a material purpose. The idea of devotion to a calling came to mean devotion to making money. The idea of self-control came to mean careful saving, spending and capital reinvestment. The Protestant ethic "escaped the cage" to become part of a new hybrid "spirit of capitalism."[8]

Comparing the origin of these motivational ideas and their ultimate destination, Weber made this significant comment:

> Today the spirit of religious asceticism—whether finally, who knows?—has escaped from the cage. But victorious capitalism, since it rests on mechanical foundations, needs its support no longer. The rosy blush of its laughing heir, the Enlightenment, seems also to be irretrievably fading and the idea of duty in one's calling prowls about in our lives like the ghost of dead religious beliefs. (1958, p. 182)

The original religious ideas jumped the churchyard fence to land in the marketplace. Luther and Calvin would have been aghast at the jump their ideas took. As Weber notes, delicately but wryly:

feel "modern." But ironically, what many are honest about is "authentic" instrumentalism. For example, Norwood tells readers honestly how to shop around for a less needy guy, preferably a man with non-alcoholic parents. Just as characters in Jane Austen's *Pride and Prejudice* shrewdly appraise the bank accounts and social lineage of their suitors, so Norwood urges women to consider their suitors' psychological capital. The difference is more than an update. Norwood's attempt to give her readers a "clear head" about love goes with a readiness to detach, to leave, to turn inward toward oneself. For Jane Austen, family and community are confining; for Norwood, they are barely there at all.

Each cool modern book offers a slightly different version of the commercial culture. Some express a theme of production, others a theme of consumption. In *Having It All,* Helen Gurley Brown (1982) does both, by focusing on the production of the body she displays as a ware. In the nearly one third of *Having It All* that she devotes to the female face, hair, body—exercise, diet—and dress, she proposes a policy of "investment" in the bodily self. Brown tells women what to do: dye your hair. Get a face lift. Diet. These practices should be done neither in the spirit of a purification rite, nor in the spirit of devotion to a particular person, but to look good to an anonymous market of men within a 30-yard radius. She helps women advertise themselves to a diversified market. The light office affairs she recommends are those of a sexual venture capitalist, a diversified, high risk, high opportunity portfolio.

In *Women Who Love Too Much,* Robin Norwood (1985) expresses more the theme of consumption. She advises women how to "spend" their nurturance in the relational marketplace. Although the language is therapeutic, the spirit is that of a shrewd investment counselor. Don't waste your love, Norwood cautions, on a poor investment. In her cautionary tales, stories of unhappy patients who "loved too much," one woman after another "wastes" her love and

lacks a return commensurate to her devotion, attention and love. "Divest," she cautions, "Cut your losses. Invest elsewhere."

In *The Cinderella Complex,* Colette Dowling (1981) takes yet a third tack. Instead of focusing as Norwood does on women who love too much, Dowling concentrates on women who need too much. Displacing the spirit of capitalism on to private life, cool modern advice books for women both reinforce and create a commercial culture of intimate life. As a result, we may have global warming, but we have a cultural cooling.

ASSIMILATING TO MALE RULES OF LOVE

The commercial spirit of intimate life is woven with a second cultural tendency—for women to assimilate to male rules of love. On one hand, cool modern advice books address women. Two-thirds are written by women and all of them address problems women have. Nearly all picture women on the covers. Further, if the author doesn't claim to be a feminist at the outset, authors refer to "progress," "struggle," "independence," "equality"—code words for core ideas of "feminism." Many portray women as victims who need to be freed from oppressive situations in love or work.

Curiously, though, such books simultaneously recycle the feeling rules that once applied to middle-class men of the 1950s. In doing so, they illustrate a pattern common to many stratification systems—of the "bottom" emulating the "top" in order to gain access to its greater respect, authority, and power. Insofar as imitation represents in part a magical solution to redistribution of respect and power, female emulation of "male" emotional folkways is useless. In addition, it also means that women are encouraged to be "cooler" while men are not urged to become "warmer." In this sense, advice books conserve the already capitalized male culture. They *conserve* the damage capitalism did to manhood instead of *critiquing* it, in the tradition set out 90 years ago by Charlotte Gilman.

In recycling male rules of love, modern advice books for women assert that it's a "feminine" practice to subordinate the importance of love, to delay falling in love until after consolidating a career, to separate love from sex, and for married women to have occasional affairs.

For one thing, these books propose that love should play an altogether less central role than it has had in the lives of women, and that women should rid themselves of ideas about the importance of love, "de-culturize" themselves in Bourdieu's terms, to unlearn the idea that "love to man is a thing apart, 'tis woman's whole existence."

Love should also occur later in life than before. In the 1950s it was middle-class men who waited until they were occupationally prepared to "fall in love and settle down." Love that occurred earlier was "too early." Wait, advice books for women now caution, until your late 20s or 30s, when you are trained in a career, until you are "ready" to fall in love. Now this delay in the timing of love, and the emotion management needed to delay, is recommended to women as well.

Just as love has been more easily separated from sex for men, so these advice books of the 1980s suggest, love can be separated from sex for women. In *Having It All,* Helen Gurley Brown tells readers how to avoid getting "too" emotionally involved with the married men at the office they sleep with. In the past, if premarital and extra-marital sex were not actually affirmed for men, they were understood as manly flaws. Now, as Dowling's Chicago woman suggests, it's a "womanly flaw" too.

Thus, in the lesser role of love, in the separation of love from sex, in the delay in the "right time" to fall in love, and in the feminization of adultery, advice books of the 1980s propose to women the emotional rules that were part of the gendered cultural capital of white middle-class men of the 1950s. We've moved from living according to two emotional codes—one for men and another for women—to a unisex code based on the old code for men. We've also moved

from a "warmer" code to a cooler one that both fits with and exacerbates the weakening of the family.

Many authors of many advice books conceive of their books as feminist, but [they] are in reality an abduction of feminism. Many advice books see their patients, their interviewees, their readers as patients. But, could it be that it's the commercial spirit of intimate life that's really sick?

EXCEPTIONS AND COUNTER-TRENDS

A look at advice books for men would surely offer a more cheerful picture, since while women have been moving toward a male norm, some men have moved in the other direction. But since the traditional "male" culture that progressive men are challenging is still associated with power and authority, I believe women's move in the direction of traditional male culture is stronger than men's move in the opposite direction.

In the 1970s and 1980s, the books pushing a pro-commercial spirit seemed to be winning. In the 1990s, with the renewal of "family values"—a phrase that means all things to all people—the anticommercial ones seem to be gaining ground. Hitting the bestseller list are such books as *Men Are from Mars, Women Are from Venus* (Gray 1992), which exaggerates the differences between men and women but offers practical tips on "inter-species" communication and commitment. In *A Woman's Worth,* Marianne Williamson proclaims women to be queens and goddesses, weirdly combining a moral social mobility—"the purpose of life as a woman is to ascend to the throne and rule with heart" (1993, p. 11)—a call for family and community, and a paradigm of distrust. While women are asked in a general way to love "our communities, our families, our friends," in the end, the only love they can really count on, according to Williamson, is God's (1993, p. 46).

Meanwhile, a smaller-sales stream of books continues the commercial spirit without a communal gloss. Joyce Vedral's *Get Rid of Him* (1993),

Susan Rabin's *How to Attract Anyone, Anytime, Anyplace* (1993), an extension of her "flirtation seminars," extend the psychological frontier of commercialism. They complement the increasingly popular mail-order video cassettes on marital sex, often authoritatively introduced by PhD psychologists in the spirit of a science class. While such videos legitimate the importance of female sexual pleasure, they would also seem to subtract something.

Both the counter-trend and the continued drumbeat of the commercial spirit of intimate life pose the question: Will the anticommercial books toss out feminism? Or will they stop the abduction of feminism, only to flatten and commercialize it? Or will they integrate it with a paradigm of trust?

CONCLUSION

In *The Second Shift* (1989), I have argued that American families are strained by the fact that they serve as a shock absorber of a stalled gender revolution. The move of masses of women into the paid workforce has constituted a revolution. But the slower shift in ideas of "manhood," the resistance to sharing work at home, the rigid schedules at work make for a "stall" in this gender revolution. It is a stall in the change of institutional arrangements of which men are the principal keepers. But if we are at the same time undergoing a cultural cooling, then we are faced with another, almost opposite, problem. It isn't simply that men are changing too slowly, but that, without quite realizing it, women are also changing in the opposite direction—in the sense of "assimilating"—too fast. Instead of humanizing men, we are "capitalizing" women. If the concept of the "stalled revolution" raises the question of how to be equal, the concept of the commercial spirit of intimate life raises the question: equal on what terms?

With an American divorce rate of 50 percent, and with 60 percent of marriages formed in the 1980s projected to end, two-thirds of them involving children, many young women today are the single mothers of tomorrow. Given this, we have to ask, isn't it *useful* for women to know how to meet their emotional needs on their own? Isn't it useful to have a defended "me" hoping to meet a defended "you"? Even if *The Cinderella Complex* is selling defective psychic armor—these days we have to ask if we don't, sadly enough, need it. Even defective armor, that helps us get around in a cool world, can be useful. But after we've asked whether "being cool" is useful, we have to ask whether "being cool" is good. Is it the best we can do? If we think not, then we have to ask the question advice books pose but don't ask—how can we rewire the broader conditions that make us need the tough armor they provide? On that we could really use good advice.

NOTES

1. I use the term "commercial spirit of intimate life" to refer not to the exchange of things for money, but to refer to the *culture* governing personal relationships that accompanies advanced capitalism. Thanks to Cas Wouters on this point. Insofar as middle-class men have already been urged to subordinate love to work—to "capitalize" love—we can see women's shift from a less to a more commercialized ethic of intimate life as a shift from female to male rules of love. Unwittingly, advice books make the "emotional investment strategy," that formerly fit middle-class heterosexual men of the 1950s seem "feminine" as well as "liberated." Many recent advice books recycle male feeling rules to women. The effect of this is likely to be double—to adapt women to an era of the fragile family, and to induce women to make it more fragile.

2. "A recent Gallup poll showed that one out of three Americans has bought a self-help book" (Wood 1988). Steven Starker, whose telephone survey of 1,000 residents of Portland found that women were

more frequent readers of self-help books than men, although he doesn't cite exact figures. He found his sample averaged 2.82 self-help books a year. Women were slightly more likely to buy a self-help book, and bought more books on love and relationships, stress and anxiety, and weight loss, while men bought more on self-improvement and motivation. Working women were nearly twice as likely as non-working women to buy books on self-improvement, motivation, and love and relationships; both working and non-working women were equally prone to buy books on stress and anxiety (10 percent vs. 11 percent) (see Starker 1989; Radway 1984; Long 1986). Simonds (1992, ch. 1) interviewed 30 readers, mostly white, employed, middle-class in income and education, two-thirds single or divorced. All of the bestsellers focused on heterosexual love; we lack data on the sexual orientation of readers.

3. In his classic book *Distinction* (1984), Pierre Bourdieu spoke of "cultural agents," or intermediaries, who actively shape, rather than passively transmit, culture. Writers of advice books are "cultural intermediaries." (Most authors of the books I studied were women, and the most common professions were psychologist, counselor, and writer.) Bourdieu applies an economizing metaphor to culture—"cultural capital"—which turns culture into something we have or we don't have—like table manners, the art of conversation and self-confidence (1984, p. 4). I use the term "culture" to refer to a set of practices and beliefs which, consciously or not, we deploy. But I also believe that we partly *are* what we "deploy."

4. Books were selected from a list of hardback or paperback trade and mass market books found in Ben Bowker's *Eighty Years of Best Sellers,* and in *Publishers Weekly.* (The criteria used by *Publishers Weekly* to determine a bestseller changed through the years and I have followed its changes.) I selected books which were addressed to women or centrally concerned women's personal or work lives. I excluded diet books, inspirational, or self-development books which did not address or directly bear on women. Books excluded from the list which I read, but didn't study, include nonbestselling advice books for women and advice books for men.

The original list includes a "core" of pure advice books modeled on psychotherapy or on a social science study based on interviews. Examples of this type are Susan Forward and Joan Torres' *Men Who Hate Women and the Women Who Love Them* (1987). Adopting the metaphors of "sickness" and "healing," which psychiatry itself adopted from medicine, these advice books tell stories of patients' emotional problems and their cures. Other books quote and interpret hundreds of interviews and report the "findings."

The list also includes a second type of book which focuses on social practices—dress, manner—with little discussion of the animating ideas or motives behind them. An example of this type would be Judith Martin's *Guide to Raising Perfect Children* (1984) or Abigail Van Buren's *The Best of Dear Abby* (1981). A more diverse third group of books includes autobiography, humor, and commentary. Examples include Bill Cosby's *Love and Marriage* (1989), Erma Bombeck's *The Grass Is Always Greener over the Septic Tank* (1976) and the Boston Women's Health Book Collective, *Ourselves and Our Children.* (For cross-cultural comparisons, see Brinkgreve 1962; Brinkgreve and Korzec 1979; Elias 1978; Wouters 1987.)

5. We may ask, for example, what is it precisely about a feeling that makes it seem wonderful or terrible? Who is on the scene during the moment? What relations are revealed, in reality or imagination? By interrogating the moment, so to speak, we ferret out the cultural premises which underlie it. Though I focus on books published between 1970 and 1990, a look back to the turn of the century reveals three types of books, of which the 1970–90 collection reflects two. The three types are traditionals, tradition-for-moderns, and moderns. By tradition-for-moderns, I refer to advice books which curiously mix a belief in male dominance with an appeal to modern goals ("increased female power") and/or an evocation of modern dilemmas. Modern advice books, as I define the term here, advocate equality between the sexes. For a study of 19th-century advice books, see Ehrenreich and English (1978). An example of a "plain" traditional advice book is Grace Dodge's (1892) *Thoughts of Busy Girls,* which explains the value of modesty, purity, altruism, dedication, capacity for moral reform,

without appeals to empowerment, freedom, equality, and without reference to the fear, once married, of being left.

6. Morgan's big moment expresses a series of basic premises: (a) that men should lead, women should obey, (b) that women benefit from patriarchy, and (c) that it's a woman's job to keep marriage happy and it is mainly her fault if the marriage is unhappy.

7. Dowling elaborates under a section of her book entitled "Springing Free." She says: "Ultimately the goal is emotional spontaneity—an inner liveliness that pervades everything we do, every work project, every social encounter, every love relationship. It comes from the conviction: 'I am the first force in my life' " (1981, p. 235).

8. Weber's thesis has attracted various criticisms. Some have argued that capitalism existed in some places before the rise of Protestantism, that there were Catholic capitalists. But these criticisms don't bear on the association I seek to focus on here—which is between Protestantism and the Spirit of Capitalism and not between either of these and Capitalism itself.

9. I assume that, for the most part, capitalism was not already "inside the cage" with early feminism. Within the complex of the last 200 years of feminist tradition, oral and written, I would argue, there is a core "warm modern" culture.

REFERENCES

Armstrong, Paul. *Conflicting Readings: Variety and Validity in Interpretation.* Chapel Hill, NC: University of North Carolina Press, 1990.

Beard, Henry. *Miss Piggy's Guide to Life.* New York: Muppet Press/Alfred A. Knopf, 1981.

Bellah, Robert, R. Madsen, M. Sullivan, A. Swidler, and S. M. Tipton. *Habits of the Heart: Individualism and Commitment in American Life.* Berkeley, CA: University of California Press, 1985.

Bourdieu, Pierre. *Outline of a Theory of Practice.* Cambridge: Cambridge University Press, 1977.

Bourdieu, Pierre. *Distinction: A Social Critique of the Judgment of Taste,* trans. R. Nice. Cambridge, MA: Harvard University Press, 1984.

Bombeck, Erma. *The Grass Is Always Greener over the Septic Tank.* New York: McGraw-Hill, 1976.

Bombeck, Erma. *If Life Is a Bowl of Cherries, What Am I Doing in the Pits?* New York: Dell, 1978.

Bombeck, Erma. *Aunt Erma's Cope Book.* New York: Fawcett Crest, 1979.

Bombeck, Erma. *Motherhood: The Second Oldest Profession.* New York: Dell, 1983.

Bombeck, Erma. *Family: The Ties that Bind . . . and Gag.* New York: McGraw-Hill, 1987.

Boston Women's Health Book Collective. *Ourselves and Our Children.* New York: Random House, 1978.

Bowker, Ben. *Eighty Years of Best Sellers.* New York: R. R. Bowker, 1977.

Brinkgreve, Christien. "On Modern Relationships: The Commandments of the New Freedom." *The Netherlands Journal of Sociology* 18 (1982), pp. 47–56.

Brinkgreve, Christien, and M. Korzec. "Feelings, Behavior, Morals in the Netherlands, 1938–1978: Analysis and Interpretation of an Advice Column." *The Netherlands Journal of Sociology* 15 (1979), pp. 123–40.

Brown, Helen Gurley. *Having It All.* New York: Pocket Books, 1982.

Cancian, Francesca. *Love in America: Gender and Self-Development.* Cambridge: Cambridge University Press, 1987.

Chodorow, Nancy. *The Reproduction of Mothering.* Berkeley, CA: University of California Press, 1978.

Cosby, Bill. *Love and Marriage.* New York: Bantam Books, 1989.

Cowan, Connell, and Melvyn Kinder. *Smart Women, Foolish Choices.* New York: Signet Books, 1985.

De Angelis, Barbara. *Secrets about Men Every Woman Should Know.* New York: Dell, 1990.

Dobson, James C. *Parenting Isn't for Cowards.* Dallas, TX: Word Publishing, 1987.

Dodge, Grace (ed.). *Thoughts of Busy Girls.* New York: Cassell Publishing, 1892.

Dowling, Colette. *The Cinderella Complex.* New York: Pocket Books, 1981.

Ehrenreich, Barbara, and Deirdre English. *For Her Own Good: 150 Years of the Experts' Advice to Women.* Garden City, NY: Anchor Press/Doubleday, 1978.

Elias, Norbert. *The History of Manners: The Civilizing Process* 1. New York: Pantheon, 1978.

Elias, Norbert. *Power and Civility: The Civilizing Process* 2. New York: Pantheon, 1982.

Featherstone, Mike. "In Pursuit of the Postmodern: An Introduction." *Theory, Culture & Society* 5 (1988), pp. 195–215.

Featherstone, Mike. "Towards a Sociology of Postmodern Culture," pp. 147–72. In Hans Haferkamp (ed.), *Social Structure and Culture.* Berlin and New York: Walter de Gruyter, 1989 (reprinted in M. Featherstone, *Consumer Culture and Postmodernism,* London: Sage, 1991).

Forest, James J. "Self-Help Books." *American Psychologist* 43, no. 7 (1988), pp. 599.

Forward, Susan, and Joan Torres. *Men Who Hate Women and the Women Who Love Them.* New York: Bantam Books, 1987.

Franklin, Benjamin. "Necessary Hints to Those Who Would Be Rich." In Jared Sparks (ed.), *The Works of Benjamin Franklin: Containing Several Political and Historical Tracts Not Included in any Former Edition and Many Letters, Official and Private Not Hitherto Published.* Boston, MA: Hillard Gray, 1938–40 (orig. 1736).

Friday, Nancy. *My Mother, My Self.* New York: Dell, 1977.

Friedman, Sonya. *Smart Cookies Don't Crumble.* New York: Pocket Books, 1985.

Fromm, Erich. *The Art of Loving.* New York: Harper, 1956.

Giddens, Anthony. *Modernity and Self-Identity.* Stanford, CA: Stanford University Press, 1991.

Gilman, Charlotte. *Women and Economics.* Boston, MA: Small, Maynard, 1899.

Gitlin, Todd. "Postmodern Culture," *Dissent* (Winter 1989), pp. 100–8.

Gray, John. *Men Are from Mars, Women Are from Venus.* New York: HarperCollins, 1992.

Greer, Germaine. *The Female Eunuch.* New York: McGraw-Hill, 1971.

Griswold, Wendy. "A Methodological Framework for the Sociology of Culture." *Sociological Methodology* 17 (1987), pp. 1–35.

Harrington, C. Lee, and Denise D. Bielby. "The Mythology of Modern Love: Representations of Romance in the 1980's." *Journal of Popular Culture* 24, no. 4 (1991), pp. 129–43.

Hochschild, Arlie Russell. *The Managed Heart.* Berkeley, CA: University of California Press, 1983.

Hochschild, Arlie Russell. "Gender Codes in Women's Advice Books." In Stephan Harold Riggins (ed.), *Beyond Goffman.* Berlin and New York: Mouton de Gruyter, 1989a.

Hochschild, Arlie Russell. *The Second Shift: Working Parents and the Revolution at Home.* New York: Viking, 1989b.

Hochschild, Arlie Russell, and Kazuko Tanaka. "Ways to See a Working Mother: American and Japanese Advice Books for Women." In Kaisa Kauppinen-Toropainen and Tuula Gordon (eds.), *Unresolved Dilemmas: Women, Work and the Family in the United States, Europe and the Former Soviet Union.* London: Aveburg Press, forthcoming.

Kaminer, Wendy. *I'm Dysfunctional, You're Dysfunctional.* Reading, MA: Addison-Wesley, 1992.

Lasch, Christopher. *Haven in a Heartless World.* New York: Basic Books, 1977.

Lerner, Harriet Goldhor. *The Dance of Anger.* New York: Harper and Row, 1985.

Long, Elizabeth. "Women, Reading and Cultural Authority: Some Implications of the Audience Perspective in Cultural Studies." *American Quarterly* (Fall 1986), pp. 591–611.

Martin, Judith. *Miss Manners' Guide to Rearing Perfect Children.* New York: Atheneum, 1984.

Molley, John. *The Women's Dress for Success Book.* New York: Warner Books, 1977.

Morgan, Marabel. *The Total Woman.* Boston, MA: G. K. Hall, 1973.

Norwood, Robin. *Women Who Love Too Much.* New York: Pocket Books, 1985.

O'Neill, Nena, and George O'Neill. *Open Marriage.* New York: Avon Press, 1972.

Rabin, Susan. *How to Attract Anyone, Anytime, Anyplace.* New York: Plume, 1993.

Radway, Janice. *Reading the Romance: Women, Patriarchy and Popular Literature.* Chapel Hill, NC: University of North Carolina Press, 1984.

Shahan, Lynn. *Living Alone and Liking It.* New York: Stratford Press, 1981.

Simonds, Wendy. *Self-Help Culture: Reading Women's Reading.* New Brunswick, NJ: Rutgers University Press, 1993.

Spock, Benjamin. *Dr. Spock's Baby and Child Care.* New York: Pocket Books, 1976.

Spock, Benjamin, and Michael B. Rothenberg. *Dr. Spock's Baby and Child Care.* New York: Pocket Books, 1985.

Starker, Steven. *Oracle at the Supermarket: The American Preoccupation with Self-Help Books.* New Brunswick, NJ: Transaction Books, 1989.

Swidler, Ann. "Culture in Action: Symbols and Strategies." *American Sociological Review* 51 (1986), pp. 273–86.

Tannen, Deborah. *You Just Don't Understand.* New York: Ballantine Books, 1990.

Tavris, Carol. "Beware the Incest-Survivor Machine." *New York Times Book Review,* January 3, 1993.

Thomas, Marlo, and Friends. *Free to Be a Family.* New York: Random House, 1987.

Van Buren, Abigail. *The Best of Dear Abby.* New York: Pocket Books, 1981.

Vedral, Joyce L. *Get Rid of Him.* New York: Time Warner, 1993.

Weber, Max. *The Protestant Ethic and the Spirit of Capitalism.* New York: Charles Scribner, 1958.

Williamson, Marianne. *A Woman's Worth.* New York: Random House, 1993.

Wood, Leonard. "The Gallup Survey: Self-Help Buying Trends." *Publishers Weekly* 234 (October 14, 1988), p. 33.

Wouters, Cas. "Developments in the Behavioral Codes between the Sexes: The Formalization of Informalization in the Netherlands, 1930–85." *Theory, Culture & Society* 4, no. 2/3 (1987), pp. 405–27.

Queer Visibility in Commodity Culture

Rosemary Hennessy

For a lesbian and gay political project that has had to combat the heteronormative tyranny of the empirical in order to claim a public existence at all, how visibility is conceptualized

Copyright © 1995 by *Cultural Critique* and Oxford University Press. Reprinted from *Cultural Critique,* Winter 1994–95 by permission of Oxford University Press, London.

matters. Like "queer," "visibility" is a struggle term in gay and lesbian circles now—for some simply a matter of display, for others the effect of discourses or of complex social conditions. In the essay that follows I will try to show that for those of us caught up in the circuits of late capitalist consumption, the visibility of sexual identity is often a matter of commodification, a process that invariably depends on the lives and labor of invisible others.

This argument needs to be prefaced, however, with several acknowledgments and qualifications. First of all, the increasing cultural representation of homosexual concerns and the recent queering of sex/gender identities undoubtedly have had important positive effects. Cultural visibility can prepare the ground for gay civil rights protection; affirmative images of lesbians and gays in the mainstream media, like the growing legitimation of lesbian and gay studies in the academy, can be empowering for those of us who have lived most of our lives with no validation at all from the dominant culture. These changes in lesbian and gay visibility are in great measure the effect of the relentless organizing efforts of lesbians and gay men. In the past decade alone groups like The National Gay and Lesbian Task Force, The Human Rights Campaign Fund, GLADD, and ACT-UP have fought ardently against the cultural abjection and civic eradication of homosexuals. Like other gay and lesbian academics now who are able to teach and write more safely about our history, I am deeply indebted to those who have risked their lives and careers on the front lines to make gay and lesbian studies a viable and legitimate intellectual concern. Without their efforts my work would not be possible.

But the new degree of homosexual visibility in the United States and the very existence of a queer counterdiscourse also need to be considered critically in relation to capital's insidious and relentless expansion. Not only is much recent gay visibility aimed at producing new and potentially lucrative markets, but as in most marketing strategies, money, not liberation, is the bottom line.[1] In her analysis of the commodification of lesbians, Danae Clark has observed that the intensified marketing of lesbian images is less indicative of a growing acceptance of homosexuality than of capitalism's appropriation of gay "styles" for mainstream audiences. Visibility in commodity culture is in this sense a limited victory for gays, who are welcome to be visible as consumer subjects but not as social subjects. The increasing circulation of gay and lesbian images in consumer culture has the effect of consolidating an imaginary class-specific gay subjectivity for both straight and gay audiences. This process is not limited to the spheres of knowledge promoted by popular culture and retail advertising but also infiltrates the production of subjectivities in academic and activist work.

Because so much of lesbian and gay studies and queer theory has all but ignored the historical relationship between (homo)sexuality and capitalism, however, one of the dangers of an analysis that sets out to address the connection between the processes of commodification and the formation of lesbian and gay identities is that it risks being misread. Drawing attention to the operations of commodity capitalism on lesbian, gay, and queer knowledges can be misconstrued to mean—*as I certainly do not*—that the material processes of commodification are only economic, and that they are all-determining and impossible to oppose. As I understand it, the materiality of social life consists of an ensemble of human practices whose complex interdeterminate relations to one another vary historically. These practices include economic divisions of labor and wealth, political arrangements of state and nation, and ideological organizations of meaning-making and value. Although capitalism is a mode of production characterized by the economic practice of extracting surplus value through commodity exchange, the processes of commodification pervade all social structures. In certain social formations under late capitalism, information has become so

much the structure in dominance that language, discourse, or cultural practice is often taken to be the only arena of social life. The challenge for social theory now is to queer-y the reigning Foucauldian materialism that reduces the social to culture or discourse and to refute misreadings of postmodern historical materialism as advocating a return to economic determinism. To examine the historical relations between homosexuality and commodification as they operate at all levels of capitalist societies does not mean dismissing the materiality of discourse and the ways culture constructs subjectivities, reproduces power relations, and foments resistance. Quite the contrary. Postmodern historical materialist critiques of sexuality are postmodern to the extent that they participate in postmodernity's historical and critical remapping of social relations, but at the same time they maintain that sexuality is a material practice that shapes and is shaped by social totalities like capitalism, patriarchy, and imperialism as they manifest differently across social formations and within specific historical conjunctures. As social practice, sexuality includes lesbian, gay, and queer resistance movements that have built social and political networks, often by way of capitalist commercial venues. That academic gay studies and queer theory have not very rigorously inquired into the relations between sexuality and capitalism is indicative of the retreat from historical materialism in social and cultural theory in the past decade. But I think it also suggests the particular class interests that have increasingly come to define lesbian and gay studies.

Although I have been using the words "queer" and "lesbian and gay" as if they were interchangeable, these are in fact contentious terms, signifying identity and political struggle from very different starting points. The now more traditional phrase "lesbian and gay" assumes a polarized division between hetero- and homosexuality and signals discrete and asymmetrically gendered identities. The more fluid and ambiguous term "queer" has recently begun to displace "lesbian and gay" in several areas of urban industrialized culture—under the signature of "queer theory" in the realm of cultural studies; in avant-garde, gay, and lesbian subcultures; and in new forms of radical sexual political activism. Lending a new elasticity to the categories "lesbian" and "gay," "queer" embraces a proliferation of sexualities (bisexual, transvestite, pre- and postop transsexual, to name a few) and the compounding of outcast positions along racial, ethnic, and class, as well as sexual lines—none of which is acknowledged by the neat binary division between hetero- and homosexual. In other words, "queer" not only troubles the gender asymmetry implied by the phrase "lesbian and gay," but potentially includes "deviants" and "perverts" who may traverse or confuse hetero–homo divisions and exceed or complicate conventional delineations of sexual identity and normative sexual practice. "Queer" often professes to define a critical standpoint that makes visible how heteronormative attempts to fix sexual identities tend to fail often because they are overdetermined by other issues and conflicts—race or national identity, for example. To the extent that "queer" tends to advance a subjectivity that is primarily sexual, it can threaten to erase the intersections of sexuality with class as well as the gender and racial histories that still situate queer men and women differently. In this respect "queer" is, as Judith Butler indicates, a "site of collective contestation" (*Bodies,* p. 228) that is only partially adequate to the collectivity it historically represents.

While in this essay I may string together the terms "lesbian and gay" and "queer," then, this is not in order to conflate them but to indicate that both expressions are being used to name homosexual identities now, even if in contesting ways. To the extent that my analysis focuses primarily on "queer" issues, this is because they are increasingly shaping postmodern reconfigurations of gay and lesbian cultural study and politics. Even though many formulations of queer theory and identity are to my mind limited, it does not follow that the viability of

"queer" as a sign of collective history and action is to be dismissed. Instead, I would argue for a renarration of queer critique as inquiry into the ensemble of social processes—systems of exploitation and regimes of state and cultural power—through which sexualities are produced. I agree with Judith Butler that the two dimensions of queering—the historical inquiry into the formation of homosexualities it signifies, and the deformative and misappropriative power the term enjoys—are both constitutive (*Bodies*). But I would add that these dimensions of queer praxis need to be marshaled as forces for collective and transformative social intervention.

. . .

IN THE LIFE(STYLE): POSTMODERN (HOMO)SEXUAL SUBJECTS

It is not accidental that homosexuals have been most conspicuous in the primary domains of the spectacle: fashion and entertainment. In 1993 no fewer than five national straight news and fashion magazines carried positive cover stories on lesbians and gays. One of the most notable among them was the cover of *New York* magazine's May 1993 issue, which featured a dashingly seductive close-up of k. d. lang dressed in drag next to the words "Lesbian Chic: The Bold, Brave World of Gay Women." Every imaginable facet of gay and lesbian life—drag, transsexuality, gay teens, gay parents—has been featured on daytime talk shows. The *New York Times* recently inaugurated "Styles of the Times" section now includes along with the engagement and marriage announcements regular features on gay and lesbian issues, here explicitly figured as one of many life "styles." The drag queens Ru Paul and Lady Bunny have both been profiled there, and in 1993 the front page of the section carried full-page stories on the Harlem balls and gay youth.

Gays and lesbians have been more visible than ever in arts and entertainment, despite the industry's still deeply entrenched investment in heteronormativity. Tony Kushner's "joyously, unapologetically, fabulously gay" play, *Angels in Amer-ica,* won the Pulitzer Prize in 1993 and was nominated for nine Tony Awards. The list of commercial film and video productions on gay subjects grows monthly and includes such notables as Neil Jordan's transvestite love story, *The Crying Game;* Sally Potter's film version of Virginia Woolf's transsexual, *Orlando;* Jonathan Demme's AIDS courtroom drama, *Philadelphia;* Barbara Streisand's film production of Larry Kramer's *The Normal Heart;* and HBO's adaptation of Randy Shilts's AIDS exposé, *And the Band Played On.* While the movie industry still fears a subject it wouldn't touch five years ago, it goes where the money is, and so far in the 90s "gay" is becoming a warmer if not a hot commodity.

Nowhere is gay more in vogue than in fashion, where homoerotic imagery is the epitome of postmodern chic. Magazines firmly situated in the middle-class mainstream like *Details, Esquire, GQ,* or *Mademoiselle* have all recently carried stories addressing some aspect of gay life and/as fashion, and it is here that gay and lesbian visibility blurs readily into a queer gender-bending aesthetic. The June 1993 issue of *Details,* for example, featured a story on couples that included one gay and one lesbian couple; another story offered a gay man's perspective on lifting the ban on gays in the military (including a graphic account of his one-night stand with a marine who is "not gay") and a favorable review by gay novelist David Leavitt of Michelangelo Signorile's book *Queer in America.* The first volume of *Esquire*'s new fashion magazine, *Esquire Gentleman,* carried a feature on "The Gay Factor in Fashion" that declared "Just about everyone dresses a little gay these days. . . . It is now a marketing given that gay sensibility sells to both gay and straight" (Martin, p. 140). *Esquire*'s regular June 1993 issue included a review of Potter's *Orlando* as well as a short story by Lynn Darling entitled "Single White Male Seeks Clue."

Darling's story is a symptomatic example of the incorporation of a queer aesthetic into the gender structure of postmodern patriarchy. "It's not easy to be the scion of a dying WASP culture," the cover blurb announces, "when women have more confidence, gay men have more style, and everyone seems to have the right to be angry with you." This is a tale of young urban professional manhood in crisis, a crisis managed through nostalgic detours into the "now vanished set of certainties" preserved in the world of boxing. As the story draws to a close, John Talbot, the single white male of the title, and his girlfriend look out of their hotel room and find in their view a gay couple "dry-humping" on a penthouse roof right below them. "Talbot was tempted to say something snide, but he checked himself. In fact, it was really sweet, he decided, and in his happiness he saw them suddenly as fellow travelers in the community of desire" (Darling, p. 104). Talbot's inclusion of gays in the diverse community of "fellow travelers" offers an interesting rearticulation of Cold War moral and political discourses that once made all homosexuals out to be communists. Here, gays are included in an elastic community of pleasure seekers and a tentatively more pliant heterosexual sex/gender system.

As Talbot's story suggests, the once-rigid links between sex, gender, and sexual desire that the invisible heterosexual matrix so firmly secured in bourgeois culture have become more flexible as the gendered divisions of labor among the middle class in industrialized countries have shifted. While these more accommodating gender codes are not pervasive, they have begun to take hold among the young urban middle class particularly. There are hints, for instance, that wearing a skirt, a fashion choice once absolutely taboo for men because it signified femaleness and femininity, is now more allowed because the gender system's heteronormative regime is loosening. The designers Betsy Johnson, Matsuda, Donna Karan, and Jean Paul Gaultier all have featured skirts on men in their spring and fall shows for the last few years. Some rock stars (among them Axl Rose of *Guns N Roses*) have worn skirts on stage. But skirts for men are also infiltrating more mundane culture. The fashion pages of my conservative local newspaper feature sarongs for men, and my 15-year-old daughter, Kate, reports that at the two-week coed camp she attended in the summer of 1993 at least one of the male counsellors wore a midcalf khaki skirt almost every day.

As middle-class women have been drawn into the professional work force to occupy positions once reserved for men, many of them are now literally "wearing the pants" in the family, often as single heads of household, many of them lesbians and/or mothers. The "new man," like Talbot, has managed the crisis of "not having a clue" where he fits anymore by relinquishing many of the former markers of machismo: he expects women of his class to work outside the home and professes to support their professional ambitions, he "helps out" with the housework and the kids, boasts one or two gay friends, may occasionally wear pink, and perhaps even sports an earring. Men of Talbot's class might also read magazines like *GQ* or *Esquire,* where the notion of the "gender fuck" that queer activists and theorists have presented as subversive cultural critique circulates as radical chic—in essays like David Kamp's piece "The Straight Queer" detailing the appropriation of gay codes by hip heteros or in spoofs like "Viva Straight Camp" that parody ultra-straight gender codes by showing up their constructedness (Powers).

Much like queer theory, the appropriation of gay cultural codes in the cosmopolitan revamping of gender displays the arbitrariness of bourgeois patriarchy's gender system and helps to reconfigure it in a more postmodern mode, where the links between gender and sexuality are looser, where homosexuals are welcome, even constituting the vanguard, and where the appropriation of their parody of authentic sex and gender identities is quite compatible with the aestheticization of everyday life into postmodern lifestyles. In itself, of course, this limited assimilation of gays into mainstream middle-class culture does not disrupt postmodern patriarchy and

its intersection with capitalism; indeed, it is in some ways quite integral to it.

Because patriarchy has become a buzzword in some postmodern/queer circles, I should explain what I mean by it here. I understand patriarchy to be a concept that explains the systematic gendered organization of all areas of social life—economic, political, and ideological—such that more social resources, power, and value accrue to men as a group at the expense of women as a group. In this sense, patriarchy is social, not merely cultural, and the privilege it accords some at the expense of others affects more than the making of meaning. Many poststructuralist critiques rightly target "the notion that the oppression of women has some singular form discernible in the universal or hegemonic structure of patriarchy or masculine domination" and remind us that any sort of monolithic theory of *the* patriarchy fails to account for the workings of gender oppression in the concrete cultural contexts in which it exists (Butler, *Gender,* p. 3). But often they also reduce patriarchy to contingent cultural forms or dismiss it as a viable concept altogether. Like capitalism, patriarchy is a politically urgent concept because it allows us to analyze and explain social hierarchies by which gender, sexuality, and their racial articulations are organized. Patriarchy is a variable and historical social totality in that its particular forms for organizing social relations like work, citizenship, reproduction, ownership, pleasure, or identity have had a persistent effect on heterogendered[2] structures in dominance at the same time these structures vary and are the sites of social struggle.

Some patriarchical formations entail kinship alliances ruled by fathers, although in industrialized countries this form of patriarchy has been unevenly and gradually displaced as the ruling paradigm by bourgeois patriarchy. In bourgeois patriarchy, kinship alliances are subordinate to a social organization split between public wage economy and unpaid domestic production, both regulated by the ideology of possessive individualism. In advanced capitalist countries, public or postmodern patriarchy has recently begun to emerge as the prevailing form. It is characterized by the hyperdevelopment of consumption and the joint wage earner family, the relative transfer of power from husbands to professionals in the welfare state, the rise of single-mother headed and other alternative households, and sexualized consumerism (Ferguson, p. 110). While any one patriarchal formation may dominate, it often co-exists with other contesting or residual forms. Policy debates like the current controversy over lifting the ban on gays in the U.S. military as well as cultural narratives of various sorts (films like *A Few Good Men, Jungle Fever,* or *The Firm,* for instance) can be read as articulations of the struggle between bourgeois patriarchal formations and their accompanying moral ideologies and postmodern patriarchy's newer forms of family, gender, sexuality, and work.

Finally, patriarchy is differential. This means that while all women as a group are positioned the same (as subordinate or other) in relation to men, they are positioned differently in relation to each other and at times in relation to men in subaltern groups. Some women have access to resources—a professional job, an urban condo, a cleaning lady, a vacation home, a fancy car— that are only possible because of the work of other women and men who do not have these resources. Because patriarchy functions in concert with a racial system of white supremacy, disproportionate numbers of people of color, men and women alike, have historically occupied these exploited, underresourced social positions. That more women than men fill the ranks of the impoverished speaks loudly to the ways class exploitation is reinforced by patriarchal structures. Similarly, some men have more patriarchal power than others, sometimes power over and at the expense of other men. This difference means that not all men benefit the same from patriarchy. Because the division of labor in general is racialized at the same time race is not necessarily congruent with class, the cultural capital

people of color might gain on entry into any class can be canceled out or undermined by the operations of racism. Consequently, the white gay psychiatrist or lawyer is not in the same patriarchal position as his white straight colleagues nor is he in the same patriarchal position as a black gay man of the same class. Some women, lesbians among them, can claim patriarchal power over other women and men by virtue of their institutional privilege. For instance, women, lesbians included, in administrative or managerial positions can make use of their institutional positions to wield power over men and other women who work for them or are affected by the policies they draft.

But even women who benefit from patriarchy in some areas of their lives are disadvantaged in a society that systematically accords men power over women. The pervasiveness of rape and wife battering across classes and races and the general invisibility of lesbians in the culture demonstrate the systematic persistence of patriarchy despite the claims of a postmodern cosmopolitanism that gender hierarchies no longer operate or are readily subverted.

In positing male and female as distinct and opposite sexes that are naturally attracted to one another, heterosexuality is integral to patriarchy. Women's position as subordinate other, as (sexual) property, and as exploited laborer depends on a heterosexual matrix in which woman is taken to be man's opposite; his control over social resources, his clear thinking, strength, and sexual prowess depend on her being less able, less rational, and never virile. As a pervasive institution within other institutions (state, education, church, media), heterosexuality helps guarantee patriarchal regulation of women's bodies, labor, and desires. Queer critiques of heterosexuality have often not acknowledged—in fact, they often disavow—the relationship between heterosexuality and patriarchy. But the struggles of lesbians in groups like Queer Nation and other gay political organizations are testimony that gender hierarchies persist between men and women even when both are fighting against heterosexuality as a regime of power (Maggenti).

The gender flexibility of postmodern patriarchy is pernicious because it casts the illusion that patriarchy has disappeared. But behind this facade corporate interests are delighting in the discovery of new markets. Among the most promising are gays and lesbians in the new professional/managerial class. Among them are "lifestyle lesbians" like the Bay area vice president of a lesbian-owned business group who announced, "Here I am, this funny, warm person that you like and I happen to be a lesbian. I am bourgeois. I have a house in the suburbs. I drive a Saab" (Stewart, p. 56). Given the increased "visibility" of this sort of gay consumer, "tolerance of gays makes sense" (Tobias). Increasingly marketers of mainstream products from books to beer are aiming ads specifically at gay men and lesbians; *Fortune* magazine contends "it's a wonderful market niche, the only question is how to reach it" (Stewart). Reaching it has so far involved manufacturing the image of a certain class-specific lesbian and gay consumer population. "Visibility is what it is all about," says David Ehrlich, of Overlooked Opinions (Gluckman and Reed, pp. 16). These stereotypes of wealthy free-spending gay consumers play well with advertisers and are useful to corporations because they make the gay market seem potentially lucrative; they cultivate a narrow but widely accepted definition of gay identity as a marketing tool and help to integrate gay people as gay people into a new marketing niche (Gluckman and Reed, pp. 17, 18). But if gay visibility is a good business prospect, as some companies argue, the question gay critics need to ask is "for whom?" Who profits from these new markets?

OUT OF SIGHT, OUT OF MIND

Commodification structures much more than the exchange of goods on the market; it affects even as it depends on the knowledges that mediate what and how we see. The commodification of gay styles and identities in the corporate and academic marketplaces is integrally related to the formation of a postmodern gay/queer subjectivity, ambivalently gender coded and in some instances flagrantly repudiating traditional, hetero and homo bourgeois culture. Nonetheless, as I have been arguing, to a great extent the construction of a new "homosexual/queer spectacle" perpetuates a class-specific perspective that keeps invisible the capitalist divisions of labor that organize sexuality and in particular lesbian, gay, queer lives. In so doing queer spectacles often participate in a long history of class-regulated visibility.[3] Beginning around the mid-19th century, the bourgeoisie mediated their experience of the working class through spatial as well as cultural/ideological arrangements. The erection of physical barriers—subway and rail construction and the siting of retail and residential districts—structured the physical arrangement of the city so as to foreclose the trauma of seeing the laboring classes (Kester, p. 73). This physical regulation of class visibility was also compounded by the consolidation of a characteristically "bourgeois" mode of perception through an array of knowledges, the philosophic and aesthetic chief among them. The notion of an autonomous aesthetic perception, first developed by 18th-century philosophers (Kant, Hume, Shaftsbury), whereby perceived objects are abstracted from the social context of their creation, provided the foundation for a way of seeing that has dominated modern culture and aesthetics through the late 20th century (Kester, p. 74). This mode of perception reinforces and is indeed historically necessary to commodity exchange and comes to function as a "phenomenological matrix" through which the bourgeoisie confront an array of daily experiences through modes of seeing that erase the differently valued divisions of labor that organize visibility (Kester, p. 75). In late 20th-century "postindustrial" societies like the United States, the (in)visibility of class divisions continues to be spatially regulated by urban planning, but it is also reinforced by changes in first world relations of production as industry has been increasingly consigned to sites in "developing countries" outside the United States. Capital has not been significantly dispersed or democratized in "first world" economies as a result, simply transferred to more profitable sectors (the so-called tertiary or service sectors, banking, finance, pension funds, etc.) (Evans, p. 43). The escalating domination of the ideological—the proliferation of information technologies, media images, codes—in postindustrial cultures has helped to reconfigure bourgeois modes of perception in first world populations, producing subjects who are more differentiated and less likely to experience capitalism collectively through production relations and more likely to experience it through relations of consumption. As a result, the neat subject–object split of Kantian aesthetics has been troubled and to some degree displaced, even as the invisibility of social relations of labor in corporate and intellectual commodity spectacles persists.

Gay-friendly corporations like Levi Strauss, for example, reinforce the gender-flexible subjects their advertising campaigns promote through gay window-dressing strategies by way of public relations programs that boast of their progressive corporate policies for lesbians and gays. Levi's gives health insurance benefits to unmarried domestic partners of its employees, has created a supportive environment for employees who test HIV+, and has a Lesbian and Gay Employees Association. Members of this association prepared a video for the company to use in its diversity training in which they, their parents, and their managers openly discuss their relationships (Stewart, p. 50). But Levi's workers in the sweatshops of Saipan who live in cramped and crowded barracks and earn as little as $2.15 an hour remain largely invisible. Although Levi's ended its contracts last year with the island's largest clothes maker after an investigation by the company found evidence of unsatisfactory treatment of workers in his factories, they still continue to make shirts at five

plants there (Shenon). Meanwhile, back in the United States, Levi's closed its San Antonio plant in 1990, laying off 1,150 workers, 92 percent of them Latino and 86 percent of them women, and moved its operations to the Caribbean, where it can pay laborers $3.80 a day, roughly half the average hourly wage of the San Antonio workforce (Martinez, p. 22). Displaying the gay-friendly policies of "progressive" U.S. corporations often deflects attention from the exploitive international division of labor they depend on in the interests of the company's bottom line—profits.[4]

The formation of a gay/queer imaginary in both corporate and academic circles also rests on the suppression of class analysis. There have been all too few books that treat the ways gay history and culture have been stratified along class lines.[5] With several notable exceptions, studies of the relationship between homosexuality and capitalism are remarkably sparse, and extended analyses of lesbian and gay poverty are almost nonexistent.[6] To ask the more pointed question of how the achievement of lesbian and gay visibility by some rests on the invisible labor of others is to expose the unspeakable underside of queer critique.

The consolidation of the professional middle class during the 1980s brought with it an array of social contradictions. The recruitment of more and more women into the workforce bolstered the legitimation of both the professional "New Woman" and of academic feminism. The increasing, albeit uneven and complicated, investiture of lesbians and gays into new forms of sexual citizenship and the relative growth of academic lesbian and gay studies accompanied and in some ways were enabled by these changes. But these were also decades when the chasm between the very rich and the very poor widened and poverty became more than ever feminized. As the 1990s began, a total of 33 million people in the United States—more than 13.5 percent of the population—were officially living in poverty. While estimates of the numbers of people who are homosexual are notoriously unreliable (ranging from the 1993 Batelle Human Research Center's 1.1 percent to the 1948 Kinsey Report's 10 percent), assuming that somewhere between 1 percent and 10 percent of the population are homosexual, it would be fair to say that there are between 1.65 and 3.3 million impoverished lesbians and gay men in the United States today.[7]

Most lesbians are leading less glamorous lives than their chic commodity images suggest, and poor lesbians of color are the most invisible and worst off. While the wage gap between women and men has supposedly narrowed in the 80s—in 1990, women earned 72 percent of what men did—much of this change is due to a drop in men's earnings, while the incomes of women have stayed the same (U.S. Bureau of the Census, 1991). Furthermore, the bulk of necessary work at home, by some estimates 70 percent, is still left up to women. In other words, women as a group do more than half of all the work in this country and make less than half of what men do (Abelda et al., p. 52). Of all poor people over 18, 63 percent are women, with 53 percent of poor families headed by women (Maciones, p. 282). While there [are] no reliable data available on the numbers of poor who are lesbian or gay, the racialized and gendered division of labor suggests that there are more lesbians than gay men living in poverty and proportionately more of them are people of color.[8]

Redressing gay invisibility by promoting images of a seamlessly middle-class gay consumer or by inviting us to see queer identities only in terms of style, textuality, or performative play helps produce imaginary gay/queer subjects that keep invisible the divisions of wealth and labor that these images and knowledges depend on. These commodified perspectives blot from view lesbians, gays, queers who are manual workers, sex workers, unemployed, and imprisoned. About a quarter to a half million homosexual and bisexual youths are thrown out of their homes and subjected to prostitution and violence in the streets [each year] (Galst). Severing queer and homo sexuality from the operations of class keeps these lives from view, forecloses consideration of the ways sexual identities are complicated by the priorities imposed by impoverishment, and keeps a queer political agenda from working collectively to address the needs of many whose historical situation is defined in terms of counterdominant sexual practices. That so little work has been done in the academy, even within lesbian and gay studies, to address these populations and the invisible social relations that maintain their marginality and exploitation speaks loudly to the ways a class-specific "bourgeois (homosexual/queer) imaginary" structures our knowledge of sexual identity, pleasure, and emancipation.

CRITIQUE-AL VISIBILITY

Critique is a political practice and a mode of reading that establishes the intimate links between the visible and the historical by taking as its starting point a systemic understanding of the social. A radical critique of sexuality understands that the visibility of any particular construction of sexuality or sexual identity is historical in that it is shaped by an ensemble of social arrangements. As a way of seeing sexuality, critique insist on making connections between the emergence of a discourse or identity in industrialized social formations and the international division of labor, between sexy commodity images and labor, the spectacle and the sweatshop, style and class. This sort of critique-al intervention into heterosexuality, therefore, does not see sexuality as just the effect of cultural or discursive practice, merely the product of ideology or institutions, but as a regulatory apparatus that spans the organization of social life in the modern world and that works in concert with other social totalities—capitalism, patriarchy, colonialism.

As a political practice, critique acknowledges the importance of "reading" to political activism. Understood broadly as all of those ways of making sense that enable one to be conscious, to be literate in the culture's codes and so to be capable of acting meaningfully in the world, reading is an activity essential to social life. Although they often go unacknowledged, modes of reading are necessary to political activism. Paying attention to how we read and considering its implications and consequences is a key component of any oppositional political work. To ignore this crucial dimension of social struggle is to risk reproducing the very conditions we seek to change. The ways of making sense available in any historical time will tend to support the prevailing social order, but they are also contested. A critical politics joins in and foments this contest not just to reframe how we interpret the world but in order to change it. It is radical in the sense that it does not settle just for a change in the style or form of commodities but demands a change in the invisible social relations that make them possible.

I have tried to show that this way of reading is not just a matter of widening the scope of what we see, but of starting from a different place in how we see. Understanding social life to be "at once global and local" requires that we analyze what presents itself on first sight as obvious in order to show its connection to social structures that often exploit and oppress. While local situations (the commodification of pleasure in suburban malls, for instance) are necessary and important places to disrupt heteronormativity, they do not exist on their own, and we read them as such only at a cost. I am suggesting that a radical sexual politics that is going to be, in Butler's words, "effectively disruptive, truly troubling" needs a way of explaining how the sexual identities we can see are systemically organized. We need a way of understanding visibility that acknowledges both the local situations in which sexuality is made intelligible as well as the ties that bind knowledge and power to commodity production, consumption, and exchange.

The critical way of reading I am proposing in this essay is indeed queer. If it is not very well received now in the academy or in activist circles—and it is not—that may be because in challenging the postmodern fetishizing of social life into discourse, culture, or local contexts, critique puts into crisis the investments of middle-class academics and professionals, queers among us, in the current social order. For this reason it is undoubtedly a risk. Perhaps it is also our best provisional answer to the question, "What is to be done?"

NOTES

1. For an astute analysis of the commodification of gay and lesbian culture, see Gluckman and Reed.
2. For an elaboration of the concept of "heterogender" and its effects on the disciplining of knowledge, see Ingraham.
3. Grant Kester's fine essay on the imaginary space of postindustrial culture prompted my analysis of the class dimensions of visibility here; the phrase "Out of Sight, Out of Mind" is in part a reference to his title.
4. I am grateful to Catherine Sustana for pointing out to me the following detail: Levi's is owned by Robert Haas, the great-great grandnephew of the company's founder; when Haas staged a successful leveraged buyout to take the company private in 1985, profits rose by a staggering 31% (Sustana).
5. Among the books that address the class dimension of lesbian and gay history and culture are Bunch, Faderman, Kennedy and Davis, Moraga, and Nestle. Essays include D'Emilio, Franzen, and Weston and Rofel.
6. On the relationship between (homo)sexuality and capitalism, see Altman, D'Emilio, and Evans. Most of the little work on gay poverty has, not accidentally, focused on lesbians and has circulated mostly in alternative/activist presses. Notable examples include Egerton, Helmbold, and Lavine.
7. The accuracy of the federally funded Batelle Institute's findings has been questioned for a number

of reasons: the study was aimed at addressing behavior related to AIDS, not homosexuality per se; the survey was based on self-reports from men; the interviewers were exclusively women who were not trained in sex research; and the questions about sex with men had a 30% nonresponse rate.

8. About 30% of the poor in the U.S. are black (U.S. Bureau of the Census, 1991).

REFERENCES

Abelda, Randy, Elaine McCrate, Edwin Melendez, June Lapidus, and the Center for Popular Economics. *Mink Coats Don't Trickle Down: The Economic Attack on Women and People of Color.* Boston: South End Press, 1988.

Butler, Judith. *Bodies That Matter: On the Discursive Limits of "Sex."* New York: Routledge, 1993.

———. *Gender Trouble: Feminism and the Subversion of Identity.* New York: Routledge, 1990.

Clark, Danae. "Commodity Lesbianism." *camera obscura* 25–26 (1991), pp. 181–201.

Darling, Lynn. "Single White Male Seeks Clue." *Esquire,* June 1993, pp. 97–104.

Evans, David T. *Sexual Citizenship: The Material Construction of Sexualities.* London: Routledge, 1993.

Ferguson, Ann. *Blood at the Root: Motherhood, Sexuality, and Male Dominance.* London: Pandora, 1989.

Galst, Liz. "Throwaway Kids." *Advocate* 29 (December 1992), p. 54.

Gluckman, Amy, and Betsy Reed. "The Gay Marketing Moment." *Dollars and Sense,* November/December 1993, pp. 16–35.

Ingraham, Chrys. "The Heterosexual Imaginary: Feminist Sociology and Theories of Gender." *Sociological Theory* 12 (July 1994), pp. 203–219.

Kester, Grant H. "Out of Sight Is Out of Mind: The Imaginary Spaces of Postindustrial Culture." *Social Text* 35 (1993), pp. 72–92.

Maciones, John J. *Sociology.* Englewood Cliffs, NJ: Prentice Hall, 1993.

Martin, Richard. "The Gay Factor in Fashion." *Esquire Gentleman,* July 13, 1993, pp. 135+.

Martinez, Elizabeth. " 'Levi's, Button Your Fly—Your Greed Is Showing.' " *Z Magazine,* January 1993, pp. 22–27.

Powers, Ann. "Queer in the Streets, Passing in the Sheets." *Village Voice,* June 29, 1993, pp. 24+.

Shenon, Philip. "Saipan Sweatshops Are No American Dream." *New York Times,* July 18, 1993, pp. 1+.

Stewart, Thomas. "Gay in Corporate America." *Fortune,* December 16, 1991, pp. 42+.

Sustana, Catherine. "The Production of the Corporate Subject." Conference on Literary/Critical Cultural Studies. University at Albany, SUNY, December 1993.

Tobias, Andrew. "Three Dollar Bills." *Time,* March 23, 1992.

PART TWO

SITES OF SUBORDINATION

CHAPTER 4

Schooling, Pedagogy, and Learning

Theorizing about schooling and learning, feminists have commonly focused on women's studies, feminist pedagogy, and women's academic community with one another. In addition, they often look at women's ways of knowing and learning. Like the work of Carol Gilligan on girls' and women's moral reasoning (see Chapter 8), the collaboration of Mary Field Belenky, Blythe McVicker Clinchy, Nancy Rule Goldberger, and Jill Mattuck Tarule on how women learn has been pathbreaking.[1] In fact, its authors say in their acknowledgments that Gilligan's (as well as William Perry's) work influenced them. Belenky and colleagues' work launches this chapter with an implicit critique of institutionalized student/teacher roles, pedagogies, and curricula.

SELF, VOICE, AND MIND

Belenky and colleagues' *Women's Ways of Knowing: The Development of Self, Voice, and Mind* emphasizes women's multiple styles of learning. Their title implies the challenges women face as students, learners, and knowers as well as their differences from men in these roles. Yet the authors avoid essentialism. Their preface refers to "ways of knowing that women have *cultivated* and *learned* to value. . . ." (emphasis added) Moreover, they say similar ways "can be found in men's thinking."[2]

Belenky and her colleagues note that only two social institutions center on human development: family and education. Within the latter they include not only academic organizations but also "invisible colleges," or "human service agencies supporting women in parenting their children." (pp. 4, 15) Based on interviews with 135 women from

153

Her observations showed Thorne that gender boundaries are ambiguous and fluid. When girls and boys spend time together, these boundaries get negotiated in ways that may bolster them or may, by disclosing their tentative character, weaken them. Thorne concedes that girls and boys interacting do often behave consistently with "the model of 'different worlds or cultures.'" Yet she sees "so many exceptions and qualifications, so many incidents that spill beyond and fuzzy up the edges, and so many conceptual ambiguities, that I have come to question the model's basic assumptions." (p. 90) In the end Thorne concludes, "The separate-and-different-cultures model has clearly outlived its usefulness." (p. 107)

In its place we should focus on *gender in context.* Thorne says that instead of assuming that girls and boys inhabit different worlds of experiencing or distinct gender subcultures, we should be asking "which boys or girls, where, when, under what circumstances?" (p. 108) We should also be looking at *crossing,* whereby girls or boys "seek access to groups and activities of the other gender." (p. 121) Crossing reveals the contradictions of gender and thus undercuts dualistic notions.

Common as it may be among children, crossing often goes unnoticed since it violates pervasive expectations about girls and boys. It may also escape attention fairly often because it falls off during adolescence as most girls and boys get heterosexualized. Becoming a normatively sexualized person—a person with a heterosexual identity, reputation, and orientation plus heterosexual erotic relationships—means becoming more patently gendered.

For girls, heterosexualization means that their looks and their boyfriends begin to overshadow other interests. Girls' social status rests more and more on "their romantic relationships with boys, but not vice versa." (p. 155) As they attune themselves to boys' perceived preferences, girls would seem to do less crossing and thus less deviating from the behavior associated with the separate-and-different-cultures model. "Paradoxically," Thorne concludes, "to create an equal world, we may sometimes need to emphasize gender, for example, by promoting strategic solidarity among girls or legitimizing alternative forms of masculinity among boys." (p. 171)

Such moves might best be school-based. As Donna Eder and her associates show, boys' athletics and girls' physical appearances anchor the gendered social hierarchy of the midwestern middle school they studied. Like the kindergarten teachers trying to stave off warrior narratives, the teachers of these middle-school students are fairly hard pressed to undercut that hierarchy. Thus, Eder and her co-researchers recommend that serious consideration be given to banning "particularly aggressive and/or violent sports" from our schools. They also emphasize that "activities like cheerleading and pom-pom teams . . . are not in the best interest of our female youth."[11]

So many school activities—formal and informal, curricular and extracurricular—are overtly gendered that almost anyone can find a starting point for degenderizing. Linda Christian-Smith, for instance, found that female students falling behind in literacy were assigned romance novels to read. If such an approach is found biased or wanting, it needs to be challenged until something better has taken its place. Yet that "if" can be surprisingly sizable. Christine Jarvis, for one, has found that using romantic fiction in various courses has "provoked reflective critical thinking, offering a stimulating focus for many" of the women taking her courses.[12] Her findings suggest how curricular materials, like gender, need to be contextualized before they can be assessed.

Such contextualizing becomes likelier as more people come to understand gender and other cultural constructions along the lines sketched in Valerie Walkerdine's *Schoolgirl Fictions*. Walkerdine proceeds from the assumption that

> femininity and masculinity are fictions linked to fantasies deeply embedded in the social world which can take on the status of facts when inscribed in the powerful practices, like schooling, through which we are regulated.[13]

From the outset, then, Walkerdine looks at schools as regulatory systems central to the relations of ruling. She argues that "individuals are produced as subjects *differently* within a variety of discursive practices. A particular individual has the potential to be 'read' within a variety of discourses." (p. 5) Walkerdine's approach thus emphasizes first "examin[ing] what elaborate fears and desires construct such fantasies and fiction" and then looking at how they get "read . . . back as fact." (p. 61) For instance, we need to understand how "constantly and continually, girls have to be proved to fail or to be inferior" in mathematics even in the face of weak, ambiguous data. Why girls get cast along such lines—as pom-pom specialists as well as weak math students—is a concern Walkerdine sees as central to feminist struggle. (pp. 62, 70)

Also central to that struggle in her judgment are critiques of how being "nice" and "kind" and "helpful" become "the most desirable characteristics for girls to possess." Walkerdine emphasizes that within the discourse of nice/kind/helpful femininity, "anger and conflict are displaced." (p. 76) At the same time, though, she stresses that girls do not

> passively adopt a female role model, but rather their adoption of femininity is at best shaky and partial: the result of a struggle in which heterosexuality is achieved as a solution to a set of conflicts and contradictions in familial and other social relations. (p. 88)

Thus does Walkerdine meet Thorne, and one might imagine the two of them meeting Kathleen Weiler and other kindred spirits along the theoretical way. Weiler studied high school teachers and administrators seen in their schools as feminists or as "sympathetic to women's interests." (p. 70)

22. Patricia Romney, Beverly Tatum, and JoAnne Jones, "Feminist Strategies for Teaching about Oppression: The Importance of Process," *Women's Studies Quarterly* 1 & 2 (Spring/Summer 1992), pp. 96, 98, 99; Erin McKenna, "Some Reflections Concerning Feminist Pedagogy," *Metaphilosophy* 27, no. 1 & 2 (January/April 1996), p. 179.

23. bell hooks, *Yearning: Race, Gender, and Cultural Politics* (Boston: South End Press, 1990), pp. 7, 8.

24. hooks, *Teaching to Transgress,* p. 91; see also Sherry Shapiro, "Re-Membering the Body in Critical Pedagogy," *Education and Society* 12, no. 1 (1994), pp. 61–79.

25. hooks, *Teaching to Transgress,* p. 92.

26. Shapiro, "Re-Membering the Body," p. 65.

27. hooks, *Killing Rage,* p. 201.

28. Satya P. Mohanty, "Colonial Legacies, Multicultural Futures: Relativism, Objectivity, and the Challenge of Otherness," *PMLA* 110, no. 1 (January 1995), pp. 110, 113.

29. Marilyn Friedman, "Multicultural Education and Feminist Ethics," *Hypatia: A Journal of Feminist Philosophy* 10, no. 2 (Spring 1995), p. 64.

30. For a discussion of "political correctness" as a media-driven phrase, see Marilyn Friedman, "Codes, Canons, Correctness, and Feminism" in Marilyn Friedman and Jan Narveson (eds.), *Political Correctness: For and Against* (Lanham, MD: Rowman & Littlefield, 1995), pp. 1–45. Charges of "male bashing" in women's studies classrooms may also be misguided or at least exaggerate its frequency; see Sue L. Cataldi, "Reflections on 'Male Bashing,'" *NWSA Journal* 7, no. 2 (Summer 1995), pp. 76–85.

31. hooks, *Talking Back,* p. 103; Romney, Tatum, and Jones, "Feminist Strategies," p. 106.

32. M. Kay Jankowski, "Catharine R. Stimpson: Charting the Course of Women's Studies Since Its Inception," *Women & Therapy* 17, no. 3/4 (1995), p. 492. For a survey of the jobs women's studies graduates have taken, see Barbara F. Luebke and Mary Ellen Reilly, *Women's Studies Graduates: The First Generation* (New York: Teachers College Press, 1995).

READING 10

What Is Feminist Pedagogy?

Carolyn M. Shrewsbury

Feminist pedagogy is a theory about the teaching/learning process that guides our choice of classroom practices by providing criteria to evaluate specific educational strategies and techniques in terms of the desired course goals or outcomes. These evaluative criteria include the extent to which a community of learners is empowered to act responsibly toward one another and the subject matter and to apply that learning to social action.

Feminist pedagogy begins with a vision of what education might be like but frequently is not. This is a vision of the classroom as a liberatory environment in which we, teacher–student and student–teacher, act as subjects, not objects. Feminist pedagogy is engaged teaching/learning—engaged with self in a continuing reflective process; engaged actively with the material being studied; engaged with others in a struggle to get beyond our sexism and racism and classism and homophobia and other destructive hatreds and to work together to enhance our knowledge; engaged with the community, with traditional organizations, and with movements for social change.

The concept of a liberatory environment suggests a new way to be with one another in the classroom. A classroom characterized as persons connected in a net of relationships with people who care about each other's learning as well as their own is very different from a classroom that is seen as comprised of teacher and students. One goal of the liberatory classroom is that members learn to respect each other's differences rather than fear them. Such a perspective is ecological and holistic. The classroom becomes an important place to connect to our roots, our past, and to envision the future. It is a place to utilize and develop all of our talents and abilities, to develop excellence that is not limited to the few. The classroom becomes a place in which integrity is not only possible but normal. The web of interrelationships in the classroom is seen to stretch to the local, regional, and global communities and, potentially, even beyond the boundaries of our earth.

Such a classroom builds on the experiences of the participants. We move on to seeing our experiences in different lights, to relating our experiences to other or new evidence, to thinking about our experiences in different ways. Under those circumstances we can integrate our new learning and modify our past understandings. But we remain grounded in our experiences, maintaining the sense of ourselves as subjects.

The vision includes a participatory, democratic process in which at least some power is shared. Learners develop independence. The classroom becomes a model of ways for people to work together to accomplish mutual or shared goals, and to help each other reach individual goals. Students are able to take risks in such a classroom. This is an active classroom, where the joy and excitement as well as the hard work of learning provide the kind of positive feedback that magnifies the effort put into learning. At its simplest level, feminist pedagogy is concerned with gender justice and overcoming oppressions. It recognizes the genderedness of all social relations and consequently of all societal institutions and structures. Thus, fundamental to a feminist perspective is a commitment to growth, to renewal, to life. The vision itself must continue to evolve.

In a feminist classroom, students integrate the skills of critical thinking with respect for and ability to work with others. Feminist pedagogy strives to help student and teacher learn to

Reprinted by permission, from Carolyn M. Shrewsbury, "What is Feminist Pedagogy?" *Women's Studies Quarterly,* 21: 3 & 4 (New York: The Feminist Press at The City University of New York, 1983), pp. 8–16. Copyright © 1993 by The Feminist Press at the City University of New York. All rights reserved.

think in new ways, especially ways that enhance the integrity and wholeness of the person and the person's connections with others (Minnich, Rutenberg). Critical thinking, then, is not an abstracted analysis but a reflective process firmly grounded in the experiences of the everyday. It requires continuous questioning and making assumptions explicit, but it does so in a dialogue aimed not at disproving another person's perspective, nor destroying the validity of another's perspective, but at a mutual exploration of explications of diverse experiences.

The vision of a feminist classroom includes an erotic dimension,

> an assertion of an empowered creative energy, the sharing of intellectual discovery, which as [Audre] Lorde says, "forms a bridge between the sharers which can be the basis of understanding much of what is not shared between them," a lessening of difference (Allen),

or difference used in a creative way, to spark increased understanding of the many dimensions of life, of incongruities or paradoxes, the complexities inherent in seemingly simple things.

Feminist pedagogy ultimately seeks a transformation of the academy and points toward steps, however small, that we can all take in each of our classrooms to facilitate that transformation. Three concepts, community, empowerment, and leadership, are central to these steps and provide a way of organizing our exploration into the meaning of feminist pedagogy.

THE THEORY: EMPOWERMENT

Of the three central concepts, empowerment has been the most frequently discussed, in part because of the early ties between feminist pedagogy and Paulo Freire's work in dialogical education. Feminist pedagogy includes a recognition of the power implications of traditional schooling and of the limitations of traditional meanings of the concept of power that embody relations of domination.

By focusing on empowerment, feminist pedagogy embodies a concept of power as energy, capacity, and potential rather than as domination. This is an image of power as the glue holding a community together, giving the people the opportunity "to act, to move, to change conditions, for the benefit of the whole population" (Lane). Under traditional conceptions of power as domination, justice requires that limits be placed on power and that a balance of power be achieved in order to mitigate the results of domination. Under conceptions of power as capability, the goal is to increase the power of all actors, not to limit the power of some.

Thus, a view of power as creative community energy would suggest that strategies be developed to counteract unequal power arrangements. Such strategies recognize the potentiality for changing traditional unequal relationships. Our classrooms need not always reflect an equality of power, but they must reflect movements in that direction.

This conception of power recognizes that people need power, both as a way to maintain a sense of self and as a way to accomplish ends (Janeway). Power can be used to enhance both autonomy and mutuality. To be empowered is to be able to "claim an education" as Adrienne Rich urges us. To be empowered is to recognize our abilities to act to create a more humane social order. To be empowered is to be able to engage in significant learning. To be empowered is to be able to connect with others in mutually productive ways.

To accomplish the empowerment of all, feminist pedagogy employs classroom strategies that: 1) enhance the students' opportunities and abilities to develop their thinking about the goals and objectives they wish and need to accomplish individually and collectively, 2) develop the students' independence (from formal instructors) as learners, 3) enhance the stake that everyone has in the success of a course and thereby make clear the responsibility of all members of the class for the learning of all,

4) develop skills of planning, negotiating, evaluating, and decision making, 5) reinforce or enhance the self-esteem of class members by the implicit recognition that they are sufficiently competent to play a role in course development and are able to be change agents, 6) expand the students' understanding of the subject matter of the course and of the joy and difficulty of intense intellectual activity as they actively consider learning goals and sequences.

Empowering strategies allow students to find their own voices, to discover the power of authenticity. At the same time, they enable individuals to find communion with others and to discover ways to act on their understanding. Empowering classrooms are places to practice visions of a feminist world, confronting differences to enrich all of us rather than to belittle some of us. Empowering pedagogy does not dissolve the authority or the power of the instructor. It does move from power as domination to power as creative energy. In such a system the teacher's knowledge and experience are recognized and are used with the students to increase the legitimate power of all. Empowering pedagogy takes seriously the goal of lifelong learning by consciously developing teaching/learning skills as well as by providing an informational subject base. It accepts the antihegemonic potential of liberatory education and provides a model of interrelationships that can be incorporated into a developing vision of a world in which hierarchical oppressive relationships are exchanged for autonomy within a community that celebrates difference.

THE THEORY: COMMUNITY

"Theories of power," Nancy Hartsock tells us, "are implicitly theories of community." And likewise, our decisions about what we image as community influence the ways in which we construct systems of power.

But, to talk about community, one needs to reexamine the gendered nature of traditional classrooms. The work of Carol Gilligan on moral development provides insights for reconceptualizing community. Gilligan identifies differences in the moral development of boys and girls and the moral conceptions of men and women. One consequence is

> the contrast between a self defined through separation and a self delineated through connection, between a self measured against an abstract ideal of perfection and a self assessed through the particular activities of care.

Women seek to build connections. They seek to maintain connections that have been built. Relationships are more than a set of interactions among people. They are the web of existence. For men, the importance of separation results in the creation of rules as the web of existence. Relationships with individual people are less important than the fabric of rules.

> These disparate visions in their tension reflect the paradoxical truths of human experience—that we know ourselves as separate only insofar as we live in connection with others, and that we experience relationships only insofar as we differentiate other from self (Gilligan).

The tragedy is that men in power have built a society that in its public aspects reflects only the morality of rights side of the tension.

Within the classroom, too, the morality of rights is dominant. By and large, students participate in our classes as individuals, taking little responsibility for the class as a whole. The classroom has a set of rules about fairness and equity but little consideration of differences in need. The rights of others in the classroom are respected, but little compassion and care is structured into the classroom.

At the core of feminist pedagogy is a re-imaging of the classroom as a community of learners where there is both autonomy of self and mutuality with others that is congruent with the developmental needs of both women and men. There are many advantages to creating such a classroom. Learning is enhanced in such environments (see Nelsen, Schmuck in Bar-Tal and Saxe, Torney-Purta, Johnson and Johnson, Schniedewind). Further, as Hannah Arendt noted, power arises from the collective self-confidence in a people's capacity to act and effect their fate. Empowerment is only possible when there is a sense of mutuality.

Decision making when there is a community of mutuality rather than a community of isolated individuals can take place by consensus as well as by formalized decision rules. Creativity is enhanced by the consensus process, for "something emerges as a desirable outcome, even though no member of the group thought about it in advance" (Thayer). Differences and diversity in a community of mutuality can be recognized and seen as a source of creative energy (Lorde, Nelsen).

The personal can be recognized as political in a classroom with some sense of mutual community. Students may find connections with themselves, their individual and collective pasts, with others, and with the future. In such a classroom there is a need and desire to move learning beyond the walls of the classroom. Theory can be extended to action, and action can come back to inform theory and that can lead again to action.

For too long community has been seen as either the polar opposite of autonomy or as the rather weak conception of an aggregate of individuals together because of some shared formality like geographic boundaries. Feminist pedagogy includes teaching strategies that are based on a reconceptualization of community with a richness that includes the autonomy and individuality of members who share a sense of relationship and connectedness with each other.

THE THEORY: LEADERSHIP

Leadership in its liberatory aspect as an active element of praxis is the third crucial concept in feminist pedagogy. Leadership is the embodiment of our ability and our willingness to act on our beliefs. Florence Howe illustrated this in noting that

a leader is someone who knows how to control her life, and who has a vision of possibilities for other lives apart from her own, for her community, for other women, for example, and who works to make that *vision* visible to others, to share it, without trampling on other persons, but engaging them, to work for that vision as well.

Feminist pedagogy focuses on the development of leadership. For example, students who take part in developing goals and objectives for a course learn planning and negotiating skills. They also learn how to develop an understanding of, and an ability to articulate, their needs. They learn how to find connections between their needs and the needs of others. They learn about groups and about the different leadership tasks in groups and take different leadership roles throughout the course period. As students struggle with evaluation methods, they learn how to evaluate actions and the connection between objectives and achievement. When things aren't working in the classroom, they learn how to analyze the problems and how to find alternatives. And the skill of the students as leaders helps all of this work more smoothly and effectively. Leadership is a special form of empowerment that empowers others.

The feminist teacher is above all a role model of a leader. S/he has helped members of the class develop a community, a sense of shared purpose, a set of skills for accomplishing that purpose, and the leadership skills so that teacher and students may jointly proceed on those tasks. There is a dynamic between leadership and followership, and effective leaders under the more modern sense of leadership are also effective followers. Between the two is a morality based upon responsibility. Individuals are responsible for their acts within the context in which they have freedom to act. They have responsibility arising out of the relationships they have with those with whom they share a community. The students' and teacher's joint responsibility for the successful conclusion of a class emphasizes the moral nature of leadership and followership activities. This is a very different perception of the classroom than that where teachers have responsibility for teaching and students for learning with the implication that each is at least partially independent. It emphasizes the moral nature of choices within a community and the necessity for agency by community members.

Leadership then is logically and intuitively connected to community and empowerment by providing the active mechanism for achieving the empowered community and for that community to continue to be effective within the broader world. It suggests that change does not take place magically but by the active exercise of agency, whether directed at ourselves or at structures.

Feminist pedagogy does not assume that all classrooms are alike. Indeed, it suggests how classrooms might differ depending, for example, on the initial competence of students . . . . It does not automatically preclude any technique or approach. It does indicate the relationship that specific techniques have to educational goals. It is not limited to any specific subject matter but it does include a reflexive element that increases the feminist scholarship component involved in the teaching/learning of any subject matter. It has close ties with other liberatory pedagogies, but it cannot be subsumed under other pedagogical approaches. It is transformative, helping us revision the educational enterprise. But it can also be phased into a traditional teaching approach or another alternative pedagogical approach. It is not all or nothing, although practitioners find that taking one step makes the next step logically compelling. It is a crucial component of a feminist revolution.

REFERENCES

Allen, Carolyn. "Feminist Teachers: The Power of the Personal." *Working Paper Series* 3 (1981). Women's Studies Research Center, University of Wisconsin.

Bar-Tal, Daniel, and Saxe, Leonard, eds. *Social Psychology of Education: Theory and Research.* New York: Hemisphere Publishing, 1978.

Freire, Paulo. *Pedagogy of the Oppressed.* New York: Seabury Press, 1968.

———. *Education for Critical Consciousness.* New York: Seabury Press, 1973.

Gilligan, Carol. *In a Different Voice: Psychological Theory and Women's Development.* Cambridge, MA: Harvard University Press, 1982.

Hartsock, Nancy. *Money, Sex, and Power: Toward a Feminist Historical Materialism.* New York: Longman, 1983.

Howe, Florence. "New Teaching Strategies for a New Generation of Students." *Women's Studies Quarterly* 11, no. 2 (1983), pp. 7–11.

Janeway, Elizabeth. *Powers of the Weak.* New York: Knopf, 1980.

Johnson, Roger T., and David W. Johnson. *Cooperative Learning: The Power of Positive Goal Interdependence.* Paper, n.d.

Lane, Ann M. "The Feminism of Hannah Arendt." *Democracy* 3, no. 3 (1983), pp. 107–17.

Minnich, Elizabeth Kamarck. "Friends and Critics: The Feminist Academy." In *Toward a Feminist Transformation of the Academy,* ed. Beth Reed, pp. 1–11. Ann Arbor, MI: Great Lakes College Association Women's Studies Program, 1978.

Nelsen, Randle W. "Reading, Writing, and Relationships: Toward Overcoming the Hidden Curriculum of Gender, Ethnicity, and Socio-economic Class." *Interchange* 12, nos. 2–3 (1981), pp. 229–42.

Rich, Adrienne. *On Lies, Secrets, and Silence.* New York: W. W. Norton, 1979.

Rutenberg, Taly. "Learning Women's Studies." In *Theories of Women's Studies,* eds. Gloria Bowles and Renate Duelli-Klein. Berkeley: Women's Studies Department, University of California, 1980.

Schniedewind, Nancy. "Cooperatively Structured Learning: Implications for Feminist Pedagogy." *Journal of Thought* 20, no. 3 (Fall 1985), pp. 74–87.

Thayer, Frederick C. *An End to Hierarchy and Competition Administration in the Post-Affluent World.* 2nd ed. New York: New Viewpoints (Franklin Watts, dist.), 1981.

Torney-Purta, Judith. "Psychological Perspectives on Enhancing Civic Education through the Education of Teachers." *Journal of Teacher Education* 34, no. 6 (November/December 1983), pp. 30–34.

READING 11

The Colonizer/Colonized Chicana Ethnographer: Identity, Marginalization, and Co-optation in the Field

Sofia Villenas

What happens when members of low-status and marginalized groups become university-sanctioned "native" ethnographers of their own communities? How is this "native" ethnographer positioned vis-à-vis her own community, the majority culture, the research setting, and the academy? While qualitative researchers in the field of education theorize about their own privilege in relation to their research participants, the "native" ethnographer must deal with her own marginalizing experiences and identities in relation to dominant society. This "native" ethnographer is potentially both the colonizer, in her university cloak, and the colonized, as a member of the very community that is made "other" in her research.

I am this "native" ethnographer in the field of education, a first-generation Chicana born in Los Angeles of immigrant parents from Ecuador. Geographically, politically, and economically, I have lived under the same yoke of colonization as the Chicano communities I study, experiencing the same discrimination and alienation from mainstream society that comes from being a member of a caste "minority."[1] I share the same ethnic consciousness and regional and linguistic experiences. The commonly used terms "Hispanic" and "Latino" do not adequately describe who I am.[2] Racially and ethnically I am *indigena,* a detribal-

ized Native American woman, descendant of the Quechua-speaking people of the South American Andes. Politically, I am a Chicana, born and raised in the American Southwest, in the legendary territories of Aztlan.[3] This story is about how these identities came into play in the process of conducting research with an emerging Latino community located in the U.S. South.

THE COLONIZER/COLONIZED DILEMMA

Rethinking the political and personal subjectivities of researcher and ethnographer has in recent times pushed the boundaries of theorizing about the multiple identities of the researcher within the research context of privilege and power. Qualitative researchers in education have called for a reexamination of the raced, gendered, aged, and classed positions of the researcher with respect to the research participants (Fine 1994; Lather 1991; Roman and Apple 1990). These researchers are also recognizing that they are and have been implicated in imperialist agendas (Pratt 1986; Rosaldo 1989) by participating in "othering" (Fine 1994) and in the exploitation and domination of their research subjects (Roman and Apple 1990).[4]

In the last decade, ethnographers and qualitative researchers have illuminated the ways in which the researched are colonized and exploited. By objectifying the subjectivities of the researched, by assuming authority, and by not questioning their own privileged positions (Crapanzano 1986; Fine 1994; Rosaldo 1989; Van Galen and Eaker 1995), ethnographers have participated as colonizers of the researched. Rosaldo (1989) uses the image of the "Lone Ethnographer" who once upon a time "rode off into the sunset in search of his 'natives'" (p. 30). After undergoing arduous fieldwork as his rite of passage, the Lone Ethnographer "returned home to write a 'true' account of the culture" (p. 30). In the texts of classic anthropology, people were depicted as "members of a harmonious, internally homogenous and unchanging culture" (p. 31), and written about in a way that "normalizes life by describing social activities as if they were always repeated in the same manner by everyone in the group" (p. 42). Rosaldo reminds us that this manner of objectifying people's lives has been the classic norm of ethnography, and that researchers have rarely asked what the researched think about how their lives are being interpreted and described in text.

Researchers are also implicated as colonizers when they claim authenticity of interpretation and description under the guise of authority. In a critique of Geertz's description of the Balinese cockfight, Crapanzano (1986) exposes the ways in which the event described is subverted and sacrificed to "a literary discourse that is far removed from the indigenous discourse of their occurrence" (p. 76). This discourse, according to Crapanzano, is ultimately masked by the authority of the author, "who, at least in much ethnography, stands above and behind those whose experiences he purports to describe" (p. 76).

As ethnographers, we are also like colonizers when we fail to question our own identities and privileged positions, and in the ways in which our writings perpetuate "othering." As Fine (1994) explains:

> When we write essays about subjugated Others as if *they* were a homogeneous mass (of vice and virtue), free-floating and severed from contexts of oppression, and as if *we* were neutral transmitters of voices and stories, we tilt toward a narrative strategy that reproduces Othering on, despite, or even "for." (1994, p. 74)

Moreover, we are like colonizers when, as Van Galen and Eaker (1995) point out, the professional and intellectual gatekeeping structures (e.g., university admissions to graduate studies, journal publication referees) from which we gain our legitimacy and privilege remain "highly inaccessible to those on whose behalf we claim to write" (p. 114).

For example, women teachers of working-class backgrounds are expected to consume a body of literature that emanates from elite universities from which they are excluded, and that thus excludes them from the production of material used for the teaching profession and their own training. Fine (1994) and Van Galen and Eaker (1995) urge ethnographers to probe the nature of their relationship to those they write about.

While we continue to push the borders of the multiple, decentered, and politicized self as researcher, we continue to analyze and write about *ourselves* in a unidirectional manner as imperialist researchers (Rosaldo 1989) and colonizers (Fine 1994) in relation to the research participants. Yet, what about the researcher as colonizer *and* colonized? Here is my own dilemma: as a Chicana graduate student in a White institution and an educational ethnographer of Latino communities, I am both, as well as in between the two. I am the coloniz*ed* in relation to the greater society, to the institution of higher learning, and to the dominant majority culture in the research setting. I am the coloniz*er* because I am the educated, "marginalized" researcher, recruited and sanctioned by privileged dominant institutions to write for and about Latino communities. I am a walking contradiction with a foot in both worlds—in the dominant privileged institutions *and* in the marginalized communities. Yet, I possess my own agency and will to promote my own and the collective agendas of particular Latino communities. I did not even consider the multiplicity of self and identity and the nuances of which such consideration meant until I had to confront my own marginality as a Chicana researcher in relation to the dominant majority culture in the research setting. In the research context of power and domination, I encountered what it means to examine closely within myself the intersectedness of race, class, gender, and other conceptual notions of identity.

I am a Chicana doctoral student, and have been conducting research in a small rural community in North Carolina, which I have named Hope City. My research project involved the educational life histories of Latina mothers who were recent immigrants to Hope City. In the telling of their stories, the women defined education—how they experienced it in their lives as learners and teachers in families, communities, and schools, and how they constructed educational models for raising their own children. I spent over two years in Hope City, teaching English as a Second Language (ESL) at the local community college and in an after-school tutorial program for elementary-school-age Spanish-speaking children. I participated in family social gatherings, and in community and church events and meetings. I also had a lot of contact with the English-speaking community of professionals who were servicing Latino families in health care and education, joining them in meetings and informal gatherings. These professionals were also formally interviewed by other colleagues involved in the Hope City project. As a team, we were funded by a child development center to investigate the beliefs about education held by the agencies and schools serving the Hope City Latino community, and by the diverse Latino community members themselves. In my own research, I systematically analyzed the public sphere and the organization of relations of power in Hope City. Through a historiographic analysis of the town's newspaper and through my observations and participant observations within the community of school and agency professionals, I found that the Latino community in Hope City was being framed as a "problem."

At the beginning of the research project, I was aware of the politics and privilege of my researcher role and my relation to the research participants. I was eager to experience the process of constructing meaning with the research participants. By talking with these Latina mothers about their beliefs and philosophies of child rearing and education, as well as my own, I hoped to engage them in conversations about how they could create a dignified space for themselves and their families in a previously biracial community that was not accustomed to Latinos. I had vague ideas about community

projects that I hoped would emerge from the research participants themselves. When I reflected later, these notions seemed arrogant, as if I thought I knew the hopes and aspirations of this Latino community. I realized I had to question all my assumptions about this southern Latino community, such as defining as problems certain aspects of their lives that, to them, were not problematic at all. I was certainly ready to learn from this Latino community, but in the process of seeking to reform my relationship with them, I failed to notice that I was being repositioned and co-opted by the dominant English-speaking community to legitimate their discourse of "Latinos as problem." In the course of working with Hope City's non-Latino school and service professionals, I discovered that while I engaged in a rethinking of my own politics and the processes of empowerment within the Latino community, I was hiding my own marginality in relation to the majority culture. I did not know then that I would have to scrutinize my own lived experiences as a Chicana daughter, mother, wife, and student in confronting the dominant community's discourses of "othering" and of difference.

In this article, I attempt to heed Fine's words in "unearthing the blurred boundaries between Self and Other" (1994, p. 72). Weis (1995) summarizes the discourse on colonialism, which takes as its central point the idea that the colonial "other" and the self (read the "Western White" self) are simultaneously co-constructed, the first being judged against the latter. Furthermore, Weis notes, "this process of 'othering' is key to understanding relations of domination and subordination, historically and currently" (p. 18). This article, then, speaks to the discourses of "othering" that jolted me out of my perceived unproblematic identity and role as a Chicana researcher in education, and into a co-construction of the "Western" self and the Chicana "other." This ongoing story involves my confrontation with my contradictory identities—as a Chicana researcher in the power structure of the dominant discourse of "other," and as a Chicana working with this marginalized Latino community. Through this story, I hope to recontextualize the ways in which qualitative researchers in education have theorized about identity and privilege to include the repositioning and manipulation of identities that can occur, particularly with native ethnographers. This recontextualization problematizes the ways in which qualitative researchers who seek to analyze privilege and the "situatedness" of each ethnographer fail to note that we as ethnographers of education are not all the same "We" in the literature of privileged ethnographers. My standpoint as a Chicana and my historical relation to Latino communities mediate and complicate my "privilege." Unveiling the ways in which the ethnographer is situated in oppressive structures is a critical task for qualitative researchers in the field of education. Even in new positions of privilege, the Chicana ethnographer cannot escape a history of her own marginalization nor her guilt of complicity.

PERSONAL HISTORY

My encounter with discourses of difference and of "othering" as a child in Los Angeles neighborhoods and schools intensified my scrutinization of my own identity and role as a Chicana in academia. Growing up in Los Angeles, I was aware of racism. As a child, I acted out the effects of colonization, refusing to speak Spanish, emphasizing that I was South American and not Mexican, as Mexicans were relegated to second-class citizenship. I grew up knowing that my culture and language were not valued, but I did not suffer direct, blatant racism. I found safety in numbers, as there were many other Latinas, Chicanas, and Mexicans with whom I could hang out.

As I grew older, our peer group continually created and celebrated our Chicano/Latino cultures and languages. As an adult, I thought I

had overcome the loss of self that comes with second-class relegation of the Spanish language and Latino cultures, and that I did not speak with the voice of a colonized person, one whose culture and language were devalued. Yet I was not as prepared for Eurocentric academia as I thought I was. In community, I had learned to manipulate my identities successfully and did not expect them to be manipulated by others. But such a manipulation is precisely what occurred when I began my professional university training in ethnographic research. At the university, I experienced the dilemma of creating my identity as a Chicana researcher in the midst of Eurocentric discourses of "other." Being an ethnographer made my contradictory position more obvious, complex, and ironic. I recognize this contradiction now, but at the university, the discourse of "othering" did not begin with my research study.

An awakening of sorts occurred for me when I attended a seminar on topics in education. On that particular day, the topic was whether public single-population schools should exist. The readings for that week centered on public and private schools for women only, for gays and lesbians, and schools based on Afrocentric or Chicanocentric curriculum. Most of my fellow classmates argued that people should not be separated, reasoning that students should be integrated so that everybody could come together to talk about societal inequities and find solutions together. They argued that single-population schools promoted separatism, and that through integrated schools, the Eurocentric curricula would be challenged. While I agreed that all people need to dialogue about oppression and work together to bring about social justice, and therefore was in favor of integrated schools, I did not agree that Afrocentric or Chicano-centric curricula and schools promoted separatism. In trying to engage in the discussion, however, I began to feel uncomfortable. I tried to explain why I felt that disenfranchised groups had the right to these curricula if they wanted them and, furthermore, why I felt they were important and necessary. I argued that people who have been stripped of their cultures through public schooling need to come together and reclaim their cultures, histories, and languages, but although I believed this, I was nevertheless buying into the discourse of fear of separatism, saying that we needed to have separate spaces before coming together to be a part of the larger group. Of course, implicit in this argument was the idea that as people of color, we were going "to come together" to join the dominant culture and integrate ourselves within it, rather than challenge the notion of a single common culture.

The discourse of this group of fellow students and friends was so powerful that it disabled me. I explained my stance apologetically, acquiescing to the notion that we would have to come back and join a mainstream culture and society rather than challenge it. Everyone else was speaking as if they were detached and removed from the topic, rationalizing the logic of their arguments, but it was different for me. The topic was personal and deeply embedded in my experiences. In this conversation, I was not the subject anymore but the object, the "other." Using Cornell West's words, hooks (1990) writes that people often engage in debates that "highlight notions of difference, marginality, and 'otherness' in such a way that it further marginalizes actual people of difference and otherness" (p. 125). Hooks likens these debates to reinscribing patterns of colonization: "When this happens . . . the 'Other' is always made object, appropriated, interpreted, taken over by those in power, by those who dominate" (1990, p. 125).

In this same manner, I felt that my experiences as a Latina going through the Eurocentric curriculum of public schools was being objectified and appropriated through a rationalized logical argument against Chicano- or Afrocentric schools. In the rational, logical arguments in that seminar, no space existed for my deeply passionate personal experience and voice, for

me to argue for the right to choose to be with Latinas/os, for us to be educated together and to center our curriculum in our diverse roots and history, to find out about ourselves and to claim ourselves in our own terms. My classmates and I talked against oppressed groups coming together to form their own schools in a way that ignored the existence of race, class, and gender privileges among the class participants. In this discussion, an aura of disinterested, detached, scientific rationalism existed that rendered me voiceless and silenced. Ellsworth (1989) describes the oppression of rational argument as putting as its opposite the irrational "other"— for example, women and people of color. In schools, she said, the rational argument has become the "vehicle for regulating conflict and the power to speak" (p. 303).

After the group dispersed, I was left feeling stripped of my identity and angry with myself for betraying my own voice. I had fallen into the trap of the dominant discourse, trying to convince the group not to worry, that we would eventually come around to integrating ourselves. But into what? I did not know, but it was implied that we would integrate ourselves into some core set of shared social and cultural ideals and belief systems, a core that evidently was the White, middle-class lifestyle. I was reminded again of Ellsworth's (1989) critique of critical pedagogy. She argues that the dialogue emphasized in critical pedagogy assumes that we could all engage in dialogue equally as if we were not raced, gendered, and classed persons with vested interests and different experiences. The seminar participants (including myself) failed to see how, in the process of discussing people of color, we silenced and marginalized the very voices of those who were supposed to have been the subjects and authors of their experiences—the voices of fellow Chicano and African American classmates.

I now realize that something else also occurred that afternoon in our seminar. The topic, as well as the disinterested, detached way in which the discussion was carried out, fueled what I wanted so desperately to express, but could not. I was the only Chicana there, and had to think and speak individualistically rather than collectively. I was without my Latino friends from home who shared the power of our activism in defying the colonization of our identities and of our people. In the absence of that collectivity, I changed my commitment and orientation from the visions my friends and I had shared. Cut off from those who collectively sustained them, I lost those visions of activism and self-determination. Deep inside, I wanted to voice what I was experiencing at that moment—the disempowerment that comes from being cut off from your own. Perez (1991) a Chicana feminist, writes what I wanted to express at that time:

> You attempt to "penetrate" the place I speak from with my Chicana/Latina hermanas. I have rights to my space. I have boundaries. . . . At times, I must separate from you, from your invasion. So call me a separatist, but to me this is not about separatism. It is about survival. I think of myself as one who must separate to my space and language of women to revitalize, to nurture and be nurtured. Then, I can resurface to build the coalitions that we must build to make the true revolution—all of us together acting the ideal, making alliance without a hierarchy of oppression. (p. 178)

Only now, as I am writing these words, do I realize what was happening. It hit me and it hurt me. I felt it in my bones, but I could not articulate it until now. The coalitions referred to by Perez imply groups of empowered and self-identified peoples who do not have to pack neatly and put away their languages and cultures in order to comply with a "standard" way of being. To be Chicanas in the myriad and infinite ways there are of being, to come as we are, poses a threat to integrated schools and to mainstream society. In the absence of collectivity in my graduate seminar, I could not be true to my vision of a Chicana.

REVEALING TENSION IN MY IDENTITY AS A CHICANA RESEARCHER

As I look back, describe, and theorize about my seminar experience, I can articulate the elements that constituted my marginalization and my complicity in the discourses of difference and "othering." The power of the dominant discourse of "other," the objectification of my experiences as the "other" through detached, rational argumentation, and the severing of a collective vision and memory that disabled me and rendered me voiceless, all constituted marginalization and complicity. These elements resurfaced when I started the process of conducting qualitative research with the Latino community in Hope City, North Carolina. There, my dilemma of being a Chicana and a researcher became problematic in ways similar to my experiences in the seminar, that is, as an accomplice to the marginalization and objectification of my identity and experiences as a Chicana, which became embedded in the power structure of the dominant and the disenfranchised.

Going into the field, my intent was to gain access to the Hope City Latino community so that I could interview Latina mothers about their beliefs on child rearing and education, particularly as their narratives played out in the context of a changing rural southern town. Yet I did not want only to take their stories and leave. I also wanted to become involved in some way with their Latino community, either through bilingual tutoring for children with their mothers or through English as a Second Language (ESL) instruction. As I sought to gain access to the community, I had to speak with numerous English-speaking institutional representatives, including educators in the elementary school, community college, and health department. From the beginning, I felt uncomfortable in my conversations with these community leaders and with their cultural views of Latino families, and of the women in particular. They constructed Latino families as "problems" tending towards violence, sexism, machismo, and low educational aspirations. In their meetings, well-meaning providers talked about showing Latina mothers models of proper child rearing. A Hope City newspaper headline read, "Program Teaches Hispanics How to Be Better Mothers." Other articles about Latino families carried headlines such as "Literacy Void." Again, the dominant discourse concerning the "other" was powerful and overwhelming—so much so that I found myself, as in the seminar, participating in it as an accomplice. I began to talk the talk.

I remember accompanying an ESL instructor from the community college to the trailer park where he gave classes. We stood in the grassy area in the middle of the park, looking out at the individual trailers, some with children and families outside them. The instructor was giving me the rundown on their living conditions and other problems. I was nodding my head, all the while gazing at the people who looked back at us. I remember ducking my head, painfully aware of my awkward position. Whose side was I on? In participating in this manner with the instructor, I was, as hooks (1989) says, "one of them in a fellowship of the chosen and superior, [it was] a gesture of inclusion in 'whiteness'" (p. 68), affirming that I had been assimilated. I felt uncomfortable, yet I participated, as in the graduate seminar, by betraying my anger and remaining silent, and by not challenging the discourse. In conversations with Hope City professionals, I had to choose my alignment in the power structure of the community—either with the leaders who were in positions to make policy, or with the disenfranchised Latino community.

Choosing to align myself with the dominant English-speaking leaders entailed sharing the same discourse and language to talk about the Latino community. To do this, I had to distance myself from the Latino community and the experiences I shared with them, and speak as the subject about the object. I could do this in the eyes of the dominant English-speaking community because I was formally educated and spoke English as well as they.

In this southern community, there were no other Chicanas/os in leadership positions. I had no one with whom to share a collective vision for the empowerment of "our" community. The ESL instructor and I spoke in a detached manner about the problems of "these people," as if I had not been socialized in a Latino family and immigrant community. I spoke as if Latino families and friends had not been the most important people in my private life. I silenced myself so that I could have further conversations with the community leaders who were the key to my accessing the educational institutions of the community. By participating in their discourse, I had to disengage myself from my experiences as an intimate participant in Latino families and communities. The dominant discourse of difference was powerful, and my experiences were again nullified through my participation in detached and rational discussions of the problems of the "other."

My uncomfortable feelings soon turned to outrage and hurt. One particular discussion with a school principal startled me out of my perceived unproblematic role as a Chicana researcher. My advisor and I went to speak with the principal about my starting a mother/child class to teach children how to read and write in Spanish. The principal, who held blatantly racist views of Latino families, told us he would play the devil's advocate and point out some problems—for example, how were we going to get mothers to come? He went on to say that we had to understand the Hispanic family. The man, he said, dictates, and the woman is subservient: "The man will not let her out of the house. They do not care about education and so it's hard to get the mothers to come to the school." An ESL teacher who was also in the room explained that these were poor people, blue-collar workers who did not have education themselves. I later responded angrily in my field notes:

> How dare you say this to me. How is it that you are telling me what Latino families are like. I was so insulted. They were talking about my "raza" so negatively as if I were not Latina myself. This

goes to show how easily I can "pass" and that in certain contexts, I am not identified as one of "them." With this conversation as in others, I have felt that I have had to put on a different persona in order to play along with well-meaning racist discourse. I have felt very uncomfortable talking to benevolent people about the "other," the exotic poor people who need our help. "Our" referring to my complicity as researcher. (Field notes, March 1994)

After that incident, I began to question my identity and my role as a Chicana researcher. It was evident that the dominant English-speaking community did not consider me a Latina, like the women we were discussing, but a middle-class, educated woman of Spanish descent. How was I to relate to this dominant discourse of difference and "othering"?

I looked to recent works on the researcher's role in disenfranchised communities in which the researcher shares the same cultural background as the research participants. Delgado-Gaitan (1993) and Delgado-Gaitan and Trueba (1991) write about an ethnography of empowerment, a framework that "provides a broad sociocultural premise and possible strategy for studying the process of disempowerment and empowerment of disenfranchised communities" (p. 391). This kind of ethnography is based on a Freirian notion of self-awareness of the social and cultural context of the nature of oppression suffered by disempowered people (Delgado-Gaitan and Trueba 1991). Such a framework calls for "the construction of knowledge through the social interaction between researcher and researched with the fundamental purpose of improving the living conditions of the communities being researched" (Delgado-Gaitan and Trueba 1991, p. 392). Delgado-Gaitan (1993) emphasizes that the researcher shapes the research participants and their environment while, at the same time, the researcher is also shaped by the participants and the dynamics of their interactions. Delgado-Gaitan's (1993) own provocative story is of the transformation of her

role with respect to her work on literacy practices in the homes and schools of a Latino community. As the parents mobilized to effect changes in the school, Delgado-Gaitan redefined her role as researcher to become involved as facilitator and informant in the process of community empowerment. As a result of her own unique experiences, Delgado-Gaitan, a Latina herself, built upon the notion of making problematic her relationship with Latino communities. By doing so, she put into practice qualitative researchers' call for the reexamination of one's identity and place within the research context of privilege and power.

My story extends this notion by problematizing the relationship between the marginalized researcher and the majority culture. The internalization of oppressive discourses relating to one's own people, especially as a product of institutionalized education and university training, can lead to a disempowerment of the researcher and the research process. The analysis can be extended then to include the empowerment of the researcher and the role of the ethnographer's culture, self-identity, and her/his raced, classed, and gendered experiences in the research process. In my case, while I naively looked for ways in which I could help Latina mothers "empower" themselves (see Le Compte and de Marrais 1992 for a critique on the discourse on empowerment), I failed to realize that I needed to help myself become empowered vis-à-vis the dominant, English-speaking community. I needed to examine my own identity in the particular cultural arena that formed the context for my research study. Not having done so, I could not engage in the process of constructing knowledge with the research participants. I needed first to ask myself, How am I, as a Chicana researcher, damaged by my own marginality? Furthermore, how am I complicit in the manipulation of my identities such that I participate in my own colonization and marginalization and, by extension, that of my own people—those with whom I feel a cultural and collective connectedness and commitment?

For these reasons, researchers must examine how their subjectivities and perceptions are negotiated and changed, not only in relation to the disenfranchised community as research participants, but also through interactions with the majority culture. In most cases, the latter are the people who espouse the dominant discourse of difference and "other," that is, the cultural views of Latino families as a "problem"—poor, disadvantaged, and language deficient. In Hope City, Latina mothers are constructed as "at risk" in the discourse of the dominant community (i.e., professionals in education, health, and social services) so that the ways in which they raise and educate their children are devalued (Swadener and Lubeck 1995). It is this "at risk" and "problem" discourse that I was being pushed hard to legitimate in Hope City. Yet this discourse concerned my own rearing, my own family, my own mother, and my own beliefs and those of my community. Through my engagement in the majority culture's "Latinos as problem" discourse, I was further marginalized and encircled in my own guilt of complicity.

IDENTITY, TENSION, AND POWER: INTERPRETING MY INSIDER/OUTSIDER PERSPECTIVE

I find it useful to appropriate Delgado-Gaitan's (1993) insider/outsider concept and apply it in a different manner to my emerging and changing identity as a Chicana researcher. In the process of conducting her study, Delgado-Gaitan (1993) learned that a researcher initially could only be an outsider to the community of research participants, but that with insight, the researcher could foster relational and reflective processes with their participants and in time become an insider. What are the particular behaviors and/or characteristics of the researcher that can make her/him an insider to the community of research participants? In a general sense, it is the sharing of collective experiences and a collective space with the research participants, such that the re-

searcher is gradually accepted as a member of that particular community. As researchers, we can be insiders and outsiders to a particular community of research participants at many different levels and at different times.

In my case, I had two layers of communities to penetrate, at least on different terms. From my perspective at the time, the irony was that I was becoming an insider to the "wrong" community—the dominant, English-speaking community of leaders with whom I felt no familial, historical, or intimate relation. I was, in fact, the outsider to the Latino community of this town, since I was not *of* their community and did not share in their everyday experiences (I did not live in Hope City). Further, I was being recruited by the institutional representatives to become an insider in the legitimization of the dominant discourse of Latinos as "problem" and "victim." The effects on me of participating in the dominant discourse in a detached manner through rational dialogue were powerful. Consequently, I had to step back and negotiate internally the ongoing recruiting efforts of the dominant, English-speaking community leaders to their discourses of difference.

I began my fieldwork on site at the beginning of the spring semester of the academic year. I discussed with my advisor how the White community might be cautious in talking with me about the Latino community, since I might be perceived as a member of this community. As I stated earlier, my advisor and I were soon proven wrong. The White community leaders were eager to talk to me about their perceptions of Latino families.

I had worked hard all semester to gain access to the Hope City Latino community and to find a niche in which to practice my profession of "maestra" (teacher), and to do research as well. My diligence paid off in that many opportunities were opened to me by English-speaking community leaders. I had received invitations to teach ESL and literacy in the churches (both the Catholic and Methodist churches), the elementary school, the community college, and the health department.

I decided to dedicate my time to teaching ESL to adults at the community college, a job in which I not only had experience but that I also thoroughly enjoyed. At the end of the semester, I looked to see what my story in terms of my research had been thus far. I had written in my field notes about my uneasy and uncomfortable feelings as I had conversations with English-speaking community leaders. Interestingly, I had also recorded my feelings of awkwardness when I talked to Latinas/os as a researcher researching "them." I was unconsciously documenting the power relations that defined the research context of which I, the dominant community leaders, and the Latino immigrant community each formed a part. Roman and Apple (1999) emphasize that a crucial task for the ethnographer should be the "elaboration of the structural power relations that formed the basis for conducting the field research and the study" (p. 60). The documentation of my feelings of anger and awkwardness formed the basis for the elaboration of my identity as a Chicana researcher in the community's power structure.

The power play in the recruitment efforts of the White power structure, and later in their efforts to appropriate me, was clearly evident. To recruit me to their discourse and narratives of difference, the community leaders had to view me as equal with them in the power structure. They appropriated my persona and appeared, at least initially, to welcome me as an equal.

I later understood this welcome to be a form of colonizing. They appropriated my persona by presuming shared assumptions of a body of experiences. For example, a community college instructor warned me about the dangers of the trailer park, implying that I shared his fear of poor people and of people of color. The community leaders also treated me as an equal by talking about Latinos as the "other" and including me in the distanced and detached conversations about the "problems of Latinos." Sharing our

detached, rational observations of Latinos made me seem objective and scientific, and seemed to put us on equal footing with each other and in a superior position to the Latino community.

I felt powerful because I could discuss "their" problems. I was even in a position to negotiate power with the elementary principal when I proposed Spanish tutoring classes for young children and their mothers. Not only did my credentials give me leverage in these negotiations, but my professional identity and language also met the criteria for inclusion and commonality with the institutional representatives. In more ways than one, I found it easier to be an insider to the community of dominant English-speaking leaders than to the Latino community.

The powerholders' recruiting efforts were intense precisely because they had a lot at stake in interpreting, structuring, and legitimating their cultural constructions of difference and diversity. The schools and agencies were interpreting Latino "cultures" and child-rearing practices. They were structuring the relationships between the Latino and English-speaking communities through the mediating force of agency bureaucracies (see Adkins, Givens, McKinney, Murillo, and Villenas 1995). And, they were legitimating the "at risk" and "problem" discourses.

Undoubtedly, as a "Hispanic" professional, I served to legitimate the "at risk" discourse and the definition of Latino child rearing as a "problem." Sleeter (1995) argues that "the discourse over 'children at risk' can be understood as a struggle for power over how to define children, families, and communities who are poor, of color, and/or native speakers of languages other than English" (p. ix).

In later months, community leaders called on me to speak about and for the Latino community. In their eyes, I was the "expert" on the educational experiences of Latino families, not because I had begun talking with Latina mothers and could possibly articulate their points of view, but because I was seen as the professional who possessed formal education, teaching experience, and spoke both Spanish and English. Indeed, they would introduce me not only by name, but also by my academic credentials and past teaching experience. On one occasion, I was asked to speak to a group of community leaders from various social service agencies about Latino families and their educational needs. I chose to speak about the strengths of language and literacy socialization in Latino families. On another occasion, I was asked to translate for and represent the Latinas from my ESL class at a meeting to organize a county chapter of a council for women. At yet another meeting, called by the county migrant education office, about 100 Latino parents met in the elementary school cafeteria, where I spoke to them about strategies to help their children in school. On all of these occasions, I was serving as the broker for and the link to the Latino community for the professional community leaders. They called me to participate in meetings and to give presentations. The stakeholders of this community clearly felt an urgent need to co-opt certain people, such as myself and other English-speaking town leaders, to represent the Latino community. It was as if in doing so, they did not have to handle the raw material. The Latino community was too foreign, too different, too working class, too brown; so they appropriated me, Sofia, the preprocessed package, wrapped in formal education and labeled in English.

Of course I did not want to be associated with the dominating power structure in the eyes of the Latino community. I had qualms about being perceived as the imperialist researcher. I felt tension with the Latino community when I was in my role as researcher, and when they saw me in company and complicity with the community leaders. I am reminded of two situations in which I felt these tensions most acutely.

It felt normal and comfortable, for example, when I visited Tienda Adrian (Adrian's Store), a Latino food store, with my husband and children. We spoke with the store owners in Span-

ish, asking about the town. However, the following week I felt uncomfortable when I revisited Tienda Adrian with my advisor and approached the store owners cloaked in my university researcher role to ask about the town. Similarly, I felt the tension of power in my researcher role when I began formal interviews with the women in the Latino community. The interviewing situation was uncomfortable for me, in contrast to the time we had engaged in informal talks about raising and educating children in Hope City.

I felt the tension of power and complicity even more directly when I engaged in social interaction with an English-speaking institutional representative and a Latina client at the same time. I felt this more acutely when service agency providers used English to talk about Latino clients in their presence. The Latina clients, who, for the most part, were new arrivals in Hope City, could not speak English. One particular service provider had the habit of introducing me to a Latina client and then giving me her personal life history right in front of her. In these situations, power was wielded through language, and English became the language of exclusion. The women's personal lives were presented to me like an open book in a language that they did not understand. In having to respond in English to the service provider, I was self-conscious and awkward about the exploitation and "othering" of the women. I did not want to be complicit with the "colonial administrator," but I was unaware that this was how I was being positioned.

My feelings of complicity and guilt, however, led me to engage in small spontaneous subversive strategies and acts of resistance. Any time a community leader spoke in English about a Latina client in her presence, I translated. Sometimes I would change the meanings somewhat so as not to cause embarrassment or hurt. On one occasion, for example, I said, "He's saying that you had gone through some rough times," even though the service agency provider said that she had had a nervous breakdown and had psychological problems. I began to translate into Spanish everything I said to community leaders when Latinos were present.

I also brought politics and subversion to the meetings at which I spoke for the community leaders. I did not always say what they wanted to hear, stirring controversy at one meeting and causing some Whites to react defensively at another. At one meeting at the elementary school, I disrupted the discourse of dominance by not accepting the seat they had saved for me in the front of the room facing the Latino audience. Instead, I took a seat among some Latino friends.

As an ESL instructor, a "maestra," in the Latino community, I am more active in dialogue and discussions with my Latino students than with the community of school and agency professionals. In being able to name and identify the situatedness of my identities, I am beginning to react to my positioning and act toward a transformation of my identity and role as a Chicana educational researcher in a Latino community.

NEGOTIATING IDENTITIES: TOWARD NEW DISCOURSES

I am in the process of my own learning, and it is not my goal to arrive at a final resolution. Rather, I am in continual discovery. Identity and self are multiple and continually remade, reconstructed, reconstituted, and renewed in each new context and situation (Stone 1992). When I left Los Angeles to attend graduate school in the South, I also left behind identities formed against the backdrop of a segregated city and against a historical context of the racial subordination and conquest of Native and Mexican peoples. In my limited and segregated experiences, I only knew Whites as living the middle-class lifestyle, and rarely as working-class people. I defined myself and was defined by this historical relationship.

In North Carolina, at first I believed I had encountered a place where a historically embedded antagonism did not exist between Mexicans and European Americans, as it exists in the Southwest. There is no territorial Alamo to remember, nor a U.S.–Mexico treaty that appropriated one-third of Mexico's land. I seemed to have forgotten the history of the genocide of American Indians and of the slavery and segregation of African Americans. Nevertheless, I believed space existed in which I could enter into new relationships with the majority culture and define new grounds and new terms. Because of this belief, I found it painful to go into the town where I was to conduct my research project, a town where a new immigrant community of Latinos were the objects of oppressive discourses. The old relationships and identities formed against these discourses were being reinscribed in me. In confronting these oppressive discourses of difference, I experienced domination and oppression, and was a party to the exercising of them.

This story demonstrates that some Chicanas/os do not move from marginalization to new positions of privilege associated with university affiliation, as if switching from one seat to another on the bus. We do not suddenly become powerful in our new identities and roles as university researchers. We do not leave one to get to the other. As Chicanas/os and ethnographers of color, we carry our baggage with us—a baggage of marginalization, complicity, and resentment, as well as *orgullo* (pride) and celebration. These are not easily cast away. No doubt it is not too difficult to embrace wholeheartedly the privileges of upward mobility, but to many of us the costs are great. Just as becoming raceless was a strategy for Black adolescents who, in Fordham's (1988) study, had to unlearn their racial identities and cultural behaviors in order to make it through high school and beyond, so must some Chicanas/os do the same. As bilingual, tricultural peoples, we "continually walk out of one culture and into another" (Anzaldúa 1987, p. 77). In Anzaldúa's images, we are straddling multiple worlds, trying to break from colonized identities formed against White supremacy and male dominance and to form a new consciousness: "I am in all cultures, at the same time" (p. 77). We learn to tolerate contradictions and ambiguities of identities and to "seek new images of identities, new beliefs about ourselves" (p. 87).

While I recognize that part of my ongoing process is seeking, forging, and negotiating new images and identities, I am also raging against postmodern renderings of the White middle-class "discovery" that politically and socially situate the ethnographer as synonymous with colonizer, imperialist, and privileged researcher. In this view, it does not matter whether we are Chicanas/os or middle-class White male ethnographers. In the name of a postmodern understanding of identity and privilege, I am led to believe that I am now the same "researcher as colonizer," that I am now privileged, and that I share the same guilt for the same exploitation of the less privileged research participants. In a sense, I was not only being recruited to legitimate the majority culture's discourse of "Latinos as problem," but I am also symbolically being co-opted to legitimate academia's declaration of the postmodern ethnographer as the socially and politically privileged colonizer. In both instances, I am being co-opted to be like the colonizer, the oppressor, in ways that ignore my own struggle as a Chicana against subjugation and marginalization.

Thus, while I recognize my contradictory position and privilege (that come from university affiliation), and while I would gladly serve as a facilitator and translator for the voices of the Latina mothers of a small rural town in North Carolina (if they would have me), I must also see myself as going beyond the role of facilitator. I must see my own historical being and space. I must know that I will not "mimic the colonizers" (Perez 1991, p. 177) and call myself the ethnographer/colonizer, for this insults my gendered, racial memory.

As I look back on my experience in the graduate seminar, I know that in the future I will not be silent, just as I could not be silent any more in the face of the dominant community's attempts to recruit me to their discourses about the Latino population in Hope City. I cannot continue to pretend that as a qualitative researcher in education, I am distanced from intimacy, hope, anger, and a historical collectivity with Latino communities. For these reasons, I cannot be neutral in the field, because to be so is to continue to be complicit in my own subjugation and that of the Latino communities. To take on only the role of facilitator is to deny my own activism. I must recognize that my own liberation and emancipation in relationship with my community are at stake, and that continued marginalization and subjugation are the perils.

I did not seek these confrontations and realizations. They came upon me while I was turned the other way, disengaging myself from the intimacy of Latina sisterhood. They came upon me as I convinced myself that I had to be careful because I was the privileged and thus the colonizer. I was attuned to seeking to reform my relationship with the research participants and to promote their empowerment, without realizing that *I* was being worked on and commodified, that *I* needed to be empowered. I suddenly found myself complicit in my own subjugation, vis-à-vis the dominant public discourse.

In the meantime, I find hope in Fine's (1994) narrative of the way her Latina niece, who was adopted into her middle-class Jewish family, moved in and out of identities as she fought a criminal case for sexual assault. Fine writes:

> Jackie mingled her autobiography with our surveilled borders on her Self and the raced and gendered legal interpretations of her Other by which she was surrounded. She braided them into her story, her deposition. . . . She slid from victim to survivor, from naive to coy, from deeply experienced young woman to child. In her deposition she dismantled the very categories I so worried we had constructed as sediment pillars around her, and she wandered among them, pivoting her identity, her self representations, and, therefore, her audiences. (1994, p. 71)

Herein I find the key: to resist "othering" and marginalization is to use our multiplicity of identities in order to tolerate and welcome the contradictions and ambiguities, as Anzaldúa (1987) writes, so that in our quest for liberation, we also dismantle the categories and the conquering language of the colonizer. In this manner, we "work the hyphen between Self and Other," as Fine (1994, p. 72) challenges us to do, yet we work from within ourselves as the Self/Other, Colonizer/Colonized ethnographer.

Thus, it is important to continue theorizing on the researchers' multiplicity of identities and the implications of this for qualitative research in education. As members of marginalized groups assume more privileged positions in the educational socioeconomic structures of hierarchy, people who were once merely the exotic objects of inquiry are now the inquirers—the ones formulating and asking the questions. As some enter the ranks of teachers, administrators, and scholars, we are becoming the enforcers and legitimators as well as the creators of official knowledge. Hence, as qualitative researchers in the field of education, we need to explore and understand the dilemmas created for Chicanas/os, African Americans, Native Americans, and scholars from other disenfranchised groups vis-à-vis the majority culture. We scholars/activists of color need to understand the ways in which we manipulate our multiple, fluid, clashing, and colonized identities and how our identities are manipulated and marginalized in the midst of oppressive discourses. Luke and Luke (1995) argue, "Only by describing and understanding how power works in oppressive social formations, how identity is shaped both through contestation and collusion with oppressive regimes of control, is it possible to lay down a systematic knowledge of marginal identities" (p. 376).

Further studies are also needed that capture the intricacies of marginalized teachers and scholars who are teaching and researching their own communities. Watson-Gegeo (1994) introduces a collection of articles that illuminate im-

portant questions dealing with "minority" teachers teaching "minority" students.[5] These excellent studies encourage further probing of the questions of resisting, negotiating, and tolerating identities in a context of power and privilege—in other words, to pay close attention to how we manipulate our identities and how our identities are manipulated by others. We need to see how Latino ethnographers, for example, become commodified in the process of research. At the same time, we also need to examine the gender, race, and class dynamics created in the university setting, where for example women of color who are professors and middle-class White students come together (see Vargas 1996). These are critical questions that need further exploration.

CONCLUSION

This story is an attempt to untangle my own multiplicity of identities played out in the terrains of privilege and power in ethnographic research. With the new generation of "native" ethnographers, including myself, increasingly working within and writing about our own communities, we are beginning to question how our histories and identities are entangled in the working of domination as we engage the oppressive discourses of "othering." In my case, while researching in a rural town in North Carolina, I had to confront both my own marginalization and my complicity in "othering" myself and my community, as I encountered the discourse that identified Latino family education and child-rearing practices as "problem" and "lacking."

At a time when qualitative researchers in education are questioning their own privilege in relation to the research participants, the "we" in the literature needs to be retheorized. My identity/role as a Chicana ethnographer cannot be collapsed in terms of "privileged" researcher in the same manner that other ethnographers are privileged in their relationships with their research participants. In failing to address the ways in which the ethnographer can be damaged by her/his own marginalization in the larger society, the literature has created a "we" that does not include my experience in the field as a Chicana ethnographer.

What might this story teach majority-culture ethnographers of education so that they too move beyond the "researcher as privileged" dilemma? I believe they also can confront their own multiplicities of identity and histories of complicity and mark the points of their own marginalization. Rosaldo (1989) and Patai (1991) write that ethnographers cannot escape their complicity in exploiting the "researched," yet I still need to ask, What is the nature of the space that I have found, and what are the possibilities for the Latino community in Hope City, North Carolina? My space is a fluid space of crossing borders and, as such, a contradictory one of collusion and oppositionality, complicity and subversion. For "Hispanos" in Hope City, surrounded by a historically violent and entrenched biracial society in which one is either Black or White, emancipatory possibilities lie in the creation of a dignified public space where they can negotiate new identities and break down the biraciality. Likewise, my challenge to majority-culture ethnographers is that they call upon their own marginalizing experiences and find a space for the emergence of new identities and discourses in the practice of solidarity with marginalized peoples.

My own journey moves me toward new transcendent discourses that are transformative and emancipatory. I hope to be, in Olson and Shopes's words, a "citizen–scholar–activist(s) rooted in the community" (cited in Van Galen and Eaker 1995, p. 120). Recognizing our multidimensional identities as colonizers, colonized, neither, and in-between, we *camaradas* in struggle must work from within and facilitate a process where Latinas/os become the subjects and the creators of knowledge. My answer to the ethnographer-as-colonizer dilemma is that I will not stop at being the public translator and facilitator for my communities, but that I am my own voice, an activist seeking liberation from

my own historical oppression in relation to my communities. We *mojado* ethnographers look anxiously to learn about the rich diversity of Latino communities in the U.S., and in doing so, create our own rich diversity of models, paradigms, and languages as we cross between our communities and "the artificial borders into occupied academic territories" (E. G. Murillo, Jr., personal communication, 1995).

NOTES

1. "Chicano" and Chicana" are self-identified terms used by peoples of Mexican origin. They are political terms of self-determination and solidarity that originated in the Chicano liberation movement of the 1960s.

2. "Hispanic" is a U.S. government term used to classify Spanish-speaking peoples of Latin America living in the United States. "Latino" refers to a collective community of Latin Americans. "Latino" is my chosen term, which I use interchangeably with the emic term "Hispano." I use "Latino" to refer to the very diverse Spanish-speaking community of Hope City (a pseudonym), North Carolina. "Latino" also refers to male members of the community, while "Latina" refers to the women. Members of the Latino community in Hope City usually refer to themselves in national terms: Mexican, Salvadoran, Guatemalan, etc. However, they have also adopted the term "Hispanos" to refer to themselves collectively as a community. It is also important to note that people self-identify differently. For this reason, when I refer to my friends, I use the various terms with which they identify themselves. Also, an "Indigenista" or "Mesocentric" (Godina 1996) perspective has spurred interest among Latinos and peoples of indigenous ancestry between themselves and tribal Native Americans. In essence, through this movement we (including myself) are saying that we *are* Native American people.

3. "Aztlan" refers to the mythical origins and ancient homelands of the Aztec civilization. Over the last 30 years, Aztlan has been popularized by the Chi-

cano liberation movement and is linked to the vast northern territories of Mexico that were invaded and annexed by the United States in 1848.

4. "Othering" refers to objectifying people who are different than the Western White self in a manner that renders them inferior.

5. This edited collection includes articles by Foster (1994) on the views of African American teachers who counter prevailing hegemonic beliefs about African American children in reform efforts to improve their achievement in schools; Watson-Gegeo and Gegeo (1994) on the ways in which a history of colonization and modernization in the Solomon Islands serves to keep teachers' cultural knowledge out of the classroom; and Lipka (1994), who examined how Yup'ik Eskimo teachers in Alaska face administrative barriers when working to include their language and culture in their classrooms.

REFERENCES

Adkins, A., G. Givens, M. McKinney, E. Murillo, and S. Villenas. *Contested Childrearing: The Social Construction of Latino Childrearing.* Paper presented at the meeting of the American Educational Studies Association, Cleveland, OH, November 1995.

Anzaldúa, G. *Borderlands/La Frontera.* San Francisco: Aunt Lute Books, 1987.

Crapanzano, V. "Hermes' Dilemma: The Masking of Subversion in Ethnographic Description." In *Writing Culture,* eds. J. Clifford and G. Marcus. Berkeley: University of California Press, 1986, pp. 51–76.

Delgado-Gaitan, C. "Researching Change and Changing the Researcher." *Harvard Educational Review* 63 (1993), pp. 389–411.

Delgado-Gaitan, C., and H. Trueba. *Crossing Cultural Borders: Education for Immigrant Families in America.* London: Falmer Press, 1991.

Ellsworth, E. "Why Doesn't This Feel Empowering: Working through the Myths of Critical Pedagogy." *Harvard Educational Review* 59 (1989), pp. 297–324.

Fine, M. "Working the Hyphens: Reinventing Self and Other in Qualitative Research." In *Handbook of Qualitative Research,* ed. N. Denzin and Y. Lincoln. Thousand Oaks, CA: Sage, 1994, pp. 70–82.

Fordham, S. "Racelessness as a Factor in Black Students' School Success: Pragmatic Strategy or Pyrrhic Victory?" *Harvard Educational Review* 58 (1988), pp. 54–84.

Foster, M. "The Role of Community and Culture in School Reform Efforts: Examining the Views of African American Teachers." *Educational Foundations* 8, no. 2 (1994), pp. 5–26.

Godina, H. *Mesocentrism: Teaching Indigenous Mexican Culture in the Classroom.* Paper presented at the annual meeting of the American Educational Research Association, New York, April 1996.

hooks, b. *Talking Back: Thinking Feminist, Thinking Black.* Boston: South End Press, 1989.

hooks, b. *Yearning.* Boston: South End Press, 1990.

hooks, b. *Teaching to Transgress: Education as the Practice of Freedom.* New York: Routledge, 1994.

Lather, P. *Getting Smart: Feminist Research and Pedagogy with/in the Postmodern.* New York: Routledge, 1991.

LeCompte, M., and K. de Marrais. "The Disempowering of Empowerment: Out of the Revolution and into the Classroom." *Educational Foundations* 6, no. 13 (1992), pp. 5–31.

Lipka, J. "Schools Failing Minority Teachers: Problems and Suggestions." *Educational Foundations* 8, no. 2 (1994), pp. 57–80.

Luke, C., and A. Luke. "Just Naming? Educational Discourses and the Politics of Identity." In *Continuity and Contradiction: The Futures of the Sociology of Education,* ed. W. Pink and G. Noblit Cresskill, NJ: Hampton Press, 1995, pp. 357–80.

Patai, D. "U.S. Academics and Third World Women: Is Ethical Research Possible?" In *Women's Words: The Feminist Practice of Oral History,* ed. S. Gluck and D. Patai. New York: Routledge, 1991, pp. 137–53.

Perez, E. "Sexuality and discourse: Notes from a Chicana survivor." In *Chicana lesbians: The girls our mothers warned us about,* ed. C. Trujillo. Berkeley, CA: Third Woman Press, 1991, pp. 158–84.

Pratt, M. "Fieldwork in Common Places." In *Writing Culture,* eds. J. Clifford and G. Marcus. Berkeley, CA: University of California Press, 1986, pp. 27–50.

Roman, L., and M. Apple. "Is Naturalism a Move Away from Positivism? Materialist and Feminist Approaches to Subjectivity in Ethnographic Research." In *Qualitative Inquiry in Education: The Continuing Debate,* ed. E. Eisner and A. Peshkin.

New York: Teachers College Press, 1990, pp. 38–73.

Rosaldo, R. *Culture and Truth: The Remaking of Social Analysis.* Boston: Beacon Press, 1989.

Sleeter, C. "Foreword." In *Children and Families "at Promise,"* ed. B. Swadener and S. Lubeck. Albany: State University of New York Press, 1995, pp. ix–xi.

Stone, L. "The Essentialist Tension in Reflective Teacher Education." In *Reflective Teacher Education: Cases and Critiques,* ed. L. Valli. Albany: State University of New York Press, 1992, pp. 198–211.

Swadener, B., and S. Lubeck. Eds. *Children and Families "at Promise."* Albany: State University of New York Press, 1995.

Van Galen, J., and D. Eaker. "Beyond Settling for Scholarship: On Defining the Beginning and Ending Points of Postmodern Research." In *Continuity and Contradiction: The Futures of the Sociology of Education,* ed. W. Pink and G. Noblit. Cresskill, NJ: Hampton Press, 1995, pp. 113–31.

Vargas, L. *When the Other is the Teacher: Implications for Teacher Diversity in Higher Education.* Paper presented at the annual meeting of the Eastern Communication Association, New York City, April 1996.

Watson-Gegeo, K. "Introduction: What's Culture Got to Do with It? Minority Teachers Teaching Minority Students." *Educational Foundations* 8, no. 2 (1994), pp. 3–4.

Watson-Gegeo, K., and D. Gegeo. "Keeping Culture out of the Classroom in Rural Solomon Islands Schools: A Critical Analysis." *Educational Foundations* 8, no. 2 (1994), pp. 27–55.

Weis, L. "Identity Formation and the Process of 'Othering': Unraveling Sexual Threads." *Educational Foundations* 9, no. 1 (1995), pp. 17–33.

CHAPTER 5

The State, Politics, and Public Policy

Most people who know of Catharine A. MacKinnon associate her with opposition to pornography, but MacKinnon, a law professor, theorizes more generally about the state and public policy. *Toward a Feminist Theory of the State,*[1] a collection of her essays, serves as a first-rate introduction to her thinking along these broader lines.

MacKinnon sees "Epistemology and politics . . . as two mutually enforcing sides of the same unequal coin." The state "participate[s] in the sexual politics of male dominance by enforcing its epistemology through law." (p. xi) Like sciences that promote male dominance through methodology and religions that enforce it through doctrine, the state cannot reach beyond society to make laws that treat women and men equally. Therefore, as we will soon see, feminist theories of the state treat "citizenship" as problematic. At the same time, they treat the law as an institution embedded in historically specific cultures that are more or less patriarchal. MacKinnon emphasizes the need to "reformulate the relation between life and law on the basis of the experience of the subordinated, the disadvantaged, the dispossessed, the silenced—in other words, to create a jurisprudence of change." (p. xiv) Such a jurisprudence

> would answer the questions: What is state power? Where, socially, does it come from? How do women encounter it? What is the law for women? How does law work to legitimate the state, male power, itself? Can law do anything for women? (p. 159)

MacKinnon's efforts to formulate a jurisprudence of change center on human sexuality. She argues that many connections, such as those between "sexual stereotyping and women's poverty," get obscured "if sexuality is cabined, less so if it roams the social hierarchy unconfined." (p. xiii)

189

MacKinnon sees gender as "a social system that divides power" and "therefore a political system." Within that system, seen historically,

> women have been economically exploited, relegated to domestic slavery, forced into motherhood, sexually objectified, physically abused, used in denigrating entertainment, deprived of a voice and an authentic culture, and disenfranchised and excluded from public life. Women, by contrast with comparable men, have systematically been subjected to physical insecurity; targeted for sexual denigration and violation; depersonalized and denigrated; deprived of respect, credibility, and resources; and silenced. (p. 160)

Thus, the law dovetails with other institutions' stances toward women, while the liberal state "constitutes the social order in the interest of men as a gender. . . ." (p. 162) From this vantage point, liberalism and liberal feminism become problematic.

RIGHTS, NEEDS, DEMOCRACY, AND THE LIBERAL STATE

"From what political perspective," asks bell hooks, "do we dream, look, create, and take action?"[2] In the thickets of that question stand invitations to consider how "the personal is political," second-wave feminism's best-known shibboleth. Formally, the political is the governmental; informally and more broadly, the political is the contested.[3] In the latter sense whatever involves the play of power is political, whether it be the politics of dating or the politics of reproductive rights.

But the liberal state, probably the most consequential and surely the most pervasive institution of modern life, defies this formal/informal dichotomy. Now a densely bureaucratized welfare state, the liberal state obfuscates issues of power even while brokering deals about rights, needs, and interests. To inquire into one's "political perspective," then, is to ask not only how one goes about being a citizen and wielding power in everyday life but also how one sees her own and others' rights, needs, and interests and whether she usually stands up for underdogs or mostly identifies with the powerful.

To inquire into one's political perspective also means to think about one's stance toward the liberalism associated with the emergence of modern democratic states. As Johanna Brenner says in Reading 12, liberalism makes two assumptions about equality. The first is that merit (and thus hierarchies based on merit) is a meaningful basis for organizing socially necessary work and allocating socially desirable rewards. Liberals deem a system fair when its unequally situated members appear to be positioned on the basis of individual characteristics such as hard work and talent, not social characteristics such as race or gender. The second liberal assumption is that in public life individuals interact as autonomous creatures capable of making contracts for themselves. Whatever dependence individuals exhibit is assumed to reside in the private sphere of kinship and friendship.

Liberalism thus entails deeply, though implicitly, gendered notions. "Merit" is woefully problematic in a world of double standards—one for men, another for women; one for white people, another for people of color; one for heterosexual people, another for bisexual, transgendered, and homosexual people. What counts as merit commonly shows up as "admission requirements," "entry requirements," "qualifications," "standards," or "credentials" demonstrably skewed to favor members of society's dominant groups.

"Independence" is no less problematic. In a society where millions of people are physically challenged, face grinding poverty, struggle with addictions, or are up against chronic under- or unemployment, regarding citizens as independent people is tantamount to disenfranchising much of the population.[4] As a matter of practical fact, we all experience various long- and short-term dependencies across the life cycle. To wit, citizens are better thought of in terms of needs alongside rights rather than mostly in terms of rights.

Yet liberal discourse marginalizes talk about what people need. It puts rights at the forefront, together with historically related notions such as interests, contracts, individual(ism), and representative government. All the while, equal access or equal opportunity serves as its main measure of fairness.[5] Many feminists, particularly in the United States, endorse some version of liberalism, treating women as one interest group among many competing "for a piece of the pie."[6] Yet women are unlike interest groups such as farmers, manufacturers, veterans, and physicians, whose *rights* as individuals are largely secured, if only because their members are mostly men.

Women, however, have not secured full rights as citizens. We remain in the grips of that historical period when "women's rights" is both a call to action and an occasion for resistance. The rights of child-abuse victims, employed parents, part-time employees, minimum-wage workers, single parents, battered spouses, old old people, rape survivors, poor people, welfare recipients, sex workers, and other disproportionately female groupings (never mind exclusively female groupings such as pregnant people) are far from established in countries like the United States. Some, including me, see that circumstance as an outgrowth of the modern state's stubborn liberalism.

As Zillah Eisenstein makes clear, liberalism and feminism fundamentally diverge. At root, liberalism is "patriarchal and individualist" while feminism is "sexual egalitarian and collectivist." Nevertheless, second-wave American feminism involves a "collaboration between the state and liberal feminism" that began roughly with the publication of Friedan's *The Feminine Mystique* (1963) and the founding of the National Organization for Women (NOW; 1966). Eistenstein says the state regards liberal feminism "as the least threatening form and, therefore, has given the liberal part of the movement the most . . . public recognition," in part "by distorting the politics of radical, socialist, and lesbian feminists in such a way as to cut them off from the majority of women."[7]

Much like other scholars, Eisenstein sees liberal feminists as committed to "freedom of choice, individualism, and equality of opportunity." Yet she differentiates among them by looking at "how self-conscious they are about the patriarchal, economic, and racial bias" of liberal ideas. On her feminist political spectrum, which comprises nine groupings, Eisenstein includes three liberal groupings.

Status quo liberal feminists like Phyllis Schlafly "operate as reactionaries today" because they treat the status quo as sufficiently gender-neutral. *Progressive liberal feminists* are less optimistic but do "accept liberal rights theory . . . with little recognition that 'rights' recognize individuals within a structure of sexual, economic, and racial inequality."[8] *Radical liberal feminists* want liberal rights theory reworked enough to take into account sexual, racial, economic, and other inequalities. In Reading 13, Patricia J. Williams articulates this position through a critique of critical legal studies (CLS) focusing on the needs and rights of black citizens. Minimally, she says, the "frame of rights reference" needs enlarging. (Brenner broaches this position in Reading 12 when she observes that "A language of rights does not have to be limited to a narrowly defined meritocratic standard. . . .")

In the end, Eisenstein sees a "real difference" between liberal feminism and liberalism, namely, "feminism is potentially subversive to liberalism and the capitalist patriarchal state."[9] All the while, though, liberal states make bureaucratic room for feminism. In fact, as Hester Eisenstein points out, "femocrat" now has international meaning. Its currency as a term designating feminist government workers is tied in with *state feminism,* which emerged as liberal states established "specific government machinery for women's affairs."[10] Such machinery is well developed in Australia, the Netherlands, Norway, and Denmark, although the United States was among the first countries with a federal agency for women: the Women's Bureau of the Department of Labor, begun in 1920.[11] Such developments parallel the emergence of the liberal welfare state.

THE WELFARE STATE

Nancy Fraser observes that "in welfare-state societies, needs-talk has been institutionalized as a major vocabulary of political discourse" alongside "talk about rights and interests at the very center of political life."[12] Generally, she says, claims about needs involve "*A* needs *x* in order to *y*," which "poses no problems when we are considering very general or 'thin' needs such as food or shelter *simpliciter*." (p. 41) More specific—that is, "thick"—needs occasion debate and controversy, if not gridlock. Most problematic of all, Fraser implies, are the *runaway* (or "leaky") needs, of particular interest to feminists because women's needs often take this shape.

Runaway needs presuppose the liberal separation of the political from the economic and the domestic. To wit, since both domestic and official-economic institutions support relations of dominance and subordination, the specific interpretations they naturalize usually tend . . . to advantage dominant groups and individuals and to disadvantage their subordinates. . . .

Family and official-economy, then, are the principal depoliticizing enclaves which needs must exceed in order to become "political" in . . . male-dominated, capitalist societies.

Thus, Fraser concludes, "Runaway needs are a species of *excess* with respect to the normative modern domestic and economic institutions." (p. 49) She uses child care as an example. Once considered a strictly domestic need—(white) children's need for the full-time attention of their (middle-class) mothers—child care has become an economic need of (female) employees for surrogates to care for their children while they are on the job.

Fraser's analysis makes several key points. "Rights" come with full-fledged citizenship, merit, and independence sufficient to entitle the individual to certain privileges and benefits; "needs" come with second-class citizenship, lack, and dependence extreme enough to qualify the individual for limited "handouts" or "charity." Fraser also implies that resistance to meeting a group's needs will find expression in a rhetoric assigning that responsibility to family, church or synagogue, community, or employers. Today's American welfare state is illustrative, particularly in its embattled relationship with moms and their kids.

The first half of the 20th century entailed two versions of feminism. One was liberal feminism aimed at "ending legal discrimination against women and removing all barriers which prevent their entry into the public sphere on equal terms with men." The other gave priority to women's "immediate material interests" or needs above and beyond "abstract notions of equal rights"; these feminists were disinclined "to place gender interests above class interests."[13] In Europe this latter strand of feminism was more influential than in the United States, where liberal feminists held sway. Both varieties of feminism were responses to a liberal state that

> is masculinist in how it constitutes the identities of workers (wage-earning or property-owning breadwinners) and citizens (rational, autonomous individuals engaging in public/political sphere activities and strong, aggressive defenders protecting their women and their nation). Conversely, it ideologically constitutes women as unpaid wives and homemakers, affective, dependent household members, and passive supporters/followers of their men and their nation.[14]

In liberal states like the United States, as Brenner indicates in Reading 12, there is

> a collective obligation to care only for those individuals who cannot legitimately be asked to care for themselves and who, through no fault of their own, *cannot be cared for within the family system.* Welfare policy has generally been constructed so as to restore the male-breadwinner family, not to substitute for it. . . . Thus men and women have had a very different relationship to

the welfare state. . . . Women have had to prove they are morally deserving (their dependence is assumed), while men have had to prove they are legitimately dependent (their independence is assumed). (emphasis added)

The welfare state is gendered as well as gendering. It both presupposes and furthers institutionalized beliefs about women and men when it channels policymakers, administrators, staffers, and recipients into gender-specific bureaucratic niches. Feminist theorists have spent the past several decades illuminating such patterns.

Linda Gordon observes that their efforts occurred in three stages. Initially, feminists documented sex discrimination in welfare programs and advanced explanations for it. Then they developed critiques of welfare programs, such as Mimi Abramovitz's *Regulating the Lives of Women* (South End Press 1988), the first book-length work of its kind in the United States. Overall, such critiques focus on the two-channel or dual-tier welfare system, wherein some government entitlements are benefits that people (mostly male) have a right to by virtue of having earned them, and others are welfare that people (mostly female) have a need for by virtue of having had their means tested and their economic situation comprehensively assessed. Finally, feminist scholars have been theorizing about women's political influence on the contemporary welfare state. This development is part of a shift away from theorizing the state to theorizing citizenship, especially as a gendered status.[15]

American welfare policy impinges more on female than male citizens and more on citizens of color than white citizens. As Gordon goes on to explain,

The relation of the welfare state to both gender and race as fundamental social divisions is bilateral. These divisions have helped create the need for welfare, but the welfare programs in turn have influenced the nature of the divisions.[16]

Gordon also emphasizes the "mystification accomplished through labeling as 'welfare' only some of those state programs that contribute to citizens' well-being." (p. 9) She thus implies how "welfare" becomes a source of stereotypes about women that build up around the collision of femininity with poverty.

Even though gender serves alongside race and class as "a major organizing principle of the system," scholars generally ignore gender when analyzing the welfare state. (p. 10) Focusing on women in discussions of welfare might disturb the relations of ruling whereby people are led to believe that compliant, other-oriented women reliably get provided for within the patriarchal nuclear family, the job market, and the divorce court. Gordon implies as much when she notes that in the rhetoric of the mass media and congressional debates, "welfare represents deplorable 'dependence,' while women's subordination to husbands is not registered as unseemly." She also notes that men themselves did not become "independent" until the modern era when "wage labor became the norm for men and voting rights were extended to all men. . . ."

Meanwhile, only some women are expected to exhibit parallel independence, namely those who are poor. Other women are still "encouraged to be dependent on their husbands. . . ." (p. 14) As you know, most females coming of age are still expected to partner with men somewhat older and bigger than themselves who also have more schooling and higher earnings. When such partners leave the picture, no system—no welfare system, no employment system, no religious system, no family system—fills in reliably. To the contrary, women on their own are seen as responsible for their own survival, as if no one had ever counseled them to put their husbands and children first, even to the point of quitting school prematurely or taking a part-time rather than a full-time job.

Before turning to welfare policy on mothers and children, let us consider one more observation Gordon makes about American "welfare." She finds that women themselves have often "campaign[ed] for welfare provisions that turned out to be quite discriminatory against women. . . ." (p. 14) Their various persuasions often put feminist activists in political tension with one another. One historical example is the tension between the National Welfare Rights Organization (NWRO) and NOW in the late 1960s and early 70s. Their limited success in working closely together points to how women's diverse circumstances shape their responses to issues like poverty. At the same time, their efforts to coordinate with one another do show how poverty is "inextricably linked to the common barriers faced by women in society, such as violence, wage discrimination, and disproportionate family responsibilities. . . ."[17]

That women of different races and classes tried to work together at all on women's poverty is a story that needs to be told. That they faced painful, sometimes insurmountable, obstacles is one of the threads weaving together its details. In our society that story developed with such force because most women are mothers and mothers are the biggest segment of the adult population affected by the American "welfare" system.

Along those lines, Virginia Sapiro makes a stark assertion: "women's poverty is increased substantially by their economic dependence brought on by the dependence for care that others place on them." Because we care for husbands and daughters and sons and aged parents, women are dramatically more prone to poverty than men. As Sapiro goes on to observe,

> Predominant beliefs and attitudes encompass a dual hierarchy of repsonsibility, one for provision and one for caring. For provision the line extends from the male "head of the family" outward, in ideological terms skipping over the female adult on the grounds that it is less demoralizing for a man to be supported by outside males (or agencies) than to be supported by a woman. For caring, the line extends from the wife and mother outward, in ideological terms skipping over the male adult on the grounds that men are not competent at caring or that their primary role is provision. Here lies another interesting assumption: a man cannot provide *and* care, a combination of efforts faced by most married women today.[18]

Those ideological lines form a thick knot in the "two-channel welfare state." In her study of Work*men*'s Compensation and Mothers' Aid, Barbara J. Nelson shows how that knot got tied early in the 20th century. Passed in 1911 and tightened in 1913, the Mothers' Aid Law in Illinois aimed to support needy mothers. By 1919, there were parallel laws in 39 states. Specifically,

> Mothers' Aid was given in return for an ongoing service rather than in response to a realized risk. For instance, the administrators of Workmen's Compensation cared if alcohol contributed to accidents (such claims were denied), but they did not care, or, more important, they could not control the beneficiary who spent all of his or her benefits on drink. The behavior of Mothers' Aid beneficiaries, on the other hand, was closely monitored. Thus it was the *capacity to care* that was supported in Mothers' Aid.[19]

Bluntly put, the states were paying mothers for nurture that would have cost more outside the home. In effect, mothers were paid for their work, not supported in their need.

Sapiro notes, "Most social policy aimed at women has been designed explicitly to benefit them in their capacity as wives and mothers and more particularly, to benefit those who depend upon them for nurturance and domestic service: husbands, children, and elderly relatives." Such policy aims to help women "to *care* for their families and not, by and large, to *provide* for them in the sense that is expected of a breadwinner." (p. 45) Sapiro concludes that the American "welfare system depends on women either being dependent or taking on what has become known as the 'double burden'" of paid employment and unpaid domestic work and child rearing. In any case, the "most economically vulnerable" women are those "who do the most to fulfill a paternalistic and patriarchal gender ideology." (p. 47)

This "welfare" system, which penalizes women with paltry payments, continual intrusions, multiple indignities, and double binds, assumes that "women are not autonomous individuals and moral agents, but that they live contingent lives." In the end, this so-called welfare system defines women "as individuals who place themselves second." (p. 51) By and large, the terms of such placement revolve around "mother."

American public policy and law treat mothers as worse than second-class citizens. Consider mother-specific crimes. First-year law students come across these in the "omission liability section" of their law casebooks, where most or all of the cases involve "mothers (or women in mothering roles) who failed to care properly for their children." Dorothy E. Roberts (the author of Reading 18) argues that these cases show how criminal law more often "impose[s] an affirmative duty on mothers than other classes of people."[20]

Over the past five years or so, I have been more and more troubled by warnings to pregnant women about smoking, drinking, and other activities capable of affecting the children they will bear. Needless to say, such warnings are important and worthy, but recurrent emphasis on them without parallel public concern for children's well-being strikes me as politically retrograde at best. Overall, such warnings seem aimed as much at controlling medical costs as promoting newborns' well-being, aimed as much at regulating pregnant women as protecting babies' health. Susan Bordo's "Are Mothers Persons?" (Reading 14) shows that just by getting pregnant, an American woman compromises her citizenship because her rights get shorn.

More generally, as Roberts (in Reading 18) and most other feminist theorists recognize, "motherhood [i]s a political institution." Its politicization shows up in divorce and child custody statutes, efforts to regulate reproductive technologies and surrogate motherhood, and continuing struggles to secure women's reproductive rights, as well as in the criminalization of pregnant women's lifestyles insofar as they impinge on their fetuses.

Motherhood also figures in "the laws governing social welfare, including Unemployment Insurance, Aid to Families with Dependent Children, and Social Security Pensions." Each of these programs "undermines the position of Mothers relative to ideal Breadwinners and thus perpetuates a status quo in which the weaker party is the one constructed as Mother."[21]

Even today, only eight of 20 major industrialized countries have established parity in women's and men's pension benefits. *Earnings sharing,* whereby married couples share equally the earnings credited for Social Security during their years of marriage, is but one option that would benefit wives, especially those who spend substantial time outside the labor force or employed part-time.[22] In the meantime, motherhood remains a risky proposition for most women, because "family" policy and welfare provisions remain patriarchy-perpetuating, not woman-friendly.[23]

Because the "role of primary caretaker for children usually brings with it a diminished earning capacity and, thus, a vulnerability to economic pressures,"[24] women who mother are generally more vulnerable than other women. Thanks to sperm donorship, the notion of "limited fathers" is gaining force.[25] Neither the law nor mainstream culture, however, allows for limited mothers. Instead, mothers routinely pay, financially and otherwise, for the nurture they provide their children. Further, women who put their children ahead of careers, community work, and other extra-domestic activities are often seen as having made no choice at all. The persistent notion that women's instincts ensure their motherhood does them a continuing disservice that gets reflected time and again in law and public policy.

THE PUBLIC/PRIVATE DIVIDE

What Carole Pateman calls "liberal social contract theory" defines the state as "a specific set of institutions that stand separate from, but regulate, as an impartial 'umpire,' the private sphere of social life."[26] Many feminist theorists, including Pateman, have severe reservations about that formulation. As this chapter shows, the state scarcely functions impartially when regulating home and hearth, let alone the job market and other aspects of the economy considered in the next chapter. As Iris Marion Young notes, "recent feminist analyses of public and private in modern political theory imply that the ideal of the civic public as impartial and universal is itself suspect." Young concludes that

> Modern normative reason and its political expression in the idea of the civic public . . . has unity and coherence by its expulsion and confinement of everything that would threaten to invade the polity with differentiation: the specificity of women's bodies and desire, the difference of race and culture, the variability or heterogeneity of the needs, the goals and desires of each individual, the ambiguity and changeability of feeling.[27]

Thus, many feminist theorists associate the public/private dichotomy with patriarchy, arguing that the distinction "exists only because of the asymmetric power relations between the sexes."[28] Prominent among such theorists is bell hooks, who characterizes the distinction as

> deeply connected . . . to ongoing practices of domination (especially thinking about intimate relationships, ways racism, sexism, and class exploitation work in our daily lives, in those private spaces—that it is there that we are often most wounded, hurt, dehumanized; there that ourselves are most taken away, terrorized, and broken). The public reality and institutional structures of domination make the private space for oppression and exploitation concrete—real.[29]

Hooks alludes to how many women's issues are anchored in the "private" sphere yet addressed in varying, though often ineffective, ways by the policymakers and legislators who oversee the "public" sphere. A swift survey of these issues demonstrates how the public sphere infiltrates the private sphere sufficiently to make the boundary between them mostly an ideological one helping to sustain the relations of ruling that disadvantage women. As V. Spike Peterson puts it,

> Liberal ideology notwithstanding, the state intervenes in private sphere . . . dynamics in part to impose centralized authority over birth rate patterns, property transmission, and reproduction of appropriately socialized family members, workers, and citizens. The means include laws circumscribing sexual behavior, control of women's reproductive rights, and the promotion (through state policies, public media, and educational systems) of gender, ethnic and race identifications, heterosexism, and particular family forms.[30]

Diane Mitsch Bush has looked at the battered women's movement (BWM) in terms pertinent to our discussion: "By the early 1970s, the BWM defined battering as the result of the gendered power structure of intimate relationships, not a private problem caused by deviant husbands or unresponsive wives." As the problem got attention from policymakers, however, that feminist definition of the situation shifted. Criminalization of battering landed shelters for women in the criminal-justice and mental-health systems. That shift diluted feminists' power to name and define the problem of women battered in their homes by men. Bush says that

> the original emphasis of the BWM on empowerment of women by shifting responsibility for violence from the woman to the perpetrator and locating his actions in a patriarchal power structure was lost as many shelters and their goals became institutionalized. Studies of the antirape movement find a similar process: as rape crisis counseling has become institutionalized, the explicitly feminist definition of the problem is less apparent.

Put differently, institutionalization precludes definitions of the situation that rock the boat by contesting entrenched assumptions. Thus, feminist definitions lose momentum as institutionalization proceeds. Bush concludes, "States do respond to women's movements, but that response is short-circuited by ideology about families as private places where love, not power, organizes interaction and by ideology about women's place in families, the polity and economy."[31]

Such short-circuiting is typical as liberal states address issues anchored in the "private" sphere. One publication powerfully documenting that principle is the Winter 1995 issue of *Hypatia,* focusing on feminist ethics and social policy. The issue looks at combat exclusion from the military, sex-selective abortion, the Family and Medical Leave Act often touted during the Clinton/Gore campaign of 1996, the rise of "unwed fathers' rights," and the needs and rights of disabled individuals.[32] In addition, it looks at immigrant women's particular vulnerability to battering and at pornography, another of those realities often hovering in the gray area between private and public.[33] For most feminists opposed to it, pornography is neither a free-speech nor a private-sphere matter. Instead, antipornography feminists propose adding it

> to the list of unprotected classes of speech, which includes personal libel, "fighting words," slander, incitement to violence, perjury, bribery, criminal solicitation, false advertisement, obscenity, and shouting "fire" without cause in a crowded movie theater.[34]

Like many feminist proposals, this one challenges established understandings about what are public concerns and what are private matters. It thus provokes keen resistance. After all, the public/private dualism reinforces the masculine/feminine one by treating "the family as focused on particularistic and hence inferior concerns, often in conflict with the superior and more universal concerns of the 'public' sphere."[35] Women's citizenship demands that we challenge such oversimplified, even mystified, notions of public and private spheres. As Young puts it,

> Extolling a public realm of manly virtue and *citizenship* as independence, generality, and dispassionate reason entailed creating the private sphere of the family as the place to which emotion, sentiment, and bodily needs must be confined. The generality of the public thus depends on excluding women, who are responsible for tending to that private realm, and who lack the dispassionate rationality and independence required of *good citizens.*[36]

Perhaps women's "good citizenship" demands no less than the oppositional politics Honi Fern Haber advocates, which treats a political theory
as viable when it

> pay[s] attention to . . . those voices or concerns that have been marginalized
> by disciplinary and normalizing power regimes. The broader the political
> sphere the more possibilities exist to give voice to those who have been mar-
> ginalized or silenced, and it is with the voicing of marginalized groups that my
> notion of oppositional politics is primarily concerned.

Haber goes on to observe, "Making the private public, and hence amenable
to political debate, is a necessary step in empowerment."[37] But this step is
not enough. Among other things, we also need reoriented notions about
citizenship. Pateman supplies clues about the sort of citizenship feminists
might help to develop:

> The essential feature of a democratic revision of the "political" is that it is no
> longer conceived as separate from everyday life. It is the area in social life in
> which citizens voluntarily cooperate together and sustain their common life
> and common undertaking.[38]

Citizenship, then, would revolve around making community with one
another. It would entail linking our households to neighborhoods and
linking our neighborhoods with other neighborhoods. The emergent picture entails a politics of community comprising a politics of difference, a
politics of commonality, and a bifocal vision of human dignity that centers on needs as well as rights. Because of our subordinate positioning in
society, our marginalization in mainstream culture, and our historical
human-rights struggle, women command the human resources to forge
such a politics. The prize for taking up that challenge is nothing less than
our full citizenship.

NOTES

1. Catharine A. MacKinnon, *Toward a Feminist Theory of the State* (Cambridge, MA: Harvard University Press, 1989).
2. bell hooks, *Black Looks: Race and Representation* (Boston: South End Press,
   1992), p. 4.
3. Nancy Fraser, "Talking about Needs," *Public Culture Bulletin* 1, no. 1 (Fall
   1988), p. 46.
4. For a deconstruction of "dependency" in "welfare" discourse, see Nancy
   Fraser and Linda Gordon, "'Dependency' Demystified: Inscriptions of Power
   in a Keyword of the Welfare State," *Social Politics* 1, no. 1 (Spring 1994),
   pp. 4–31.
5. Mary Dietz, "Context Is All: Feminism and Theories of Citizenship" in
   Chantall Mouffe (ed.), *Dimensions of Radical Democracy: Pluralism, Citizenship, Community* (London: Verso, 1992), p. 68.
6. Hester Eisenstein, *Inside Agitators: Australian Femocrats and the State*
   (Philadelphia: Temple University Press, 1996), p. xviii.

7. Zillah R. Eisenstein, *The Radical Future of Liberal Feminism* (New York and London: Longman, 1981), pp. 3, 177.
8. *Ibid.,* pp. 229, 230, 231.
9. *Ibid.,* p. 248.
10. H. Eisenstein, *Inside Agitators,* pp. xii, xvi. Eisenstein (p. 217) notes that "Norwegian social scientist and senior public servant Helga Hernes" coined the phrase "state feminism" in a 1987 book. Also see Hester Eisenstein, *Gender Shock: Practicing Feminism on Two Continents* (Boston: Beacon Press, 1991), where she analyzes state feminism, femocrats, and various "feminist interventions" in the political arena.
11. Amy G. Mazur and Dorothy McBride Stetson, "Conclusion: The Case for State Feminism" in Dorothy McBride Stetson and Amy G. Mazur (eds.), *Comparative State Feminism* (Thousand Oaks, CA: Sage, 1995), pp. 276–7; Dorothy McBride Stetson and Amy Mazur, "Introduction" in *ibid.,* p. 2. On the Women's Bureau, see Dorothy McBride Stetson, "The Oldest Women's Policy Agency: The Women's Bureau in the United States" in *ibid.,* pp. 254–71.
12. Fraser, "Talking about Needs," pp. 39–40.
13. Jennifer Dale and Peggy Foster, *Feminists and State Welfare* (London: Routledge & Kegan Paul, 1986), pp. 5–6, 8.
14. V. Spike Peterson, "The Politics of Identification in the Context of Globalization," *Women's Studies International Forum* 19, no. 1/2 (January/April 1996), p. 9.
15. Linda Gordon, "The New Feminist Scholarship on the Welfare State" in Linda Gordon (ed.), *Women, the State, and Welfare* (Madison: University of Wisconsin Press, 1990), pp. 18, 19, 23; Ann Curthoys, "Feminism, Citizenship and National Identity," *Feminist Review* 44 (Summer 1993), p. 34. Sylvia Walby illustrates this shift in "Is Citizenship Gendered?" *Sociology* 28, no. 2 (May 1994), pp. 379–96.
16. Gordon, "The New Feminist Scholarship," pp. 9, 13; also Gwendolyn Mink, "The Lady and the Tramp: Gender, Race, and the Origins of the American Welfare State" in Gordon, *Women, the State, and Welfare,* pp. 92–122.
17. Martha F. Davis, "Welfare Rights and Women's Rights in the 1960s," *Journal of Policy History* 8, no. 1 (1996), pp. 144, 145.
18. Virginia Sapiro, "The Gender Basis of American Social Policy" in Gordon, *Women, the State, and Welfare,* pp. 48, 49.
19. Barbara J. Nelson, "The Origins of the Two-Channel Welfare System" in Gordon, *Women, the State, and Welfare,* pp. 133, 139, 141.
20. Dorothy E. Roberts, "Motherhood and Crime," *Social Text* 42 (Spring 1995), p. 99.
21. M. M. Slaughter, "The Legal Construction of 'Mother'" in Martha Albertson Fineman and Isabel Karpin (eds.), *Mothers in Law: Feminist Theory and the Legal Regulation of Motherhood* (New York: Columbia University Press, 1995), p. 87.
22. Dana Carol Davis Hill and Leann M. Tigges, "Gendering Welfare State Theory: A Cross-National Study of Women's Public Pension Quality," *Gender & Society* 9, no. 1 (February 1995), pp. 103, 109, 115. For a broader look at these issues, see Diane Sainsbury (ed.), *Gendering Welfare States* (Thousand Oaks, CA: Sage, 1994); see also Drude Dahlerup's efforts toward a typology of welfare states in "Learning to Live with the State—State, Market, and

Civil Society: Women's Need for State Intervention in East and West," *Women's Studies International Forum* 17, no. 2/3 (1994), pp. 117–27.

23. Cf. Patricia Spakes, "Equality and Family Policy in International Perspective: Toward a Feminist Theory of the State," *Journal of Sociology and Social Welfare* XXIII, no. 2 (March 1996), pp. 113–30.

24. Slaughter, "The Legal Construction," p. 79.

25. See, for instance, Kate Harrison, "Fresh or Frozen: Lesbian Mothers, Sperm Donors, and Limited Fathers" in Fineman and Karpin, *Mothers in Law,* pp. 167–201.

26. Carole Pateman, *The Problem of Political Obligation: A Critical Analysis of Liberal Theory* (Chichester and New York: John Wiley & Sons, 1979), p. 173.

27. Iris Marion Young, "Impartiality and the Civic Public: Some Implications of Feminist Critiques of Moral and Political Theory" in Seyla Benhabib and Drucilla Cornell (eds.), *Feminism as Critique: On the Politics of Gender* (Minneapolis: University of Minnesota Press, 1987), pp. 66, 67. See also Nancy Fraser, "Rethinking the Public Sphere: A Contribution to the Critique of Actually Existing Democracy," *Social Text* 25/26, pp. 56–80. There she criticizes the conflation of "state apparatus" with "public sphere" and advocates Jurgen Habermas's framework, which bypasses that problem.

28. Gillian Rose, *Feminism and Geography: The Limits of Geographical Knowledge* (Minneapolis: University of Minnesota Press, 1993), p. 16; Joni Lovenduski and Vicky Randall, *Contemporary Feminist Politics: Women and Power in Britain* (Oxford and New York: Oxford University Press, 1993), p. 5.

29. bell hooks, *Talking Back: Thinking Feminist, Thinking Black* (Boston: South End Press, 1989), p. 2.

30. V. Spike Peterson, "The Politics of Identification," p. 8.

31. Diane Mitsch Bush, "Women's Movements and State Policy Reform Aimed at Domestic Violence against Women: A Comparison of the Consequences of Movement Mobilization in the U.S. and India," *Gender & Society* 6, no. 4 (December 1992), pp. 593, 599, 603.

32. See Judith Wagner Decew, "The Combat Exclusion and the Role of Women in the Military," pp. 56–73; Eva Feder Kittay, "Taking Dependency Seriously: The Family and Medical Leave Act Considered in the Light of the Social Organization of Dependency Work and Gender Equality," pp. 8–29; Mary L. Shanley, "Fathers' Rights, Mothers' Wrongs? Reflections on Unwed Fathers' Rights and Sex Equality," pp. 74–103; and Anita Silvers, "Reconciling Equality to Difference: Caring (f)or Justice for People with Disabilities," pp. 30–55, all in *Hypatia: A Journal of Feminist Philosophy* 10, no. 1 (Winter 1995).

33. In the same issue of *Hypatia* cited in note 32, see Uma Narayan, "'Male-Order' Brides: Immigrant Women, Domestic Violence and Immigration Law," pp. 104–19; Alisa L. Carse, "Pornography: An Uncivil Liberty?" pp. 155–82.

34. *Ibid.,* pp. 160–61. For recent critiques of this position, see Katherine J. Patterson, "Pornography Laws as Censorship: Linguistic Control as (Hetero)Sexist Harness," *Feminist Issues* 14, no. 2 (Fall 1994), pp. 91–115; Ellen Willis, "Porn Free: MacKinnon's Neo-Statism and the Politics of Speech," *Transition* 63 (1994), pp. 4–23.

35. Virginia Held, "Birth and Death" in Cass R. Sunstein (ed.), *Feminism and Political Theory* (Chicago: University of Chicago Press, 1990), p. 102.
36. Iris Marion Young, "Polity and Group Difference: A Critique of the Ideal of Universal Citizenship" in Sunstein, *Feminism and Political Theory,* p. 121. See also Carole Pateman, *The Disorder of Women: Democracy, Feminism and Political Theory* (Cambridge: Polity Press, 1989). Pateman says the private/public dichotomy "is, ultimately, what the feminist movement is about." (p. 118)
37. Honi Fern Haber, *Beyond Postmodern Politics: Lyotard, Rorty, Foucault* (New York: Routledge, 1994), pp. 2, 5.
38. Pateman, *The Disorder of Women,* p. 174.

READING 12

Feminist Political Discourses: Radical versus Liberal Approaches to the Feminization of Poverty and Comparable Worth

Johanna Brenner

. . .

A liberal discourse on equality operates with two interrelated assumptions. The first assumption involves issues of organization and allocation: that is, how necessary social functions—governance, education, the production of goods, services, and knowledge—should be organized (hierarchy) and how resources and labor time should be allocated (differential rewards). The second assumption involves the issue of dependence and the related separation of the public and private spheres. Liberal thought assumes that social relationships of economy and polity are created by autonomous, independently contracting individuals. I will lay out each of these assumptions and then show how they are fundamental to feminist political discourse on women's poverty and gendered pay inequity.

A liberal discourse on equality centers on the ideal of meritocracy. Liberal political thought accepts the notion of inequality and hierarchy: some will have more, some less; some will command, others follow; some will create, others only implement. Equality is defined as equal opportunity, and thus, from a liberal perspective, fairness exists when the distribution of individuals within unequal positions reflects their individual qualities—their differential motivation, talent, intelligence, and effort—and not their gender, race, religion, or family background. Liberal demands have changed over time—in the 18th century, they were tied to the free market and unregulated competition; in the 20th century, they are compatible with state intervention in the economy. But there is a continuity in liberal goals and argument. The free market was rejected when it became clear that the market alone would not distribute people in a meritocratic way. Inequalities in familial economic and social status and historic prejudices led to unfair outcomes for meritorious individuals. State intervention was required to ensure equality of opportunity. The goal of 20th-century policy is still a just distribution of individuals within a hierarchy of rewards and power.

. . .

In contrast to the assumptions underlying liberal political thought, socialists (and many radical and socialist feminists) have contended that hierarchy brings out the worst, not the best, in individuals, and that while those at the bottom suffer particularly, everyone is distorted and narrowed by competitive striving. They also contend that collective decision making and responsibility are workable alternative forms of social organization, even in an advanced industrial society, and that such forms promote the full development of individual talents and offer the greatest individual freedom (Ferguson 1984; Mason 1982; Rothschild-Whitt 1979).

The second fundamental assumption of liberal political thought is that dependence belongs in the private sphere—there is no place for dependent individuals either in the notion of economic contract or in the concept of the citizen. Indeed, political citizenship is defined by independence, by the capacity to make choices based on individual self-interest, free from control by others on whom one is dependent. Similarly, wage laborers own their own persons and can sell their labor power as independent contractors. As Daniel Bell so nicely puts it:

> The liberal theory of society was framed by the twin axes of individualism and rationality. The unencumbered individual would seek to realize

Johanna Brenner, "Feminist Political Discourses: Radical versus Liberal Approaches to the Feminization of Poverty and Comparable Worth." *Gender & Society* 1, 4 (December 1987): 447–465. Copyright © 1987 by *Sociologists for Women in Society*. Reprinted by Permission of Sage Publications, Inc.

his own satisfactions on the basis of his work—he was to be rewarded for effort, pluck, and risk—and the exchange of products with others was calculated by each so as to maximize his own satisfactions. Society was to make no judgments between men—only to set the procedural rules—and the most efficient distribution of resources was the one that produced the greatest net balance of satisfactions. (1972, p. 58)

The contribution of women within the family in reproducing the male breadwinner and replacing his labor over a generation is of course hidden in liberal economic theory. The dependence of the whole society, the economy, and political system, on the family and women's work within the family is ignored. As Linda Gordon (1986, p. 81) argues, "Liberal political and economic theory rests on assumptions about the sexual division of labor and on notions of citizens as heads of families." A society of "freely contracting" male citizens relies on the prior existence of the noncontractual relationships of the family. Women and children (and other nonearners) are regarded as dependents of men. How they fare depends on the "effort" and "pluck" of their male protector. Barrett and McIntosh (1982, pp. 48–49) argue that "in order to elevate the morality of the market into an entire social ethic it is necessary to ignore all those members of society who do not themselves enter the market. . . . Those who cannot earn a living are subsumed under those who can." Women's dependence within the family makes them noncitizens (Okin 1979), and their family commitments make them politically suspect (Pateman 1980).

Welfare-state intervention is justified within a political framework that retains the notion of the independent citizen. Just as the society has an obligation to promote the conditions for a free and fair exchange between competing individuals but no obligation to secure their livelihood, the society has a collective obligation to care only for those individuals who cannot legitimately be asked to care for themselves and who, through no fault of their own, cannot be cared

for within the family system. Welfare policy has generally been constructed so as to restore the male-breadwinner family, not to substitute for it (Lewis 1983; Zaretsky 1982). Thus men and women have had a very different relationship to the welfare state and different ways of legitimating their claims to state support. Women have had to prove they are morally deserving (their dependence is assumed); while men have to prove they are legitimately dependent (their independence is assumed). For example, the rules and regulations of workmen's compensation, disability programs, and unemployment insurance, developed primarily in response to the demands and needs of male workers, require that workers prove either that they are no longer "able-bodied" (in the first two instances) or that they are without work through no fault of their own (Nelson 1984).

ALTERNATIVE FRAMEWORKS

The radical alternative to the liberal framework has argued for interdependence and the legitimate claim of each individual on the community to meet his or her needs for good and productive work, physical sustenance, emotional support, and social recognition. Radical and socialist feminists have further argued that men are as dependent on women's unpaid labor (including women's emotional work) as women are on men's income and that parenthood is a social contribution and should be recognized as such. Socialist feminists have envisioned a society in which the right to contribute and the right to be cared for are equally shared by men and women. This depends on a reformulation of individual and collective responsibilities and the redistribution of material resources such that the care of dependent individuals is no longer primarily a private responsibility of the family (Barrett and McIntosh 1982).

Feminists have of course been divided on how to approach the state: whether to demand "a fair field and no favor" or "protection" (Kessler-Harris

1982; Lewis 1986). The comparable worth campaign is organized around the first approach—it is essentially a campaign to rectify distortions of the market, which has failed to reward women according to the value of their work. It therefore appeals directly to the liberal principle of meritocracy. The feminization-of-poverty campaign is organized around the second approach—it aims to rectify men's failure to provide for their wives through refusal of child and spousal support (in the case of divorced women) or through lack of life insurance (in the case of widows). Women's claims on the state for support are justified by their lack of a male breadwinner. In the rest of this article, I will discuss the ways in which the feminization-of-poverty and comparable worth campaigns reflect a liberal political discourse, outline the likely consequences, and suggest an alternative approach.

FEMINIZATION OF POVERTY

Two central assertions of the feminization-of-poverty campaign—"Divorce produces a single man and a single mother," "40 percent of ex-husbands contribute nothing to their children's support"—link women's poverty primarily to men's failure to support their families. They also picture women's poverty as something that happens even to good middle-class people. In this regard, the campaign shares with earlier feminist campaigns, such as the campaigns for women's legal right of separation and for mothers' pensions, an imagery of female victimization. While attempting to provide women an alternative to marriage, these campaigns operated within ideological terms and political limits that assumed rather than undermined the male-breadwinner family (Boris and Bardaglio 1983; Pleck 1983).

Like those campaigns, the feminization-of-poverty campaign responds to a real problem facing women and has a potentially radical side. On the other hand, also like those campaigns, in seeking to legitimize their demands and to be most effective in gathering political support, feminists have appealed to broadly held liberal political values and assumptions. As Folbre (1984) argues, the increasing pauperization of motherhood reflects a consensus that AFDC mothers are not among the "deserving" poor. The feminization-of-poverty campaign attempts to change this perception. Portraying poor women as innocent victims of men's irresponsibility may win sympathy for the plight of poor women but at the cost of failing to challenge deeply held notions about feminine dependence on a male breadwinner and distinctions between the deserving and the nondeserving poor, in particular between the "good" woman who is poor because her husband refuses support and the "bad" woman who is poor because she has had a child outside of marriage or has married a poor man who cannot provide.

The feminization-of-poverty literature often assumes that women of all races and classes have a common destiny as poor single heads of families following divorce or widowhood. It is true that generally women's standard of living declines after divorce, while their ex-husbands' standard of living rises (Weitzman 1985). But relative deprivation is not impoverishment. Some women, for example, those with more affluent ex-husbands, those employed during marriage, and those with marketable job skills, are less likely to end up poor or near-poor (Weiss 1984; Weitzman 1985). Race and ethnic differences are quite striking in this regard. The 1983 median income for Black and Hispanic women maintaining families was only 60 percent of the median income of white women maintaining families—$7,999 and $7,797 compared with $13,761. The unemployment rate for Black and Hispanic women maintaining families is double that of white women—18.7 percent and 16.7 percent compared with 8.6 percent (Alliance against Women's Oppression 1983). While many white women are "only a husband away from poverty," many minority women *with* a husband are poor: 13.8 percent of all Black married-couple families were below the poverty level, compared with 6.3 percent of all white married-couple families (Bureau of the Census 1984a).

A study comparing separated and divorced women with children whose family income when married had been in the upper, middle, or lower third of the income distribution showed that while divorce and separation had a leveling effect, significant differences in postdivorce or separation income remained among women even after five years. Women who when married had a family income in the top third lost the most (50 percent of family income); women in the poorest third experienced the least drop (22 percent of family income). But women from the highest third income bracket had postdivorce or separation incomes twice that of women from the lowest third, and 131 percent of the income of women from the middle third, because women from more affluent marriages were more likely to receive alimony and child support (Weiss 1984). Women from the lowest third income bracket were most likely to be eligible for welfare and food stamps (71 percent in the first year). In the first year, only one-fourth of the women from marriages in the middle third income bracket received welfare or food stamps, dropping to one-eighth by the fifth year.

In addition to ignoring class and race differences among women, the feminization-of-poverty campaign denies the poverty of men, especially minority men. Women make up an increasing proportion of the poor because more women are falling into poverty, not because more men are getting out. As Malvaux (1985) argues, the slogan that "by the year 2,000 all the poor will be women and children," is true only if genocide (or full employment) is planned for minority men.

One reason poor women outnumber poor men is that men have a shorter life span: after age 65 there are 1.5 women for every one man. However, older Black men are twice as likely to be poor as older white women (and three times more likely to be in poverty than older white men). Hispanic men over 65 are also more im-

poverished than white women—20.7 percent compared with 7.2 percent (Bureau of the Census 1984a). In 1984, white widows had a mean family income of $23,469 and an average income per family member of $8,331, compared with a mean family income of $13,464 and $3,663 per family member for widowed Black women, and $15,503 and $4,515 per family member for widowed Hispanic women (Bureau of the Census 1984b).

The astonishing growth in families headed by a woman between 1970 and 1984 (from 11.5 percent to 22.9 percent overall and from 33 percent to 56 percent among Blacks) and the consequent increasing poverty of women may be the result, at least in part, of the economic structure rather than men's neglect of their familial responsibilities. Many Black men do not have access to steady employment and higher paid work. Stack (1975) describes the cross-household survival networks that organize family life among poor Blacks. Black fathers may contribute to their children's support while living in a different female-headed household. In 1979, 15 percent of Black men aged 25–60 were living in households in which they were not the head, compared with 6 percent of white men in the same age group (Bureau of the Census 1980). For the underclass, minority or white, poverty is not simply a problem of women without men—it includes their sons, husbands and ex-husbands, and fathers.

When the feminization-of-poverty campaign focuses on the increased standard of living of divorced men compared with that of their ex-wives and looks to child-support enforcement legislation as a solution to women's poverty, it fails to address this reality. By 1984, in the United States, never-married women constituted one-half of the household heads among Black women-headed families. Sixty percent of these women are under 30; Black men between the ages of 15 and 29 (who are most likely to be the fathers of these women's children) do not make enough money to support them—a substantial proportion have no income and a majority make less than $10,000 a year (Simms 1985/6). A California study found that half of the ex-husbands of women in the welfare system made incomes under $15,000 a year (Women's Economic Agenda Project n.d.).

There is surely a fine but very important line between the feminist demand that men take responsibility for their children and the antifeminist demand that men have the obligation to be the family breadwinner. The new right recognized the poverty of abandoned women. Their solution is to force men to support women and children by making divorce more difficult (in order to tie men to their families), to force women on welfare to name the child's father and how to find him, and so forth (Ehrenreich and Stallard 1982). The claim that women's poverty is caused by deadbeat fathers, similar to the claim that black poverty is caused by teenage mothers, is not only factually incorrect but looks to the restoration of the nuclear family as the solution to the problem of dependent care (Darity and Myers 1980; Sarvasy and Van Allen 1984).

In the face of political opposition and constricted government budgets, expanded public services for single mothers—increased eligibility for means-tested benefits, inexpensive quality child care—will not be easy to win. The desperate need of poor women may seem to justify the use of whatever arguments appear politically effective. However, we ought to be alerted to the dangers of this temptation by the way that previous reform campaigns (for example, for protective legislation for women workers) appealed to prevailing gender ideals and thereby contributed to perpetuating a gender ideology that justified women's exclusion from public life (Brenner and Ramas 1984; Kessler-Harris 1982).

The alleviation of women's poverty ought to be incorporated in a broader program of social and economic change. The familistic ideology and state policy that denies collective responsibility for dependent individuals, forces women to take on the burdens for caring, and assumes

that only men have a claim to economic independence and citizenship, must be transformed. For instance, a comprehensive system of supplements to low-income households, regardless of their composition, would benefit all the poor and near-poor, including women-headed families. Paid parental leave (for meeting the needs of older children as well as infants) would benefit single mothers as well as help men and married women to combine wage work and care giving.

In the longer run, a living wage, quality child care, and good work are necessary for everyone, but especially for women who choose not to share child care with a man. A program that incorporates short-term reforms into the larger goal of expanded social responsibility for caring would counteract both the stereotypical dependence of women as care givers and the stereotypical independence of men as citizen–workers. This approach would frame the feminization-of-poverty issue in a way that connects it to the movements of working-class people and people of color (Sarvasy and Van Allen 1984).

COMPARABLE WORTH

As its proponents have argued, comparable worth focuses attention on the systematic devaluation of women's work and the roots of that devaluation in a general cultural denigration of women and womanly activities. Unlike equal pay and affirmative action programs, comparable worth offers the possibility of raising the wages of the vast majority of women working in jobs that have traditionally been held mostly by women. Trade unions, especially in the public sector, have embraced comparable worth as a strategy for raising their members' wages, and many working women have been brought into union activities around the issue.

Because it has been taken up by trade unions and because it has met resistance from employers, employer organizations, and conservatives, comparable worth advocates have tended to assume that the issue has radical or potentially radical force. Hartmann and Treiman (1983, p. 416) argue: "Claims of comparable worth force explicit discussion about relative pay rates. As such, they politicize wage setting in a new, possibly even revolutionary, way." Similarly, Feldberg (1984, p. 313) argues that comparable worth "has radical implications because it initiates an end to women's economic dependency and questions the market basis of wages."

Comparable worth is often referred to as the civil rights issue of the 80s. Yet the significance of comparable worth as a remedy to women's low pay and to occupational segregation is limited. Its application has been most effective in public-worker settings because these workers are often unionized and because it is possible for these unions to bring pressure through legislatures or elected officials. The state of Washington finally bargained a comparable worth settlement with the American Federation of State, County and Municipal Employees even though the union's comparable worth lawsuit had lost on appeal. San Francisco was forced to give comparable worth raises to women and members of minority groups, a step Mayor Diane Feinstein resisted, after voters approved a ballot measure directing city officials to resolve the pay inequities (*New York Times* 1987). Without such political pressure, the chances for imposing comparable worth on the private sector through the courts are slim, at least in the near future, since such suits are rarely won (Hutner 1986) and only a small proportion of women employees in the private sector are unionized (*Monthly Labor Review* 1986).

While a demand for recognition of the value of their work and higher pay is a possible strategy for all women workers, raising wages by equating women's and men's wages in comparable jobs will not work in industries, such as insurance, in which men are employed mostly at the top and middle and women at the bottom (Remick 1984a). Affirmative action remains crucial to encouraging women's employment in nontraditional occupations and management. Furthermore, as even its supporters (Feldberg 1984; Malvaux 1985/6) point out, comparable worth will not improve the access of women of color to jobs and education.

As a political discourse, comparable worth's fundamental claim to legitimacy reinforces an existing ideology: the necessity and validity of meritocratic hierarchy. Rather than questioning the market as an arbiter of wages, comparable worth, as two of its most prominent advocates say, attempts to:

> pay a fair market wage to jobs historically done by women. This means that the wage rate should be based on the productivity-based job content characteristics of the jobs and not on the sex of the typical job incumbent. . . . Comparable worth advocates seek to disentangle and remove discrimination from the market. (Remick and Steinberg 1984, p. 289)

Job evaluations use wage surveys to fix a dollar value to the factor points for benchmark jobs, which are then used to establish a salary scale. Job evaluations measure only the traits of jobs; the money value of the traits is determined by the wages prevailing in the labor market (Aldrich and Buchele 1986). Thus comparable worth aims primarily to rationalize the existing sorting and selecting of individuals into unequal places and does *not* eliminate market criteria from job evaluation.

From this point of view, comparable worth is a relatively conservative approach to women's low pay in that it situates its rationale firmly within the hegemonic liberal political discourse. A radical approach to women's low pay would not only challenge the existing inequalities between women's and men's pay for comparable jobs, but would also contest the notion that people's income should be determined primarily by where they fit in an occupational hierarchy. If jobs are assessed in terms of their necessity to an integrated labor process, it is equally important that *all* jobs be done consistently and well. Anyone who contributes his or her best efforts in a particular job is as deserving as any other individual.

Western contemporary society will not accept "from each according to his/her ability, to each according to his/her need" as a standard of fairness. Nonetheless, the claim that everyone who labors deserves to live decently has been, particularly in periods of working-class mobilization, a central value. Of course, historically, the trade union movement appealed to the right of the working *man* to make a family wage. Perhaps because the strategy has served to institutionalize women's marginalization in wage labor, feminists have preferred to address the problem of women's low pay in terms other than women's life needs as individuals and as mothers. Perhaps also because it relies on broadly shared meritocratic values, comparable worth may appear to be a practical approach to raising women's pay. But so long as comparable worth efforts remain within that liberal discourse, they risk eventually increasing racial and occupational divisions among working women.

The heart of the comparable worth strategy is the job evaluation. Certain dimensions of every job are measured and given a numerical rating: knowledge and skill, effort, responsibility, and working conditions are the major dimensions used. These dimensions are weighted. Typically, skill and responsibility are given higher weights than working conditions. In the Hay study on which an Idaho State employee's comparable worth adjustment was based, the weight given the dimension of responsibility was 42 times the weight given to working conditions (Treiman 1984). Supervision of other people and responsibility for money or expensive equipment are measures that may not reflect responsibilities typical of women's jobs.

McArthur (1985) argues that important dimensions of jobs are left out of most job evaluations. Opportunity for advancement, job security, and how boring a job is might also be considered as compensable factors; jobs might deserve higher compensation not only for poor physical working conditions but for poor psychological conditions. Of course, as she also reports, the more desirable a job is, the higher people judge its monetary worth, not the other way around. Therefore, the impact of a job evaluation scheme on a given work force will depend on how the evaluations are constructed. Treiman (1984) demonstrates that evaluation methods that put a low value on working conditions and physical strength will tend to assign higher scores to jobs typically done by whites. He concludes:

> The choice of factors and factor weights in job evaluation schemes should not be regarded as a technical issue beyond the purview of affected parties but rather as an expression of the values underlying notions of equity and hence as a matter to be negotiated as part of the wage-setting process. (p. 89)

To evaluate the probable impact of comparable worth, then, we need to consider who will participate in the negotiations over the factors and factor weights and with what sorts of assumptions. Since less than one-fifth of the U.S. work force and only 13 percent of all U.S. women workers are unionized (*Monthly Labor Review* 1986), we can expect that in most cases, technical experts and management will formulate the evaluation policies. We can further expect that existing cultural biases in factors and factor weights will be replicated. Acker (1986) demonstrates how difficult it is to overcome experts' and managers' resistance to altering evaluation systems even in a unionized and public setting, especially when alterations might change the rank order of jobs or undermine pay differentials between management and nonmanagement employees.

Malvaux (1985/6) contends that Black men and women will benefit from comparable worth adjustments, because the jobs held by Black women and men tend to be even more underpaid relative to comparable white men's jobs than are white women's jobs. However, the implementation of a job evaluation scheme that all parties agree is equitable may legitimize large differences in pay among employees by race and occupation. Even after the implementation of comparable worth among Washington State employees, one of the highest nonmanagement women's jobs will pay 149 percent of one of the lowest women's jobs (calculated from Remick 1984a). Estimating the impact of comparable worth adjustments under different conditions, Aldrich and Buchele (1986) found the earnings gap between women workers by quintiles would be reduced by at most 6.5 percent. Since women are not distributed proportionately by race within job categories, large inequalities by race will remain, but appear to be reflections of differential merit and thus ultimately difficult to challenge.

Comparable worth may also exacerbate hierarchies in women's jobs. For example, hospital administrations do not currently award differential salaries among nursing specialties, although there is a clear hierarchy of rewards to medical specialties. Remick (1984b, p. 97) predicts that job evaluation systems may expose "internal squabbles that will have to be dealt with by the nursing profession." At hearings conducted by the U.S. Equal Employment Opportunities Commission in 1980, the American Nurses Association testified to the similarities between intensive care unit nurses and doctors (Eyde 1983). Comparable worth adjustments may encourage nurses with such specialties to claim higher pay.

Comparable worth may very well open up discussion of how society values work, but that discussion must be framed by a broader challenge to the prevailing culture. The superior value of mental over manual skills and the greater importance of supervisory over other kinds of responsibility should not be assumed but questioned. Otherwise, we can expect comparable worth to readjust women's and men's pay but to change very little, perhaps even to solidify, the existing divisions in the work force:

divisions between whites and minority workers, between designated professionals and nonprofessionals, between white-collar and blue-collar workers. These divisions cut across gender and have been an important source of trade-union disunity. Yet any radical potential for "politicizing the wage-setting process" depends on the strength of worker organization.

Gender divisions within the work force have played an important part in perpetuating women's low pay. Male-dominated trade unions have been willing to take up the issue only as women workers have become organized. The kind of strategies used for raising the pay of women workers can undermine or aggravate men's resistance, increase or decrease the possibilities for overcoming employer opposition, and create a more unified—or more divided—work force.

Job evaluation studies often find men's job classes "overpaid" for the content of their jobs, especially craft jobs, which tend to be held by white men (Farnquist et al. 1983). Since market realities may be felt to require relatively higher wages in order to recruit and hold those workers and it may be illegal to equalize pay scales by lowering men's wages, most plans attempt to achieve equity over a long run by gradually increasing women's wages. Some plans freeze men's wages; others simply raise men's wages more slowly, for example, giving all workers a cost-of-living raise and women workers an equity bonus. The plan selected influences the impact of a comparable worth settlement on relationships between the men's and women's sections of a work force. Freezing men's wages is divisive, but because it is cheaper, comparable worth adjustments will probably take that route, except when worker organization and union leadership mount effective opposition.

A less divisive strategy is to adjust women's wages to a level commensurate with the intrinsic value of their work. In the strike by women clericals at Yale, the union demanded higher pay on the ground that the women made an important

Mason, Ronald M. *Participatory and Workplace Democracy: A Theoretical Development in Critique of Liberalism.* New York: Basic Books, 1982.

McArthur, Leslie Zebrowitz. "Social Judgment Biases in Comparable Worth Analysis." In *Comparable Worth: New Directions for Research,* ed. H. I. Hartmann. Washington, DC: National Academy Press, 1985, pp. 53–70.

Monthly Labor Review. "Union Membership for Employed Wage and Salary Workers, 1985." 109 (1986), pp. 44–6.

Nelson, Barbara J. "Women's Poverty and Women's Citizenship: Some Political Consequences of Economic Marginality." *Signs* 10 (1984), pp. 209–31.

New York Times. "San Francisco Agrees to Pay Raise for Women." (March 20, 1987).

Okin, Susan. *Women in Western Political Thought.* Princeton, NJ: Princeton University Press, 1979.

Pateman, Carole. "'The Disorder of Women': Women, Love, and the Sense of Justice." *Ethics* 91 (1980), pp. 20–34.

Pleck, Elizabeth. "Feminist Responses to 'Crimes Against Women,' 1868–1896." *Signs* 8 (1983), pp. 451–70.

Remick, Helen. "Major Issues in *a priori* Applications." In *Comparable Worth and Wage Discrimination,* ed. Helen Remick. Philadelphia: Temple University Press, 1984a, pp. 99–117.

———. "Dilemmas of Implementation: The Case of Nursing." In *Comparable Worth and Wage Discrimination,* ed. Helen Remick. Philadelphia: Temple University Press, 1984b, pp. 90–8.

——— and Ronnie J. Steinberg. "Technical Possibilities and Political Realities: Concluding Remarks." In *Comparable Worth and Wage Discrimination,* ed. Helen Remick. Philadelphia: Temple University Press, 1984, pp. 285–302.

Rothschild-Whitt, Joyce. "The Collectivist Organization: An Alternative to Rational Bureaucratic Models." *American Sociological Review* 44 (1979), pp. 509–27.

Sarvasy, Wendy, and Judith Van Allen. "Fighting the Feminization of Poverty: Socialist-Feminist Analysis and Strategy." *Review of Radical Political Economics* 16 (1984), pp. 89–110.

Simms, Margaret C. "Black Women Who Head Families: An Economic Struggle." *Review of Black Political Economy* 14 (1985/6), pp. 140–51.

Stack, Carol B. *All Our Kin: Strategies in a Black Community.* New York: Harper & Row, 1975.

Treiman, Donald J. "Effect of Choice of Factor and Factor Weights in Job Evaluation." In *Comparable Worth and Wage Discrimination: Technical Possibilities and Political Realities.* Philadelphia: Temple University Press, 1984, pp. 79–89.

Weiss, Robert S. "The Impact of Marital Dissolution on Income and Consumption in Single-Parent Households." *Journal of Marriage and the Family* 24 (1984), pp. 115–27.

Weitzman, Lenore J. *The Divorce Revolution: The Unexpected Social and Economic Consequences for Women and Children in America.* New York: Free Press, 1985.

Women's Economic Agenda Project. *Women's Economic Agenda.* Oakland, CA: Author, n.d.

Zaretsky, Eli. "The Place of the Family in the Origins of the Welfare State." In *Rethinking the Family: Some Feminist Questions,* ed. Barrie Thorne with Marilyn Yalom. New York: Longman, 1982, pp. 188–220.

READING 13

The Pain of Word Bondage (a tale with two stories)

Patricia J. Williams

Some time ago, Peter Gabel and I taught a contracts class together. (He was one of the first to bring critical theory to legal analysis and so is considered a "founder" of Critical Legal Studies [CLS].) Both recent transplants from California to New York, each of us hunted for apartments in between preparing for class. Inevitably, I suppose, we got into a discussion of trust and distrust as

Reprinted by permission of the publishers from *The Alchemy of Race and Rights* by Patricia J. Williams, Cambridge, MA: Harvard University Press. Copyright © 1991 by President and Fellows of Harvard College.

factors in bargain relations. It turned out that Peter had handed over a $900 deposit in cash, with no lease, no exchange of keys, and no receipt, to strangers with whom he had no ties other than a few moments of pleasant conversation. He said he didn't need to sign a lease because it imposed too much formality. The handshake and the good vibes were for him indicators of trust more binding than a form contract. At the time I told Peter he was mad, but his faith paid off. His sublessors showed up at the appointed time, keys in hand, to welcome him in. There was absolutely nothing in my experience to prepare me for such a happy ending. (In fact I remain convinced that, even if I were of a mind to trust a lessor with this degree of informality, things would not have worked out so successfully for me: many Manhattan lessors would not have trusted a black person enough to let me in the door in the first place, paperwork, references, and credit check notwithstanding.)

I, meanwhile, had friends who found me an apartment in a building they owned. In my rush to show good faith and trustworthiness I signed a detailed, lengthily negotiated, finely printed lease firmly establishing me as the ideal arm's-length transactor.

As Peter and I discussed our experiences, I was struck by the similarity of what each of us was seeking, yet with such polar approaches. We both wanted to establish enduring relationships with the people in whose houses we would be living; we both wanted to enhance trust of ourselves and to allow whatever closeness was possible. This similarity of desire, however, could not reconcile our very different relations to the tonalities of law. Peter, for example, appeared to be extremely self-conscious of his power potential (either real or imagistic) as white or male or lawyer authority figure. He therefore seemed to go to some lengths to overcome the wall that image might impose. The logical ways of establishing some measure of trust between strangers were an avoidance of power and a preference for informal processes generally.[1]

On the other hand, I was raised to be acutely conscious of the likelihood that no matter what degree of professional I am, people will greet and dismiss my black femaleness as unreliable, untrustworthy, hostile, angry, powerless, irrational, and probably destitute.[2] Futility and despair are very real parts of my response. So it helps me to clarify boundary; to show that I can speak the language of lease is my way of enhancing trust of me in my business affairs. As black, I have been given by this society a strong sense of myself as already too familiar, personal, subordinate to white people. I am still evolving from being treated as three-fifths of a human, a subpart of the white estate. I grew up in a neighborhood where landlords would not sign leases with their poor black tenants, and demanded that rent be paid in cash; although superficially resembling Peter's transaction, such informality in most white-on-black situations signals distrust, not trust. Unlike Peter, I am still engaged in a struggle to set up transactions at arm's length, as legitimately commercial, and to portray myself as a bargainer of separate worth, distinct power, sufficient *rights* to manipulate commerce.

Peter, I speculate, would say that a lease or any other formal mechanism would introduce distrust into his relationships and he would suffer alienation, leading to the commodification of his being and the degradation of his person to property.[3] For me, in contrast, the lack of formal relation to the other would leave me estranged. It would risk a figurative isolation from that creative commerce by which I may be recognized as whole, by which I may feed and clothe and shelter myself, by which I may be seen as equal— even if I am stranger. For me, stranger–stranger relations are better than stranger–chattel.

The unifying theme of Peter's and my discussions is that one's sense of empowerment defines one's relation to the law, in terms of trust/distrust, formality/informality, or rights/no-rights ("needs"). In saying this I am acknowledging points that are central in most CLS literature—

that rights may be unstable and indeterminate. Despite this recognition, however, and despite a mutual struggle to reconcile freedom with alienation, and solidarity with oppression, Peter and I found the expression of our social disillusionment lodged on opposite sides of the rights/needs dichotomy.

On a semantic level, Peter's language of circumstantially defined need, of informality, solidarity, overcoming distance, sounded dangerously like the language of oppression to someone like me who was looking for freedom through the establishment of identity, the formulation of an autonomous social self. To Peter, I am sure, my insistence on the protective distance that rights provide seemed abstract and alienated.

Similarly, while the goals of CLS and of the direct victims of racism may be much the same, what is too often missing is acknowledgment that our experiences of the same circumstances may be very different; the same symbol may mean different things to each of us. At this level, the insistence of certain scholars that the "needs" of the oppressed should be emphasized rather than their "rights" amounts to no more than a word game. The choice has merely been made to put needs in the mouth of a rights discourse—thus transforming need into a new form of right. "Need" then joins "right" in the pantheon of reified representations of what it is that you, I, and we want from ourselves and society.

Although rights may not be ends in themselves, rights rhetoric has been and continues to be an effective form of discourse for blacks. The vocabulary of rights speaks to an establishment that values the guise of stability, and from whom social change for the better must come (whether it is given, taken, or smuggled). Change argued for in the sheep's clothing of stability ("rights") can be effective, even as it destabilizes certain other establishment values (segregation). The subtlety of rights' real instability thus does not render unusable their persona or stability.

What is needed, therefore, is not the abandonment of rights language for all purposes, but an attempt to become multilingual in the semantics of evaluating rights. One summer when I was about six, my family drove to Maine. The highway was straight and hot and shimmered darkly in the sun. My sister and I sat in the back seat of the Studebaker and argued about what color the road was. I said black, she said purple. After I had harangued her into admitting that it was indeed black, my father gently pointed out that my sister still saw it as purple. I was unimpressed with the relevance of that at the time; but with the passage of years, and much more observation, I have come to see endless overheated highways as slightly more purple than black. My sister and I will probably argue about the hue of life's roads forever. But the lesson I learned from listening to her wild perception is that it really is possible to see things—even the most concrete things—simultaneously yet differently; and that seeing simultaneously yet differently is more easily done by two people than one, but that one person can get the hang of it with time and effort.

In addition to our different word usage, Peter and I had qualitatively different experiences of rights. For me to understand fully the color my sister saw when she looked at a road involved more than my simply knowing that her "purple" meant my "black." It required as well a certain slippage of perception that came from my finally experiencing how much her purple felt like my black:

> Wittgenstein's experiments in some of the passages of his *Zettel* teach us about multiple perception, ellipsis and hinging, as well as about seeing and saying. He speaks of "entering the picture" . . . and indeed his tricks try out our picture as our thought. . . . Ambivalence is assumed. It is as if the imagination were suddenly to be stretched: "Suppose someone were to say: 'Imagine this butterfly exactly as it is, but ugly instead of beautiful'?! . . . The transfer we are called upon to make includes a . . . stretching not just of the imagination, but of the transfer point. . . . "It is

as if I were told: here is a chair. Can you see it clearly?—Good—now translate it into French!"[4]

In Peter's and my case, such a complete transliteration of each other's experience is considerably harder to achieve. If it took years for me to understand my own sister, probably the best that Peter and I can do—as friends and colleagues, but very different people—is to listen intently to each other so that maybe our children can bridge the experiential distance. Bridging such gaps requires listening at a very deep level, to the uncensored voices of others. To me, therefore, one of the most troubling positions advanced by some in CLS is that of rights' *disutility* in political advancement. The CLS disutility argument is premised on the assumption that rights' rigid systematizing may keep one at a permanent distance from situations that could profit from closeness and informality: "It is not just that rights-talk does not do much good. In the contemporary United States it is positively harmful."[5] Furthermore, any marginal utility to be derived from rights discourse is perceived as being had at the expense of larger issues, rights being pitted against, rather than asserted on behalf of, agendas of social reform. This line of reasoning underlies much of the rationale for CLS's abandonment of rights discourse and for its preference for informality— for restyling, for example, arguments about rights to shelter for the homeless into arguments about the needs of the homeless.[6]

Such statements, however, about the relative utility of needs over rights discourse overlook that blacks have been describing their needs for generations. They overlook a long history of legislation *against* the self-described needs of black people. While it is no longer against the law to teach black people to read, there is still within the national psyche a deep, self-replicating strain of denial of the urgent need for a literate black population. ("*They're* not intellectual," "*They* can't . . .") In housing, in employment, in public and private life, it is the same story: the undesired needs of black people transform them into those-without-desire. ("*They're* lazy," "*They* don't want to . . .")

For blacks, describing needs has been a dismal failure as political activity. It has succeeded only as a literary achievement. The history of our need is certainly moving enough to have been called poetry, oratory, epic entertainment— but it has never been treated by white institutions as the statement of a political priority. (I don't mean to undervalue the liberating power for blacks of such poetry, oratory, and epic; my concern is the degree to which is has been compartmentalized by the larger culture as something other than political expression.[7]) Some of our greatest politicians have been forced to become ministers or blues singers. Even white descriptions of "the blues" tend to remove the daily hunger and hurt from need and abstract it into a mood. And whoever would legislate against depression? Particularly something as rich, soulful, and sonorously productive as black depression.

It may be different when someone white is describing need. Shorn of the hypnotic rhythmicity that blacks are said to bring to their woe, white statements of black needs suddenly acquire the sort of stark statistical authority that lawmakers can listen to and politicians hear. But from blacks, stark statistical statements of need are heard as strident, discordant, and unharmonious. Heard not as political but only against the backdrop of their erstwhile musicality, they are again abstracted to mood and angry sounds. (Mythologically speaking, black anger inspires white fear and fear is the one mood to which legislators have responded, but that story has nothing to do with black need.)

For blacks, then, the battle is not deconstructing rights, in a world of no rights; nor of constructing statements of need, in a world of abundantly apparent need. Rather the goal is to find a political mechanism that can confront the *denial* of need. The argument that rights are disutile, even harmful, trivializes this aspect of black experience specifically, as well as that of any person or group whose vulnerability has been truly protected by rights.

This difference of experience from whites is not, I think, solely attributable to such divisions as positive/negative, bourgeois/proletariat; given our history, it is a difference rooted in race and in the unconsciousness of racism. It is only in acknowledging this difference, however, that one can fully appreciate the underlying common ground of the radical left and the historically oppressed: the desire to heal a profound existential disillusionment. Wholesale rejection of rights does not allow for the expression of such difference.

The white left is perhaps in the position of King Lear, when he discovered in himself a "poor, bare, forked animal" who *needed* no silks, furs, or retinue, only food, water, and straw to sleep on. The insight of this experience also freed him to see the weight, the constrictions, that his due as king had imposed on him. Similarly, the white left may feel that words and rights "have only the meaning that power wishes them to have." In this context, relationships of trust (which require neither speech nor rights) are replaced by the kind of "sufferance with which force condescends to weakness."[8] From this perspective, the Olympus of rights discourse may indeed to an appropriate height from which those on the resourced end of inequality, those already rights-empowered, may wish to jump.

Blacks, however, may symbolize that King Lear who was pushed to the point of madness: who did not find his essential humanity while retaining some reference point to an identity as social being temporarily lost in the wilderness— and who ultimately lost everything including a sense of self. The black slave experience was that of lost languages, cultures, tribal ties, kinship bonds, even of the power to procreate in the image of oneself and not that of an alien master. That sort of confrontation with the utter powerlessness of status which is the true and full condition of the wilderness is what ultimately drove Lear from insight into madness. Reduced to the basic provisions of food, water, and straw pallet, kings may gain new insight into those needs they share with all humankind. For others, however—slaves, sharecroppers, prisoners, mental patients—the experience of poverty and need is fraught with the terrible realization that they are dependent "on the uncertain and fitful protection of a world conscience,"[9] which has forgotten them as individuals. For the historically disempowered, the conferring of rights is symbolic of all the denied aspects of their humanity: rights imply a respect that places one in the referential range of self and others, that elevates one's status from human body to social being. For blacks, then, the attainment of rights signifies the respectful behavior, the collective responsibility, properly owed by a society to one of its own.

Another way of describing the dissonance between blacks and CLS is in terms of the degree of moral utopianism with which blacks regard rights. For blacks, the prospect of attaining full rights under law has been a fiercely motivational, almost religious, source of hope ever since arrival on these shores. It is an oversimplification to describe that hope as merely a "compensation for . . . feelings of loss," rights being a way to "conceal those feelings."[10] Black loss is not of the sort that can be compensated for or concealed by rights assertion. It must be remembered that *from the experiential perspective of blacks,* there was no such thing as "slave law."[11] The legal system did not provide blacks, even freed blacks, with structured expectations, promises, or reasonable reliances of any sort. If one views rights as emanating from either slave "legal" history or from that of modern bourgeois legal structures, then of course rights would mean nothing because blacks have had virtually nothing under either. And if one envisions rights as economic advantages over others, one might well conclude that "because this sense of illegitimacy [of incomplete social relations] is always threatening to erupt into awareness, there is a need for 'the law.'"[12]

But where one's experience is rooted not just in a sense of illegitimacy but in *being* illegitimate, in being raped, and in the fear of being murdered, then the black adherence to a scheme of both positive and negative rights—to the self, to the sanctity of one's own personal boundaries—makes sense.[13]

The individual unifying cultural memory of black people is the helplessness of living under slavery or in its shadow. I grew up living in the past: the future, some versions of which had only the vaguest possibility of happening, was treated with the respect of the already-happened, seen through the prismatic lenses of what had already occurred. Thus, when I decided to go to law school, my mother told me that "the Millers were lawyers so you have it in your blood." (Of course Mother did not mean that law was literally part of my genetic makeup; she meant that law was an intimate part of the socially constructed reality into which I had been born. She meant that dealing with law and lawyers was something with which my ancestors were all too familiar.) Now the Millers were the slaveholders of my maternal grandmother's clan. The Millers were also my great-great-grandparents and great-aunts and who knows what else. My great-great-grandfather Austin Miller, a 35-year-old lawyer, impregnated my 11-year-old great-great-grandmother Sophie, making her the mother of Mary, my great-grandmother, by the time she was 12.

In ironic, perverse obeisance to the rationalism of this bitter ancestral mix, the image of this self-centered child molester became the fuel for my survival in the dispossessed limbo of my years at Harvard, the *Bakke* years, when everyone was running around telling black people that they were very happy to have us there but, after all, they did have to lower the standards and readjust the grading system. (I do not mean this as a criticism of affirmative action, but of those who tried to devalue the presence and contribution of us, the affirmatively active.) And it worked. I got through law school, quietly driven by the false idol of white-man-within-me, and absorbed much of the knowledge and values that had enslaved my foremothers.

I learned about images of power in the strong, surefooted arm's-length transactor. I learned about unique power-enhancing lands called Whiteacre and Blackacre, and the mystical fairy rings encircling them, called restrictive covenants. I learned that excessive power overlaps generously with what is seen as successful, good, efficient, and desirable in our society.

I learned to undo images of power with images of powerlessness; to clothe the victims of excessive power in utter, bereft, naiveté; to cast them as defenseless supplicants pleading defenses of duress, undue influence, and fraud. A quick review of almost any contracts text will show most successful defenses feature women, particularly if they are old and widowed; illiterates; blacks and other minorities; the abjectly poor; and the old and infirm. A white male student of mine once remarked that he couldn't imagine "reconfiguring his manhood" to live up to the "publicly craven defenselessness" of defenses like duress and undue influence.[14]

I learned that the best way to give voice to those whose voice had been suppressed was to argue that they had no voice.[15]

Some time ago, I taught a property class in which we studied the old case of *Pierson v. Post*:

> Post, being in possession of certain dogs and hounds under his command, did, "upon a certain wild and uninhabited, unpossessed and waste land, called the beach, find and start one of those noxious beasts called a fox," and whilst there hunting, chasing and pursuing the same with his dogs and hounds, and when in view thereof, Pierson, well knowing the fox was so hunted and pursued, did, in the sight of Post, to prevent his catching the same, kill and carry it off.[16]

One day a student gave me a version of the case as reinterpreted by her six-year-old, written from the perspective of the wild fox. In some ways it resembled Peter Rabbit with an unhappy ending; most important, it was a tale retold from the doomed prey's point of view, the hunted reviewing the hunter. It was about this time that I began studying something that may have been the contract of sale of my great-great-grandmother as well as a census accounting that does list her, along with other, inanimate evidence of wealth, as the "personal property" of Austin Miller.

In reviewing those powerfully impersonal documents, I realized that both she and the fox shared a common lot, were either owned or unowned, never the owner. And whether owned or unowned, rights over them never filtered down to them; rights to their persons were never vested in them. When owned, issues of physical, mental, and emotional abuse or cruelty were assigned by the law to the private tolerance, whimsy, or insanity of an external master. And when unowned—free, freed, or escaped—again their situation was uncontrollably precarious, for as objects *to be* owned, they and the game of their conquest were seen only as potential enhancements to some other self. (In *Pierson,* for example, the dissent described the contest as between the "gentleman" in pursuit and the "saucy intruder." The majority acknowledged that Pierson's behavior was "uncourteous" and "unkind" but decided the case according to broader principles of "peace and order" in sportsmanship.) They were fair game from the perspective of those who had rights; but from their own point of view, they were objects of a murderous hunt.

This finding of something that could have been the contract of sale of my great-great-grandmother irretrievably personalized my analysis of the law of her exchange. Repeatedly since then, I have tried to analyze and undo her situation employing the tools of adequacy of valuable consideration—how much value, I wonder. Just how did the value break down? Did they haggle? Was it a poker game, a trade, a promissory note? How much was she *worth?* The New York Public Library's Shomberg Center has in its archives a contract in which a

young woman was sold for a dollar. In contrast, a review of the literature on the slave trade from Africa shows that the death of one-fourth to two-thirds of every cargo ship's population still provided "a good return on their investment." With what literalism must my philosophizing be alloyed: "There's something in me which might have been great, but due to the unfavorable market, I'm only worth a little."[17]

I have tried to rationalize and rescue her fate using defenses to formation, grounds for discharge and remedies (for whom?). That this was a dead-end undertaking is obvious, but it was interesting to see how the other part of my heritage, Austin Miller the lawyer and his confreres, had constructed their world so as to nip quests like mine in the bud.

The very best I could do for her was to throw myself upon the mercy of an imaginary, patriarchal court and appeal for an exercise of its extraordinary powers of conscionability and "humanitarianism." I found that it helped to appeal to the court's humanity, not to stress the fullness of hers. I found that the best way to get anything for her, whose needs for rights were so overwhelmingly manifest, was to argue that she, poor thing, had no rights.[18] It is this experience of having, for survival, to argue for our own invisibility in the passive, unthreatening rhetoric of "no-rights" which, juxtaposed with the CLS abandonment of rights theory, is both paradoxical and difficult for minorities to accept.

My discussion may prompt the argument that this last paradox is the direct product of rights discourse itself. So, in addition, I tried arguing my great-great-grandmother's fate in terms more direct, informal, descriptive, and substantive. I begged, pleaded, "acted out," and cried. I prayed loudly enough for all to hear, and became superstitious. But I didn't get any relief for Sophie's condition, my most silver-tongued informality got her nothing at all.

The problem, as I came to see it, is not really one of choosing rhetoric, of formal over informal, of structure and certainty over context, of right over need.[19] Rather it is a problem of appropriately choosing signs within any system of rhetoric. From the object-property's point of view (that of my great-great-grandmother and the nameless fox), the rhetoric of certainty (of rights, formal rules, and fixed entitlement) has been enforced at best as if it were the rhetoric of context (of fluidity, informal rules, and unpredictability). Yet the fullness of context, the trust that enhances the use of more fluid systems, is lost in the lawless influence of cultural insensitivity and taboo. So while it appears to jurisdictionally recognized and invested parties that rights designate outcomes with a clarity akin to wisdom, for the object-property the effect is one of existing in a morass of unbounded irresponsibility.

But this failure of rights discourse, much noted in CLS scholarship, does not logically mean that informal systems will lead to better outcomes. Some structures are the products of social forces and people who wanted them that way. If one assumes, as blacks must, not that the larger world wants to overcome alienation but that many heartily embrace it, driven not just by fear but by hatred and taboo, then informal systems as well as formal systems will be run principally by unconscious or irrational forces: "Human nature has an invincible dread of becoming more conscious of itself."[20] (By this I do not mean to suggest a Hobbesian state of nature, but a crust of cultural habit and perception whose power shelters as it blinds.)

This underscores my sense of the importance of rights: rights are to law what conscious commitments are to the psyche. This country's worst historical moments have not been attributable to rights *assertion* but to a failure of rights commitment. From this perspective, the problem with rights discourse is not that the discourse is itself constricting but that it exists in a constricted referential universe. The body of private laws epitomized by contract, including slave contract, is problematic because it denied the object of contract any rights at all.

The quintessential rule of contract interpretation, the parol evidence rule, illustrates the mechanics by which such constriction is achieved. It says: "Terms with respect to which the confirmatory memoranda of the parties agree . . . may not be contradicted [by extrinsic evidence] . . . but may be explained or supplemented . . . by evidence of consistent additional terms."[21] If this rule is understood as a form of social construction, the words could as well read: "Terms with respect to which the constructed reality (or governing narrative) of a given power structure agree, may not be contradicted, but only supplemented or explained."

Such a social construction applied to rights mythology suggests the way in which rights assertion has been limited by delimiting certain others as "extrinsic" to rights entitlement: "Europe during the Discovery era refused to recognize legal status or rights for indigenous tribal peoples because 'heathens' and 'infidels' were legally presumed to lack the rational capacity necessary to assume an equal status or exercise equal rights under the European's medievally-derived legal world-view."[22] The possibility of a broader referential range of considered types of rights may be found by at least adding to, even contradicting, traditional categories of rights recipients.

Imagine, for example, a world in which a broader range of inanimate objects (other than corporations) were given rights—as in cases of the looting of American Indian religious objects: spurred by a booming international art market and virtually no fear of prosecution, raiders have taken "ceremonial objects and ancient tools [as well as] the mummified remains of Anasazi children . . . the asking price for quality specimens starts at $5,000. The best of these are said to have been preserved by casting them into acrylic blocks, an expensive, high-tech procedure. . . . 'To us,' says Marcus Sekayouma, a Hopi employee of the Bureau of Indian Affairs, 'the removal of any old object from the ground is the equivalent of a sacrilege.'"[23]

Such expanded reference—first made controversial by Christopher Stone's famous article "Should Trees Have Standing?"—is premised on the degree to which rights do empower and make visible:

We are inclined to suppose the rightlessness of rightless "things" to be a decree of Nature, not a legal convention acting in support of some status quo. It is thus that we defer considering the choices involved in all their moral, social and economic dimensions. . . . The fact is that each time there is a movement to confer rights onto some new "entity," the proposal is bound to sound odd or frightening or laughable. This is partly because until the rightless thing receives its rights, we cannot see it as anything but a thing for the use of "us"—those who are holding rights at the time.[24]

One consequence of this broader reconfiguration of rights is to give voice to those people or things that, by virtue of their object relation to a contract, historically have had no voice. Allowing this sort of empowering opens up the *egoisme à deux* of traditional contract and increases the limited bipolarity of relationship that characterizes so much of western civilization.[25] Listening to and looking for interests beyond the narrowest boundaries of linear, dualistically reciprocal encounters is characteristic of gift relationships, networks of encompassing expectation and support. As my colleague Dinesh Khosla describes it, "In the circularity of gift, the wealth of a community never loses its momentum. It passes from one hand to another; it does not gather in isolated pools. So all have it, even though they do not possess it and even though they do not own it."[26]

Such an expanded frame of rights reference underlies a philosophy of more generously extending rights to all one's fellow creatures, whether human or beast. Think how differently might have been the outcome in the Tuskegee syphilis experiment, in which illiterate black men were deliberately allowed to go untreated from 1932 until 1972, observed by doctors from the U.S. Public Health Service. Approximately 400 diseased men with 200 more as controls were allowed to degenerate and die; doctors told them only that they had "bad blood."[27]

Similarly, every year one reads in the newspapers about millions of cattle who are periodically destroyed for no other purpose than to drive up the price of milk or beef. One also reads about the few bleeding hearts who wage a mostly losing war to save the lives of the hapless animals. Yet before the Reformation, the bleeding heart was the Christian symbol of one who could "feel the spirit move inside all property. Everything on earth is a gift and God is the vessel. Our small bodies may be expanded; we need not confine the blood." Today, on the other hand, the "'bleeding heart' is . . . the man of dubious mettle with an embarrassing inability to limit his compassion."[28]

One lesson I never learned in school was the degree to which black history in this nation is that of fiercely interwoven patterns of family, as conceived by white men. Folklore notwithstanding, slaves were not treated "as though" they were part of the family (for that implies a drawing near, an overcoming of market-placed distance); too often the unspoken power of white masters over slaves was the covert cohesion *of* family.[29] Those who were, in fact or for all purposes, family were held at a distance as strangers and commodities: strangers in the sense that they were excluded from the family circle at the hearth and in the heart, and commodities in the sense that they could be sold down the river with no more consideration than the bales of cotton they accompanied.

In the thicket of those relations, the insignificance of family connection was consistently achieved through the suppression of any image of blacks as capable either of being part of the family of white men or of having family of their own: in 1857 the Supreme Court decided the seminal case of *Dred Scott v. Sandford,* in which blacks were adjudged "altogether unfit to associate with the white race, either in social or political relations; and so far inferior, that they had no rights which the white man was bound to respect; and that the negro might justly and lawfully be reduced to slavery for his benefit."[30] A popular contemporary pamphlet likened blacks to "ourang outangs" and determined them to be descendants of Canaan. (In the Bible, Noah condemns his son's son Canaan to be a "servant of servants.")

Moreover, "Since slaves, as chattels, could not make contracts, marriages between them were not legally binding. . . . Their condition was compatible only with a form of concubinage, voluntary on the part of the slaves, and permissive on that of the master. In law there was no such thing as fornication or adultery between slaves; nor was there bastardy, for, as a Kentucky judge noted, the father of a slave was 'unknown' to the law. No state legislature ever seriously entertained the thought of encroaching upon the master's rights by legalizing slave marriages."[31] Antimiscegenation laws also kept blacks outside the family of those favored with rights; and laws restricting the ability of slaveholders to will property or freedom to blacks suspended them in eternal illegitimacy.

The recognition of such a threshold is the key to understanding slavery as a structure of denial—a denial of the generative independence of black people. A substitution occurred: instead of black motherhood as the generative source for black people, master-cloaked white manhood became the generative source for black people. Although the "bad black mother" is even today a stereotypical way of describing what ails the black race, the historical reality is that of careless white fatherhood. Blacks are thus, in full culturally imagistic terms, not merely unmothered but badly fathered, abused and disowned by whites. Certainly the companion myths to this woeful epic are to be found in brutalized archetypes of black males (so indiscriminately generative as to require repression by castration) and of white females (so discriminately virginal as to wither in idealized asexuality).[32]

To say that blacks never fully believed in rights is true. Yet it is also true that blacks believed in them so much and so hard that we gave them life where there was none before; we held onto them, put the hope of them into our wombs, mothered them and not the notion of them. And this was not the dry process of reification, from which life is drained and reality fades as the cement of conceptual determinism hardens round—but its opposite. This was the resurrection of life from ashes 400 years old.[33] The making of something out of nothing took immense alchemical fire—the fusion of a whole nation and the kindling of several generations. The illusion became real for only a few of us; it is still elusive for most. But if it took this long to breathe life into a form whose shape had already been forged by society, and which is therefore idealistically if not ideologically accessible, imagine how long the struggle would be without even that sense of definition, without the power of that familiar vision. What hope would there be if the assignment were to pour hope into a timeless, formless futurism? The desperate psychological and physical oppression suffered by black people in this society makes such a prospect either unrealistic (experienced as unattainable) or other-worldly (as in the false hopes held out by many religions of the oppressed).

It is true that the constitutional foreground of rights was shaped by whites, parceled out to blacks in pieces, ordained from on high in small favors, random insulting gratuities. Perhaps the predominance of that imbalance obscures the fact that the recursive insistence of those rights is also defined by black desire for them—desire fueled not by the sop of minor enforcement of major statutory schemes like the Civil Rights Act, but by knowledge of, and generations of existing in, a world without any meaningful boundaries—and "without boundary" for blacks meant not untrammeled vistas of possibility but the crushing weight of total—bodily and spiritual—*intrusion.* "Rights" feels new in the mouths of most black people. It is still deliciously empowering to say.

It is the magic wand of visibility and invisibility, of inclusion and exclusion, of power and no power. The concept of rights, both positive and negative, is the marker of our citizenship, our relation to others.

In many mythologies, the mask of the sorcerer is also the source of power. To unmask the sorcerer is to depower.[34] So CLS's unmasking of rights mythology in liberal America is to reveal the source of much powerlessness masquerading as strength; it reveals a universalism of need and oppression among whites as well as blacks. In those ancient mythologies, however, unmasking the sorcerer was only part of the job. It was impossible to destroy the mask without destroying the balance of things, without destroying empowerment itself. The mask had to be donned by the acquiring shaman and put to good ends.

The task for critical legal studies, then, is not to discard rights but to see through or past them so that they reflect a larger definition of privacy and property: so that privacy is turned from exclusion based on self-regard into regard for another's fragile, mysterious autonomy; and so that property regains its ancient connotation of being a reflection of the universal self.[35] The task is to expand private property rights into a conception of civil rights, into the right to expect civility from others. In discarding rights altogether, one discards a symbol too deeply enmeshed in the psyche of the oppressed to lose without trauma and much resistance. Instead, society must *give* them away. Unlock them from reification by giving them to slaves. Give them to trees. Give them to cows. Give them to history. Give them to rivers and rocks. Give to all of society's objects and untouchables the rights of privacy, integrity, and self-assertion; give them distance and respect. Flood them with the animating spirit that rights mythology fires in this country's most oppressed psyches, and wash away the shrouds of inanimate-object status, so that we may say not that we own gold but that a luminous golden spirit owns us.

NOTES

1. See generally Richard Delgado et al., "Fairness and Formality: Minimizing the Risk of Prejudice in Alternative Dispute Resolution," *Wisconsin Law Review* 6 (1985), p. 1359.
2. "Whatever else they learned in school, black children came to understand, as their parents had, that their color marked them as inferior in the eyes of whites, no matter how they conducted themselves. 'We came to understand,' a black woman would recall of her youth, 'that no matter how neat and clean, how law abiding, submissive and polite, how studious in school, how church-going and moral, how scrupulous in paying our bills and taxes we were, it made no essential difference in our place.'" Leon Litwack, "'Blues Falling Down Like Rain,'" in *New Perspectives on Race and Slavery in America,* ed. Robert Abzug and Stephen Maizlish (Lexington: University of Kentucky Press, 1986), p. 118.
3. Peter describes the law of formalized hierarchical social arrangements as deriving from "externalized" and "totemic source[s] of unification" in which each person experiences his or her authentic being as a privatized non-self that is denied recognition and that is therefore "invisible" or unconscious: "it is known or comprehended only though the experienced bodily tension that derives from not being-oneself and through a continual obsessive and pre-conscious fantasy life that reaches a dim awareness in moments of distraction. . . . The 'visible' or conscious self that is enacted in behavior is experienced as a 'public' or 'outer' synthesis of as-if performances which is at once lived as passively undergone to the degree that it lacks any sense of its own agency and yet is 'owned' to the degree that each person feels this self as 'I.'" Peter Gabel, "The Bank Teller," *TIKKUN* 2 (1987), pp. 48–49.
4. Mary Ann Caws, "Literal or Liberal: Translating Perception," *Critical Inquiry* 13 (1986), p. 55.
5. Mark Tushnet, "An Essay on Rights," *University of Texas Law Review* 62 (1982), p. 1386.
6. Demanding that needs "be satisfied—whether or not satisfying them can today persuasively be characterized as enforcing a right—strikes me as more likely to succeed than claiming that existing rights to food and shelter must be en-

forced" (*ibid.*, p. 1394). See also Alan Freeman, "Legitimizing Racial Discrimination through Anti-Discrimination Law: A Critical Review of Supreme Court Doctrine," *Minnesota Law Review* 62 (1978), p. 1049.

7. For a discussion of the transformative significance of black music and literature, see Mari Matsuda, "Looking to the Bottom." *Harvard Civil Rights— Civil Liberties Law Review* 22 (1987), p. 335.

8. Michael Ignatieff, *The Needs of Strangers* (London: Chatto and Windus, 1984), p. 38.

9. *Ibid.*, p. 53.

10. Gabel, "The Bank Teller," p. 28.

11. Mark Tushnet, *The American Law of Slavery* (Princeton: Princeton University Press, 1981), pp. 37–42. Tushnet's analysis is premised, in part, on an understanding of the law of slaveholders as creating a system of enforceable expectations and limited rights for slaves.

12. Gabel, "The Bank Teller," p. 29.

13. "In the discussion of law, there is an everrenewed conflict between those who see it as a functional necessity and others who invest it with hope and promise. The former accept law as a given, as fact, at best as an instrument of practical problem-solving. For the legal idealist, on the other hand, law connotes a larger moral achievement." Phillip Selznick, "Law, Society and Moral Evolution," in *Cohen and Cohen's Readings in Jurisprudence and Legal Philosophy,* ed. Phillip Schuman (Boston: Little, Brown, 1979), p. 930.

14. See Mary Jo Frug, "Reading Contracts: A Feminist Analysis of a Contracts Casebook," *American Law Review* 34 (1985), p. 1065; Karl Klare, "Contracts, Jurisprudence and the First-Year Casebook," *New York University Law Review* 54 (1979), p. 876.

15. See Catherine MacKinnon, "Feminism, Marxism, Method and the State: An Agenda for Theory," *Signs: Journal of Women in Culture and Society* 7 (1982), p. 515; Frances Olsen, "The Family and the Market: A Study of Ideology and Legal Reform," *Harvard Law Review* 96 (1983), p. 1497.

16. 3 Cal. R. 175 (N.Y. Sup. Ct. 1805).

17. Søren Kierkegaard, cited in Karl Jaspers, *Existentialism from Dostoevsky to Sartre* (New York: New American Library, 1972), p. 176.

18. See Derrick Bell, "Social Limits on Basic Protections for Blacks," in *Race, Racism and American Law* (Boston: Little, Brown, 1980), p. 230.

19. See William Simon, "Legal Informality and Redistributive Politics," *Special Issue, Clearinghouse Review* 19 (1985), p. 384; E. Johnson, "The Justice System of the Future: Four Scenarios for the Twenty-First Century," in *Access to Justice and the Welfare State,* ed. Mauro Cappalletti (Alphen aan den Rijn: Sijthoff, 1981), p. 183; Jerold Auerbach, *Justice without Law?* (New York: Oxford University Press, 1983).

20. Carl Jung, *Psyche and Symbol: A Selection from the Writing of C. J. Jung* (Garden City: Doubleday Anchor Books, 1958), p. 214.

21. §2-202, Uniform Commercial Code, in *Selected Commercial Statutes.*

22. Robert Williams, "The Algebra of Federal Indian Law: The Hard Trail of Decolonizing and Americanizing the White Man's Indian Jurisprudence," *Wisconsin Law Review* 7 (1986), p. 290; see also *Dred Scott v. Sandford,* 60 U.S. 383 (1857).

23. Derek Goodwin, "Raiders of the Sacred Sites," *New York Times Magazine,* December 7, 1986, p. 65.

24. Christopher Stone, "Should Trees Have Standing?—Toward Legal Rights for Natural Objects," *Southern California Law Review* 45 (1972), pp. 453, 455.

25. See generally, John M. Brockman, "Bitburg Deconstruction," *Philosophical Forum* 7 (1986), p. 160.

26. Dinesh Khosla and Patricia Williams, "Economies of Mind: A Collaborative Reflection," *Nova Law Review* 10 (1986), p. 621.

27. James Jones, *Bad Blood* (New York: Free Press, 1981).

28. Lewis Hyde, *The Gift: Imagination and the Erotic Life of Property* (New York: Vintage, 1983), p. 139.

29. Kenneth Stampp, *The Peculiar Institution* (New York: Knopf, 1956), pp. 250–1.

30. *Dred Scott v. Sandford,* 60 U.S. 383 (1857), at p. 407.

31. Stampp, *The Peculiar Institution,* p. 198.

32. See generally, Winthrop Jordan, *White over Black* (Chapel Hill: University of North Carolina Press, 1968), pp. 136–78; John Dollard, *Caste and Class in a Southern Town* (Garden City: Doubleday, 1957), pp. 134–72.

33. "You must teach your children that the ground beneath their feet is the ashes of our grandfathers.

So that they will respect the land, tell your children that the earth is rich with the lives of our kin." Chief Seattle of the Suquamish, 1854 speech in response to a U.S. offer to enter into a treaty for tribal lands, in Williams, "The Algebra of Federal Indian Law," p. 292.

34. Almost every culture in the world has its share of such tales: Plains Indian, Inuit, Celtic, Siberian, Turkish, Nigerian, Cameroonian, Brazilian, Australian, and Malaysian stories—to name a few—describe the phenomenon of the power mask or power object. Moreover, the unmasking can occur in a number of less-than-literal ways: killing the totemic animal from whom the sorcerer derives power; devaluing the magician as merely the village psychotic; and, perhaps most familiarly, in our culture, incanting sacred spells backwards. See Joan Halifax, *Shamanic Voices* (New York: Dutton, 1979); James Frazer, *The Golden Bough* (London: Macmillan, 1963); Claude Lévi-Strauss, *The Raw and the Cooked* (New York: Harper & Row, 1969); Michael Taussig, *Shamanism, Colonialism, and the Wild Man* (Chicago: University of Chicago Press, 1987); Weston La Barre, *The Ghost Dance* (New York: Dell, 1978).

35. "In exactly the same way that the South imagines that it 'knows' the Negro, the North imagines that it has set him free. Both camps are deluded. Human freedom is a complex, difficult—and private—thing. If we liken life, for a moment, to a furnace, then freedom is the fire which burns away illusion." James Baldwin, *Nobody Knows My Name* (New York: Dell, 1970), p. 99.

READING 14

Are Mothers Persons?
Reproductive Rights
and the Politics of Subject-ivity

Susan Bordo

. . .

EMBODIED SUBJECTS
AND DE-SUBJECTIFIED BODIES

Our legal tradition officially places a high—some might say inordinately high—value on bodily integrity. As the United States Supreme Court acknowledged over 100 years ago:

> No right is held more sacred, or is more carefully guarded, by the common law, than the right of every individual to the possession and control of his own person, free from all restraint or interference of others, unless by a clear and unquestionable authority of law. As well said by Judge Cooley, "The right to one's person may be said to be a right of complete immunity: to be let alone."[1]

Bodily integrity and the "right to one's person" are philosophically knit together by the Cartesian conception of the human body as the "home" of the person—the "ghost in the machine," as Gilbert Ryle has called it[2]—the self-conscious, willing, desiring, dreaming, creating "inner" self, the "I." The historical influence of this construction on Western modernity, especially on legal conceptions of bodily integrity, privacy, and personhood, has been sweeping and profound. Yet, as we will see, the "ghost in the machine" is not always the legislating metaphor in concrete social practice; sometimes entirely mechanistic conceptions of the body dominate, conceptions from which all concern for the inner self have vanished. In practice, our legal tradition divides the human world as Descartes divided all of reality: into conscious subjects and mere bodies (*res extensa*). And in the social expression of that duality, some groups have clearly been accorded subject-status and its protections, while others have regularly been denied those protections, becoming for all medical and legal purposes pure *res extensa*, bodies stripped of their animating, dignifying, and humanizing "subject-ivity."

From Susan Bordo, "Are Mothers Persons? Reproductive Rights and the Politics of Subject-ivity." Pp. 71–97, and 310–317 in *Unbearable Weight: Feminism, Western Culture, and the Body*. Berkeley: University of California Press, 1993. Reprinted by permission of the Regents of the University of California and the University of California Press. Copyright © 1993 by the Regents of the University of California. All rights reserved.

First let us examine the tradition regarding embodied subjects. This is one in which bodily integrity is privileged so highly that judges have consistently refused to force individuals to submit without consent to medical treatment even though the life of another hangs in the balance. So, for example, in the case of *McFall v. Shimp* (1979), Shimp's bodily integrity was legally protected to the extent that he was permitted to refuse a procedure (a bone-marrow extraction and donation) that could have prevented his cousin's otherwise certain death from aplastic anemia. (McFall did indeed die two weeks after the decision was handed down.) Other similar suits have been equally unsuccessful, including highly publicized ones such as that pressed by a Seattle woman to have the father of her leukemic child donate his marrow, and that of an Illinois father who sued the mother of his son's twin half-siblings to have tests done to see if their marrow matched his son's.[3] Many of us—and I include myself—may find Shimp's action and similar refusals morally repugnant. They are, however, thoroughly sanctioned by law, which insists on *informed consent* for any medical procedure, and which permits us to be Bad Samaritans in the interests of preserving *principles* that are viewed as constituting (in the words of the *McFall* decision) "the very essence . . . of our society."[4]

The doctrine of informed consent is, in a very real sense, a protection of the *subjectivity* of the person involved—that is, it is an acknowledgment that the body can never be regarded merely as a site of quantifiable processes that can be assessed objectively, but must be treated as invested with personal meaning, history, and value that are ultimately determinable only by the subject who lives "within" it. According to the doctrine of informed consent, even when it is "for the good" of the patient, no one else—neither relative nor expert—may determine for the embodied subject what medical risks are worth taking, what procedures are minimally or excessively invasive, what pain is minor. When that meaning-bestowing function is in danger of being taken away from the subject, the prevailing ideology (and the accompanying legal response) conceptualizes the situation as a violent invasion of the personal space of the body. For example, physicians performing unconsented-to treatment are legally guilty of battery.[5] Or consider the impassioned justification for his decision given by the judge who ruled on *McFall v. Shimp:*

> For a society which respects the rights of *one* individual, to sink its teeth into the jugular vein or neck of one of its members and suck from it sustenance for *another* member, is revolting to our hard-wrought concepts of jurisprudence. Forcible extraction of living tissue causes revulsion to the judicial mind. Such would raise the specter of the swastika and the Inquisition, reminiscent of the horrors this portends.[6]

The key metaphor of this description, vampirism, not only evokes the pulsing flowing, *vital* nature of the human body but suggests that to invade it is tantamount to parasitism, a stealing of the inner essence of the person. The body here, clearly, is no mere physical entity but a self embodied, or (to put it the other way around) a body suffused with subjectivity. The system which would countenance its invasion is likened to Nazi Germany and the Inquisition, or (as in *Rochin v. California* (1952)), to medieval torture:

> Illegally breaking into the privacy of the petitioner, the struggle to open his mouth and remove what was there, the forcible extraction of his stomach contents—this course of proceeding by agents of government to obtain evidence is found to offend even hardened sensibilities. They are methods too close to the rack and the screw to permit of constitutional differentiation.[7]

Rochin, a suspected drug dealer, had merely been made to regurgitate two capsules he had swallowed. Moreover, the invasion of Rochin's privacy falls within a clearly recognized category of possible exception to the protection of bodily integrity: invasion of a minimal nature may be permitted when it is required to promote the state's interest in the prosecution of criminals.[8] So, for example, blood-alcohol tests may be required of drivers suspected of intoxication.[9] But even for suspected criminals, the law has emphatically drawn the line at major surgery. In *Winston v. Lee* (1985), law-enforcement authorities needed a bullet, lodged in the defendant's chest, as evidence against him. Both the circuit court and the Supreme Court ruled against the state, the Supreme Court arguing that "surgery without the patient's consent, performed under a general anesthetic to search for evidence of a crime, involves a virtually total divestment of the patient's ordinary control over surgical probing beneath his skin." Both the circuit court and the Supreme Court, interestingly, were especially emphatic concerning the degrading and "demeaning" nature of "dragging" this citizen "into a state of unconsciousness" against his will.[10]

In contrast to all this privileging of the hallowed ground of "the subject's" body[11] is the casual and morally imperious approach medicine and law have taken to nonconsensual medical interference in the reproductive lives of women—particularly when they are of non-European descent, poor, or non-English-speaking. In this arena we see racism, classism, and sexism interlock virulently, whether we are looking at the history of involuntary sterilization in this country, the statistics on court-ordered obstetrical intervention, or the Supreme Court's *Rust v. Sullivan* decision, which forbids doctors in federally funded clinics to discuss or offer information about abortion or to indicate where such information might be available, even when a woman has no other access to medical advice.[12]

The history of involuntary sterilization, overwhelmingly aimed at the "mentally defective" ("feeble-minded," "retarded," "mentally ill") and one of the most blatant examples of medical and legal disregard for the personhood of certain groups in this country, has been strongly shaped by the politics of race, class, and gender. From 1900 to 1960, 60,000 persons in the United States were sterilized without their consent, many never even informed of the nature of the operation.[13] Initially fueled by 19th-century versions of

evolutionary theory (almost invariably racist) and the eugenics-inspired vision of a society purged of "defective genes," the history of involuntary sterilization of the "mentally defective" in this country has in practice largely affected those groups considered genetically suspect and racially inferior: those convicted of crimes, the poor, African Americans, Native Americans, Spanish Americans, and Puerto Ricans.[14]

Less often noted is the overwhelming gender-bias that began to develop in the 1930s and 1940s, as the Depression shifted the concerns of those officials empowered to sterilize from the prevention of genetic defect to the prevention of parenthood in those individuals deemed unable to *care* adequately for their children. Philip Reilly, in *The Surgical Solution,* notes the change in ideology and the increasingly glaring disparity between the number of men and of women sterilized.[15] He fails, however, to see the connection between the two. Today, virtually all sterilization abuse (as well as proposals for less drastic bodily invasions, such as the use of Norplant) is directed against women on welfare, and is rationalized by the "inability to care" model. Often, as in the case of *Rust,* the reproductive rights of poor women are threatened without outright legal deprivation of those rights. In *Walker v. Pierce,* for example, the defendant admitted that his practice was to require consent for postpartum sterilization of his Medicaid patients who came to him pregnant with a third child. If consent was not given, he would refuse to treat the patient, and on occasion he threatened to try to have their state assistance terminated. He did not insist on these conditions for patients *not* on Medicaid, no matter how many children they had.[16]

Turning to court-ordered obstetrical interventions—and these include forced cesarean sections, detention of women against their will, and intrauterine transfusions—the statistics make clear that in this culture the pregnant poor woman (especially if she is of non-European descent) comes as close as a human being can get to being regarded, medically and legally as "mere body," her wishes, desires, dreams, religious scruples of little consequence and easily ignored in (the doctor's or judge's estimation of) the interests of fetal well-being. In 1987, the *New England Journal of Medicine* reported that of 21 cases in which court orders for obstetrical intervention were sought, 86 percent were obtained. Eighty-one percent of the woman involved were black, Asian, or Hispanic.[17]

In one of the most extreme and revealing of the forced-cesarean cases, George Washington University Hospital won a court order requiring that a cesarean section be performed on a terminally ill patient, Angela Carder, before her fetus was viable, and against the wishes of the woman, her husband, and the doctors on the staff. Both the woman and her baby died shortly after the operation. The District of Columbia Court of Appeals, in affirming the order against a requested stay, ruled that the woman's right to avoid bodily intrusion could justifiably be put aside, as she had "at best two days left of sedated life."[18] Here, clearly, a still living human subject had become, for all legal purposes, dead matter, a mere fetal container. A woman whom *no court in the country would force to undergo a blood transfusion for a dying relative* had come to be legally regarded, when pregnant, as a mere life-support system for a fetus.

It is important to emphasize here that the legal analogues to cases such as these are *not* interventions such as those involved, for example, when a Johovah's Witness is ordered to permit a dependent child to receive a blood transfusion, but precisely cases such as *McFall v. Shimp,* in which the *body* of the person subject to the court order is required for the intervention. This is why the protection of bodily integrity is an issue in cases of this latter sort, but not in cases solely involving the overriding of parental wishes, where the body of the parent is not itself involved. With the correct moral analogues in mind, it is clear that even granting full personhood to the fetus does not mute the force and

depth of the legal and moral inconsistency here. On the one hand, we have Shimp's refusal to submit to a procedure that could have saved his cousin's life, a refusal which was upheld by law on the grounds that to do otherwise would be a gross invasion of the privileged territory of the subject's own body. On the other hand, we have numerous cases in which judges not only have ordered pregnant women to submit to highly invasive procedures[19] but have conceptualized these interventions as the protection of the fetus's right against the inappropriate and selfish maternal evaluations of the physical, emotional, and religious acceptability of those procedures.

Consider the language of court orders for medical treatment of pregnant women. These orders, in striking contrast to the rhetoric of violent subjugation, the metaphors of the rack and the screw, the analogies with fascist regimes employed in the rulings on *McFall v. Shimp* and *Rochin v. California,* often dismiss the proposed intervention as minor, inconsequential, of significance only as an individual whose desires for personal freedom and "convenience" are excessive. So, the judge in *Taft v. Taft* (1982), in issuing an order for cervical surgery against the will of the woman (the order had been sought by her husband), referred to the procedure as "the operation of a *few sutures* . . . to hold the pregnancy."[20] This is clearly to sidestep utterly, in the case of the pregnant woman, the doctrine of informed consent, which requires that the individual affected be the final judge of the degree of invasiveness and risk that is acceptable. Without that requirement, informed consent has no meaning at all.

Even, however, if we are likely to agree that cerclage is a minimally invasive procedure,[21] let us not forget the judicial horror expressed at even less intrusive procedures carried out on the bodies of suspected criminals (such as the forced regurgitation that was the issue in *Rochin*). The discomfort, risk, and invasiveness of cesareans are another matter. The court record has made it abundantly clear (cf. *Winston*) that major surgery without consent is an extreme and demeaning violation of bodily integrity and control; it is also risky, no matter how "routine" the procedure. If marrow transfusions and even blood tests have not been required, surely a refusal to undergo the "massive intrusion"[22] of a major surgical procedure such as a cesarean section should be honored. Yet when Ayesha Madyun refused a cesarean on religious grounds, the judge ruled that for him *not* to issue a court order forcing her to have the operation would be to "indulge" Madyun's "desires" at the expense of the safety of her fetus.[23]

As a number of analysts have pointed out, there are no legal justifications for the discrepancies between the treatment accorded pregnant women and that given to nonpregnant persons.[24] Rather, to explain such contradictions we must leave the realm of rationality and enter the realm of gender ideology (and, in many cases, of racial prejudice as well). These decisions, clearly, are mediated by normative conceptions of the pregnant woman's appropriate role and function. Note the judge's choice, in the *Madyun* case, of the term *desires* (over, for example, the more legally conventional *wishes*). The idea of female "desire" is potent and threatening in our culture, with its sexual overtones and suggestions of personal gratification and capricious self-interest—particularly when paired with the notion of indulgence, as in this judge's ruling. Madyun's objections, we should remember, were religious (as are most maternal refusals of obstetrical intervention).[25] For the judge, however, religious scruples are on a par with the flightiest of personal whims when they come into conflict with the supreme role the pregnant woman should be playing: that of incubator to her fetus. In fulfilling that function, the pregnant woman is *supposed* to efface her own subjectivity, if need be. When she refuses to do so, that subjectivity comes to be construed as excessive, wicked. (The cultural archetype of the cold, selfish, mother—the evil goddesses, queens, and stepmothers of myth and fairy tale—clearly lurks in the imaginations of many of the judges issuing court orders for obstetrical intervention.)

Thus, ontologically speaking, the pregnant woman has been seen by our legal system as the mirror-image of the abstract subject whose bodily integrity the law is so determined to protect. For the latter, subjectivity is the essence of personhood, not to be sacrificed even in the interests of the preservation of the life of another individual. Personal valuation, choice, and consciousness itself (remember the *Winston* court's horror at unconsented-to anesthesia) are the given values, against which any claims to state interest or public good must be rigorously argued and are rarely granted. The essence of the pregnant woman, by contrast, is her biological, purely mechanical role in preserving the life of another. In her case, *this* is the given value, against which her claims to subjectivity must be rigorously evaluated, and they will usually be found wanting insofar as they conflict with her life-support function. In the face of such a conflict, her valuations, choices, consciousness are expendable.[26]

Intersecting with this gender ideology, in cases such as *Madyun,* are our historical tradition of effacement of the personhood of people of color, racist beliefs about their "irresponsibility," and disdain for religious and cultural diversity. These elements can come into play at both ends of the spectrum of reproductive abuse—coerced sterilization, and coerced cesareans. In coerced-sterilization cases the mediating racist image is often that of the promiscuous breeder, populating the world irresponsibly, like an unspayed animal. One of the witnesses in *Walker v. Pierce* said that Pierce lectured her. "And, he said, 'Listen here young lady . . . this is my tax money paying for something like this. . . . I am tired of people going around here having babies and my tax money paying for it.'"[27] In forced-cesarean cases like *Madyun,* the mediating racist image may be that of the ignorant, uncivilized primitive whose atavistic religious beliefs are in conflict with the enlightened attitudes of modern science.

FETAL SUPER-SUBJECTS
AND MATERNAL INCUBATORS

As a one-time cocaine abuser, Debbie abused her son in the womb. Now, thanks to support from Alliance, she's learned how to be the responsible parent little Ricky needs.
—From the 1991 *United Way* brochure

Clearly, there has been one legal tradition for those who occupy the cultural location of the subject and another for those who are marked as "other." Some acknowledgment of the injustice of forced cesareans was finally made when the District of Columbia Court of Appeals, in a widely publicized decision, set aside the original ruling on Angela Carder's case and even raised the question of whether "there could ever be a situation extraordinary or compelling enough to justify a massive intrusion into a person's body, such as a cesarean section, against that person's will." (It is not to depreciate the court's ruling to note that Angela Carder was a white woman.) The appeal had been filed by the American Medical Association and 39 other organizations, whose consciousness had been significantly raised by the efforts of Lynn Paltrow of the American Civil Liberties Union, George Annas of the Boston University School of Medicine, and several others who brought the Carder case and others to national attention.[28] In 1987, 47 percent of the obstetricians surveyed by the *New England Journal of Medicine* had approved of forced cesareans and had agreed that the precedent set by the courts in cases requiring emergency cesarean sections for the sake of the fetus should be extended to include other procedures such as intrauterine transfusion.[29] Since the Angela Carder case, these attitudes may be changing. Yet there are extremely vocal and powerful advocates of pervasive obstetrical intervention,[30] and pregnant women continue to be treated as fetal incubators in other ways as well. The past few years have seen increasing numbers of cases in which brain-dead pregnant women have been

kept alive for as long as seven or eight weeks, until the fetus is mature enough to deliver by cesarean section,[31] and the Catholic church has declared life-sustaining treatment to be mandatory for a pregnant patient, "if continued treatment may benefit her unborn child."[32]

Indeed, I believe the ideology of woman-as-fetal-incubator is stronger than ever and is making ever greater encroachments into pregnant women's lives. The difference is that today it is most likely to emerge in the context of issues concerning the "lifestyles" of pregnant women. In 1986, Lawrence Nelson and his colleagues warned that "compelling pregnant women to undergo medical treatment sets an unsavory precedent for further invasion of a woman's privacy and bodily integrity." As though imagining the horrifying terrain of a future dystopia (such as that depicted in Margaret Atwood's *The Handmaid's Tale*), they list such potential intrusions:

> [These] could include court orders prohibiting pregnant women from using alcohol, cigarettes, or other possibly harmful substances, forbidding them from continuing to work because of the presence of fetal toxins in the workplace, forcing them to take drugs or accept intrauterine blood transfusions, requiring pregnant anorexic teenagers to be force-fed, forcing women to undergo prenatal screening and diagnostic procedures such as amniocentesis, sonography, or fetoscopy, or mandating that women submit to *in utero* or extra-uterine surgery for the fetus. . . . The prospect of courts literally managing the lives of pregnant women and extensively intruding into their daily activities is frightening and antithetical to the fundamental role that freedom of action plays in our society.[33]

Just five years later, this landscape no longer seems so futuristic. Although the Supreme Court has banned employers from adopting "fetal protection" policies that would bar women of childbearing age from hazardous jobs, this decision seems almost anomalous in the contemporary zeitgeist, within which the protection of fetal rights has burgeoned into a national obsession. Prosecutions and preventive detentions of pregnant women for fetal endangerment, once a rarity, are becoming more and more common. Since the Pamela Rae Stewart case of 1985, in which Stewart was charged with criminal neglect of her child for failing to follow medical advice during pregnancy, such cases have multiplied. In 1989, a Florida judge sentenced 23-year-old Jennifer Johnson to 15 years' probation on her conviction of delivering illegal drugs via the umbilical cord to her two babies. A Massachusetts woman who miscarried after an automobile accident in which she was intoxicated was prosecuted for vehicular homicide of her fetus. A Connecticut woman was charged with endangering her fetus by swallowing cocaine as police moved to arrest her. A Washington judge sent Brenda Vaughan to jail for nearly four months to protect her fetus, because a drug test, taken after she was arrested for forging a check, revealed cocaine use.[34] In 1990, a Wyoming woman was charged by the police with the crime of drinking while pregnant and was prosecuted for felony child abuse. In South Carolina, a dozen women have been arrested after the hospitals they went to for maternity care tested them for cocaine use and turned them in to the police for fetal abuse.[35]

In some ways even more disturbing than these legal actions are changes in the everyday attitudes of people. In March 1991, two waiters were fired from their jobs when they tried to persuade a nine-months-pregnant customer not to order a rum daiquiri because drinking alcohol could harm her fetus.[36] Soon after, they appeared on the Oprah Winfrey show, where many members of the audience indicated their strong support for the waiters' action. As might be expected, the customer's action was construed as reckless and "selfish," even though it is highly unlikely that one drink at her advanced stage of pregnancy could affect the fetus's health. Audience members were insistent, as was columnist Cal Thomas, that pregnant women who engage in *any* activities that have even the *slightest* risk

are behaving "selfishly" and that others are only acting responsibly in pointing this out to them. In Thomas's condemnation of the customer, all distinctions—between levels of harm, between fetuses and children, between prohibitions that affect the deployment of the mother's own body and those that do not—are effaced:

> What if the woman had come in a month from now with her newborn child and ordered two drinks, one for her and one to put in the baby's bottle, because the child had been crying and the mother thought this was a good way to get it to sleep? Would the waiter have been justified in refusing service to the baby because it is underage? Of course. Then what's the difference between wanting to protect a child that is newly born and one that is about to be born?[37]

Once again the specter of the evil mother looms large. The biting injustice is that pregnant women are in general probably the Best Samaritans of our culture. The overwhelming majority will suffer considerable person inconvenience, pain, risk, and curtailment of their freedom to do what their doctors advise is in the best interests of their fetuses. As one obstetrical surgeon put it, most of the women he sees "would cut off their heads to save their babies."[38] In the specific case of the customer who ordered the daiquiri, by her own account she had been extremely careful throughout her pregnancy and thought hard before ordering the drink:

> I was a week overdue . . . and I thought it would be safe to have just this one drink, which I ordered with dinner. . . . I've always made it a point to read everything I could find about alcohol in pregnancy. I felt guilty enough as it was for ordering the drink. . . . They tried to make me feel like a child abuser.[39]

Most poignant about this quote is the woman's internal sense of transgression, which I interpret as an indication, not of her recognition of the *actual* threat of one drink to her fetus's health, but of the extraordinary levels of vigilance now expected of and taken upon themselves by pregnant women. Yet at the same time as supererogatory levels of care are demanded of the pregnant woman, neither the father nor the state nor private industry is held responsible for any of the harms they may be inflicting on developing fetuses, nor are they required to contribute to their care. Fathers' drug habits, smoking, alcoholism, reckless driving, and psychological and physical treatment of pregnant wives are part of the fetus's "environment," too—sometimes indirectly, through their effect on the mother's well-being, but sometimes directly as well (through the effects of secondhand smoke and crack dust in the air, physical abuse, and alcohol's deleterious effect on the quality of sperm, to give a few examples). But fathers are nonetheless off the hook, as is the health system that makes it so difficult for poor women to obtain adequate prenatal care and for addicted mothers to get help.[40] As Katha Pollitt points out:

> Judges order pregnant addicts to jail, but they don't order drug treatment programs to accept them, or Medicaid, which pays for heroin treatment, to cover crack addiction—let alone order landlords not to evict them, or obstetricians to take uninsured women as patients, or the federal government to fund fully the Women, Infants, and Children supplemental feeding program, which reaches only two-thirds of those who are eligible. The policies that have underwritten maternal and infant health in most of the industrialized west since World War II—a national health service, paid maternity leave, direct payments to mothers, government-funded day care, home health visitors for new mothers, welfare payments that reflect the cost of living—are still regarded in the United States by even the most liberal as hopeless causes, and by everyone else as budget-breaking giveaways to the undeserving, pie-in-the-sky items from a mad socialist's wish list.[41]

While public service announcements on television target the smoking and alcohol habits of pregnant women as though they were the sole causes of low birth weight and infant disability, a task force commissioned by the government concluded that "if we just delivered routine clinical care and social services to pregnant women, we could prevent one-quarter to one-third of infant mortality." As things now stand, one out of every three pregnant women gets insufficient prenatal care (a situation that is not helped, of course, if drug-addicted mothers avoid seeking medical help, for fear they will be turned in to the police). Among other improvements, the task force recommends a public information campaign and a "nurturing approach" to pregnant women's needs, with home visits by nurses, social workers, and other counselors. The Bush White House, however, acted on none of this, withholding most of the report from Congress in the interests of preserving "the confidentiality of the deliberative process" in the Executive branch.[42]

Only the pregnant woman, apparently, has the "duty of care."[43] Indeed, according to the construction examined in the first section of this essay, this is her essential function. That it is framed, moreover, in entirely mechanistic terms—as fleshy incubator—is revealed by the exclusive attention given to her physiological state. The facts that a drink now and then might relax and soothe her, and that continual vigilance over the "environment" she is providing (if not the threat of public scrutiny and condemnation itself) may make her perpetually tense and worried, and that such factors may also affect the well-being of the fetus are not considered. Rather, a crudely mechanistic portrayal of her bodily connection with the fetus prevails. One daiquiri taken by the mother is imagined as equivalent to serving the fetus a cocktail. This image is so distasteful that it is then easy to leap to the further equation: one drink = fetal alcohol syndrome.

Sometimes the womb is described not as incubator but as prison. "The viable unborn child is literally captive within the mother's body," argued the dissenting judge in the appeal of the Carder case. Antichoice spokesperson Barnard Nathanson describes the fetus as "bricked in, as it were, behind . . . an impenetrable wall of flesh, muscle, bone and blood."[44] Perhaps such images can be dismissed as those of an ideologue. Michael Harrison's description, then, will serve as an example of the increasing *justification* of fetal being. For, strikingly, as the personhood of the pregnant woman has been drained from her and her function as fetal incubator activated, the subjectivity of the *fetus* has been elevated:

> The fetus could not be taken seriously as long as he remained a medical recluse in an opaque womb; and it was not until the last half of this century that the prying eye of the ultrasonogram rendered the once opaque womb transparent, stripping the veil of mystery from the dark inner sanctum, and letting the light of scientific observation fall on the shy and secretive fetus. . . . The sonographic voyeur, spying on the unwary fetus, finds him or her a surprisingly active little creature, and not at all the passive parasite we had imagined. . . . The fetus has come a long way— from biblical "seed" and mystical "homunculus" to an individual with medical problems that can be diagnosed and treated, that is, a patient. Although he cannot make an appointment and seldom complains, this patient will at all times need a physician.[45]

The gender ideology that permeates this quotation is various and obvious, and need not be belabored here. Here, I need only highlight the duality Harrison constructs between the "opaque," impenetrable womb, a territory itself bereft of the light of consciousness, a cave, a place merely to sleep, and the psychologically complex, fully personified fetus, at once "shy and secretive" and vitally "active." (And, of course, unlike his mother, he "seldom complains"—an ideal "patient"!) Ruth Hubbard notes, as well, the remarkable arrogance of the assumption that before developments in ultrasound, "we" had imagined the fetus to be a "passive parasite." Who is this "we"? she asks. "Surely not," she points out, "women who have been awakened by the painful kicks of a fetus!"[46] Those women, of course, have been rendered metaphorically unconscious by Harrison; only their inert, shrouded wombs remain.

Of course, the increasingly routine use of ultrasound *has* made the fetus seem more of a person, both to the doctor and to the mother.[47] Because of such changes in the perception of the fetus's status, combined with the advancing technologies that enable the doctor to treat the fetus directly, as an autonomous patient, doctors have come to feel confused, angry, and, perhaps, morally outraged when mothers refuse a recommended treatment. I can understand their discomfort and frustration. But the disturbing fact remains that increased empathy for the fetus has often gone hand in hand with decreased respect for the autonomy of the mother.[48] And, in general, the New Reproductive Technology has been a confusingly mixed bag as far as the subjectivity of women is concerned. On the one hand, women now have a booming technology seemingly focused on fulfilling *their* desires: to conceive, to prevent miscarriage, to deliver a health baby at term. On the other hand, proponents and practitioners continually encourage women to treat their bodies as passive instruments of those goals, ready and willing, "if they want a child badly enough," to endure however complicated and invasive a regime of diagnostic testing, daily monitoring, injections, and operative procedures may be required. Thus, one element of women's subjectivity is indeed nurtured, while all other elements (investment in career, other emotional needs, importance of other personal relationships, etc.) are minimized, marginalized, and (when they refuse to be repressed) made an occasion for guilt and self-questioning.

One of the most disturbing examples is presented by Dr. Stefan Semchyshyn. Semchyshyn argues for an extremely aggressive approach to the prevention of miscarriage, dismissing the (generally accepted) belief that many early miscarriages are the inevitable result of genetic defect and ought not to be rigorously prevented. He reassures readers that genetic testing (amniocentesis and ultrasound) will pick up those defects at the beginning of the second trimester, when the woman can still elect to have an abortion.[49] Semchyshyn is, I presume, aware of the physical pain and (well-documented) psychological trauma involved in a second-trimester abortion; yet, apparently, these factors are too trivial for him to mention even as possible considerations.[50] In our present cultural context, the New Reproductive Technologies *do* cater to women's desires (that is, to the desires of women who can afford them), but only when they are the *right* desires, desires that will subordinate all else (even in the face of technological success rates which continue to be very discouraging) to the project of producing a child.

Gradually over the last century, and steeply accelerated over the decade of the 1980s, the legal status of the fetus has been greatly enhanced as well.[51] For over half a century, the *Dietrich* rule (1884), which established that damages (for instance, accidental death or injury) incurred on a fetus were not separately recoverable, because the fetus was "a part of the mother," prevailed.[52] Then, in 1946, in what has been described as "the most spectacular abrupt reversal of a well settled rule in the whole history of the law of torts,"[53] a federal district court in *Bonbrest v. Kotz* held that there may be recovery for injury to a viable fetus subsequently born alive.[54] Nelson points that even this change, however, did not recognize the fetus as a person with full legal rights; the point of the ruling was to allow damaged *born* persons in need of special medical treatment, schooling, and so forth to be compensated for injuries wrongly suffered when they were not yet legal persons.

The same intent, on Nelson's analysis, is behind the New Jersey Supreme Court's unfortunately worded statement, in *Smith v. Brennan* (1960) that "a child has a legal right to begin life with a sound mind and body." *Smith*, recognizing a child's cause of action for negligently inflicted prenatal injury, explicitly denies that this entails recognition of fetal personhood. The point is simply to establish the legitimacy of the *live-born* child's injury claim.[55] Yet the phrase taken by itself (out of context of the decision) *is* problematic, not only suggesting an unprece-

dented scope of rights, but ambiguous concerning to whom they belong. Over the past 30 years this ambiguity has been frequently exploited at the expense of the intent of the ruling, as advocates of obstetrical intervention have freely invoked the *fetus's* right to "begin life with a sound mind and body" as justification for their suits. The slippage here, from a live-born child's right to bring action against injuries suffered when in the fetal state to the right of the *fetus* to force its mother to accept treatment against her will, is profound and pernicious.

But let us, for the sake of argument, lay aside the issue of misapplication of tort law. Let us grant a fetus's right to be born healthy and sound and to be provided with a safe, healthy environment to promote this end. If we grant this, we are obliged to recognize also that this gives the fetus rights that *no one else* in this society has. Here we are once again confronted with the strange set of affairs entailed by fetal-rights arguments, that a two-year-old child has far fewer rights than a six-month-old fetus![56]

My point here is *not* to deny protection or dignity to the fetus or to suggest that it is no more than tissue or an appendage to the mother. In fact, I will later argue very strongly against such perspectives. Rather, my object is to bring attention to the ontological construction that is entailed (but never openly acknowledged) by the fetal-rights position, a position that is increasingly becoming conventional wisdom in many quarters of our culture. Very simply put, that construction is one in which pregnant women are not subjects at all (neither under the law nor in the zeitgeist) while fetuses are *super*-subjects. It is as though the subjectivity of the pregnant body were siphoned from it and emptied into fetal life.

. . .

RECLAIMING REPRODUCTIVE SUBJECTIVITY

The future of *Roe v. Wade* is now the central cultural arena for the battle over reproductive control. In this essay, however, I have emphasized the necessity of locating the struggle for abortion rights in a broader context. What gets obscured when abortion rights are considered in abstraction from issues involving forced medical treatment, legal and social interference in the management of pregnancy, and so forth, is the fact that it is not only women's reproductive rights that are currently being challenged but women's status as *subjects,* within a system in which—for better or worse—the protection of the "subject" remains a central value. What also may be obscured are the interlocking and mutually supporting effacements of subjectivity that are involved when the woman is perceived as a racial or economic "other" as well. So long as the debate over reproductive control is conceptualized solely in the dominant terms of the abortion debate—that is, as a conflict between the fetus's right to life and the woman's right to choose—we are fooled into thinking that it is only the fetus whose ethical and legal status is at issue. The pregnant woman (whose ethical and legal status as a person is not constructed as a question in the abortion debate, and which most people wrongly assume is fully protected legally) is seen as fighting, not for her *personhood,* but "only" for her right to control her reproductive destiny.

The nature of pregnancy is such, however, that to deprive the woman of control over her reproductive life—whether by means of involuntary or coerced sterilization, court-ordered cesarean, or forbidden abortion—is necessarily also to mount an assault on her personal integrity and autonomy (the essence of personhood in our culture) and to treat her merely as pregnant *res extensa,* material incubator of fetal subjectivity. Unfortunately, feminists have in the past sometimes colluded in such constructions, arguing the reproduction and pregnancy are "functions" that are disengageable from the being of the subject and—like all alienated labor—amenable to being sold or rented to another. Over time, the severe limitations of this model, crystallized for many feminists by the "Baby M"/Mary Beth Whitehead surrogacy case, have become clear. It is crucial, I believe, that we now shift our discourse and strategies away from an abstract rhetoric of choice to one focused on (1) exposing the contradictions in our legal tradition regarding bodily integrity and insisting that women's equal protection under the law requires that they be resolved,[57] and (2) challenging the fetal-container conception, by reclaiming (from the right wing, which now holds a monopoly on such ideas) the view of pregnancy and abortion as *experientially* profound events. Only on the basis of such a reclamation can we assert women's moral authority, not only by virtue of our distinctive embodiment but also by virtue of our social histories, to adjudicate the complex ethical dilemmas that arise out of our reproductivity.

The foregoing contains several notions that may give contemporary feminists pause, and that require some further explanation. First, there is the problematic notion of women's "experience," and the concomitant danger of essentializing the experiences of some groups of women while effacing the histories and experience of others. Although I acknowledge that danger, I believe that invoking women's embodied experience need not be equivalent to an alliance with "essentialism," so long as we remain mindful of the historical, racial, and cultural diversity of that experience—for example, so long as we recognize the different social histories within which the freedom and economic conditions that permit women to *have* children have been as tenuous as the right *not* to have them. At the same time, consciousness of our diversity ought not to be permitted to dilute recognition that, *as women,* we *all* have an "authority of experience" that men lack, and that gives us "a privileged critical location from which to speak" concerning reproduction.[58] Women's varied historical experiences of reproduction and birth—such as those described by Emily Martin[59] and Angela Davis,[60] and including the experiences of the infertile and the voluntarily childless—provide such locations of authority for us. So, too, do more philosophical, reconstructive accounts, such as Iris Young's study of "pregnant embodiment."[61]

Feminists may be made queasy, too, by the idea of emphasizing the experiential significance of pregnancy and birth, out of a fear of the conceptual proximity of such notions to constructions of mothering as the one true destiny for women. I believe, however, that we stand a better chance of successfully contesting such ideology if we engage in the construction of a public, feminist discourse on pregnancy and birth rather than leaving it in the hands of the "pro-lifers." It now seems to me, for example, that feminists should never have permitted debate over the status of the fetus to have achieved center stage in the public imagination, but ought, rather, to have attempted to preempt that debate with a strong *feminist* perspective acknowledging and articulating the ethical and emotional value of the fetus.[62] (I suspect that we would have developed such a perspective if African American women, with their historical experience of having not only their bodies but their children appropriated from them, had played a more central role in framing the rhetoric and arguments of earlier feminist politics.) Granting value, even personhood, to the fetus does not make social control of women's reproduction any less problematic, as I have argued in this essay. Attempts to *devalue* fetal life, on the other hand, have fed powerfully into the right-wing imagination of a possible world in which women would be callously and casually scraping fetuses out of their bodies like leftovers off a plate. This image—so cruelly unrepresentative of most women's experiences—must be challenged, must be shown to be a projection of "evil mother" archetypes, reflective of deep cultural *anxieties* about women's autonomy rather than the *realities* of its exercise.

And, finally, there is the currently problematic status of concepts such as authority and the subject, concepts which have played a crucial role in Western modernity but are now in various philosophical and literary quarters being declared decentered, dying, or dead. This is not the place to detail those arguments. But it is easy, I believe, to call for the wholesale deconstruction of concepts such as subjectivity, authority, and identity only so long as we remain on the plane of high theory, where they function as abstractions. Once we begin to examine the role played by such concepts as they are institutionally and socially embedded in contexts such as law and medicine, in which the philosophical blueprint is transformed into real social architecture, a different agenda may suggest itself. This is what I have argued in this essay with regard to the politics and rhetoric of subjectivity as they are played out in the arena of the current legal and social battle over reproductive control.

Within this battle, we cannot afford, whether in the interests of theoretical avant-gardism or political correctness, to abandon conceptions such as subjectivity, authority, embodied consciousness, and personal integrity. But this does not mean that we will be reproducing them in precisely the form in which we have inherited them. We need to remember that when poststructuralist writers declare that the "author" or "man" (or "metaphysics" or "philosophy") is dead, they refer to conceptions that were historically developed by European men, under conditions of their cultural dominance. Under those conditions, subjectivity took a very particular form by virtue of the experiences excluded from it. Iris Young's study of pregnant embodiment, for example, suggests that pregnancy makes uniquely available (although it does not guarantee) a very different experience of the relationship between mind and body, inner and outer, self and other than that presumed by Descartes, Hobbes, Locke, and other architects of the modernist subject. The conception of autonomy assumed by that model, for example is challenged by an embodiment that literally houses "otherness" within the self.

Young's argument makes us aware of the fact that invoking the authority of marginalized subjects may ultimately result in a reconstruction of subjectivity itself. This is not to say that the (historical) subjectivities of subordinate groups have developed fully *outside* of or unaffected by dominant constructions of the subject. (It is not as though, for example, women have not sought autonomy or cherished possibilities for individuation and self-development.) But our relation to these values has been different: more ambivalent, less purely identified; one could even say, less oppressed.[63] Historically excluded from participation in the making of philosophy, law, and politics, we have nonetheless created culture in our own assigned "spheres," and these cultures now provide a valuable resource for us as we begin to make philosophy, law, and politics in the public arena.

NOTES

1. *Union Pacific Railway v. Botsford,* 141 U.S. 250, 251 (1891).
2. Gilbert Ryle, *The Concept of Mind* (New York: Barnes and Noble, 1949), passim.
3. Stephen Wermiel, "Legal Beat: Bone Marrow Test," *The Wall Street Journal,* October 1, 1990, p. 16.
4. *McFall v. Shimp,* No 78-17711 (C. P. Allegheny County, Pa., July 16, 1978), quoted in Lawrence J. Nelson, Brian P. Buggy, and Carol Weil, "Forced Medical Treatment of Pregnant Women: 'Compelling Each to Live as Seems Good to the Rest,'" *Hastings Law Journal* 37 (May 1986), p. 255. Many newspaper commentaries that appeared before the Illinois decision (cf. note 3, above) emphatically echoed such sentiments, insisting that "one person's right to life stops where another person's body starts" (Lynn Baker, "Are We Safe in Our Own Skins?" *New York Times,* August 21, 1990, p. 27) and declaring the father's efforts to have the twins forced to become donors "a potentially dangerous precedent for allowing bodily invasions without the consent of the donor" (editorial, *New York Times,* August 29, 1990, p. 20).

5. Nelson et al., "Forced Medical Treatment," p. 723.
6. *McFall v. Shimp,* quoted in Nelson et al., "Forced Medical Treatment," p. 755.
7. 342 U.S. 165 (1952), quoted in Nancy Rhoden, "The Judge in the Delivery Room: The Emergence of Court-Ordered Cesareans," *California Law Review* 74 (1986), p. 1983.
8. Other bodily invasions that have been constitutionally permitted are compulsory vaccinations and nonconsensual treatment of institutionalized persons. The former have been permitted because they serve a broad public interest and are required of all members of the society reciprocally. The history of nonconsensual treatment of institutionalized persons (one aspect of which—sterilization abuse—will be discussed briefly later in this essay) is a scandal in itself. Those who have been deemed "mentally defective" or "mentally ill" clearly represent another major category of persons whose rights to bodily integrity and informed consent have regularly been ignored and effaced. It is outside the scope of this essay to discuss that effacement except insofar as it intersects with the specific themes developed here, but this limited treatment should not be understood as minimizing its relevance or importance.
9. *Schmerber v. California,* 384 U.S. 757 (1966).
10. *Winston, Sheriff, et al. v. Lee,* 470 U.S. 753 (1985).
11. Even the subjectivity of persons in persistent vegetative states is respected; determination of the wishes of such patients is always one of the central issues raised in decisions involving termination of their life support (e.g., the Nancy Cruzan and Helga Wanglie cases). And our cultural horror of unconsented-to bodily intrusion extends, as well, to *dead* bodies; cadavers are legally protected against the unconsented-to use of their organs and tissues, even when their use could save the lives of others. Here, respect is extended to the "subjectivity" of corpses far beyond the value placed on those *living* beings who could be benefited if a purely mechanistic, depersonalizing attitude toward body parts prevailed.
12. *Rust v. Sullivan,* 59 USLW 4451 (1991).
13. Philip R. Reilly, *The Surgical Solution* (Baltimore: Johns Hopkins University Press, 1991), p. xiii.

14. Angela Davis, *Women, Race, and Class* (New York: Vintage, 1983), pp. 215–21.
15. Reilly, *The Surgical Solution, pp. 94–5.*
16. *Walker v. Pierce,* 560 F.2d 609 (1977). Pierce won the case, but with an extremely strong dissent from one of the circuit court judges, who argued that beyond doubt Dr. Pierce's policy pertaining to sterilization was based on economic factors instead of the health of his Medicaid patients.
17. Veronika Kolder et al., "Court-Ordered Obstetrical Interventions," *New England Journal of Medicine* 316, no. 19 (May 7, 1987), p. 1192.
18. In re: A. C. Appellant, 523 2d 611 (1987).
19. These procedures, moreover, may turn out not to have been essential to the life of the fetus. In *Jefferson v. Griffin Spaulding Hospital Authority* (GA 86, 274 S.E. 2d 457 1981), Mrs. Jefferson, suffering from placenta previa, was ordered to undergo a cesarean. The order was never enforced, and she wound up uneventfully delivering a healthy child vaginally.
20. *Taft v. Taft,* 446 N.E. 2d 395 (Mass. 1983).
21. Performed when there is high risk of third-trimester miscarriage due to weakness of the cervix (often described as "incompetent cervix"), cerclage involves suturing the cervix closed in order to maintain the pregnancy.
22. So the District of Columbia Court of Appeals described it, in overturning the circuit court's decision on Angela Carder (too late, unfortunately, to affect Carder, but extremely meaningful nonetheless, as I will shortly discuss).
23. Tamar Lewin, "Courts Acting to Force Care of the Unborn," *New York Times,* November 28, 1988, p. 1.
24. See Nelson et al., "Forced Medical Treatment," and Rhoden, "Judge in the Delivery Room," and also Janet Gallagher, "Prenatal Invasions and Interventions: What's Wrong with Fetal Rights," *Harvard Women's Law Journal* 10 (1987), pp. 9–58.
    Some judges *have* attempted to offer a legal rationalization for such contradictions. The dissenting judge in the District of Columbia Court of Appeals overturn of the A. C. ruling, for example, argued that the third-trimester pregnant woman belongs to a "unique category of persons," by virtue of her having "undertaken to bear another human being" and having carried it to viability, and thus having "placed herself" in a special class of persons, those upon whom another's life is totally dependent. Against such arguments, it might reasonably be asked why such a commitment, if indeed it can be said to exist, ends with the birth of the child, and why it does not apply as well to the father of the child. That it does not so apply, legally, is manifest in the decisions that have consistently refused to order parents to donate marrow and organs to their children (even when their lives are "totally dependent" on the donation). I suspect, too, that the element of voluntarily "undertaking" the preservation of the life of another would hold no legal water against broken commitments to donate organs or marrow or to take blood tests. Finally, the question remains: Does the undertaking to care for another entail a commitment to do so *at all costs?*
25. Nelson et al., "Forced Medical Treatment," p. 714.
26. This construction seems to be in the background of the many frequent misapplications of *Roe v. Wade,* arguing in favor of forced cesareans on the basis of the "state's interest in protecting the life of the fetus." The *Roe* decision does indeed acknowledge that this interest increases as pregnancy advances. However, it emphasizes that it is never to supersede that of the life and health of the mother, right up to term. Rather, as *American College of Obstetricians and Gynecologists v. Thornberg* made clear, "the woman's life and health must always prevail over the fetus's life and health when they conflict" (737 F.2d 283 [1984], quoted in Nelson et al., "Forced Medical Treatment," p. 744). The slippage from state interest in fetal life (which *Roe* grants) to the elevation of that interest above the preservation of maternal health (which neither *Roe* nor its progeny accept) converts the protection of fetal life into a doctrine of maternal self-sacrifice. (For an interesting discussion of the misapplications of *Roe,* see Susan Behuniak-Long, "Reproductive Issues and the Applicability of *Roe v. Wade:* Limits and Essence," in *Biomedical Technology and Public Policy,* ed. Robert Black and Miriam Mills [New York: Greenwood Press, 1990].)
27. *Walker v. Pierce.*
28. District of Columbia Court of Appeals No. 87-609 In Re: A. C., April 26, 1990, p. 1142.

29. Kolder et al., "Court-Ordered Obstetrical Interventions."

30. See, for example, Robertson, "The Right to Procreate and In Utero Fetal Therapy," *Journal of Legal Medicine* 333 (1982), pp. 351–61.

31. What is most chilling about these cases is how rarely they occasion real moral controversy, and how casually newspapers describe the procedures in terms that utterly dehumanize the mother. In Syracuse this year, a brain-dead woman who had suffered a brain aneurysm was kept alive for more than seven weeks until her baby could be delivered by cesarean section. The family, acting in proxy, claimed certitude that this would have been her wish. My point here is not to challenge their interpretation. It is striking, however, that *no one* did. In the local newspaper the case was reported purely as a technological achievement, with no suggestion that there might be any sort of ethical conflict involved. Throughout the piece the brain-dead woman was described simply as a *body:* "Aubry said the woman's body probably would go into labor on its own"; "It would be better to deliver before the mother really deteriorates"; etc. (Amber Smith, "Brain-dead Pregnant Woman Kept Alive so Her Baby Could Be Born," *Syracuse Herald-American,* November 3, 1991, p. 1.) My strong suspicion is that even if the family had made their case without reference to the woman's wishes, their request would still have been viewed as morally unproblematic.

Compare this to the highly publicized controversy occasioned in 1989 when Martin Klein (acting in concert with his wife's family) sought a court order appointing him guardian of comatose Nancy Klein, in order to authorize an abortion for her (an abortion doctors deemed necessary to the recovery of the 17-weeks-pregnant woman, and after which she did indeed regain consciousness). In the face of *that* family's claim, right-to-life activists created a national furor and initiated legal proceedings (which ultimately failed) to stay Klein's court order ("Court OKs Abortion for Comatose Woman," *Syracuse Herald Journal,* February 11, 1989, pp. A1–A4). Later that year, a father easily won an order—passionately contested by his wife's family—to sustain his brain-dead pregnant wife's life for seven and a half weeks; she was disconnected from the life-support system immediately after the delivery. In that case, unlike the more recent one, the woman's wishes were not even an issue for the father's case; his claim was argued simply on the basis of *his* desire that the baby be born. I am not suggesting that he had no moral argument. What I *am* pointing out are the dramatic inconsistencies in our moral responses to proxy actions and interpretations affecting the lives of the comatose and the brain-dead. Because the fetal-incubator construction is so normative within cultural attitudes, treating a pregnant comatose woman as mere body simply does not rouse the moral qualms that other such cases do (see also note 11, above).

32. *Guidelines for Legislation on Life-Sustaining Treatment,* National Conference of Catholic Bishops Administrative Committee, November 10, 1984, as reported in "New York State's Health Care Proxy Law: A Catholic Perspective," pamphlet produced by New York State Catholic Conference, Albany, n.d.

33. Nelson et al., "Forced Medical Treatment," pp. 756–7.

34. Eileen McNamara, "Fetal Endangerment Cases on the Rise," *Boston Globe,* October 3, 1989, p. 1.

35. Ellen Goodman, "Pregnant and Prosecuted," *Finger Lakes Times,* February 9, 1990.

36. Robb London, "Two Waiters Lose Jobs for Liquor Warning to Woman," *New York Times,* March 30, 1991, p. 7.

37. Cal Thomas, "Watch What You Say to a Pregnant Woman," *Syracuse Herald Journal,* April 18, 1981.

38. Rhoden, "Judge in the Delivery Room," p. 1959.

39. "Two Waiters Lose Jobs," p. 7.

40. Often waiting lists for drug treatment programs are as much as six months long, and a 1989 New York City survey found that of the existing 78 treatment centers, 54% did not accept pregnant woman and 87% would not treat pregnant women on Medicaid addicted to crack cocaine ("Fetal Endangerment Cases on the Rise").

41. Katha Pollitt, "Fetal Rights: A New Assault on Feminism," *The Nation,* March 26, 1990, p. 410.

42. Robert Pear, "The Hard Thing about Cutting Infant Mortality Is Educating Mothers," *New York Times,* August 12, 1990, p. 5.

43. Discussed in Pollitt, "Fetal Rights," p. 415, a "duty of care" has been proposed by fetal-rights advocates as ethically justifying the obstetrical and lifestyle interventions they argue for.

44. Quoted in Gallagher, "Prenatal Invasions," p. 58.

45. Michael Harrison, "Unborn: Historical Perspective of the Fetus as Patient," *Pharos* (Winter 1982), pp. 19–24, quoted in Ruth Hubbard, *The Politics of Women's Biology* (New Brunswick: Rutgers University Press, 1990), pp. 175–6.

46. Hubbard, *The Politics of Women's Biology,* p. 176.

47. See Rosalind Petchesky, "Fetal Images: The Power of Visual Culture in the Politics of Reproduction," in Michelle Stanworth, ed., *Reproductive Technologies* (Minneapolis: University of Minnesota Press, 1987), pp. 57–80, for an extremely insightful and balanced discussion of this issue.

48. "A lot of doctors," says George Annas, "identify more with the fetus than with a woman who is different from them" (quoted in Lewin, "Courts Acting," p. B10). Especially interesting about this identification is its apparently greater significance than, for example, *racial* "differences" between fetus and doctor, which pale (so to speak) beside deep psychic sources of sympathy with the fetus's state of helpless dependence on the mother.

49. Stefan Semchyshyn and Carol Colman, *How to Prevent Miscarriage and other Crises of Pregnancy* (New York: Macmillan, 1989), p. 5.

50. I hasten to emphasize here that this criticism is not directed against women who choose to take such risks, but toward the discourse that effaces or minimizes those risks.

51. See Nelson et al., "Forced Medical Treatment," pp. 732–45, for an excellent discussion of these changes.

52. *Dietrich v. Inhabitants of Northhampton,* 138 Mass. 14 (1884).

53. W. Prosser, quoted in Nelson et al., "Forced Medical Treatment," p. 733.

54. 65 F. Supp. 138 (D.D.C. 1946).

55. 31 N.J. 353, 157 A.2d 497 (1960), quoted in Nelson et al., "Forced Medical Treatment," p. 734.

56. And this is not to mention the disparity between the respect afforded fetuses and grown women: in Minnesota, the same state that has ordered numerous medical procedures sanctioning the unconsented-to invasion of living women's bodies, a law went into effect in 1990 requiring hospitals and clinics to bury or cremate already dead fetuses, to preserve their "dignity" ("Law Says Cremate or Bury Fetuses," *Syracuse Herald Journal,* October 1, 1990, p. 2).

57. It could be argued that what is required is to bring the social and legal system into line with the treatment of pregnant women, not the other way around. That is, *everyone* (not only pregnant women) should be required to be Good Samaritans toward those who require our aid. It is beyond the scope of this essay to evaluate such an ideal beyond suggesting that those for whom such a transformation is genuinely the goal (and is not merely being paid lip service to, with the covert goal of justifying current inequities) need to demonstrate their good faith by requiring some social care and sacrifice from sources other than pregnant women. A good place to start would be with a national health system that would give poor, pregnant women the care *they* need.

58. The phrases in quotes are from bell hooks's discussion of the reclamation of "black subjectivity," a discussion that is applicable as well to the reclamation of other marginalized and desubjectified identities, including women's reproductive identities: "Contemporary African-American resistance struggle must be rooted in a process of decolonization that continually opposes re-inscribing notions of 'authentic' black identity. This critique should not be made synonymous with a dismissal of the struggle of oppressed and exploited people to make ourselves subject. Nor should it deny that in certain circumstances this experience affords us a privileged critical location from which to speak. This is not a re-inscription of modernist master narratives of authority which privilege some voices by denying voice to others. Part of our struggling for radical black subjectivity is the quest to find ways to construct self and identity that are oppositional and liberatory. The unwillingness to critique essentialism on the part of many African-Americans is rooted in the fear that it will cause folks to lose sight of the specific history and experience of African-Americans and the unique sensibilities and culture that arise from that experience. An adequate response to this concern is to critique essentialism while emphasizing

the significance of 'the authority of experience.' There is a radical difference between a repudiation of the idea that there is a black 'essence' and recognition of the way black identity has been specifically constituted in the experience of exile and struggle." (*Yearning* [Boston: South End Press, 1990], pp. 28–9.)

59. Emily Martin, *The Woman in the Body* (Boston: Beacon Press, 1989), pp. 139–65.

60. Davis, *Women, Race, and Class,* pp. 20–1.

61. Iris Young, "Pregnant Embodiment: Subjectivity and Alienation," *Journal of Medicine and Philosophy* 9 (January 1984), pp. 45–62.

62. I used to argue that this issue should be avoided, insisting that the fetus's status is not simply *there,* "in nature," awaiting an accurate reading, but is a matter of human decision, shaped according to the conventions of particular communities. I still believe all this. But I no longer believe that such meta-considerations remove the responsibility to participate in the public process of shaping those conventions. We retreat into the disembodied haven of meta-discourse only at great risk. For whether or not we choose to engage in the process, cultural determinations and imaginations of the fetus are being made, and currently they have begun to endow the fetus not merely with human status but (as I have shown in this essay) with superhuman status.

63. As Nancy Miller insists: "[T]he postmodernist decision that the Author is dead . . . does not necessarily work for women and prematurely forecloses the question of identity for them. Because women have not had the same historical relation of identity to origin, institution, production, that men have had, women have not, I think, (collectively) felt burdened by too much Self, Ego, Cognito, etc. Because the female subject has juridically been excluded from the polis, and hence decentered, 'disoriginated,' deinstitutionalized, etc., her relation to integrity and textuality, desire and authority, is structurally different." ("Changing the Subject," in Teresa de Lauretis, ed., *Feminist Studies, Critical Studies* [Bloomington: Indiana University Press, 1986], p. 106.)

CHAPTER 6

The Economy, Work, and Money

By 1980 American women held "70 percent of the jobs at all levels of government *concerned with social services,* which was a quarter of all female employment and about half of all professional jobs occupied by women."[1] Thus, cutbacks in welfare mean constricted opportunities for women in an area of employment where they occupy a significant niche. Many women will also face increased domestic labor as caretakers.[2] Such circumstances point to how contemporary capitalism, the liberal state, and the patriarchal nuclear family interact to shape most women's work (and most men's, for that matter). Most of us understand that the capitalist economy and the welfare state join hands in producing these effects, but the nuclear family also lends its institutional force to the equations setting the terms of women's work lives.

Understanding these institutional linkages necessitates distinguishing among four types of work. The most recognized and rewarded (though often not the most rewarding) is paid work, or *productive labor,* which takes a person into the labor market to sell her skills, time, and energy to an employer, such as Intel, Wendy's, Dade County, a dentist, or a parent paying for in-house child care.

A second type of work is *reproductive labor,* the efforts invested in raising one or more members of the next generation to adulthood. This work consists of the commonplaces of child care—feeding, tucking in, snuggling, transporting, helping with homework, bathing, cheering, and endless listening. Some theorists include all domestic work in this category, but that lumps together responsibilities that merit conceptual separation.

Thus, a third type of work is *maintenance labor,* the routine as well as periodic chores necessary to maintain oneself and, for many women, any

243

other adult(s) one serves in this broad, pervasive way. Cooking, paying bills, taking out the garbage, food shopping, mowing the yard, and doing laundry fit here. Sometimes they overlap with reproductive labor, as when cooking feeds one's child as well as oneself (and one's partner).

The fourth type of labor involves men as well as women but would seem to fall squarely in many more women's laps. As Nona Y. Glazer describes it, this labor is

> *unwaged work* . . . directly appropriated by firms and exploited by the state. Private firms and the government have reorganized various activities to draw increasingly upon the work of consumers (users, patients, customers, and clients). . . . For example, the organization of retail sales . . . experienced a major change from a service-intensive to a self-service industry.[3]

Contemporary women commonly do all four kinds of work, often pursuing them simultaneously over long sweeps of their lives. Indeed, many women juggling four distinct sets of work responsibilities are also part- or full-time students who manage to participate in church or synagogue, stay in touch with friends, and much else that got trivialized during the 1996 presidential campaign with the class-loaded phrase "soccer moms." This chapter focuses on how these four kinds of work intertwine in women's lives to their overall disadvantage. Before looking at second-wave theorizing on these matters, however, this one time we turn to first-wave feminist theorizing that still undergirds feminist thinking about the economy, work, and money.

FIRST-WAVE FOUNDATIONS

The first two decades of the 20th century occasioned powerful theorizing about women's economic situations. Three theorists stand out. The first is Olive Schreiner, the novelist whose *Women and Labor* (1911) opens this way:

> In that clamor which has arisen in the modern world, where now this, and then that, is demanded for and by large bodies of modern women, he who listens carefully may detect as a keynote . . . a demand which may be embodied in such a cry as this: *Give us labor and the training which fits for labor!*[4]

Much of Schreiner's treatise concerns the historical changes whereby women's labor got shifted to the home, deprived of its *recognized* economic value, and taken for granted as an expression of women's nature. Schreiner also discussed *sex-parasitism,* what today's theorists call economic dependence among wives working solely or primarily in the home without wages. As Schreiner saw it, women can either gain access to new kinds of work or slip more and more into sex-parasitism. (p. 75) Speaking for the universal "woman" now recognized as deeply problematic, Schreiner concludes, "We claim, to-day, all labor for our province!" (p. 203)

Published about the same time as Schreiner's volume was a work on marriage as a means of livelihood for women. In *Marriage as a Trade* (1909), little-known Cicely Hamilton documented the "infinite importance" of how a "woman earns her bread and the economic conditions under which she enters the family."[5] Hamilton advanced a constructionist view long before theorists had named that perspective, and hers had a materialist bent. She theorized that women's characteristics largely reflect the conditions of their labor. (p. vi) Further, she anticipated Adrienne Rich's notion of "compulsory heterosexuality" (see Chapter 7), observing that for women marriage is "a trade that is practically compulsory." (p. 20)

Hamilton argued that women are "a class persistently set apart for the duties of sexual attraction, house-ordering and the bearing of children" (p. 52), and thus they have little choice but to partner with men as domestic workers. For such labor, they get "essentially a wage of subsistence, regulated by the idea of what is necessary for subsistence in the particular class to which [a given woman] may happen to belong." (p. 95) Hamilton thus pointed to how a homemaker's economic status reflects her husband's earnings, not the merits of her domestic work. In that vein she anticipates post-World War II writings, including Betty Friedan's *Feminine Mystique,* about homemakers' frustrations. Like Friedan and other theorists, Hamilton gave no attention to women of color and Euro-American immigrant women who sometimes longed for the choice to stay home with their children or otherwise opt out of the paid labor force.

Of singular significance among these first-wave theorists is Charlotte Perkins Gilman, who in a series of books between 1898 and 1923 advanced a remarkably modern framework. Her main points remain theoretical cornerstones for conceptualizing women's work so as to render it fully visible and soundly valued. A hundred years ago, for example, she saw the need to recognize the full sweep of women's work: "For a certain percentage of persons to serve other persons, in order that the ones so served may produce more, is a contribution not to be overlooked."[6]

In *The Home: Its Work and Influence* (1903), Gilman challenges the naturalized nuclear family by announcing, "The home is a human institution."[7] She goes on to describe how that institution has not kept pace with other institutions. As the main sources of its cultural lag, Gilman points to the perpetuation of "primitive industries" in the economy and "the confinement of women to those industries and their limited area of expression." (p. 10) Having linked dead-end jobs outside the home to the institutional lethargy of the domestic institution, Gilman insists we can "all have homes to love and grow in without the requirement that half of us shall never have anything else." (p. 12)

In 1914, Gilman's *The Man-Made World or, Our Androcentric Culture* appeared. Dedicated to the sociologist Lester F. Ward, this work takes its inspiration from Chapter XIV of his *Pure Sociology,* where "the Androcentric

Theory of Life is fairly defined and contrasted with the Gynaecocentric Theory."[8] Here Gilman argues that the family's purpose is "the care and nurture of the young." (pp. 26–7) The male-centered culture distorts that purpose, however:

> What man has done to the family . . . is to change it from an institution for the best service of the child to one modified to his own service, the vehicle of his comfort, power, and pride. (p. 27)

Gilman rejects such culturally blessed machinations: "Friendship does not need 'a head.' Love does not need 'a head.' Why should a family?" (p. 43) Yet the abolition of the "head of the household" will be no easy task. Two social movements are necessary to its demise: "The great woman's movement and labor movement of to-day are parts of the same pressure, the same world-progress." (p. 260) That progress also requires cultural shifts capable of raising consciousness. For example, in *His Religion and Hers* (1923), Gilman argues that "'masculinization,' which is precisely as regular in form and which describes a far more common fact [than 'feminization'], we do not yet recognize."[9]

These important first-wave theorists laid foundations for seeing the family as a social construction disproportionately benefiting men in capitalist societies. Much that preoccupied them still concerns feminist theorists. Above all, wives' primary responsibility for housework and mothers' primary responsibility for child care remain theoretical preoccupations.

REPRODUCTION AND MAINTENANCE

Julie A. Nelson observes that

> Analyzing phenomena fraught with connection to others (e.g., responsibility for children), tradition (e.g., the division of household tasks), and relations of domination (e.g., labor market discrimination) with only the language of individual agency, markets, and choice is very likely to create a feeling of distortion; a feeling that that which is most important has been left out.[10]

In large measure, that state of affairs reflects "the 'emotionalisation' of housework which justifies the large amount of time and energy women are expected to devote to homemaking."[11] As Nancy Hartsock says in Reading 15, feminist theorists had to struggle even "to argue that what are held to be acts of love instead must be recognized as work." Sandra Lee Bartky, who also emphasizes that "forms of emotional caregiving . . . are among the commonest ways we show affection," goes on to say that

> the woman in intimacy may set her own needs to one side in order better to attend to his. She does this not because she is "chauvinized" or has "false consciousness," but because *this is what the work requires*.[12]

No woman who has pursued caretaking over the long term needs to be told that it is indeed work. It is hard, hard work to care well for another human being—to be thoughtful, patient, supportive, encouraging. Yet such efforts usually go unrecognized as work. Even the typology of work serving as a launchpad here neglects the caretaking woven into the maintenance labor women typically do in their homes. Alongside their cooking and laundering and all else is the emotional labor of being a "good" partner. Granted, the caretaking built into reproductive labor is recognized. Even there, though, its being *work* is muted (beyond the company of mothers, who know that it is, however joyful and unutterably rewarding at times).

What follows from all this is that a concern with women's work necessitates the phrase *family–household system,* which points to both the "family ideology and the material structure of the household" comprising parent(s) and child(ren). Less obvious, though implied between the lines above, is that housework or homemaking "is a socially constructed job for women."[13] Its construction is rooted in the Industrial Revolution, which looks different from when you and I first learned about it—when it had to do with men and factories, the geographic displacement of the rural peasantry, and the gradual dissolution of the family as an economically productive unit.

Seen through feminist lenses, industrialization established homemaking as women's proper work. Carol Pateman, among others, describes a historical transformation whereby "masters and servants become employers and employees, husbands become worker/breadwinners, and wives become housewives." As Carol Johnson sees it, capitalism jeopardized "the patriarchal 'marriage' contract; a threat that had to be met by male workers mobilising to exclude or marginalise female labour from the employment contract."[14]

Whether or not one postulates that male workers or male capitalists (or both) moved to constrict women's employment opportunities and whether or not one postulates a design for that outcome, the political fact is that such machinations cannot readily sustain social transformation. Ideologies making people want to do what the powerful mean them to do are essential. Thus, over time came the separate-spheres ideology naturalizing the public sphere as masculine and the domestic one as feminine; the breadwinner/homemaker ideology naturalizing the patriarchal nuclear family; and the cult-of-true-womanhood ideology emphasizing the inherent fragility and moral superiority of white bourgeois women.

Such historical constructions as housewifery for women reflect the relations of ruling in multiple ways. As Johanna Brenner and Barbara Laslett emphasize, "systems of social reproduction" like breadwinner/homemaker derive from "class and gender struggles—struggles that are often about sexuality and emotional relations as well as political power and economic resources."[15] Brenner and Laslett's depiction of the social construction of homemaking focuses on the early 20th century in middle-American society:

> Increasing participation in education and wage work, especially for unmarried women, encouraged a greater emphasis on middle-class women's sexual and personal autonomy. Women's low wages, however, put economic autonomy

Yet most men earn incomes "at least sufficient to support a one-adult household," while substantial numbers of mothers fall below that threshold. Janet Siltanen defines a full-wage job as one that lets a person "take sole responsibility for maintaining an independent household, a responsibility that in some cases includes financial maintenance of other household members not in waged work"; a component-wage job fails to do that. Focusing on British society, Siltanen finds that women typically "earn component-wages, manual men earn full-wages for a one-adult household, and nonmanual men earn full-wages for a two-adult, two-child household."[34] On those bases she analyzes the social obligations that various workers can realistically handle.

In the process she shows how hiring and pay discrimination undermines women's capacity to form the households they really want rather than the ones they get by default. Siltanen thus theorizes the connections between most women's subordination in the workplace and their subordination at home. She also points out that across the class structure women are hard pressed to "maintain their married standard of living as single persons."[35] Bluntly put, mothers bear the primary responsibility for financially supporting their children in the event of divorce. Thus, even those with decent full-wage jobs live less comfortably after divorce.

What stands on the theoretical horizon is the question of how patriarchal family forms correlate with capitalist economic forms. At the broadest level, some feminist theorists treat patriarchy and capitalism as a single male-dominated system that disadvantages women. Dual-systems theorists, by contrast, see them as distinct but complementary enterprises. Brenner and Laslett summarize the differences between the two stances:

> Within the dual-systems—or capitalist–patriarchy—framework, socialist-feminists have argued that the state mediates between the conflicting interests of male capitalists and workers, on the one hand, and their common interests as white men on the other. They point out that state policy with regard to both services . . . and regulation . . . reflects and perpetuates women's marginalization in paid labor and their assignment to unpaid labor in the home. From this perspective, state provision for women and children is understood as a "negotiated settlement" among contending groups of men. The development of the welfare state, rather than providing women access to income and services as an alternative to their dependence on men for support, established a "public patriarchy" that reinforced women's dependence on the male-breadwinner family and on a male-controlled state.

Brenner and Laslett support a socialist-feminist, "single-system" model emphasizing "that production and social reproduction are two domains of an integrated process of species reproduction."[36]

Alternatively, Walby argues that "patriarchy is never the only mode in a society but always exists in articulation with another, such as capitalism." For her, the state does "represent patriarchal as well as capitalist interests," but institutions distinct from the capitalist economy and the state also bolster patriarchy. Among them is heterosexuality, "without [which] the patriarchal mode of production could not exist."[37]

Typical household inequities illustrate that state of affairs. An employed wife may have a decent income and her own benefits, yet as a matter of course in most heterosexual-couple households, she works two shifts to her husband's one. From Ann Oakley's *The Sociology of Housework* (1974) to Arlie Hochschild's *The Second Shift* (1989), that domestic situation has been documented in detail. In practical terms, "the overall labour contribution of women consistently outstrips that of men" and "men . . . are assumed to have an automatic right to leisure, not women." Kynaston concludes that

> while variation can clearly occur, the exploitative core of the patriarchal mode of production nevertheless remains remarkably resilient. Variation, then, is apt to be structured around this core rather than in defiance of it. In short, men's lives continue to be consistently enhanced by their appropriation of female labour.[38]

Glazer describes this socioeconomic situation in terms of "a female underclass whose members also serve as a family underclass—increasingly the custodial partner, the sole adult responsible for raising the next generation."[39]

ECONOMICS, WORK, AND WOMEN'S SUBORDINATION

Like other systems of knowledge bolstering the relations of ruling, economics neglects women. Even when it does carve out space for us, its accommodations are far from commodious. Like most other disciplines, economics developed as a male-monopolized, male-centered enterprise.[40] One sign of its persistent biases is the absence of attention to families in its dominant models. As Nelson reports, Gary Becker and other "New Home Economists" are important exceptions to that rule.[41]

Among the major applications of economics are the national and international accounting systems whereby people's labor gets measured. By now, some economists want to correct the exclusion of household economies from those systems, but Lois Bryson sees masculinist biases infiltrating their efforts. For starters, money remains the main measure for estimating the value of unpaid work, when time might be a better yardstick. Even then, though, women's unpaid labor is commonly mismeasured, in part because they often do multiple tasks simultaneously and in part because some of what passes as women's leisure involves reproductive or maintenance work.[42] A poignant example of such neglect and bias is breast-feeding. Even though mothers' milk "is the most satisfying food supply for infants, at least for the first four to six months of life," it "has not usually been considered or classified as a food. . . ." After all, it is neither "grown agriculturally nor purchased in a processed container."[43]

Even some of women's paid work escapes notice in such systems. One example is the street food trade. "Like other micro-enterprises, [it] was generally dismissed as insignificant economic activity by development economists." Even when the informal sector of economies began getting attention, rarely did it include micro-entrepreneurs. So "women entrepreneurs, who tend to be clustered at the smallest end of the informal sector, remained invisible." Similarly, "Women's work in subsistence agriculture was reflected neither in definitions . . . nor in statistics. . . ." Thus, stereotypes of women as economically dependent or nonproductive got perpetuated, while male-centered programs for economic development got justified.[44]

These patterns are part of a much bigger picture wherein

> women's "comparative disadvantages" in the labor market in any given country can, at some time, be translated into "comparative advantages" for companies, capitals, and governments in the international markets.

As Lourdes Arizpe and Josefina Aranda go on to note, when women thus disadvantaged organize on their own behalf, "the 'comparative advantages' are lost and investments go elsewhere."[45]

Thus, women's economic situations need to be addressed at the microcosmic level of the family–household system, at the macrocosmic level of the national economy and the state, and at the geocosmic level of the global economy, where capital gets internationalized in search of cheap labor that often comes from women. Carol S. Robb, the author of Reading 16, puts it in a nutshell when she flatly announces that "the economy is structured for men."[46] Reading 15 could have been placed in Chapter 8, where feminist ethics gets attention. I put it here, however, because Robb's feminist economic ethics captures costs women commonly incur as workers. By showing that injustices such as sexual harassment are expensive, Robb points to the costs of patriarchy itself.

Its costs far exceed the dollars and cents economists are finally calculating. The costs also include daily challenges revolving around questions of what can wait, what corners can be cut, and what deadline can be renegotiated. Yet as Bartky implies and many women's lives demonstrate, women do manage to lead meaningful, rewarding lives; they do manage to undercut the unfairnesses in their lives; they do what much of this chapter implies cannot readily be done. As a matter of practical fact, what many women do cannot be done easily. It can, however, be done with more than a little satisfaction.

One wonderful source of stories about how women of various ages, races, ethnicities, sexual orientations, and social classes have prevailed, especially as mothers and workers of diverse sorts, is a volume entitled *The Conversation Begins: Mothers and Daughters Talk about Living Feminism.* Its tales show women "combin[ing] motherhood with a passionate commitment to a broader life."[47] Among the mothers contributing to that volume is Alix Kates Shulman, the author of *Memoirs of an Ex-Prom Queen* (among other works). Shulman's thoughts offer an apt conclusion to this chapter:

Feminism gave me back my defiant voice, enabling me again to stand up and be active in the world instead of passively accepting the marginality I had felt condemned to once I had children. Feminism gave me a way to understand, perhaps escape, my predicament and be a mother with pride and honor. . . . Feminism was the tool with which I could mend my life and rejoin the world. (p. 89)

Before long Shulman adds,

I never felt any conflict between the movement and motherhood. Feminism healed my conflicts. Once I joined the movement I never again felt I had to sacrifice anything or choose between being a mom and having my own independent life. To me, all the sacrifice and compromise preceded feminism, and feminism reversed them. In fact, it was as a mother that I most deeply engaged with feminism.

For those facing the hard question of how to combine motherhood with paid work of one sort or other, then, there *is* support to be had as well as practical wisdom. Feminism takes shape from the day-in, day-out efforts of women hard at work in their everyday lives. They make it a virtual support system as well as an empowering perspective on women's lived experiences.

NOTES

1. Carole Pateman, *The Disorder of Women: Democracy, Feminism and Political Theory* (Cambridge: Polity Press, 1989), p. 181.
2. V. Spike Peterson, "The Politics of Identification in the Context of Globalization," *Women's Studies International Forum* 19, no. 1/2 (January/April 1996), p. 12.
3. Nona Y. Glazer, "Paid and Unpaid Work: Contradictions in American Women's Lives Today" in Kathryn M. Borman, Daisy Quarm, and Sarah Gideonse (eds.), *Women in the Workplace: Effects on Families* (Norwood, NJ: Ablex Publishing, 1984), p. 180; emphasis added. More recently, George Ritzer has documented this phenomenon in detail; see his *McDonaldization of Society: An Investigation into the Changing Character of Contemporary Social Life,* revised ed. (Thousand Oaks, CA: Pine Forge Press, 1996).
4. Olive Schreiner, *Women and Labor* (New York: Frederick A. Stokes Company, 1911), p. 27.
5. Cicely Hamilton, *Marriage as a Trade* (New York: Moffat, Yard and Company, 1909), p. v.
6. Charlotte Perkins Gilman, *Women and Economics: A Study of the Economic Relation between Men and Women as a Factor in Social Evolution* (Boston: Small, Maynard & Co., 1898), p. 13.
7. Charlotte Perkins Gilman, *The Home: Its Work and Influence* (New York: McClure, Phillips & Co., 1903), p. 4.
8. Charlotte Perkins Gilman, *The Man-Made World or, Our Androcentric Culture* (New York: Charlton Co., 1914), Preface.
9. Charlotte Perkins Gilman, *His Religion and Hers: A Study of the Faith of Our Fathers and the Work of Our Mothers* (Westport, CT: Hyperion Press, 1976 (orig. 1923)), p. 83.

10. Julie A. Nelson, *Feminism, Objectivity and Economics* (New York: Routledge, 1996), p. 67.

11. Janeen Baxter, *Work at Home: The Domestic Division of Labour* (Queensland, Australia: University of Queensland Press, 1993), p. 16.

12. Sandra Lee Bartky, *Femininity and Domination: Studies in the Phenomenology of Oppression* (New York: Routledge, 1990), pp. 103, 114.

13. Baxter, *Work at Home,* pp. 16, 35. Baxter draws "family–household system" from Michelle Barrett's *Women's Oppression Today.*

14. Carole Pateman, "A Comment on Johnson's *Does Capitalism Really Need Patriarchy?*," *Women's Studies International Forum* 19, no. 3 (1996), p. 203; Carol Johnson, "Does Capitalism Really Need Patriarchy? Some Old Issues Reconsidered," *Women's Studies International Forum* 19, no. 3 (1996), p. 195.

15. Johanna Brenner and Barbara Laslett, "Gender, Social Reproduction, and Women's Self-Organization: Considering the U.S. Welfare State," *Gender & Society* 5, no. 3 (September 1991), p. 315.

16. Betty Friedan, *The Feminine Mystique* (New York: Dell Publishing Co., 1963).

17. Chris Kynaston, "The Everyday Exploitation of Women: Housework and the Patriarchal Mode of Production," *Women's Studies International Forum* 19, no. 3 (1996), pp. 228, 232–3.

18. Sylvia Walby, *Patriarchy at Work: Patriarchal and Capitalist Relations in Employment* (Cambridge: Polity Press, 1986), pp. 52–3, 54, 66.

19. Margaret Benston, "The Political Economy of Women's Liberation" in Ellen Malos (ed.), *The Politics of Housework* (London: Allison & Busby Ltd., 1980), p. 121.

20. Mariarosa Dalla Costa and Selma James, "The Power of Women and the Subversion of the Community" in Malos, *The Politics of Housework,* pp. 168, 169. Like Walby and Brenner and Laslett, Dalla Costa and James also pay attention to heterosexuality, describing it as institutionalized "sexual, economic, and social discipline"; p. 172.

21. Wanda Minge, "The Industrial Revolution and the European Family: 'Childhood' as a Market for Family Labor" in Eleanor Leacock, Helen I. Safa, and Contributors, *Women's Work: Development and the Division of Labor by Gender* (South Hadley, MA: Bergin & Garvey Publishers, 1986), pp. 13, 14, 24.

22. Walby, *Patriarchy at Work,* p. 248.

23. Bartky, *Femininity and Domination,* pp. 98, 119.

24. Caroline Bird, *The Two-Paycheck Marriage: How Women at Work Are Changing Life in America* (New York: Wade Publishers, 1979), p. 4; *Enterprising Women* (New York: W. W. Norton & Co., 1976), p. 13.

25. Eileen Janes Yeo, "Conflicts between the Domestic and Market Economy in Britain: Past and Present" in Barbara Einhorn and Eileen Janes Yeo (eds.), *Women and Market Societies: Crisis and Opportunity* (Aldershot, UK: Edward Elgar, 1995), p. 137.

26. Pateman, "Comment," p. 204.

27. For commentaries on such legislation, see Kim M. Blankenship, "Bringing Gender and Race In: U.S. Employment Discrimination Policy," *Gender & Society* 7, no. 2 (June 1993), pp. 204–26; Cynthia Deitch, "Gender, Race, and Class Politics and the Inclusion of Women in Title VII of the 1964 Civil Rights Act," *Gender & Society* 7, no. 2 (June 1993), pp. 183–203; Martha W. Griffiths, "Requisites for Equality" in Juanita M. Kreps (ed.), *Women and*

the American Economy: A Look to the 1980s (Englewood Cliffs, NJ: Prentice-Hall, 1976), pp. 146–54; Vicki Schultz, "Women 'before' the Law: Judicial Stories about Women, Work, and Sex Segregation on the Job" in Judith Butler and Joan W. Scott (eds.), *Feminists Theorize the Political* (New York: Routledge, 1992), pp. 297–338.

28. Glazer, "Paid and Unpaid Work," p. 183.
29. Lisa Peattie and Martin Rein, *Women's Claims: A Study in Political Economy* (Oxford: Oxford University Press, 1983), p. 73.
30. Pateman, "Comment," pp. 203–4.
31. Lois Bryson, "Revaluing the Household Economy," *Women's Studies International Forum* 19, no. 3 (1996), p. 209.
32. Anne Phillips, *Hidden Hands: Women and Economic Politics* (London: Pluto Press, 1983), p. 75.
33. Blankenship, "Bringing Gender and Race In," p. 214.
34. Janet Siltanen, *Locating Gender: Occupational Segregation, Wages and Domestic Responsibilities* (London: UCL Press, 1994), pp. 77–8, 99, 115, 194.
35. Bird, *The Two-Paycheck Marriage,* p. 13.
36. Brenner and Laslett, "Gender, Social Reproduction," pp. 311–2, 313, 329.
37. Walby, *Patriarchy at Work,* pp. 50, 57, 66. On the connections between patriarchy and capitalism, see Zillah R. Eisenstein (ed.), *Capitalist Patriarchy and the Case for Socialist Feminism* (New York and London: Monthly Review Press, 1979); Karen V. Hansen and Ilene J. Philipson (eds.), *Women, Class, and the Feminist Imagination: A Socialist-Feminist Reader* (Philadelphia: Temple University Press, 1990).
38. Kynaston, "Everyday Exploitation," pp. 230, 231, 233.
39. Glazer, "Paid and Unpaid Work," p. 184.
40. For a fine overview, see Michele A. Pujol, *Feminism and Anti-Feminism in Early Economic Thought* (Aldershot, England: Edward Elgar, 1992).
41. Nelson, *Feminism, Objectivity and Economics,* p. 61; also see Peattie and Rein, *Women's Claims,* p. 51. They say the New Home Economists treat the household like a "small factory."
42. Bryson, "Revaluing," pp. 208, 211, 212, 214, 215.
43. Marilyn Waring, *If Women Counted: A New Feminist Economics* (San Francisco: Harper & Row, 1988), pp. 206, 207, 208.
44. Irene Tinker, "The Urban Street Food Trade: Regional Variations of Women's Involvement" in Esther N. Chow and Catherine Berheide White (eds.), *Women, the Family, and Policy: A Global Perspective* (Albany: State University of New York Press, 1994), pp. 166, 167.
45. Lourdes Arizpe and Josefina Aranda, "Women Workers in the Strawberry Agribusiness in Mexico" in Leacock, Safa et al., *Women's Work,* p. 193.
46. Carol S. Robb, *Equal Value: An Ethical Approach to Economics and Sex* (Boston: Beacon Press, 1995), p. 1.
47. Christina Looper Baker and Christina Baker Kline, "Introduction" in Christina Looper Baker and Christina Baker Kline (eds.), *The Conversation Begins: Mothers and Daughters Talk about Living Feminism* (New York: Bantam Books, 1996), p. xiv.

READING 15

The Feminist Standpoint: Toward a Specifically Feminist Historical Materialism

Nancy C. M. Hartsock

The different understandings of power put forward by women who have theorized about power implicitly pose the question of the extent to which gender is a worldview-structuring experience. In this paper I explore some of the epistemological consequences of claiming that women's lives differ systematically and structurally from those of men. In particular, I suggest that, like the lives of proletarians according to Marxian theory, women's lives make available a particular and privileged vantage point on male supremacy, a vantage point that can ground a powerful critique of the phallocratic institutions and ideology that constitute the capitalist form of patriarchy. I argue that on the basis of the structures that define women's activity as contributors to subsistence and as mothers, the sexual division of labor, one could begin, though not complete, the construction of a feminist standpoint on which to ground a specifically feminist historical materialism. I hope to show how just as Marx's understanding of the world from the standpoint of the proletariat enabled him to go beneath bourgeois ideology, so a feminist standpoint can allow us to descend further into materiality to an epistemological level at which we can better understand both why patriarchal institutions and ideologies take such perverse and deadly forms and how both theory and practice can be redirected in more liberatory directions.

The reader will remember that the concept of a standpoint carries several specific contentions. Most important, it posits a series of levels of reality in which the deeper level both includes and explains the surface or appearance. Related to the positing of levels are several claims:

1. Material life (class position in Marxist theory) not only structures but sets limits on the understanding of social relations.
2. If material life is structured in fundamentally opposing ways for two different groups, one can expect that the vision of each will represent an inversion of the other, and in systems of domination the vision available to the rulers will be both partial and perverse.
3. The vision of the ruling class (or gender) structures the material relations in which all parties are forced to participate and therefore cannot be dismissed as simply false.
4. In consequence, the vision available to the oppressed group must be struggled for and represents an achievement that requires both science to see beneath the surface of the social relations in which all are forced to participate and the education that can only grow from struggle to change those relations.
5. As an engaged vision, the understanding of the oppressed, the adoption of a standpoint exposes the real relations among human beings as inhuman, points beyond the present, and carries a historically liberatory role.

Because of its achieved character and its liberatory potential, I use the term "feminist" rather than "women's standpoint." Like the experience of the proletariat, women's experience and activity as a dominated group contains both negative and positive aspects. A feminist standpoint picks out and amplifies the liberatory possibilities contained in that experience.

Women's work in every society differs systematically from men's. I intend to pursue the suggestion that this division of labor is the first, and in some societies the only, division of labor; moreover, it is central to the organization of social labor more generally.[1] On the basis of an account of the sexual division of labor, one should be able to begin to explore the oppositions and differences between women's and men's activity and their consequences for epistemology. While I cannot attempt a complete account, I put forward a schematic and simplified account of the sexual division of labor and its consequences for epistemology. I sketch out a kind of ideal type of the social relations and world view characteristic of men's and women's activity in order to explore the epistemology contained in the institutionalized sexual division of labor. In so doing, I do not mean to attribute this vision to individual women or men (any more than Marx or Lukács meant their theory of class consciousness to apply to any particular worker or group of workers). My focus is instead on institutionalized social practices and on the specific epistemology and ontology manifested by the institutionalized sexual division of labor. Individuals, as individuals, may change their activity in ways that move them outside the outlook embodied in these institutions, but such a move can be significant only when it occurs at the level of society as a whole.

I discuss the "sexual division of labor" rather than "gender division of labor" to stress, first, my desire not to separate the effects of "nature and nurture," or biology and culture, and my belief that the division of labor between women and men cannot be reduced to simply social dimensions. One must distinguish between what Sara Ruddick has termed "invariant and *nearly* unchangeable" features of human life, and those that, despite being "*nearly* universal," are "certainly changeable."[2] Thus the fact that women and not men *bear* children is not (yet) a social choice, but that women and not men *rear* children in a society structured by compulsory heterosexuality and male dominance is clearly a societal choice. A second reason to use the term "sexual division of labor" is to keep hold of the bodily aspect of existence, perhaps to grasp it overfirmly in an effort to keep it from evaporating altogether. There is some biological, bodily

component to human existence. But its size and substantive content will remain unknown until at least the certainly changeable aspects of the sexual division of labor are altered.

On the basis of a schematic account of the sexual division of labor, I begin to fill in the specific content of the feminist standpoint and begin to specify how women's lives structure an understanding of social relations, that is, begin to follow out the epistemological consequences of the sexual division of labor. In addressing the institutionalized sexual division of labor, I propose to lay aside the important differences among women and instead to search for central commonalities across race and class boundaries. I take some justification from the fruitfulness of Marx's similar strategy in constructing a simplified, two-class, two-man model in which everything was exchanged at its value. Marx's schematic account in volume I of *Capital* left out of account such factors as imperialism; the differential wages, work, and working conditions of the Irish; the differences between women, men, and children; and so on. While all these factors are important to the analysis of contemporary capitalism, none changes either Marx's theories of surplus value or alienation, the two most fundamental features of the Marxian analysis of capitalism. My effort here takes a similar form, in an attempt to move toward a theory of the extraction and appropriation of women's activity and women themselves. Still, I adopt this strategy with some reluctance, since it contains the danger of making invisible the experience of lesbians or women of color.[3] At the same time, I recognize that the effort to uncover a feminist standpoint assumes that there are some things common to all women's lives in Western class societies.

The feminist standpoint that emerges through an examination of women's activities is related to the proletarian standpoint, but deeper-going. Women and workers inhabit a world in which the emphasis is on change rather than stasis, a world characterized by interaction with natural substances rather than separation from nature, a world in which quality is more important than quantity, a world in which the unification of mind and body is inherent in the activities performed. Yet there are some important differences, differences marked by the fact that the proletarian (if male) is immersed in this world only during the time his labor power is being used by the capitalist. If, to paraphrase Marx, we follow the worker home from the factory, we can once again perceive a change in the dramatis personae. He who before followed behind as the worker, timid and holding back, with nothing to expect but a hiding, now strides in front, while a third person, not specifically present in Marx's account of the transactions between capitalist and worker (both of whom are male) follows timidly behind, carrying groceries, baby, and diapers.

Given what has been said about the life activity of the proletarian, one can see that, because the sexual division of labor means that much of the work involved in reproducing labor power is done by women, and because much of the male worker's contact with nature outside the factory is mediated by a woman, the vision of reality which grows from the female experience is deeper and more thoroughgoing than that available to the worker.

THE SEXUAL DIVISION OF LABOR

Women's activity as institutionalized has a double aspect: their contribution to subsistence and their contribution to childrearing. Whether or not all women do both, women as a sex are institutionally responsible for producing both goods and human beings, and all women are forced to become the kinds of persons who can do both. Although the nature of women's contribution to subsistence varies immensely over time and space, my primary focus here is on capitalism, with a secondary focus on the class societies that preceded it.[4] In capitalism, women contribute both production for wages and pro-

duction of goods in the home, that is, they, like men, sell their labor power and produce both commodities and surplus value, and produce use values in the home. Unlike men, however, women's lives are institutionally defined by their production of use values in the home.[5] Here we begin to encounter the narrowness of Marx's concept of production. Women's production of use values in the home has not been well understood by socialists. It is no surprise to feminists that Engels, for example, simply asks how women can continue to do the work in the home and also work in production outside the home. Marx, too, takes for granted women's responsibility for household labor. He repeats, as if it were his own, the question of a Belgian factory inspector: If a mother works for wages, "how will [the household's] internal economy be cared for; who will look after the young children; who will get ready the meals, do the washing and mending?"[6]

Let us trace both the outlines and the consequences of women's dual contribution to subsistence in capitalism. Women's labor, like that of the male worker, is contact with material necessity. Their contribution to subsistence, like that of the male worker, involves them in a world in which the relation to nature and to concrete human requirement is central, both in the form of interaction with natural substances whose quality, rather than quantity, is important to the production of meals, clothing, and so forth and in the form of close attention in a different way from men's. While repetition for both the wages and even more in household production involves a unification of mind and body for the purpose of transforming natural substances into socially defined goods [*sic*]. This, too, is true of the labor of the male worker.

There are, however, important differences. First, women as a group work more than men. We are all familiar with the phenomenon of the "double day," and with indications that women work many more hours per week than men.[7] Second, a larger proportion of women's labor time is devoted to the production of use values than men's. Only some of the goods women produce are commodities (however much they live in a society structured by commodity production and exchange). Third, women's production is structured by repetition in a different way from men's. While repetition for both the woman and the male worker may take the form of production of the same object, over and over—whether apple pies or brake linings— women's work in housekeeping involves a repetitious cleaning.[8]

Thus the man, in the process of production, is involved in contact with necessity and interchange with nature as well as with other human beings, but the process of production or work does not consume his whole life. The activity of a woman in the home as well as the work she does for wages keeps her continually in contact with a world of qualities and change. *Her* immersion in the world of use—in concrete, many-qualitied, changing material processes—is more complete than his. And if life itself consists of sensuous activity, the vantage point available to women on the basis of their contribution to subsistence represents an intensification and deepening of the materialist world view available to the producers of commodities in capitalism, an intensification of class consciousness. The availability of this outlook to even nonworking-class women has been strikingly formulated by a novelist: "Washing the toilet used by three males, and the floor and walls around it, is, Mira thought, coming face to face with necessity. And that is why women were saner than men, did not come up with the mad, absurd schemes men developed: they were in touch with necessity, they had to wash the toilet bowl and floor."[9]

The focus on women's subsistence activity rather than men's leads to a model in which the capitalist (male) lives a life structured completely by commodity exchange and not at all by production, and at the farthest distance from contact with concrete material life. The male worker marks a way station on the path to the other extreme—the constant contact with material necessity present in women's contribution to subsistence. There are of course important differences along the lines of race and class. For example, working-class men seem to do more domestic labor than men higher up in the class structure—car repairs, carpentry, and the like. And until very recently, the wage work done by most women of color replicated the housework required by their own households. Still, there are commonalities present in the institutionalized sexual division of labor that makes women responsible for both housework and wage work.

Women's contribution to subsistence, however, represents only a part of women's labor. Women also produce/reproduce men (and other women) on both a daily and a long-term basis. This aspect of women's "production" exposes the deep inadequacies of the concept of production as a description of women's activity. One does not (cannot) produce another human being in anything like the way one produces an object such as a chair. Much more is involved, activity that cannot easily be dichotomized into play or work. Helping another to develop, the gradual relinquishing of control, the experiencing of the human limits of one's actions—all these are important features of women's activity as mothers. Women, as mothers, even more than as workers, are institutionally involved in processes of change and growth, and more than workers, must understand the importance of avoiding excessive control in order to help others grow.[10] The activity involved is far more complex than instrumentally working with others to transform objects. (Interestingly, much of women's wage work— nursing, social work, and some secretarial jobs in particular—requires and depends on the relational and interpersonal skills women learned by being mothered by someone of the same sex.)

This aspect of women's activity, too, is not without consequences. Indeed, it is in the production of men by women and the appropriation of this labor, and women themselves, by men, that the opposition between feminist and masculinist experience and outlook is rooted, and it is here that features of the proletarian vision are enhanced and modified for the woman and diluted for the man. Women's experience in reproduction represents a unity with nature that goes beyond the proletarian experience of interchange with nature. As another theorist has put it, "reproductive labor might be said to combine the functions of the architect and the bee: Like the architect, parturitive woman knows what she is doing; like the bee, she cannot help what she is doing." And just as the worker's acting on the external work changes both the world and the worker's nature, so too "a new life changes the world and the consciousness of the woman."[11] In addition, in the process of producing human beings, relations with others may take a variety of forms with deeper significance than simple cooperation with others for common goals—forms that range from a deep unity with another through the many-leveled and changing connections mothers experience with growing children. Finally, women's experience in bearing and rearing children involves a unity of mind and body more profound than is possible in the worker's instrumental activity.

Motherhood in the large sense, that is, motherhood as an institution rather than an experience, including pregnancy and the preparation for motherhood almost all female children receive in being raised by a woman, results in the construction of female existence as centered within a complex relational nexus.[12] One aspect of this relational existence is centered on the experience of living in a woman's rather than a man's body. There are a series of what our culture treats as boundary challenges inherent in female physiology, challenges that make it difficult to maintain rigid separation from the object world. Menstruation, coitus, pregnancy, childbirth, lactation—all represent challenges to bodily boundaries.[13] Adrienne Rich has described the experience of pregnancy as one in which the embryo was both inside and yet "daily more separate, on its way to becoming separate from

me and of-itself. In early pregnancy the stirring of the fetus felt like ghostly tremors of my own body, later like the movements of a being imprisoned in me; but both sensations were *my* sensations, contributing to my own sense of physical and psychic space."[14]

In turn, the fact that women but not men are primarily responsible for young children means that the infant first experiences itself as not fully differentiated from the mother and then as an *I* in relation to an *It* that it later comes to know as female.[15] Nancy Chodorow and Jane Flax have argued that the object-relations school of psychoanalytic theory puts forward a materialist psychology, one that I propose to treat as a kind of empirical hypothesis. If the account of human development provided by object relations is correct, one ought to expect to find consequences—both psychic and social.[16] According to object-relations theory, the process of differentiation from a woman, by both boys and girls, reinforces boundary confusion in women's egos and boundary strengthening in men's. Individuation is far more conflictual for male than for female children, in part because both mother and son experience the other as a definite "other." The experience of oneness on the part of both mother and infant seems to last longer with girls.[17]

The complex relational world inhabited by women has its start in the experience and resolution of the oedipal crisis, cleanly resolved for the boy, whereas the girl is much more likely to retain both parents as love objects. The nature of the crisis itself differs by sex: The boy's love for the mother is an extension of mother–infant unity and thus essentially threatening to his ego and independence. Masculine ego formation necessarily requires repressing this first relation and negating the mother.[18] In contrast, the girl's love for the father is less threatening both because it occurs outside this unity and because it occurs at a later stage of development. For boys, the central issue to be resolved concerns gender identification; for girls, the issue is psychosexual development.[19] Chodorow concludes that girls' gradual emergence from the oedipal period takes place in such a way that empathy is built into their primary definition of self, and they have a variety of capacities for experiencing another's needs or feelings as their own. Put another way, girls, because of female parenting, are less differentiated from others than boys, more continuous with and related to the external object world. They are differently oriented to their inner object world as well.[20]

The more complex female relational world is reinforced by the process of socialization. Girls learn roles from watching their mothers; boys must learn roles from rules that structure the life of an absent male figure. Girls can identify with a concrete example present in daily life; boys must identify with an abstract set of maxims only occasionally concretely present in the form of the father. Thus, not only do girls learn roles with more interpersonal and relational skills, but the process of role learning itself is embodied in the concrete relation with the mother. The male, in contrast, must identify with an abstract, cultural stereotype and learn abstract behaviors not attached to a well-known person. Masculinity is idealized for boys, whereas femininity is concrete for girls.[21]

Women and men, then, grow up with personalities affected by different boundary experiences, differently constructed and experienced inner and outer worlds, and preoccupations with different relational issues. This early experience forms an important ground for the feminine sense of self as connected to the world and the masculine sense of self as separate, distinct, and even disconnected. By retaining the preoedipal attachment to the mother, girls come to define and experience themselves as continuous with others. In sum, girls enter adulthood with a more complex layering of affective ties and a rich, ongoing inner set of object relations. Boys, with a simpler oedipal situation and a clear and early resolution, have repressed ties to another. As a result, women define and experience themselves relationally, and men do not.[22]

Chodorow's argument receives interesting support from Robert Stoller's work on sexual excitement and his search for the roots of adult sexual behavior in infant experience. Attempting to understand why men are more perverse than women (i.e., why men's sexual excitement seems to require more gross hostility than women's) led him to suggest that boys may face more difficulties in individuating than girls.[23] He puts forward a theory of what he terms "primary femininity." Because the male infant is merged with the mother, who is a woman, the boy may experience himself as female. Stoller suggests that it may be that the boy does not start out as heterosexual, as Freud thought, but must separate himself to achieve heterosexuality. The oneness with the mother must be counteracted.[24] Thus, "masculinity in males starts as a movement away from the blissful and dangerous, forever remembered and forever yearned for, mother–infant symbiosis."[25] To become masculine, the boy must separate himself both externally from his mother's body, and within himself, from his own already formed primary identification with femininity.[26] This requires the construction of barriers to femininity directed both inward and outward. The mother may be represented as an evil creature, a witch, to counteract the wish to merge with her. Or the barrier may be constructed and sustained by fantasies of harming the mother.[27] Inwardly, the boy must develop a character structure that forces the feminine part of himself down and out of awareness.[28]

Yet this individuation has a certain fragility, marked by what Stoller terms symbiosis anxiety—the fear that one will not be able to remain separate from the mother, the desire to return to the original oneness.[29] Symbiosis anxiety in males takes a variety of forms and is memorialized in such things as the fear of changing gender found frequently among male psychotics and infrequently among females; the greater fear of homosexuality among men than women; and *machismo,* an excessive resistance to unacceptable temptations or a great sensitivity about one's masculinity.[30]

Fantasies of harming the mother may help the continual shoring up of these barriers.[31] And Stoller speculates that in erotic fantasies the fetish and its isolation represent the fetishist's efforts to isolate his mother and depict her as no longer being in contact with him, and therefore no longer threatening to merge with him and thus destroy his identity as a separate person. Then he can succumb in scripted and staged form to the temptation to merge again with his mother.[32] Thus, Stoller's account too supports the contention that boys', but not girls', individuation takes place in terms of the building of both inner and outer barriers, barriers sustained in part by making the other (the mother) into a thing.

ABSTRACT MASCULINITY AND THE FEMINIST STANDPOINT

This excursion into psychoanalytic theory has served to point to the differences in men's and women's experience of self resulting from the sexual division of labor in childrearing. These different psychic experiences both structure and are reinforced by the differing patterns of men's and women's activity required by the sexual division of labor, and are thereby replicated as epistemology and ontology. This differential life activity in class society leads on the one hand toward a feminist standpoint and on the other toward an abstract masculinity.

Because the problem for the boy is to distinguish himself from the mother and protect himself against the real threat she poses for his identity, his conflictual and oppositional efforts lead to the formation of rigid ego boundaries. The way Freud takes for granted the rigid distinction between the "me and not-me" makes the point well: "Normally, there is nothing of which we are more certain than the feeling of ourself, of our own ego. This ego appears to us as something autonomous and unitary, marked off distinctly from everything else." At least toward the outside, "the ego seems to maintain clear and sharp lines of demarcation."[33] Thus,

the boy's construction of self in opposition to unity with the mother, his construction of identity as differentiation from the mother, sets a hostile and combative dualism at the heart of both the community men construct and the masculinist worldview by means of which they understand their lives.

I do not mean to suggest that the totality of human relations can be explained by psychoanalysis. Rather, I want to point to the ways masculine but not feminine experience and activity replicates itself in both the hierarchical and dualist institutions of class society, in the frameworks of thought these societies have generated in the West, and in our cultural construction of sexuality. It is interesting to read Hegel's account of the relation of self and other as a statement of masculine experience: The relation of the two (unhappy) consciousnesses takes the form of a trial by death. As Hegel describes it, "each seeks the death of the other." "Thus, the relation of the two self-conscious individuals is such that they provide themselves and each other through a life and death struggle. They must engage in this struggle, for they must raise their certainty *for themselves* to truth, both in the case of the other and in their own case."[34]

The construction of the self in opposition to another who threatens one's very being reverberates throughout the construction of both class society and the masculinist worldview and results in a deep-going and hierarchical dualism. First, the man's experience is characterized by the duality of concrete versus abstract.[35] Material reality as experienced by the boy in the family provides no model, and is unimportant in the attainment of masculinity. Nothing of value to the boy occurs within the family, and masculinity becomes an abstract ideal to be achieved over the opposition of daily life.[36] Masculinity must be attained by means of opposition to the concrete world of daily life, by escaping from contact with the female world of the household into the masculine world of politics or public life. This experience of two worlds, one valuable, if abstract and deeply unattainable, the other useless and demeaning, if concrete and necessary, lies at the heart of a series of dualisms—abstract/concrete, mind/body, culture/nature, ideal/real, stasis/change. And these dualisms are overlaid by gender; only the first of each pair is associated with the male.

Dualism, along with the dominance of one side of the dichotomy over the other, marks phallocentric society and social theory. These dualisms appear in a variety of forms—in philosophy, sexuality, technology, political theory, and the organization of class society itself. One can, for example, see them very clearly worked out in Plato, although they appear in many other forms.[37] There, the concrete/abstract duality takes the form of an opposition of material to ideal, and a denial of the relevance of the material world to the attainment of what is of fundamental importance: love of knowledge, or philosophy (masculinity). The duality of nature and culture takes the form of a devaluation of work, or necessity, and the primacy instead of purely social interaction for the attainment of undying fame. Philosophy itself is separate from nature, and indeed exists only on the basis of the domination of (at least some of) the philosopher's own nature.[38] Abstract masculinity, then, can be seen to have structured Western social relations and the modes of thought to which they give rise at least since the founding of the *polis*.

The oedipal roots of these hierarchical dualisms are memorialized in the overlay of masculine and feminine connotations. It is not accidental that women are associated with quasi-human and nonhuman nature, that the woman is associated with the body and material life, that the lives of women are systematically used as examples to characterize the lives of those ruled by their bodies rather than their minds.[39]

Both the fragility and fundamental falseness of the masculinist ideology and the deeply problematic nature of the social relations from which it grows are apparent in its reliance on a series of counterfactual assumptions and contentions.

Consider how the following contentions run counter to lived experience: The body is both irrelevant and in opposition to the (real) self, an impediment to be overcome by the mind; the female mind either does not exist (Do women have souls?) or works in such incomprehensible ways as to be unintelligible (the "enigma of woman"); what is real and primary is imperceptible to the senses and impervious to nature and natural change. What is remarkable is not only that these contentions have absorbed a great deal of philosophical energy but, along with a series of other counterfactuals, have structured social relations for centuries.

Interestingly enough, the epistemology and society constructed by men, suffering from the effects of abstract masculinity, have a great deal in common with the society and ideology imposed by commodity exchange. The separation and opposition of social and natural worlds, of abstract and concrete, of permanence and change, the effort to define only the former of each pair as important, the reliance on a series of counterfactual assumptions—all this is shared with the exchange abstraction. Abstract masculinity shares still another of its aspects with the exchange abstraction: It forms the basis for an even more problematic social synthesis. Hegel's analysis makes clear the problematic social relations available to the self that maintains itself by opposition: Each of the two subjects struggling for recognition tries to kill the other. But if the other is killed, the subject is once again alone. In sum, then, masculine experience when replicated as epistemology leads to a world conceived as (and in fact) inhabited by a number of fundamentally hostile others whom one comes to know by means of opposition (even death struggle) and yet with whom one must construct a social relation in order to survive.

Women's construction of self in relation to others leads in an opposite direction—toward opposition to dualisms of any sort; valuation of concrete, everyday life; a sense of a variety of connectednesses and continuities both with other persons and with the natural world. If material life structures consciousness, women's relationally defined existence, bodily experience of boundary challenges, and activity of transforming both physical objects and human beings must be expected to result in a worldview to which dichotomies are foreign. Women experience others and themselves along a continuum whose dimensions are evidenced in Adrienne Rich's argument that the child carried for nine months can be defined *"neither* as me or as not-me,"* and she argues that inner and outer are not polar opposites but a continuum.[40] What the sexual division of labor defines as women's work turns on issues of change rather than stasis—the changes involved in producing both use values and commodities, but more profoundly in the activity of rearing human beings who change in both more subtle and more autonomous ways than any inanimate object. Not only the qualities of things but also the qualities of people are important in women's work; quantity becomes peripheral. In addition, far more than the instrumental cooperation of the workplace is required; the mother–child relation and the maintenance of the family, while it has instrumental aspects, is not defined by them. Finally, the unity of mental and manual labor and the directly sensuous nature of much of women's work leads to a more profound unity of mental and manual labor, social and natural worlds, than is experienced by the male worker in capitalism. The unity grows from the fact that women's bodies, unlike men's, can be themselves instruments of production: In pregnancy, giving birth, or lactation, arguments about a division of mental from manual labor are fundamentally foreign.

That this is indeed women's experience is documented in both the theory and practice of the contemporary women's movement and needs no further development here.[41] The more important question here is whether women's experience and the world view constructed by women's activity can meet the criteria for a standpoint. If we return

to the five claims carried by the concept of a standpoint it seems clear that women's material life activity has important epistemological and ontological consequences for both the understanding and construction of social relations. Women's activity, then, does satisfy the first requirement for a standpoint.

I can now take up the second claim made by a standpoint: that women's experience not only inverts that of men but forms a basis on which to expose abstract masculinity as both partial and fundamentally perverse, as not only occupying only one side of the dualities it has constructed but reversing the proper valuation of human activity. The partiality of the masculinist vision and of the societies that support this understanding is evidenced by its confinement of activity proper to the man to only one side of the dualisms. Its perverseness, however, lies elsewhere. Perhaps the most dramatic (though not the only) reversal of the proper order of things characteristic of masculine experience is the substitution of death for life.

The substitution of death for life results at least in part from the sexual division of labor in childrearing. The self surrounded by rigid ego boundaries, certain of what is inner and what is outer, the self experienced as walled city, is discontinuous with others. Georges Bataille has made brilliantly clear the ways in which death emerges as the only possible solution to this discontinuity and has followed the logic through to argue that reproduction itself must be understood, not as the creation of life, but as death. The core experience to be understood is that of discontinuity and its consequences. As a consequence of this experience of discontinuity and aloneness, penetration of ego boundaries, or fusion with another, is experienced as violent. The pair "lover–assailant" is not accidental. Nor is the connection of reproduction and death.

"Reproduction," Bataille argues, "implies the existence of *discontinuous* beings." This is so because "beings which reproduce themselves are distinct from one another, and those reproduced are likewise distinct from each other, just as they are distinct from their parents. Each being is distinct from all others. His birth, his death, the events of his life may have an interest for others, but he alone is directly concerned in them. He is born alone. He dies alone. Between one being and another, there is a *gulf,* a discontinuity."[42] (Clearly the gulf of which he speaks is better characterized as a chasm.) In reproduction, sperm and ovum unite to form a new entity, but they do so from the death and disappearance of two separate beings. Thus, the new entity bears death with itself.

Although death and reproduction are intimately linked, Bataille stresses that "it is only death which is to be identified with [the transition to] continuity"; he holds to this position despite his recognition that reproduction is a form of growth. The growth, however, he dismisses as not "ours," as being only "impersonal."[43] This is not the female experience, in which reproduction is hardly impersonal, nor experienced as death. It is, of course, in a literal sense, the sperm that is cut off from its source and lost. Perhaps we should not wonder, then, at the masculinist preoccupation with death, and the feeling that growth is "impersonal," not of fundamental concern to oneself. Beneath Bataille's theorization of continuity as death lies the conflictual individuation of the boy: Continuity with another, continuity with the mother, carries not just danger but inevitable death as a separate being. But this complete dismissal of the experience of another bespeaks a profound lack of empathy and refusal to recognize the very being of another. It manifests the chasm that separates each man from every other being and from the natural world, the chasm that marks and defines the problem of community.

The preoccupation with death instead of life appears as well in the argument that it is the ability to kill (and for centuries, the practice) that sets humans above animals. Even Simone de Beauvoir has accepted that "it is not in giving life but in risking life that man is raised above the animal: that is why superiority has been accorded in humanity not to the sex that brings forth but to that which kills."[44] That superiority has been accorded to the sex which kills is beyond doubt. But what kind of vision can take reproduction, the creation of new life, and the force of life in sexuality, and turn it into death, not just in theory but in the practice of rape and sexual murder? And why give pride of place to killing? That is not only an inversion of the proper order of things but also a refusal to recognize the real activities in which men as well as women are engaged. The producing of goods and the reproducing of human beings are certainly life-sustaining activities. And even the deaths of the ancient heroes in search of undying fame were pursuits of life and represented the attempt to avoid death by attaining immortality. The search for life, then, represents the deeper reality that lies beneath the glorification of death and destruction.

Yet one cannot dismiss the substitution of death for life as simply false. Men's power to structure social relations in their own image means that women too must participate in social relations that manifest and express abstract masculinity. The most important life activities have consistently been held by the powers that be to be unworthy of those who are fully human, most centrally because of their close connections with necessity and life: motherwork (the rearing of children), housework, and until the rise of capitalism in the West, any work necessary to subsistence. In addition, these activities in contemporary capitalism are all constructed in ways that systematically degrade and destroy the minds and bodies of those who perform them.[45] The organization of motherhood as an institution in which a woman is alone with her children, the isolation of women from each other in domestic labor, the female pathology of loss of self in service to others—all mark the transformation of life into death, the distortion of what could have been creative and communal activity into oppressive toil, and the destruction of the possibility of community present in women's relational self-definition. The ruling gender's and class's interest in maintaining social relations such as these is evidenced by the fact that when women set up other structures in which the mother is not alone with her children, isolated from others, as is frequently the case in working-class communities or the communities of people of color, these arrangements are described as pathological deviations.

The real destructiveness of the social relations characteristic of abstract masculinity, however, is now concealed beneath layers of ideology. Marxian theory needed to go beneath the surface to discover the different levels of determination that defined the relation of capitalist and (male) worker. These levels of determination and laws of motion or tendency of phallocratic society must be worked out on the basis of female experience. This brings me to the fourth claim for a standpoint: its character as an achievement of both analysis and political struggle occurring in a particular historical space. The fact that class divisions should have proved so resistant to analysis and required such a prolonged political struggle before Marx was able to formulate the theory of surplus value indicates the difficulty of this accomplishment. And despite the time that has passed since the theory was worked out, rational control of production has yet to be achieved.

Feminists have only begun the process of revaluing the female experience, searching for the common threads that connect the diverse experiences of women, and searching for the structural determinants of these experiences. The difficulty of the problem faced by feminist theory can be illustrated by the fact that it required a struggle even to define household labor, if not done for wages, as work, to argue that what are held to be acts of love instead must be recognized as work.[46] Both the revaluation of women's experience and the use of this experience as a ground for critique are required.

That is, the liberatory possibilities present in women's experience must be, in a sense, read out and developed. Thus, a feminist standpoint may be present on the basis of the commonalities within women's experience, but it is neither self-evident nor obvious.

Finally, because it provides a way to reveal the perverseness and inhumanity of human relations, a standpoint forms the basis for moving beyond these relations. Just as the proletarian standpoint emerges out of the contradiction between appearance and essence in capitalism, understood as essentially historical and constituted by the relation of capitalist and worker, the feminist standpoint emerges both out of the contradiction between the systematically differing structures of men's and women's life activity in Western cultures. It expresses women's experience at a particular time and place, located within a particular set of social relations. Capitalism, Marx noted, could not develop fully until the notion of human equality achieved the status of universal truth.[47] Despite women's exploitation, both as unpaid reproducers of the labor force and as a sex-segregated labor force available for low wages, then, capitalism poses problems for the continued oppression of women. Just as capitalism enables the proletariat to raise the possibility of a society free from class domination, so too it provides space to raise the possibility of a society free from all forms of domination. The articulation of a feminist standpoint based on women's relational self-definition and activity exposes the world men have constructed and the self-understanding that manifests these social relations as both partial and perverse. More important, by drawing out the potentiality available in the actuality and thereby exposing the inhumanity of human relations, it embodies a distress that requires a solution. The experience of continuity and relation—with others, with the natural world, of mind with body—provides an ontological base for developing a nonproblematic social synthesis, a social synthesis that need not operate through the denial of the body, the attack on nature, or the death struggle between the self and other, a social synthesis that does not depend on any of the forms taken by abstract masculinity.

What is necessary is the generalization of the potentiality made available by the activity of women—the defining of society as a whole as propertyless producer both of use values and of human beings. To understand what such a transformation would require, we should consider what is involved in the partial transformation represented by making the whole of society into propertyless producers of use values: socialist revolution. The abolition of the division between mental and manual labor cannot take place simply by means of adopting worker self-management techniques, but instead requires the abolition of private property, the seizure of state power, and lengthy post-revolutionary class struggle. Thus I am not suggesting that shared parenting arrangements can abolish the sexual division of labor. Doing away with this division of labor would of course require institutionalizing the participation of both women and men in childrearing. But just as the rational and conscious control of the production of goods and services requires a vast and far-reaching social transformation, so too the rational and conscious organization of reproduction would entail the transformation both of *every* human relation and of human relations to the natural world. The magnitude of the task is apparent if one asks what a society without institutionalized gender differences might look like.

Generalizing the human possibilities present in the life activity of women to the social system as a whole would raise, for the first time in human history, the possibility of a fully human community, a community structured by a variety of connections rather than separation and opposition. One can conclude then that women's life activity does form the basis of a specifically feminist materialism, a materialism that can provide a point from which to both critique and work against phallocratic ideology and institutions.

NOTES

1. This is Iris Young's point. I am indebted to her persuasive arguments for taking what she terms the "gender differentiation of labor" as a central category of analysis. See Young, "Dual Systems Theory," *Socialist Review* 50, no. 51 (March/June 1980), p. 185. My use of this category, however, differs to some extent from hers. Young focuses on the societal aspects of the division of labor and chooses to use the term "gender division" to indicate that focus. I want to include the relation to the natural world as well. In addition, Young's analysis of women in capitalism does not seem to include marriage as a part of the division of labor. She is more concerned with the division of labor in capitalism in the productive sector.

2. See Sara Ruddick, "Material Thinking," *Feminist Studies* 6, no. 2 (Summer 1980), p. 364.

3. See, for a discussion of this danger, Adrienne Rich, "Disloyal of Civilization: Feminism, Racism, Gynephobia," in *On Lies, Secrets, and Silence* (New York: Norton, 1979), pp. 275–310; Elly Bulkin, "Racism and Writing: Some Implications for White Lesbian Critics," *Sinister Wisdom*, no. 6 (Spring 1980); bell hooks, *Ain't I a Woman* (Boston: South End Press, 1981), p. 138.

4. Some cross-cultural evidence indicates that the status of women varies with the work they do. To the extent that women and men contribute equally to subsistence, women's status is higher than it would be if their subsistence work differed profoundly from that of men; that is, if they do none or almost all of the work of subsistence, their status remains low. See Peggy Sanday, "Female Status in the Public Domain," in Michelle Rosaldo and Louise Lamphere (ed.), *Woman, Culture and Society* (Stanford, CA: Stanford University Press, 1974), p. 199. See also Iris Young's account of the sexual division of labor in capitalism, mentioned in note 1.

5. It is irrelevant to my argument here that women's wage labor takes place under different circumstances than men's—that is, their lower wages, their confinement to only a few occupational categories, etc. I am concentrating instead on the formal, structural features of women's work. There has been much effort to argue that women's domestic labor is a source of surplus value, that is,

to include it within the scope of Marx's value theory as productive labor, or to argue that since it does not produce surplus value it belongs to an entirely different mode of production, variously characterized as domestic or patriarchal. My strategy here is quite different from this. See, for the British debate, Mariarosa Dalla Costa and Selma James, *The Power of Women and the Subversion of the Community* (Bristol: Falling Wall press, 1975); Wally Secombe, "The Housewife and Her Labor under Capitalism," *New Left Review* 83 (January/February 1974); Jean Gardiner, "Women's Domestic Labour," *New Left Review* 89 (March 1975); and Paul Smith, "Domestic Labour and Marx's Theory of Value," in Annette Kuhn and Ann Marie Wolpe (eds.), *Feminism and Materialism* (Boston: Routledge and Kegan Paul, 1978). A portion of the American debate can be found in Ira Gerstein, "Domestic Work and Capitalism," and Lisa Vogel, "The Earthly Family," *Radical America* 7, nos. 4/5 (July/October 1973); Ann Ferguson, "Women as a New Revolutionary Class," in Pat Walker (ed.), *Between Labor and Capital* (Boston: South End Press, 1979).

6. Frederick Engels, *Origins of the Family, Private Property and the State* (New York: International Publishers, 1942); Karl Marx, *Capital* (New York: International Publishers, 1967) 1, p. 671. Marx and Engels have also described the sexual division of labor as natural or spontaneous. See Mary O'Brien, "Reproducing Marxist Man," in Lorenne Clark and Lynda Lange (ed.), *The Sexism of Social and Political Thought* (Toronto: University of Toronto Press, 1979).

7. For a discussion of women's work, see Elise Boulding, "Familial Constraints of Women's Work Roles," in Martha Blaxall and B. Reagan (ed.), *Women and the Workplace* (Chicago: University of Chicago Press, 1976), esp. pp. 111, 113. An interesting historical note is provided by the fact that Nausicaa, the daughter of a Homeric king, did the household laundry. See M. I. Finley, *The World of Odysseus* (Middlesex, England: Penguin, 1979), p. 73. While aristocratic women were less involved in actual labor, the difference was one of degree. And as Aristotle remarked in the *Politics*, supervising slaves is not a particularly uplifting activity. The life of leisure and philosophy, so much the goal for aristocratic Athenian men, then, was almost unthinkable for any woman.

8. Simone de Beauvoir holds that repetition has a deeper significance and that women's biological destiny itself is repetition. See *The Second Sex,* trans. H. M. Parshley (New York: Knopf, 1953), p. 59. But see also her discussion of housework in *ibid.,* pp. 423 ff. There, her treatment of housework is strikingly negative. For her the transcendence of humanity is provided in the historical struggle of self with other and with the natural world. The oppositions she sees are not really stasis vs. change, but rather vs. transcendence, escape from the muddy concreteness of daily life.

9. Marilyn French, *The Women's Room* (New York: Jove, 1978), p. 214.

10. Sara Ruddick, "Maternal Thinking," presents an interesting discussion of these and other aspects of the thought which emerges from the activity of mothering. Although I find it difficult to speak the language of interests and demands she uses, she brings out several valuable points. Her distinction between maternal and scientific thought is very intriguing and potentially useful (see esp. pp. 350–3).

11. Mary O'Brien, "Reproducing Marxist Man," p. 115, n. 11.

12. It should be understood that I am concentrating here on the experience of women in Western culture. There are a number of cross-cultural differences that can be expected to have some effect. See, for example, the differences that emerge from a comparison of child rearing in ancient Greek society with that of the contemporary Mbuti in central Africa. See Philip Slater, *The Glory of Hera* (Boston: Beacon, 1968); and Colin Turnbull, "The Politics of Non-Aggression," in Ashley Montagu (ed.), *Learning Non-Aggression* (New York: Oxford University Press, 1978). See also Isaac Balbus, *Marxism and Domination* (Princeton, NJ: Princeton University Press, 1982).

13. See Nancy Chodorow, "Family Structure and Female Personality," in Rosaldo and Lamphere, *Women, Culture, and Society,* p. 59.

14. Adrienne Rich, *Of Woman Born* (New York: Norton, 1976), p. 63.

15. I rely on the analyses of Dinnerstein and Chodorow but there are difficulties in that they are attempting to explain why humans, both male and female, fear and hate the female. My purpose here is to invert their arguments and to attempt to put forward a positive account of the epistemological consequences of this situation. What follows is a summary of Nancy Chodorow, *The Reproduction of Mothering* (Berkeley: University of California Press, 1978).

16. See Chodorow, *Reproduction;* and Jane Flax, "The Conflict between Nurturance and Autonomy in Mother–Daughter Relations and in Feminism," *Feminist Studies* 6, no. 2 (June 1978).

17. Chodorow, *Reproduction,* pp. 105–9.

18. This is Jane Flax's point.

19. Chodorow, *Reproduction,* pp. 127–31, 163.

20. *Ibid.,* p. 166.

21. *Ibid.,* pp. 174–8. Chodorow suggests a correlation between father absence and fear of women (p. 213), and one should, treating this as an empirical hypothesis, expect a series of cultural differences based on the degree of father absence. Here the ancient Greeks and the Mbuti provide a fascinating contrast. (See above, note 12.)

22. *Ibid.,* p. 198. The flexible and diffuse female ego boundaries can of course result in the pathology of loss of self in responsibility for and dependence on others (the obverse of the male pathology of experiencing the self as walled city).

23. He never considers that single-sex childrearing may be the problem and also ascribes total responsibility to the mother for especially the male's successful individuation. See Robert Stoller, *Perversion* (New York: Pantheon, 1975), pp. 154, 161, for an awesome list of tasks to be accomplished by the mother.

24. *Ibid.,* pp. 137–8.

25. *Ibid.,* p. 154. See also his discussion of these dynamics in chap. 2 of Robert Stoller, *Sexual Excitement* (New York: Pantheon, 1979).

26. Stoller, *Perversion,* p. 99.

27. *Ibid.,* pp. 150, 121 respectively.

28. *Ibid.,* p. 150.

29. *Ibid.,* p. 149.

30. *Ibid.,* pp. 149–51.

31. *Ibid.,* p. 121.

32. Stoller, *Sexual Excitement,* p. 172.

33. Sigmund Freud, *Civilization and Its Discontents* (New York: Norton, 1961), pp. 12–3.

34. G. W. F. Hegel, *Phenomenology of Spirit,* trans. A. V. Miller (New York: Oxford University press, 1979), p. 114. See also Jessica Benjamin's very interesting use of this discussion in "The Bonds of Love: Rational Violence and Erotic Domination," *Feminist Studies* 6, no. 1 (June 1980).

35. I use the terms abstract and concrete in a sense much influenced by Marx. "Abstraction" not only refers to the practice of searching for universal generalities but also carries derogatory connotations of idealism and partiality. By "concrete," I refer to respect for complexity and multidimensional causality, and mean to suggest as well a materialism and completeness.

36. Alvin Gouldner has made a similar argument in his contention that the Platonic stress on hierarchy and order resulted from a similarly learned opposition to daily life rooted in the young aristocrat's experience of being taught proper behavior by slaves who could not themselves engage in this behavior. See Gouldner, *Enter Plato* (New York: Basic Books, 1965), pp. 351–5.

37. One can argue, as Chodorow's analysis suggests, that their extreme form in his philosophy represents an extreme father-absent (father-deprived?) situation. A more general critique of phallocentric dualism occurs in Susan Griffin, *Woman and Nature* (New York: Harper & Row, 1978).

38. More recently, of course, the opposition to the natural world has taken the form of destructive technology. See Evelyn Fox Keller, "Gender and Science," *Psychoanalysis and Contemporary Thought* 1, no. 3 (1978).

39. See Elizabeth Spelman, "Metaphysics and Misogyny: The Soul and Body in Plato's Dialogues" (mimeo). One analyst has argued that its basis lies in the fact that "the early mother, monolithic representative of nature, is a source, like nature, of ultimate distress as well as ultimate joy. Like nature, she is both nourishing and disappointing, both alluring and threatening. . . . The infant loves her . . . and it hates her because, like nature, she does not perfectly protect and provide

for it. . . . The mother, then—like nature, which sends blizzards and locusts as well as sunshine and strawberries—is perceived as capricious, sometimes actively malevolent." Dorothy Dinnerstein, *The Mermaid and the Minotaur* (New York: Harper & Row, 1976), p. 95.

40. Rich, *Of Woman Born*, pp. 64, 167. For a similar descriptive account, but a dissimilar analysis, see David Bakan, *The Duality of Human Existence* (Boston: Beacon Press, 1966).

41. My arguments are supported with remarkable force by both the theory and practice of the contemporary women's movement. In theory, this appears in different forms in the work of Dorothy Riddle, "New Visions of Spiritual Power," *Quest: A Feminist Quarterly* 1, no. 3 (Spring 1975); Griffin, *Woman and Nature,* esp. Book IV, "The Separate Rejoined"; Rich, *Of Woman Born,* esp. pp. 62–8; Linda Thurston, "On Male and Female Principle," *The Second Wave* 1, no. 2 (Summer 1971). In feminist political organizing, this vision has been expressed as an opposition of leadership and hierarchy, as an effort to prevent the development of organizations divided into leaders and followers. It has also taken the forms of an insistence on the unity of the personal and the political, a stress on the concrete rather than on abstract principles (an opposition to theory), and a stress on the politics of everyday life. For a fascinating and early example, see Pat Mainardi, "The Politics of Housework," in Leslie Tanner (ed.), *Voices of Women's Liberation* (New York: New American Library, 1970).

42. Georges Bataille, *Death and Sensuality* (New York: Arno Press, 1977), p. 12; italics mine.

43. *Ibid.,* pp. 95–6.

44. de Beauvoir, *The Second Sex,* p. 58.

45. Consider for example, Rich's discussion of pregnancy and childbirth, chaps. 6–7 in *Of Woman Born*. And see also Charlotte Perkins Gilman's discussion of domestic labor in *The Home* (Urbana, IL: University of Illinois Press, 1972).

46. The Marxist–feminist efforts to determine whether housework produces surplus value and the feminist political strategy of demanding wages for housework represent two (mistaken) efforts to recognize women's activity as work.

47. Marx, *Capital,* 1 p. 60.

READING 16

Principles for a Woman-Friendly Economy

Carol S. Robb

While I was editing with Beverly Harrison her article "Sexuality and Social Policy," she startled me one day when I had spoken of sexual ethics as if it were personal ethics; she said sexual ethics is *social* ethics. At the time I was a single woman, a campus minister, funded ecumenically, and wanting to have a baby. Imagine what it would be like for a single female campus minister to be pregnant, have a baby, and *keep* it! Someone from among the supporting denominations would call into question the morality of sustaining in ministry such a role model on a college campus, and either I would lose my job or the campus ministry collective with whom I worked would lose one or more major sources of funding. From my personal experience I knew that sexual ethics is a social force, affecting economic distributions. In time I decided to document several ways sexuality is an economic matter in women's lives. Demonstrating the connection between women's sexuality and economic vulnerability would be one way to underscore why sexuality is a justice issue, why sexual ethics is social ethics, and conversely, why economic ethics has important implications for the way we live in our body selves. I see this work as deeply influenced by Beverly's contributions to theological ethics, probably in more ways than I could ever identify. Most obvious are her focus on the structural changes necessary for a just economy, her witness to the asymmetrical power relations among women and men, and her insight that power derived from economic sources is often unjustly expressed as control of others' body space.

From Carol S. Robb, "Principles for a Woman-Friendly Economy." *Journal of Feminist Studies in Religion,* 9, 1–2 (Spring/Fall 1993): 147–160. Reprinted by permission of Scholars Press.

In this research I have been probing women's experiences which, at face value, seem to have little to do with the public world of the economy but are more often associated with intimate private space. Those experiences include childbirth and child rearing, domestic violence, sexual harassment, and lesbian identity. What links women's experience in these four arenas is that our sexuality is, in effect, a liability to our capacity to live out our life plans, a liability that does not so consistently appear in men's life stories (with the exception of gay men). In these instances what is owed to women because we participate in creating social value is denied us because our sexuality is not ours but public (i.e., male) property.

The focus of this essay is to explore principles for economic ethics that are informed by women's experiences of vulnerability due to our sexual experiences. What kind of economic order would it take to support women and enable us to contribute to the common good, as well as to have access to the material conditions for a life with dignity for ourselves and our children? This question itself reflects Harrison's influence in justice theory. She, among others, is challenging the liberal view of human rights as negative only, and replacing that view with the notion that human rights (another way of describing what is owed to people) are the minimal conditions that ought to exist in society to ground personal human well-being,[1] or human dignity.[2] My question is another way of asking, What today are the principles and policies that constitute an approximation of economic justice for our time?

This article will suggest how sexuality functions to undermine women's economic stability—not that gender is the *only* cause of class stratification (it isn't; the class structure in the United States is heavily racialized, for instance), but gender is *one* important component of economic stratification.[3] I will review a valuable religious tradition for challenging the economic vulnerability of women. That tradition is Roman Catholic social teachings, which I use because they contain a moral language for evaluating economics that is rich and more explicit than Protestant teachings, even though Protestants appropriated the Catholic social teachings. Nevertheless, I will also argue that this religious inheritance cannot sufficiently criticize the economic injustices women experience unless it is itself transformed by a commitment to gender, racial, and social equality. And, finally, I will propose some principles for evaluating economic systems that are consistent with this religious inheritance but take on new meaning as a result of attention to women's economic vulnerability. I will also suggest some public policies that might satisfy these principles, or appear to move toward conformity with them. While my point of departure is a critical perspective on the economic vulnerability of women, my vision is one of economic reciprocity in a context of a sustainable relationship with the biosphere.

WAYS WOMEN PAY THE PRICE

It is fairly easy to draw the conclusion that ours is not a woman-friendly economy. Whatever their class or race, women pay a gender tax, although in different ways depending on our race and class location. For instance, women in the United States pay $31 billion annually in earnings lost because of childbirth. That's a high tax.[4] Childbirth, however, *increases* sex-role differentiation (as measured by earnings and labor market behavior) for whites and *decreases* it for African Americans, largely because African American women do not take as much time out of the labor force as white women, and because the racism in the labor force deprives African American men of jobs, compelling African American women to continue earning.[5]

Sexual harassment also exacts a gender tax. Sexual harassment makes women self-conscious, humiliated, anxious, depressed about going to work, eager to get away from the job; they suffer stress symptoms such as sleeplessness, nervous stomach, ulcers, and headaches.

Fifty percent of all working women report experiencing harassment[6]—75 percent of women in male-dominated occupations[7]—which only rarely can be litigated. The cumulative effect of these "micro-inequalities," the daily minutiae of sexism, is to erect serious barriers to women's educational and economic advancement.[8]

Domestic violence works in three ways to make and keep women economically vulnerable. In violent relationships, male partners often actively discourage women from working, getting an education, or getting job training, in order to maintain the woman's economic dependence. When a woman stays in an abusive relationship, she loses the self-respect and self-confidence that enable her to enter the job market, learn new skills, and meet challenges. And if she leaves an abusive relationship before she has the social support system to help her establish stability in a new living environment, she may end up on the street with all the pressures of having no home and no social claim on the rest of the community. Between 40 and 50 percent of homeless women and children are fleeing domestic violence.[9]

Women who are lesbians pay a gender tax and also a homophobia tax. Most lesbians have stable work histories, tend to be higher achievers than heterosexual women, and have a serious commitment to work, giving it priority because they support themselves. The percentage of lesbians with advanced education or professional degrees is nine times greater (28.9 percent) than in the general adult female population (3 percent).[10] Yet between 50 and 75 percent of lesbians fear losing their jobs, and many of those who do not feel this threat are either self-employed, working in feminist agencies, or working in a small number of occupations in which lesbianism is tolerated. Nearly one-quarter of lesbians in a recent study report actual instances of formal or informal job discrimination, including not being hired for a job or being fired from a job solely because they were lesbians.[11]

It seems that the pressure to stay closeted has been greater for lesbians who have high-income professional jobs than for lesbians in a workplace that has a predominance of women, has a female boss, is small, and whose work requires little supervisory responsibility and does not involve children.[12] Gay men also seem to be more closeted if their positions are economically powerful or high-status.[13] In this respect both lesbians and gay men are vulnerable to homophobia, and the trade-off is between increased levels of financial independence *or* openness at work about one's identity, a trade-off heterosexual men and women do not face. In addition to homophobia, lesbians as women experience the wage gap, job segregation, child-care stresses, sexual harassment, and racism described above.

A RELIGIOUS INHERITANCE FOR ECONOMIC ETHICS

Religious social ethicists help the culture keep alive a memory of right relationship and nourish energy for change toward a future that we can only imagine today. We don't come empty-handed to the effort to imagine a woman-friendly economy (that is, one that does not exact more from women than men). There are principles for economic justice that constitute a "religious inheritance," though establishing the structural underpinnings for "partnership" between women and men has not been the dominant concern of these traditions. We must, therefore, be cautious about the moral weight we give to these social teachings, while recognizing that together they constitute a significant confrontation with the dominant liberal capitalist economic culture, which lets the market determine accessibility to the goods and services necessary for human dignity.

What are these teachings? They are most sharply articulated in a body of statements whose origin is usually identified as Pope Leo XIII's *Rerum Novarum*, written in 1891 primarily to preserve the "one true faith" at a time when working-class Catholics were disaffiliating from the church and turning to socialist labor politics. Although Leo and other popes have been accused of wanting to preserve an "organic" society in which the church would remain dominant, the Catholic church was in fact less quickly seduced into an uncritical perspective on free market liberal capitalism than Protestantism was. From the repository of potentially critical principles I will select a few examples to illustrate the contributions of Roman Catholic social teaching to a critical evaluation of free market absolutism.

The accountability of capital to justice in productive relations. Because of the power differential between employers and workers, contracts between employers and employees are not "freely" negotiated. Contracts must be subject to moral constraints in addition to freedom, particularly the constraints of justice. Capitalists should provide workers a just wage, sufficient for family needs and sufficient to allow the accumulation of some property for family needs and sufficient to allow the accumulation of some property by the workers. Capitalists should not permit working conditions that are degrading or threaten workers' health. Private property cannot be amassed or used in ways that are contrary to distributive justice and the dignity of all persons.

The accountability of private property to the common good. Private property is necessary for people's capacity to exercise autonomy in their lives, substantiating and giving a base to their responsibility for themselves and their families. The right to private property, however, is not an absolute right, for it is accountable to the common good. Leo said,

No one is commanded to distribute to others that which is required for [one's] own necessities and those of [one's] household; nor even to give away what is reasonably required to keep up becomingly [one's] condition in life; for no one

ought to live unbecomingly. But when necessity has been supplied, and one's position fairly considered, it is a duty to give to the indigent out of that which is left over.[14]

A corollary to this principle is therefore the just entitlement of the poor to necessities from the luxury of the nonpoor.

The duty of government to protect the poor. Since it is through the labor of the poor that material well-being is constructed and since the poor are most vulnerable to exploitation and least able to protect themselves, the duty of justice requires governments to protect the interest of the poor. Governments fulfill their obligation when the poor are housed, clothed, and enabled to support life. If there is a conflict between the rights of the poor and the rights of the not-poor, it is the duty of the public authority to give special consideration to the poor.

The obligation to make payment on the social mortgage. The *social mortgage* is the debt all must pay back to the society in recognition that one inherits wealth in the form of goods or knowledge or technology from those who have gone before or who walk with us now. No one receives wealth debt-free, because of the social origin of wealth. The social mortgage is a principle of return. It is paid in various ways; for example by providing low- or no-interest loans for low-income housing out of a portion of one's holdings, contributing fully one's share of taxes used to support social programs, or dedicating a percentage of income directly to services for the poor and otherwise vulnerable.

The principle of subsidiarity. The state and the law must protect communities, families, and individuals. Social problems must be dealt with at the lowest possible level of social and political organization where they can be addressed successfully, which protects the autonomy of small and intermediate-sized social groupings. Yet we must involve ever-higher levels of social and political organization until issues *can* be addressed appropriately. If issues can be addressed successfully in the family or neighborhood, they should be. But if the school system or parish involvement is necessary, then we must involve them, or the city, or state, the federal government, or the international world order.

Participation as an aspect of economic justice. In the 1986 U.S. bishops' pastoral letter, *Economic Justice for All,* the bishops viewed participation in the economy to be exercised primarily through employment and widespread ownership of property.[15] The principle of participation is antithetical to paternalism, and is consistent with and implied in the principle of subsidiarity.

A LEGACY TO OVERCOME

In addition to the above principles, the social teaching also contains some aspects that make the struggle for economic justice for women very difficult to wage within the churches. One principle is particularly ignoble: *the principle of inequality.* Leo's agenda in *Rerum Novarum* was to renounce socialism, so the encyclical assumes capitalism, though capitalism with a human face. Leo denounced socialism in part because of its challenge to religious authority. He was reacting, in part, to socialist activists who exposed class conflict and encouraged working people to develop a loyalty to their own class rather than to their employers or their employers' church. In addition he was reacting to a mistaken notion that a socialist program would collectivize all property. And finally, he was reacting to the expressed commitment of socialist movements to social equality for all.

> Humanity must remain as it is. It is impossible to reduce human society to a level. The Socialists may do their utmost, but all striving against nature is vain. There naturally exist among mankind innumerable differences of the most important kind. People differ in capability, in diligence, in health, and in strength; and thus inequality in fortune is a necessary result of inequality in condition. Such inequality is far from being disadvantageous either to individuals or to the community. Social and public life can go on only by the help of various kinds of capacity and the playing of many partners, and each man, as a rule, chooses the part which peculiarly suits his case.[16]

One wonders if the special duty of government to consider the interests of the poor is an easier principle to promote than to advocate removing the structural conditions allowing the rich to emerge as a class, while a great many other people become poor.

While Roman Catholic social teachings have provided clearer principles for evaluating economic systems than have Protestant social teachings, there is an amazing quantity of shared tradition, particularly in the "mainline" denominational documents on economic ethics. One shared principle is the principle of inequality.[17] From the time of the early church it has been claimed that the poor have just entitlement to goods to satisfy their necessities, even if they must take it from the rich,[18] yet this claim has always rested on the assumption of some form of a class society, where there would always be the rich and the poor. There is also a strand of economic and political egalitarianism which surfaced socially, for instance, in the 16th-century Anabaptists. But it is quite likely that Protestants and Catholics alike remember the Anabaptists only in terms of "excesses," and not as having had a *legitimate* interpretation of the social implications of Luther's *sola gratia, sola fide,* and *sola scriptura* (salvation by grace alone, by faith alone, with scripture the only authority).[19]

THE INHERITANCE EVALUATED IN TERMS OF WOMEN'S EXPERIENCE

What *changes* in this moral language if we use as our point of departure not the authority of church or tradition, but, rather, the experience of women who are vulnerable economically?

Some of these principles do not change at all. The duty of the government to protect the poor, for instance, has an immediate relevance to our contemporary context, where housing is in increasingly short supply and the homeless, abused women and their children among them, are those least able to compete for it in the market. Instead of decreasing governmental involvement in housing, as presidents Reagan and Bush did, there should be a renewed commitment to governmental support for low- and moderate income housing stock.

Some of these principles take on new meaning or specificity when viewed in light of women's economic vulnerability. For instance, *the principle of subsidiarity* has new meaning in relationship to the provision of high-quality child care. High-quality child care requires caregiver stability, yet child-center staff positions are among the highest in turn-over. Caregiver stability requires good working conditions and livable salaries, yet caregivers are among the lowest paid. High-quality child care requires a low child-to-caregiver ratio (three-to-one or four-to-one for children under one year old) and small group size (eight-to-twelve infants and twelve toddlers). In other words, high-quality child care is expensive. Child care cannot be left to market forces as advocated by those who value consumer freedom and dislike government involvement; the market will always attempt to decrease the cost per child, hence what's good for the market is bad for the child. The principle of subsidiarity stipulates that social problems must be dealt with at the lowest possible level of society where they can be addressed successfully. The solution to the child-care problem must occur on a combination of levels: family, neighborhood, city, county, state, and nation. We have the benefit of successful efforts in other industrialized countries which finance good quality child care by combining national, state, and local subsidies with parent fees. Making individual choices in an impersonal market may yield satisfactory results for the wealthy, but to

provide good care for all our children policy guaranteeing social support is required.

To give another example of the way traditional principles require historical specification: the accountability of private property to the common good in our circumstances means, among other things, *the accountability of capital to community stability.* This principle is antithetical to economic policies promoting the mobility of capital, over the interests of the labor force. We need to reverse this latter dynamic. If companies want our markets, then we have something to bargain with; and I believe we should be debating the most effective accountability structures, rather than negotiating free trade agreements. Until we are serious about holding capital accountable for its effects on community stability, we will have no hope for stable communities. Lacking stable industries, our communities are deprived of the tax base they need to undergird social programs, like childcare and women's shelters. Lacking stable industries we have high unemployment rates, particularly among workers who traditionally entered the labor force through manufacturing. When men go into the underground economy they are less likely to marry or to support their offspring, leaving women financially dependent often before they finish the education they need to compete in the labor market.

Local community stability is also necessary for entrepreneurs and others to pay their social mortgage. Any production of wealth occurs in a *place* where people live, where there is a geography and an ecology. When business is not held accountable for its effects on particular communities, or when people in the communities are itinerant, temporary, and incapable of developing or sustaining roots, then there is little social authority to collect on the social mortgage, and little motivation for businesses to pay it. Also, the social mortgage is a principle of return not only to people but also to other species. We are now looking for appropriate methods of guaranteeing that people don't take from other species more than can be paid back to them, since we are destroying species' habitats, thus threatening to destroy the species themselves.

Local community stability should serve as a criterion for evaluating economic policies. Women have a stake in local community stability, particularly when these communities exercise the self-rule prescribed by the principle of subsidiarity. In such communities, not only is there a capacity to *plan* for social programs, such as childcare and emergency and second-stage shelters, but in social situations characterized by local control, women are frequently leaders along with men. When power is hierarchalized, women seem always to lose participation rights. The economic basis for such community self-rule will involve a measure of *decentralization,* not deregulation. Self-rule requires access to raw materials for community life *from* the community and its immediate area, so solar and wind energy rather than nuclear and fossil fuel energy, plus moderate and small-farm agriculture rather than factory farming, will probably be hallmarks of such decentralized economies. Decentralization is seen here to be necessary, though not sufficient, to support *participation* of women in the community's economic policymaking.

The principle of *sustainability* has appeared in Catholic and Protestant religious economic ethics only recently, but I find it a useful way of specifying the requirements of accountability of power and private property to the common good. Sustainability involves living within the regenerative capacities of the earth. It is a principle of return, like payment on the social mortgage. Work and all other contributions women traditionally make to society are not recognized or valued commensurate with men's contributions. Yet the reproduction of life and its nurturance is absolutely necessary and "productive" for the economy and community well-being. Sustainability as a principle requires a new way of calculating consequence and growth, beyond GNP to what Herman Daly and John Cobb, Jr.

call the *index of sustainable welfare.*[20] This principle connects ecological integrity to economic justice for women.

CHALLENGING INEQUALITY

These are illustrations of how the religious inheritance of standards for economic justice takes on new meaning or specificity in light of reflection on the failure of the economy to serve women and children. But, perhaps more significantly, reflection on women's experience in the economy leads us to challenge one principle in the tradition: the principle of inequality. Principles for economic justice should incorporate the principle of equality if the goal is truly the *common* good rather than men's good solely. Gender equality would redress each of the problem areas discussed earlier.

In terms of childbearing, it is not fair to treat women who have young children equally, that is, the *same* as, women and men who do not, because there are morally relevant differences in their situations. And yet it is also not fair to treat all women as though we are mothers of young children, especially since protective social policies nearly always result in inequality, because they function as disincentives for employers to hire women. Justice for all women requires parental or family policies that men can and do use for child-rearing purposes. We need family policies that give economic stability to women who are single parents and at the same time encourage fathers to be parents. This is a move toward *gender equality,* yet one that depends on recognizing the need for special support, that is, *difference in treatment,* for parents and others with significant dependent care.

Reflecting on the causes and effects of domestic violence, it is very clear to me that the reason our culture has not mobilized more effectively to punish violent men and to protect vulnerable women is that we are still living the cultural memory of a time when women were property. We are not committed to women as moral equals with men; we still believe in some corner of our collective psyche that men know better than women what is good for women and thus have the right to control us. The fractures caused by domestic violence can only be healed in relationships marked by equality. The church should be committed to equality for women at every level, for nearly every branch of the church believes it should be involved in a ministry of health and healing.

Reflecting on sexual harassment, I think it is significant that the immobilizing effects of this behavior are best prevented in sexually desegregated work groups. When at least one-third of the group is women, sexual harassment either does not occur or can be neutralized before it becomes significant to any person targeted. This requires the sexual desegregation of the labor force so that the supervisor, as well as the supervisee, is as likely to be a woman as a man. Equality once again is an economic factor, a concrete criterion of relations that will assure women justice.

Reflecting on the effects of lesbian identity, we see that for morally irrelevant reasons, lesbians and gay men are economically vulnerable. Recognition of their contributions depends so often on their hiding their identities, otherwise their work is not evaluated on equal terms with that of heterosexuals. The social stigma of homosexual identity is an artificial barrier to economic justice for lesbians and gay men.

The egalitarianism here affirmed is not the "simple equality" that requires totalitarianism to sustain it, nor is it simply "equality of opportunity" that coexists, though uncomfortably, with extreme racial and economic inequality. Political philosophers such as Carol Gould and Michael Walzer are trying to help us "remember" a commitment to democracy in the economic realm to accompany democracy in the political realm, a memory sustained for Christians and Jews by certain scriptural themes, particularly covenant and jubilee.[21] Until we believe economic democracy is right and valuable

to struggle for, we will not experience anything near egalitarianism in the *political* realm, because of the collusions of owners of great amounts of capital and their collective ability to call upon the support of state officials.[22] Thus economic equality involves a commitment to economic *reciprocity*.

Reciprocity seems to me to be a way of talking about what mutuality might mean in economic relations. Whereas as I conceive *mutuality* to be equal regard, *reciprocity* implies structures of fair distribution that flow from interdependence in production and reproduction. The distribution, production, and reproduction systems must have the marks of reciprocity even if equal regard is missing.

The principle of reciprocity might be the moral language we need to reflect on economies from the standpoint of women. Reciprocity is the opposite of exploitation. Exploitation is a nonreciprocal relationship in which the owner benefits at the expense of labor because the owner controls the conditions of labor and the activity of the workers and does not give equivalent return to the workers.[23] Reciprocity, on the other hand, amounts to a requirement of workers' self-management—or worker control—in the economy. Such worker control is suggested as an *option* in the U.S. bishops' pastoral letter as a way of honoring the principle of participation. Here I suggest it should be a major way to organize production.

When workers elect their own management councils that produce policy with the professional management, there seems to be a high level of worker involvement in problem solving and innovation, and hence a decreased need for the layer of the workforce known as supervisors. The workers supervise themselves and each other. Productivity is often very high. The workers are producing in order to create a product they are proud of, to support themselves and their families, and to insure ongoing stability for their own workplace. They are essentially supporting only themselves and their communities rather than an elite group of management or a class of capitalists whose highest priority is to turn a profit for themselves and their stockholders.

If workers do not have to support this essentially wasteful and superfluous stratum, they can then work fewer hours. The 30-hour workweek should be a social priority for our churches. Particularly when parents can spell each other for child care (whether they are married to each other or not), the 30-hour workweek decreases the contradiction between work and nurturance that so many parents experience today. Worker self-management as one index of reciprocity has an immediate connection to freeing time for the "reproductive" sphere of our lives.

In addition, reciprocity is one of the principles underlying comparable pay for comparable work—a policy measure to address the wage gap. Women are paid less for their work, not because it is less productive, less skilled, or less responsible, but solely because it is work *women* do. *Comparable pay* is another way of specifying what reciprocity in the economic arena might mean.

TOWARD A WOMAN-FRIENDLY ECONOMY

In sum, when we take as a starting point for moral reflection a commitment to the dignity and well-being of economically vulnerable women, some new specificity and moral insight emerges that adds to our understanding about what economic justice requires:

1. The principle of *subsidarity* requires moving child-care policy from the private realm and the market to the social realm.
2. Enforcing accountability of capital to community stability is a contemporary way of honoring the accountability of power and private property to the *common good.*
3. *Community stability* involves self-rule and decentralization of major aspects of the economy, including energy and agriculture.

4. *Sustainability* is another measure of accountability to the common good, and involves calculating health, biodiversity, and children's security and well-being as measures of social welfare, thus eliminating economic growth as the sole indicator of economic well-being.
5. The principle of *equality*—gender, racial, and social equality—as a measure of economic justice moves to ascendancy.
6. *Reciprocity* in the labor force is the relationship that challenges all forms of exploitation, and suggests worker control as the major mode of organizing production. It is also the principle underlying comparable pay for comparable work, and erasing the gender and race taxes in wages; and through worker self-management may result in the 30-hour workweek.

While the work of sexual ethics is not collapsed into economic ethics, there is a very important connection between them in the "lived-world experience" of every woman and every man. As Harrison says,

> economic justice as access to and genuine participation in the production, distribution, and determination of the use of a society's wealth is also a condition of sexual freedom. All distortions of power in society reveal themselves in the inequality of power dynamics in interpersonal life.[24]

I have tried to imagine how to remove the distortions of power created by the economy that result in women's vulnerability. The economic principles I have proposed are both principles for evaluating and criticizing the current economic order and pointers to an alternative economic system. If we can nourish the political will to reorganize the economy to serve *these* principles rather than principles such as freedom without accountability, and the market as the sole measure of value, then a commonwealth would emerge where distortions of power from the economic realm could be avoided, and women's sexual self-determination would have a material basis.

NOTES

1. Beverly Wildung Harrison, *Our Right to Choose, Toward a New Ethic of Abortion* (Boston: Beacon, 1984), p. 196.
2. David Hollenbach, *Claims in Conflict, Retrieving and Renewing the Catholic Human Rights Tradition* (New York: Paulist, 1979), p. 59.
3. The ratio of female-to-male earnings has remained in the neighborhood of 60% for full-time workers between 1900 and 1980. In 1989 the annual wage gap was 68%. See Heidi Hartmann and Roberta Spalter-Roth, "Improving Employment Opportunities for Women," Testimony about H.R. 1, Civil Rights Act of 1991 before the U.S. House of Representatives, February 27, 1991. Available from the Institute for Women's Policy Research, 1400 20th St. N.W., Suite 204, Washington, DC 20036.
4. It may be a convenience to refer to a *gender tax* exacted from women though not from men, just as there is a *race tax,* exacted from racial ethnic people though not Caucasians, perhaps an *age tax,* and other "taxes" in addition to those collected by the Internal Revenue Service. Like the race tax, the gender tax is a distributive mechanism that sustains an extremely wealthy elite at the expense of 95% of the population. Ronald Pacquarillo, *Tax Justice* (Lanham, MD: University Press of America and the Churches' Center for Theology and Public Policy, 1985), p. 32. The use of the terms *race tax* and *gender tax* does not adequately communicate the ways race, class, and gender oppression are interstructured; they imply an additive dynamic. I use gender tax as a heuristic device to emphasize for the moment the pervasive importance of gender in social structure.
5. Roberta M. Spalter-Roth and Heidi I. Hartmann, *Unnecessary Losses: Costs to Americans of the Lack of Family and Medical Leave* (Washington, DC: Institute for Women's Policy Research, 1990), pp. 17–9. Though both African American and white mothers suffer losses in earnings in the two postbirth years, new African American mothers earn more than new white mothers, and also report more unemployment than white mothers in those years, reflecting the special need of new black mothers to stay in the labor force and earn a living.
6. Edward Lafontaine and Leslie Tredau, "The Frequency, Sources, and Correlates of Sexual Harassment among Women in Traditional Male Occupations," *Sex Roles* 15, no. 7/8 (1986), pp. 435–6.
7. Gilda Berger, *Women, Work and Wages* (New York: Franklin Watts, 1986), p. 94.
8. Mary P. Rowe, "Dealing with Sexual Harassment," *Harvard Business Review* 59, no. 3 (May/June 1981).
9. For a review of studies linking homelessness to domestic violence, see Joan Zorza, "Woman Battering: A Major Cause of Homelessness," *Clearinghouse Review* (Special Issue, 1991).
10. Virginia R. Brooks, *Minority Stress and Lesbian Women* (Lexington, MA: Lexington Books, 1981), p. 62. Brooks used 1975 census figures.
11. Martin P. Levine and Robin Leonard, "Discrimination against Lesbians in the Work Force," in *The Lesbian Issue: Essays from Signs,* ed. Estelle Freedman, Barbara C. Gelpi, Susan L. Johnson, and Katherine M. Weston (Chicago: University of Chicago Press, 1985).
12. Beth Schneider, "Peril and Promise: Lesbians' Workplace Participation," in *Women-Identified Women,* ed. Trudy Darty and Sandee Potter (Palo Alto, CA: Mayfield, 1984), p. 221.
13. Schneider, p. 214.
14. Pope Leo XIII, *Rerum Novarum,* no. 36.
15. U.S. Bishops' pastoral letter, *Economic Justice for All,* no. 91.
16. *Rerum Novarum,* no. 26.
17. For an interesting discussion of egalitarianism and whether it is consistent with Calvin and/or the Reformed tradition, see Robert L. Stivers (ed.), *Reformed Faith and Economics* (Lanham, MD: University Press of America, 1989), particularly Christian T. Iosso, "Reformed Economic Ethics in Presbyterian General Assembly Statements, 1900–1987," Ronald H. Stone, "The Reformed Economic Ethics of John Calvin," and David Little, "Economic Justice and the Ground for a Theory of Progressive Taxation in Calvin's Thought."
18. Prentiss L. Pemberton and Daniel Rush Finn, *Toward a Christian Economic Ethic* (Minneapolis: Winston Press, 1985), pp. 36–40.
19. I am indebted to Christopher Ocker for pointing out to me the work of Peter Blickle in *The Revolution of 1525: The German Peasants' War from a New Perspective* (Baltimore and London:

Johns Hopkins University Press, 1981), particularly pp. 137–61.

20. Herman E. Daly and John B. Cobb, Jr., *For the Common Good* (Boston: Beacon, 1989).

21. Carol C. Gould, *Rethinking Democracy* (Cambridge: Cambridge University Press, 1988); Michael Walzer, *Spheres of Justice: A Defense of Pluralism and Equality* (New York: Basic Books, 1983).

22. Walzer, p. 301.

23. Gould, pp. 135–43.

24. Beverly Wildung Harrison in *Making the Connections: Essays in Feminist Social Ethics,* Carol S. Robb (ed.) (Boston: Beacon, 1985), p. 90.

CHAPTER 7

Partnering, Parenting, and Family Making

From the beginning, second-wave feminists looked in detail at motherhood and, with it, women's sexualities and sexual partnerships. Focusing on the 1960s and early 1970s, Lauri Umansky shows that these feminists usually treated motherhood positively:

> Motherhood minus "patriarchy," theorists have claimed, holds the truly spectacular potential to bond women to each other and to nature, to foster a liberating knowledge of self, to release the very creativity and generativity that the institution of "motherhood" in our culture denies to women.[1]

As Robin Morgan observed in 1978, a maternal-feminist synthesis had already taken shape around "the concept of 'mother-right,' the affirmation of childbearing and/or child rearing when it is a woman's *choice*."[2]

For most women in the world, though, motherhood remains a requirement, not an option. Even among women who do choose the terms of their motherhood, such as when to conceive, motherhood is sometimes experienced as a have-to because pressures on women to become mothers persist throughout American society. In everyday life the very tones often used to utter "childless" signal those pressures, as does the pervasive assumption that womanhood entails motherhood. As a matter of pervasive, practical fact, whether and how one mothers significantly defines one's femininity during much of adulthood.

Its complexity, diversity, and far-flung ramifications make motherhood a topic that defies balanced analysis. One move that ensures less imbalance is to focus on the *institution* of motherhood rather than its ideals or possibilities. An institution is a set of socially regulated practices culturally reserved for certain types of people. Institutions de-individualize social practices by standardizing them so that they have a predictable shape within a cultural community. They concern members' shared patterns of behavior, not individuals' distinct styles. Like Adrienne Rich, whose work will concern us soon, most feminist theorists focus on the institution of motherhood, not women's personal experiences of mothering. For the institution they have lots of criticism, especially insofar as it routinely dovetails with the institutions of heterosexuality, marriage, and the family, which favor men. Like all other institutions, these quash most people's awareness that lovemaking or birthing could really be different.

Perhaps no institution in American life better illustrates these principles than heterosexuality. Most people, including many social scientists, even fail to grasp its institutionalized character. In fact, the most reliable sign of an institution's strength is how much it *naturalizes* in people's consciousness—that is, how much people come to see a given set of social practices as an expression of human nature or how things "naturally" are. To say the least, heterosexuality is grossly naturalized in American culture.

HETEROSEXUALITY: THE INSTITUTION

Over most of her life cycle, no other relation says as much about a woman's femininity as the one she has with a male significant other—boyfriend, lover, male cohabitant, husband. Unlike the child-mother relation, this one requires her to be both sexually desirable and strongly other-oriented. Since being desirable to men and oriented to others' needs are at the core of mainstream femininity, a female's heterosexual relationship singularly expresses the nature of her femininity.

Only participation in the *institution* of heterosexuality confirms a woman's unadulterated femininity. The more she departs from its mandates, the more questionable her femininity becomes. This institution lays out a series of subordinating circumstances and activities for its female participants. They are to partner with males more powerful than themselves, who in turn generally expect that their priorities and preferences will hold sway. Like other unequal relationships, institutionalized heterosexuality puts the emotional weight of the relationship on its subordinate member. Thus, it sets women up for emotional inequality. Typically, a girl or woman feeds her partner's ego and tends his wounds[3] more often and more thoroughly than he emotionally supports and nurtures her.

Then, too, women's and men's sexual needs weigh differently in institutionalized heterosexuality. From the outset the female's charge is to await the male's signals of interest. Even in the 1990s young adults follow preadolescents and adolescents in making dutch-treat dating a minor blip in the routines of heterosexual coupling. From preadolescence onward, heterosexual females who want to be "normal" walk a fine line between seeming naive and inexperienced, on the one side, or worldly and whorish, on the other.[4] Heterosexual intercourse remains a male-defined enterprise, with "foreplay" often treated as a warm-up before the aerobics get under way.

All these institutionalized inequalities guarantee that women (and often their partners) who discernibly insist on equality in their sexual relationships with men pay some price. As Carol Siegel puts it, heterosexuality "becomes a battle site for women who refuse passivity."[5] They may be called man-haters or nymphomaniacs; they may be charged with henpecking or castrating their partners; they face ridicule, scorn, or worse. Overall, women who deviate from the institution of heterosexuality are called to account; the institution that has failed them gets off scot-free.

Often women who insist on something other than a typical heterosexual relationship for themselves face a comment like "You must be one of those feminists." That reaction to their deviance, while stereotypical, does make some sense. By and large, feminists are as interested in transforming the institution of heterosexuality as they are in transforming institutions such as education, science, and religion. Thus, combining feminism with institutionalized heterosexuality is no easy task. Few women succeed at it. Instead, heterosexual feminists often forge sexual partnerships beyond the confines of the institution aimed at regulating their primary relationship.

Nowhere is this better seen than in *Heterosexuality: A Feminism & Psychology Reader,* which includes (among other things) statements from 21 heterosexual academic feminists (including Sandra Lee Bartky) about how their sexual orientation affects their work. One theme there is that *heterosexual privilege,* the array of taken-for-granted prerogatives and legal entitlements tied to heterosexuality, is not equally shared among female and male heterosexuals. Both are, to be sure, privileged by belonging to society's dominant sexual group, but women's mandated subordination within that group deflates their heterosexual privilege. Feminism further deflates it. As Caroline Ramazanoglu puts it, "Feminist heterosexuality in my experience is politically sensitive, personally painful, and insufficiently studied." Speaking as young women, Rosalind Gill and Rebecca Walker say that

> To be white, heterosexual feminists in the 1990s is to live inside contradictions—of which the contradiction between recognizing patriarchal oppression in all its subtle and pernicious forms and yet wanting to have profound friendships and sexual relationships with men is only the most obvious example.

Moreover, they live with the realization that feminist discourse "has not *displaced* the other discourses, it has not stopped us wanting (no, craving) things which we know are unsound."[6] Not surprisingly, then, one straight feminist attributes her feminism to her heterosexuality. In that vein, another sees her heterosexuality as "a continual struggle to assert my autonomy, get my needs met and have my subjective experience recognized." Another says her heterosexuality became "especially focused for me since becoming a parent,"[7] thus implying the institutional linkages among heterosexuality, parenthood, and family.

Women's clear-cut disadvantages within this institution may necessitate massive efforts to engage women in it voluntarily. To wit, "heterosexuality may not be a 'preference' at all but something that has had to be imposed, managed, organized, propagandized, and maintained by force. . . ." Because it is deeply naturalized in people's consciousness, that idea may seem untenable. As Sue Wilkinson and Celia Kitzinger go on to concede, the very idea of heterosexuality as socially imposed—indeed, the very idea of heterosexuality as an institution—"is an immense step to take if you consider yourself freely and 'innately' heterosexual. . . ."[8]

These theorists make another point likely to jar those unattuned to the institutionalized character of heterosexuality: "'Heterosexual' and 'lesbian' are *not* opposite ends of the same continuum." The latter is "intrinsically politicized" inasmuch as it departs from "deviant" as well as institutionalized heterosexuality. Wilkinson and Kitzinger say that "what is needed is not the depoliticization of lesbianism . . . but the politicization of the category 'heterosexual.'"[9] With that sweeping recommendation they open a theoretical window of opportunity on female sexualities.

DESIRE, AGENCY, AND FEMALE SEXUALITIES

In her classic delineation of *compulsory heterosexuality* (the social law that everyone be heterosexual or practically commit psychological suicide trying), Adrienne Rich introduced the *lesbian continuum*. Its gradations concern a woman's bonds with other women. At one end of the continuum are bonds involving genital sexuality as well as intense emotions. As one moves toward the other end, physical bonding gradually disappears but emotional ties with women remain significant. Rich's continuum encompasses all women whose emotional satisfactions derive mostly from other women.[10] It thus includes many women with heterosexual identities—women whose most satisfying talks are with other women, who get their greatest support from women, whose most honest moments are usually with women.

Rich thus contributed to the move among feminist theorists to politicize heterosexuality. Less obviously, she contributed to the burgeoning recognition that sexism and heterosexism work together or, alternatively, that the matrix of domination revolves around a *heteropatriarchy*[11] whereby elite men institutionally dominate gay men and all women. Rich's continuum theoretically complicates women's "sexual orientations" by giving their social–emotional needs and sexual desires enormous weight alongside their sexual activities. Just as significantly, she lays grounds for thinking about sexualities and sexual identities beyond binary categories such as gay/straight or monosexual/bisexual. Overall, Rich implies that definitions of women's sexual identities must consider much more than their sexual activity. Yet her theorizing also implies what Julia Penelope later put this way: "An adequate definition [of 'lesbian'] must include our sexuality without making it the only deciding factor."[12]

Conceptually ignoring women's sexual behavior would land us back in the 19th century, when only socially degraded women (lesbians, nymphomaniacs, prostitutes) were seen as sexualized.[13] Thanks to the madonna/whore dualism and its ideological cousins, good women (especially mothers) were thoroughly desexualized. Deemed to have sex with their husbands only as a matter of duty, they were culturally shorn of sexual desires. Not unlike slave women, they had no real "right to love 'big,'" let alone any "entitlement to desire."[14] A century later, unadulterated sexual desire among women still evokes ambivalence or scorn. Theorizing "heterosexual coercion," Nicola Gavey observes that "dominant discourses on women's sexuality are structured around consent and . . . neglect more active notions such as desire. . . ."[15]

Michelle Fine has documented this state of affairs by theorizing about sex education and school-based health clinics. She finds three sexual discourses at work in American curricula for adolescents: one treats (hetero)sexuality as violence; another as victimization of females; another as individual morality. No discourse of desire has taken hold in our public schools; hence, no "naming of desire, pleasure, or sexual entitlement, particularly for females. . . ." What Fine says about young women applies to women in general:

> A genuine discourse of desire would invite [them] to explore what feels good and bad, desirable and undesirable, grounded in experiences, needs, and limits. Such a discourse would release females from a position of receptivity, enable an analysis of the dialectics of victimization and pleasure, and would pose [them] as subjects of sexuality, initiators as well as negotiators.[16]

A discourse of desire would, then, deinstitutionalize the heterosexuality that now casts women not as "subjects at all but rather objects of male prerogative."[17] Deinstitutionalization would make women "the guardians of our own bodies and the explorers of our own desire," eventuating in the "erotic self-possession" that Joan Nestle[18] associates with lesbian living. French feminist Luce Irigaray states the fundamentals that would become less uncommon:

> To know how to be separate and how to come back together. Each to go, both he and she, in quest of self, faithful to the quest, so that they may greet one another, come close, make merry, or seal a covenant.[19]

Deinstitutionalization might also burst open our notions of sexual orientation and sexual identity. Judith Roof implies that, in effect, women's lived experiences do that now insofar as "desire and sexual orientation already destabilize any binary system." Moreover, a grouping as broad as "lesbians" exhibits "vast polymorphous diversity."[20] Much of Gayle Rubin's work centers on such points:

> The fact that *categories leak and can never contain all the relevant "existing things"* does not render them useless, only limited. Categories like "woman," "butch," "lesbian," or "transsexual" are all imperfect, historical, temporary, and arbitrary. We use them, and they use us.[21]

Like Roof, Rubin notes the dramatic diversity among lesbians, where "Drag, cross-dressing, passing, transvestism, and transsexualism are all common . . . , particularly [among] those not attempting to meet constricted standards of political virtue." Lillian Faderman makes a more diffuse observation about various lesbian subcultures that "not only had little in common with each other but [whose] members often distrusted and even disliked one another." Beverly Burch notes the "great diversity" among heterosexuals as well as lesbians.[22]

Burch thinks that to meaningfully theorize sexual orientation we should use not only the gender(s) of a person's sexual partners but also how "restricted and rigid" or "open and flexible" her sexual identity is.[23] Here Burch opens a theoretical door that Eve Kosofsky Sedgwick flies through to great theoretical effect. Sedgwick reminds us that

> It is a rather amazing fact that, of the very many dimensions along which the genital activity of one person can be differentiated from that of another (dimensions that include preference for certain acts, certain zones or sensations, certain physical types, a certain frequency, certain symbolic investments, certain relations of age or power, a certain species, a certain number of participants, etc.), precisely one, the gender of object choice, emerged from the turn of the century, and has remained, as *the* dimension denoted by the now ubiquitous category of "sexual orientation."[24]

Similarly amazing is theorists' neglect of how much this diversity *among* individuals shows up *within* individuals as we move through the life cycle. Even now, attention to sexual diversity—whether within sexual categories or within individuals' lives—remains unusual.

All the while, feminist theorists have moved in that direction. Led by lesbian feminist theorists, by now they often acknowledge the fluidity of our sexual feelings, desires, and activities. Moreover, feminist theorists tend not to assume that "we inherently strive for congruence between our sexual feelings, activities, and identities"; indeed, "permanent congruence may not be an achievable state." Perhaps "pressure[s] to be congruent and to proclaim an identity . . . in line with [one's] sexual activities" come more from the outside than from within.[25]

Diversity stamps feminist theory itself. Debates continue and dissensus prevails over matters such as sadomasochistic sex, pornography, and even bisexuality. Only over the past 10 years or so has women's bisexuality gotten much attention from feminist theorists, perhaps in part because bisexual women were often unwilling to talk about their experiences. Their reluctance, still operative today, often reflects their rejection by monosexuals insistent that bisexual women are *really* lesbians trying to hold onto however much heterosexual privilege they can.[26] As Julia Penelope notes, in lesbian communities bisexual women are sometimes called "bluffs" (a combination of "butch" and "fluff") or switch-hitters.[27]

Today some feminist theorists point to the "subversive potential" of women's bisexuality. Elisabeth Daumer, for instance, treats bisexuality "as an epistemological as well as ethical vantage point from which we can examine and deconstruct the bipolar framework of gender and sexuality." She claims, "Because bisexuality occupies an ambiguous position *between* identities, it is able to shed light on the gap and contradictions of all identity, on what we might call the difference *within* identity."[28] Rebecca Shuster, whose thinking resonates with Daumer's, says bisexuals anchor their sexual identity in "particular personal relationships rather than as an abstract gender preference." Thus, bisexuality implies "a continuum of sexual choices, a continuum that is threatening to those who have imposed a categorical definition on their sexuality. . . ."[29] What emerges, then, is a continuum covering people's lived sexualities.

What also emerges, perhaps, is a distinct set of values arrayed on that continuum. Treating the "sacredness of pleasure" as "a position we as bis need to take," for example, Starhawk says that bisexuals' "struggle is . . . about affirming pleasure, variety, diversity, fluidity, as sacred values. . . ."[30] Understandably, then, Paula C. Rust, who no longer sees herself " 'as' anything" sexually, concludes that the bisexual movement may be "the final revolution on the wheel of sexual identity politics."[31]

This recent theorizing implies what Rubin, a leading spokesperson among lesbian sadomasochists, says explicitly:

> Individuals should be allowed to navigate their own trails through the possibilities, complexities, and difficulties of life in postmodern times. Each strategy and each set of categories has its capabilities, accomplishments, and drawbacks. None is perfect, and none works for everyone all the time.[32]

Moreover, many theoretical and practical difficulties derive from "characterizing *persons* rather than *acts, moments, relationships, encounters, attractions, perspectives, insights, outlooks, connections,* and *feelings.* . . ." In that vein, lesbian feminist philosopher Joyce Trebilcot says, "I am not primarily sexual and so do not like being named with a word that means 'sex' to most people; defining women in terms of sex is a trick men play on women and I don't want to play it on myself."[33]

As we all already knew, sexual labels say too much and too little. However we name ourselves, we should be unashamed of whatever label suits us. At the same time, we should be aware that "no position or approach—transgender, bisexual, or queer—can be said to be either progressive or regressive per se." Indeed, as we saw with feminism and the media, "Perpetuation *and* disruption of dominant gender-sexuality constructs are not always mutually exclusive."[34] We must move past, as feminists have been trying to do for years, such notions as the "lavender menace" (lesbians) or women who "sleep with the enemy" (female heterosexuals).[35] We need always to bear in mind what Gloria Steinem said in "The Politics of Supporting Lesbianism": "we are attempting . . . a revolution, not a public relations movement."[36] With that revolution in mind, let us move to the matter of mothering.

MOTHERING AND FAMILY MAKING

Motherhood comes to harsh and glowing light in Rich's *Of Woman Born,* a classic of autobiographical revelation and feminist analysis. Rich says, "If rape has been terrorism, motherhood has been penal servitude"—harsh light, indeed. Immediately, however, she adds that "*It need not be.*" Anticipating reactions to her piercing analysis, Rich insists her "book is not an attack on the family or on mothering, *except as defined and restricted under patriarchy.*"[37] Rich had her children during the decade focusing Friedan's *Feminine Mystique*:

> I became a mother in the family-centered, consumer-oriented, Freudian-American world of the 1950s. My husband spoke eagerly of the children we would have; my parents-in-law awaited the birth of their grandchild. I had no idea of what *I* wanted, what *I* could or could not choose. I only knew that to have a child was to assume adult womanhood to the full, to prove myself, to be "like other women." (p. 5)

Before long, the domestic part of Rich's life began colliding with the part where her poetry, plus "fantasies of travel and self-sufficiency," sustained her. She developed a "sense of acting a part," which stimulated "a curious sense of guilt, even though it was a part demanded for survival." (p. 6) Rich was pregnant again two years after having her first child and then again in two more years. Her husband remained

> a sensitive, affectionate man who wanted children and who—unusual in the professional, academic world of the 50s—was willing to "help." But it was clearly understood that this "help" was an act of generosity; that *his* work, *his* professional life, was the real work in the family; in fact this was for years not even an issue between us. I understood that my struggles as a writer were a kind of luxury, a peculiarity of mind. (p. 7)

In 1996, this same poet won a prestigious MacArthur Fellowship of several hundred thousand dollars, but her talents scarcely affected the expectations she faced as a mother. Conceding that we may have an "organic or developed gift for nurture"—an essential or constructed facility for caring—Rich notes that it works like a boomerang. (p. 289) That boomerang might be called the *24-hour rule:* Mothers in particular, but also wives to a substantial extent, are supposed to be available to work 24 hours a day. Most fathers "help" to some degree, but wives and mothers often work two shifts and are on call for a third one. Since their charges typically accompany them on vacation, many young mothers have no real vacation for years at a time. Mothering remains, then, a full-time, year-round activity; fathering, by sharp contrast, refers mostly to impregnation, not child nurturing.

An interesting companion piece to Rich's book is Nancy Chodorow's *The Reproduction of Mothering: Psychoanalysis and the Sociology of Gender,* published two years later (see Reading 15). Chodorow's broad focus is how family dynamics, centered on women's mothering, "affect unconscious psychic structure and process."[38] She theorizes that women's emotionally intense mothering and men's emotionally distant fathering, on average, establish a masculinity "defined more in terms of denial of relation and connection (and denial of femininity)" and a femininity revolving around "a fundamental definition of self in relationship." (p. 169) Put differently, girls develop greater "relational potential" than boys. (p. 166) Because of males' shortcomings in this area, women's heterosexuality gets less firmly formed than men's. Even for women heterosexually identified, then, men "tend to remain *emotionally* secondary." (p. 167)

Here Chodorow's thinking intersects with Rich's. Where Rich sees a lesbian continuum, however, Chodorow sees a maternal one. Deeming the prohibitions against homosexuality profoundly effective, Chodorow says women seeking emotional closeness "come to want and need primary relationships to children." (pp. 200, 203) Julia Kristeva maps out conceptual grounds between Rich's and Chodorow's by postulating a "homosexual facet of motherhood" or a homosexual–maternal facet linking the daughter who gives birth with her own mother, the two being "the same continuity differentiating itself."[39]

For Chodorow, a deterministic circle is set up whereby women's mothering reproduces the conditions wherein women typically need to mother in efforts to satisfy their emotional needs. At the same time, women's mothering "prepares men for participation in a male-dominant family and society, for their lesser emotional participation in family life, and for their participation in the capitalist world of work." (p. 181) Not surprisingly, Chodorow (p. 215) concludes that equality between women and men necessitates "a fundamental reorganization of parenting, so that primary parenting is shared between men and women." Like most feminist theorists, she emphasizes that

> women's mothering . . . benefits many people. It is a major feature of the sex–gender system. It creates heterosexual asymmetries which reproduce the family and marriage, but leave women with needs that lead them to care for children, and men with capacities for participation in the alienated work world. It creates a psychology of male dominance and fear of women in men. (p. 219)

Where exactly change might originate is unclear in Chodorow's theory. One can infer that individual mothers, especially those doing paid as well as unpaid work, must demand greater participation from their children's coparent. Yet if that coparent is a man, by Chodorow's account he is probably emotionally unfit to nurture children well. Also, mothers' emotional satisfactions from their intense bonding with daughters and sons make them unlikely to want their partners to bond equally strongly with their children. To say the least, we have hit upon a theoretical conundrum. In Reading 17 Diane Ehrensaft analyzes this theoretical impasse.

Both Rich and Chodorow offer sharp insights into the dense dynamics of mothering and family making. By and large, they focus on the *dominant ideology of motherhood* comprising "the dominant ideals against which women's lives are judged." Women (including those who do not bear or adopt at least one child) falling short of these ideals face more or less harsh judgments, but the harshest judgments fall on those women considered unfit to mother at all. As Marlee Kline notes, this circumstance has applied at various times to

> disabled women, Black women, First Nation women, immigrant women, Jewish women, lesbian women, sole-support women, poor women, unmarried women, young women, and others. . . . For these women, procreation has often been devalued and discouraged. The ideology of motherhood, therefore, speaks not only to gender roles and behavior. It also constructs some locations within social relations of race, class, sexuality, ability, and so on as more appropriate for motherhood than others.[40]

Thus, beyond the "professional, academic world" that Rich vicariously inhabited as a young mother or the white, middle-class one that focuses Chodorow's analysis lie experiences their frameworks ignore. Beyond such safe harbors, mothering means facing empty cupboards and worrying about eviction; it means losing your daughter to her convicted-murderer father because you are making a home with the woman you love (as happened with Mary Ward of Pensacola, Florida, in 1996); it means being seen as a child raising a child rather than as a teenage mother struggling against the odds such imagery exacerbates; it means not being able to support your children because of job discrimination against handicapped people, especially women; it means being stared at because your child is of another race with national origins different from your own; it means your addictions impair your child nurturing. Mothering commonly entails much more messiness and many more headaches than these theorists address. The sad irony is that for women belonging to other subordinated groups in society, motherhood is often their "main source of dignity and self-respect."[41]

In Reading 18, Dorothy E. Roberts makes that point about black teenage moms, for instance. More generally, she shows how racism interacts with patriarchy in cultural constructions of motherhood. She picks up on some of Rich's points while setting maternal constructions in a rich Afrocentric context. Roberts has the theoretical wisdom to see that mothers from "outcast" groups have a great deal to tell us about the liberation of motherhood.[42] She also has the practical wisdom to emphasize that the work–family conflict is largely experienced in middle-class circles, where mothers often expect more parenting options than women in lower classes—disproportionately women of color—expect. Throughout her analysis, then, Roberts points to how social class interacts with race and gender to construct distinct versions of motherhood.

Not only various racial/ethnic groups and various social classes but also lesbigay people construct distinctive families in response to their material, sociocultural, political–legal, and historical circumstances. The diverse familial forms that are viable (as well as observable in our society) make a travesty of the family-values rhetoric that right-wing traditionalists ply from pulpits, lecterns, and soapboxes in our society today. By now "family values" is a "mantra" widely used by "keepers of the patriarchy" (or "patriarchalists") bent on keeping the home and family "inviolate from prying eyes."[43] The "family" thus valorized is a common site of girls' and women's violation, emotionally and sexually.

No contemporary theorist better speaks to the linkages between the heteropatriarchal family and female oppression than Colette Guillaumin, who emphasizes that "Relations of domination, exploitation, inequality are held as socially necessary and, furthermore, are sometimes dressed up in terms of 'complementarity.' "[44] Guillaumin's central concept is *sexage,* the "relation of appropriation" whereby men as a class take control of or have ultimate say about women's time, the products of their bodies, their sexuality, and their care of babies, children, and sick and infirm people "as well as the *healthy members of the group of the male sex.*"[45] Her rich theorizing also delineates how female family members besides the wife get drawn into serving the "head of the household" and how all these phenomena in the so-called private sphere are knotted up with the dynamics of job markets, body languages, and much else.

One of the few social realities Guillaumin neglects is women's friendships. How these relationships can further men's appropriation of women's sexuality, labor, time, and attention is the focus of Stacy J. Oliker's *Best Friends and Marriage,* which shows how a wife's female friends often "help" her stay in a miserable marriage. Yet the picture is vastly more complicated:

> Women's friendships do accommodate them to strained marriages. But by serving as a repository for marital ideals of reciprocity, emotional communion, and interdependent individuality, they do considerably more than accommodate some women to unequal, emotionally unsatisfying, and identity-submerging marriages. Friends' shared recognition of realities of gender power and their exchange of emotional self-awareness sustain a vision of gender power struggle and a strategic mode of thought about marriage.[46]

Thus, women help their female friends struggling with marital woes in diverse, tangled ways. Their circumstances make it inordinately difficult, however, to encourage swift departure from the hell of a painful marriage:

> When marriage represents most women's only opportunity to provide decently for their children, when women's opportunities to establish new heterosexual relationships decrease dramatically with age, when married women friends are powerless to share their material means of survival, the costs of resistance can be high.[47]

Some women pay those costs. Yet "women suffering at the hands of men are only ever advised to leave *him,* never to leave *them.*"[48]

In the end the challenges of partnering, parenting, and family making invite social and cultural changes alongside shifts in individuals' consciousness. Gender equality has little chance of emerging "unless work is reorganized to meet the demands of daily life, caring work becomes as valued as producing profits, and the issue of male power is directly confronted."[49] Even a reorganization of work and a revaluation of caring and a collective confrontation of male power will have only ambiguous results, however, for women wanting to live apart from men and to mother without a male coparent. For such women, community is as much an issue as family. Indeed, once one leaves the social space covered by the institution of heterosexuality, "family" and "community" commonly become coextensive. They are the people with whom we figure things out, share our news and our love, and forge our future.

Both concepts remain profoundly problematic, especially among non-feminist theorists. The next chapter focuses on "community." Let us leave this chapter with one particularly important illustration of how problematic "family" can be from a feminist perspective. Martha Albertson Fineman, who sees it as fundamental to patriarchy, has given up on the idea of liberating women by reforming the traditional family. To promote "unsubjugated motherhood," she proposes making the mother/child dyad the "basic family paradigm" while rendering voluntary, adult sexual relationships and interactions "of no concern to the state."[50] In this model, which allows anyone to "mother," lies great promise, I believe—the promise of nurturance as the real hallmark of "family" rather than dominance or exploitation.

NOTES

1. Lauri Umansky, *Motherhood Reconceived: Feminism and the Legacies of the Sixties* (New York: New York University Press, 1996), p. 3.
2. Robin Morgan, *Going too Far: The Personal Chronicle of a Feminist* (New York: Vintage Books, 1978), p. 8.
3. See the last chapter ("Feeding Egos and Tending Wounds") of Sandra Lee Bartky, *Femininity and Domination: Studies in the Phenomenology of Oppression* (New York: Routledge, 1990).
4. For particularly poignant data along these lines, see Donna Eder with Catherine Colleen Evans and Stephen Parker, *School Talk: Gender and Adolescent Culture* (New Brunswick, NJ: Rutgers University Press, 1995). This middle-school ethnography details the sexual pressures and harassment girls face at school.
5. Carol Siegel, "Compulsory Heterophobia: The Aesthetics of Seriousness and the Production of Homophobia," *Genders* 21 (1995), p. 329.
6. Caroline Ramazanoglu, "Love and the Politics of Heterosexuality" in Sue Wilkinson and Celia Kitzinger (eds.), *Heterosexuality: A Feminism & Psychology Reader* (Newbury Park, CA: Sage, 1993), p. 59; Rosalind Gill and Rebecca Walker, "Heterosexuality, Feminism, Contradiction: On Being Young, White, Heterosexual Feminists in the 1990s" in *ibid.*, pp. 68, 69.
7. Alison M. Thomas, "The Heterosexual Feminist: A Paradoxical Identity?" in Wilkinson and Kitzinger, *Heterosexuality*, p. 83; Tamsin Wilton, "Sisterhood in the Service of Patriarchy: Heterosexual Women's Friendships and Male Power" in *ibid.*, p. 273; Susie Orbach, "Heterosexuality and Parenting" in *ibid.*, p. 48.

8. Sue Wilkinson and Celia Kitzinger, "Editorial Introduction" in Wilkinson and Kitzinger, *Heterosexuality,* p. 3.

9. *Ibid.,* p. 8.

10. Adrienne Rich, "Compulsory Heterosexuality and Lesbian Existence," *Signs: Journal of Women in Culture and Society* 5 (1980), pp. 631–60.

11. See Shane Phelan, *Identity Politics: Lesbian Feminism and the Limits of Community* (Philadelphia: Temple University Press, 1989), p. 47; Julia Penelope, *Call Me Lesbian: Lesbian Lives, Lesbian Theory* (Freedom, CA: The Crossing Press, 1992), p. xiii.

12. Penelope, *Call Me Lesbian,* p. 34.

13. Carol Groneman, "Nymphomania: The Historical Construction of Female Sexuality" in Jennifer Terry and Jacquiline Urla (eds.), *Deviant Bodies: Critical Perspectives on Difference in Science and Popular Culture* (Bloomington: Indiana University Press, 1995), p. 234.

14. Ann duCille, *The Coupling Convention: Sex, Text, and Tradition in Black Women's Fiction* (New York: Oxford University Press, 1993), p. 5.

15. Nicola Gavey, "Technologies and Effects of Heterosexual Coercion" in Wilkinson and Kitzinger, *Heterosexuality,* p. 105.

16. Michelle Fine, "Sexuality, Schooling, and Adolescent Females: The Missing Discourse of Desire" in Michelle Fine (ed.), *Disruptive Voices: The Possibilities of Feminist Research* (Ann Arbor: University of Michigan Press, 1992), pp. 33–5, 35–6.

17. Wendy Lee-Hampshire, "Decisions of Identity: Feminist Subjects and Grammars of Sexuality," *Hypatia: A Journal of Feminist Philosophy* 10, no. 4 (Fall 1995), p. 37.

18. Joan Nestle, "Desire Perfected: Sex after Forty" in Barbara Sang, Joyce Warshow, and Adrienne J. Smith (eds.), *Lesbians at Midlife: The Creative Tension* (San Francisco: Spinsters Book Co., 1991), p. 181.

19. Luce Irigaray, *An Ethics of Sexual Difference* (Ithaca, NY: Cornell University Press, 1993), trans. Carolyn Burke and Gillian C. Gill (orig. 1984), p. 71. Irigaray (p. 68) also lists cultural tasks required for recognizing *two* who are to experience *oneness.*

20. Judith Roof, *A Lure of Knowledge: Lesbian Sexuality and Theory* (New York: Columbia University Press, 1991), pp. 50, 250.

21. Gayle Rubin, "Of Catamites and Kings: Reflections on Butch, Gender, and Boundaries" in Joan Nestle (ed.), *The Persistent Desire: A Butch–Femme Reader* (Boston: Alyson Publications, 1992), p. 477.

22. *Ibid.,* p. 468; Lillian Faderman, *Odd Girls and Twilight Lovers: A History of Lesbian Life in Twentieth-Century America* (New York: Penguin Books, 1992), p. 160; Beverly Burch, *On Intimate Terms: The Psychology of Difference in Lesbian Relationships* (Urbana: University of Illinois Press, 1993), p. 11.

23. Burch, *On Intimate Terms,* p. 24.

24. Eve Kosofsky Sedgwick, *Epistemology of the Closet* (Berkeley: University of California Press, 1990), p. 8.

25. Carla Golden, "Diversity and Variability in Women's Sexual Identities" in Boston Lesbian Psychologies Collective (ed.), *Lesbian Psychologies: Explorations and Challenges* (Urbana: University of Illinois Press, 1987), pp. 29, 31.

26. For accounts of such experiences, see Loraine Hutchins and Lani Kaahumanu (eds.), *Bi any other Name: Bisexual People Speak Out* (Boston: Alyson Publications, 1991).

27. Penelope, *Call Me Lesbian,* p. 2. Faderman reports on the status of bisexual women in lesbian communities; see *Odd Girls,* pp. 234–5, 296–97; see also Sharon Dale Stone, "Bisexual Women and the 'Threat' to Lesbian Space, or What if All the Lesbians Leave?" *Frontiers* XVI, no. 1 (1996), pp. 101–16.

28. Elisabeth D. Daumer, "Queer Ethics; or, The Challenge of Bisexuality to Lesbian Ethics," *Hypatia* 7 (Fall 1992), pp. 97–8.

29. Rebecca Shuster, "Sexuality as a Continuum: The Bisexual Identity" in Boston Lesbian Psychologies Collective, *Lesbian Psychologies,* p. 62.

30. Starhawk, "The Sacredness of Pleasure" in Naomi Tucker (ed.), *Bisexual Politics: Theories, Queries, and Visions* (New York: The Haworth Press, 1995), p. 327.

31. Paula C. Rust, *Bisexuality and the Challenge to Lesbian Politics: Sex, Loyalty, and Revolution* (New York: New York University Press, 1995), p. 259.

32. Rubin, "Of Catamites and Kings," p. 477.

33. Ruth Ginzberg, "Audre Lorde's (Nonessentialist) Lesbian Eros," *Hypatia* 7 (Fall 1992), p. 82; Joyce Trebilcot, "Not Lesbian Philosophy," *Hypatia* 7 (Fall 1992), p. 42.

34. Clare Hemmings, "From Lesbian Nation to Transgender Liberation: A Bisexual Feminist Perspective," *Journal of Gay, Lesbian, and Bisexual Identity* 1, no. 1 (1996), p. 39.

35. The former characterization is associated with Betty Friedan when she led NOW; the latter with radical lesbian feminists, especially during the late 1960s and early 1970s.

36. Cited in Faderman, *Odd Girls,* p. 213.

37. Adrienne Rich, *Of Woman Born: Motherhood as Experience and Institution* (New York: Bantam Books, 1977 (orig. 1976)), p. xvi.

38. Nancy Chodorow, *The Reproduction of Mothering: Psychoanalysis and the Sociology of Gender* (Berkeley: University of California Press, 1978), p. 49.

39. Julia Kristeva, *Desire in Language: A Semiotic Approach to Literature and Art* (New York: Columbia University Press, 1980 (orig. 1977)), trans. Thomas Gora, Alice Jardine, and Leon S. Roudiez.

40. Marlee Kline, "Complicating the Ideology of Motherhood: Child Welfare Law and First Nation Women" in Martha Albertson Fineman and Isabel Karpin (eds.), *Mothers in Law: Feminist Theory and the Legal Resolution of Motherhood* (New York: Columbia University Press, 1995), pp. 119, 120–1; see also Sharon Hays, *The Cultural Contradictions of Motherhood* (New Haven, CT: Yale University Press, 1996).

41. Karen Anderson, *Changing Women: A History of Racial Ethnic Women in Modern America* (New York: Oxford University Press, 1996), p. 94. Anderson was referring to Chicanas in this instance.

42. Along these lines, another theorist argues that the African American institution of "othermothering" implies how mothering in general might be socially transformed; the same might be said of the Latina institution of *comadres.* See Stanlie M. James, "Mothering: A Possible Black Feminist Link to Social Transformation?" in Stanlie M. James and Abena P. A. Busia (eds.), *Theorizing Black Feminisms: The Visionary Pragmatism of Black Women* (London and New York: Routledge, 1993), p. 45.

43. Marcia Ann Gillespie, "Family Values," *Ms.* (July/August 1994), p. 1; Marilyn French, *The War against Women* (New York: Ballantine Books, 1992), p. 196.

44. Colette Guillaumin, "Sexism, A Right-Wing Constant of any Discourse: A Theoretical Note" in *Racism, Sexism, Power and Ideology* (London and New York: Routledge, 1995), p. 172; trans. Caroline Kunstenaar.

45. Colette Guillaumin, "The Practice of Power and Belief in Nature: Part I, The Appropriation of Women" in Guillaumin, *Racism, Sexism,* p. 181, trans. Linda Murgatroyd.

46. Stacey J. Oliker, *Best Friends and Marriage: Exchange among Women* (Berkeley: University of California Press, 1989), p. 157.

47. *Ibid.,* p. 164.

48. Wilton, "Sisterhood in the Service," p. 274.

49. Joan Acker, "Women, Families, and Public Policy in Sweden" in Esther Ngan-ling Chow and Catherine White Berheide (eds.), *Women, the Family, and Policy: A Global Perspective* (Albany: State University of New York Press, 1994), p. 48,

50. Martha Albertson Fineman, *The Neutered Mother, the Sexual Family, and Other Twentieth Century Tragedies* (New York: Routledge, 1995), pp. 27, 229–30, 233.

Feminists Fight (for) Fathers

Diane Ehrensaft

You've come a long way, baby—until you have one. And left feminists are now among the surge of women "having them." At the birth of the contemporary women's movement, few feminists were themselves giving birth. Those of us who were politically involved then pondered new gender and parenting roles, but mostly from armchairs, rather than from the nursery floor. In fact, for many, motherhood was "out," even politically incorrect. As the movement matured, so did its early members. Now motherhood is "in," and many of us, both gay and straight, single and coupled, have chosen motherhood.

The pressure is on to develop a viable feminist strategy for parenting. Like millions of other women in this country, we face the survival issue of balancing work and family in a society that offers meager support to do either—work or mother—adequately. For over 20 years feminists have struggled to develop a politics of motherhood. The mission was once charged with revolutionary and ideological fervor and was voiced in the demand that men pick up the diaper pin so women could pick up a paycheck. But now it has increasingly shifted to a politics of personal experience and self-interest. And while we have struggled to release women from the oppressive shackles of traditional motherhood, the women's movement has repeatedly found itself in a muddle when it reaches the question of how men should be involved in that process.

We have not resolved the seeming dilemmas between fathers' involvement and mothers' op-

pression. On issue after issue feminists have been polarized between a view of men and fathers as the ultimate patriarchal robbers of mother rights (as when fathers take child custody away from their lesbian ex-wives) and the stance that women will only stand to gain from a reconstruction of parenting in which men and women fully share both parental rights and responsibilities. It is time for left feminists to reframe this polarized view into a dialectical understanding of fatherhood as both oppressive to women and as bearing potential for women's liberation, in order to develop a politics of parenting that takes both sides of the dialectic into account. This article is meant to be a step in that direction, toward sifting through our history, sorting out confusions, and solidifying a cohesive position on father involvement and feminist change.

FRIEDAN ON FATHERING

Dr. [Selma] Fraiberg would not go back herself, from her fine, well-paying professional position as a psychoanalyst who is also a mother. If she is indeed ready to take arms "in defense of mothering" . . . [l]et her concern herself with institutional changes and social innovations which are needed now so men and women can better share the burdens—and joys—of parenting.

—Betty Friedan, 1981[1]

You would hope that in any situation of parenting there would be mutual joy and a mutual sharing of responsibilities. But in the last analysis, until technology makes it possible for a man to carry for nine months and go through the risk and the pain of giving birth, then finally the risk and the bond belong to the mother.

—Betty Friedan, 1987[2]

One feminist, two positions on fathering and mothering. In carving out a feminist position on the role of men as fathers, conflicts, contradictions, and controversy have been rampant among different segments of the women's movement, as well as *within* each of us. Thus in 1981 Betty Friedan can wage a militant campaign for fa-

Diane Ehrensaft, "Feminists Fight (for) Fathers," *Socialist Review* 90/4 (vol. 20, no. 4; Oct.-Dec. 1990). Copyright © 1990, Center for Social Research and Education. Reprinted by permission of Duke University Press.

thers' *equal* involvement in parenting as essential to the "second stage" of feminism, and then in 1987, to support Mary Beth Whitehead's right to Baby M, do an about-face and argue for the biological supremacy of mothers over fathers.

It is not simply a matter of a change in Friedan's thinking from 1981 to 1987. For in 1989 she again vehemently advocates fathers' equal involvement in parenting in her attack of Felice Schwartz's proposal in the *Harvard Business Review* for separate corporate tracks for "career primary" and "career and family" women.[3] In her vacillation, one of the earliest prime movers of modern feminism becomes a spokeswoman for many of her sisters, and her words give us pause. Even on an issue fraught with deep emotions and childhood memories, we cannot have it both ways, arguing for the rights of mothers over fathers because of biology from one side of our mouths while demanding from the other that fathers ought to tend to the diapers as much as mothers.

It was not a random choice to open this piece on fathering and feminism with a renowned feminist's contradictory positions on two recent social events, the Baby M case and the "mommy track" debate. The feminist responses to each of these events reveal how the Baby M case forced to the surface the chronic conflicts among feminists on fatherhood (and motherhood) while the brouhaha surrounding Schwartz's proposed "mommy track" finally pushed feminists to speak in one unified public voice on the issue. Both events also bring to the fore three essential questions for a political movement whose bedrock has been a critique of the family and the stereotypic gender roles within it: (1) Do we want or need men to be involved in children's lives? (2) If yes, how? and (3) Who can (or should) "mother"? These are questions for both lesbian and heterosexual women, and all implicitly challenge the accepted hegemony of the heterosexual nuclear family as the bastion of American childrearing. Whether they live alone or in couples or in communes, with men or with women, feminists have yet to tackle the unre-

solved dilemma regarding fathering: Do we want the men, or don't we?

. . .

ARE FATHERS NECESSARY?

"We don't need the men," Malvina Reynolds sang. Do we or don't we? Regarding fathering and families, that has been the major dividing force among feminists over the past 20 years—between lesbians and heterosexual women, between women of different classes and colors, and between radical and socialist or liberal feminists. The debate rages both in theory—around "who can mother?" and the role of patriarchy—and in practice—around personal life and the political campaigns waged over family issues.

"Who can mother?" Even the wording of the question has been cause for dispute. Some feminists argue for the word "parenting" rather than "mothering," because the former avoids representing child care responsibilities as only women's work and includes men in the concept. Others object that this is a form of "post-feminist" liberalism or reformism which assumes that gender relationships have already changed, and merely plays into the hands of those who would wish to deny that women have had a unique and special hand in the nurturing of other human beings.[4] My own recent work on shared parenting, like Sarah Ruddick's *Maternal Thinking,* represents a third feminist response which treats "mother" as a verb, rather than as a description of social position. We both argue that at this moment in history mothering is the correct term for it embodies all the tasks of nurturing and empathy that have historically been women's domain and now must also be taken up by men if there is to be a healthy society.[5]

But then the question becomes, If women do this work better than men, why would we want fathers to do it? The early radical feminist response to this query was definitive: We wouldn't. It is not just that fathers can't mother, but that they *shouldn't.* In her 1973 *Lesbian Nation,* Jill

Johnston argued that "the overthrow of mother-right was the *world defeat of the female sex.*" As she explained it, men claimed rights over women through paternity, and so patriarchy began. To free women of patriarchy, we need to eliminate fatherhood, and create a society of mothers, "an order which would naturally correspond to the biological situation of women as parent prime." Men can be sons, but never fathers, neither traditional ones nor new mothering figures.[6] In a segment of the women's movement which was both revolutionary and declared the structure of patriarchy as *the* source of women's oppression, the early call for separatism and the elimination of men from positions of power, including fatherhood, was the obvious strategy.

Most radical feminists of the early 1970s were not seriously considering having children themselves. Yet their theoretical argument that a child could grow up well if not better in a family without a father would later come to support the move of both lesbian and straight women of all persuasions in the 1980s to choose motherhood without fathers, a choice made more possible by the availability of both artificial insemination and single-parent adoption. In the meantime, the radical feminist argument against fatherhood throughout the 1970s was two-fold: essentialist, in that women = nature = parent prime, and structuralist, in that patriarchy = father's power = women's oppression. So "down with fatherhood" was the battle cry.

This critique of fathering did not sit well with either liberal or socialist feminists. In formulating a program for the 1970s, they, like radical feminists, were consistent in their critique of the traditional family as oppressive to women. But socialist feminists recognized class as well as the gender system as the source of oppression and the locus of change, and saw men not just as their oppressors but also as their brothers in a larger political struggle for a more democratic and humane society. Liberal feminists accepted the overall system but believed men and women genuinely desired and deserved more harmonious and intimate relationships that could be

fought for through a reform movement. When it came to fathering, socialist and liberal feminists joined hands in demanding the equal involvement of men and women in household work, including childcare.

Liberal feminism, whose voice was consolidated in Betty Friedan's *The Second Stage,* insisted that we must look at the family as it really is today and that for real trade-offs in gender divisions and power to take place, "the sharp demarcation between family and home as 'woman's world' and work (and politics and law) as 'man's world' will have to be redrawn."[7] Socialist feminists believed that only a radical transformation rather than reform of both the class and gender system would truly make this possible, and that until such time we must persist in a radical critique of personal relationships and sexual politics, one which encompasses a vital tension between androgynous and female-centered visions.[8]

By the late 1970s the left feminist demand for father involvement was crystallized in two publications, Nancy Chodorow's *The Reproduction of Mothering* and Dorothy Dinnerstein's *The Mermaid and the Minotaur.*[9] Chodorow argued that the only reason females can mother better than males is that they are raised by women, their same-sex parent, while sons, raised by an opposite-sex parent, never get the opportunity to develop the empathy and nurturance that are the prerequisites of mothering. Dinnerstein demonstrated that gender warfare is directly related to female-centered childrearing, because males spend the rest of their lives desperately trying symbolically to undo their tie to an archaic, infantile image of an overwhelmingly powerful female (a.k.a. "Mother"). From both of these works came the conclusion that if we want to eliminate the personality and social schisms between men and women and rear males who are capable of mothering, we *must* get fathers equally involved in parenting from infancy on. Men as traditional fathers will no longer do. We must place them alongside women as equal mothering figures. The envisioned results of male involvement in early childrearing were seen as potentially far-reaching and revolutionary.

Many feminists, myself included, embraced Chodorow's social-psychological theory because it demonstrated that it is not biology, but the social structure of families that is destiny. We also lauded both her and Dinnerstein for providing a theoretical rationale to back the political demand that men get involved in parenting for the larger good of society and gender relationships. Chodorow's book, in fact, was the stimulus for my own work on shared parenting, which set out to demonstrate that men can and indeed *do* share parenting in certain U.S. subcultures, and that shared parenting benefits children, men, and women alike.[10]

Yet several radical feminists vitriolically attacked Chodorow's arguments on fathering. Pauline Bart, another feminist sociologist, decried Chodorow's theory as playing right into the hands of the patriarchal order that takes children away from women who choose to parent without a man—divorced mothers, single mothers, lesbian mothers. Chodorow, Bart argued, was unwittingly providing patriarchal forces the psychological ammunition needed to do their dirty work against nontraditional mothers. Moreover, Bart saw Chodorow kowtowing to the liberals by providing a solution, bringing men into childrearing, that was far less threatening to the social order than the more radical stance of Adrienne Rich or Judith Arcana that *woman bonding* is the solution to the oppressive nature of motherhood as an institution. "Requiring adults of both genders to raise children reinforces heterosexuality and the nuclear family." According to Bart, who is adamant that liberal and socialist feminists have failed to deal with the misogyny of the culture, this is not what feminism should be about.[11]

But it is Bart herself who misses the point that relegating men to a back seat in parenting in no way tears down heterosexism and the oppressive nuclear family but instead reinforces the chains of bondage that keep women tied to hearth and home. The real problem with Chodorow's work is not that she advocates male involvement in parenting, but that she im-

plies that this is the *only* way to insure healthy development and dismantle oppressive gender relationships. The theory tends to reduce all social change related to gender to change within the family, and to the heterosexual nuclear family at that. A corrective would be to advocate that shared parenting between men and women in heterosexual families is one extremely important means of both preparing males for the tasks of mothering and establishing more gender harmony in the culture, but not the *only* avenue to healthy gender relationships and societal functioning.

Regardless of their veracity, the intensity of Pauline Bart's attacks reflects how deeply the issue of fathering and feminism hits the core of our thinking and feeling about men, women, and the sex/gender system, and also how deep the schisms have run among feminists between the view of men as the enemy versus that of men as comrades. To make matters more complicated in the recent history of fathering and feminism, Alice Rossi, a well-respected feminist scholar who made her mark in 1964 with her early article "Equality between the Sexes: An Immodest Proposal," in 1974 published "A Biosocial Perspective on Parenting."[12] Shocked and betrayed, feminists of all ilks were appalled by her argument that men are simply genetically disadvantaged when it comes to mothering, and that the differences between the sexes come from biology, not deeply ingrained social and psychological forces. Rossi uprooted the feminist stance that human personality is an interaction of biology and culture, but with culture the overwhelmingly more powerful influence, and she came to represent a new form of "conservative" feminism in the late 1970s. Recognizing the ammunition Rossi provided for antifeminist backlash, Wini Breines, Margaret Cerullo, and Judith Stacey, three socialist feminists, responded:

The ultimate effect of what the *Daedalus* editors aptly term Rossi's "immodest interpretation" is to roll back one of the major intellectual gains of the women's movement—that which transferred the family and sex roles from the realm of biology to that of society and history. . . . In Rossi's restoration the world of fatherhood and men is once again the world of culture while women and motherhood are returned to their identification with nature.[13]

But whose rug was Rossi really rolling back? For her identity of women and nature is really not that different from Jill Johnston's or Adrienne Rich's before her. Rossi's intent was not to celebrate women as nature but to assert what she knew would be perceived within feminist discourse as both a renegade and conservative position on genetics and biology. The outcome, however, is that her work has been used not only by conservative thinkers but by her radical feminist sisters in supporting the argument that mothers and nature go together, while fathers and nature do not.

By the early 1980s, the lines of response to the question, "Can men mother?" were clearly drawn. While the distinctions between radical, liberal, and socialist feminists become less relevant as the second wave of feminism rolled in with a more issue-oriented politics, the legacy of those tendencies was a lasting schism among feminists on the issue of gender and parenting. Regarding men and "mothering," one set of feminists argue that nature dictates that men cannot or should not; another that the primacy of nurture over nature dictates men can and should. Herein lies the major paradox of these two positions: If you support men as fathers you can be said to oppress women; if you do not support men you can be accused of oppressing women. As the women's movement faced the 80s, we see this paradox in action when we take a look at the actual feminist *practice* on two issues: alternative families and divorce/custody.

FATHER ABSENCE/FATHER PRESENCE

A major task for feminists has been to fight for a woman's right to have a child when she wants and with whom she wants. Society takes particular offense if the "with whom" does not include a man. Lesbian and single mothers have been the special targets of attack. Particularly for a lesbian mother, it is not just that she cannot find a live-in father for her child or has lost one, but that she does not want one. She may have had her child in a previous marriage or through adoption, a sexual union with a man, or artificial insemination, with a known or unknown donor, with a lesbian partner or alone. If an ex-husband is in the picture, he will likely get custody of the children if he files suit.[14] If there is a lesbian co-parent, she presently cannot obtain the same rights as a father or even a stepfather, because no state in this country recognizes the legal rights of a nonbiological parent who is not married to the child's natural or adoptive parent, and no state allows marriage between same-sex partners.

Two main questions, actually thinly veiled accusations, are repeatedly posed by opponents of lesbian parenting. One, do you think it is fair to bring a child into the world who will have to face the stigma of being from a "different" family? Two, isn't it unhealthy for a child to be raised without the presence of a father? After all, feminists themselves have said that sex-typing will only be broken down when children are exposed equally to both men and women.

In fact, hostility has built up among lesbian parents toward their heterosexual feminist sisters because of the latter's unwillingness to respond strongly to these accusations. Lesbians believe that worse yet, heterosexual feminists play into the hands of those who condemn lesbian parenting by insisting that it is in the best interests of children to have both fathers and mothers active in mothering.

Lesbians' own response to the accusations, with at least some feminist support, has been that a child raised without a father will be a healthy child as long as there are loving parents in the home, regardless of their sex or sexual preference, a position that I strongly support. Further, raising children with one or two mothers does not mean there will be no exposure to men or to their own fathers. Many lesbian mothers have chosen gay or heterosexual male friends to be the biological fathers of their children, with the commitment to joint involvement in parenting after the child's birth.[15] Others have established commitments from male friends or relatives to take on a fathering or avuncular role. Finally, lesbians argue that the concerns about "man-hating" are misdirected at lesbian mothers. Loving a woman in no way is equated with condemning men. If people are really worried about the hostility of mothers toward men or fathers, they would better aim their inquiry at heterosexual families where the growing incidence of open warfare or violence between mothers and fathers can hardly contribute to the health and welfare of the children.

These arguments provide support not only for lesbian mothers, but for divorced and single mothers as well. In the meantime, organizations such as the Lesbian Rights Project in San Francisco have been pushing for both legal decisions and legislation that would allow coparent adoptions and insure parental rights to the nonbiological mother in lesbian families. Their argument is that any individual who has provided long-time physical and psychological nurturance to a child should be considered a "de facto" parent. Or to put it in one lesbian co-parent's words (a woman who has been turned down by a California court in her suit for joint custody or even visitation of the children raised by her and her ex-partner): "To sit there and say with a straight face that someone who has stayed up all night nursing a child, swabbing her chicken pox, taking joy in her every advancement, picking her up every time she's skinned her knee, or singing her to sleep is not a mother is an absurdity."[16]

Ironically, even though lesbian feminists have been bolstered by the radical feminist stance that children can thrive with mothers and no fathers, they have, for political and legal purposes, fallen into becoming the most staunch supporters of the social construction (as opposed to the essentialist) approach to parenthood. To equate women

with nature, as in the original radical feminist doctrines which argued for the banishment of fathers, would be tantamount to squashing their own struggle for the legal recognition of nonbiological parents in lesbian and gay families. In carving out a new legal definition of family, lesbian activists are now implicitly advocating that *any* individual, regardless of gender or biological role in parenthood, is entitled to the recognized status of parent if he or she fully engages in the social and emotional tasks of raising a child.

We can now identify the link between the campaign to legitimate families where children are being raised without fathers and the political battle waged by heterosexual feminists to insist that men as well as women take equal responsibility for childcare. The new alternative family is the shared-parenting family and the underlying premise, as with lesbian parenting, is that parenting is a social, not a biological, act. The main feminist argument is that, although easier said than done (because of socialized gender splits in parenting willingness and ability), co-parenting by men and women should be done. As with the battles around lesbian parenting, there are no doubt self-interest politics at work here: women who are in relationships with men or plan to be recognize their liberation will come only when women are released from primary parenting. But there is also an underlying vision of change that involves an integration, rather than a separation of female and male, a left and liberal feminist vision that has always been and remains at political odds with the original radical feminist vision of overthrowing patriarchy through mother supremacy.

Regardless of vision, the "pro-fathering" movement has had to take pause as it is buffeted about by a series of events all having the effect of calling its very base into question. First, pro-fathering *is* in fact being used against lesbian and single mothers by both conservatives and liberals in antifeminist backlash. Second, the insistence that men can mother has been used for its own purposes by a social system that values men over women. Just as men make better chefs, men will now make better parents (witness Dustin Hoffman outdoing Meryl Streep in *Kramer vs. Kramer*). Third, the insistence on fathers' involvement has led to the worst nightmare yet, as fathers have indeed disempowered mothers in brutal child-custody battles across the country. Lastly, some feminists are looking at the rising incidence of revealed sexual abuse of children by their fathers and saying that feminists had better think twice about the blanket demand, with no qualifiers, for more involvement by fathers. In certain instances, given the gender realities of our culture, fathering is downright dangerous for children (and their mothers). Perhaps it is true that feminists who fight for father involvement are naive about the true roots of misogyny in this society.

However, this is no reason to throw out the baby with the bath water, so to speak, and the real solution is to develop a more sophisticated analysis that can identify when father involvement is in a woman's (and a child's) best interests and when it is potentially destructive, given the social fabric of U.S. society. From there, carefully planned strategies can be developed accordingly, with a clear rationale for each. For example, I see no contradictions in arguing for the equal involvement of fathers in parenting, but *only* if they are capable of the true nurturance and support that is required for "mothering," which would exclude abusive or gender-power-hungry men who use children as collateral.

THE CUSTODY QUESTION

Feminists who have supported shared parenting have also been obvious supporters of shared custody: following a divorce a father should have equal access to his children. The premise was that he would also have been involved prior to the divorce. It has been shocking to witness what has in fact happened to women in the courts. Using the children as collateral, men have waged ruthless custody battles against the

mothers of their children through the legal system. Over 200 men's rights groups have sprung up across the country supporting fathers as nurturing caregivers; books have been written advising men of good strategies to win custody of their children, including accusations of lesbianism or techniques for kidnapping a child from a custodial mother.[17] In approximately two-thirds of contested custody cases before a judge, a father will win. [18]

Some men are genuinely fighting to remain connected to the children they have cared for and are strongly attached to and to whom it is the child's best interest to stay connected—I have seen their pain in my consulting office. But a large majority of the men who challenge their ex-wives in custody suits are not interested in the care, but rather in the control of their children. They sue for custody as a way to avoid paying child support or as a club over their ex-wives' heads, often in retaliation for the women's quest for autonomy and equal rights. They will likely wrest the child from the mother's arms only to hand their son or daughter over to another woman (their next wife) to care for, rather than take responsibility themselves. Conservative judges are only too happy to support the men: "You ladies wanted to be liberated. Well, I guess you'll just have to live with the consequences."[19] Laurels now go to the "new father": the prize is the children.

Feminist lawyers did not see it coming. They believed the trend away from assuming mother rights in the early 1970s would generate a new gender-neutral inquiry in assigning custody to the person or persons who had actually been caring for the children, regardless of sex. Instead, they found the courts devaluing the work of the actual childraiser and invoking other criteria such as financial status, the nicer home, even the new spouse a father would more likely have to grant custody to the men.[20] From a radical feminist perspective, Phyllis Chesler sees it as no surprise: "Our culture overvalues men, fathers, and money and undervalues women, mothers, and maternal–child bonding.[21]

Chesler does not hold feminists responsible for what the courts do, but she too recognizes the feminist confusion between rights and responsibilities: "many feminists have confused their *desire* for male coparenting with the male *right* to custody.[22] She argues that any law which values legal paternity over biological motherhood and/or over maternal primary childcare degrades and violates women and children. From a left feminist perspective, Chesler's response is too simple. It again conflates birthing labor with mothering and ignores the other compelling and competing reality that many women (along with their children) stand to benefit from a system, which if forced to be equitable, would both grant shared rights to *and* demand shared care responsibilities from the father and the mother, in as well as out of a marriage.

FEMINISM, FATHERING, AND THE FUTURE

In the contradictory positions on fathering within the women's movement, one woman's solution becomes another woman's problem. As more and more mothers enter the workforce and find themselves strapped with two jobs for the price of one, an obvious remedy is to insist that men be involved in childrearing. But such a remedy also becomes a vicious weapon in the hands of a male-dominated power system out to punish any woman who parents without a man, whether through divorce, personal choice, sexual preference, or demographics.

The lesson to be learned is that the issue of men's involvement in the rearing of children is a true dialectic. The historical tension resides between the desire to restructure family so that childrearing is seen as a *parental* not a *mother's* responsibility and the reality that women are having their parental authority and maternal influence taken away from them both by the "new" father and by the political power structure that embodies traditional male values.

We cannot escape the differences among feminists in their vision for change. Shared parenting as opposed to mother supremacy are simply incompatible constructs. In the new age of issue-oriented politics, the incompatibilities reflect not just political disagreements, but also strikingly different personal interests among diverse groups of women—married women, lesbians, single mothers. These interests, concerning a very central part of our lives, children and motherhood, promote very different visions. We need to understand that whatever common gender interests we as women have, we may also be struggling with extremely different life and family situations that call for divergent if not contradictory social transformations.

In that context, there are dangers in the strategies emanating from each of these visions when not placed in the context of a *combined* androgynous and female-centered approach. The feminist position that celebrates mother as nature and holds that men should be sons but not fathers has unwittingly served the patriarchal power structure which aims to keep women in secondary status as "mother" and argues for her rightful place in the home. The exclusive demand for the full involvement of men in the rearing of children, by failing to address the problem of taking the power of the hearth away from women without simultaneously offering them more equality in the public sphere, is also doomed to backfire on women. It leaves women bereft of ascendancy anywhere. The intent was that women would move over to make room for the men; the reality is that women often find themselves squeezed out in both places. A viable feminist approach to fathering must insure male responsibility while simultaneously protecting women's rights and ascendancy. We cannot dodge the reality that different groups of women will have competing interests regarding fathers and families.

But as we march into the last decade of the century, a poll conducted by the *New York Times* shows that women today indeed see the balancing of work and family as one of their main concerns, one which crosses class and racial lines "far more clearly than some of the grander philosophical issues of the 1960s and 1970s.[23] The poll indicated that while black women still see finding a good job as more important, they now join hands with white women in asking, "Who will raise the children?" The women's movement has responded by putting greater emphasis on a work and family agenda. This is a hopeful direction, one that bridges the gap between the attitudes and needs of women of different classes and color and sexual orientation and proceeds with a practical program that overrides philosophical differences. The program could be directed toward demanding government subsidized daycare, flex-time, parental leave policies, recognition of nonbiological or unmarried parents of either gender in work health plans and leave policies, and any other institutional support and recognition for families of all types so that they can better combine work and family and facilitate men's involvement, when appropriate, in mothering.

The issue of gender and family is no longer simple philosophical musing. It is a survival issue for a growing number of women in this country, the majority of whom now work and parent simultaneously. Seen as an ideological charge for women in the late 1960s, the involvement of fathers has become an economic necessity for many families in the 1990s. As feminists have witnessed women's increased participation in the world of "work," the women's movement has, out of necessity, revved up its questions about men in "the home." At the same time, as feminists have both seen and supported the proliferation of alternative family structures, we have broached a new question, "What is a home, anyway?"

Feminist mothers and non-mothers all share a common goal: to remove sexism and eliminate the oppression of women. If we really want this

to happen, there is no question that feminists must stop fighting fathers and stop fighting each other about fathers. Instead, it is time to fight for men's equitable involvement in family life where it is beneficial to our common goal, but to block that involvement when it rides on the crest of the male-dominated sex/gender system that squashes, rather than liberates, women.

NOTES

1. Betty Friedan, *The Second Stage* (New York: Summit Books, 1981), p. 86.
2. Betty Friedan, quoted in Iver Peterson, "Feminists Discern a Bias in Baby M Custody Case," *New York Times,* March 20, 1987.
3. Felice Schwartz, "Management Women and the New Fact of Life," *Harvard Business Review,* January/February 1989, pp. 65–76.
4. Susan Rae Peterson, "Against 'Parenting,'" in Joyce Trebilcot (ed.), *Mothering: A Feminist Theory* (Totowa, NJ: Rowman and Allenhead, 1984), pp. 62–9.
5. See Diane Ehrensaft, "When Women and Men Mother," *Socialist Review* 49 (January/February 1980), and *Parenting Together* (New York: The Free Press, 1987); and Sarah Ruddick, *Maternal Thinking* (Boston: Beacon, 1989).
6. Jill Johnston, *Lesbian Nation* (New York: Touchstone, 1973).
7. Friedan, *The Second Stage,* p. 60.
8. For a summation of the socialist–feminist perspective on the need for radical transformation of capitalism to eliminate gender divisions in both productive and reproductive labor, see "The Berkeley–Oakland Women's Union Statement," in Zillah R. Eisenstein (ed.), *Capitalist Patriarchy and the Call for Socialist Feminism* (New York: Monthly Review Press, 1977), pp. 355–61. See also Judith Stacey, "The New Conservative Feminism," *Feminist Studies* 9, no. 3 (Fall 1983), pp. 559–83.
9. Nancy Chodorow, *The Reproduction of Mothering* (Berkeley, CA: University of California

Press, 1978); Dorothy Dinnerstein, *The Mermaid and the Minotaur* (New York: Harper & Row, 1976).

10. See D. Ehrensaft, *Parenting Together,* and D. Ehrensaft, "When Women and Men Mother."

11. Pauline Bart, review of Chodorow's *The Reproduction of Mothering* in *Off Our Backs* 11, no. 1 (January 1981).

12. Alice Rossi, "A Biosocial Perspective on Parenting," *Daedalus* (Spring 1977), pp. 1–31.

13. Wini Breines, Margaret Cerullo, and Judith Stacey, "Social Biology, Family Studies, and Anti-Feminist Backlash," *Feminist Studies* 4, no. 1 (February 1978), pp. 43–67.

14. In the 1970s no lesbian ever successfully won custody of her children in a court battle against her ex-husband (Del Martin and Phyllis Lyon, *Lesbian Woman* (New York: Bantam, 1972), chap. 5, "Lesbians Are Mothers, Too"). By the 1980s the situation has improved somewhat, with civil rights actions being taken so that except in those states where sodomy laws still exist courts can no longer use sexual preference as a determination of custody (Philip S. Gates, "Homosexuals Winning Some Custody Cases," *New York Times,* January 21, 1987). But courts can still get around such injunctions by calling on other criteria, such as the importance of a father in a child's life. They can also use medical issues to override factors of sexual preference, as has been done recently when gay men have lost custody or visitation privileges with their children because they have AIDS. One can be assured that if lesbian parents, too, began contracting AIDS, the same discriminatory criteria would be used against *them.*

15. Unfortunately, the spread of AIDS in the gay community has eliminated this option of biological fathering for many lesbian mothers who now turn to sperm banks where they acquire medically tested AIDS-free sperm from an unknown donor.

16. David Margolick, "Lesbian and Custody Fights Test Family Law Frontier," *New York Times,* July 4, 1990.

17. Titles of such books include *How to Win Custody* (by Louis Kiefer), *The Lion's Share: A Combat Manual for the Divorcing Male* (by J. Alan Orenstein), and *How to Avoid Paying Alimony* (by Maurice Franks).

18. Statistic reported in Sharon Johnson, "The Odds on Custody Change," *New York Times,* March 17, 1986. Also refer to the findings in Phyllis Chesler, *Mothers on Trial: The Battle for Children and Custody* (New York: McGraw-Hill, 1986). Her book included an in-depth study of 60 mothers challenged for the custody of their children between 1960 and 1981. All the mothers had been the primary caretaker of the child prior to the custody fight; among the fathers, 87% had not been directly involved in childcare before seeking custody, 67% had not paid child-support upon separation. Nonetheless, permanent custody was awarded to 70% of the fathers. Even when it comes to visitation, the courts have ignored the pleas of mothers to protect their children from the sexual molestation or abuse by their fathers. Elizabeth Morgan, a physician, has defied the mandate of the courts and let herself be jailed rather than reveal the whereabouts of her child, who she insists has been consistently molested on visits to her ex-husband. See Marianne Szegedy-Maszak, "Who's to Judge?" *New York Times Magazine,* May 21, 1989.

19. Statement from a judge quoted in Marianne Takas, "Divorce: Who Gets the Blame in 'No Fault'?" *Ms.,* February 1986.

20. See Takas, "Divorce: Who Gets the Blame in 'No Fault'?" for a discussion of the unexpected consequences for women and children in the direction the courts were taking in advancing men's custody rights. Also refer to "Beneath the Surface: The Truth about Divorce, Custody, and Support," *Ms.,* February 1986.

21. Quoted in "Beneath the Surface." Also see Chesler, *Mothers on Trial.*

22. Chesler, in "Beneath the Surface."

23. Lisa Bilken, "Bars to Equality of Sexes Seen as Eroding, Slowly," *New York Times,* August 20, 1989. See also Alison Leigh Cowan, "Poll Finds Women's Gains Have Taken Personal Toll," *New York Times,* August 21, 1989, and E. J. Dionne, Jr., "Struggle for Work and Family Fueling Women's Movement," *New York Times,* August 22, 1989, for further reporting on the results of *New York Times* poll.

READING 18

Racism and Patriarchy in the Meaning of Motherhood

Dorothy E. Roberts

. . .

Racism and patriarchy are not two separate institutions that intersect only in the lives of Black women. They are two interrelated, mutually supporting systems of domination, and their relationship is essential to understanding the subordination of all women. Racism makes the experience of sexism different for Black women and white women. But it is not enough to note that Black women suffer from both racism and sexism, although this is true. Racism is patriarchal. Patriarchy is racist. We will not destroy one institution without destroying the other. I believe it is the recognition of that connection—along with the recognition of difference among women—that is truly revolutionary.

This essay explores how racism and patriarchy interact in the social construction of motherhood. Feminist thinking has established that motherhood is a role through which women often experience gender subordination. My aim is to show how any feminist account of motherhood as gender oppression must also include an account of race oppression.

Adrienne Rich distinguishes between the "experience of motherhood"—the relationship between a woman and her children—and "motherhood as enforced identity and political institution." (Rich 1979, p. 196) This is a particularly useful distinction, as it begins with a conception of "motherhood" as contested and not essentialized. An unwed Black teenager, for example, may experience motherhood as a rare source of self-affirmation, while society deems her motherhood to be illegitimate and deviant. She may experience caring for her child as a determined struggle against harsh circumstances, while society sees in her mothering the pathological perpetuation of poverty. Some women may experience mothering as debilitating and intrusive, even though patriarchal ideology defines it as woman's instinctive vocation. Some women may experience fulfillment and happiness in mothering, even though some feminist theory calls it oppressive.

There are joys and sorrows that most mothers share: the pleasure of nursing her baby; the exhaustion from chasing after her toddler; the gratification of watching her child achieve whatever goal; the terror of unwanted pregnancy; the despair of surrendering yet another dream in order to care for her child. There are also experiences mothers do not share, in part because of race. Most white mothers do not know the pain of raising Black children in a racist society. It is impossible to explain the depth of sorrow felt at the moment a mother realizes she has birthed her precious brown baby into a society that regards her child as just another unwanted Black charge. Black mothers must perform the incredible task of guarding their children's identity against innumerable messages that brand them as less than human.[1]

There are features of motherhood as a political institution that subordinate women because we are women: our status as childbearer determines our identity; we are assigned the enormous responsibility of childrearing; our work is unpaid and degraded; and, to the extent our role as mother is valued, it is only when it "is attached to a legal father." (Rich 1979, pp. 196–7) Adrienne Rich argues that motherhood in its present form denies women their potential as full human beings. She writes:

> Institutionalized motherhood demands of women maternal "instinct" rather than intelligence, selflessness rather than self-realization, relation to others rather than the creation of self. Motherhood is

From *Mothers in Law,* edited by Martha Albertson Fineman and Isabel Karpin. Copyright © 1995 by Columbia University Press. Reprinted with permission of the publisher.

"sacred" so long as its offspring are "legitimate"—that is, as long as the child bears the name of a father who legally controls the mother. (Rich 1976, p. 42)

Society's construction of mother, its image of what constitutes a good mother and a bad mother, facilitates male control of all women. Women who fail to meet the ideal of motherhood (unwed mothers, unfit mothers, and women who do not become mothers) are stigmatized for violating the dominant norm and are considered deviant or criminals. Martha Fineman calls motherhood "a colonized [concept]—an event physically practiced and experienced by women but occupied, defined, and given content and value by the core concepts of patriarchal ideology." (Fineman 1995a, p. 217)

This is patriarchy's meaning of motherhood, one designed to serve the interests of men. The meaning of motherhood in America, however, is shaped on the basis of race as well as gender. Patriarchy does not treat Black and white motherhood identically. In America, the image of the Black mother has always diverged from, and often contradicted, the image of the white mother.

There are several areas to be examined in the study of racism and patriarchy in the meaning of motherhood. This essay is directed to a diverse community of feminist thinkers. It concerns the construction of motherhood by those in power. The essay also raises issues for discussion within the Black community, issues that Black feminist scholars are continuing to address, including: the meaning of motherhood within communities of color (Austin 1989, p. 553); sexism by Black men (Crenshaw 1989, pp. 160–6; hooks 1981, pp. 87–117); and the need for Black women to confront our own differences and to develop solidarity among ourselves. Audre Lorde writes about black women's need for one another: "There are two very different struggles involved here. One is the war against racism in white people, and the other is the need for Black women to confront

and wade through the racist constructs underlying our deprivation of each other. And these battle are not at all the same." (Lorde 1984, p. 164) Black mothers' self-definition is a critical aspect of the meaning of motherhood, as well, an aspect that influences both the dominant society's construction and the feminist reconstruction of mother. (Collins 1990, p. 91–113)

In this essay I explore the social meaning of motherhood during various periods of American history, from slavery to contemporary poverty discourse. While a complete historical analysis is beyond its scope, my review indicates that the social definition of mother changes along with other social developments. The systems of patriarchy and racism interact in different ways throughout history to produce diverse constructions of motherhood. The dynamic quality of subordination and resistance suggests that my inquiry will not produce a grand theory of the relationship between patriarchy and racism. Rather, my inquiry seeks a better understanding of how racism and patriarchy shape the meaning of motherhood in particular contexts, the ways in which women resist those meanings, and the implications for future action.

SLAVERY: THE FOUNDATION OF RACIST PATRIARCHY IN AMERICA

The intimate intertwining of race and gender in the very structure of slavery makes it practically impossible to speak of one without the other. The social order established by white slaveowners was founded on two inseparable ingredients: the dehumanization of Africans on the basis of race, and the control of women's sexuality and reproduction. The American legal order is rooted in this horrible combination of race and gender oppression. America's first laws concerned the status of children born to slave mothers and fathered by white men: a 1662 Virginia statute made these children slaves. (Marcus 1988, pp. 217–8; Higginbotham 1978, p. 252)

The experiences of Black women during slavery provide the most brutal examples of the denial of autonomy over reproduction. Female slaves were commercially valuable to their masters not only for their labor but also for their capacity to produce more slaves. White masters, therefore, could increase their wealth by controlling their slaves' reproductive capacity—by rewarding pregnancy; punishing slave women who did not bear children; forcing them to breed; and raping them. (Jones 1985, pp. 34–5; Sterling 1984, pp. 24–6) Racism created for white slaveowners the possibility of unrestrained reproductive control. As Henry Louis Gates, Jr., writes about the autobiography of a slave named Harriet A. Jacobs, she "charts in vivid detail precisely how the shape of her life and the choices she makes are defined by her reduction to a sexual object, an object to be raped, bred, or abused." (Gates 1987, p. 12) The radical feminist model of motherhood, which is characterized by the patriarchal male's use of woman's body for reproduction, is epitomized in slavery. (J. Allen 1984, p. 317) Slavery allowed the perfection of patriarchal motherhood. Patriarchy devised the most dehumanizing form of slavery.

Compulsory childbirth was a critical element of the oppression of both Black and white women of the time. A *racist* patriarchy required that both Black and white women bear children, although these women served different and complementary functions. Black women produced children who were legally Black to replenish the master's supply of slaves. (Davis 1983, p. 7) White women produced white children to continue the master's legacy. The racial purity of white women's children was guaranteed by a violently enforced taboo against sexual relations between white women and Black men and by antimiscegenation laws that punished interracial marriages. (Collins 1990, p. 50) There was a critical difference in the white patriarch's relationship to these two classes of women. White men accorded some degree of respect and protection to white women, who were their wives, mothers, daughters, and sisters. White patriarchs,

however, owed nothing to their female slaves, who were denied even the status of "woman." (Fox-Genovese 1988, p. 293; Omolade 1987, pp. 242–3) Black mothers reproduced for white patriarchy, but gained nothing from it.

Paradoxically, the role of Black slave women—who were forced to serve white patriarchy—often contradicted the fundamental structure of patriarchy. First, the sexual relationship between female slaves and their white masters impugned the value that white women held under patriarchy as wives and mothers. For example, some Southern white women cited in their divorce actions their husbands' "affection" for slave women as the cause for the dissolution of the marriage. (Clinton 1985, pp. 29–30) Some denounced slavery because of their anger and humiliation at their husbands' sexual exploitation of Black women. (hooks 1981, p. 28) Second, giving children born of the union between white masters and Black women the status of slaves violated a central tenet of patriarchy: that the status of the child follow the male line. The slave's *mother* determined her child's identity as slave. Thus, Frederick Douglass saw no hope for freedom in a biological tie to his master:

> The whisper that my master was my father, may or may not be true; and, true or false, it is of little consequence to my purpose whilst the fact remains in all its glaring odiousness, that slaveholders have ordained, and by law established, that the children of slave women shall in all cases follow the condition of their mothers. (Douglass 1982, p. 49)

Maintaining racial hierarchy required that the patriarchal bloodline be broken, that white men deny their own sons' entitlement to patriarchal power.

THE VALUE OF MOTHERHOOD

Society exerts structural and ideological pressures upon women to become mothers. In this way, motherhood under patriarchy is virtually compulsory. As Fineman has argued, however, only certain kinds of motherhood are valued.

(Fineman 1995a) Nevertheless, the performance of an idealized conception of motherhood is women's major social role. All women are socially defined as mothers or potential mothers. No woman achieves her full position in society until she gives birth to a child. Pronatalism is so deeply imbedded in our consciences that even feminist reproductive freedom discourse usually centers on the timing of births and the social arrangements surrounding motherhood; it does not question the assumption that all women will eventually be mothers. (Gimenez 1984, p. 290) Historically, the sanctity of motherhood not only encouraged women to become mothers, it also relieved some of the pain women experienced from their exploitation under patriarchy. (Gimenez 1984, p. 304) Women's labor in the home has been compensated by the ideological rewards of motherhood, rather than economic remuneration or the opportunity for self-determination. Thus the voluntary motherhood advocates in the 19th century opposed birth control partly because they realized that motherhood was the only source of dignity for women of their time. (Gordon 1992, p. 140)

Compulsory motherhood under patriarchy is complicated, however, by racism. Contemporary society views childbearing by white women as desirable. Procreation by Black mothers, on the other hand, is devalued and discouraged. (Austin 1989, pp. 549–58; Roberts 1991, pp. 1436–50) The devaluation of Black motherhood is a way of undermining Black humanity. The value society places on individuals determines whether it sees them as entitled to perpetuate themselves in their children. Denying a woman the right to bear children deprives her of a basic part of her humanity. Patriarchy values white women primarily for their procreative capacity, but it denies to Black women even this modicum of value. Black women are deemed not even worthy of the dignity of childbearing. Discouraging black procreation is also a means of subordinating the entire race; under patriarchy, it is accomplished through the regulation of Black women's fertility.

A popular mythology about Black women, rooted in slavery, portrays them as less deserving of motherhood. (Roberts 1991, pp. 1436–50) One of the most prevalent images of slave women was as the character of Jezebel, a woman governed by her sexual desires. (White 1985, p. 28–9) The ideological construct of the licentious Jezebel legitimated white men's sexual abuse of black women and defined Black women as the opposite of the ideal mother. Jezebel contradicted the prevailing image of the True Woman, who was virtuous, pure, and white. The myth of the sexually loose, impure Black women was deliberately and systematically perpetuated after slavery ended and persists in American culture today. (Omolade 1987, p. 16)

If the "bad" Black Jezebel represented the opposite of ideal motherhood, the asexual and maternal Black Mammy was the embodiment of the patriarchal ideal. (Austin 1989, p. 570; hooks 1981, pp. 84–5) Mammy was both the perfect mother and the perfect slave: whites saw her as a "passive nurturer, a mother figure who gave all without expectation of return, who not only acknowledged her inferiority to whites but who loved them." (hooks 1981, p. 85) It is important to recognize, however, that Mammy did not reflect any virtue in Black women as the mothers of their own children. Rather, patriarchy "claimed for the white family the ultimate devotion of black women, who reared the children of others as if they were their own." (Fox-Genovese 1988, p. 292) Because of racism, Black mothers could not be moral authorities as white mothers were in relation to their children. Mammy, while she cared for the master's children, remained under the moral supervision of her white mistress. (Ferguson 1984, p. 171)

This ideological devaluation of Black motherhood has been manifested in many ways throughout American history. During slavery, Black women were systematically denied the rights of motherhood, including any legal claim to their children. (A. Allen 1990, p. 140, n. 9) Slave masters owned both Black women and their children. Slaveowners alienated slave women from their children through the sale of either mother or child to other slaveowners and through the control of child rearing. In *Beloved,* Toni Morrison recounts a slave mother's experience of separation from her loved ones:

> Anybody Baby Suggs knew, let alone loved, who hadn't run off or been hanged, got rented out, loaned out, bought up, brought back, stored up, mortgaged, won, stolen or seized. . . . What she called the nastiness of life was the shock she received upon learning that nobody stopped playing checkers just because the pieces included her children. Halle she was able to keep the longest. Twenty years. A lifetime. Given to her, no doubt, to make up for *hearing* that her two girls, neither of whom had their adult teeth, were sold and gone and she had not been able to wave goodbye. (Morrison 1987, p. 23)

Patriarchy denied to Black mothers the authority, the joy, and the gratification of mothering that it allowed white mothers. Once again, patriarchy was perfected in the treatment of slave women.

A contemporary example of the way in which society devalues Black motherhood is the welfare system's disproportionate denial of Black mothers' parental rights. (Gray and Nybell 1990, p. 513) Malcolm X called foster care a system of legalized slavery. (Little 1965, p. 21–2) He described the state's disruption of his own family in terms that mirror white slavemasters' control of slave families:

> Soon the state people were making plans to take over all of my mother's children. . . . A judge . . . in Lansing had authority over me and all of my brothers and sisters. We were "state children," court wards; he had the full say-so over us. A white man in charge of a black man's children! Nothing but legal, modern slavery—however kindly intentioned. . . . I truly believe that if ever a state social agency destroyed a family, it destroyed ours. (Little 1965, pp. 21–2)

The state intervenes more often in Black homes in part because Black mothers are more likely to be supervised by social workers, because child welfare workers apply culturally biased standards to Black families, and because the state is more willing to intrude upon the autonomy of Black mothers. (Stack 1983–84, p. 541) Government bureaucrats often mistake Black child-rearing patterns as neglect when they diverge from the norm of the nuclear family. (Hill 1977; Stack 1974, pp. 62–107)

One of the most extreme forms of devaluation of Black motherhood is the coerced sterilization of Black women. (Davis 1983, pp. 215–21) The disproportionate sterilization of Black women enforces society's determination that we do not deserve to be mothers. Black women have experienced sterilization abuse in the form of blatant coercion, trickery, and subtle influences on their decision to be sterilized. (Petchesky 1979, p. 32) The procedure is performed by individual doctors who encourage Black women to be sterilized because they view Black women's family sizes as excessive and believe we are incapable of using contraceptives. (Roberts 1991, p. 1443) It is also accomplished through government policies that penalize women on welfare for having babies, but make sterilization the only publicly funded birth control method readily available to them. (Roberts 1991, pp. 1443–4)

Currently, the image of the undeserving black mother legitimizes the prosecution of poor Black women who use drugs during pregnancy. Although prenatal substance abuse cuts across racial and socioeconomic lines, the vast majority of women charged with such crimes are poor and Black. (Roberts 1991, pp. 1432–6) These women are more likely to be detected and reported to government agencies, in part because of the racist attitudes of health care professionals. (Roberts 1991, pp. 1432–4) On a deeper level, it is their failure to meet society's image of the ideal mother that makes their prosecution acceptable. The state does not punish poor crack addicts simply because they may harm their unborn children. Rather, the state punishes them for having babies because it deems them unworthy of procreating. (Roberts 1991, p. 1472)

Angela Harris uses the example of beauty to demonstrate the qualitative difference between white and Black women's failure to meet patriarchal standards. (Harris 1990, pp. 596–8) She observes that Black women's frustration at being unable to look like the "All-American" woman is not simply a more intense form of white women's frustration. This is because beauty is constructed according to race, as well as gender. (hooks 1991, p. 4) Thus, the despair felt by Pecola Breedlove, the character in Toni Morrison's *The Bluest Eye* who spends her childhood praying for blue eyes, is something other than the disappointment felt by a little white girl who despises her features (Morrison 1970). Pecola Breedlove despairs "not because she's even further away from the ideal of beauty than white women are, but because Beauty [sic] *itself* is white, and she is not and can never be, despite the pair of blue eyes she eventually believes she has." (Harris 1990, p. 597)

Similarly, Black women can never attain the ideal image of motherhood, no matter how much we conform to middle-class convention, because ideal motherhood is white. The maternal standards created to confine women are not sex-based norms that Black women happen to fail. They are created out of raced, as well as gendered, components.

MOTHERHOOD AND DOMESTICITY

During the 19th century, the ideology of separate spheres for men and women reinforced women's devotion to motherhood within the orbit of patriarchy. Under this construct, the husband sustained the family economically and represented the family in the public sphere; the wife cared for the private realm of the home. (Olsen 1983, pp. 1498–1501) The separate spheres ideology gave women a place, role, and importance in the home, while preserving male dominance over women. "The cult of domesticity" legitimized the confinement of women to the private sphere by defining women as naturally suited for motherhood and naturally unfit for public life. . . .

The gendered division of labor continues to be an aspect of women's subordination. The American wage labor system is structured as if workers have no child care responsibilities. (Frug 1979, p. 56–61) This assumption systematically disadvantages women, because they are assigned the task of childrearing. Men have the privilege of performing as ideal workers (i.e., workers with no child care responsibilities) and consequently earn more money. . . . Although most mothers now engage in wage labor, typically they must limit their work commitments to accommodate their child care duties. According to Joan Williams, this gendered system results in the economic marginalization of women workers who are mothers because, by virtue of their mothering, they fail to perform as ideal workers. Often this "failure" is what makes it possible for their husbands to perform that role, while mothers ensure that their children receive high-quality care. (Williams 1989, p. 823–4)

Black women have historically defied the norm that defines motherhood in opposition to wage labor. The separate-spheres ideology dissolved within slavery. While Victorian roles required white women to be nurturing mothers, housekeepers, and companions to their husbands, the slave women's role required strenuous labor. (D. White 1985, p. 27–9)

Slave women's lives of hard physical labor shattered the myth that women were weaker than men and unfit for the public sphere. Thus, in 1851 Sojourner Truth could present to a women's rights convention in Akron, Ohio, a unique denunciation of male justifications for the disenfranchisement of women. Unlike most of the white women's rights advocates, she could point to her personal experience of field labor as proof that women could perform the same work as men:

Dat man ober dar say dat women needs to be helped into carriages, and lifted ober ditches, and to have de best place every whar. Nobody eber help me into carriages, or ober mud puddles, or gives me any best place . . . and ar'n't I a woman? Look at me! Look at my arm! . . . I have plowed, and planted, and gathered into barns, and no man could head me—and ar'n't I a woman? I could work as much and eat as much as a man (when I could get it), and bear de lash as well—and ar'n't I a woman? I have borne 13 chilern and seen em mos all sold off into slavery, and when I cried out with a mother's grief, none but Jesus heard—and ar'n't I a woman? (Gilbert 1878, p. 134)

Sojourner Truth not only attacked patriarchal images of women, she also challenged white feminists to relinquish their racial privilege. (Crenshaw 1989, p. 154) As bell hooks notes, "White women saw black women as a direct threat to their social standing—for how could they be idealized as virtuous, goddesslike creatures if they associated with black women who were seen by the white public as licentious and immoral?" (hooks 1981, p. 31) In this way, the construction of an ideal mother that excluded Black women actually encouraged white women's allegiance to an oppressive concept of their own womanhood. In order to embrace Ms. Truth's message, the white women present had to reject the racist assumption that because Black women were unworthy of the title "woman" their experiences had no bearing on true womanhood. In fact, at an antislavery rally in Indiana, Sojourner Truth bared her breasts to prove that she was indeed a woman. (hooks 1981, p. 159) The women present had to accept Ms. Truth as truly woman and to sacrifice their personal stake in the white ideal of womanhood.

After slavery, Black women continued to work in patterns that diverged drastically from those of white women. Black women joined the wage-earning labor force in proportions three or four times higher than white women. (Ferguson 1984, p. 179, n. 12) After the Civil War, Black women were encouraged by white politicians and entrepreneurs, as well as by the depressed wages of Black men, to earn a living outside the home. (Omolade 1987, p. 252) In 1880, 50 percent of Black women were in the labor force, compared to only 15 percent of white women.

(Omolade 1987, p. 252) The racial disparity among married women was even greater: in 1870 in the rural South, more than four out of 10 Black married women had jobs, mostly as field laborers, while 98.4 percent of white wives were housekeepers. (Jones 1985, p. 63) In Southern cities, Black married women worked outside the home five times more often than white married women. (Jones 1985, p. 113)

The demands of labor within white homes undermined Black women's own roles as mothers and homemakers. (Jones 1985, p. 127) Black domestics, of course, were unable to attend to their children during the day. They returned home late in the evening (if not on weekends) and had to entrust their children to the care of a neighbor, relative, or older sibling, or leave them to wander in the neighborhood. (Jones 1985, p. 129) The preoccupation with the virtue of white women justified not only the persecution of Black men but also the condemnation of "insolent" Black female servants. (Jones 1985, p. 149) Black women holding menial jobs were portrayed as unfeminine in order to justify subjecting them to working conditions that conflicted with the image of delicate womanhood: "The image of Mammy, 'Aunt Jemima,' Beulah, and even the emasculating matriarch is that of an overweight, rotund female, devoid of the curves that are indicative of the more seductive examples of her sex. Outfitted in an unflattering dress, apron, and scarf (a 'headrag'), she is always ready for work and never ready for bed." (Austin 1989, p. 583)

Women of color continue to do most of the domestic service in America, filling jobs such as maids, child-care workers, nurse's aides, sewing machine operators, and food preparation workers. (National Committee for Pay Equity [NCPE] 1987, pp. 20–6) In the early century, nearly two-thirds of all employed Black women in the North were domestic servants and laundresses. (Jones 1985, p. 164) It was not until 1970 that Black women were no longer employed primarily as domestic workers or farm laborers. (Omolade

1987, pp. 258–9) Nevertheless, these jobs remain segregated on the basis of both race and gender, and they pay the lowest wages. (NCPE 1987, pp. 20–6; hooks 1981, pp. 132–6)

The experience of Black working mothers complicates the feminist response to domesticity in two ways. First, white feminists' view of work, as resistance to motherhood and a liberating force for women, does not account for Black women's experiences. This ideology often focuses on a romanticized, middle-class quest for entrance into an elite workforce rather than on the women who have always been exploited as a source of cheap surplus labor. (hooks 1981, p. 146) Black women historically experienced work outside the home as an aspect of racial subordination and the family as a site of solace and resistance against white oppression. (Davis 1983, pp. 16–7; Spelman 1988, p. 132) Black women's attention to domestic duties within their homes has defied the expectation of total service to whites. Elizabeth Spelman has observed that the oppressive nature of the "housewife" role must be understood in relation to women's other roles, which are raced as well as gendered: "The work of mate/mother/nurturer has a different meaning depending on whether it is contrasted to work that has high social value and ensures economic independence or to labor that is forced, degrading, and unpaid." (Spelman 1988, p. 123)

Second, Black mothers' work experience raises one way in which racial privilege has helped to maintain the gendered division of domestic work. The employment of black women as domestic servants in white homes reproduced the mistress–houseslave relationship. (Davis 1983, pp. 90–1) White mothers who could afford it reduced the burdens of childrearing by shifting their duties to Black maids. (Palmer 1989, pp. 65–87) Judith Rollins found in her study of domestics and the women who employ them that the increased participation of middle-class women in the workplace did not change their attitudes toward their role in the home. According to Judith Rollins:

The middle-class women I interviewed were not demanding that their husbands play a greater role in housekeeping; they accepted the fact that responsibility for domestic maintenance was theirs, and they solved the problem of their dual responsibilities by hiring other women to assist. (Rollins 1985, p. 104)

Thus, white middle-class women gained entry to the male public sphere by assigning female domestic tasks to Black women, rather than by demanding a fundamental change in the sexual division of labor. (Crenshaw 1989, p. 154 and n. 5)

SINGLE MOTHERHOOD AND POVERTY

The sharp increase in the number of single mothers is changing the practice of motherhood in America. As more and more women raise children without husbands (Wegman 1989, pp. 944–5), the state has responded by increasing its interference in their families and by instituting programs and policies designed to restore the traditional nuclear family through reinstatement of the missing male. (Fineman 1995a).

Contemporary welfare reform measures exemplify this effort. Martha Fineman demonstrates how the new poverty rhetoric blames single mothers for perpetuating poverty and how it proposes as the solution the coupling of poor single mothers with financially secure males. (Fineman 1995a, 205–6) She links the representation of single motherhood as pathological to patriarchal ideology that defines mother and child by their relationship to fathers. (Fineman 1995a) Single mothers are considered deviant because they reject the primacy of sexual affiliation as the basic organizing concept of the family. Fineman concludes that the condemnation of single mothers in current poverty reform discourse is primarily a reflection of patriarchy. Indeed, she declares: "The ideology of patriarchy is the most instrumental force in the creation and acceptance of discourses about mothers in our society." (Fineman 1995a, p. 207)[2]

Race is very much implicated both in the correlation between poverty and single motherhood and in the discourses that explain it. While the proportion of poor families maintained by women has risen in all racial and ethnic groups, the proportion of poor Black families headed by women is far larger. (Rowe 1991, p. 74) Black single motherhood also has a unique history. During slavery, masters forcibly separated many Black mothers from their husbands. (Omolade 1987, p. 242) Some slave men escaped to freedom or purchased themselves from their masters, leaving their women and children behind. (Omolade 1987, p. 248) For example, Mississippi marriage registration records from 1864 show that nearly one in five Black women aged 30 and older were separated from their husbands by force. (Gutman 1976, p. 146) One study of slave women in Georgia revealed that over half of the women known to have been mothers appeared to have been living apart from their husbands. (Wood 1987, p. 609)

Suzanne Lebsock's research on free Black women in early 19th-century Petersburg, Virginia, revealed that the most common household structure among free Blacks was the female-headed family containing one woman and her children. (Lebsock 1982, pp. 285–6) Lebsock notes that free Black women had a unique incentive to remain single, arising from their ability to retain legal control over their property.

> For the woman who hoped to buy an enslaved relative, legal wedlock meant that her plan could be sabotaged at any time by her husband or by her husband's impatient creditors. The common-law disabilities of married women added an ironic twist to chattel slavery's strange fusion of persons and property: [m]atrimony could pose a threat to the integrity of the free black woman's family. (Lebsock 1982, p. 285)

This pattern of Black single motherhood continued after Emancipation. Between 1880 and 1915, 25 to 30 percent of all urban Black families were headed by women. (Jones 1985, p. 113)

Ideologically, in America single motherhood is Black. The current condemnation of unwed mothers is rooted in the myth of the Black matriarch, the domineering female head of the Black family. White sociologists have held Black "matriarchs" responsible for the disintegration of the Black family and the consequent failure of Black people to achieve success in America. (Giddings 1984, pp. 325–35)[3] Senator Daniel Patrick Moynihan of New York popularized this theory in his 1965 report, *The Negro Family: The Case for National Action* (Moynihan 1965). According to Moynihan:

> At the heart of the deterioration of the fabric of Negro society is the deterioration of the Negro family. It is the fundamental cause of the weakness of the Negro community. . . . In essence, the Negro community has been forced into a matriarchal structure which, because it is too out of line with the rest of the American society, seriously retards the progress of the group as a whole. (Moynihan 1965, pp. 5, 29)

Thus, Moynihan attributes the cause of Black people's inability to overcome the effects of racism largely to the independence and dominance of Black mothers.

Underlying the current campaign against poor single mothers is the image of the lazy welfare mother who breeds children at the expense of taxpayers in order to increase the amount of her welfare check. (Collins 1991, p. 77; Fineman 1995b, pp. 117–8) In society's mind, that mother is Black. Writers in the 1980s, most notably Charles Murray, author of *Losing Ground,* claimed that welfare induces poor Black women to refrain from marriage and to have babies. (Murray 1984, pp. 154–66) Society penalizes Black single mothers not only because they depart from the norm of marriage as a prerequisite to pregnancy but also because they represent rebellious Black culture. (Austin 1989, p. 557; Solinger 1992a, p. 25) To some extent, society punishes white single mothers because they are acting too much like Black women. (Collins 1991, p. 74)

. . .

In some ways, white mothers' lives are becoming structurally more similar to the lives of Black mothers.[4] Patriarchy in the modern capitalist welfare state is marked by an increased devaluation of motherhood that cuts across racial lines. Indications of this change include: the rise in "illegitimate" single motherhood for both Black and white women; the abandonment of the moral mother ideology and women's diminished control over child-rearing; the replacement of the father by the patriarchal welfare state; the decrease in the amount of mothers doing domestic work and the increase in the numbers of women in the labor force; and the growing isolation of mothers. (Ferguson 1984, pp. 172–5) In late 20th-century America, more and more white mothers will occupy social positions that have been historically defined for Black mothers only. Just as Black women must identify and oppose patriarchy in the social control of families, white women must identify and oppose the operation of racism in the social control of families.

It may be in the lives of those most outcast by patriarchy that we will catch a glimpse of a liberated motherhood. (Rich 1979, pp. 271–3; West 1988, pp. 47–8) Those mothers considered the most deviant may help us to imagine what motherhood might be like in a society where women are "free to develop a sense of self that is our own, and not a mere construct of patriarchy." (Cain 1990, p. 212) In other words, we could move from deconstructing society's view of these women to actually claiming their oppositional insights as part of our reconstruction of motherhood. Regina Austin challenges us to consider whether Black single motherhood is an example of resistance against patriarchy.

> A black feminist jurisprudential analysis . . . must seriously consider the possibility that young, single, sexually active, fertile, and nurturing black women are being viewed ominously because they have the temerity to attempt to break out of the rigid economic, social, and political categories that a racist, sexist, and class-stratified society would impose upon them. (Austin 1989, p. 555)

Of course, this is risky territory. It is difficult to identify the emancipatory moments that spark within the vast realm of subordination. How can we claim what is liberating in the lives of the oppressed without denying all that remains oppressive? How can we discern the transformative potential in what is basically a response to subjugation? We must do the hard work of distinguishing between self-destructive and self-affirming behavior, between resistance and accommodation, between what merely reproduces illegitimate hierarchy and what destroys it.

DISLOYALTY TO FEMINISM

What does this connection between racism and patriarchy mean for the feminist project? How does it test our commitment to a feminist vision of motherhood and of society in general? What does it tell us about the requirements for unity among women who are different? In this section, I explore the ways in which the interaction between racism and patriarchy tempts both white and Black women to be "disloyal" to feminism.[5]

White Women and White Privilege

One of the most painful parts of recognizing the relationship between racism and patriarchy is confronting white women's participation in the racial subordination of Black women. During slavery, for example, most white women either silently co-operated with the practice of owning Africans as chattel or actively abused the slaves in their households. (Clinton 1985, pp. 28–32; hooks 1984, p. 49) Elizabeth Fox-Genovese explains that, although Southern white women grumbled in private about certain aspects of slavery, they were not willing to attack the entire system that benefited them in many ways: "Slavery, with all its abuses, constituted the fabric of their beloved country—the warp and woof of their social position, their personal relations, their very identities." (Fox-Genovese 1988, p. 334) Some white women used their power over the slaves their husbands owned as compensation for their own subjugated position in marriage. (hooks 1981, p. 153) Bell hooks suggests that the cruelty that white men inflicted on female slaves in the presence of white women served as a warning to their wives, sisters, and daughters to remain obedient.

> Surely, it must have occurred to white women that . . . [if] . . . enslaved black women were not available to bear the brunt of such intense antiwoman male aggression, they themselves might have been the victims. . . . Their alliance with white men on the common ground of racism enabled them to ignore the antiwoman impulse that also motivated attacks on black women. (hooks 1981, pp. 38–9)

Thus, the subjugation of Black women encouraged white women's allegiance to the patriarchy. This is a critical lesson about the relationship between racism and patriarchy: racism did not perfect patriarchy only by allowing slavemasters the possibility of unrestrained control of Black women. It also secured the compliance of white women by promising them the privileges denied to slaves and threatening them with the punishments meted out to slaves.

Black feminists at the turn of the century criticized white women for allowing their affiliation with white men and their interest in the system to limit their opposition to white supremacy. Ida B. Wells, for example, saw the patriarchal idealization of white womanhood as license for white women's willing or unwilling silence. (Harris 1990, pp. 599–660) Anna Julia Cooper charged the contemporary women's movement with opposing only women's domestic confinement rather than the entire system of racial patriarchy. (Harris 1990, p. 600, n. 88) My intention here is not to assess the level of white women's guilt but to show how white women's stake in patriarchy largely determined their complicity in institutions of white supremacy. This complicity, in turn, enabled their acquiescence in their own inferior status.

Racism within feminist advocacy concerning motherhood in particular has neglected and even harmed Black women. The feminist birth control movement in the early 20th-century collaborated with the racist eugenics movement of the time. (Davis 1983, pp. 213–5; Gordon 1976, pp. 274–90 and 329–40) Leading advocates of birth control, such as Margaret Sanger, made accommodations with eugenicists and used racist rhetoric urging the reduction of the birthrates of "undesirables." (Gordon 1976, pp. 274–90) For example, in "Why Not Birth Control in America?," published in *Birth Control Review* in 1919, Sanger stated as the feminist movement's objective, "More children from the fit, less from the unfit—that is the chief issue of birth control." (Gordon 1976, p. 281) In *The Pivot of Civilization,* published in 1922, Sanger advocated society's use of stockbreeding techniques, warning that uncontrolled procreation by the illiterate and "degenerate" might destroy "our way of life." (Gordon 1976, p. 281)

Feminists during this period advocated birth control, not as a means of self-determination for all women but as a tool of social control by the white elite. (Gordon 1976, pp. 276–86) Their private birth control clinics evaluated clients based on their eugenic worth and advised them on the desirability of their procreative decisions. (Gordon 1976, p. 286–7) The first publicly funded birth control clinics were established in the South in the 1930s as a way of lowering the Black birthrate (Gordon 1976, pp. 314–29), and during the Depression, birth control was promoted as a means of lowering welfare costs. (Gordon 1976, pp. 329–40) In 1939 the Birth Control Federation of America proposed a "Negro Project" designed to reduce reproduction by Blacks who "still breed carelessly and disastrously, with the result that the increase among Negroes, even more than among whites, is from that portion of the population least intelligent and fit, and least able to rear children properly." (Gordon 1976, p. 332)[6]

The focus of contemporary reproductive rights discourse on abortion also neglects the broader range of reproductive health issues that affect Black women. White middle-class women concern themselves mainly with laws restricting choices otherwise available to them, such as statutes making it more difficult to obtain an abortion. Poor women of color, however, remain primarily concerned with the material conditions of poverty and oppression restricting their choices.[7] For example, the denial of access to safe abortions through lack of government funding, as well as the lack of resources necessary for a healthy pregnancy and parenting relationship, limits the reproductive freedom of poor women of color. Because of racism, it is more likely that the government will interfere with their reproductive decisions; because of their poverty, they are more likely to need the government's assistance to facilitate those decisions.

The mainstream opposition to sterilization reform in the 1970s exemplifies how the focus on "choice" has contradicted the interests of Black women. The Committee to End Sterilizaiton Abuse introduced, in New York City, guidelines designed to prevent sterilization abuse by requiring informed consent and a 30-day waiting period. (Roberts 1991, p. 1461, n. 213) Planned Parenthood and the National Abortion Rights Action League openly opposed the guidelines on the grounds that they restricted women's access to sterilization.

Women's false hope in white privilege continues to thwart any radical assault on gender hierarchy. I have discussed earlier in this essay how many white women gained entry into the white male working world by shifting female domestic work to Black women rather than by demanding a fundamental change in the sexual division of labor. Dolores Janiewski describes how racism prevented unity among Southern working women in the 1930s:

White women prized the tangible benefits of their privileged position as workers and sometimes employers of black women. The intangible benefits of white supremacy's pseudo-homage to white womanhood remained deeply entrenched in these women's notions of self-respect and respectability. Taught to view themselves as "lady-like" when

they refrained from heavy labor but to call black women "lazy" when they made the same claims, these women resisted any imputation of "social equality" which would place them on the same level with those they regarded as unclean, immoral and unlike themselves. Black women's demands for equal treatment threatened white women's deeply held beliefs in a natural, God-given order that established their moral as well as economic superiority over their black co-workers. Organized, whenever such organization was successful, by unions that failed to confront white domination, these women never met their black counterparts on equal terms in the workplace, the community, or the union. (Janiewski 1983, pp. 33–4)

Privileged racial identity has always provided whites with a powerful incentive to leave the existing social order intact. (Bell 1990, pp. 402–3) W. E. B. DuBois explained white resistance to labor reform during Reconstruction, for example, by the fact that "the white group of laborers, while they received a low wage, were compensated in part by a sort of public and psychological wage." (Du Bois 1976, pp. 700–1) Similarly, the white laboring class never demanded free public education during slavery because they relied on the possibility of becoming slaveholders themselves as their means of social advancement. (Du Bois 1976, p. 64) Freed slaves, not working whites, led the first mass movement for publicly funded education in the South. Women's common oppression has not been any more successful than workers' common oppression at overcoming the stifling effect of racial privilege on movements for radical social change.

Sojourner Truth's challenge to the women's movement of her time was to relinquish any perceived advantage in the cult of white womanhood. Her challenge—the racial challenge to feminism—is the giant step necessary for radical change. To point out white women's racial privilege is not to deny that white women are oppressed. (Hurtado 1989, p. 834) Indeed, it is to point out a principal means by which white women remain oppressed. Adrienne Rich sees the need to confront racism as a white woman because she understands that only by giving up white privilege will white women be fully capable of dismantling patriarchy. Otherwise, Rich argues, white feminists "might still possess the capacity to delude themselves into some compromise of inclusion into patriarchy, into the white male order." (Rich 1979, p. 309)

Black Women and Black Nationalism

Catharine MacKinnon has recently suggested that some Black women may be disloyal to feminism because of our common struggle with Black men for racial justice.

> I sense here that people feel more dignity in being part of any group that incudes men than in being part of a group that includes that ultimate reduction of the notion of oppression, that instigator of lynch mobs, that ludicrous whiner, that equality coat-tails rider, that white woman. It seems that if your oppression is also done to a man, you are more likely to be recognized as oppressed, as opposed to inferior. Once a group is seen as putatively human, a process helped by including men in it, an oppressed man falls from a human standard. (MacKinnon 1987, pp. 21–2)

I would imagine that most Black women would find it farfetched to seek a greater claim to humanity (in the eyes of the dominant culture) by identifying with black men, who are also viewed as less than human. Our unity with men in the struggle for Black liberation is grounded in the reality that being Black in America is part of *our* identity, critical to what it means for us to be women. We are bound to Black men through the day-to-day struggles of living in a racist society. We know that our liberation as women is linked to the liberation of Black people as a group.

Black women may be guilty of another kind of disloyalty, however. Some of us remain silent about sexism in our own communities or decline to align with white feminists because of the response of Black men. We fear we will be charged with betraying our common interests as a people. Nationalist and Afrocentric accounts of the African past and of ideal gender relations often propose a conservative utopian model of Black family life that discounts conflict between Black men and women. (White 1990, pp. 73–7) This model expects Black women to accept an unequal, "complementary" role that will arguably help to further the nationalist struggle. Audre Lorde has explained that "[t]he necessity for and history of shared battle have made us, Black women, particularly vulnerable to the false accusation that anti-sexist is anti-Black." (Lorde 1984, p. 120)

The relationship between racism and patriarchy, then, also holds a challenge for Black women. It calls upon Black feminists to inform our communities that patriarchy contributes to Black men's oppression and that feminism is essential to the struggle for the liberation of all Black people. E. Frances White describes, for example, "the emergence of a black feminist discourse that attempts to combine nationalist and feminist insights in a way that counters racism but tries to avoid sexist pitfalls." (E. White 1990, p. 74)

Perhaps women who occupy different social positions possess differing abilities to identify particular aspects of oppression in each instance of domination. Perhaps some feminists see more clearly the patriarchy in discourses about single mothers, for example, while others see more clearly their racism. We can help each other to understand how the discourses really contain both. We can remind each other that, whatever attraction racist patriarchy holds for us, it is not *our* order. Comparing oppressions ("I experience sexism the same way you experience racism," or "I experience sexism more painfully than you experience racism," or vice versa) can only be destructive. These comparisons lead us to think, "What you are experiencing is only [or less than] what I have experienced, and therefore I do not need to listen to your story." (Grillo and Wildman 1991, p. 409, n. 36) Recognizing the connection between different forms of subordination leads to a more productive response: "What you are experiencing is linked to what I have experienced, and therefore I need to listen to your story to better understand my own (and our) oppression."

FEMINISM AND ANTIRACISM

> In the past, I don't care how poor this white woman was in the South she still felt like she was more than us. In the North, I don't care how poor or how rich this white woman has been, she still felt like she was more than us. But coming to the realization of the thing, her freedom is shackled in chains to mine, and she realizes for the first that she is not free until I am free.
>
> —Fannie Lou Hamer, "The Special Plight and Role of Black Women" (Lerner 1973, p. 611)

Understanding the connection between racism and patriarchy expands the feminist project. Its goal cannot be to liberate women without taking issues of race into consideration. Racism subordinates women. (Spelman 1988, pp. 14–5) "If feminism is to be a genuine struggle to improve the lives of *all* women, then all feminists must assume the responsibility for eliminating racism." (Kline 1989, p. 117) The struggle against racism is also a necessary part of uniting women in political solidarity. Racism divides women. (hooks 1981, p. 156) Some feminists may find their motivation to oppose racism within the dreams of feminism: "It can spring from a heartfelt desire for sisterhood and the personal, intellectual realization that racism among women undermines the potential radicalism of feminism." (hooks 1981, pp. 157–8) I do not mean that feminists should see opposition to racism as an important extracurricular project. Racism is part of the structure of patriarchy in America, and opposition to racism is critical to dismantling it.

Difference is such a pleasant word. It applies to everyone. It does not call anyone to action. We need only acknowledge that it exists and then move on with our preconceived plans. *Racism* is quite different. It destroys. It condemns. It speaks of power. It demands a response. Adrienne Rich calls on feminists to use the word *racism*:

If black and white feminists are going to speak of female accountability, I believe the word *racism* must be seized, grasped in our bare hands, ripped up out of the sterile or defensive consciousness in which it so often grows, and transplanted so that it can yield new insights for our lives and our movement. (Rich 1979, pp. 301–4)

Acknowledging each other's differences is not enough. Relationships of power produce some of our differences. We must face the awful history and reality of racism that helps to create those differences. We do not need to focus less on gender; we need to understand how gender relates to race. If we see feminism as a "liberation project" that seeks the emancipation of all women we must address the complexity of forces that bind us. (Romany 1991, p. 23) Bell hooks describes the feminist project that embraces this holistic understanding of oppression:

> To me feminism is not simply a struggle to end male chauvinism or a movement to ensure that women will have equal rights with men; it is a commitment to eradicating the ideology of domination that permeates Western culture on various levels—sex, race, and class, to name a few—and a commitment to reorganizing U.S. society so that the self-development of people can take precedence over imperialism, economic expansion, and material desires. (hooks 1981, pp. 194–5)

When we not only acknowledge our differences but also take up the struggle they demand, we stand a chance of creating that world.

NOTES

· · ·

1. Patricia Williams mused about a lawsuit brought by a white woman against a clinic that negligently sold her a Black man's sperm: "I ponder this case about the nightmare of giving birth to a black child who is tormented so that her mother gets to claim damages for emotional distress. I think about whether my mother shouldn't bring such a suit, both of us having endured at least the pain of

my maturation in the racism of the Boston public school system. Do black mothers get to sue for such an outcome, or is it just white mothers?" (Williams 1991, pp. 186–7)

2. I credit this declaration as the inspiration for my article. . . .

3. Hooks explains how white male scholars assume that Black men vacate their parenting roles because of domineering Black women. As hooks points out, the term *matriarch* does not accurately describe the Black woman's role in our society. As the most socially and economically marginalized group in America, Black women do not hold the power the term *matriarch* implies (hooks 1981, pp. 70–83).

4. Statistics demonstrate that since 1980 there has been a 40% increase in the number of births to unmarried white women, thereby narrowing the gap between the percentage of Black unmarried mothers and white unmarried mothers (Fineman 1995, pp. 124–5).

5. This phrase is a play on the title of Adrienne Rich's essay, "Disloyal to Civilization: Feminism, Racism, Gynephobia," in which Rich refers to women's disloyalty to patriarchy (Rich 1979, p. 295).

6. It is arguable that a contemporary version of the "Negro Project" (not connected to feminist reproductive rights advocacy) can be seen in recent attempts to implement incentives for welfare mothers to use the long-term contraceptive Norplant. For more information on this see "Poverty and Norplant: Can Contraception Reduce the Underclass?" The *Philadelphia Inquirer,* December 12, 1990, p. A18 (suggesting that Black women on welfare be given incentives to use the contraceptive Norplant), and Tamar Lewin, "Implanted Birth Control Device Renews Debate over Forced Contraception," *New York Times,* January 10, 1991, p. A20 (reviewing the debate on forced use of Norplant).

7. Thus, the prochoice movement remained relatively complacent about the effective denial of access to abortions for poor women with the Supreme Court's decisions in *Maher v. Roe,* 432 U.S. 464 (1977) and *Harris v. McRae,* 448 U.S. 297 (1980), which upheld the denial of public funding for abortion. See Stearns 1989, p. 7. The belated mobilization of the prochoice movement triggered by the Supreme Court's decision in *Webster v. Reproductive Health Services,* 492 U.S. 490 (1989) (upholding the state's ability to restrict access to abortion services), and the resulting spate of state restrictions on abortion seemed motivated by their threat to the reproductive rights of affluent women (pp. 7–9).

REFERENCES

Allen, Anita. "Surrogacy, Slavery, and the Ownership of Life." *Harvard Journal of Law and Public Policy* 13 (1990), p. 139.

Allen, Jeffner. "Motherhood: The Annihilation of Women." In *Mothering: Essays in Feminist Theory,* ed. Joyce Treblicot. Totowa, NJ: Rowman and Allanheld, 1984. Also published in *Lesbian Philosophy: Explorations,* ed. Jeffner Allen. Palo Alto, CA: Institute for Lesbian Studies, 1988.

Austin, Regina. "Sapphire Bound." *Wisconsin Law Review,* 1989, p. 539.

Bell, Derrick. "After We're Gone: Prudent Speculations on America in a Post-Racial Epoch." *Saint Louis University Law Journal* 34: (1990), p. 393.

Cain, Patricia. "Feminist Jurisprudence: Grounding the Theories." *Berkeley Women's Law Journal* 4 (1990), p. 191.

Clinton, Catherine. "Caught in the Web of the Big House: Women and Slavery." In *The Web of Southern Social Relations,* ed. Walter J. Raser. Athens: University of Georgia Press, 1985, pp. 19–34.

Collins, Patricia Hill. *Black Feminist Thought: Knowledge, Consciousness, and the Politics of Empowerment.* Boston: Unwin Hyman, 1990.

Crenshaw, K. "Demarginalizing the Intersection of Race and Sex: A Black Feminist Critique of Antidiscrimination Doctrine, Feminist Theory, and Antiracist Politics." *University of Chicago Legal Forum,* 1989, pp. 139–67.

Davis, Angela Y. *Women, Race, and Class.* New York: Vintage, 1983.

Douglass, Frederick. *Narrative of the Life of Frederick Douglass: An American Slave.* Ed. Houston A. Baker, Jr. New York: Penguin, 1982.

Du Bois, W. E. B. *Black Reconstruction.* Milwood, NY: Kraus-Thompson, 1976.

Ferguson, Ann. "On Conceiving Motherhood and Sexuality: A Feminist Materialist Approach." In

Mothering: Essays in Feminist Theory, ed. Joyce Treblicot, 1984, pp. 153–82.

Fineman, Martha A. "Images of Mothers in Poverty Discourse." In Martha Albertson Fineman and Isabel Karpin, eds. *Mothers in Law: Feminist Theory and the Legal Regulation of Motherhood.* New York: Columbia University Press, 1995a, pp. 205–23.

———. *The Neutered Mother, the Sexual Family, and other Twentieth-Century Tragedies.* New York: Routledge, 1995b.

Fox-Genovese, Elizabeth. *Within the Plantation Household: Black and White Women of the Old South.* Chapel Hill: University of North Carolina Press, 1988.

Frug, Mary Joe. "Securing Job Equality for Women: Labor Market Hostility to Working Mothers." *Buffalo University Law Review* 59 (1979), p. 55.

Gates, Henry Louis Jr. "To Be Raped, Bred, or Abused." Review of *Incidents in the Life of a Slave Girl* by Harriet Jacobs, ed. by J. Yelin. *New York Times Book Review* (November 22, 1987), p. 12.

Giddings, Paula. *When and Where I Enter: The Impact of Black Women on Race and Sex in America.* New York: Marrow, 1984.

Gilbert, Olive. *Narrative of Sojourner Truth: A Bondswoman of Olden Time.* Battle Creek, MI: privately printed, 1878.

Gimenez, Martha E. "Feminism, Pronatalism, and Motherhood." In *Mothering: Essays in Feminist Theory,* ed. Joyce Treblicot. 1984, pp. 290–304.

Gordon, Linda. *Woman's Body, Woman's Right: A Social History of Birth Control in America.* New York: Grossman, 1976.

———. "Why Nineteenth-Century Feminists Did Not Support Birth Control and Twentieth-Century Feminists Do: Feminism, Reproduction, and the Family." In *Rethinking the Family: Some Feminist Questions,* ed. B. Thorne and M. Yalom. Boston: Northeastern University Press, 1992, pp. 140–54.

Gray, Silvia Sims, and Lynn M. Nybell. "Issues in African-American Family Preservation." *Child Welfare* 69 (1990), p. 513.

Grillo, Trina, and Stephanie M. Wildman. "Obscuring the Importance of Race: The Implications of Making Comparisons between Racism and Sexism (or Other -isms)." *Duke Law Journal,* 1991, p. 397.

Gutman, Herbert G. *The Black Family in Slavery and Freedom.* New York: Pantheon, 1976.

Harris, Angela P. 1990. "Race and Essentialism in Feminist Legal Theory." *Stanford Law Review* 42 (1990), p. 581.

Higginbotham, Leon A. *In the Matter of Color.* New York: Oxford University Press, 1979.

Hill, Robert B. *Informal Adoption among Black Families.* Washington, DC: National Urban League, 1977.

hooks, bell. *Ain't I a Woman: Black Women and Feminism.* Boston: South End, 1981.

———. *Feminist Theory: From Margin to Center.* Boston: South End, 1984.

———. "Theory as Liberatory Practice." *Yale Journal of Law and Feminism* 4 (1991), pp. 1–4.

Hurtado, Aida. 1989. "Relating to Privilege: Seduction and Rejection in the Subordination of White Women and Women of Color." *Signs: Journal of Women in Culture and Society* 14 (1989), p. 833.

Janiewski, Dolores. 1983. "Sisters under Their Skins: Southern Working Women." In *Sex, Race, and the Role of Women in the South,* ed. Joanne V. Hawks and Sheila L. Skemp. Jackson: University of Mississippi Press, 1983, pp. 13–35.

Jones, Jacqueline. *Labor of Love, Labor of Sorrow: Black Women, Work, and the Family from Slavery to the Present.* New York: Basic Books, 1985.

Kline, Marlee. "Race, Racism, and Feminist Legal Theory." *Harvard Women's Law Journal* 12 (1989), p. 115.

Lebsock, Suzanne. "Free Black Women and the Question of Matriarchy: Petersburg, Virginia, 1784–1820." *Feminist Studies* 8 (1982), p. 271.

Lerner, Gerda. *Black Women in White America: A Documentary History.* New York: Vintage, 1973.

Lewin, Tamar. "Implanted Birth Control Device Renews Debate over Forced Contraception." *New York Times* (January 10, 1991), p. A20.

Little, Malcolm. *The Autobiography of Malcolm X.* New York: Grove, 1965.

Lorde, Audre. *Sister Outsider: Essays and Speeches.* New York: Crossing, 1984.

MacKinnon, Catharine A. *Feminism Unmodified: Discourses on Life and Law.* Cambridge: Harvard University Press, 1987.

Marcus, Isabel, et al. "Looking toward the Future: Feminism and Reproductive Technologies." *Buffalo Law Review* 37 (1988), p. 203.

Morrison, Toni. *The Bluest Eye.* New York: Holt, Rinehart, and Winston, 1970.

———. *Beloved.* New York: Knopf, 1987.

Moynihan, Daniel Patrick. *The Negro Family: The Case for National Action.* Washington, DC: Department of Labor, Office of Policy Planning and Research, 1965.

Murray, Charles M. *Losing Ground: American Social Policy, 1950–1980.* New York: Basic Books, 1984.

National Committee for Pay Equity (NCPE). *Pay Equity: An Issue of Race, Ethnicity, and Sex.* Washington, DC: National Committee on Pay Equity, 1987.

Olsen, Frances E. "The Family and the Market: A Study of Ideology and Legal Reform." *Harvard Law Review* 96 (1983), p. 1497.

Omolade, Barbara. "The Unbroken Circle: A Historical Study of Black Single Mothers and Their Families." *Wisconsin Women's Law Journal* 3 (1987), p. 239.

Palmer, Phyllis. *Domesticity and Dirt: Housewives and Domestic Servants in the United States, 1920–1945.* Philadelphia: Temple University Press, 1989.

Petchesky, Rosalind P. "Reproduction, Ethics, and Public Policy: The Federal Sterilization Regulations." *Hastings Center Report* 9 (1979), p. 29.

Rich, Adrienne. *Of Woman Born: Motherhood as Experience and Institution.* New York: Norton, 1976.

———. "Motherhood: The Contemporary Emergency and the Quantum Leap." In *On Lies, Secrets, and Silence.* New York: Norton, 1979.

Roberts, Dorothy E. "Punishing Drug Addicts Who Have Babies: Women of Color, Equity, and the Right of Privacy." *Harvard Law Review* 104 (1991), p. 1419.

Rollins, Judith. *Between Women: Domestics and Their Employers.* Philadelphia: Temple University Press, 1985.

Romany, Selina. "Ain't I a Feminist?" *Yale Journal of Law and Feminism* 4 (1991), p. 23.

Rowe, Audrey. "The Feminization of Poverty: An Issue for the 90s." *Yale Journal of Law and Feminism* 4 (1991), p. 73.

Spelman, Elizabeth V. *Inessential Woman: Problems of Exclusion in Feminist Thought.* Boston: Beacon Press, 1988.

Stack, Carol B. *All Our Kin: Strategies for Survival in a Black Community.* New York: Harper & Row, 1974.

———. "Cultural Perspectives on Child Welfare." *New York University Review of Law and Social Change* 12 (1983–84), p. 539.

Stearns, Nancy. "*Roe v. Wade.* Our Struggle Continues." *Berkeley Women's Law Journal* 4 (1989), p. 1.

Sterling, Dorothy. *We Are Your Sisters: Black Women in the Nineteenth Century.* New York: Norton, 1984.

Wegman, Myron E. "Annual Summary of Vital Statistics: 1988." *Pediatrics* 84 (1989), p. 943.

West, Robin. "Jurisprudence and Gender." *University of Chicago Law Review* 55 (1988), p. 1.

White, Deborah. *Ar'n't I a Woman? Female Slaves in the Plantation South.* New York: Norton, 1985.

White, E. Frances. "Africa on My Mind: Gender, Counter Discourse, and African-American Nationalism." *Journal of Women's History* 2 (1990), p. 73.

Williams, Joan C. "Deconstructing Gender." *Michigan Law Review* 87 (1989), p. 797.

———. "Sameness, Feminism, and the Work/Family Conflict." *New York Law School Law Review* 35 (1990), p. 347.

Williams, Patricia. *The Alchemy of Race and Rights: Diary of a Law Professor.* Cambridge, MA: Harvard University Press, 1991.

Wood, Betty. "Some Aspects of Female Resistance to Chattel Slavery in Low Country Georgia, 1763–1815." *History Journal* 30 (1987), pp. 603–9.

PART THREE

PROSPECTS FOR EMPOWERMENT

CHAPTER 8

Caring and Community

This chapter explores the rich sensibilities feminists bring to matters of ethics, spirituality, and community. Overall, the chapter invites us to ponder our needs for connecting, appreciate our diverse resources for doing so, and use them with as much imagination as determination. To a large extent the theorists considered in this chapter work on the boundary where theory and praxis most openly hold hands and thus where empowerment takes shape as a vivid prospect. For the most part these theorists work as feminist ethicists, ecofeminists, and feminist communitarians.

MORAL REASONING AND THE ETHIC OF CARE

Carol Gilligan's *In a Different Voice* is a theoretical hub for feminist ethics and a good deal of other feminist theorizing, especially about identity (see Chapter 9). Although her influence is far-reaching, Gilligan is best known in connection with the ethic of care that inspires much feminist theorizing. Yet her most famous work focuses not on ethics as such but on psychology. *In a Different Voice* is subtitled *Psychological Theory and Women's Development*. In this work Gilligan addresses core psychological issues, particularly about "women's identity *formation* and their moral *development* in adolescence and adulthood."[1]

Gilligan found that women and men favor different imagery about human relationships. Women incline toward the image of the web; men, toward that of hierarchy. Gilligan theorizes that these images

> inform different modes of assertion and response: the wish to be alone at the top and the consequent fear that others will get too close; the wish to be at the center of connection and the consequent fear of being too far out on the edge. These

disparate fears of being stranded and being caught give rise to different portrayals of achievement and affiliation, leading to different modes of action and *different ways of assessing the consequences of choice.* (p. 62; emphasis added)

In general, women develop an ethic of care (or responsibility); men, an
ethic of rights. Women feel responsible for noticing and responding to
people's suffering and problems. Men typically feel responsible for noticing and respecting people's rights, including their rights to privacy and
"self-fulfillment" (or what Abraham Maslow called self-actualization).
(p. 100) Gilligan points out that

> The morality of rights is predicated on equality and centered on the under-
> standing of fairness, while the ethic of responsibility [or care] relies on the
> concept of equity, the recognition of differences in need. While the ethic of
> rights is a manifestation of equal respect, balancing the claims of other and
> self, the ethic of responsibility rests on an understanding that gives rise to
> compassion and care. (pp. 164–5)

Women's developmental progress, then, results in treating care as an
ethical touchstone, "as the most adequate guide to the resolution of conflicts in human relationships." (p. 105) This ethic of care presupposes that
people inescapably depend on one another. Developing an awareness of
that circumstance entails insights into human relationships and social interaction. Moral judgments come to hinge on care as a principle "that remains psychological in its concern with relationships and response but becomes universal in its condemnation of exploitation and hurt."

At first, Gilligan may seem to be describing an ethic of self-sacrifice.
Throughout her work, though, she emphasizes a developmental sequence
wherein women learn to include themselves in the orbit of their caring. In
that vein Gilligan credits feminism. She says "changes in women's rights
change women's moral judgments, seasoning mercy with justice by enabling women to consider it moral to care not only for others but for themselves." As women begin to think about rights alongside responsibilities,
their moral judgments become more flexible and less universalist. (p. 149)
Along these broad lines Gilligan theorizes a distinct point of view among
women as well as a distinct set of priorities. (p. 22) Overall, her work suggests that women's moral agency revolves around "a plurality of moral interests, contextual decision making, nonadversarial accommodation of diverse interests, personhood as relational, and the body as moral agent."[2]

By and large, feminist ethicists build up their frameworks around such
characteristics commonly associated with women. Collaterally with care,
"connection" gets to the heart of most feminist theorizing about moral judgments and ethical living. In Reading 19, Gilligan talks about her work in
terms of "theorizing connection." That focus reorients our ideas about
moral agents. No longer, says Gilligan, can we abide by dominant conceptions of "the separate self, the individual acting alone, the possessor of natural rights, the autonomous moral agent." Instead of seeing individuals

along liberal lines (see Chapter 5), we need to consider people in their dense contexts, where home, workplace, school, church or temple, neighborhood, the mall, and the gym are experienced mostly through the social relations built up there. In those face-to-face relationships, whether intimate or superficial, moral agency either passes or fails its most important tests.

Feminist theorists suggest several conditions for passing such tests. Feelings and desires, "valuable aspects of the wise person's epistemic repertoire," are also crucial for one's moral repertoire, where "appropriate affect" is essential. One cannot launch a moral endeavor without knowing that a situation invites it. Often, though, what moral agents need to know is not readily observable, as Margaret Olivia Little says:

> Think of what is really involved in seeing what is morally relevant. Often it means noticing what is *not* present: noticing that a student is not in class; spotting in a busy crowd that a child, though surrounded by adults, is not *accompanied* by any of them. Or again, noticing subtle patterns: that a patient asks for more pain medication on the nights after she has had a visit from her husband. Or again, noticing what is so pervasive that it tends to be invisible (notice how the movie *Fatal Attraction* or the actions of Lorena Bobbitt draw immediate and dramatic public moralizing, while the ubiquitous violence against women in film and reality continues with still too little comment).[3]

Thus, moral agency requires a great deal more than honoring one's own and others' rights, assessing one's responsibilities, and applying one's resources. It requires emotional attunement to one's daily situations as well as an abiding commitment to rid them of unfairness and cruelty.

Alongside feelings and desires that are morally motivating we need self-knowledge. Sarah Lucia Hoagland argues, for instance, that ethics presupposes not altruism but self-knowledge. She means not the navel-gazing sort of self-preoccupation that passes for self-awareness in some circles but hard-won insights into self. She also means knowing one's power-from-within, which is a matter of centering and remaining steady in

> our environment as we choose how we direct our energy. "Power-from-within" is the power of ability, of choice and engagement. It is creative; and hence it is an affecting and transforming power, but not a controlling power.[4]

For Hoagland, then, "moral agency involves enacting choice in limited situations, avoiding de-moralization, and working within boundaries rather than trying to rise above them."[5]

More implicitly, feminist theorists point to resistance as a condition of women's moral agency. Broadly, this entails "taking responsibility for resisting the language and thought and practices that . . . maintain our subordination."[6] In many respects the opposite of resistance is self-sacrifice, habitually giving other people's needs and preferences priority over one's own. Often we see self-sacrifice "In the provision of housework and child care, in the domain of sexuality, and in the maintaining of relationships between family members and friends" where women "give more than we receive."[7]

Gilligan decries self-sacrifice. In Reading 19 she distinguishes between a *feminine* ethic of care, which emphasizes "special obligations and interpersonal relationships," and a *feminist* ethic of care, which only starts with "connection, theorized as primary and . . . fundamental in human life." The feminist ethic of care extends outward from its center of connectedness. It involves women bringing

> themselves and their concerns about relationship into the public arena, placing high on the political agenda relationships with children, family relationships, relationships with the environment, relationships with the future as developed through education and health care, and above all, the problem of violence in domestic as well as national and international relationships.

A common paradigm for this embracing ethic of care is mothering, or the mother–child relationship. Part of its appeal lies in the relative absence of domination in mothering. Instead, maternal caring involves "being vulnerable to the needs and pains of the child" and "fearing the loss of the child before the child is ready for independence."[8] One of the first proponents of a maternal paradigm in feminist moral theory was Caroline Whitbeck, whose ideas began appearing in the early 1970s.[9] The best-known proponent, however, is Sara Ruddick, whose work focuses on "maternal thinking" (see Reading 26).

A number of theorists question or even reject a maternalist basis for feminist ethics. Some dislike how "the 'masculinist' individualist ethics and the feminist, relational ethics of care implicitly rely on the public–domestic distinction"[10] that operates as a problematic in much feminist theorizing, as we have seen. Others emphasize justice, even though some feminist theorists regard it a "traditionally masculine concern."[11] A few fear that an ethic of care promotes paternalism while feeding perceptions that those receiving care are dependent.[12]

It may strike you that one strategy for addressing these concerns is to combine the ethic of rights with the ethic of care, thus circumventing the either/or. Yet Joy Kroeger-Mappes makes a strong case for the impossibility of doing that. She notes that "people cannot be made to care, to love. To say that people have a right to another's caring is jarring. . . ." Caring cannot be made obligatory in the ways feeding or clothing someone can be.[13]

Nevertheless, care may be a broad enough moral framework to accommodate justice.[14] One concept pointing in that theoretical direction is Kathleen Jones's *compassionate authority,* which leaves room for rules and rights but "detach[es] them . . . from private, possessive moorings."[15]

Another way to move toward fitting justice and rights into a care-centered framework is to use female friendship as a paradigm or, more generally, feminist community. Later in this chapter we will look at that theoretical strategy. Anticipating that section, let us first consider Hoagland's ethics, which promotes community alongside individuals' moral agency. Her ethics "encourages not vulnerability but intimacy" and "recognizes power not as controlling but enabling"; her ethics emphasizes "neither merging nor estranging but interacting" and "encourages not binding but engaging"; her ethics "treats moral agency . . . as acting one among many and as making choices within situations"; her ethics "has as its axis not the antagonism of dominance and subordination but a form of cooperation. . . ."[16]

ECOFEMINISM AND THE POLITICS OF SPIRITUALITY

In important respects ecofeminism represents feminist ethics at its most ambitious. Its core principle is that the matrix of domination extends well past the human world to domination over other beings such as animals and over the rest of the natural world (humankind of course belonging to the natural world). Ecofeminists insist on close linkages between the subordination of women and the exploitation of other beings and "nature."

Significantly, much ecofeminist theorizing uses the ethic of care as a point of departure. Also significant is the virtual consensus among ecofeminists about the literal destructiveness of dualisms such as nature/culture and female/male and the costly absurdity of defining humanity in contrast with nature and femininity.[17] Eugenie Gatens-Robinson is scarcely alone, then, in contending that

> the most central ecological responsibility consists in taking on the necessary work of transforming consciousness in ways that eliminate the alienation between human culture and nature, body and mind, the masculine and feminine.[18]

She goes on to observe that feminist theorists often argue "that the moral and the epistemological cannot be separated." For instance, then, "the philosophy of science must incorporate a connection between how we choose to know the natural world and what that makes of us in a spiritual sense." (p. 214) As you probably sense, ecofeminist theory often addresses spirituality as well as ethics, religion as well as politics, epistemology as well as ecology.

It may be no historical accident that *WomanSpirit,* a magazine about women's spirituality, first appeared in 1974. In fact, ecofeminism emerged in close company with the women's spirituality movement during the 1970s. Adrienne Rich's *Of Woman Born* dovetails with both developments. On the one side she asks us to "imagine a world" where

> Women will truly create new life, bringing forth not only children (if and as we choose) but the visions, and the thinking, necessary to sustain, console, and alter human existence—a new relationship to the universe.[19]

On the other side, "her visions of women's strengths, women's values, and women's love for women, for themselves holds much to inspire all women's quests,"[20] especially those spiritual journeys sometimes associated with mothering. Another contemporary classic appearing only two years later was Susan Griffin's *Woman and Nature: The Roaring inside Her.* Like Rich's work, Griffin's embraces a maternalist/feminist perspective.[21] Yet other ecofeminists reject that stance, as I mentioned earlier.

After we examine ecofeminism's main themes, looking at women's spirituality and moral vegetarianism will shed light on such disagreements.

These theorists see us as "latecomers to the planet"[22] who must change our ways as fast as we can. Their theorizing concerns itself with ecology, whose Greek origins have to do with *oikos,* or home. It thus deals with "learning to become a native of a place."[23] As Karen J. Warren summarizes it,

> What makes ecological feminism *ecological* is its understanding of and commitment to the importance of valuing and preserving ecosystems (whether understood as organisms, individuals, populations, communities and their interactions, or as nutrient flows among entities "in a biospherical net of relationships"). This includes the recognition of human beings as ecological beings (as "relational and ecological selves"), and of the necessity of an environmental dimension to any adequate feminism or feminist philosophy.[24]

Warren goes on to say that ecofeminism's *feminist* character lies in its commitment to ending male-gender bias. (p. 1) She adds that ecofeminist theory is not only ecological and feminist but also multicultural insofar as it resists ethnocentrism, colonialism, racism, and other systems of domination besides sexism. (p. 2)

According to Ellen Cronan Rose, the most influential ecofeminists "accept and affirm the woman–nature connection." These theorists—Griffin, for instance—"believe women should proudly assert their difference from men and reclaim their 'natural' creativity, intuition, emotion, and spirituality."[25] Typically, they assume that women are "'closer' to nature than men and . . . that women's voices thus ought to be privileged in ethical discussions of interspecies relations. This thesis has been called 'nature feminism' . . ."[26]

Warren is one of the ecofeminist theorists taking issue with that position, which resonates with Gilligan's notion of a "different voice" and with Belenky and her colleagues' work on "women's ways of knowing." She contrasts an eco*feminine* with an eco*feminist* position, much as Gilligan contrasts a feminine with a feminist ethic of care. Warren associates so-called nature feminism with an ecofeminine stance that "glorifies the feminine as a *principle* rather than a gender role" and "assumes women have some special understanding of nature."[27]

That stance puts Warren and like-minded ecofeminists in conflict with much of the women's spirituality movement and its theorists. In fact, Warren has analyzed that movement, which overlaps a great deal with ecofeminism. She describes three broad positions ecofeminists adopt toward spirituality. One treats earth-based spiritualities as crucial or precious; another sees a spiritual orientation as likely to undermine the ecofeminist movement; the last acknowledges the importance of women's spiritualities but treats them as neither necessary nor sufficient for ecofeminist progress. Warren emphasizes that ecofeminist spirituality itself entails great diversity. Its participants differ about such matters as whether mainstream religious traditions can be reconceived or reinterpreted to provide environmentally responsible and nonsexist practices and theologies; . . . whether an earth-based spirituality promotes harmful gender-stereotypical views of women . . . ; whether any specific environmental practice (vegetarianism, bans on hunting and animal experimentation, organic farming, population control) is mandated by a given ecofeminist spirituality; whether ecofeminist spiritualities inappropriately mystify and romanticize nature; and whether a given ecofeminist spirituality is an expression of ethical colonialism, co-opting indigenous cultural practices as part of an otherwise unchanged dominant Western worldview.[28]

Lest we lose sight of what these ecofeminists largely agree on, let us take swift note of their coming together around the idea that "the same dominant mind-set that separates humans from the rest of nature divides politics from spirituality, as though humans are not a part of nature and politics is not integrally related to spirituality." As Gloria Feman Orenstein puts it, ecofeminists usually see "no contradiction between spiritual and political practice."[29] She mentions Starhawk, whose books you may find interesting, as someone exemplifying that position.

Another influential theorist of women's spirituality as well as feminist theology is Mary Daly, who by 1968 "had contrasted the holistic, communalistic potential of a female-centered religion with the alienating and destructive thrust of patriarchal religions." In 1973, the publication of *Beyond God the Father* brought her ideas to the attention of many feminists. By 1976, women's spirituality occasioned a national conference in Boston. Its focus was the goddess.[30]

Most feminist theorizing about women's spirituality focuses on female- and goddess- and earth-centered spiritualities, though a substantial minority of it does center on religious traditions such as Buddhism, Judaism, and Christianity. The former work commonly assumes that "gynocentric spiritualities (such as Goddess worship and the practice of Wicca) share an earth-based focus and basic metaphysical assumptions with Native sprituality. . . ."[31] A great deal of ecofeminist spirituality thus draws from indigenous cultures such as Native American ones. Some Native American feminist theorists approve of that propensity. Arguing that white American feminism is rooted in Native American cultures, for example, Paula Gunn Allen generalizes that

> If American society judiciously modeled the traditions of the various Native Nations, the place of women in society would become central, the distribution of goods and power would be egalitarian, the elderly would be respected, honored, and protected as a primary social and cultural resource, the ideals of physical beauty would be considerably enlarged (to include "fat," strong-featured women, gray-haired and wrinkled individuals, and others who in contemporary American culture are viewed as "ugly"). Additionally, the destruction of the biota, the life sphere, and the natural resources of the planet would be curtailed, and the spiritual nature of human and nonhuman life would become a primary organizing principle of human society.[32]

Much ecofeminist spirituality revolves around such core beliefs. Orenstein's discussion of shamanism illustrates their appeal. She says that the shamanism associated with earth-based spiritualities in indigenous cultures emphasizes the earth's sacredness, the "interconnected web of life," and the spiritual dimension of matter.[33]

Sometimes, though, efforts to theorize a feminist spirituality inspired by indigenous cultures raise the specter of cultural misappropriation or exploitation. *Whiteshamanism* is the name for such abuses. It generally refers to white individuals' efforts to convey a sense of "Indian-ness," usually for commercial purposes such as increasing their readership or attracting clients. Some Native American feminists decry such moves as cultural mockery and worse.[34]

As you would expect, white feminist theorists also express reservations about the selective appropriation of what suits non-Indian women in their quests to feel more connected with the earth, more holistically spiritual, and less constrained by patriarchal forms of spirituality. Carol J. Adams's voice is perhaps representative. In "syncretistic ecofeminist spiritualities" she sees great meaning. At the same time she emphasizes that

> *How* to incorporate diverse cultural and religious traditions within ecofeminism is an important ethical/political question to raise about these syncretistic efforts. The more diverse the sources for envisioning ecofeminist spiritualities, the more opportunities exist for either succumbing to racism or exposing racism in this syncretism.[35]

Historically, the crudest expression of such racism is the "noble savage" stereotype of native peoples, which romanticizes them as more innocent yet wiser than materially well-off but alienated people.

Other ecofeminist spiritualities are theorized as "a return to a mode of earth-based spiritual life which actually existed in the Neolithic period." Often these draw from the ideas of the archaeologist Marija Gimbutas. Without rendering a judgment about the empirical or historical validity of such approaches, Gatens-Robinson emphasizes that like other feminist spiritualities, they usually seek not historical or empirical truth but a spiritual or social-psychological truth "that heals severed connections, not only with nature but with the human religious past, a past in which women have been oppressed. . . ." In line with most feminist theorizing about spirituality, Gatens-Robinson concludes that each of us must find our place "in a healing and empowering way in the intricate networks of histories of which we are a part."[36]

As I noted earlier, some ecofeminist theorists situate themselves within religious traditions like Judaism. In direct and indirect ways, they contribute to "green worship."[37] Such theorists include the ecofeminist theologian Rosemary Radford Ruether, who says that ecofeminist spirituality treats God as "the immanent source of life that sustains the whole planetary community. God is neither male nor anthropomorphic." Another is Elisabeth Schussler Fiorenza, who, like Ruether, advocates "the biblical tradition as a resource for ecofeminist sensibilities."[38]

Gatens-Robinson holds out the ideas of one writer as an important resource for those wanting to theorize a nonexploitive, syncretistic spirituality revolving around women's diverse experiences and needs. She considers naturalist Annie Dillard, whose work you may already value, "a model for transforming our experience of nature in a deeply *religious* way independent of the tradition of ritual and symbol we choose."[39] When I first came across this suggestion, rich memories of *Pilgrim at Tinker Creek* flooded my consciousness. Whatever the theoretical possibilities it holds, this work may be spiritually expansive enough to inspire renewed theoretical efforts.

So, too, may be the work of Carol J. Adams and others theorizing moral vegetarianism as a spiritual/political part of their ecofeminism. In *The Sexual Politics of Meat: A Feminist-Vegetarian Theory,* Adams traces ecofeminism back to feminist-vegetarian communities. In fact, her book originated as a paper for Mary Daly's course on feminist ethics at Boston College in the mid-1970s.

Theoretically, Adams treats meat as a social construction that is pervasively naturalized. Animals, she says, "are made absent *as animals* for meat to exist."[40] Adams's points seem irrefutable, especially in a society where animal-companions are key members of many households. A quiet, entrenched hierarchy of animals first divides these creatures into edible and nonedible. Then edible animals get rendered as filets, drumsticks, Buffalo wings, or ground round as they move from slaughterhouse to supermarket to dinner plate; they get rendered as groceries or dog food. They become mere meat, not the dead bodies of their former selves.

Among the diverse reasons ecofeminist theorists like Adams theorize vegetarianism as a spiritual responsibility are the waste of planetary resources in "meat" production and the environmental devastation wrought by the "meat" industry. Adams (p. 130) points out, for instance, that about half the water used in the United States goes to crops for livestock and that more than half of water pollution comes from wastes associated with the livestock industry. (Note how some animals get socially constructed as "livestock" on their way to becoming "meat.")

Influenced by Adams's work, Deane Curtin argues that if there is any "compelling" context for moral vegetarianism "as an expression of an ecological ethic of care, it is for economically well-off persons in technologically advanced countries." More generally, he cites ecofeminists' moral concern with the question of what should count as food. Curtin concludes that choosing one's diet is "one way of politicizing an ethic of care."[41] So, too, is choosing one's community and helping to construct it as ecologically sound and woman-friendly.

FEMINIST COMMUNITARIANISM

Over the centuries, communitarianism has been a rich vein of social and political thought. Its core idea is that human beings are social or interdependent creatures whose well-being requires stable communities. Enlightenment thinkers added "democratic" communities to that calculus, but their notions of democracy historically excluded women, men without property, and slaves. "Community" remains the knotty problematic of this tradition of social thought.

In the past decade or so, *communitarianism* has come to refer not only to a historically sweeping body of social thought but also to a contemporary intellectual and social movement to theorize "community" in ways that are viable in practice. Contemporary communitarians launched their own journal, *Responsive Community,* in 1991. Major figures in this group are Amitai Etzioni, Robert N. Bellah, Michael Sandel, and Jean Bethke Elshtain. By and large, these communitarians are critical of liberalism as well as committed to social action; their theorizing often invokes ethics or morality; they tend to talk about responsibilities as well as rights. In "The Responsive Communitarian Platform: Rights and Responsibilities," for example, Etzioni points to all this and more.[42]

One might suppose that these thinkers find a lot of value in feminist theorizing about the family, the ethic of care, the state and public policy, and community itself. For the most part, though, they remain pointedly nonfeminist. In fact, contemporary communitarian thinkers largely fall into nonfeminist or feminist groupings. Penny A. Weiss offers a superb overview of the theoretical differences between the two.[43]

More often than not, feminist communitarians theorize community using sisterhood, friendship, and solidarity as their models. All the while the "ideal of community" remains "politically problematic," entailing issues of difference as well as tension between individualism and community.[44]

On the face of it, sisterhood might seem most capable of accommodating differences. This metaphor conventionally implies, however, women of the same race and generation as well as the same family. Thus, it is implicitly exclusionary. Moreover, second-wave white feminists may have lifted "Sister" out of its African American context and shaped it to their own rhetorical and political purposes.[45] Not surprisingly, then, the "ideal of sisterhood" only "briefly held sway"[46] among feminist communitarians, even though it is far from defunct.

Marilyn Friedman observes that friendship is an appealing model because of its voluntaristic character. As Janice Raymond puts it, "Female friendship is a political statement that women come together not by default (because men oppress women), but because there is an intrinsic vitality in their coming together."[47] Yet friendship is ultimately an insufficient model for community, as Friedman implies. Some of its limitations parallel those of the mother–child bond as a model. Diverse individuals probably cannot expect to establish, let alone sustain, either the emotional richness friends share or their holistic sense of one another.

By now, then, solidarity in various conceptual guises has become the model of choice among feminist communitarians. One variant is implied in Latino/a usages of *companero*. As Maria Lugones emphasizes, this term connotes "the egalitarianism . . . of companionship and participation in common struggle."[48] It connotes, then, coming together around common values, goals, and activities—a kind of moral companionship based on struggle. Lugones's position resonates with those of bell hooks and Ann Ferguson, among others, who theorize about "communities of resistance" as enterprises in solidarity. Ferguson also calls these "oppositional communities," which people choose in order to gain acceptance of who they are, support for who they want to become, and allies in undermining the matrix of domination. Ferguson understands that these communities, like all others, necessitate an "ethics of disagreement" capable of curtailing divisiveness without denying differences.[49]

These feminist notions about community often do not address the matter of *where* we are to build the communities we need and want for ourselves. But in today's cybernetic world, location is less an issue than it once had to be. At least at some junctures or during some passages in our lives, we can make together something meaningful and sustaining called a *community of consciousness*. This means being a woman "in concert with other women, wherever they may be"; it means "people who do not inhabit a cohesive physical space" but who do make together "a community of ideas, emotions, perspectives, and goals."

This is the kind of community that feminist mothers make with and for their daughters "even when the immediate geographical community ma[kes] life difficult."[50] This is the kind of community feminist students and staff and faculty make together in many universities, the kind we often experience in a women's bookstore, the kind we participate in while listening to the music of Chris Williamson, Patti LaBelle, or Holly Near. This is the kind of community Verta Taylor and Leila J. Rupp theorize in Reading 20, where they show that lesbian feminist communities support "a rich and complex resistance culture and style of politics that nourishes rather than betrays the radical feminist vision."

A community of consciousness is what people are getting at when they mindfully refer to the Chicano/a community, the black community, or the gay community. This is what bell hooks is getting at when she says, "I take my community where I find it." In the same vein, hooks mentions "learning to be nourished" wherever she experiences a "sense of community"; she says "this way of thinking has enlarged my community."[51] Such theorizing implies an imaginative praxis that takes shape around attention to shared values and goals, attunement to "what kept us apart or works to keep us apart," and acceptance of the likelihood that "communities of choice cannot help but be partial." Above all, this praxis of community entails Hillel's three questions joined with the one Adrienne Rich adds:

If I am not for myself, who will be for me?
If I am only for myself, what am I?
If not now, when?

If not with others, how?[52]

NOTES

1. Carol Gilligan, *In a Different Voice: Psychological Theory and Women's Development* (Cambridge, MA: Harvard University Press, 1993 (orig. 1982)), p. 3; emphasis added.
2. Deane Curtin, "Toward an Ecological Ethic of Care," *Hypatia: A Journal of Feminist Philosophy* 6, no. 1 (Spring 1991), p. 65.
3. Margaret Olivia Little, "Seeing and Caring: The Role of Affect in Feminist Moral Epistemology," *Hypatia* 10, no. 3 (Summer 1995), pp. 118, 121.
4. Sarah Lucia Hoagland, *Lesbian Ethics: Toward New Value* (Palo Alto, CA: Institute of Lesbian Studies, 1988), pp. 70, 118.
5. *Ibid.,* p. 198. By "de-moralization" Hoagland refers to how one's capacity to make choices and her awareness of that capacity get undermined; p. 213.
6. Virginia Held, *Feminist Morality: Transforming Culture, Society, and Politics* (Chicago: University of Chicago Press, 1993), p. 15.
7. *Ibid.,* p. 165.
8. Held, *Feminist Morality,* p. 209.
9. Kathryn Pyne Addelson, *Moral Passages: Toward a Collectivist Moral Theory* (New York: Routledge, 1994), p. 20.
10. *Ibid.,* p. 21.
11. Ann Ferguson, "Twenty Years of Feminist Philosophy," *Hypatia* 9, no. 3 (Summer 1994), p. 206.
12. Anita Silvers, "Reconciling Equality to Difference: Caring (f)or Justice for People with Disabilities," *Hypatia* 10, no. 1 (Winter 1995) p. 40.
13. Joy Kroeger-Mappes, "The Ethic of Care vis-à-vis the Ethic of Rights: A Problem for Contemporary Moral Theory," *Hypatia* 9, no. 3 (Summer 1993), p. 122. Kroeger-Mappes notes that Ruddick and Whitbeck make similar points.
14. Virginia Held, "The Meshing of Care and Justice," *Hypatia* 10, no. 2 (Spring 1995), p. 131.
15. Kathleen B. Jones, *Compassionate Authority: Democracy and the Representation of Women* (New York: Routledge, 1993), pp. 141, 244.
16. Hoagland, *Lesbian Ethics,* p. 297.
17. Val Plumwood, "Nature, Self, and Gender: Feminism, Environmental Philosophy, and the Critique of Rationalism," *Hypatia* 6, no. 1 (Spring 1991), p. 11.
18. Eugenie Gatens-Robinson, "Finding Our Feminist Ways in Natural Philosophy and Religious Thought," *Hypatia* 9, no. 4 (Fall 1994), p. 211.
19. Adrienne Rich, *Of Woman Born: Motherhood as Experience and Institution* (New York: Bantam Books, 1976), p. 292.
20. Carol P. Christ, *Diving Deep and Surfacing: Women Writers on Spiritual Quest,* 2nd ed. (Boston: Beacon Press, 1986), p. 96.

21. Lauri Umansky, *Motherhood Reconceived: Feminism and the Legacies of the Sixties* (New York: New York University Press, 1996), pp. 146, 150.
22. Rosemary Radford Ruether, "Ecofeminism: Symbolic and Social Connections of the Oppression of Women and the Domination of Nature" in Carol J. Adams (ed.), *Ecofeminism and the Sacred* (New York: Continuum, 1993), p. 21.
23. Gatens-Robinson, "Finding Our Feminist Ways," p. 207.
24. Karen J. Warren, "Introduction" in Karen J. Warren (ed.), *Ecological Feminism* (London and New York: Routledge, 1994), p. 2.
25. Ellen Cronan Rose, "The Good Mother: From Gaia to Gilead" in Adams, *Ecofeminism and the Sacred,* p. 150.
26. Deborah Slicer, "Wrongs of Passages: Three Challenges to the Maturing of Ecofeminism" in Warren, *Ecological Feminism,* p. 33.
27. Warren, "Introduction," pp. 20, 22, 26.
28. Karen J. Warren, "A Feminist Philosophical Perspective on Ecofeminist Spiritualities" in Adams, *Ecofeminism and the Sacred,* pp. 119, 124.
29. Carol J. Adams, "Introduction" in Adams, *ibid.,* p. 2; Gloria Feman Orenstein, "Toward an Ecofeminist Ethic of Shamanism and the Sacred" in Adams, *Ecofeminism and the Sacred,* p. 173.
30. Umansky, *Motherhood Reconceived,* p. 122.
31. Adams, "Introduction," p. 3.
32. Paula Gunn Allen, *The Sacred Hoop: Recovering the Feminine in American Indian Traditions* (Boston: Beacon Press, 1986), pp. 211, 215.
33. Orenstein, "Toward an Ecofeminist Ethic," p. 172.
34. Two superb examples are Wendy Rose, "The Great Pretenders: Further Reflections on Whiteshamanism" in Mary F. Rogers (ed.), *Multicultural Experiences, Multicultural Theories* (New York: McGraw-Hill, 1996), pp. 99–115; Andy Smith, "For All Those Who Were Indian in a Former Life" in Adams, *Ecofeminism and the Sacred,* pp. 168–71.
35. Adams, "Introduction," p. 3.
36. Gatens-Robinson, "Finding Our Feminist Ways," pp. 221, 223. See Janet E. McCrickard's "Born-Again Moon: Fundamentalism in Christianity and the Feminist Spirituality Movement," *Feminist Review* 37 (Spring 1991), pp. 1–22, for an account of her parallel experiences with evangelical Christianity and Goddess revival.
37. See Beth Baker, "Green Worship," *Common Boundary* 14, no. 5 (September/October 1996), pp. 40–6. On ecofeminism and Buddhism, see Stephanie Kaza, "Acting with Compassion: Buddhism, Feminism, and the Environmental Crisis" in Adams, *Ecofeminism and the Sacred,* pp. 50–69; Anne C. Klein, "Presence with a Difference: Buddhists and Feminists on Subjectivity," *Hypatia* 9, no. 4 (Fall 1994), pp. 112–30; on ecofeminist Judaism, see Judith Plaskow's "Feminist Judaism and Repair of the World" in Adams, *Ecofeminism and the Sacred,* pp. 70–83.
38. Ruether, "Ecofeminism," p. 21; Gatens-Robinson, "Finding Our Feminist Ways," pp. 223, 224.
39. *Ibid.,* p. 225.
40. Carol J. Adams, "Ecofeminism and the Eating of Animals," *Hypatia* 6, no. 1 (Spring 1991), pp. 126–7; 135; 136, emphasis added.
41. Curtin, "Toward an Ecological Ethic of Care," pp. 68, 70, 71.
42. Amitai Etzioni, "The Responsive Communitarian Platform: Rights and Responsibilities," *Responsive Community* 2, no. 1 (Winter 1991/1992), pp. 4–20.

43. Penny A. Weiss, *Gendered Community: Rousseau, Sex, and Politics* (New York: New York University Press, 1993).

44. Iris Marion Young, "The Ideal of Community and the Politics of Difference" in Linda J. Nicholson (ed.), *Feminism/Postmodernism* (New York: Routledge, 1990), pp. 300, 306.

45. This is Pat Alake Rosezelle's contention; see Maria C. Lugones with Pat Alake Rosezelle, "Sisterhood and Friendship as Feminist Models" in Penny A. Weiss and Marilyn Friedman (eds.), *Feminism and Community* (Philadelphia: Temple University Press, 1995), pp. 139–41.

46. Sara Ruddick, *Maternal Thinking: Toward a Politics of Peace* (Boston: Beacon Press, 1989), p. 239.

47. Marilyn Friedman, "Feminism and Modern Friendship: Dislocating the Community," *Ethics* 99 (January 1989), pp. 275–90; Janice Raymond, "Female Friendship and Feminist Ethics" in Barbara Hilkert Andolsen, Christine E. Gudorf, and Mary D. Pellauer (eds.), *Women's Consciousness, Women's Conscience: A Reader in Feminist Ethics* (San Francisco: Harper & Row, 1987), p. 165.

48. Lugones with Rosezelle, "Sisterhood," p. 138.

49. Bell hooks in bell hooks and Cornel West, *Breaking Bread: Insurgent Black Intellectual Life* (Boston: South End Press, 1991), p. 17; Ann Ferguson, "Feminist Communities and Moral Revolution" in Weiss and Friedman, *Feminism and Community,* pp. 371–72, 381.

50. Rose L. Glickman, *Daughters of Feminists* (New York: St. Martin's Press, 1993), pp. 50, 49.

51. Hooks in hooks and West, *Breaking Bread,* pp. 90–1.

52. Marilyn Frye, "Lesbian Community: Heterodox Congregation" in Weiss and Friedman, *Feminism and Community,* p. 157; Hilde Lindemann Nelson, "Resistance and Insubordination," *Hypatia* 10, no. 2 (Spring 1995), p. 36; Adrienne Rich, "If Not with Others, How?" in Weiss and Friedman, *Feminism and Community,* p. 405.

READING 19

Hearing the Difference: Theorizing Connection

Carol Gilligan

When I began the work that led to *In a Different Voice* (1982), the framework was invisible. To study psychology at that time was like seeing a picture without seeing the frame, and the picture of the human world had become so large and all-encompassing that it looked like reality or a mirror of reality, rather than a representation. It was startling then to discover that women for the most part were not included in research on psychological development, or when included were marginalized or interpreted within a theoretical bias where the child and the adult were assumed to be male and the male was taken as the norm.

Bringing women's voices into psychology posed an interpretive challenge: how to listen to women in women's terms, rather than assimilating women's voices to the existing theoretical framework. And this led to a paradigm shift. Men's disconnection from women, formerly construed as the separation of the self from relationships, and women's dissociation from parts of themselves, formerly interpreted as women's selflessness in relationships, now appeared problematic. Framed within an ethic of care, disconnections and dissociations which had been taken as foundational to conceptions of self and morality appeared instead to be careless and harmful. This is what I meant by a different voice, on a theoretical level.

It is said that a tuning fork, tuned to a particular pitch, will stop the vibrations in eight or nine others that are tuned to a different frequency.

Carol Gilligan, "Hearing the Difference: Theorizing Connection." *Hypatia* 10, 2 (Spring 1995): 120–127. Copyright © 1995 by Carol Gilligan. Reprinted with permission of the author.

(Noel 1995) Listening to human voices, Noel finds that one voice, speaking in a particular emotional register, can stop the emotional vibrations in a group of people so that the environment in the room becomes deadened or flat. When this happens, she observes, it looks like silence but in fact the feelings and thoughts—the psychological energy—often move into the only place they can still live, and vibrate in silence, in the inner sense, until it becomes possible to bring them back into the world. (Noel 1995)

I began writing about a different voice when I heard what George Eliot called the "still, small voice" speaking in a different psychological register. The voice that set the dominant key in psychology, in political theory, in law and in ethics, was keyed to separation: the separate self, the individual acting alone, the possessor of natural rights, the autonomous moral agent. Because the paradigmatic human voice conveyed this sense of separation as foundational, it was difficult to hear connection without listening under the conversation.

I was listening at the time to women who were pregnant and thinking about abortion in the immediate aftermath of the *Roe v. Wade* decision. Women's concerns were often driven by experiences of disconnection which rendered relationships difficult to maintain, but their voices carried a sense of connection, of living and acting in a web of relationships which went against the grain of the prevailing discourse of individual rights and freedom. Speaking of connection, of responsiveness and responsibility in relationships, women heard themselves sounding either selfish or selfless, because the opposition of self and other was so pervasive and so powerfully voiced in the public discourse. It was as if women's experience of connection was unnatural, unhealthy, or unreal. But it was also ironic, because the Supreme Court had given women a legal voice in a matter of relationship and at the same time had framed that voice within a discourse of rights which made it impossible to speak about relationship, except in terms of justice—equality, fairness, reciprocity—or in terms of contractual obligation, neither of which had much bearing on many women's situation. In developing a different voice as a key to a new psychology and politics, I found that human voices and also relationship became more resonant and more vibrant.

On a theoretical and political level, on a personal and psychological level, this change in voice seemed essential. The existing paradigm was patriarchal; it was built on a disconnection from women which became part of the psychology of women and men. Theories of psychological and political development took this separation as foundational to the development of a sense of self, and as a result, the separate self and the selfless woman—the artifacts of a patriarchal psychology and politics—appeared natural and inevitable, necessary and good.

I come then to a crucial distinction: the difference between a feminine ethic of care and a feminist ethic of care. Care as a feminine ethic is an ethic of special obligations and interpersonal relationships. Selflessness or self-sacrifice is built into the very definition of care when caring is premised on an opposition between relationships and self-development. A feminine ethic of care is an ethic of the relational world as that world appears within a patriarchal social order: that is, as a world apart, separated politically and psychologically from a realm of individual autonomy and freedom which is the realm of justice and contractual obligation.

A feminist ethic of care begins with connection, theorized as primary and seen as fundamental in human life. People live in connection with one another; human lives are interwoven in a myriad of subtle and not so subtle ways. A feminist ethic of care reveals the disconnections in a feminine ethic of care as problems of relationship. From this standpoint, the conception of a separate self appears intrinsically problematic, conjuring up the image of rational man, acting out a relationship with the inner and outer world. Such autonomy, rather than being the bedrock for solving psychological and moral

problems itself becomes the problem, signifying a disconnection from emotions and a blindness to relationships which set the stage for psychological and political trouble. This reframing of psychology in terms of connection changes the conception of the human world; in doing so, it establishes the ground for a different philosophy, a different political theory, a change in ethics and legal theory.

From this perspective, it becomes easier to see how the disconnection of the self from relationships and the separation of the public world from the private world define a realm of human activity which can only be maintained as long as someone cares about relationships, takes care of the private world, and feels bound to other people. Historically this labor of caring has been the special obligation and unpaid labor of women, or the poorly paid labor of women who by virtue of class or caste difference are doubly excluded from the general domain of human freedom. Women living in patriarchal families, societies, and culture are bound internally and externally by obligations to care without complaint, on pain of becoming a bad woman: unfeminine, ungenerous, uncaring. Following women's psychological development, I found that for a woman to free herself from these moral strictures generally involves undoing a process of psychological dissociation and retrieving a voice that has been driven into silence. (Gilligan 1982; Gilligan, Rogers, and Noel 1992; Jack 1991; Linklater 1976) When this inner voice surfaces and comes into relationships, it sets off different vibrations and resonances. Then a discourse of relationship can replace the patriarchal construction of relationships. The tension between a relational psychology and a patriarchal social order is caught by a paradox: living within the structures of patriarchy, women find themselves giving up relationship in order to have relationships. (Gilligan 1990b; Gilligan n.d.b; Miller 1988) A feminist ethic of care became the voice of the resistance.

This brings me to my central point. Theorizing connection as primary and fundamental in human life directs attention to a growing body of supporting evidence which cannot be incorporated within the old paradigm. Studies of the infant as a member of a couple refute the depiction of the infant as locked up in egocentrism and provide compelling data showing that the desire for relationship, pleasure in connection, and the ability to make and maintain relationship are present at onset of development. Research on women and girls provides evidence of psychological capacities and relational knowledge that raises the most fundamental questions about the nature of cognitive and emotional and social development; otherwise, it would seem impossible that women and girls know what they know. These psychological studies of infants and women recast the understanding of the developmental process in relational terms; they have relied on new research methods and they demonstrate the power of a relational approach in research as well as in psychotherapy. (Murray and Trevarthen 1985; Stern 1985; Tronick 1989; Brown and Gilligan 1992; Gilligan 1982; Gilligan, Kreider, and O'Neill n.d.; Jordan et al. 1991; Miller and Stiver 1994; Relke 1993)

In *History after Lacan,* Brennan describes the ending of the ego's era. It began with the joining of the Cartesian self and capitalism in the 17th century. Brennan characterizes the separate self or the autonomous ego as a foundational fantasy which does not appear as a fantasy as long as the ego's omnipotence and control are socially constructed as reality, wrapping the imperial "I" in a cultural cocoon.

To allow that my feelings physically enter you, or yours me, to think that we both had the same thought at the same time because it was literally in the air, is to think in a way that really puts the subject in question. In some ways, the truly interesting thing is that this questioning has begun. (Brennan 1993, p. 41)

I am interested in women's relationship to this societal and cultural transformation because the history of this relationship is in danger of being buried. Listening to women's voices clarified the ethic of care, not because care is essentially associated with women or part of women's nature, but because women for a combination of psychological and political reasons voiced relational realities that were otherwise unspoken or dismissed as inconsequential. A patriarchal social order depends for its regeneration on a disconnection from women, which in women takes the form of a psychological dissociation: a process of inner division that makes it possible for a woman not to know what she knows, not to think what she thinks, not to feel what she feels. Dissociation cuts through experience and memory, and when these cuts become part of cultural history, women lose the grounds of their experience and with it, their sense of reality.

In studies of girls' psychological development, my colleagues and I have witnessed the onset of dissociative processes at adolescence. (Brown and Gilligan 1992; Gilligan, Brown, and Rogers 1990; Rogers 1993) Girls at this time face a relational crisis or developmental impasse which has its parallel in the relational crisis of boys' early childhood. Freud called this crisis the Oedipus complex and theorized it as a turning point in psychological development, marking a definitive intersection between psychological development and the requisites of civilization. The resolution of the Oedipus complex structures the connection between inner and outer worlds.

I have come to theorize a similar crisis in girls' lives at adolescence as a crisis of voice and relationship, also marking a definitive joining between psychological development and civilization. This is the time when girls are pressed from within and without to take in and take on the interpretive framework of patriarchy and to regulate their sexuality, their relationships, their desires, and their judgments in its terms. As for boys in early childhood, this internalization of a patriarchal voice leads to a loss of relationship or a compromise between voice and relationships, leaving a psychological wound or scar. The asymmetry I have posited between boys' and girls' development finds confirmation in the considerable evidence showing that boys are more psychologically at risk than girls throughout the childhood years and that girls' psychological strengths and resilience are suddenly at risk in adolescence. (see Gilligan n.d.a; Debold 1994)

Girls' initiation into womanhood has often meant an initiation into a kind of selflessness, which is associated with care and connection but also with a loss of psychological vitality and courage. To become selfless means to lose relationship or to lose one's voice in relationships. This loss of relationship leads to a muting of voice, leaving inner feelings of sadness and isolation. In effect, the young woman becomes shut up within herself.

When the release of women's voices in the 1970s put an end to this house arrest and brought the disconnection from women out into the open, women revealed the startling omission of women from psychology and from history and also discovered the extent of women's dissociation: women's ignorance of their bodies, themselves, and other women. The association of women with care became problematic for many women because when care is framed as an ethic of selflessness and self-sacrifice in relationships it enjoins these inner divisions in women and catches women in a psychological and political trap. Claiming human status, women brought themselves and their concerns about relationship into the public arena, placing high on the political agenda relationships with children, family relationships, relationships with the environment, relationships with the future as developed through education and health care, and above all, the problem of violence in domestic as well as national and international relationships. In this way, women reframed women's problems as human concerns.

Any discussion of a care ethic, then, has to begin with the issue of framing. What is the framework within which we will compare and contrast justice and care? When I hear care discussed as a matter of special obligations or as an ethic of interpersonal relationships, I hear the vestiges of patriarchy. When I listen to care versus justice debated as if there was no framework, I hear the implicit patriarchal framework silently slipping back into place.

In analyzing psychological theory and women's psychological development, I have attempted to show how a feminist ethic of care repudiates a feminine ethic of care on the grounds that a feminine ethic of care rests on a faulty notion of relationship. This fault erupts in women's lives in the form of a psychological crisis. A paradox then becomes evident: women are "doing good and feeling bad" (Miller 1976); women are silencing themselves in order to be with other people; women are giving up relationship for the sake of having relationships, and then missing themselves and missing relationship or feeling stranded in a confusing isolation which is often filled with self-condemnation. (Gilligan 1977; Gilligan 1982; Gilligan 1990b; Jack 1991; Miller 1988; Miller 1991; Stern 1991)

Hearing the difference between a patriarchal voice and a relational voice means hearing separations which have sounded natural or beneficial as disconnections which are psychologically and politically harmful. Within a relational framework, the separate self sounds like an artifact of an outmoded order: a disembodied voice speaking as if from nowhere. In the absence of relational resonances, the exposure of an inner voice is psychologically dangerous because its openness to vibrations heightens vulnerability. Hearing a relational voice as a new key for psychology and politics, I have theorized both justice and care in relational terms. Justice speaks to the disconnections which are at the root of violence, violation and oppression, or the unjust use of unequal power. Care speaks to the dissociations which lead people to abandon themselves and others: by not speaking, not listening, not knowing, not seeing, not caring, and ultimately not feeling by numbing themselves or steeling themselves against the vibrations and the resonances which characterize and connect the living world.

The talking cure or cure through relationship which Freud and Breuer discovered to be so psychologically powerful and effective finds its analogue in the public arena which Arendt saw as essential to the health of a democratic society: a place where people can come and speak freely. The antidote to psychological repression is the antidote to totalitarianism. When a relational voice sets the key for psychology, political theory, law, ethics, and philosophy, it frees the voices of women and men and also the voices of the disciplines from patriarchal strictures.

Hope is a dangerous emotion because it creates such vulnerability to disappointment, and the process of change is never straightforward. The desire for relationship may jeopardize relationships; the desire to speak will heighten vulnerability and may lead to psychological harm. The psychological knowledge that has been gained in the past quarter century provides a map for the resistance and a guide to relationship, marking the pitfalls of disconnection and dissociation. However arduous the terrain and however conflicted the journey, however strong the pulls toward repetition and return, a different voice has been heard and a new direction charted.

REFERENCES

Belenky, Mary F., Blythe Clinchy, Nancy Goldberger, and Jill M. Tarule. *Women's Ways of Knowing.* New York: Basic Books, 1986.

Bordo, Susan. *Unbearable Weight: Feminism, the Body and Western Culture.* New York: Routledge, 1994.

Brennan, Teresa. *History after Lacan.* New York: Routledge, 1993.

Brown, Lyn Mikel, and Carol Gilligan. "Listening for Voices in Narratives of Relationship." In *Narrative and Storytelling: Implications for Understanding Moral Development,* ed. M. Tappan and M. Packer. New Directions for Child Development. San Francisco: Jossey-Bass, 1991.

———. *Meeting at the Crossroads: Women's Psychology and Girls' Development.* New York: Ballantine Books, 1992.

Debold, Elizabeth. "Toward an Understanding of Gender Differences in Psychological Distress: A Foucauldian Integration of Freud, Gilligan, and Cognitive Development Theory." Qualifying Paper, Harvard Graduate School of Education. Cambridge, MA, 1994.

Freud, Sigmund, and Josef Breuer. *Studies on Hysteria.* London: Penguin Books, 1974 (orig. 1895).

Freud, Sigmund. *The Interpretation of Dreams.* London: Penguin Books, 1899/1900.

Gilligan, Carol. "In a Different Voice: Women's Conceptions of Self and Morality. *Harvard Educational Review* 47 (1977), pp. 481–517.

———. *In a Different Voice: Psychological Theory and Women's Development.* Cambridge: Harvard University Press, 1982.

———. "Teaching Shakespeare's Sister: Notes from the Underground of Female Adolescence." In *Making Connections,* ed. Gilligan, Lyons, and Hamner. Cambridge: Harvard University Press, 1990a.

———. "Joining the Resistance: Psychology, Politics, Girls and Women." *Michigan Quarterly Review* 29, no. 4 (1990b), pp. 501–36.

———. "The Centrality of Relationship in Human Development: A Puzzle, Some Evidence, and a Theory." In *Development and Vulnerability in Close Relationships,* ed. G. Noam and K. Fischer. NJ: Erlbaum, n.d.a.

———. "Remembering Iphigenia: Voice, Resonance, and a Talking Cure." In *The Inner World in the Outer World,* ed. E. Shapiro. New Haven, CT: Yale University Press, n.d.b.

Gilligan, Carol, Lyn Mikel Brown, and Annie G. Rogers. "Psyche Embedded: A Place for Body, Relationships, and Culture in Personality Theory." In *Studying Persons and Lives,* ed. Albert Rabin et al. New York: Springer, 1990.

Gilligan, Carol, Annie G. Rogers, and Deborah Tolman, eds. *Women, Girls and Psychotherapy:*

Reframing Resistance. Birmingham, NY: Haworth Press, 1991.

Gilligan, Carol, Annie G. Rogers, and Normi Noel. "Cartography of a Lost Time: Women, Girls and Relationships." Paper presented at the Lilly Conference on Youth and Caring, Daytona Beach, Florida, and at the Harvard Conference, Learning From Women, April 1993.

Gilligan, Carol, Holly Kreider, and Kate O'Neill. n.d. "Transforming Psychological Inquiry: Clarifying and Strengthening Connections." *Psychoanalytic Review.* In press.

Jack, Dana Crowley. *Silencing the Self: Depression and Women.* New York: HarperCollins, 1991.

Jordan, Judith V., Jean Baker Miller, Irene P. Stiver, and Janet Surrey. *Women's Growth in Connections.* New York: Guilford Press, 1992.

Linklater, Kristin. *Freeing the Natural Voice.* New York: Drama Book Publishers, 1976.

Miller, Jean Baker. *Toward a New Psychology of Women.* Boston: Beacon Press, 1976.

———. "The Development of Women's Sense of Self." In *Women's Growth in Connections,* ed. Jordan et al. New York: Guilford Press, 1991.

———. "Connections, Disconnections and Violations." Wellesley, MA: Stone Center Works in Progress, 1988.

Miller, Jean Baker, and Irene P. Stiver. "A Relational Reframing of Therapy." Wellesley, MA: Stone Center Works in Progress, 1994.

Murray, Lynne, and Colwyn Trevarthen. "Emotional Regulation of Interactions between Two-Month-Olds and Their Mothers." In *Social Perception in Infants,* ed. T. Field and N. Fox. NJ: Ablex, 1985.

Noel, Normi. Personal Communication, 1995.

Nussbaum, Martha C. *The Fragility of Goodness.* Cambridge, England: Cambridge University Press, 1986.

Relke, Diana M. "Foremothers Who Cared: Paula Heimann, Margaret Little and the Female Tradition in Psychoanalysis." *Feminism and Psychology* 3, no. 1 (1993), pp. 89–109.

Rogers, Annie. "Voice, Play and a Practice of Ordinary Courage in Girls' and Women's Lives." *Harvard Educational Review* 63, no. 3 (1993), pp. 265–95.

Rogers, Annie G. "Exiled Voices: Dissociation and Repression in Women's Narratives of Trauma." Wellesley, MA: Stone Center Works in progress, 1995.

Stern, Daniel. *The Interpersonal World of the Infant.* New York: Basic Books, 1985.

Stern, Lori. "Disavowing the Self in Female Adolescence." In *Women, Girls, and Psychotherapy: Reframing Resistance,* ed. Carol Gilligan et al. Birmingham, NY: Haworth Press, 1991.

Taylor, Jill McLean, Carol Gilligan, and Amy Sullivan, eds. n.d. *Holding Difference, Sustaining Hope: Women and Girls, Race and Relationship.* Cambridge: Harvard University Press. In press, n.d.

Tronick, Edward Z. "Emotions and Emotional Communication in Infants." *American Psychologist* 44, no. 2 (1989), pp. 112–9.

READING 20

Women's Culture and Lesbian Feminist Activism: A Reconsideration of Cultural Feminism

Verta Taylor and Leila J. Rupp

The rise of cultural feminism within the U.S. women's movement, according to the current feminist orthodoxy, spelled the death of radical feminism. Because cultural feminism is based on an essentialist view of the differences between women and men and advocates separatism and institution building, it has, say its critics, led feminists to retreat from politics to "life-style." Alice Echols, the most prominent critic of cultural feminism, credits Redstockings member Brooke Williams with introducing the term *cultural feminism* in 1975 to describe the depoliticization of radical feminism. (Echols 1989, p. 301) "Cultural feminism is the belief that

Verta Taylor and Leila J. Rupp, "Women's Culture and Lesbian Feminist Activism: A Reconsideration of Cultural Feminism." *Signs: Journal of Women in Culture and Society* 19, 1 (1993): 33–37 and 41–61. Copyright © 1993 by The University of Chicago Press. Reprinted with permission of the publisher and authors.

women will be freed via an alternate women's culture. It . . . has developed at the expense of feminism, even though it calls itself 'radical feminist.'" (Williams 1978, p. 79)[1] Since 1975, denunciations of cultural feminism have become commonplace. From all sides—from socialist feminists, black feminists, postmodern feminists, and especially from radical feminists who reject cultural feminism as a betrayal of their early ideas—come charges that cultural feminism represents the deradicalization and demobilization of the women's movement.[2] In Echols's words, "radical feminism was a political movement dedicated to eliminating the sex–class system, whereas cultural feminism was a countercultural movement aimed at reversing the cultural valuation of the male and the devaluation of the female." (1989, p. 6)

Implicit in most discussions of cultural feminism is the centrality of lesbianism to the process of depoliticization. The critique of cultural feminism sometimes is a disguised—and within the women's movement more acceptable—attack on lesbian feminism. By *lesbian feminism,* we mean a variety of beliefs and practices based on the core assumption that a connection exists between an erotic and/or emotional commitment to women and political resistance to patriarchal domination. Cultural feminism's three greatest "sins"—essentialism, separatism, and an emphasis on building an alternative culture—are strongly associated with the lesbian feminist communities that grew up in U.S. cities and towns in the 1970s and 1980s. Williams, herself lesbian, identified the development of cultural feminism with the growth of lesbianism; later critics have strengthened this association. Echols sees cultural feminism as growing out of lesbian feminism but modifying it, "so that male values rather than men were vilified and female bonding rather than lesbianism was valorized." (1989, p. 244) In the context of the 1980s "sex wars"— the struggle over sexual expressiveness and regulation between, on one side, feminists who emphasized the dangers of sexuality and the need to fight pornography as a form of violence against

women and, on the other side, those who stressed its pleasures—cultural feminism came to stand for an "antisex" variety of lesbian feminism.[3] Although lesbian voices are among those raised in condemnation of cultural feminism, the boundary in common usage between cultural feminism and lesbian feminism is highly permeable, if it exists at all.

Our goal here is to reposition what has been called "cultural feminism" as one tendency within dynamic and contested contemporary U.S. lesbian feminist communities. By shifting our focus from the ideology of cultural feminism to concrete social movement communities, we make explicit the central role of lesbians in what is often euphemistically called the "women's community" and we emphasize that a movement's culture is more than a formal ideological position.[4] To understand the culture of any group requires attention to the contexts in which it is produced, so we turn our gaze to the communities that give birth to "women's culture."

Lesbian feminist communities in the United States are made up of women with diverse views and experiences. They encompass "cultural feminists"—significantly, this is not a label that any women, as far as we know, apply to themselves—and their critics, as well as "antisex" and "pro-sex" feminists and separatists and antiseparatists. In contrast to critics who view lesbian feminist communities as embodying the evils of cultural feminism, we see the debate over essentialism, separatism, sexuality, and so on taking place within these communities. As Jan Clausen has pointed out, even critics of the racism and Eurocentrism of "the women's community" remain identified with it. (1992, p. 9)

Our intent is not to defend the ideological position that has been described as "cultural feminism" but to change the terms of the debate by focusing on the consequences for feminist activism of lesbian feminist culture and communities. We identify four elements of lesbian feminist culture that promote survival of the women's movement during periods of waning activity: female values, separatism, the primacy of women's relationships, and feminist ritual. The culture of lesbian feminist communities both serves as a base of mobilization for women involved in a wide range of protest activities aimed at political and institutional change and provides continuity from earlier stages of the women's movement to the future flowering of feminism. Rather than de-politicizing the radical feminist attack on the multiple roots of women's oppression, lesbian feminist communities preserve that impulse.

Our argument is shaped by historical analyses of women's culture and by theories of social movement continuity. From a historical perspective, Echols's and others' indictment of cultural feminism is curious, given that women's culture and intimate bonds between women have generally played a benevolent role in the development of the women's movement.[5] As Estelle Freedman explains in her classic article "Separatism as Strategy," the decline of the U.S. women's movement in the 1920s can be partly attributed to the devaluation of women's culture and the decline of separate women's institutions. (1979) And Blanche Cook argues persuasively that female networks of love and support were vital to women's political activism in the early 20th century. (1977) Although no monolithic women's culture has developed across lines of race, class, and ethnicity, women involved in a wide array of collective action—from food riots in immigrant neighborhoods, to labor strikes, to protests against the lynching of African-American men, to suffrage demonstrations—have shaped oppositional cultures that sustained their struggles.[6] These women were motivated by what Nancy Cott has distinguished as three forms of consciousness: feminist consciousness, female consciousness, and communal consciousness. (1989)[7] The lesbian feminist culture we explore here is such an oppositional culture.

Recent work on social movements by sociologists also points to a positive relationship between the culture of lesbian feminist communities and the persistence of feminist activism. Focusing on the 60s, scholars have documented the role that preexisting organizations and activist networks from earlier rounds of protest played in the emergence of all of the so-called new social movements such as the civil rights, student, and gay rights movements.[8] These studies illuminate the importance of studying movements in differing stages of mobilization and in various organizational forms. To conceptualize periods of the U.S. women's movement that previously have been overlooked, we draw on the concept of "abeyance stages" in social movements. (Taylor 1989b) The term *abeyance* depicts a holding process by which activists sustain protest in a hostile political climate and provide continuity from one stage of mobilization to another. Abeyance functions through organizations that allow members to build their lives around political activity. Such groups ensure the survival of a visionary core of the movement, develop a strategy or project for realizing the movement's vision, and allow activists to claim an identity that opposes the dominant order. We see lesbian feminist communities as fulfilling this function for the radical branch of the women's movement in the 1980s and early 1990s.

The argument we develop here is based on preliminary research for a larger study of lesbian feminist communities and on our own extensive participation in the Columbus, Ohio, lesbian feminist community. Although we use published movement writings, formal and informal interviews with members of various communities, and participant observation in Columbus and at national events, we see this article as less an empirical study than a conceptual piece.[9] Our perspective is, of course, shaped by our identities as white, middle-class, academic lesbians immersed in the issues we discuss. But we try to use our experience to reproduce for nonparticipants the flavor of involvement in a lesbian feminist community. Much of what we report will be familiar to other participants, even those from quite different communities. Columbus is a noncoastal but urban community where developments in New York, Washington, D.C.,

Boston, San Francisco, and Los Angeles are played out later and on a smaller scale. In that sense, Columbus both reflects national trends and typifies smaller communities that have been less studied by feminist scholars.[10]

. . .

THE CULTURE OF LESBIAN FEMINIST COMMUNITIES

Lesbian feminist communities do show signs of the essentialism, separatism, and "life-style politics" that cultural feminism's critics view as anathema to radical feminism. But a closer examination of the ideas, separatist strategies, primary relationships, and symbolic practices of community members reveals that these elements of lesbian feminist culture are what sustain and nourish feminist activism.

Female Values

The question of whether women are fundamentally different from men is central throughout the women's movement. Although a variety of individuals and groups assert the existence of "female values," this position is closely associated with contemporary lesbian feminists, who are more forthright than earlier feminists in proclaiming the superiority of women's values over men's. This is also the aspect of cultural feminism that is most disputed, in part because the notion of universal female values sits uneasily with the recognition of differences among women.

Critics of cultural feminism denounce belief in female values as essentialist, that is, based on biological determinism. According to Linda Alcoff, "cultural feminism is the ideology of a female nature or female essence reappropriated by feminists in an effort to revalidate undervalued female attributes." (1988, p. 408) Some lesbian feminists do see female values as linked to women's biological capacity to reproduce, but others take a social constructionist position and attribute differences between female and male values to differences in women's and men's so-

cialization and prescribed roles. Explanations aside, belief in fundamental differences between female and male values permeates lesbian feminist communities. Indeed, this emphasis on difference serves to justify the existence of a "women's community."

Lesbian feminists find support for the belief in female values in a large body of scholarly and popular writing that valorizes egalitarianism, collectivism, an ethic of care, respect for knowledge derived from experience, pacifism, and cooperation as female traits. In contrast, an emphasis on hierarchy, oppressive individualism, an ethic of individual rights, abstraction, violence, and competition are denounced as male. Not all such works are written by lesbian women or by women who would identify with the lesbian feminist community, but they set forth positions embraced by lesbian feminists.[11]

On one end of the female values continuum lies Mary Daly's later work, which dismisses men as death-dealing necrophiliacs draining female energy, both figuratively and literally, in order to stay alive. (Daly 1978, 1984; Daly and Caputi 1987) Audre Lorde, in an open letter to Daly, criticizes what she sees as Daly's assumption that all women suffer the same oppression and calls for recognition of the creative function of differences among women. (Lorde 1984a) In a spoof of arguments such as Daly's, Margot Sims's *On the Necessity of Bestializing the Human Female* purports to prove that women and men belong to different species. (1982) The biological underpinnings of Daly's work, or of Adrienne Rich's early work on motherhood, fuel the charge of essentialism hurled by cultural feminism's critics. (Rich 1976)

But an essentialist view of female values is only one perspective. To move to the other end of the continuum, Patricia Hill Collins, whose work is influential in the academic sector of the lesbian feminist community, draws parallels between the standpoints of African-American and white feminists, suggesting that both share values that are different from, and superior to, those of the dominant white male culture. (1989, 1990) Although this is a social constructionist argument, to critics of cultural feminism it might still smack of an unwarranted emphasis on difference between women and men, or at least between women and white men.

Exposed to these intellectual debates through books, periodicals, and women's studies classes, lesbian feminists often find support for their belief in superior female values. As one community member explained, "We've been acculturated into two cultures, the male and the female culture. And luckily we've been able to preserve the ways of nurturing by being in this alternative culture."[12] Even women who intellectually reject the notion of male and female difference are apt to use *male* as a term of derision. It is common in the Columbus community to hear everything from controlling and aggressive behavior to impersonal relationships and hierarchical organizational structures characterized in casual conversation as "male." Our point here is that while most lesbian feminists do not embrace biological explanations of sex differences, such drawing of boundaries between male and female values promotes the kind of oppositional consciousness necessary for organizing one's life around feminism.

Separatism

Lesbian feminist communities advocate both separatism as strategy and separatism as goal, but it is total separation from men as an end in itself that has proven most controversial and that has given the impression that radical feminism has evolved into a politics of identity.[13] Some groups have attempted to withdraw from all aspects of male control by forming rural self-sufficient communes, but these are the exception. Sally Gearhart glorifies such communities in her popular fiction, which portrays separatist communities of women fighting the death-dealing patriarchy with extraordinary and distinctively female mental and physical powers. (1978, 1991) Critics of such total separatism point to the race and class bias inherent in the assumption that women want to and can separate from men in this way. (Jaggar 1983; hooks 1984)

In general, however, the lesbian feminist community endorses temporally and spatially limited separatism. The Columbus Women's Action Collective statement of philosophy asserted plainly that "the work of the women's movement must be done by women. Our own growth can only be fostered by solving our problems among women."[14] Often men, and even male children over a very young age, are explicitly excluded from participation in groups and events. Some early lesbian feminist communes included male children but barred them from decision making and social events on the grounds that "male energy" violates women's space.[15] This tradition continues at the annual Michigan Womyn's Music Festival in Hart, Michigan, where male children over the age of three are not permitted in the festival area but must stay at a separate camp. Men were not permitted to attend any sessions at the National Lesbian Conference in Atlanta in 1991. (Stevens 1991) In Columbus, the annual Take Back the Night march welcomes men at the kickoff rally but permits only women to march, a source of ongoing controversy. Supporters of this policy maintain that women gain a liberating sense of power specifically from separating from men for the march, reclaiming the right to walk the streets at night with no vestiges of male "protection."

The importance of such limited separatism is asserted even by critics of total separation from men and boys. Lesbian women of color, working-class lesbian women, and Jewish lesbian women with an interest in working politically within their own racial, class, and ethnic communities argue for separate space to organize and express solidarity apart both from men and from lesbian women who are white or middle-class or Christian.[16] The very structure of the National Women's Studies Association embodies separatism as strategy: caucuses for women of color, lesbian women, Jewish women, and working-class and poor women reflect women's different and competing interests. The need for this kind of organizing within the lesbian feminist community was illustrated at the National Lesbian Conference in Atlanta, at which women of color caucused separately in an attempt to make the conference deal more directly with issues of racism. (Sharon, Elliott, and Latham 1991) Separatism in the lesbian feminist community has come to mean organizing around one's identity.

Separately organized caucuses or groups may, then, work politically with women of different interests or with men. Although some lesbian feminist groups, especially in the early years of the community, refused to work at all with heterosexual women, coalitions across the lines of both sexual identity and gender are increasingly common. Barbara Epstein argues that lesbian feminists have played a significant role in mixed-gender nonviolent direct action since the mid-1970s because the lesbian feminist movement has matured and succeeded in creating space for lesbianism within the broader radical community. (1991)[17] Many participants in lesbian communities consider the women's movement their primary allegiance but work actively in movements for gay and lesbian rights, AIDS education and advocacy, Latin American solidarity, environmental causes, peace, animal rights, reproductive freedom, and labor unions, and movements against racism, apartheid, and nuclear weapons. Nevertheless, separatist events and caucuses remain important for women who are disenchanted with the politics of the mainstream; separatism is a means of both drawing sustenance and maintaining feminist identity.

The Primacy of Women's Relationships

Lesbian feminist communities view heterosexuality as an institution of patriarchal control and lesbian relationships as a means of subverting male domination. Relationships between women are considered not only personal affairs but also political acts, as captured in the often-repeated slogan, "Feminism is the theory and lesbianism is the practice."[18] The statement of philosophy of the Columbus Women's Action Collective, for example, defined lesbianism as a challenge to male domination.[19] It was no accident that the coming out of a large number of radical feminists in Columbus coincided with the founding of the Women's Action Collective and Women Against Rape. That lesbian women were central in the antirape movement undoubtedly shaped the feminist analysis of rape as an act representing one end of the continuum of what Susan Cavin calls "heterosex." (1985)

For some community members, lesbianism is defined by overriding identification with women and by resistance to patriarchy rather than by sexual attraction to or involvement with women. As one woman put it, lesbianism is "an attempt to stop doing what you were taught—hating women."[20] Rich's classic article "Compulsory Heterosexuality and Lesbian Existence" introduced the notion of the "lesbian continuum," which embraces women who resist male control but are not sexual with women. (1980) Earlier writers had also accepted what were originally known in the movement as "political lesbians." Ti-Grace Atkinson, for example, denounced married women who engaged in sexual relations with women as "collaborators" and praised women who had never had sex with women but who lived a total commitment to the women's movement as "lesbians in the political sense." (1973, p. 12) More recently, Marilyn Frye, in an address to the 1990 National Women's Studies Association conference titled "Do You Have to Be a Lesbian to Be a Feminist?" equated lesbianism with rebellion against patriarchal institutions. Frye was willing to imagine truly radical feminist women—what she called "Virgins" in the archaic sense of autonomous women—in erotic relationships with men, but she insisted that they would be exceptional. (1990)

Lesbian feminist communities indeed include some women who are oriented toward women emotionally and politically but not sexually; they are sometimes referred to as "political dykes" or "heterodykes." (Clausen 1990; Smeller 1992; Bart 1993) Some are women in the process of coming out, and some are "going in," or moving from lesbian to heterosexual relationships. For example, singer and political activist Holly Near explains in her autobiography that she continues to call herself lesbian even though she is sometimes heterosexually active because of the importance of lesbian feminism as a political identity. (1990) In the same vein, a feminist support group sprang up in 1989 at Ohio State University for "Lesbians Who Just Happen to Be in Relationships with Politically Correct Men." What is significant is that lesbian identity is so salient to involvement in the women's community that even women who are not, or no longer, involved sexually with women claim such an identity.

Most lesbians are, of course, erotically attracted to other women, and a strong current within the community criticizes those who downplay sexuality. The popularity of lesbian sex expert JoAnn Loulan, who spoke to a large and enthusiastic audience in Columbus in 1991, signals that the erotic aspects of lesbian relationships have not been completely submerged. (Loulan 1990) The "sex wars" of the early 1980s have spawned feminist community. (Stein 1989; Echols 1991) Advocates of sexual expressiveness, including champions of "butch–femme" roles and sadomasochism (S/M), challenge the less sexual style of what S/M practitioners call "vanilla lesbians" and denounce any notion of "politically correct" sex (see, e.g., Califia 1981; Dimen 1984). The lines are explicitly drawn by the very titles of the periodicals associated with each camp: *off our backs,* the classic radical feminist newspaper, now confronts the magazine *On Our Backs* with its sexual "bad girl" style. But the role of politics in structuring relationships is undisputed, even for those who emphasize sexual pleasure over the use of (hetero)sexuality as a means of social control of women. The defense of S/M, for example, argues the superi-

ority of sexual interactions and relationships that explicitly play with power. (Califia 1979, 1980; Samois 1979)[21]

In other words, the lesbian feminist community incudes both women who emphasize relationships between women as a form of political resistance and women who stress the sexual pleasures of lesbianism. The sex wars are fought within the community over who best deserves the label "feminist." Although advocates of lesbian S/M and associated sexual practices experience exclusion from some community events, the nature of lesbian sexuality is contested openly at community conferences and in movement publications. (Califia 1981) Even smaller communities have been affected by the national debate. In Columbus, when a gay bar placed ads featuring S/M imagery in a local gay/lesbian publication, lesbian members of Columbus's women's S/M group, Briar Rose, came to blows, metaphorically, with antipornography lesbian feminists offended by the depiction of what they perceived as violence.[22]

Although lesbian feminist communities are riven by conflict over the nature and proper expression of lesbian sexuality, relationships hold communities together. Highly committed activists tend to form partnerships with each other because, as one women noted, otherwise "there's too much political conflict."[23] Political organizing, meetings, and conferences become occasions for meeting potential lovers or for spending time with a partner. Even an academic women's studies conference can provide a safe place to show affection in public. Women's relationships often structure their entire social worlds. Within the community, lesbian couples or groups of single and paired lesbian women construct family-like ties with one another, together celebrating holidays, birthdays, commitment ceremonies, births, and anniversaries. Former lovers are often part of lesbian networks, at least in smaller communities like Columbus. In contrast to the New Left in the 1960s, where women no longer in relationships with male leaders often found themselves marginalized in the movement, lesbian feminists' tendency to remain friends with their ex-lovers provides stability in the lesbian world. (Pearlman 1987; Epstein 1991, pp. 181–2)

Lesbian feminist communities make explicit—and sexual—the ties that bind women. The contemporary antifeminist charge that one "has to be a lesbian to be a feminist" is in an odd way an acknowledgment of the central role that lesbians play in the contemporary women's movement and that women with primary bonds to other women played in earlier stages of feminism.[24] It is no coincidence that self-identified "gay women" who reject the label "lesbian" often associate it with feminism and political activism.[25] Women's relationships are especially crucial to the maintenance of the women's movement when mass support for feminism ebbs; such bonds tie together groups of women who are unlikely to find acceptance for their relationships outside the movement. Furthermore, lesbian feminist communities provide fertile ground for recruiting young lesbian women into feminism. Thus, the relationship between activism and woman-bonding (lesbian or otherwise) is a symbiotic one: women with primary commitments to other women find support within the women's movement and, in turn, pour their energies into it.

Feminist Ritual

Among lesbian feminists, both public and private rituals are important vehicles for constructing feminist models of community and expressing new conceptions of gender. Public rituals are local or national cultural events such as concerts, films, poetry readings, exhibitions, plays, and conferences. Most prominent nationally is the annual Michigan Womyn's Music Festival, a five-day celebration that attracts several thousand women for musical performances, workshops, support groups, political strategy sessions, "healing circles," and the sale of woman-made crafts,

clothing, and other goods. The National Women's Studies Association (NWSA) conference is another annual cultural event; it goes far beyond the usual parameters of an academic conference by providing a forum for feminist performances and by featuring open and often highly charged debate over issues central to the women's movement.[26] Dozens of specialized national and regional conferences and festivals take place each year. Other local events, such as antiviolence marches and pro-choice rallies, occur in much the same way in different communities. Publicity in national publications and participation in national demonstrations foster a common culture of protest across the country; chants and songs, for example, spread from one community to another. Lesbian feminist events in Columbus mirror those in both larger and smaller communities. The Women's Action Collective for many years sponsored an annual Famous Feminist Day to raise money and educate the community about feminist foremothers; Stonewall Union or Women's Outreach to Women bring nationally known performers to town (as the Women's Music Union did until 1990); the Lesbian Business Association puts on an annual Ohio Lesbian Festival; and Take Back the Night continues to sponsor an annual march and rally.

What is known among contemporary feminists as "women's culture"—women's music, literature, and art—plays a central role in recruiting women and raising their feminist consciousness.[27] Musicians such as Meg Christian, Near, and Sweet Honey in the Rock, as well as dozens of other feminist performers, have introduced issues as well as songs to communities across the country. For example, in Columbus as in other areas, Near introduced the lesbian feminist community to sign language interpretation of concerts. Now no feminist—or even mainstream—event is without such interpretation for the hearing impaired. Likewise, Christian brought discussion of alcoholism and the recovery movement to the Columbus community by performing such songs as "Turning It Over" and talking of the Alcoholism Center for Women in Los Angeles. And Sweet Honey in the Rock exposed Columbus audiences composed primarily of white women to an Afrocentric perspective and African-American history and culture. Women in local communities read many of the same lesbian novels and poetry and listen to the same music. At the 1979 gay/lesbian march in Washington, women at the rally joined in to sing and sign when lesbian performers came on stage, while gay men in the crowd, lacking such unifying rituals, seemed to wonder how all of the women knew the words.

Private ritual or the politicization of everyday life is, in many respects, the hallmark of the lesbian feminist community and the most damning aspect of cultural feminism in the eyes of its critics. Through the tenet that "the personal is political," every aspect of life—where one lives, what one eats, how one dresses—can become an expression of politics. (Hanisch 1978) The sale at feminist bookstores, conferences, concerts, and festivals of feminist T-shirts, jewelry (especially labryses), books, music, and bumper stickers means that women can adorn and surround themselves with their politics.

The most significant displays challenge conventional standards of gender behavior that subordinate women. In the early years of lesbian feminism, comfortable, practical, less "feminine" styles of dress, unshaved legs and armpits, and extremely short hair were de rigueur. Although flannel shirts, jeans, and boots are no longer a uniform, the dominant mode of presentation is still unisex or what Holly Devor has termed a deliberate "gender blending." (1989) In the Columbus community, attire at cultural events has changed markedly over the past 15 years. What was once a fairly monolithic crowd has become more diverse. Although most women remain "gender blended," some appear in leather and mohawks and some in skirts, lipstick, and long hair. At one feminist event, billed as "Girls Just Want to

Have Fun," members of the community participated in a fashion show, albeit one that included political commentary on style. The use of the term *girls* (previously anathema), the emphasis on fun rather than serious politics, the reference to a mainstream popular song (Cyndi Lauper's "Girls Just Want to Have Fun") rather than women's music, and attention to clothing, including traditional women's attire, all marked this event as a new departure for the community.

Such changes in self-presentation are in part a consequence of the sex wars and in part an expression of the preferences of working-class women, women of color, and young women. "Antifeminine" styles associated with the downplaying of sexuality are under attack from advocates of sexual expressiveness who sometimes adopt fashions associated with the sex trade. (Stein 1989) "Pro-sex" lesbian feminists sport high-heeled shoes, short skirts, low-cut tops, and other items of clothing denounced by "antisex" lesbian feminists as the paraphernalia of oppression. In addition, some working-class women and women of color criticize the "politically correct" styles of the dominant faction as an imperialist imposition of white, middle-class standards. And young lesbian feminist women have brought their own ideas on fashion and self-presentation, including the grunge and punk styles, to the community.

The intensity of the debate over cultural expression is an indication of the significance of ritual for distinguishing who is and is not a feminist—just as lesbian women historically have developed cultural codes to identify one another while remaining "hidden" to the mainstream culture that stigmatized them (see, e.g., Faderman 1991). Feminist ritual reaffirms commitment to the community and openly embraces resistance to the dominant society. Thus, what Echols and other critics of cultural feminism have denounced as a "profoundly individualistic" retreat to lifestyle has political consequences. (Echols 1989, p. 251)

CONCLUSION: THE POLITICAL FUNCTIONS OF LESBIAN FEMINIST COMMUNITIES

Our reconsideration of cultural feminism in the context of lesbian feminist communities suggests a number of interpretations that run counter to the standard view. First, cultural feminism, as it has been defined by its critics, represents just one ideological position within lesbian feminist communities. Second, these communities have forged a rich and complex resistance culture and style of politics that nourishes rather than betrays the radical feminist vision. Third, the dynamics of lesbian feminist communities are shaped at least in part by the politics of the Right that dominated the period of abeyance or maintenance in which the women's movement found itself in the 1980s. And, finally, the lesbian feminist community intersects with many contemporary struggles for political and institutional change and carries a feminist legacy that will shape the future of the women's movement itself.

In our earlier collaborative work on the U.S. women's rights movement in the period from 1945 to the 1960s, we argued that a small group of white, well-educated, economically privileged old women, primarily recruited to the women's movement during the suffrage struggle, greatly influenced the resurgent liberal branch of the women's movement. We showed that the women's rights movement that hung on in the doldrum years provided activist networks, the ultimately unifying goal of the Equal Rights Amendment, and a feminist identity that maintained a focus on women's subordination. Yet this group of committed feminists sustained their vision in a homogeneous community that did not and could not attract women of color, working-class women, or young women. Although the women's movement that blossomed in the 1960s differed in fundamental ways from the more limited women's rights movement that preceded it, the legacy, both positive and negative, of that early activism lingered. (Rupp and Taylor 1987)

In the same way, lesbian feminist communities both sustain the women involved in them now and also have consequences for the next round of mass feminist activism. Perhaps a new wave of the women's movement is already taking shape; witness the groundswell of outrage at Anita Hill's treatment in the U.S. Senate confirmation hearings for Supreme Court Justice Clarence Thomas in October 1991 and the huge turnout for the pro-choice march on Washington, D.C., in April 1992. Since the presidential election of 1992 and the passage of antigay/lesbian legislation in Colorado, the National Organization for Women has decided to make lesbian and gay rights a priority in the 1990s.[28]

Our discussion of the culture of lesbian feminist communities has emphasized how belief in female difference, the practice of limited or total separatism, belief in the primacy of women's relationships, and the practice of feminist ritual create a world apart from the mainstream in which women can claim feminism as a political identity. At the same time, of course, the ideas and practices of lesbian feminist communities can exclude potential participants. Most heterosexual feminists may not find the lesbian world congenial. The association of feminism and lesbianism, as several scholars have found, alienates some young heterosexual women from feminist identification.[29] Our experience suggests that there is, even among older women, a widespread sense of the "lesbianization" of the women's movement. The revelation by Patricia Ireland, president of the National Organization for Women, that she lives with a "female companion" undoubtedly reinforced that perception. (Minkowitz 1992) One feminist quoted in the *Washington Post* commented on the public view of NOW as "a gay front group." (*off our backs* 1992a) Participants at the 1992 NOW conference report that it had the feel of a lesbian conference.[30] The 1992 Bloomington (Indiana) Women's Music Festival offered a workshop on "Networking for Straight Women in a Lesbian World."[31] At the local level, one lesbian-affirming heterosexual Columbus woman went to a local NOW meeting with a profeminist male friend involved in a men against rape group and reported feeling completely unwelcome because of her association with a man.[32] Equally as important, the dominance of white, middle-class, Christian women creates barriers to the achievement of a truly multicultural lesbian feminist community despite the ongoing community dialogue about race, class, ethnic, and other differences. As Judit Moschkovich, a Jewish Latina, put it, the assumption that she should reject her Latin culture means accepting "the American culture of French Fries and Hamburgers (or soyburgers), American music on the radio (even if it's American women's music on a feminist radio show), not kissing and hugging every time you greet someone." (Moschkovich 1981)

Our point is not that the lesbian feminist community is a pure expression of radical feminism. Rather, we want to highlight its political and transformative functions. A wide variety of struggles have been influenced by the involvement of lesbian feminists or by ideas and practices characteristic of the community. (Whittier 1991, esp. chap. 7) Direct action movements concerned with peace and other issues have adopted from the lesbian feminist community a view of revolution as an ongoing process of personal and social transformation, an emphasis on egalitarianism and consensus decision making, an orientation toward spirituality, and a commitment to shaping present action according to the values desired in an ideal future world. (Epstein 1991; *off our backs* 1992b) Similarly, the ongoing dialogue in the lesbian feminist community about diversity has carried over into the gay/lesbian movement, and the radical feminist analysis of rape shapes the struggle against antigay/lesbian violence. (Vaid 1991) Further, the AIDS movement has been driven by the radical feminist definition of control of one's body and access to health care as political issues. (Hamil-

ton 1991) Lesbians also have played a leading role in the development of the recovery movement for survivors of incest. (Galst 1991) In short, lesbian feminist cultures of resistance have had political impact not only by sheltering battle-weary feminists but also by influencing the course of other social movements.

Finally, lesbian feminist communities affect a younger generation of women who hold the future of the women's movement in their hands. In our research on women's rights activists of the 1940s and 1950s, we found these women longing for "young blood" but unwilling to accept the new ideas and new strategies that young women brought with them. (Rupp and Taylor 1987) An aging generation of activists may always long for fresh recruits who will be drawn to their cause but will not change anything about their movement; such an inclination, in part, lies behind the cultural clash between Meg Christian fans and Madonna devotees within the lesbian feminist community. (Echols 1991; Yollin 1991; Starr 1992; Stein 1993) The next round of the women's movement is likely to take a different course, but it will not be untouched by the collective processes, consciousness, and practices of lesbian feminism. One of the major mechanisms of transmittal is women's studies, which mobilizes young women who identify as feminists. (Dill 1991; Houppert 1991; Kamen 1991)

. . .

In the climate of the 1980s and early 1990s, then, the culture of lesbian feminist communities has not just served to comfort, protect, and console activists in retreat. It also has nourished women involved in myriad protests, both within and outside the women's movement, whose vision of feminist transformation goes beyond political and economic structures to a broad redefinition of social values. Rather than squelching mobilization, we see lesbian feminist communities as sustaining the radical feminist tradition and bequeathing a legacy, however imperfect, to feminists of the future.

NOTES

1. Redstockings was a radical feminist action group founded in New York City in 1969. On cultural feminism versus radical feminism, see also Echols 1983a, 1983b, 1984.

2. For a critique of total separatism from a socialist feminist perspective, see Jaggar 1983; for a black feminist critique of the race and class bias of cultural feminism, see hooks 1984; for postmodern critiques, see Alcoff 1988—juxtaposing the cultural feminist and poststructuralist answers to the problem of defining the category of women—and Young 1990—rejecting the ideal of "community" as unable to encompass difference. For attacks on cultural feminism as a betrayal of radical feminism, from a radical feminist perspective, see Atkinson 1984; Willis 1984; and Ringelheim 1985. Other commentaries on cultural feminism can be found in Eisenstein 1983 (she does not use the term *cultural feminism* but warns of reactionary tendencies in what she calls "the new essentialism" [p. xvii]); Donovan 1985 (she traces cultural feminism to its 19th-century roots); and Buechler 1990 (he identifies cultural feminism as a variant of radical feminism).

3. The "sex wars" became a national issue after the 1982 "Scholar and the Feminist IX" conference at Barnard College, New York City. The conference, which focused on women's sexual autonomy, choice, and pleasure, included speakers who advocated sadomasochism, sexual role-playing, and pornography, provoking an attack by Women against Pornography, Women against Violence against Women, and New York Radical Feminists. See the discussion and bibliography in Vance 1984, pp. 441–53; and see Segal and McIntosh 1993. The two major feminist anthologies associated with the "pro-sex" position (Snitow, Stansell, and Thompson 1983; Vance 1984) both included essays by Alice Echols in which she looked critically at the development of cultural feminism; see Echols 1983b, 1984. See also Echols 1991.

4. Our thinking on movement culture is influenced by Rick Fantasia's study of emergent cultures of resistance within the labor movement. (1988)

5. The basic positions on the nature of women's culture and its relationship to feminism are clearly stated in an exchange between Ellen DuBois and Carroll Smith-Rosenberg. (DuBois et al. 1980) DuBois defines women's culture as "the broad-based commonality of values, institutions, relationships, and methods of communication, focused on domesticity and morality and particular to late 18th- and 19th-century women." (p. 29) For her, women's culture and feminism stand in a dialectical relationship. In contrast, Smith-Rosenberg questions the use of the term *women's culture* to describe the acceptance of mainstream cultural values and insists that a culture must have "its own autonomous values, identities, symbolic systems, and modes of communication." (p. 58) Eschewing the word *culture,* she argues that feminism cannot develop outside a "female world" in which women create rituals and networks, form primary ties with other women, and develop their own worldview. (p. 61)

6. Scholars of African-American and working-class women, in particular, have rejected the notion of a universal women's culture. But their evidence suggests that various groups of women—enslaved African-American women, mill workers, and working-class housewives—did create "women's cultures," albeit multiple ones that often supported men of their groups. See Hewitt 1985. See Pascoe 1990 for a recent work that attacks the idea that there is a women's culture based on women's values.

7. Feminist consciousness involves a critique of male supremacy, the will to change it, and the belief that change is possible. (Cott 1989 draws on Gordon 1986, p. 29, in defining feminist consciousness.) Female consciousness, which Cott bases on Kaplan's (1982) exploration of working-class food protests and strikes, is rooted in women's acceptance of the division of labor by sex. Communal consciousness is based on solidarity with men of the same group. Feminist consciousness is necessarily oppositional, while female and communal consciousness can support the status quo or can lead women to engage in a variety of kinds of protest.

8. For a discussion of "new social movements," see Klandermans and Tarrow 1988. On the civil rights movement, see Morris 1984; McAdam 1988. On the New Left, see Gittlin 1987; Isserman 1987; Whalen and Flacks 1987; and Hayden 1988. On the gay rights movement, see D'Emilio 1983.

9. Written sources include books, periodicals, and narratives by community members, and newsletters, position papers, and other documents from lesbian feminist organizations. We also have made use of 21 in-depth, open-ended interviews with informants from Provincetown, Boston, and the rural Berkshire region of western Massachusetts; Portland, Maine; Washington, D.C.; New York City; St. Petersburg, Fla.; Columbus, Yellow Springs, Cleveland, and Cincinnati, Ohio; Minneapolis; Chicago; Denver; and Atlanta, conducted between 1987 and 1989, mostly by Nancy E. Whittier (1988) but also by Verta Taylor (Taylor and Whittier 1992). In addition, we have both been a part of the lesbian feminist community in Columbus since the late 1970s, have attended national events such as conferences, cultural events, and marches in Washington, D.C., and have over the past 15 years interviewed informally lesbian feminists in a variety of communities across the country. All of these interviews were conducted with the understanding that quotations would not be attributed to named individuals.

10. Columbus is the largest city in Ohio, the state capital, and the home of the largest university campus in the country, Ohio State University. The lesbian feminist community is overwhelmingly, although not exclusively, white and middle class, with a large proportion of students and professionals. Most scholarship on the women's movement focuses on developments in large cities. See, e.g., Freeman 1975; Cassell 1977; Wolf 1979; Echols 1989; Staggenborg 1991; Ryan 1992. A notable exception is Krieger 1983.

11. See, e.g., Walker 1974; Rich 1976; Chodorow 1978; Daly 1978, 1984; Dworkin 1981; Gilligan 1982; Cavin 1985; Johnson 1987; MacKinnon 1987.

12. Interview conducted by Nancy Whittier, August 1987, Stockbridge, Mass.

13. On separatism, see Frye 1983; Hoagland and Penelope 1988.

14. Women's Action collective "Statement of Philosophy," adopted by consensus May 21, 1974, in the personal papers of Teri Wehausen, Columbus, Ohio.

15. Interview conducted by Verta Taylor, April 1989, Columbus, Ohio.

16. See, for a variety of perspectives, Beck 1980; Moraga and Anzaldúa 1981; Hull, Scott, and Smith 1982; Smith 1983; Bulkin, Pratt, and Smith 1984; Lorde 1984a, 1984b; Anzaldúa 1990; Trujillo 1991.

17. See also Cavin 1990; Whittier 1991; and Gorman 1992.

18. This statement is attributed to Ti-Grace Atkinson in Koedt 1973. Echols points out that Sidney Abbott and Barbara Love record the original version of this remark quite differently: in 1970, Atkinson addressed the lesbian group Daughters of Bilitis in New York and commented that "Feminism is a theory; but Lesbianism is a practice." (Abbott and Love 1972, p. 117; Echols 1989, p. 238) In any case, the phrase has been widely quoted within lesbian feminist communities.

19. Women's Action Collective "Statement of Philosophy."

20. Interview conducted by Nancy Whittier, September 1987, Washington, D.C.

21. For the opposing position, see Linden et al. 1982.

22. Interview conducted by Leila Rupp, May 1992, Columbus, Ohio.

23. Interview conducted by Verta Taylor, May 1987, Columbus, Ohio.

24. See Faderman 1981, 1991; Rupp 1989a, 1989b; Lützen 1990.

25. Interviews conducted by Verta Taylor and Leila Rupp, April 1992, Columbus, Ohio.

26. The issue of racism within the organization blew apart the twelfth annual NWSA conference, "Feminist Education: Calling the Question," held in Akron, Ohio, June 20–24, 1990. See Ruby, Elliott, and Douglas 1990.

27. Zimmerman 1990 analyzes the impact of lesbian fiction on the development of the lesbian community.

28. Communication from Jo Reger, Columbus, Ohio, 1992.

29. See Schneider 1986, 1988; Dill 1989; Kamen 1991.

30. Interview conducted by Verta Taylor and Leila Rupp, February 1992, Columbus, Ohio.

31. Communication from Suzanne Staggenborg, Bloomington, Ind., 1992.

32. Interview conducted by Verta Taylor, May 1992, Columbus, Ohio.

REFERENCES

Abbott, Sidney, and Barbara Love. *Sappho Was a Right-on Woman: A Liberated View of Lesbianism.* New York: Stein & Day, 1972.

Alcoff, Linda. "Cultural Feminism versus Post-Structuralism: The Identity Crisis in Feminist Theory." *Signs: Journal of Women in Culture and Society* 13, no. 3 (1988), pp. 405–36.

Anzaldúa, Gloria. *Making Face, Making Soul— Haciendo Caras: Creative and Critical Perspectives by Women of Color.* San Francisco: Aunt Lute, 1990.

Atkinson, Ti-Grace. "Lesbianism and Feminism." In *Amazon Expedition: A Lesbian Feminist Anthology,* ed. Phyllis Birkby et al. New York: Times Change Press, 1973, pp. 11–4.

———. "Le nationalisme feminin." *Nouvelles-questions feministes* 6–7 (1984), pp. 35–54.

Bart, Pauline B. "Protean Woman: The Liquidity of Female Sexuality and the Tenaciousness of Lesbian Identity." In *Heterosexuality: A Feminism and Psychology Reader,* ed. Sue Wilkinson and Celia Kitzinger. London: Sage, 1993, pp. 246–52.

Beck, Evelyn Torton. *Nice Jewish Girls: A Lesbian Anthology.* Watertown, MA: Persephone, 1980.

Buechler, Steven M. *Women's Movements in the United States.* New Brunswick, NJ: Rutgers University Press, 1990.

Bulkin, Elly, Minnie Bruce Pratt, and Barbara Smith. *Yours in Struggle: Three Feminist Perspectives on Anti-Semitism and Racism.* Brooklyn, NY: Long Haul Press, 1984.

Califia, Pat. "A Secret Side of Lesbian Sexuality." *Advocate,* December 27, 1979, pp. 19–23.

———. *Sapphistry: The Book of Lesbian Sexuality.* Tallahassee, FL: Naiad, 1980.

———. "Feminism and Sadomasochism." *Heresies* 12 (1981), pp. 30–4.

Cassell, Joan. *A Group Called Women: Sisterhood and Symbolism in the Feminist Movement.* New York: McKay, 1977.

Cavin, Susan. *Lesbian Origins.* San Francisco: Ism Press, 1985.

———. "The Invisible Army of Women: Lesbian Social Protests, 1969–1988." In *Women and Social Protest,* ed. Guida West and Rhoda Lois Blumberg. New York: Oxford University Press, 1990, pp. 321–32.

Chodorow, Nancy. *The Reproduction of Mothering: Psychoanalysis and the Sociology of Gender.* Berkeley: University of California Press, 1978.

Clausen, Jan. "My Interesting Condition." *Outlook* 7 (Winter 1990), pp. 10–21.

———. "A Craving for Community." *Women's Review of Books* 9 (March 1992), pp. 8–9.

Collins, Patricia Hill. "The Social Construction of Black Feminist Thought." *Signs: Journal of Women in Culture and Society* 14, no. 4 (1989), pp. 745–73.

———. *Black Feminist Thought: Knowledge, Consciousness, and the Politics of Empowerment.* Boston: Unwin Hyman, 1990.

Cook, Blanche Wiesen. "Female Support Networks and Political Activism: Lillian Wald, Crystal Eastman, Emma Goldman." *Chrysalis* 3 (1977), pp. 43–61.

Cott, Nancy F. "What's in a Name? The Limits of 'Social Feminism'; or, Expanding the Vocabulary of Women's History." *Journal of American History* 76, no. 3 (1989), pp. 809–29.

Daly, Mary. *Gyn-Ecology: The Metaethics of Radical Feminism.* Boston: Beacon, 1978.

———. *Pure Lust: Elemental Feminist Philosophy.* Boston: Beacon, 1984.

Daly, Mary, in cahoots with Jane Caputi. *Websters' First New Intergalactic Wickedary of the English Language.* Boston: Beacon, 1987.

D'Emilio, John. *Sexual Politics, Sexual Communities: The Making of a Homosexual Minority in the U.S., 1940–1970.* Chicago: University of Chicago Press, 1983.

Devor, Holly. *Gender Blending: Confronting the Limits of Duality.* Bloomington: Indiana University Press, 1989.

Dill, Kim. "Qualified Feminism and Its Influence on College Women's Identification with the Women's Movement." Unpublished manuscript, Columbus, OH, 1989.

———. "Feminism in the Nineties: The Influence of Collective Identity and Community on Young Feminist Activists." M.A. thesis, Ohio State University, 1991.

Dimen, Muriel. "Politically Correct? Politically Incorrect?" In Vance 1984, pp. 138–48.

Donovan, Josephine. *Feminist Theory: The Intellectual Traditions of American Feminism.* New York: Ungar, 1985.

DuBois, Ellen, Mari Jo Buhle, Temma Kaplan, Gerda Lerner, and Carroll Smith-Rosenberg. "Politics and Culture in Women's History." *Feminist Studies* 6, no. 1 (1980), pp. 26–64.

Dworkin, Andrea. *Pornography: Men Possessing Women.* New York: Perigee, 1981.

"Dyke Manifesto." Flyer handed out at the March on Washington for Lesbian, Gay, and Bisexual Rights and Liberation, April 25, 1993, in possession of the authors.

Echols, Alice. "Cultural Feminism and the Anti-Pornography Movement." *Social Text* 7 (1983a), pp. 34–53.

———. "The New Feminism of Yin and Yang." In Snitow, Stansell, and Thompson 1983, pp. 439–59.

———. "The Taming of the Id: Feminist Sexual Politics, 1968–83." In Vance 1984, pp. 50–72.

———. *Daring to Be Bad: Radical Feminism in America, 1967–1975.* Minneapolis: University of Minnesota Press, 1989.

———. "Justifying Our Love? The Evolution of Lesbianism through Feminism and Gay Male Politics." *Advocate,* March 26, 1991, pp. 48–53.

Eisenstein, Hester. *Contemporary Feminist Thought.* Boston: G. K. Hall, 1983.

Epstein, Barbara. *Political Protest and Cultural Revolution: Nonviolent Direct Action in the 1970s and 1980s.* Berkeley and Los Angeles: University of California Press, 1991.

Faderman, Lillian. *Surpassing the Love of Men.* New York: Morrow, 1981.

———. *Odd Girls and Twilight Lovers: A History of Lesbian Life in Twentieth-Century America.* New York: Columbia University Press, 1991.

Fantasia, Rick. *Cultures of Solidarity: Consciousness, Action, and Contemporary American Workers.* Berkeley and Los Angeles: University of California Press, 1988.

Freedman, Estelle. "Separatism as Strategy: Female Institution Building and American Feminism, 1870–1930." *Feminist Studies* 5, no. 3 (1979), pp. 512–52.

Freeman, Jo. *The Politics of Women's Liberation.* New York: Longman, 1975.

Frye, Marilyn. "Some Reflections on Separatism and Power." In her *The Politics of Reality: Essays in Feminist Theory.* Trumansburg, NY: Crossing Press, 1983, pp. 95–109.

———. "Do You Have to Be a Lesbian to Be a Feminist?" *off our backs* 20 (August/September 1990), pp. 21–23.

Galst, Liz. "Overcoming Silence." *Advocate,* December 3, 1991, pp. 60–63.

Gearhart, Sally Miller. *The Wanderground: Stories of the Hill Women.* Watertown, MA: Persephone, 1978.

———. "The Chipko." *Ms.* (September–October 1991), pp. 64–69.

Gilligan, Carol. *In a Different Voice.* Cambridge, MA: Harvard University Press, 1982.

Gittlin, Tod. *The Sixties.* New York: Bantam, 1987.

Gordon, Linda. "What's New in Women's History." In *Feminist Studies/Critical Studies,* ed. Teresa de Lauretis. Bloomington: Indiana University Press, 1986.

———. "On 'Difference.'" *Genders* 10 (Spring 1991), pp. 91–111.

Gorman, Phyllis. "The Ohio AIDS Movement: Competition and Cooperation between Grassroots Activists and Professionally Sponsored Organizations." Ph.D. dissertation, Ohio State University, 1992.

Hamilton, Amy. "Women in AIDS Activism." *off our backs* 21 (November 1991), pp. 4–5.

Hanisch, Carol. "The Personal Is Political." In *Feminist Revolution,* ed. Redstockings of the Women's Liberation Movement. New York: Random House, 1978, pp. 204–15.

Hayden, Tom. *Reunion.* New York: Random House, 1988.

Hewitt, Nancy A. "Beyond the Search for Sisterhood: American Women's History in the 1980s." *Social History* 10 no. 3 (1985), pp. 299–321.

Hoagland, Sarah Lucia, and Julia Penelope. *For Lesbians Only: A Separatist Anthology.* London: Onlywomen, 1988.

hooks, bell. *Feminist Theory: From Margin to Center.* Boston: South End, 1984.

Houppert, Karen. "Wildflowers among the Ivy: New Campus Radicals." *Ms.* 2 (September/October 1991), pp. 52–58.

Hull, Gloria T., Patricia Bell Scott, and Barbara Smith. *All the Women Are White. All the Blacks Are Men, but Some of Us Are Brave: Black Women's Studies.* Old Westbury, NY: Feminist Press, 1982.

Isserman, Maurice. *If I Had a Hammer: The Death of the Old Left and the Birth of the New Left.* New York: Basic Books, 1987.

Jagger, Alison M. *Feminist Politics and Human Nature.* Totowa, NJ: Rowman & Allanheld, 1983.

Johnson, Sonia. *Going Out of Our Minds: The Metaphysics of Liberation.* Freedom, CA: Crossing Press, 1987.

Kamen, Paula. *Feminist Fatale: Voices from the "Twentysomething" Generation Explore the Future of the Women's Movement.* New York: Donald I. Fine, 1991.

Kaplan, Temma. "Female Consciousness and Collective Action: The Case of Barcelona, 1910–1918." *Signs* 7, no. 3 (1982), pp. 545–66.

Klandermans, Bert, and Sidney Tarrow. "Mobilization into Social Movements: Synthesizing European and American Approaches." In *From Structure to Action: Comparing Social Movement Research across Cultures,* ed. Bert Klandermans, Hanspeter Kriesi, and Sidney Tarrow. International Social Movement Research, vol. 1. Greenwich, CT: JAI, 1988, pp. 1–38.

Koedt, Anne. "Lesbianism and Feminism." In *Radical Feminism,* ed. Anne Koedt, Ellen Levine, and Anita Rapone. New York: Quadrangle, 1973, pp. 246–58.

Krieger, Susan. *The Mirror Dance: Identity in a Women's Community.* Philadelphia: Temple University Press, 1983.

Lewis, Sasha Gregory. *Sunday's Women.* Boston: Beacon, 1979.

Linden, Robin Ruth, Darlene R. Pagano, Diana E. H. Russell, and Susan Leigh Star. *Against Sadomasochism: A Radical Feminist Analysis.* East Palo Alto, CA: Frog in the Well, 1982.

Lockard, Denyse. "The Lesbian Community: An Anthropological Approach." In *The Many Faces of Homosexuality,* ed. Evelyn Blackwood. New York: Harrington Park, 1986, pp. 83–95.

Lorde, Audre. "An Open Letter to Mary Daly." In her *Sister Outsider: Essays and Speeches.* Trumansburg, NY: Crossing Press, 1984a, pp. 66–71.

———. "The Master's Tools Will Never Dismantle the Master's House." In her *Sister Outsider: Essays and Speeches.* Trumansburg, NY: Crossing Press, 1984b, pp. 110–13.

Loulan, JoAnn Gardner. *The Lesbian Erotic Dance: Butch, Femme, Androgyny, and other Rhythms.* San Francisco: Spinsters, 1990.

Luker, Kristin. *Abortion and the Politics of Motherhood.* Berkeley and Los Angeles: University of California Press, 1984.

Lützen, Karin. *Was das Herz begehrt: Liebe und Freundschaft zwischen Frauen.* Hamburg: Ernst Kabel, 1990.

McAdam, Doug. *Freedom Summer.* New York: Oxford University Press, 1988.

McCormick, Kelly. "Moms without Dads: Women Choosing Children." Ph.D. dissertation, Ohio State University, 1992.

MacKinnon, Catharine A. *Feminism Unmodified: Discourses on Life and Law.* Cambridge, MA: Harvard University Press, 1987.

Minkowitz, Donna. "The Newsroom Becomes a Battleground." *Advocate,* May 19, 1992, pp. 31–37.

Moraga, Cherrié, and Gloria Anzaldúa, eds. *This Bridge Called My Back: Writings by Radical Women of Color.* Watertown, MA: Persephone, 1981.

Morris, Aldon. *The Origins of the Civil Rights Movement: Black Communities Organizing for Change.* New York: Free Press, 1984.

Moschkovich, Judit. "'But I Know You, American Woman.'" In Moraga and Anzaldúa 1981, pp. 79–84.

Near, Holly. *Fire in the Rain, Singer in the Storm.* New York: Morrow, 1990.

off our backs. "The News That 'Rocked the Feminist Community.'" *off our backs* 22 (January, 1992a), p. 2.

———. "Queer Notions." *off our backs,* October 1992b, pp. 12–15.

Pascoe, Peggy. *Relations of Rescue: The Search for Female Moral Authority in the American West, 1874–1939.* New York: Oxford University Press, 1990.

Pearlman, Sarah F. "The Saga of Continuing Clash in Lesbian Community, or Will an Army of Ex-Lovers Fail?" In *Lesbian Psychologies: Explorations and Challenges,* ed. Boston Lesbian Psychologies Collective. Urbana: University of Illinois Press, 1987, pp. 313–26.

Rich, Adrienne. "Compulsory Heterosexuality and Lesbian Existence." *Signs* 5 no. 4 (1980), pp. 631–60.

———. *Of Woman Born.* New York: Norton, 1976.

Ringelheim, Joan. "Women and the Holocaust: A Reconsideration of Research." *Signs* 10, no. 4 (1985), pp. 741–61.

Ruby, Jennie, Farar Elliott, and Carol Anne Douglas. "NWSA: Troubles Surface at Conference." *off our backs* 1 (August/September 1990), pp. 10–16.

Rupp, Leila J. "Feminism and the Sexual Revolution in the Early Twentieth Century: The Case of Doris Stevens." *Feminist Studies* 15 no. 2 (1989a), pp. 289–309.

———. "'Imagine My Surprise': Women's Relationships in Mid-Twentieth Century America." In *Hidden from History: Reclaiming the Gay and Lesbian Past,* ed. Martin Bauml Duberman, Martha Vicinus, and George Chauncey, Jr. New York: New American Library, 1989b, pp. 395–410.

Rupp, Leila J., and Verta Taylor. *Survival in the Doldrums: The American Women's Rights Movement, 1945 to the 1960s.* New York: Oxford University Press, 1987.

Ryan, Barbara. "Ideological Purity and Feminism: The U.S. Women's Movement from 1966 to 1975." *Gender and Society* 3, no. 2 (1989), pp. 239–57.

———. *Feminism and the Women's Movement.* New York: Harper Collins, 1992.

Samois. *What Color Is Your Handkerchief? A Lesbian S/M Sexuality Reader.* Berkeley, CA: Samois, 1979.

Schneider, Beth. "Feminist Disclaimers, Stigma, and the Contemporary Women's Movement." Unpublished manuscript, Santa Barbara, CA, 1986.

———. Political Generations in the Contemporary Women's Movement." *Sociological Inquiry* 58, no. 1 (1988), pp. 4–21.

Segal, Lynne, and Mary McIntosh. *Sex Exposed: Sexuality and the Pornography Debate.* New Brunswick, NJ: Rutgers University Press, 1993.

Sharon, Tanya, Farar Elliott, and Cecile Latham. "The National Lesbian Conference." *off our backs,* June 1991, pp. 1–4, 18–19.

Sims, Margot. *On the Necessity of Bestializing the Human Female.* Boston: South End, 1982.

Smeller, Michele M. "Crossing Over: The Negotiation of Sexual Identity in a Social Movement Community." Unpublished manuscript, Columbus, OH, 1992.

Smith, Barbara. *Home Girls: A Black Feminist Anthology.* New York: Kitchen Table; Women of Color Press, 1983.

Snitow, Ann, Christine Stansell, and Sharon Thompson. *Powers of Desire: The Politics of Sexuality.* New York: Monthly Review Press, 1983.

Staggenborg, Suzanne. *The Pro-Choice Movement.* New York: Oxford University Press, 1991.

Starr, Victoria. "The Changing Tune of Women's Music." *Advocate,* June 2, 1992, pp. 68–71.

Stein, Arlene. "All Dressed Up but No Place to Go? Style Wars and the New Lesbianism." *Out/Look* 1, no. 4 (1989), pp. 34–42.

———. *Sisters, Sexperts, Queers: Beyond the Lesbian Nation.* New York: Plume, 1993.

Stevens, Robin. "Style vs. Substance at the National Lesbian Conference." *Out/Look* 14 (1991), pp. 51–53.

Taylor, Verta. "The Future of Feminism: A Social Movement Analysis." In *Feminist Frontiers II: Rethinking, Sex, Gender, and Society,* ed. Laurel Richardson and Verta Taylor. New York: Random House, 1989a, pp. 473–90.

———. "Social Movement Continuity: The Women's Movement in Abeyance." *American Sociological Review* 54 (October 1989b), pp. 761–75.

Taylor, Verta, and Nancy E. Whittier. "Collective Identity in Social Movement Communities: Lesbian Feminist Mobilization." In *Frontiers of Social Movement Theory,* ed. Aldon Morris and Carol Mueller. New Haven, CT: Yale University Press, 1992, pp. 104–29.

Trujillo, Carla. *Chicana Lesbians: The Girls Our Mothers Warned Us About.* Berkeley, CA: Third Woman, 1991.

Vaid, Urvashi. "Let's Put Our Own House in Order." *Out/Look* 14 (Fall 1991), pp. 55–7.

Vance, Carole S., ed. *Pleasure and Danger: Exploring Female Sexuality.* Boston: Routledge & Kegan Paul, 1984.

Walker, Alice. *In Search of Our Mothers' Gardens.* New York: Harcourt Brace Jovanovich, 1974.

Whalen, Jack, and Richard Flacks. *Beyond the Barricades: The Sixties Generation Grows Up.* Philadelphia: Temple University Press, 1987.

Whittier, Nancy E. "The Construction of a Politicized Collective Identity: Ideology and Symbolism in Contemporary Lesbian Feminist Communities." M.A. thesis, Ohio State University, 1988.

———. "Feminists in the 'Post-Feminist' Age: Collective Identity and the Persistence of the Women's Movement." Ph.D. dissertation, Ohio State University, 1991.

Williams, Brooke. "The Retreat to Cultural Feminism." In *Feminist Revolution,* ed. Redstockings of the Women's Liberation Movement. New York: Random House, 1978.

Willis, Ellen. "Radical Feminism and Feminist Radicalism." In *The '60's without Apology,* ed. Sonya Sayres, Anders Stephanson, Stanley Aronowitz, and Fredric Jameson. Minneapolis: University of Minnesota Press, 1984.

Wolf, Deborah Goleman. *The Lesbian Community.* Berkeley and Los Angeles: University of California Press, 1979.

Yollin, Patricia. "Painting the Town Lavender." *Image* (San Francisco *Examiner*), March 10, 1991, pp. 18–29.

Young, Iris Marion. "The Ideal of Community and the Politics of Difference." In *Feminism/Postmodernism,* ed. Linda J. Nicholson. New York: Routledge, 1990, pp. 300–23.

Zimmerman, Bonnie. *The Safe Sea of Women: Lesbian Fiction, 1969–1989.* Boston: Beacon, 1990.

CHAPTER 9

Identity and Selfhood

Feminist theorists have dramatically advanced our insights into the project of identity and the challenges of selfhood. Broadly, they posit a social self drawn to other people not for life's extras but for its essentials. This portrayal collides, however, with modern Western masculinist ideas about selfhood. Conceptualized as individualism of one sort or another, these other ideas emphasize a creature whose individuating trajectory leads to autonomy, independence, and self-sufficiency. These hegemonic ideas about selfhood disconnect the individual from other individuals, at least to the extent of subordinating people's relationships to their psyches.

As we have already seen, feminist theorists commonly deconstruct those ideas as mystifying and misleading. By skeptically scrutinizing the idea of autonomy, they arrive at sociologically dense notions about identity and selfhood. At the same time they disclose how the tasks of selfhood can become pathways to empowerment.

AUTONOMY RECONCEIVED

Sarah Lucia Hoagland is one of many feminist theorists who dislike the notion of autonomy. She says that it "encourages us to believe that connecting and engaging with others limits us . . . and undermines our sense of self." Hoagland has little patience with such balderdash. She reconceptualizes selfhood as a complex venture comprising both separation and connection. She theorizes "a self who is terrified neither of solitude nor of gatherings, a self who is both elemental and related, who has a sense of herself making choices within a context created by community." This is a *self in community*, or what some theorists call the *self-in-*

relation.[1] This self stands in conceptual opposition to the highly individuated, independent self conceptualized as whole and complete apart from
his relationships with other people. This conceptually rebellious self lays
bare the masculine character of most psychological models of selfhood
while laying grounds for reconceptualizing "autonomy."

By and large, feminist theorists have emphasized how psychological
models typically exclude not only most women but also many men (poor
men, for example). Further, they exaggerate the independence of privileged
men. As Jean Baker Miller observes, few men become as self-sufficient as
dominant models make them out to be: "They are usually supported by
wives, mistresses, mothers, daughters, secretaries, nurses, and other women
(as well as other men who are lower than they in the socioeconomic hierarchy)." Naomi Scheman makes the point this way: "men have been free to
imagine themselves as self-defining only because women have held the intimate social world together."[2]

With insights like these, feminists theorists have reoriented the idea of
autonomy. Among the first book-length contributions to that effort is Diana
T. Meyers's *Self, Society, and Personal Choice* (1989). Meyers treats autonomy as a set of skills central to a well-examined, well-connected life.
As a complex competency, autonomy involves coordinating one's goals,
projects, values, emotions, and conduct in adaptive fashion. It thus concerns self-governance; it requires getting clear about what one wants and
then acting on that clarity. Thus, autonomy presupposes a habitual "dispo-
sition to consult the self."[3]

Meyers steers past dualistic thinking by emphasizing autonomy as a
matter of degree (p. 205), with selfhood requiring some measure of it. Autonomy, she says, bolsters one's sense of self-worth as well as one's "commitment to his or her projects." (pp. 212, 213) To that extent it is a crucial
set of skills. Meyers's portrait of self-respecting people points toward that
conclusion:

> Self-respecting people have due regard for their dignity as agents. Not obse-
> quious, not imperious, they neither belittle nor overrate the importance of their
> own inclinations. They take their own desires to be worthy of consideration, but
> they give these desires only their proper weight in deliberation. Conscious of
> their powers of choice and of the significance of choosing well, self-respecting
> people . . . are not rigid. (p. 214)

Yet "their sense of their own identity precludes chameleonlike change."
That same sense of self promotes reliable insights about their prospects
and awareness of the limits of their influence. (p. 244) This is what we
came across in the last chapter as power-from-within.

When Meyers talks about self-contempt—the defeat of self-respect—
the conceptual resonance between autonomy and power-from-within
intensifies. She says people become vulnerable to self-contempt when
their self-regard fails to extend past this or that narrow sphere of their lives.

Self-contempt thus sits on the existential horizon when self-regard derives only from one's "achievement or occasional self-expression within an assigned activity." (p. 245) Diverse projects, commitments, and opportunities stave it off and enhance self-respect. Meyers's greatest theoretical moment comes when she links her reworked notion of autonomy with the idea of equal opportunity: "Without equal opportunity, autonomy is severely constrained, but without autonomy, equal opportunity is a sham." (p. 248)

Meyers's framework complements the ideas of many feminist theorists aiming to illuminate selfhood and community, identity and membership, individuality and sociality. Whether or not they try to salvage the concept of autonomy—that is, whether or not they keep the term—these theorists postulate a dialectical selfhood comprising close connections with other people *as well as* strong senses of who one is, what one needs and values, and where one wants to apply her energies and devote her attention. In my theoretical judgment that amounts to a revitalized notion of autonomy, one that respects people's lived experiences and everyday challenges. I part company, then, with those feminist theorists who discard the idea of autonomy and join hands with those who aim to reconstruct it.[4]

Before considering what selfhood may demand in the way of emotional freedom of expression, let us look at some formulations feeding into feminist reconceptualizations of autonomy. Janet L. Surrey theorizes "relationship and empowerment" so as to imply an enriched notion of autonomy. She observes that hegemonic models treat human relationships as something people *have* after work and on weekends. She rejects the disjuncture between "relating" and "acting" or "working." Surrey conceptualizes relationships as "opportunities for action," not just support systems or growth mechanisms.[5]

From a different theoretical perspective, Shane Phelan offers resonant notions. What she calls the *liberal sentiment* strikes me as nothing more and nothing less than acknowledgment of another person's autonomy:

> The bearer of such a sentiment need not abstract from the particulars of my existence to respect me; neither must she agree that my understanding of a good life is the true, the best, the purest. What she need do is believe that I mean what I say; that is, she must agree to treat me as a being competent to speak of my own desires and motives directly, even if she suspects that I am not.[6]

Hoagland herself also offers ideas capable of reorienting our thinking about autonomy. In large measure she does this by emphasizing balance between independence and dependence alongside substantial self-awareness. She advances these ideas in the context of discussing love and intimacy:

> If I pursue the closeness of intimacy, of greater understanding, and embrace the risk of change, if I let go of control (which does not mean therefore being out of control), I will less likely restrict my growth through distance ("independence") from you or restrict yours through manipulation ("dependence") for fear of losing something valuable in my life.[7]

In that one thick sentence, Hoagland uproots hegemonic ideas while exploring alternatives worthy of careful attention. For starters, she links interpersonal closeness with movement toward greater understanding as well as the "risk of change." Getting closer enlarges consciousness, then, and challenges one's current modus operandi. Hoagland also disentangles losing control from forswearing control. Most importantly, she indicates what unadulterated independence and dependence mean in practical terms—social distance and interpersonal manipulation, respectively—while also suggesting how people who cherish intimacy can overcome their fear of losing it.

Hoagland then extends her discussion of how intimacy and understanding work together: "Intimacy involves deep understanding of another and another's deep understanding of us." She continues,

> The prerequisite for that is self-awareness: If you are going to understand me intimately, then I must understand myself so that I am not threatened by your understanding of me. For before I am really able to respond to you, I need to be clear on at least some things about my self. (p. 113)

In some respects Hoagland's ideas, like those of Surrey and Phelan, extend Gilligan's ideas about an ethic of care that is self-nurturant as well as other-oriented. Overall, these theorists imply that *sharing* is often harder than giving[8] and that balance is trickier to achieve than the gender-typed extremes predominating in nonfeminist models of human development. Such, too, is the upshot of the work that Gilligan, perhaps significantly, pursues mostly in connection with other scholars.

In research on teenagers in danger of dropping out of school, becoming mothers, and sinking (often further) into poverty, Jill McLean Taylor, Carol Gilligan, and Amy M. Sullivan observe that "when the pendulum of voice or silence swings too far in either direction, each poses a risk."[9] Voice is not everything, then, even though selfhood requires it. Via language, voice "joins psyche and culture." To experience a self means to have a voice. Voice also joins self with others so that "the sounds of one's voice change in resonance depending on the relational acoustics: whether one is heard or not heard. . . ." To say the very least, voice is "polyphonic and complex."[10]

This vibrant metaphor might well serve as a gateway to the idea of autonomy, now understood as a set of skills essential for individuals making and sharing a world together. By now, autonomy seems akin to the art of attuning oneself to what is while keeping one's eye on the prize of what might be. To that extent autonomy entails the art of improvisation, a prospect explored in the chapter's last section.

THE POLITICS OF EMOTIONAL EXPRESSION

The personal is thus artful as well as political; it involves aesthetics as well as power. Put differently, developing a self means establishing one's own style of acting and interacting. That style finds expression in what one wears and what one cooks, in how one shops and how one shares, in where one lives and where one spends her precious little leisure time. Above all, one's personal style gets expressed in what feminist theorists mean by *voice*, a person's distinctive way of getting others to take her into account. Voice thus entails some empowerment. As we have seen, it also entails some autonomy that leaves one diversely connected with other people. Feminist theorists imply that voice also involves some emotional clarity and freedom. Women's voices, in particular, require some skill at expressing the emotions commonly considered out of feminine bounds. Anger is the most widely theorized of these emotions.

Expressing anger casts a woman beyond the company of *nice* women she is supposed to keep. Such expression ranks high among all the mundane ways a woman can violate mainstream femininity. It commonly strikes people as unseemly, nasty, or downright ugly. Often such perceptions translate into stereotypes about bad girls, castrating bitches, uppity women, or queen bees.

Not surprisingly, then, many women are hard pressed to express anger and other "negative" or "antisocial" emotions effectively, as we saw in Chapter 1. Besides whatever emotional inhibitions they have learned and whatever other penalties they face during interaction, some women risk physical retaliation if they lose their temper in front of a patriarch in residence such as a tradition-minded father or husband.[11] Under these complex circumstances, making one's voice and securing one's sense of self are no small enterprises. They become big projects demanding as much courage as stamina.[12] A good deal of feminist theorizing illuminates these micropolitical projects centered on emotional expression and freedom.

Arlie Russell Hochschild was among the first scholars to show how extensively today's individuals, particularly employed women, are expected to manage their emotions. The "happy face" is an icon showing what mainstream women are expected to deliver each day—on the paid job and the unpaid one, in public and private. Hochschild uses the metaphor of the "managed heart" to underscore the emotional control women, in particular, are supposed to exhibit.

Basing her theorizing on flight attendants' training and job demands, Hochschild emphasizes that women are specialists in emotional labor who incur considerable costs for doing such work; this labor "affects the degree to which we listen to feeling and sometimes our very capacity to feel."[13] She implies that many, perhaps most, women have had the kinds of training she observed among Delta flight attendants, who were taught "that an obnoxious person could be reconceived in an honest but useful way." Such lessons were part and parcel of their "anger-desensitization." (p. 25)

Reflective of the broader culture that routinely denies women their real and rightful anger, the flight attendants faced a curriculum where one's right to be angry is "smuggled out of discourse." (p. 112) The discourse of mainstream femininity, which insists on a *nice* demeanor, involves that same smuggling. As Jean Baker Miller puts it, women are "allowed anger *in the interest of someone else*" but not in their own right.[14]

Hochschild develops that idea by observing that in mainstream American culture there is a

> form of false self: the altruist, the person who is overly concerned with the needs of *others*. In our culture, women—because they have traditionally been assigned the task of tending to the needs of others—are in great danger of overdeveloping the false self and losing track of its boundaries. (p. 195)

Alongside the problems culture poses are conceptual problems, too. Hochschild emphasizes that how we manage our emotions is bound up with what emotions we experience; the management and the emotion are inseparable, though analytically distinct. Put differently, "how we manage or express feeling" is not separate from the feeling but part of it. (p. 27) Thus, over time people trained to micromanage their anger experience it less and less. In its stead they may experience depression, anxiety, or sadness; they may eat or drink to numb their anger; they may aerobicize it away; they may turn it inward. The point is that "unexpressed emotion" is an anomaly. The emotion finds expression *in some form*, even though that form may occlude the initial feeling. Crying when one is angry is illustrative, as is jogging when one is spitting mad.

Hochschild's and others' work implies, then, that people trained to habitually squelch certain of their emotions stand to lose clear-cut experience of those emotions. As we saw in Chapter 1, Naomi Scheman joins other feminist theorists who explore how women's anger gets thwarted. Concerned with many women's difficulty "synthesizing the pieces and naming the puzzle of our feelings," Scheman looks for reasons in the relations of ruling, especially dominant ideologies. There she finds three notions widely promulgated in American culture that inhibit women's expressions of anger.

The first is the idea that women's emotions are (like women themselves) "irrational or nonrational storms." The second is that one must "trust one's own reactions and take oneself to be in a position to judge." Taught to second-guess themselves and orient to others' feelings, some women translate their anger toward a growling husband or a mean-spirited co-worker into generous speculations about what might be accounting for their maddening behavior. Finally, according to Scheman, another "thing keeping us from seeing ourselves as angry is the picture we are likely to have of what the good life for a woman consists in." To the extent that one's circumstances and achievements reflect that picture one's anger becomes problematic, for the good life is supposed to promote satisfaction, not rage.

Like Hochschild, then, Scheman gives enormous weight to those mechanisms whereby women's anger gets smuggled out of the picture.

Scheman concludes that an angry woman and a nonangry one may differ more in what they are prepared to treat as anger than in what they are actually feeling.[15]

Scheman goes on to cite another important impediment to women's expression of their anger. She notes how autonomy "is *less an individual achievement than a socially recognized right*" (p. 28) to interpret one's own experiences and account for oneself on one's own terms. Those who appropriate the interpretation of women's experiences seem never to cite their own behavior or neglect as the reason for our short tempers or frustrated frenzy.

What Scheman points to is what Sue Campbell theorizes as *being dismissed*. This happens "when what we say or do . . . is either not taken seriously or not regarded at all in the context in which it is meant to have its effect." Campbell says that in both the theoretical and the practical realms, women need to come to terms with all the "techniques of interpretive dismissal" used against us "as much as with our own reluctance to get angry." Conceptualizing *expression* as how we variously articulate our subjective experiences, Campbell says,

> We require a theory of affect that has a strong focus on the communicative nature of emotional encounters, one that does not regard the failures and achievements of expression as independent of an interpretive requirement.[16]

In the course of her theorizing, Campbell cites a sad commonplace associated with the denial of women's autonomy. She notes that when people refuse to "forgive and forget," it is often because of the sinner's "failure. . . . to listen and act."[17] Put differently, we often find ourselves unable to forgive because no one has sought our forgiveness, even implicitly, by taking us seriously and trying to do better.

As we saw in Chapter 1, theorists like Audre Lorde know the awesome power-from-within that anger can unleash. Lorde says that when anger is sharply focused, it can promote progress and growth by clarifying our consciousness and strengthening our wills.[18] Hoagland theorizes in the same direction. She says that for oppressed people, anger renders a political judgment and thus bespeaks political awareness. Like Lorde, Hoagland sees anger as transformative of consciousness. It can also transform culture and social structure insofar as "getting angry is the beginning of fighting back." Anger, says Hoagland, is one stimulus for community, for collective movement toward a less oppressive world.[19]

Needless to say, anger is only one of the emotions whereby we either set ourselves back or move ourselves forward. It is many women's most problematic emotion and thus the one that feminists most theorize, but it does have a close competitor. Its name is love, and it is often conceptualized not as a social bond but as a web of intensely romantic feelings impelling the individual toward thoughts of and interactions with the beloved. Long tomes have been written about this heady experience—its ideology, its modernity, its power, its gendered ways. Yet love remains a big compound of feelings, not a single steady feeling like that associated with anger or joy.

I leave it for you to explore that theoretical byway on your own, perhaps by reading or rereading Zora Neale Hurston's novel *Their Eyes Were Watching God*. Much that feminist theorists have written about love (and friendship) finds powerful expression in the experiences of its indomitable heroine, Janey Crawford. Hurston's novel also plows the depths of what "identity" means in practical, sustainable terms. To that concept we now turn.

IDENTITY AS PERPETUAL PROJECT

Since the 1960s, the notion of identity has taken on more and more of a performative cast. A self capable of multiple mutations, an improvisational self, a protean self, and multiple selves have dominated the theoretical landscape over the last several decades. By now, the notion of performance or performativity holds such thinking in theoretical place. Also focusing such ideas is the postmodernist perspective that emphasizes the provisional, decentered, localized, fluid character of lived realities such as identity.

That perspective, which is at work in Reading 21 by Judith Butler, has a dense root system. Michel Foucault's work is a central part of that system, as is the social constructionism that became ascendant in social theory during the late 1960s and early 1970s. Also part of that root system is that sociological perspective known as ethnomethodology, which focuses on the artful practices whereby mundane actors make together the very understandings they commonly take for granted as they pursue their projects. Two ethnomethodological theorists whose ideas resonate with those of Butler and other postmodernist thinkers are Candace West and Don H. Zimmerman. Their work on "doing gender" holds insights not only into how femininity and masculinity get done but also into how people "do" their identities while going about their daily business.

West and Zimmerman emphasize that gender is "a routine, methodical, and recurring *accomplishment*." It grows out of acts that get gendered when people use the frames or schemas culture offers as sense-making resources. Cultural communities "cast particular pursuits as expressions of masculine and feminine 'natures,'" and members act and interact in ways that routinely reflect those understandings. West and Zimmerman conclude that gender is not part of what one *is* but "something that one *does*, and does recurrently, in interaction with others."[20]

How West and Zimmerman theorize gender applies to identity at large. It is a social and psychological process whereby we enact our selfsameness, establishing it for the time being in and through actions taken to be expressive of who we *are*. Like social structure and culture, identity can neither originate nor maintain itself. Its roots and its sustenance lie in individuals' actions and interactions. As phenomenologists put it, identity is the current sedimentation of an individual's past actions. Its horizon is our future acts, which may or may not continue the particulars currently characteristic of our selfsameness.

One's identity is not only processual but also multiple. Even though "identity politics" revolves around a single core identity taken as definitive or at least central (as we will see in Chapter 11), each of us has an identity that is really a set of identi*ties*. We inhabit diverse social locations within the matrix of domination and pass through diverse social situations during a typical week, all of which elicit distinctive reactions.

Not surprisingly, those aggregated reactions—that *set* of identities—comprise inconsistencies and paradoxes. Such lapses of consistency, inevitable in the selves we fashion, are the stuff of resistance and creativity. As Sandra Harding implies, "traitorous identities" (what Bonnie Zimmerman calls "perverse identities") derive their possibility from the unevenness and contradictions we build into our identities.

In those inconsistencies are the resources necessary for choosing marginality, for "willfully refusing to do what the culture of the center expects [one] to do."[21] As Amy Mullin has argued, the diversity within one's very self can, when affirmed, lead to identification with and recognition of one's affinities with diverse groups.[22] All these ideas lead to the postmodernist perspective on selfhood and identity.

Judith Butler is one of the leading theorists helping to develop that perspective. Her work is embracing. It does pay particular attention, though, to the identity work women and nonheterosexual men undertake in reaction to their subordination. In Reading 21, Butler questions whether identity is fundamentally experiential. At the same time she suggests that it may operate more as a "normative ideal." People's identities do typically reflect the values, preferences, and tastes definitive of mainstream culture or respectable society. That much is fairly obvious.

Where Butler goes with those insights is less obvious. She emphasizes that the hegemonic culture makes some actions and appearances *intelligible*. These are the actions and appearances whose meanings members take for granted as "just there," "natural," "obvious," or "what everyone knows." These, then, are *naturalized* actions and appearances. They invite no particular notice or scrutiny; they require no accounts or explanations.

In American culture, for example, a woman who shows up at the office in a dress is doing gender in pervasively intelligible ways that evoke no particular notice. A man showing up in that same attire, however, has left the arena of intelligibility. Is it Halloween? Did he lose a bet? Is this a joke? Has he lost his mind? Questioning of this sort signals the loss or at least the diminution of intelligibility. As Butler points out, some people's gender identities depart from the norms ensuring considerable intelligibility. Rather than leading us to recognize people's gender diversity, however, such identities get interpreted as "deviant" or "sick" or "abnormal." As Butler puts it, "they appear only as developmental failures or logical impossibilities from within that domain" of cultural intelligibility.

In her book *Gender Trouble: Feminism and the Subversion of Identity*, the source of Reading 21, Butler goes on to underscore gender's performative character; it "is always a doing." She theorizes that gender "identity is performatively constituted by the very 'expressions' that are said to be its results."[23] Identity thus comprises historically specific, culturally mandated "acts that create the appearance of a naturalistic necessity." (p. 33) Moreover, identity comes to serve as a "regulatory practice" (p. 32), an array of enacted ideas about who one is that functions to channel behavior along those very lines. Put differently, identity often regulates behavior not only out of sheer force of habit but also out of misplaced attributions about where "identity" lies—namely, that it lies "inside" the person rather than taking shape from her embodied actions and everything that conditions them.

What does this all mean for that much used one-letter, first-person pronoun? It means there is no "I" independent of or apart from discourses and other significations. As Butler (p. 143) puts it,

> the enabling conditions for an assertion of "I" are provided by the structure of signification, the rules that regulate the legitimate and illegitimate invocation of that pronoun, the practices that establish the terms of intelligibility by which that pronoun can circulate.

Identity is "a signifying practice," then, and its significations grow out of regulated repetitions. Butler concludes that "agency" can then "be located within the possibility of a variation on that repetition." (p. 145)

In other terms, what is *self*-expressive lies in the individual's capacity to step outside the regulated repetitions that express her identity. Agency thus has to do with the resourcefulness of the individual making her very own way in the world, enacting a biography and living a life distinct from all others. It has to do with the individual's enactment of possibilities beyond intelligibility's current reach. "I" steps out of line, then—neither easily nor regularly, perhaps, but she expresses and secures her *self* in such steps. With reference to feminist identities, Butler puts it this way:

> The critical task . . . is not to establish a point of view outside of constructed identities. . . . The critical task is, rather, to locate strategies of subversive repetition enabled by those constructions, to affirm the local possibilities of intervention through participating in precisely those practices of repetition that constitute identity and, therefore, present the immanent possibility of contesting them. (p. 147)

Much to her theoretical credit, Butler inveighs against "celebrat[ing] each and every new possibility *qua* possibility. . . ." Rather the challenge is to seize those possibilities that "exist within cultural domains designated as culturally unintelligible and impossible." (pp. 148–49) The projects of selfhood and identity invite us, in sum, to demonstrate the possibilities buried under what culture has deemed impossible or inconceivable. These projects require de-sedimentation, then. To secure our selves and enact our identities in liberated ways requires bringing to the cultural surface what lies buried beneath its institutionalized sedimentations, that is, its relations of ruling. In lieu of seizing those challenges, we can remain queued up in the lines of society's matrix of domination. We can remain what culture has named us rather than what we name ourselves.

Another way of approaching these notions is to talk about selfhood and identity in terms of transformative processes. As bell hooks observes, "A culture of domination demands of all its citizens *self*-negation. The more marginalized, the more intense the demand."[24] We have seen how the matrix of domination demands that men of privilege deny their dependence on women and lower-status men. That same matrix typically makes central to one's identity the grounds for one's subordination:

> If there is no experience of oppression (or just as importantly, no recognition of oppression), the identity may not achieve central importance. This lack of experiences or recognition of oppression might explain why few heterosexuals claim a central sexual identity, why so few white people have a sense of racial identity, and why women are often more aware of their gender than men.[25]

In practical terms, then, oppression shapes lived identities more than privilege does. It shapes them by demanding that women and other subordinated people deny the validity and worthwhileness of their experiences; that they excessively curtail their emotional expressions; that they forgo their dreams in service to someone else's. For individuals to cultivate their full distinctiveness, then, they must transform the social shapes given to them into the shapes fitting their experiences and aspirations. They must repeatedly insist in action that a "wholeness of being" can be achieved.[26]

Such insistence is most efficacious when enacted with other individuals also struggling to become whole—that is, fully developed rather than underdeveloped along socially prescribed lines. Chapter 11 looks at such collective struggles. Anticipating its considerations, we should keep in mind that selfhood and identity are as much at stake in those struggles as are social change and cultural transformation.

At the same time, we need to see that all these reworked notions of selfhood and identity often express romanticism's emphasis on the unique self apart from any social role. Pauline Johnson says that feminism should override this "romantic formulation" by adopting a different stance toward the "struggle between self and role." She emphasizes that as individuals establish their individuality, they tend to transform social roles by interpreting their significance within the concrete circumstances of their own situations.[27] Johnson's points complement Rebecca Kukla's, which also warn of shortsighted formulations of self and identity. Kukla finds particularly disappointing those that tend toward "asserting [an] opposite, rather than articulating a real alternative" to hegemonic conceptions.[28]

In Reading 22 on self-definition, Patricia Hill Collins steers past romanticism to depict practical alternatives to masculinist notions of selfhood and identity. Focusing on African American women, she demonstrates how women can make their full personhood intelligible through their bonds with one another as well as through their interactions at those institutional sites where they have a reliable chance of being heard.

Collins also shows us how women have created their own cultural resources for defining themselves in defiance of mainstream culture's definitions; for underscoring the rightfulness of their claims to respect and their quests for self-affirmation; and for celebrating their independence and resourcefulness. Collins shows us how women can be culturally and socially "generous with ourselves" for the sake of becoming positively "self-full"[29] as individuals in communities with one another. She points, then, toward how women can make "a home in ourselves"[30] that is secure and satisfying and big enough to accommodate intimacy and promote community. Collins thus joins Taylor and Rupp (Reading 20) on those feminist grounds where theory and practice embrace.

NOTES

1. Sarah Lucia Hoagland, *Lesbian Ethics: Toward New Value* (Palo Alto, CA: Institute of Lesbian Studies, 1988), pp. 144–5; see also Judith V. Jordan, Alexandra G. Kaplan, Jean Baker Miller, Irene P. Stiver, and Janet L. Surrey, *Women's Growth in Connection: Writings from the Stone Center* (New York: The Guilford Press, 1991).
2. Jean Baker Miller, "The Development of Women's Sense of Self" in Jordan et al., *Women's Growth*, pp. 11–2; Naomi Scheman, *Engenderings: Constructions of Knowledge, Authority, and Privilege* (New York: Routledge, 1993), p. 51.
3. Diana T. Meyers, *Self, Society, and Personal Choice* (New York: Columbia University Press, 1989), pp. 55, 58, 84.
4. Trudy Govier, "Self-Trust, Autonomy, and Self-Esteem," *Hypatia: A Journal of Feminist Philosophy* 8 (Winter 1993), p. 104.
5. Janet L. Surrey, "Relationship and Empowerment" in Jordan et al., *Women's Growth*, p. 162.
6. Shane Phelan, *Identity Politics: Lesbian Feminism and the Limits of Community* (Philadelphia: Temple University Press, 1989), p. 155.
7. Hoagland, *Lesbian Ethics*, p. 112.
8. Mary Catherine Bateson, *Composing a Life* (New York: Penguin Books, 1990), p. 131.
9. Jill McLean Taylor, Carol Gilligan, and Amy M. Sullivan, *Between Voice and Silence: Women and Girls, Race and Relationship* (Cambridge: Harvard University Press, 1995), p. 67.
10. Lyn Mikel Brown and Carol Gilligan, *Meeting at the Crossroads: Women's Psychology and Girls' Development* (Cambridge: Harvard University Press, 1992), pp. 20, 21, 23.
11. Demie Kurz shows that women separating from or divorcing their husbands are especially vulnerable to violence; see "Separation, Divorce, and Woman Abuse," *Violence against Women* 2, no. 1 (March 1996), pp. 63–81.

12. For superb insights into such "ordinary courage," see Annie G. Rogers, "Voice, Play and a Practice of Ordinary Courage in Girls' and Women's Lives," *Harvard Educational Review* 63, no. 3 (1993), pp. 265–95.

13. Arlie Russell Hochschild, *The Managed Heart: Commercialization of Human Feeling* (Berkeley: University of California Press, 1983), pp. 20, 21.

14. Jean Baker Miller, "The Construction of Anger in Women and Men" in Jordan et al., *Women's Growth*, p. 184.

15. Scheman, *Engenderings*, pp. 25–6.

16. Sue Campbell, "Being Dismissed: The Politics of Emotional Expression," *Hypatia* 9, no. 3 (Summer 1994), pp. 49, 54, 56.

17. *Ibid.*, p. 51.

18. Audre Lorde, *Sister Outsider: Essays and Speeches* (Freedom, CA: The Crossing Press, 1984), p. 127.

19. Hoagland, *Lesbian Ethics*, p. 188.

20. Candace West and Don H. Zimmerman, "Doing Gender," *Gender & Society* 1 (June 1987), pp. 126, 127, 140.

21. Sandra Harding, "Who Knows? Identities and Feminist Epistemology" in Joan E. Hartman and Ellen Messer-Davidow (eds.), *(En)Gendering Knowledge: Feminists in Academe* (Knoxville: University of Tennessee Press, 1991), pp. 107, 109.

22. Amy Mullin, "Selves, Diverse and Divided: Can Feminists Have Diversity without Multiplicity?" *Hypatia* 10, no. 4 (Fall 1995), p. 22.

23. Judith Butler, *Gender Trouble: Feminism and the Subversion of Identity* (New York: Routledge, 1990), p. 25.

24. bell hooks, *Black Looks: Race and Representation* (Boston: South End Press, 1992), p. 19.

25. Michele J. Eliason, "An Inclusive Model of Lesbian Identity Assumption," *Journal of Gay, Lesbian, and Bisexual Identity* 1, no. 1 (1996), p. 16.

26. bell hooks, *Talking Back: Thinking Feminist, Thinking Black* (Boston: South End Press, 1990), p. 30.

27. Pauline Johnson, "The Quest for the Self: Feminism's Appropriation of Romanticism," *Thesis Eleven* 41 (1995), p. 91.

28. Rebecca Kukla, "Decentering Woman," *Metaphilosophy* 27, no. 1/2 (January/April 1996), p. 31.

29. Nett Hart, *Spirited Lesbians: Lesbian Desire as Social Action* (Minneapolis: Word Weavers, 1989), p. 33.

30. *Ibid.*, p. 111.

READING 21

Identity, Sex, and the Metaphysics of Substance

Judith Butler

. . .

Whereas the question of what constitutes "personal identity" within philosophical accounts almost always centers on the question of what internal feature of the person establishes the continuity or self-identity of the person through time, the question here will be: To what extent do *regulatory practices* of gender formation and division constitute identity, the internal coherence of the subject, indeed, the self-identical status of the person? To what extent is "identity" a normative ideal rather than a descriptive feature of experience? And how do the regulatory practices that govern gender also govern culturally intelligible notions of identity? In other words, the "coherence" and "continuity" of "the person" are not logical or analytic features of personhood but, rather, socially instituted and maintained norms of intelligibility. Inasmuch as "identity" is assured through the stabilizing concepts of sex, gender, and sexuality, the very notion of "the person" is called into question by the cultural emergence of those "incoherent" or "discontinuous" gendered beings who appear to be persons but who fail to conform to the gendered norms of cultural intelligibility by which persons are defined.

"Intelligible" genders are those which in some sense institute and maintain relations of coherence and continuity among sex, gender, sexual practice, and desire. In other words, the

spectres of discontinuity and incoherence, themselves thinkable only in relation to existing norms of continuity and coherence, are constantly prohibited and produced by the very laws that seek to establish causal or expressive lines of connection among biological sex, culturally constituted genders, and the "expression" or "effect" of both in the manifestation of sexual desire through sexual practice.

The notion that there might be a "truth" of sex, as Foucault ironically terms it, is produced precisely through the regulatory practices that generate coherent identities through the matrix of coherent gender norms. The heterosexualization of desire requires and institutes the production of discrete and asymmetrical oppositions between "feminine" and "masculine," where these are understood as expressive attributes of "male" and "female." The cultural matrix through which gender identity has become intelligible requires that certain kinds of "identities" cannot "exist"—that is, those in which gender does not follow from sex and those in which the practices of desire do not "follow" from either sex or gender. "Follow" in this context is a political relation of entailment instituted by the cultural laws that establish and regulate the shape and meaning of sexuality. Indeed, precisely because certain kinds of "gender identities" fail to conform to those norms of cultural intelligibility, they appear only as developmental failures or logical impossibilities from within that domain. Their persistence and proliferation, however, provide critical opportunities to expose the limits and regulatory aims of that domain of intelligibility and, hence, to open up within the very terms of that matrix of intelligibility rival and subversive matrices of gender disorder.

Before such disordering practices are considered, however, it seems crucial to understand the "matrix of intelligibility." Is it singular? Of what is it composed? What is the peculiar alliance presumed to exist between a system of compulsory heterosexuality and the discursive

Reprinted from *Gender Trouble: Feminism and the Subversion of Identity* by Judith Butler (1990) by permission of the publisher, Routledge: New York and London.

categories that establish the identity concepts of sex? If "identity" is an *effect* of discursive practices, to what extent is gender identity, construed as a relationship among sex, gender, sexual practice, and desire, the effect of a regulatory practice that can be identified as compulsory heterosexuality? Would that explanation return us to yet another totalizing frame in which compulsory heterosexuality merely takes the place of phallogocentrism as the monolithic cause of gender oppression?

Within the spectrum of French feminist and poststructuralist theory, very different regimes of power are understood to produce the identity concepts of sex. Consider the divergence between those positions, such as Irigaray's, that claim there is only one sex, the masculine, that elaborates itself in and through the production of the "Other," and those positions, Foucault's, for instance, that assume that the category of sex, whether masculine or feminine, is a production of a diffuse regulatory economy of sexuality. Consider also Wittig's argument that the category of sex is, under the conditions of compulsory heterosexuality, always feminine (the masculine remaining unmarked and, hence, synonymous with the "universal"). Wittig concurs, however paradoxically, with Foucault in claiming that the category of sex would itself disappear and, indeed, *dissipate* through the disruption and displacement of heterosexual hegemony.

The various explanatory models offered here suggest the very different ways in which the category of sex is understood depending on how the field of power is articulated. Is it possible to maintain the complexity of these fields of power and think through their productive capacities together? On the one hand, Irigaray's theory of sexual difference suggests that women can never be understood on the model of a "subject" within the conventional representational systems of Western culture precisely because they constitute the fetish of representation and, hence, the unrepresentable

as such. Women can never "be," according to this ontology of substances, precisely because they are the relation of difference, the excluded, by which that domain marks itself off. Women are also a "difference" that cannot be understood as the simple negation or "Other" of the always-already-masculine subject. As discussed earlier, they are neither the subject nor its Other, but a difference from the economy of binary opposition, itself a ruse for a monologic elaboration of the masculine.

Central to each of these views, however, is the notion that sex appears within hegemonic language as a *substance,* as, metaphysically speaking, a self-identical being. This appearance is achieved through a performative twist of language and/or discourse that conceals the fact that "being" a sex or a gender is fundamentally impossible.

. . .

In this sense, *gender* is not a noun, but neither is it a set of free-floating attributes, for we have seen that the substantive effect of gender is performatively produced and compelled by the regulatory practices of gender coherence. Hence, within the inherited discourse of the metaphysics of substance, gender proves to be performative—that is, constituting the identity it is purported to be. In this sense, gender is always a doing, though not a doing by a subject who might be said to preexist the deed. The challenge for rethinking gender categories outside of the metaphysics of substance will have to consider the relevance of Nietzsche's claim in *On the Genealogy of Morals* that "there is no 'being' behind doing, effecting, becoming; 'the doer' is merely a fiction added to the deed—the deed is everything." In an application that Nietzsche himself would not have anticipated or condoned, we might state as a corollary: There is no gender identity behind the expressions of gender; that identity is performatively constituted by the very "expressions" that are said to be its results.

READING 22

The Power of Self-Definition

Patricia Hill Collins

FINDING A VOICE: COMING TO TERMS WITH CONTRADICTIONS

"To be able to use the range of one's voice, to attempt to express the totality of self, is a recurring struggle in the tradition of [Black women] writers" maintains Black feminist literary critic Barbara Christian. (1985, p. 172) African-American women have certainly expressed our individual voices. Black women have been described as generally outspoken and self-assertive speakers, and as a consequence of an Afrocentric expectation that both men and women participate in the public sphere, Black women communicate more nearly as equals with Black men. (Stanback 1985) But despite this tradition, the overarching theme of finding a voice to express a self-defined Black women's standpoint remains a core theme in Black feminist thought.

Why this theme of self-definition should preoccupy African-American women is not surprising. Black women's lives are a series of negotiations that aim to reconcile the contradictions separating our own internally defined images of self as African-American women with our objectification as the Other. The struggle of living two lives, one for "them and one for ourselves" (Gwaltney 1980, p. 240) creates a peculiar tension to extract the definition of one's true self from the treatment afforded the denigrated categories in which all Black women are placed.

Much of the best of Black feminist thought reflects this effort to find a self-defined voice and express a fully articulated Afrocentric feminist standpoint. Audre Lorde observes that "within this country where racial difference creates a constant, if unspoken, distortion of vision, Black women have on the one hand always been highly visible, and so, on the other hand, have been rendered invisible through the depersonalization of racism." (1984, p. 42) Lorde also points out that the "visibility which makes us most vulnerable"—that accompanying being black—"is that which is also the source of our greatest strength." (p. 42) The category of "Black woman" makes all Black women especially visible and open to the objectification afforded Black women as a category. This group treatment renders each Black woman invisible as a fully human individual. But paradoxically, being treated as an invisible Other gives Black women a peculiar angle of vision, the outsider-within stance that has served so many African-American women intellectuals as a source of tremendous strength.

Resolving contradictions of this magnitude takes considerable inner strength. In describing the development of her own racial identity, Pauli Murray remembers: "My own self-esteem was elusive and difficult to sustain. I was not entirely free from the prevalent idea that I must prove myself worthy of the rights that white individuals took for granted. This psychological conditioning along with fear had reduced my capacity for resistance to racial injustice." (1987, p. 106) Murray's quest was for constructed knowledge (Belenky et al. 1986), a type of knowledge essential to resolving contradictions. To learn to speak in a "unique and authentic voice, women must 'jump outside' the frames and systems authorities provide and create their own frame." (p. 134) Unlike white women's images attached to the cult of true womanhood, the controlling images applied to Black women are so uniformly negative that they almost necessitate resistance if Black women are to have any positive self-images. For Black women, constructed knowledge of self emerges from the struggle to reject controlling images and

Reprinted from *Black Feminist Thought, Knowledge, Consciousness, and the Politics of Empowerment* by Patricia Hill Collins (1990) by permission of the publisher, Routledge: New York and London.

integrate knowledge deemed personally important, usually knowledge essential to Black women's survival.[1]

SAFE SPACES AND FINDING A VOICE

While domination may be inevitable as a social fact, it is unlikely to be hegemonic as an ideology within that social space where Black women speak freely. This realm of relatively safe discourse, however narrow, is a necessary condition for Black women's resistance. Extended families, churches, and African-American community organizations are important locations where safe discourse potentially can occur. Sondra O'Neale describes the workings of this Black women's space: "Beyond the mask, in the ghetto of the black women's community, in her family, and, more important, in her psyche, is and has always been another world, a world in which she functions—sometimes in sorrow but more often in genuine joy . . .—by doing the things that 'normal' black women do." (1986, p. 139) This space is not only safe—it forms a prime location for resisting objectification as the Other. In this space Black women "observe the feminine images of the 'larger' culture, realize that these models are at best unsuitable and at worst destructive to them, and go about the business of fashioning themselves after the prevalent, historical black female role models in their own community." (O'Neale 1986, p. 139) By advancing Black women's empowerment through self-definition, the safe spaces housing this culture of resistance help Black women resist the dominant ideology promulgated not only outside Black communities but within African-American institutions.

These institutional sites where Black women construct independent self-definitions reflect the dialectical nature of oppression and activism. Institutions controlled by the dominant group such as schools, the media, literature, and popular culture are the initial source of externally defined, controlling images. African-American women have traditionally used Black families and community institutions as places where they

could develop a Black women's culture of resistance. But African-American institutions such as churches and extended families can also perpetuate this dominant ideology. The resulting reality is much more complex than one of an external white society objectifying Black women as the Other with a unified Black community staunchly challenging these external assaults through its "culture of resistance." Instead, African-American women find themselves in a web of cross-cutting relationships, each presenting varying combinations of controlling images and Black women's self-definitions.

. . .

Black Women's Relationships with One Another

Black women's efforts to find a voice have occurred in at least three safe spaces. One location involves Black women's relationships with one another. In some cases, such as friendships and family interactions, these relationships are informal, private dealings among individuals. In others, as was the case during slavery (D. White 1985), in Black churches (Gilkes 1985), or in Black women's organizations (Gilkes 1982; Giddings 1988), more formal organizational ties have nurtured powerful Black women's communities. As mothers, daughters, sisters, and friends to one another, African-American women affirm one another. (Myers 1980)

The mother/daughter relationship is one fundamental relationship among Black women. Countless Black mothers have empowered their daughters by passing on the everyday knowledge essential to survival as African-American women. (Joseph 1981; Collins 1987) Mothers and mother figures emerge as central figures in autobiographies such as Maya Angelou's *I Know Why the Caged Bird Sings* (1969), Bebe Moore Campbell's *Sweet Summer* (1989), and Mamie Garvin Fields and Karen Fields's *Lemon Swamp and other Places* (1983). Alice Walker attributes the trust she has in herself to her mother. Walker "never doubted her powers of judgment because her mother assumed that they were sound; she never questioned her right to follow her intellectual bent, because her mother implicitly entitled her to it." (Washington 1984, p. 145) By giving her daughter a library card, Walker's mother knew the value of a free mind.

In the comfort of daily conversations, through serious conversation and humor, African-American women as sisters and friends affirm one another's humanity, specialness, and right to exist. Black women's fiction, such as Toni Cade Bambara's short story "The Johnson Girls" (1981) and Toni Morrison's novels *Sula* (1974), *The Bluest Eye* (1970), and *Beloved* (1987), is the primary location where Black women's friendships are taken seriously. In a dialogue with four other Black women, Evelyne Hammond describes this special relationship that Black women can have with one another: "I think most of the time you have to be there to experience it. When I am with other black women I always laugh. I think our humor comes from a shared recognition of who we all are in the world." (Clarke et al. 1983, p. 114)

This shared recognition often operates among African-American women who do not know one another but who see the need to value Black womanhood. Marita Golden describes her efforts in 1968 to attend a college which was "nestled . . . in the comfortable upper reaches of northwest Washington, surrounded by . . . the manicured, sprawling lawns of the city's upper class." To enter this world, Golden caught the bus downtown with "black women domestic workers who rode to the end of the line to clean house for young and middle-aged white matrons." Golden describes her fellow travelers' reaction to her acquiring a college education:

> They gazed proudly at me, nodding at the books in my lap. . . . I accepted their encouragement and hated America for never allowing them to be selfish or greedy, to feel the steel-hard bite of ambition. . . . They had parlayed their anger, brilliantly shaped it into a soft armor of survival. The spirit of those women sat with me in every class I took. (Golden 1983, p. 21)

My decision to pursue my doctorate was stimulated by a similar experience. In 1978 I offered a seminar as part of a national summer institute for teachers and other school personnel. After my Chicago workshop, an older Black woman participant whispered to me, "Honey, I'm real proud of you. Some folks don't want to see you up there [in the front of the classroom] but you belong there. Go back to school and get your PhD and then they won't be able to tell you nothing!" In talking with other Black women, I have discovered that many of us have had similar experiences.

This issue of Black women being the ones who really listen to one another is an important one, particularly given the importance of voice in Black women's lives. (hooks 1989)[2] Audre Lorde describes the importance of voice in self-affirmation: "Of course I am afraid, because the transformation of silence into language and action is an act of self-revelation, and that always seems fraught with danger." (1984, p. 42) One can write for a nameless, faceless audience, but the act of using one's voice requires a listener. For African-American women the listener most able to move beyond the invisibility created by objectification as the Other in order to see and hear the fully human Black woman is another Black woman. This process of trusting one another can seem dangerous because only Black women know what it means to be Black women. But if we will not listen to one another, then who will?

While social science research on Black women's relationships remains scarce, Black women writers have recognized their importance. Mary Helen Washington points out that one distinguishing feature of Black women's literature is that it is about African-American women. Women talk to one another, and "their friendships with other women—mothers, sisters, grandmothers, friends, lovers—are vital to their growth and well being." (1987, p. xxi) This emphasis on Black women's relationships is so striking that novelist Gayl Jones suggests that women writers select different themes from those of their male counterparts. In the work of many Black male writers, the significant relationships are those that involve confrontation with individuals outside the family and community. But among Black women writers, relationships within the family and community, between men and women, and among women are treated as complex and significant. (Tate 1983, p. 92)

Black women writers have explored themes such as the difficulties inherent in affirming Black women in a society that denigrates African-American women (Claudia's use of her relationship with her sister in searching for positive Black women's images in Toni Morrison's *The Bluest Eye*); of how Black women's relationships can support and renew (the relationship between Celie and Shug in Alice Walker's *The Color Purple*); or how such relationships can control and repress (Audre Lorde's relationship with her mother in *Zami* [1982]). Perhaps Ntozake Shange best summarizes the importance that Black women can have for one another in resisting oppressive conditions. Shange gives the following reason for why she writes: "When I die, I will not be guilty of having left a generation of girls behind thinking that anyone can tend to their emotional health other than themselves." (in Tate 1983, p. 162)

The Black Women's Blues Tradition

African-American music as art has provided a second location where Black women have found a voice. "Art is special because of its ability to influence feelings as well as knowledge," suggests Angela Davis. (1989, p. 200) Davis contends that the dominant group failed to grasp the social function of music in general and particularly the central role music played in all aspects of life in West African society. As a result, "Black people were able to create with their music an aesthetic community of resistance, which in turn encouraged and nurtured a political community of active struggle for freedom." (1989, p. 201) Spirituals, blues, jazz, and the progressive raps of the 1980s all form part of a "continuum of struggle which is at once aesthetic and political." (p. 201)

Afrocentric communication maintains the integrity of the individual and his or her personal voice, but does so in the context of group activity. (Smitherman 1977; Kochman 1981; Asante 1987; Cannon 1988; Brown 1989) In music one effect of this oral mode of discourse is that individuality, rather than being stifled by group activity or being equated with specialization, actually flourishes in a group context. (Sidran 1971)[3] "There's something about music that is so penetrating that your soul gets the message. No matter what trouble comes to a person, music can help him face it," claims Mahalia Jackson. (1985, p. 454) "A song must do something for me as well as for the people that hear it. I can't sing a song that doesn't have a message. If it doesn't have the strength it can't lift you." (p. 446)

The blues tradition is an essential part of African-American music.[4] Blues singer Alberta Hunter explains the importance of the blues as a way of dealing with pain: "To me, the blues are almost religious . . . almost sacred—when we sing the blues, we're singing out of our own hearts . . . our feelings." (Harrison 1978, p. 63) Black people's ability to cope with and even transcend trouble without ignoring it means that it will not destroy us. (Cone 1972)

Traditionally, blues assumed a similar function in African-American oral culture as that played by print media for white, visually based culture. Blues was not just entertainment—it was a way of solidifying community and commenting on the social fabric of Black life in America. Sherley Anne Williams contends that "the blues records of each decade explain something about the philosophical basis of our lives as black people. If we don't understand that as so-called intellectuals, then we don't really understand anything about ourselves." (in Tate 1983, p. 208) For African-American women, blues seemed to be everywhere. Mahalia Jackson describes its pervasiveness during her childhood in New Orleans: "The famous white singers like Caruso—you might hear them when you went by a white folk's house, but in a colored house you heard blues. You couldn't help but hear blues—all through the thin partitions of the houses—through the open windows—up and down the street in the colored neighborhoods—everybody played it real loud." (1985, p. 447)

Black women have been central in maintaining, transforming, and recreating the blues tradition of African-American culture. (Harrison 1978, 1988; Russell 1982) Michele Russell asserts that the "blues, first and last, are a familiar idiom for Black women, even a staple of life." (1982, p. 130) Blues has occupied a special place in Black women's music as a site of the expression of Black women's self-definitions. The blues singer strives to create an atmosphere in which analysis can take place, and yet this atmosphere is intensely personal and individualistic. When Black women sing the blues, we sing our own personalized, individualistic blues while simultaneously expressing the collective blues of African-American women.

. . .

The Voices of Black Women Writers

During the summer of 1944, recent law school graduate Pauli Murray returned to her California apartment and found the following anonymous note from the "South Crocker Street Property Owner's Association" tacked to her door: "We . . . wish to inform you the flat you now occupy . . . is restricted to the white or Caucasian race only. . . . We intend to uphold these restrictions, therefore we ask that you vacate the above mentioned flat . . . within seven days." (1987, p. 253) Murray's response was to write. She remembers: "I was learning that creative expression is an integral part of the equipment needed in the service of a compelling cause; it is another form of activism. Words poured from my typewriter." (p. 255)

Increased literacy among African-Americans has provided new opportunities for Black women to transform former institutional sites of domination such as scholarship and literature into institutional sites of resistance. Trudier Harris (1988) suggests that a community of Black women writers has emerged since 1970, one in

which African-American women engage in dialogue among one another in order to explore formerly taboo subjects. Black feminist literary criticism is documenting the intellectual and personal space created for African-American women in this emerging body of ideas. (Washington 1980, 1982; Tate 1983; Evans 1984; Christian 1985; McDowell 1985; Pryse and Spillers 1985; O'Neale 1986) Especially noteworthy are the ways in which this emerging community of Black women writers builds on former themes and approaches of the Black women's blues tradition (Williams 1979) and of earlier Black women writers. (Cannon 1988) Also key are the new themes raised by contemporary Black women writers. For example, Trudier Harris (1988) contends that a variety of taboos are violated in contemporary Black women's literature, among them the taboos that Black women were not allowed to leave their children, have interracial affairs, have lesbian relationships, be the victims of incest, or generally escape the confining image of "long-suffering commitment to Black people." In all, the emerging work of this growing community potentially offers another safe space where Black women can articulate a self-defined standpoint.

Not everyone agrees that Black women writers are using the full range of their voices to create safe spaces. In discussing the potential for systems of domination to harness the creative potential of Black music, Angela Davis observes, "some of the superstars of popular-musical culture today are unquestionably musical geniuses, but they have distorted the Black music tradition by brilliantly developing its form while ignoring its content of struggle and freedom." (1989, p. 208) Black literary critic Sondra O'Neale suggests that a similar process may be affecting Black women's writing. "Where are the Angela Davises, Ida B. Wellses, and Daisy Bateses of black feminist literature?" she asks. (1986, p. 144) O'Neale contends that one of the tasks of the Black woman critic is to assess whether contemporary Black women's literature reveals those strengths that have furthered Black women's survival. "Lamentably," O'Neale points out, "we are still seeing the black women in roles that the prevailing cultural manipulators ascribe to her—always on the fringes of society, always alone." (p. 153)

The specialized thought of contemporary Black feminist writers and scholars should be able to draw on the long-standing Afrocentric tradition of struggle in order to produce "progressive art." As Angela Davis observes, "progressive art can assist people to learn not only about the objective forces at work in the society in which they live, but also about the intensely social character of their interior lives. Ultimately it can propel people toward social emancipation." (1989, p. 200) This type of art is emancipatory because it fuses thought, feeling, and action and helps its participants see their world differently and act to change it. Traditionally, everyday thought expressed in Black women's music approximated this definition of *progressive*. It remains to be seen whether the specialized thought generated by contemporary Black feminist thinkers in very different institutional locations is capable of creating safe spaces that will carry African-American women even further.

CONSCIOUSNESS AS A SPHERE OF FREEDOM

Taken together, Black women's relationships with one another, the Black women's blues tradition, and the emerging influence of Black women writers coalesce to offer an alternative worldview to that embedded in institutional locations of domination. These three sites offer safe spaces that nurture the everyday and specialized thought of African-American women and where Black women intellectuals can absorb ideas and experiences for the task of rearticulating Black women's experiences and infusing them with new meaning. More important, these new meanings offer African-American women potentially powerful tools to resist the controlling images of Black womanhood. Far from being a secondary concern in bringing about so-

cial change, challenging controlling images and replacing them with a Black women's standpoint is an essential component in resisting systems of race, gender, and class oppression. (Thompson-Cager 1989) What are some of the fundamental themes developed in these safe spaces?

The Importance of Self-Definition

"Black groups digging on white philosophies ought to consider the source. Know who's playing the music before you dance," cautions poet Nikki Giovanni. (1971, p. 126) Her advice is especially germane for African-American women. Giovanni suggests: "We Black women are the single group in the West intact. And anybody can see we're pretty shaky. We are . . . the only group that derives its identity from itself. I think it's been rather unconscious but we measure ourselves by ourselves, and I think that's a practice we can ill afford to lose." (1971, p. 144) Black women's survival is at stake, and creating self-definitions reflecting an independent Afrocentric feminist consciousness is an essential part of that survival.

The issue of the journey from internalized oppression to the "free mind" of a self-defined, Afrocentric feminist consciousness is a prominent theme in the works of Black women writers. Author Alexis DeVeaux notes that there is a "great exploration of the self in women's work. It's the self in relationship with an intimate other, with the community, the nation, and the world." (in Tate 1983, p. 54) Far from being a narcissistic or trivial concern, this placement of self at the center of analysis is critical for understanding a host of other relationships. DeVeaux continues, "you have to understand what your place as an individual is and the place of the person who is close to you. You have to understand the space between you before you can understand more complex or larger groups." (p. 54)

Black women have also stressed the importance of self-definition as part of the journey from victimization to a free mind in their blues. Sherley Anne Williams's analysis of the affirmation of self in the blues make a critical contribution in understanding the blues as a Black women's text. In discussing the blues roots of Black literature, Williams notes, "the assertion of individuality and the implied assertion—as action, not mere verbal statement—of self is an important dimension of the blues." (1979, p. 130)

The assertion of self usually comes at the end of a song, after the description or analysis of the troublesome situation. This affirmation of self is often the only solution to that problem or situation. Nina Simone's (1985) classic blues song "Four Women" illustrates this use of the blues to affirm self. Simone sings of three Black women whose experiences typify controlling images— Aunt Sarah, the mule, whose back is bent from a lifetime of hard work; Sweet Thing, the Black prostitute who will belong to anyone who has money to buy; and Saphronia, the mulatto whose Black mother was raped late one night. Simone explores Black women's objectification as the Other by invoking the pain these three women actually feel. But Peaches, the fourth woman, is an especially powerful figure, because Peaches is angry. "I'm awfully bitter these days," Peaches cries out, "because my parents were slaves." These words and the feelings they invoke demonstrate her growing awareness and self-definition of the situation she encountered and offer to the listener, not sadness and remorse, but an anger that leads to action. This is the type of individuality Williams means—not that of talk but self-definitions that foster action.

While the theme of the journey also appears in the work of Black men, African-American women writers and musicians explore this journey toward freedom in ways that are characteristically female (Thompson-Cager 1989). Black women's journeys, though at times embracing political and social issues, basically take personal and psychological forms and rarely reflect the freedom of movement of Black men who "hop trains," "hit the road," or in other ways physically travel in order to find that elusive sphere of freedom from racial oppression. Instead, Black women's journeys often involve "the transformation of silence into language and action." (Lorde 1984, p. 40) Typically tied

to children and/or community, fictional Black women characters search for self-definition within close geographical boundaries. Even though physical limitations confine the Black heroine's quest to a specific area, "forming complex personal relationships adds depth to her identity quest in lieu of geographical breadth." (Tate 1983, p. xxi) In their search for self-definition and the power of a free mind, Black heroines may remain "motionless on the outside . . . but inside?"

Given the physical limitations on Black women's mobility, the conceptualization of self that is part of Black women's self-definitions is distinctive. Self is not defined as the increased autonomy gained by separating oneself from others. Instead, self is found in the context of family and community—as Paule Marshall describes it, "the ability to recognize one's continuity with the larger community." (Washington 1984, p. 159) By being accountable to others, African-American women develop more fully human, less objectified selves. Sonia Sanchez points to this version of self by stating, "we must move past always focusing on the 'personal self' because there's a larger self. There's a 'self' of black people." (Tate 1983, p. 134) Rather than defining self in opposition to others, the connectedness among individuals provides Black women deeper, more meaningful self-definitions.[5]

This journey toward self-definition has political significance. As Mary Helen Washington observes, Black women who struggle to "forge an identity larger than the one society would force upon them . . . are aware and conscious, and that very consciousness is potent." (1980, p. xv) Identity is not the goal but rather the point of departure in the process of self-definition. In this process Black women journey toward an understanding of how our personal lives have been fundamentally shaped by interlocking systems of race, gender, and class oppression. Peaches's statement, "I'm awfully bitter these days because my parents were slaves," illustrates this transformation.

The journey toward self-definition offers a powerful challenge to the externally defined, controlling images of African-American women. Replacing negative images with positive ones can be equally problematic if the function of stereotypes as controlling images remains unrecognized. John Gwaltney's (1980) interview with Nancy White, a 73-year-old Black woman, suggests that ordinary Black women can be acutely aware of the power of these controlling images. To Nancy White the difference between the controlling images applied to African-American and white women are those of degree, not of kind:

> My mother used to say that the black woman is the white man's mule and the white woman is his dog. Now, she said that to say this: we do the heavy work and get beat whether we do it well or not. But the white woman is closer to the master and he pats them on the head and lets them sleep in the house, but he ain't gon' treat neither one like he was dealing with a person. (p. 148)

Although both groups are objectified, albeit in different ways, the function of the images is to dehumanize and control both groups. Seen in this light, it makes little sense in the long run for Black women to exchange one set of controlling images for another even if positive stereotypes bring better treatment in the short run.

The insistence of Black female self-definition reframes the entire dialogue from one of protesting the technical accuracy of an image—namely, refuting the Black matriarchy thesis—to one stressing the power dynamics underlying the very process of definition itself. By insisting on self-definition, Black women question not only what has been said about African-American women but the credibility and the intentions of those possessing the power to define. When Black women define themselves, we clearly reject the assumption that those in positions granting them the authority to interpret our reality are entitled to do so. Regardless of the actual content of Black women's self-definitions, the act of insisting on Black female self-definition validates Black women's power as human subjects.

Self-Valuation and Respect

While self-definition speaks to the power dynamics involved in rejecting externally defined, controlling images of Black womanhood, the theme of Black women's self-valuation addresses the actual content of these self-definitions. Through relationships with one another, music, and literature, African-American women create self-valuations that challenge externally defined notions of Black womanhood.

Many of the controlling images applied to African-American women are actually distorted renderings of those aspects of our behavior that threaten existing power arrangements. (Gilkes 1983a; White 1985) For example, strong mothers are threatening because they contradict elite white male definitions of femininity. To ridicule strong, assertive Black mothers by labeling them matriarchs reflects an effort to control a dimension of Black women's behavior that threatens the status quo. African-American women who value those aspects of Black womanhood that are stereotyped, ridiculed, and maligned in scholarship and the popular media challenge some of the basic ideas inherent in an ideology of domination.

The significance of self-valuation is illustrated through the emphasis that Black feminist thinkers place on respect. In a society in which no one is obligated to respect African-American women, we have long admonished one another to have self-respect and to demand the respect of others. Black women's voices from a variety of sources resonate with this demand for respect. Katie G. Cannon (1988) suggests that Black womanist ethics embraces three basic dimensions of "invisible dignity," "quiet grace," and "unstated courage," all qualities essential for self-valuation and self-respect. Black feminist critic Claudia Tate (1983) reports that the issue of self-esteem is so primary in the writing of Black women that it deserves special attention. Tate claims that what the writers seem to be saying is that "women must assume responsibility for strengthening their self-esteem by learning to love and appreciate themselves." (p. xxiii) Her analysis is certainly borne out in Alice Walker's comments to an audience of women. Walker cautioned, "please remember, especially in these times of group-think and the right-on chorus, that no person is your friend (or kin) who demands your silence, or denies your right to grow and be perceived as fully blossomed as you were intended. Or who belittles in any fashion the gifts you labor so to bring into the world." (Walker 1983, p. 36) The right to be Black *and* female *and* respected pervades everyday conversations among African-American women. In describing the importance self-respect has for her, elderly domestic worker Sara Brooks notes, "I may not have as much as you, I may not have the education you got, but still, if I conduct myself as a decent person, I'm just as good as anybody." (Simonsen 1986, p. 132)

Respect from others—especially from Black men—is a recurring theme in Black women's writing. In describing the things a woman wants out of life, middle-class Marita Bonner lists "a career as fixed and as calmly brilliant as the North Star. The one real thing that money buys. Time . . . And of course, a husband you can look up to without looking down on yourself." (Bonner 1987, p. 3) Black women's belief in respect also emerges in the works of a variety of Black women blues singers. Perhaps the best-known popular statement of Black women's demand for self-respect and that of others is found in Aretha Franklin's (1967) rendition of the Otis Redding song "Respect." Aretha sings to her man:

> What you want? Baby I got it.
> What you need? You know I got it.
> All I'm asking for is a little respect when you
>   come home.

Even though the lyrics can be sung by anyone, they take on special meaning when sung by Aretha in the way that she sings them. On one level the song functions as a metaphor for the condition of African-Americans in a racist society. But Aretha's being a Black woman enables the song to tap a deeper meaning. Within the blues tradition, the listening audience of African-American women assumes "we" Black women,

even though Aretha as the blues singer sings "I." Sherley Ann Williams describes the power of Aretha's blues: "Aretha was right on time, but there was also something about the way Aretha characterized respect as something given with force and great effort and cost. And when she even went so far as to spell the word 'respect,' we just knew that this sister wasn't playing around about getting Respect and keeping it." (Williams 1979, p. 124)

June Jordan suggests that this emphasis on respect is tied to a distinctive Black feminist politic. For Jordan, a "morally defensible Black feminism" is verified in the ways Black women present ourselves to others, and in the ways in which Black women treat people different from ourselves. While self-respect is essential, respect for others is key. "As a Black feminist," claims Jordan, "I cannot be expected to respect what somebody else calls self-love if that concept of self-love requires my suicide to any degree." (1981, p. 144)

Self-Reliance and Independence

In her 1831 essay Black feminist thinker Maria Stewart not only encouraged Black women's self-definition and self-valuations but linked Black women's self-reliance with issues of survival:

> We have never had an opportunity of displaying our talents; therefore the world thinks we know nothing. . . . Possess the spirit of independence. The Americans do, and why should not you? Possess the spirit of men, bold and enterprising, fearless and undaunted: Sue for your rights and privileges. . . . You can but die if you make the attempt; and we shall certainly die if you do not. (Richardson 1987, p. 38)

Whether by choice or circumstance, African-American women have "possessed the spirit of independence," have been self-reliant, and have encouraged one another to value this vision of womanhood that clearly challenges prevailing notions of femininity. (Steady 1987) These beliefs apparently find wide support among African-American women. For example, when asked what they admired about their mothers, the women in Gloria Joseph's (1981) study of the Black mother/daughter relationship recounted their mothers' independence and ability to provide in the face of difficulties. Participants in Lena Wright Myers's (1980) study of Black women's coping skills respected women who were resourceful and self-reliant. Black women's autobiographies, such as Shirley Chisholm's *Unbought and Unbossed* (1970) and Maya Angelou's *I Know Why the Caged Bird Sings* (1969), typify Black women's self-valuation of self-reliance. As elderly domestic worker Nancy White cogently explains, "most black women can be their own boss, so that's what they be." (Gwaltney 1980, p. 149)

The works of prominent Black women blues singers also counsel the importance of self-reliance and independence for African-American women. In her classic ballad "God Bless the Child That Got His Own," Billie Holiday sings:

> The strong gets more, while the weak ones fade,
> Empty pockets don't ever make the grade;
> Mama may have, Papa may have,
> But God bless the child that got his own!
> —(*Billie Holiday Anthology* 1976, p. 12)

In this mournful song Billie Holiday offers an insightful analysis of the need for autonomy and self-reliance. "Money, you got lots of friends, crowdin' round the door," she proclaims. But "when you're gone and spendin' ends they don't come no more." In these passages Holiday admonishes Black women to become financially independent because having one's "own" allows women to choose their relationships. In "Tain't Nobody's Business if I Do," Holiday offers a vision of the type of freedom Black women will have if we become self-reliant and independent:

> If I should take a notion to jump into the ocean,
> If I dislike my lover and leave him for another,
> If I go to church on Sunday then cabaret on
>   Monday,
> If I should get the feeling to dance upon the ceilin',
> Tain't nobody's business if I do!
> —(*Billie Holiday Anthology* 1976, p. 119)

The linking of economic self-sufficiency as one critical dimension of self-reliance with the demand for respect permeates Black feminist thought. For example, in "Respect" when Aretha sings, "your kisses sweeter than honey, but guess what, so is my money," she demands respect on the basis of her economic self-reliance. Perhaps this connection between respect, self-reliance, and assertiveness is best summarized by Nancy White, who declares, "there is a very few black women that their husbands can pocketbook to death because we can do for ourselves and will do so in a minute!" (Gwaltney 1980, p. 149)

Self, Change, and Empowerment

"The master's tools will never dismantle the master's house. They may allow us temporarily to beat him at his own game, but they will never enable us to bring about genuine change." (Lorde 1984, p. 112) In this passage Audre Lorde explores how independent self-definitions empower Black women to bring about social change. By struggling for a self-defined Afrocentric feminist consciousness that rejects the "master's" images, African-American women change ourselves. This changed consciousness in turn is a fundamental factor in empowering Black women to change the conditions of our lives.

Nikki Giovanni illuminates these connections among self, change, and empowerment. She admonishes that people are rarely powerless, no matter how stringent the restrictions on our lives: "We've got to live in the real world. If we don't like the world we're living in, change it. And if we can't change it, we change ourselves. We can do something." (in Tate 1983, p. 68) Giovanni recognizes that effective change occurs through action. The multiple strategies of resistance that Black women have employed, such as withdrawing from postemancipation agricultural work in order to return their labor to their families, ostensibly conforming to the deference rituals of domestic work, protesting male bias in African-American organizations, or creating the progressive art of Black women's blues all represent physical actions to bring about change. Here is the connected self and the empowerment that comes from change in the context of community.

But change can also occur in the private, personal space of an individual woman's consciousness. Equally fundamental, this type of change is also empowering. If a Black woman is forced to remain "motionless on the outside," she can always develop the "inside" of a changed consciousness as a sphere of freedom. Becoming empowered through self-knowledge, even within conditions that severely limit one's ability to act, is essential. In Black women's literature

> this type of change . . . occurs because the heroine recognizes, and more importantly respects her inability to alter a situation. . . . This is not to imply that she is completely circumscribed by her limitations. On the contrary, she learns to exceed former boundaries but only as a direct result of knowing where they lie. In this regard, she teaches her readers a great deal about constructing a meaningful life in the midst of chaos and contingencies, armed with nothing more than her intellect and emotions. (Tate 1983, p. xxiv)

In this passage Claudia Tate demonstrates the significance of rearticulation. But rearticulation does not mean reconciling Afrocentric feminist ethics and values with opposing Eurocentric masculinist ones. Instead, as Chezia Thompson-Cager contends, rearticulation "confronts them in the tradition of 'naming as power' by revealing them very carefully." (1989, p. 590) Naming daily life by putting language to everyday experience infuses it with the new meaning of an Afrocentric feminist consciousness and becomes a way of transcending the limitations of race, gender, and class subordination.

Black women's literature contains many examples of how Black women are empowered by a changed consciousness. Barbara Christian maintains that the heroines of 1940s Black women's literature, such as Lutie Johnson in Ann Petry's *The Street* (1946) and Cleo Judson in Dorothy West's *The Living Is Easy* (1948), are defeated not only by social reality but by

their "lack of self-knowledge." In contrast, the heroines from the 1950s to the present represent a significant shift toward self-knowledge as a sphere of freedom. Christian dates the shift from Gwendolyn Brooks's *Maud Martha* (1953) and claims, "because Maud Martha constructs her own standards, she manages to transform that 'little life' into so much more despite the limits set on her. . . . [She] emerges neither crushed nor triumphant." (1985, p. 176)

No matter how oppressed an individual woman may be, contemporary African-American women writers place the power to save the self within the self. (Harris 1988) Other Black women may assist a Black woman in this journey toward empowerment, but the ultimate responsibility for self-definitions and self-valuations lies within the individual woman herself. An individual woman may use multiple strategies in her quest for the constructed knowledge of an independent voice. Like Celie in Alice Walker's *The Color Purple,* some women write themselves free. Sexually, physically, and emotionally abused, Celie writes letters to God when no one else will listen. The act of acquiring a voice through writing, of breaking silence with language, eventually moves her to the action of talking with others. Other women talk themselves free. In *Their Eyes Were Watching God,* Janie tells her story to a good friend, a prime example of the rearticulation process essential for Black feminist thought. (Hurston 1937) Ntozake Shange's *For Colored Girls* (1975) also captures this journey toward self-definition, self-valuation, and an empowered self. At the end of the play the women gather around one women who shares the pain she experienced by seeing her children killed. They listen until she says "I found God in myself and I loved her fiercely." These words, expressing her ability to define herself as worthwhile, draw them together. They touch one another as part of a Black women's community that heals the member in pain, but only after she has taken the first step of wanting to be healed, of wanting to make the journey toward finding the voice of empowerment.

Persistence is a fundamental requirement of this journey from silence to language to action. Black women's blues contains numerous messages to Black women to keep on pushing despite the difficulties. When Sweet Honey in the Rock (1985) sing the traditional African-American song "We'll Understand It Better By and By," they sing of hope in times of trouble. When Aretha Franklin (1967) sings that change has been a "long time comin'" but that she knows her "change is gonna come," she acknowledges the difficulties of the present and holds out hope for the future, but only for those who persist. These songs tap deep roots in African-American women. The message is to continue the connectedness of self with others, to persist through the responsibilities of hard times, because understanding and change will come.

Black women's persistence is fostered by the strong belief that to be Black and female is valuable and worthy of respect. In a song "A Change Is Gonna Come," Aretha Franklin (1967) expresses this feeling of enduring in spite of the odds. She sings that there were times that she thought that she would not last for long. She sings of how it has been an "uphill journey all the way" to find the strength to carry on. But in spite of the difficulties, Aretha "knows" that "a change is gonna come."

Actions to bring about change, whether the struggle for an Afrocentric feminist consciousness or the persistence needed for institutional transformation, empower African-American women. Because our actions change the world from one in which we merely exist to one over which we have some control, they enable us to see everyday life as being in process and therefore amenable to change. By persisting in the journey toward self-definition we are changed, and this change empowers us. Perhaps this is why so many African-American women have managed to persist and "make a way out of no way." Perhaps they knew the power of self-definition.

NOTES

1. Belenky et al. (1986) suggest that achieving constructed knowledge requires self-reflection about and distancing from familiar situations, whether psychological and/or physical. For Black women intellectuals, being outsiders within may provide the distance from and angle of vision on the familiar that can be used to "find a voice" or create constructed knowledge. Belenky et al. describe this process as affecting individuals. I suggest that a similar argument can be applied to Black women as a group.

2. Belenky et al. (1986) report that women repeatedly use the metaphor of voice to depict their intellectual and ethical development: "The tendency for women to ground their epistemological premises in metaphors suggesting speaking and listening is at odds with the visual metaphors (such as equating knowledge with illumination, knowing with seeing, and truth with light) that scientists and philosophers most often use to express their sense of mind." (p. 16) This emphasis on voice in women's culture parallels the importance of oral communications in African-American culture. (Sidran 1971; Smitherman 1977)

3. Sidran (1971) suggests that to get one's own "sound" is a key part of vocalized Black music. Black theologian James Cone has also written about Black music as carrier of the values of African-American culture. Cone notes that Black music is "unity music. It unites the joy and the sorrow, the love and the hate, the hope and the despair of black people. . . . Black music is unifying because it confronts the individual with the truth of black existence and affirms that black being is possible only in a communal context. Black music is fundamental. Its purposes and aims are directly related to the consciousness of the black community." (1972, p. 5) Note the both/and orientation of Cone's description, an analysis rejecting the either/or dichotomous thinking of Western societies.

4. Black women have participated in all forms of Black music but have been especially central in vocal music such as spirituals, gospel, and the blues. (Jackson 1981) I focus on the blues because of its association with the Black women's secular tradition. Though a more recent phenomenon,

gospel music is also "a Black feminine musical tradition." (Jackson 1981) With roots in the urban Black folk church, the text of gospel songs could also be examined. Another emerging location for Black women's voice is in the works of African-American women filmmakers. Julie Dash's *Illusions* and *Diary of an African Nun,* Michelle Parkerson's *Gotta Make That Journey: Sweet Honey in the Rock,* Ayoka Chenzira's satiric *Hair Piece,* and Kathleen Collins's *Losing Ground* all explore different facets of Black women's reality. For information on Black women filmmakers, see Campbell (1983). More general information on Black women in film can be found in Mapp (1973).

5. Afrocentric scholars have examined this conceptualization of the self in African and African-American communities. See Smitherman (1977), Asante (1987), Myers (1988), and Brown (1989). For feminist analyses of women's development of self as a distinctive process, see especially Evelyn Keller's (1985) discussion of dynamic autonomy and how it relates to relationships of domination, and Benhabib and Cornell's (1987) discussion of the unencumbered self.

REFERENCES

Angelou, Maya. *I Know Why the Caged Bird Sings.* New York: Bantam, 1969.

Asante, Molefi Kete. *The Afrocentric Idea.* Philadelphia: Temple University Press, 1987.

Bambara, Toni Cade. "The Johnson Girls." 1981.

Belenky, Mary Field, Blythe McVicker Clinchy, Nancy Rule Goldberger, and Jill Mattuck Tarule. *Women's Ways of Knowing.* New York: Basic Books, 1986.

Benhabib, Seyla, and Drucilla Cornell. "Introduction: Beyond the Politics of Gender." In *Feminism as Critique,* ed. Seyla Benhabib and Drucilla Cornell. Minneapolis: University of Minnesota Press, 1987, pp. 1–15.

Billie Holiday Anthology/Lady Sings the Blues. Ojai, CA: Creative Concepts Publishing, 1976.

Bonner, Marita O. "On Being Young—A Woman—and Colored." In *Frye Street and Environs: The Collected Works of Marita Bonner,* ed. Joyce Flynn and Joyce Occomy Stricklin. Boston: Beacon, 1987, pp. 3–8.

Brooks, Gwendolyn. *Maud Martha.* Boston: Atlantic Press, 1953.

Brown, Elsa Barkley. "African-American Women's Quilting: A Framework for Conceptualizing and Teaching African-American Women's History." *Signs: Journal of Women in Culture and Society,* no. 4 (1989), pp. 921–9.

Campbell, Loretta. "Reinventing Our Image: Eleven Black Women Filmmakers." *Heresies* 4, no. 4 (1983), pp. 58–62.

Campbell, Bebe Moore. *Sweet Summer: Growing Up with and without My Dad.* New York: Putnam, 1989.

Cannon, Katie G. *Black Womanist Ethics.* Atlanta: Scholars Press, 1988.

Chisholm, Shirley. *Unbought and Unbossed.* New York: Avon, 1970.

Christian, Barbara. *Black Feminist Criticism, Perspectives on Black Women Writers.* New York, Pergamon, 1985.

Clarke, Cheryl, Jewell L. Gomez, Evelyn Hammonds, Bonnie Johnson, and Linda Powell. "Conversations and Questions: Black Women on Black Women Writers." *Conditions: Nine* 3, no. 3 (1983), pp. 88–137.

Collins, Patricia Hill. "The Meaning of Motherhood in Black Culture and Black Mother/Daughter Relationships." *Sage: A Scholarly Journal on Black Women* 4, no. 2 (1987), pp. 4–11.

Cone, James H. *The Spirituals and the Blues: An Interpretation.* New York: Seabury Press, 1972.

Davis, Angela Y. *Women, Culture, and Politics.* New York: Random House, 1989.

Evans, Mari, ed. *Black Women Writers (1950–1980).* Garden City, NY: Anchor, 1984.

Fields, Mamie Garvin, and Karen Fields. *Lemon Swamp and Other Places: A Carolina Memoir.* New York: Free Press, 1983.

Franklin, Aretha. *I Never Loved a Man the Way I Love You.* Atlantic Recording Corp., 1967.

Giddings, Paula. *In Search of Sisterhood: Delta Sigma Theta and the Challenge of the Black Sorority Movement.* New York: William Morrow, 1988.

Gilkes, Cheryl Townsend. "From Slavery to Social Welfare: Racism and the Control of Black Women." In *Class, Race, and Sex: The Dynamics of Control,* ed. Amy Swerdlow and Hanna Lessinger. Boston: G. K. Hall, 1983a, pp. 288–300.

———. "Going Up for the Oppressed: The Career Mobility of Black Women Community Workers." *Journal of Social Issues* 39, no. 3 (1983b), pp. 115–39.

———. 1985. " 'Together and in Harness': Women's Traditions in the Sanctified Church." *Signs* 10, no. 4 (1985), pp. 678–99.

Gilkes, Cheryl Townsend. "Successful Rebellious Profiles: The Black Woman's Professional Identity and Community Commitment." *Psychology of Women Quarterly* 6, no. 3 (1982), pp. 289–311.

Giovanni, Nikki. *Gemini.* New York: Penguin, 1971.

Golden, Marita. *Migrations of the Heart.* New York: Ballantine, 1983.

Gwaltney, John Langston. *Drylongso, A Self-Portrait of Black America.* New York: Vintage, 1980.

Harris, Trudier. *From Mammies to Militants: Domestics in Black American Literature.* Philadelphia: Temple University Press, 1982.

———. *Transcending Guilt: The Creation of a New Universe in the Works of Toni Cade Bambara, Alice Walker, and Toni Morrison.* Cincinnati: Women's Studies Program, University of Cincinnati Colloquium, 1988.

Harrison, Daphne Duval. "Black Women in the Blues Tradition." In *The Afro-American Woman: Struggles and Images,* ed. Sharon Harley and Rosalyn Terborg-Penn. Port Washington, NY: Kennikat Press, 1978, pp. 58–73.

Harrison, Daphne Duval. *Black Pearls: Blues Queens of the 1920s.* New Brunswick, NJ: Rutgers University Press, 1988.

hooks, bell. *Talking Back: Thinking Feminist, Thinking Black.* Boston: South End Press, 1989.

Hurston, Zora Neale. *Their Eyes Were Watching God.* Greenwich, CT: Fawcett, 1937.

Jackson, Irene V. "Black Women and Music: From Africa to the New World." In *The Black Woman Cross-Culturally,* ed. Filomina Chioma Steady. Cambridge, MA: Schenkman, 1981, pp. 383–401.

Jackson, Mahalia. "Singing of Good Tidings and Freedom." In *Afro-American Religious History,* ed. Milton C. Sernett. Durham, NC: Duke University Press, 1985, pp. 446–57.

Jordan, June. *Civil Wars.* Boston: Beacon, 1981.

Joseph, Gloria. "Black Mothers and Daughters: Their Roles and Functions in American Society." In *Common Differences,* ed. Gloria Joseph and Jill Lewis. Garden City, NY: Anchor, 1981, pp. 75–126.

Keller, Evelyn Fox. *Reflections on Gender and Science.* New Haven, CT: Yale University Press, 1985.

Kochman, Thomas. *Black and White Styles in Conflict.* Chicago: University of Chicago Press, 1981.

Lorde, Audre. *Zami, A New Spelling of My Name.* Trumansberg, NY: The Crossing Press, 1982.

———. *Sister Outsider.* Trumansberg, NY: The Crossing Press, 1984.

Mapp, Edward. "Black Women in Films." *Black Scholar* 4, no. 6–7 (1973), pp. 42–6.

McDowell, Deborah E. "New Directions for Black Feminist Criticism." In *The New Feminist Criticism,* ed. Elaine Showalter. New York: Pantheon, 1985, pp. 185–99.

Morrison, Toni. *The Bluest Eye.* New York: Pocket Books, 1970.

———. *Sula.* New York: Random House, 1974.

———. *Beloved.* New York: Random House, 1987.

Murray, Pauli. *Song in a Weary Throat: An American Pilgrimage.* New York: Harper & Row, 1987.

Myers, Lena Wright. *Black Women: Do They Cope Better?* Englewood Cliffs, NJ: Prentice-Hall, 1980.

Myers, Linda James. *Understanding an Afrocentric World View: Introduction to an Optimal Psychology.* Dubuque, IA: Kendall/Hunt, 1988.

O'Neale, Sondra. "Inhibiting Midwives, Usurping Creators: The Struggling Emergence of Black Women in American Fiction." In *Feminist Studies/ Critical Studies,* ed. Teresa de Lauretis. Bloomington: Indiana University Press, 1986, pp. 139–56.

Petry, Ann. *The Street.* Boston: Beacon, 1946.

Pryse, Marjorie, and Hortense J. Spillers, eds. *Conjuring: Black Women, Fiction, and Literary Tradition.* Bloomington: Indiana University Press, 1985.

Richardson, Marilyn, ed. *Maria W. Stewart, America's First Black Woman Political Writer.* Bloomington: Indiana University Press, 1987.

Russell, Michele. "Slave Codes and Liner Notes." In *But Some of Us Are Brave,* ed. Gloria T. Hull, Patricia Bell Scott, and Barbara Smith. Old Westbury, NY: Feminist Press, 1982, pp. 129–40.

Shange, Ntozake. *For Colored Girls Who Have Considered Suicide/When the Rainbow is Enuf.* New York: Macmillan, 1975.

———. *Sassafrass, Cypress and Indigo.* New York: St. Martin's Press, 1982.

Sidran, Ben. *Black Talk.* New York: Da Capo Press, 1971.

Simone, Nina. *Backlash.* Portugal: Movieplay Portuguesa Recording, 1985.

Simonsen, Thordis, ed. *You May Plow Here: The Narrative of Sara Brooks.* New York: Touchstone, 1986.

Smitherman, Geneva. *Talkin and Testifyin: The Language of Black America.* Boston: Houghton Mifflin, 1977.

Stanback, Marsha Houston. "Language and Black Women's Place: Evidence from the Black Middle Class." In *For Alma Mater: Theory and Practice of Feminist Scholarship,* ed. P. A. Trechler, Cheris Kramarae, and R. Shafford. Urbana: University of Illinois Press, 1985, pp. 177–93.

Steady, Filomina Chioma. "African Feminism: A Worldwide Perspective." In *Women in Africa and the African Diaspora,* ed. Rosalyn Terborg-Penn, Sharon Harley, and Andrea Benton Rushing. Washington, DC: Howard University Press, 1987, pp. 3–24.

Sweet Honey in the Rock. *Feel Something Drawing Me On.* Chicago: Flying Fish Records, 1985.

Tate, Claudia, ed. *Black Women Writers at Work.* New York: Continuum Publishing, 1983.

Thompson-Cager, Chezia. "Ntozake Shange's *Sassafras, Cypress and Indigo:* Resistance and Mythical Women of Power." *NWSA Journal* 1, no. 4 (1989), pp. 589–601.

Walker, Alice. *The Color Purple.* New York: Washington Square Press, 1982.

———. *In Search of Our Mothers' Gardens.* New York: Harcourt Brace Jovanovich, 1983.

Washington, Mary Helen, ed. *Midnight Birds.* Garden City, NY: Anchor, 1980.

———. "Teaching *Black-Eyed Susans:* An Approach to the Study of Black Women Writers." In *But Some of Us Are Brave,* ed. Gloria T. Hull, Patricia Bell Scott, and Barbara Smith. Old Westbury, NY: Feminist Press, 1982, pp. 208–17.

———. "I Sign My Mother's Name: Alice Walker, Dorothy West and Paule Marshall." In *Mothering the Mind: Twelve Studies of Writers and Their Silent Partners,* ed. Ruth Perry and Martine Watson Broronley. New York: Holmes & Meier, 1984, pp. 143–63.

———, ed. *Invented Lives: Narratives of Black Women 1860–1960.* Garden City, NY: Anchor, 1987.

West, Dorothy. *The Living Is Easy.* New York: Arno Press/*New York Times,* 1948.

White, Deborah Gray. *Ar'n't I a Woman? Female Slaves in the Plantation South.* New York: W. W. Norton, 1985.

Williams, Sherley A. "The Blues Roots of Afro-American Poetry." In *Chant of Saints: A Gathering of Afro-American Literature, Art and Scholarship,* ed. Michael S. Harper and Robert B. Steptoe. Urbana: University of Illinois Press, 1979, pp. 123–35.

CHAPTER 10

Embodied Consciousness

Feminist theory parallels women's lived experiences, and no parallel is stronger than the one between feminists' theorizing about women's bodies and women's bodily experiences. Like most women in modern everyday life, feminist theorists approach women's bodies as more or less problematic within mainstream culture. In a nutshell, those women wanting to pass unquestioned as feminine persons or go unnoticed as women must attend to their bodies to some substantial degree. That degree varies with their age, race, sexual orientation, and social class.

Put differently, feminized bodies convey signs of one's compliance with the sex/gender system. In practical terms, that system depends a lot on ideas about women's bodies and biological dispositions. As we have seen, people learn such ideas at home, at church or synagogue, and at school as well as from popular culture. A lot of learning also derives from what people are able to make of one another's bodies—what the body implies, what skills it exhibits, what care has observably been taken with it. Feminist theorists thus devote a great deal of attention to how women regard, care for, manage, control, alter, and otherwise treat their bodies. Such actions give telltale evidence of women's practical claims to this or that style of femininity. We announce our femininity with our bodies; conversely, we challenge mainstream femininity with our bodies. The particulars of our body awareness can thus oppress or empower us.

Feminist theorizing along these broad lines often starts from some notion of *embodied consciousness*, the existential circumstance that our grasp of and engagement with the world are both mindful *and* fleshy. Practitioners of complementary medicine or alternative healing, in particular, often refer to this as *bodymind*. With that concept they remind us, as do feminist theorists more diffusely, that our beliefs often find expression more in our physical appearance and gesticulations (that is, nonverbal communication) than in our speechifying and interacting, no matter how intense or inspired.

What sociologist Erving Goffman called *demeanor*—our mode of claiming a given status for ourselves by how we posture, glance, and costume ourselves—thus represents a central concern among feminist theorists. Inclined to consider feminine demeanor across a variety of settings, such theorists are also inclined to reject the mind/body dualism tied in with other gendered, hierarchical dualisms such as light/dark, spiritual/material, science/arts, written/oral, and rational/intuitive.

Let us look at the bodymind along axes feminist theorists often address. Drawing on cultural schemas at work in such institutions as government, economy, medicine, advertising, and religion, we might think of the bodymind as productive, reproductive, aesthetic, and ludic. Along these axes the feminine and masculine bodyminds get constructed as radically divergent, with the *human* bodymind remaining elusive in Western mainstream cultures. Yet the feminine bodymind is also decidedly elusive, for it gets no consistent recognition in medical research and health care practice, in ethical systems and theologies, in boot camps and school athletics. What gets socially constructed as a feminine bodymind—that is, bodyminds that get feminized—exists as Other, as "different," as a deviation from the masculine standard.

PRODUCTIVE BODIES

Despite the millions of women who have known slavery, sweatshops, drudgery, and workdays too long to allow for leisure, women's bodies in our culture are widely portrayed as nonproductive or even antiproductive. Mass advertising and popular culture make female bodies icons of conspicuous consumption as well as symbols of leisure, perhaps epitomized by having the time to paint, sculpt, and decorate one's body. Women's sweat is likelier to be shown in connection with a no pain, no gain workout than as an outcome of work. For the most part, though, women's sweat has little public visibility.

Feminist theorists offer correctives to such distortions. Approaching women's bodies as extremely productive, they emphasize that women do most of the world's work. As we saw in Chapter 6, they count the unpaid as well as (under)paid work that nonelite women routinely do. Although many women are expected to provide "extras" in the workplace such as organizing office birthday parties or ordering flowers for hospitalized co-workers, most of women's unpaid work revolves around family and home or the so-called private sphere, where labor becomes invisible to all but a few.

Most sharply contrasting with popular images of women's nonproductive bodies is the health care work more and more female family members are doing in our economy. As we have seen in more general terms (Chapter 6), much of that work derives from *work transfers* whereby "waged workers are eliminated or given new tasks, and the work that they did before is transferred to . . . family members" who are overwhelmingly women.[1] Shortened hospital stays account for much of women's medical work in their homes. To that extent women experience these duties much as they experience other aspects of being female; namely, parental status, race, household income, and age affect the impact medical work transfers have on them. Mothers of minor children, women of color, and women in lower-income households are likelier than other women to do home-based medical work. The same is true of older women partnered with senior-citizen men, who find that Medicare provides them no nocturnal relief from their duties.[2] Like countless other women, they come up against the 24-hour rule.

Many caregivers, especially those tending to chronically ill loved ones, do a great deal of hard, heartrending work. As Nona Y. Glazer points out, they

> use and clean equipment such as infuser pumps, intermittent positive pressure breathing equipment, and nasal–gastric tubes, which are becoming common in home care. Patients and their family caregivers learn to care for tracheotomies, administer oxygen, do "wet-and-dry" wound treatments, and change dressings on still-draining wounds (which are infected easily), give injections, do peritoneal dialysis, turn patients to prevent bed sores, use a Foley catheter to empty bladders, and refill infusion pumps with morphine packs and check for accurate dosage. Family caregivers learn to give intravenous treatments, which include cleaning tubes inserted into the chest wall, irrigating catheters inserted in veins that allow drawing blood or giving nutrition, chemotherapy, or antibiotics into the heart.[3]

The experiences of disabled women, like those of family health care providers, poignantly illustrate realities about women's bodies that get glossed by popular imagery. First, their bodies seldom even figure in imagery of "dependent" people needing care. Instead, a "separation of 'women' from disabled and older people is evident [even] in most of the feminist research on caring. . . ." Jenny Morris associates this neglect with a failure "to identify with the subjective experiences of those who need some form of care." More generally, she emphasizes the paucity of cultural resources for arriving at such insights and sensitivities.[4]

Second, disabled women's "underinvolvement" in sexual relationships with men or women cannot be explained by their perceived or inferred "unattractiveness." If heterosexual men sought only the "passive, doll-like" woman portrayed in fashion magazines and mass advertising, "disabled women might do, but the doll must be functional as well as decorative."[5]

Therein lies the cruel paradox of popular representations of female bodies. Not only do they promote images beyond the practical reach of flesh-and-blood girls and women, but they also mask the pervasive expectation that women will work hard and long in this world, both as paid workers and as loving partners, mothers, *comadres*, othermothers, grand-mothers, daughters, sisters, aunts, and friends. Cultural representations distort female corporeality by homing in on thin, white, able-bodied women with flawless skin and gleaming teeth, whose images obscure the productivity of women's lived bodies.

Yet more than women's manual labor gets masked. Because cultural representations of women still hover around "dumb blond," "dizzy dame," "bimbo," and "airhead"—stereotypes downplaying or denying women's intelligence—women's mental labor also gets glossed over by popular imagery. Put differently, female body*minds* seldom infiltrate popular culture except as rare deviations from the norm (for example, Sigourney Weaver playing Dian Fossey in *Gorillas in the Mist* or Emma Thompson playing Dora Carrington in *Carrington)*. The usual fare portrays women more in terms of embodiment than consciousness.

In the end, then, women's productivity gets denied in fantastic mass images. These images promote a sense that what women, especially het-erosexual women not yet middle-aged, produce is above all their bodies.[6] And the bodies they are mandated to produce are aesthetic ones capable of reproduction, not productive bodies as such. Historical resistance to dress reform—even in the face of "six to eight heavy petticoats, long, dragging skirts, constraining corsets, and tight sleeves"[7]—conveys that message. Contemporary reactions to comfortable, practical women's clothing are less severe but still a far cry from enthusiastic.

REPRODUCTIVE BODIES

Judith Butler sees in gender "a corporeal style" and in gendered bodies "so many 'styles of the flesh.'"[8] Feminine styles of the flesh center on women's secondary sex characteristics. In practice, then, the social construction of *feminine* bodies "heterosexualizes the female body."[9] Typically, girls and women learn to "discipline their bodies" so as to "experienc[e] themselves as sexual objects for heterosexual male viewing, pleasure," and procre-ation.[10] Their breasts become "boobs, knockers, knobs" often treated as "toys to be grabbed, squeezed, handled." Their bras are designed mostly to "normalize the breasts, lifting and curving [them] to approximate the one and only breast ideal" of the day."[11]

Objectifying and normalizing women's breasts occurs even among pro-fessionals and volunteers working with postmastectomy women. For women 45 to 64 years old, breast cancer is the leading cause of death, and surgical removal of one or both breasts (mastectomy) is a common treat-ment. Sue Wilkinson and Celia Kitzinger show that an "emphasis on sex-uality and body image—meaning being attractive to men and engaging in sexual intercourse with them—is a major preoccupation of the psychiatric and psychological literature on mastectomy." Few other issues get dis-cussed; moreover, prostheses are pressed upon patients soon after surgery, and "breast reconstruction" is widely promoted.[12]

Such patterns intensify whatever sexual misgivings and other painful emotions a postmastectomy woman may experience in a culture that fetishizes women's breasts. Patients like Audre Lorde, the African American lesbian poet, are likely to face multiple assaults on their identities. After her mastectomy Lorde got a visit from a volunteer with the American Cancer Society's Reach for Recovery program, who encouraged her to wear the temporary prosthesis she had brought. The prosthesis was "white."[13]

Even activism on behalf of breast-cancer patients involves cultural imagery that distorts women's experiences and priorities. Such activists, who are often breast-cancer survivors, find that their effectiveness depends on a proper feminine, heterosexual demeanor. Like other women facing diverse challenges, they learn how much "women continue to be damned if we do gender and damned if we don't."[14]

Social constructions of women's reproductive bodies even affect women's experiences with male impotence and infertility. Given how women's bodies get heterosexualized, for instance, many men being treated for impotence assume intravaginal intercourse is necessary to women's sexual satisfaction and fear their wives might leave them because they cannot participate in it. When interviewed separately, "the wives are often surprised and offended" by such ideas.[15]

More stunning are some women's reactions to their husbands' "reproductive impairment." Even when the infertility is really *his*, some wives still define it as their own problem, "harbor[ing] the suspicion that their bodies must also be working imperfectly" and that they themselves must be infertile.[16] Such experiences make sense only in a cultural context where women's bodies are deemed inherently problematic by virtue of being "different" and deemed valuable only insofar as they are properly reproductive and aesthetic.

The recent medicalization of menopause and the massive marketing of hormone replacement therapy (HRT) further illustrate how women's reproductive bodies fare in mainstream culture. By definition, menopause involves the cessation of women's capacity to conceive. Rendering it a physical and psychological problem thus means treating women's loss of reproductive capacity as deeply consequential, implying that women's value and sense of well-being depend heavily on their reproductive potential. Women's aging thus gets defined mostly in terms of their reproductive bodies. Unlike men, women don't simply age. Instead, we become premenopausal, hot-flash our way through menopause, and settle into the postmenopausal part of our lives. Aging is thus a gendered process linked to women's reproductive and (as we will see) aesthetic bodies.

As such, aging can become big business. It seems that a "veritable assault on midlife women" is under way where the main "message is that only with the help of powerful hormones . . . taken for the rest of our lives can women cope with" menopause and its aftermath. The assault might be called the *menopause industry*, after the title of Sandra Coney's book.[17] Symptomatically, the book that first popularized the idea of a hormone (estrogen) preventing the symptoms of women's aging was titled *Feminine Forever*, thus equating femininity with youthfulness. Published in 1966, *Feminine Forever* was perhaps symptomatic in a second way. Its author "was funded by Wyeth-Ayerst, the manufacturer of the menopausal estrogen product Premarin. . . ."[18]

Needless to say, some women do experience severe symptoms during the passage from a reproductive to a nonreproductive body, just as some women experience severe premenstrual and menstrual symptoms. Safe, effective means to counteract those symptoms are unquestionably important. Yet the safety of some antidotes is far from consistent, as evidenced by silicone breast implants, the Dalkon shield, thalidomide, and other measures that have proven catastrophic for some women (and for their children in the case of thalidomide). Moreover, that *some* women have symptoms scarcely means that virtually *all* women in certain groupings should be advised to use available antidotes regardless of their side effects. Clearly, too, less intrusive, nonmedical antidotes such as diet, exercise, herbs, and meditation may be just as effective and less costly.

Responses to aging need to be as diverse as women's lived experiences of getting older. Until such diversity takes hold in the medical establishment, feminist theorizing about the medicalization of women's bodies, especially their reproductive bodies, will probably continue to parallel theorizing about the institution of heterosexuality. To wit, feminists will keep theorizing around the core principle that there is not just *one* way—the hegemonic, normalized, institutionalized one—to age or to be heterosexual. Women can demand more options based on recognition that their bodies are so richly inscribed with lived experiences as to defy meaningful assignment to this or that (dualistic) niche. For theorists, this means promoting insights into our lived experiences while disclosing cultural misrepresentations of our bodies, reproductive and otherwise.

AESTHETIC BODIES

Prominent among the theorists illuminating the cultural containment of women's reproductive bodies is Luce Irigaray, who also emphasizes the cultural construction of women's bodies as aesthetic objects. Emphasizing that women have more than just "*one* sex organ," Irigaray considers "breasts, pubis, clitoris, labia, vulva, vagina, neck of the uterus, womb . . . [*sic*]" as the precious bases of women's "sexual multiplicity." Yet cultural arrangements are such that even if a woman "plays to perfection the role of femininity in all its bourgeois perversity," that multiplicity cannot find expression in her unadulterated sexual agency. It is, in other words, almost impossible for her to enter "the system of exchange as something other than an 'object.' "[19] That object is decidedly aesthetic as well as fundamentally reproductive.

The sexual economy wherein women's value gets assessed ensures multidimensional objectification. Irigaray says

> *we may question whether woman has a choice of being vain about her body* if she is to correspond to the "femininity" expected of her. Does not her sexual "usefulness" depend upon her being concerned about the qualities or "properties" of her body? If she is to solicit, support, and even swell the sexual pleasure of the male consumer? (pp. 113–4)

Irigaray goes on,

> The "physical vanity" of woman, the "fetishization" of her body . . . are mandatory if she is to be a desirable "object" and if he is to want to possess her. But no doubt she will in her turn seek to secure an increase in her price. The cosmetics, the disguises of all kinds that women cover themselves with are intended to deceive, to promise more value than can be delivered. . . . Is there pleasure in this for women? (p. 114)

Irigaray thus theorizes what women's magazines and self-help peddle: endless guidance about how to make our bodies sexier, tighter, firmer, smoother, prettier, and younger looking. Sizable industries have developed around such concerns—the fashion, beauty, diet, and fitness industries, for instance. Moreover, cosmetic or "corrective" surgery remains a fast-growing medical specialization. As of 1990, its most popular form was liposuction, followed by breast augmentation.[20]

As we have seen, feminism is not prescriptive at the level of the individual. Rather, feminists challenge cultural prescriptions for women and explore their connections with women's collective subordination. Feminist theorists do commonly criticize the aforementioned industries, then, while forswearing criticism of those individuals who use their goods and services. All the while, feminists theorize that what many women "opt" for is a regimen that seems more or less compulsory in order to feel good, look attractive, and be happy.

Feminists deconstruct the cultural equation of feeling good and looking attractive and being happy while disclosing the disciplinary character and compulsory feel of many women's body projects. Especially among young women, where "jock chic" may hold sway and "working out" is one of "the new markers of feminine sexuality, desirability, and status,"[21] the felt *need* to discipline the body may become intense. It feeds the pursuit of defatted, defeminized styles of the flesh and introduces ambivalence into whatever pleasures do come with cultivating one's body. For instance, Dolores, a woman quoted in Wendy Chapkis's *Beauty Secrets*, observes that preventing wrinkles means avoiding the sun. It also means: "Don't move your face and don't touch it. Don't make any really big expressions with your face." Kathay, another of the women Chapkis quotes, reports "when I arrived in the domain of thinness, it suddenly felt like [I] had a right to exist."

Alternatively, Diana "refuse[s] to be identified by [her] appearance." Instead, her appearance signals, "I will not accept my place, my role, my slot."[22] Diana pursues what some feminist theorists call "oppositional" or "deviant" dress, which announces the wearer's individuality while challenging, consciously or not, the codes for women of her class, age, sexual orientation, or race.[23] Such a stance assumes that choices about our appearance can be more or less feminist. It brings "the personal is political" into one's drawers and closets while attesting, perhaps, to RuPaul's assertion that "we're born naked and the rest is drag."[24]

In general, how we dress and adorn our bodies can bolster our sense of efficacy in the world. Moreover, "the pursuit of beauty often gives [us] access to a range of individuals who administer to [our] bod[ies] in a caring way. . . ."[25] Theorizing such outcomes enriches our insights into the appeal—indeed, the pleasures—of bodily practices from applying lipstick to styling one's hair. As Gloria Steinem observes, however, "beauty is less about looks than about behavior." She goes on to note that it is *really about what society wants us to do or not to do*."[26] Hers is a spin on beauty capable of orienting theories about its diverse functions in women's lives; hers is a standpoint reminding us that beauty often regulates those it seems to empower.

Such notions make more obvious sense with respect to women's eating and various refusals to eat. Consider, for example, anorexia nervosa, a disease "that emerged from the distinctive economic and social environments of the late 19th century."[27] Whatever its causes and dynamics, this gendered eating disorder may reflect some females' reactions to cultural mandates for women, to women's subordination, or to their own sexual or other traumas. Becky Thompson's research illustrates the latter eventualities, just as Lillene Fifield's notion of "oppression sickness" allows for drug and alcohol abuse (as well as various forms of self-abuse) as responses to oppression.[28] Such a stance resonates with that of bell hooks, who writes about how often she has seen other African Americans "gobbling up junk food morning, noon, and night." Hooks says that the feeling they get

> when stuffing Big Macs, Pepsi, and barbecue potato chips down their throats is similar to the ecstatic, blissful moment of the narcotics addict. So if we want to talk about dealing with addiction in Black communities we are going to have to talk about consumption on all levels, the construction of desire, and the problems of unmediated, unfulfilled desire.[29]

Hooks goes on to talk about consumption as providing a sense of agency, much as other feminist theorists talk about women's beauty regimens as providing that same sense. As we will see in the next section, other pleasures also enter into such activities. The concerns of feminist theorists are whether such pleasures are sustainable, how likely they are to promote individuals' development and well-being, and whose interests they seem ultimately to serve.

Illustrative of such concerns is Leslie Heywood's study of modernity's anorexic aesthetic. Like many feminist theorists, Heywood includes her own experiences in her analysis. When Heywood was a member of a university track team, she and her teammates routinely had their body-fat percentages measured. Their coach wanted the percentages below 10, even though the typical female percentages run 22 to 25 percent. Heywood reports that they were weighed twice weekly, and their weights were called out loud.[30] She talks about how common "anorexic logic" is among high-achieving women (and men) who identify with mainstream values centering on masculinity and achievement. Anorexic logic revolves not around "a desire to transcend" the body but around "a fight between two bodies, male and female, where one remains as the common standard for the body and the other should disappear altogether."[31]

That fight reflects many things—above all, "the status quo of dieting as a normative, feminine, lifelong preoccupation."[32] As Sharlene Hesse-Biber sees it, many women's preoccupation with their food intake (that is, their pursuit of lean bodies) entails such intensity and focus that it results in "behavior associated with culthood—ritualistic performance and obsession with a goal or ideal." Hesse-Biber points to all the major players helping to construct this cult:

> Being female is the primary criterion for membership in the Cult of Thinness. The object of worship is the "perfect" body. The primary rituals are dieting and exercising with obsessive attention to monitoring progress—weighing the body at least once a day and constantly checking calories. The advertising industry and the media provide plenty of beautiful-body icons to worship. There are numerous ceremonies—pageants and contests—that affirm the ideal.
>
> And there are plenty of guides and gurus along the way. Often it is the mother who initiates the young novice. . . . Some of the most revered oracles have celebrity as their major qualification. Jane Fonda, Cindy Crawford, and Oprah Winfrey are among those who advise their fans on the virtues or pitfalls of certain diets and exercises.
>
> Other sages have medical qualifications and have produced "sacred texts." . . . The diet gurus can also be psychologists. Some make motivational audiotapes for their patients. Others have special phone-in hours for those who have fallen off their diets or provide a special "intensive care" line for those in dire need.
>
> Diet clubs and 12-step weight loss programs introduce even more fervor toward shedding pounds.[33]

Susan Bordo (the author of Reading 14) says that slenderness is closely associated with "autonomy, will, discipline, conquest of desire, enhanced spirituality, purity, and transcendence of the female body. . . ." She generalizes that the most pervasive conceptions of femininity

> require that women learn to feed others, not the self, and to construe any desires for self-nurturance and self-feeding as greedy and excessive. Thus, women must develop a totally other-oriented emotional economy. In this economy, the control of female appetite for food is merely the most concrete expression of the general rule governing the construction of femininity: that female hunger—for public power, for independence, for sexual gratification—be contained, and the public space that women be allowed to take up be circumscribed, limited.[34]

Reading 23 focuses on emotional economy, women's appetites, and the racism woven into discussions of anorexia and other eating disorders. Doris Witt's "What (N)ever Happened to Aunt Jemima" is subtitled "Eating Disorders, Fetal Rights, and Black Female Appetite in Contemporary American Culture." Witt's theoretical reach is ambitious. It embraces women's reproductive and aesthetic embodiment without neglecting our productive contributions and ludic possibilities. By exposing racism as well as classism and heterosexism in academic and popular approaches to eating disorders, Witt illustrates that imaginative theorizing often involves looking for absences and erasures. As she shows, who is missing often comments powerfully on social structure and culture.

LUDIC BODIES

Cultural constructions of our aesthetic bodies cast shadows on our ludic bodies, which are meant to play and find expression in what is fun. Another woman quoted in Chapkis's book is 79-year-old Keetje, whose improvisational stance toward her body illustrates ludic possibilities. She claims to have always been attuned to fashion because she hated "not being noticed." Keetje tells how she once saw

> a pair of short white leather boots with low heels in a store window. I thought they'd be fantastic under long pants, so I went in and asked to see them. The sales clerk took them out of the window and handed them to me. But when I said I'd like to try them on, she sputtered, "surely they're not for you!" "No," I replied, "they're for my grandmother, but don't worry, we wear the same size."[35]

Keetje's is a style of the flesh women are discouraged from pursuing. Instead, the productive, reproductive, and aesthetic styles of the flesh that women are widely pressured to pursue pare down their chances for pleasure, bodily self-acceptance, and comfortable expressions of desire. Those styles of the flesh revolve around negation—negation of women's productive work, their reproductive wonder, their aesthetic diversity.

Reading 24 by Myra Dinnerstein and Rose Weitz says a great deal about the negation of women's aesthetic diversity. Focusing on Jane Fonda and Barbara Bush as prominent public figures, Dinnerstein and Weitz treat the two as virtual agemates whose responses to aging seem radically divergent. They show, though, that both public figures illustrate not the futility but the constricted potential of *individual* resistance to this or that social construction of women's bodies.

Theirs is thus an exploration of how individuals' *agency*, their capacity to enact their preferences and effectively register their presence in the world, interacts with *social control*, the system of regulatory mechanisms set up to channel people's choices and actions. Theirs is also a look at cultural codes that shows, as in the case of breast-cancer activists, that women are damned if they comply with the codes of femininity and damned if they defy them. Commonly, then, femininity entails *double binds*, where the individual's options are few and each carries substantial penalties or disadvantages. Women's bodies, as Dinnerstein and Weitz show, are the locus of the double binds we most often experience.

What the two readings on the horizon and the materials cited in this chapter have in common is some notion of female bodies as sites of contestation or struggle. Contemporary feminism, in both theory and practice, has aimed for "sexual and bodily self-determination for women," as evidenced in classic works such as Kate Millett's *Sexual Politics* and the "feminist antiviolence campaign against rape, incest, battering, sexual harassment, and pornography. . . ."[36] It has also dealt with "right-wing strategies to control and contain female bodies, bodies of people of color, gay and lesbian bodies, and bodies of third-world peoples of all racial descriptions, sexualities, and genders"; how female adolescents' bodies represent a "public site . . . commented on and monitored by others"—a "nexus of race, class, and gender politics"; how "somatophobia" underlies the mind/body dualism; how powerful people are entitled to deny their bodies; and how, conversely, oppressed people "share in the minds of the privileged *a defining connection to the body*. . . ."[37]

Our bodies emerge, then, as cultural constructions, not fixed expressions of "nature." Indeed, feminists' (especially ecofeminists) theoretical attention to embodiment reveals nature itself as a cultural construction, a product of discourses promulgated in centers of power and taken up in the hum and buzz of everyday life. "Nature" shows profoundly how things get culturally constructed to justify the uses powerful people have in mind for them. As Heywood found on the track team, athletics promises "women a 'healthy' sense of our own value and power" but can actually "function, with our enthusiastic cooperation, to make us destroy ourselves instead." She observed similar disjunctures between what female bodybuilding appears to be and how it actually often works:

> Female bodybuilding, often read as the obverse of anorexia, is a sport in which many anorexics participate after their recoveries. Concerned with building up the body, rather than eliminating it, and said to present an image of female power, the female bodybuilder seems to offer a hopeful alternative to anorexia and anorexic logic.[38]

Using a photo essay in a bodybuilding magazine to illustrate her point, Heywood concludes that female bodybuilding "is often consumed by the structure it most seeks to subvert." More generally, she concludes that "Anorexia is . . . based on the same values as high modernist literary art so that the text of the anorexic body stands as the literalization of the modernist fascination with disembodiment, the desire not to desire."[39]

Heywood thus treats anorexia and its aesthetic as squelching desire. Anorexia emotionally collapses ludic possibilities; its aesthetic speaks to the feminized body as desirable but not desiring. It poignantly illustrates that "Although feminine bodies share with masculine bodies the feature of being socially constructed, they are constructed as inferior to them."[40]

That inferiority is densely multidimensional, but perhaps its ultimate locus is the negation of women's ludic possibilities. Unlike masculinized bodies, feminized bodies are not culturally licensed for fun, play, and the pleasures of fiercely active, wondrously nonproductive physicality. Ours are bodies emptied of desire on culture's main stage.

It may well be, then, that women's empowerment "begins with their ability to reclaim their own experience and claim their bodies as the site of *their own* desires."[41] In sum, cultural transformation may well originate with and in our bodies, now experienced as bodyminds whose health and development take precedence over the dictates of consumerist culture and heteropatriarchal institutions.

NOTES

1. Nona Y. Glazer, "The Home as Workshop: Women as Amateur Nurses and Medical Care Providers," *Gender & Society* 4, no. 4 (December 1990), p. 484.
2. *Ibid.*, p. 493.
3. *Ibid.*, p. 489.
4. Jenny Morris, "Feminism and Disability," *Feminist Review* 43 (Spring 1993), pp. 60, 61, 68; see also Jenny Morris, "Creating a Space for Absent Voices: Disabled Women's Experience of Receiving Assistance with Daily Living Activities," *Feminist Review* 51 (Autumn 1995), pp. 68–93.
5. Adrienne Asch and Michelle Fine, "Beyond Pedestals: Revisiting the Lives of Women with Disabilities" in Michelle Fine (ed.), *Disruptive Voices: The Possibilities of Feminist Research* (Ann Arbor: University of Michigan Press, 1992), p. 156.
6. Cf. Jane Gaines, "Introduction" in Jane Gaines and Charlotte Herzog (eds.), *Fabrications: Costume and the Female Body* (New York: Routledge, 1990), p. 9.
7. See, for example, Lois Banner, *American Beauty* (Chicago: University of Chicago Press, 1983), pp. 147ff; Amy Kesselman, "The 'Freedom Suit': Feminism and Dress Reform in the United States, 1848–1875," *Gender & Society* 5, no. 4 (December 1991), pp. 495–510.
8. Judith Butler, *Gender Trouble: Feminism and the Subversion of Identity* (New York: Routledge, 1990), p. 139.
9. Gaines, "Introduction," p. 7.
10. Janet Lee, "Menarche and the (Hetero)Sexualization of the Female Body," *Gender & Society* 8, no. 3 (September 1994), p. 344.
11. Iris Marion Young, *Throwing Like a Girl and other Essays in Feminist Philosophy and Social Theory* (Bloomington: Indiana University Press, 1990), pp. 190, 195.
12. Sue Wilkinson and Celia Kitzinger, "Whose Breast Is It Anyway? A Feminist Consideration of Advice and 'Treatment' for Breast Cancer," *Women's Studies International Forum* 16, no. 3 (May/June 1993), pp. 229, 230, 231.
13. Audre Lorde, *The Cancer Journals* (Freedom Cross, CA: The Freedom Press, 1984).
14. Theresa Montini, "Gender and Emotion in the Advocacy for Breast Cancer Informed Consent Legislation," *Gender & Society* 10, no. 1 (February 1996), p. 21.

15. Leonore Tiefer, "The Medicalization of Impotence: Normalizing Phallocentrism," *Gender & Society* 8, no. 3 (September 1994), p. 370.
16. Arthur L. Greil, Thomas A. Leitko, and Karen L. Porter, "Infertility: His and Hers," *Gender & Society* 2, no. 2 (June 1988), pp. 183, 184.
17. See Renate Klein and Lynete J. Dumble, "Disempowering Midlife Women: The Science and Politics of Hormone Replacement Therapy (HRT)," *Women's Studies International Forum* 17, no. 4 (July/August 1994), p. 327.
18. Nancy Worcester and Mariane H. Whatley, "The Selling of HRT: Playing on the Fear Factor," *Feminist Review* 41 (Summer 1992), p. 3; see also Margaret Morganroth Gullette, "Menopause as Magic Marker: Discursive Consolidation/Strategies for Cultural Combat," *Discourse* 17, no. 1 (Fall 1994), pp. 93–123; Jane Lewis, "Feminism, the Menopause and Hormone Replacement Therapy," *Feminist Review* 43 (Spring 1993), pp. 38–56.
19. Luce Irigaray, *Speculum of the Other Woman* (Ithaca, NY: Cornell University Press, 1985 (orig. 1974)), trans. Gillian C. Gill, pp. 233, 114.
20. Kathryn Pauly Morgan, "Women and the Knife: Cosmetic Surgery and the Colonization of Women's Bodies," *Hypatia: A Journal of Feminist Philosophy* 6, no. 3 (Fall 1991), pp. 28, 29.
21. Laurie Schulze, "On the Muscle" in Gaines and Herzog, *Fabrications*, p. 60.
22. See Wendy Chapkis, *Beauty Secrets: Women and the Politics of Appearance* (Boston: South End Press, 1986), pp. 101, 158, 110, 111.
23. Elizabeth Wilson discusses "oppositional dress" and feminism; see her "All the Rage" in Gaines and Herzog, *Fabrications*, p. 32. See also Elizabeth Wilson, "Deviant Dress," *Feminist Review* 35 (Summer 1990), pp. 67–74. Wilson talks about how lesbian styles sometimes challenge some feminists' assumptions, thus representing a way of dressing that is oppositional not to patriarchal culture but to some feminists' preconceptions.
24. Andrea Benton Rushing, "Becoming a Feminist: Learning from Africa, Part Two," *Sage* IX, no. 2 (Summer 1995), p. 62.
25. Gaines, "Introduction," p. 6; Morgan, "Women and the Knife," p. 34; see also Dorothy E. Smith, *Texts, Facts, and Femininity: Exploring the Relations of Ruling* (New York: Routledge, 1990), pp. 175–202. There Smith discusses the "agency" expressed in women's shopping, dressing, and use of makeup as well as the social construction of women's bodies less as sexual objects than as objects in need of repair, correction, adjustment, or transformation.
26. Gloria Steinem, *Revolution from Within: A Book of Self-Esteem* (Boston: Little, Brown, 1992), p. 220. Naomi Wolf builds her *Beauty Myth* (New York: William Morrow, 1991) around this very idea.
27. Joan Jacobs Brumberg, *Fasting Girls: The History of Anorexia Nervosa* (New York: New American Library, 1989), p. 3.
28. See Becky Thompson, *A Hunger so Wide and Deep: American Women Speak Out on Eating Problems* (Minneapolis: University of Minnesota Press, 1994). Fifield's ideas are cited in Les K. Nicoloff and Eloise A. Stiglitz, "Lesbian Alcoholism: Etiology, Treatment, and Recovery" in Boston Lesbian Psychologies Collective (ed.), *Lesbian Psychologies: Explorations and Challenges* (Urbana: University of Illinois Press, 1987), pp. 285–6.
29. bell hooks and Cornel West, *Breaking Bread: Insurgent Black Intellectual Life* (Boston: South End Press, 1991), p. 98.
30. Leslie Heywood, *Dedication to Hunger: The Anorexic Aesthetic in Modern Culture* (Berkeley: University of California Press, 1996), p. 5.

31. *Ibid.*, pp. 29, 67.
32. Sylvia Kathleen Blood, "The Dieting Dilemma—Factors Influencing Women's Decision to Give Up Dieting," *Women & Therapy* 18, no. 1 (1996), p. 118.
33. Sharlene Hesse-Biber, *Am I Thin Enough Yet? The Cult of Thinness and the Commercialization of Identity* (New York: Oxford University Press, 1996), pp. 5, 10. On the "helping discourses" of NutriSystem, Overeaters Anonymous, and feminist psychoanalytic therapy, see Catherine Hopwood, "My Discourse/My-Self: Therapy as Possibility (for Women Who Eat Compulsively)," *Feminist Review* 49 (Spring 1995), pp. 66–82.
34. Susan Bordo, *Unbearable Weight: Feminism, Western Culture, and the Body* (Berkeley: University of California Press, 1993), pp. 68, 171.
35. Chapkis, *Beauty Secrets*, p. 186.
36. Patricia Searles and Ronald J. Berger, "The Feminist Self-Defense Movement: A Case Study," *Gender & Society* 1, no. 1 (March 1987), p. 61.
37. Julia Epstein and Kristina Straub, "Introduction: The Guarded Body" in Julia Epstein and Kristina Straub (eds.), *Body Guards: The Cultural Politics of Gender Ambiguity* (New York: Routledge, 1991), p. 17; Michelle Fine and Pat Macpherson, "Over Dinner: Feminism and Adolescent Female Bodies" in Fine, *Disruptive Voices*, p. 185; Vicky Kirby, "Corporeal Habits: Addressing Essentialism Differently," *Hypatia* 6, no. 3 (Fall 1991), p. 10; bell hooks, *Teaching to Transgress: Education as the Practice of Freedom* (New York: Routledge, 1994), p. 137; Naomi Scheman, *Engenderings: Constructions of Knowledge, Authority, and Privilege* (New York: Routledge, 1993), p. 88.
38. Heywood, *Dedication to Hunger*, pp. 5, 35.
39. *Ibid.*, p. 144.
40. Margaret McLaren, "Possibilities for a Nondominated Female Subjectivity," *Hypatia* 8 (Winter 1993), p. 156.
41. Janet Holland, Caroline Ramazanoglu, Sue Sharpe, and Rachel Thompson, "Power and Desire: The Embodiment of Female Sexuality," *Feminist Review* 46 (Spring 1994), p. 35; emphasis added.

What (N)ever Happened to Aunt Jemima: Eating Disorders, Fetal Rights, and Black Female Appetite in Contemporary American Culture

Doris Witt

It occurred to me that the black woman is herself a symbol of nourishment. . . .

—Alice Walker, "Giving the Party"

On April 27, 1989, the Chicago-based Quaker Oats Company announced plans to "update" its Aunt Jemima trademark for the 1990s. The two-page news release begins:

> Aunt Jemima, one of America's oldest packaged food trademarks and a symbol of quality breakfast products for 100 years, will be given a new look this year. The facial appearance is unchanged. Noticeably different, however, is a new, stylish, grey-streaked hairdo, and her headband has been removed. Other changes include cosmetic touches such as a different style of collar and the addition of earrings.
>
> "We wanted to present Aunt Jemima in a more contemporary light, while preserving the important attributes of warmth, quality, good taste, heritage and reliability," said Barbara R. Allen, Vice President of Marketing for Quaker Oats Company's Convenience Foods Division, makers of Aunt Jemima products. "Based on the results of consumer research over a five-month period, we think the new design does that." ("Aunt Jemima," p. 1)

This preemptive strike was intended to fortify the corporate line on the trademark's symbolic meaning several weeks before the altered image

was itself actually "released" into the American marketplace—or into an ideological background, to be more precise, where efforts to "preserve" and valorize the iconography of slavery are fiercely contested. Given the context, the public relations staff at Quaker Oats was obviously not about to comment on *why* the company "wanted" to update the trademark image in the first place.[1]

What are we to make of the longevity of the Aunt Jemima trademark and of the ambiguity of the symbolic attributes which Quaker Oats wants to preserve by keeping it? After all, "warmth" is surely a characteristic of Aunt Jemima as cook; "good taste," of Aunt Jemima food products. "Quality," "heritage," and "reliability" could refer to either. One might infer from this symbolic slippage that the trademark is intended to signify both cook and food. Like her precursors, the big-breasted mammies of post-Civil War lore, Aunt Jemima *prepares* and *is* food; she/it is the ever-smiling source of sustenance for infants and adults.[2] Yet one obstacle faced by Quaker Oats in trying to maintain this dual symbolic meaning, while presenting the visual image of Aunt Jemima in a more "contemporary" light, is that the new picture could be said to represent not so much a servant producer as a middle-class consumer. Ex cathedra pronouncements of Barbara Allen notwithstanding, the 1990s' Jemima looks more like a "Mrs." than an "Aunt." And viewed from this perspective, "good taste" should be her attribute as a discriminating shopper, not as a stack of pancakes.[3]

Of course, one assumption I am begging here is that a middle-class black matron has a "look" which we all readily recognize. This is a problem that Jean-Christophe Agnew neatly skirts. Near the end of a December 1989 *Village Voice* review of Susan Strasser's *Satisfaction Guaranteed: The Making of the American Mass Market,* Agnew pauses momentarily in an attempt to resolve the contradictions posed by the upscale Aunt Jemima:

For instance, what are we now to make of a figure like Aunt Jemima, whose 100-year-old kerchief was finally removed from her head during her most recent makeover last July? Now she is said to *look like* Oprah Winfrey. But then again, Oprah's face and body have themselves been inducted into the Wiz's vast warehouse of interchangeable cultural signifiers. (Emphasis added) (p. 30)[4]

By invoking the instability of Winfrey as a referent, Agnew dismisses the possibility of making meaning of Aunt Jemima at all ("looks like" ad infinitum).[5] In particular he would appear to be alluding to the highly publicized sixty-seven-pound weight loss in 1988 of the popular talk show hostess and television producer, and perhaps also to tabloid allegations that an August 1989 *TV Guide* cover picture of the newly slim Winfrey depicted her face atop Ann-Margret's body.[6]

What, then, ever happened to Aunt Jemima? Nothing and everything. On the one hand, the trademark is where it has been for the last century, on grocery store shelves, and the same (conflicted) fears and desires which gave rise to it in 1889 surely underwrite its retention today.[7] Yet without going so far as to label Aunt Jemima and Oprah Winfrey interchangeable, one might well conclude, on the other hand, that the updated trademark needs also to be interpreted in new ways. Neither the cultural work performed by African-American women nor the manner in which they are interpellated as subjects is today precisely what it was a century ago. For if Aunt Jemima foregrounds one axis of American desire for black women to be the ever-smiling *producers* of food, to be nurturers who themselves have no appetite and make no demands, then Oprah Winfrey surely also foregrounds another, complementary axis, one which has been latent in popular fascination with the Aunt Jemima trademark from its inception: that is, American fear of what black women *consume,* or perhaps more precisely American obsession with black female appetites. This concern has played itself out on numerous levels, from gastronomic to sexual to economic. The (foreclosed) question,

What does Aunt Jemima eat?, quickly mutates to encompass other aspects of black female consumption, including access to the wealth and power that can satisfy desire. One surely suspects, after all, that popular interest in Winfrey's eating habits is in no small part a function of her enormous wealth. She earned $98 million dollars in 1992 and 1993 alone, making her the top-earning entertainer in America. (Newcomb and Gubernick, p. 97)

Much fine work has been done on this Mammy/Jezebel dichotomy by scholars ranging from Angela Davis, Barbara Christian, bell hooks, and Deborah Gray White to Hortense Spillers, Deborah McDowell, Patricia Hill Collins, K. Sue Jewell, and many others.[8] My own contribution differs, however, in its literalization of "consumption." I take dietary practices to be fundamental to the ways we come to understand ourselves as embodied, sexed, gendered, raced, classed, religious, local, regional, and national subjects. I take the dietary practices of African-American women, moreover, to be fundamental to the making of American subjectivities. To appropriate for my working hypothesis one of the more famous dicta of French gastrophile Jean Anthelme Brillat-Savarin, tell me what African-American women are said to eat, and I shall tell you what Americans fear they are.[9]

In the remainder of this essay I will attempt to unpack this overarching claim by looking more specifically at the relationship between (1) the construction of black female appetite in contemporary American culture and (2) debates over the boundaries and ontological status of the "embodied" subject. In particular, I will focus on the interlocking domains of "eating disorders" and "fetal rights." African-American women have, by and large, been perceived as absences in both discourses of eating disorders and in the specularization of the anorexic and bulimic body; African-American women have been very much a presence both in the discourses of fetal rights and in the specularization of fetal and neonate bodies—especially the purported epidemics of "fetal alcohol syndrome" and "crack babies" in the 1980s. Each of these topics has generated a tremendous amount of discussion in both popular and academic circles, but for the most part not in the same breath. What follows, then, is a conjectural cross-mapping.

I. "FAT IS A BLACK WOMAN'S ISSUE"

I begin with the former. Anorexia nervosa refers to self-imposed starvation; bulimia is also called the binge–purge cycle. Since the late 1960s and early 1970s—the period of Black Power, second-wave feminism, Stonewall, and other liberatory social movements—both have been widely construed in popular and academic discourses as symptoms displayed by young, presumptively heterosexual white women from middle- and upper-class nuclear families. In addition to the multitude of articles on dieting and body image in popular young women's magazines, I have in mind here mainly the work of white feminist scholars such as Kim Chernin, Joan Jacobs Brumberg, and, to a lesser extent, Susan Bordo. Less well known among humanists would be the clinical research of psychiatrists and other medical professionals who publish their findings in the *International Journal of Eating Disorders,* founded in 1981. Here, too, with a very few exceptions the object of their gaze has been young, bourgeois, female, and white.[10] As readers who are familiar with this subject will realize, there are significant differences in the models proposed for interpreting eating disorders: Chernin and Bordo basically view disorderly eating as normative female behavior. Chernin from a feminist psychoanalytic perspective and Bordo from a feminist Foucauldian perspective. Brumberg sets forth an explanatory model in which biology, psychology, and culture interact, and she is more receptive to biomedical analyses of eating disorders as a "pathology" which can be treated with a combination of drugs and therapy than are Chernin and Bordo.

My initial question in approaching this topic was "Why are African-American women absent from these discourses about eating disorders?" Diverse students, friends, and colleagues with whom I discussed the topic concluded that black women do not "get" eating disorders. Two of my African-American women students reached this conclusion even in the context of telling me about their experiences with Slim-Fast and Dexatrim.[11] My early inquiries having thus led me to believe that this was a topic worth pursuing, I reframed the question. Rather than assuming that African-American women were absent from discourses about eating disorders, I began asking, "Where are African-American women?" "How are they present?" One answer was in the index and footnotes—literally, in Brumberg's otherwise meticulously researched history of anorexia, *Fasting Girls.* The sole entry in her index on African-American women reads: "Blacks, as anorectics, 284*n14.*" (p. 361) Needless to say, there is no comparable entry reading "Whites, as anorectics, everything but 284*n14.*"

What intrigued me was why someone who interrogates the cultural construction of white female appetite with such brilliance would relegate women of color to a footnote. There Brumberg repeats the claim of medical researcher George Hsu that "the rarity among blacks of anorexia nervosa and bulimia is the result of cultural differences that protect young black women from the negative self-image and intense pressure for slimness that are part of the white middle-class experience" (see note 10). Brumberg then comments: "These data, if correct, are telling evidence of the separateness of black culture and white culture and their differential strengths." (p. 284) Black women protected from a negative self-image? Is *The Bluest Eye's* Pecola Breedlove then solely a product of Toni Morrison's vivid imagination, created out of whole cloth? The proviso "if correct" surely indicates that Brumberg recognized the inadequacy of such an analysis, particularly in its conflation of "negative self-image" with "intense pressure for slimness." One reason for her reluctance to pursue this issue, I would speculate, is that to ask about the appetites, dietary practices, and bodies of African-American women is tantamount to making the domain of eating disorders—as she and many others have constructed it—collapse. Black women are not just a footnote but a constitutive footnote; they are not just an absence in eating disorders but a constitutive absence, and this is an important distinction.

For whereas the creation of mammy/cook figures such as Aunt Jemima entailed a naturalization and/or biologization of black female cooking skills, these discourses of eating disorders have also relied upon a naturalization of black female appetite. This is particularly true of the work of Kim Chernin. In her book *The Obsession: Reflections on the Tyranny of Slenderness,* Chernin argues that "women" have not been allowed to have a "natural" relationship to "our" appetites and bodies.[12] She claims that Western culture fears fully developed womanhood and that the emergence of anorexia nervosa and bulimia in conjunction with the rise of second-wave feminism is a sign of women's conflicted feelings about "our" mothers and about inhabiting adult women's bodies. In effect, the anorectic attempts to resolve these conflicts by retaining the body of a child. Chernin argues that "large size, maturity, voluptuousness, massiveness, strength, and power are not permitted if we wish to conform to our culture's ideal. Our bodies, which have knowledge of life, must undo this fullness of knowing and make themselves look like the body of a precocious child if we wish to win the approval of our culture." (p. 94) For Chernin, "large size, maturity, voluptuousness, massiveness, strength, and power" are valorized terms, ideals to which "we" have not been "permitted" to aspire. But given that traits such as "strength" and "power" have historically been attributed to African-American women in the context of an indictment of black matriarchy—as exemplified most notoriously by Daniel Moynihan's 1965 report *The Negro Fam-*

ily: The Case for National Action—one might well question what relationship black women have had to Chernin's "we."[13]

Viewed from this perspective, Chernin's complaint seems to be that the hegemonic subject positions available to bourgeois white women have not been constituted in the same way as the positions available to black women, particularly those of the lower classes. Yet she never explicitly addresses the fact that her model for the anorectic is an adolescent white female. Indeed, Chernin even includes a chapter in *The Obsession* called "The Matriarch" which invokes a mythic past of female power and has no reference to race.[14] Intriguingly, however, at the very start of the book she quotes from a poem collected in *Passion,* by black feminist essayist and poet June Jordan. After acknowledging that "Nothing fills me up at night," the poem's speaker proceeds to detail her sleep-interrupting desire for food ("cherry pie hot from the oven with Something like Vermont/Cheddar Cheese," etc.) as a symptom of other emotional needs. (Chernin, p. 12) She concludes with a self-admonition to be "writing poems, writing poems" rather than rummaging around in her refrigerator "in the middle of the night. . . ." (p. 12) In a subsequent annotation of the poem, Chernin refers to Jordan as a "woman" and never questions her relationship to ideals such as "massiveness, strength, and power." To have acknowledged Jordan's race, class, and historical location would have disrupted the models of female development Chernin was setting up. It would have denaturalized them by forcing her to confront the ways in which her conceptions of the "natural"—"natural bodies" and "natural appetites"—are already inscribed by differences of gender, race, class, sexuality, sexual orientation, and historicity.

Of course, as the subject matter of Jordan's poem would tend to suggest, one is by no means hard-pressed to locate writings by African-American women which foreground their own appetites, dietary practices, and bodies. These topics appear repeatedly in the work of Jordan's peers—contemporary African-American fiction writers such as Alice Walker, Gloria Naylor, and Carolyn Ferrell.[15] Furthermore, several contributors to *The Black Women's Health Book* incorporate discussion of dietary practices into a more comprehensive agenda to improve the mental and physical health of African-American women, as does black feminist scholar bell hooks in *Sisters of the Yam: Black Women and Self-Recovery.*[16] In these works food is treated in conjunction with drugs and alcohol, as a habit-forming substance which African-American women can and do abuse. Similar themes are sounded in popular culture. To cite one of the more intriguing examples, in 1989 *Essence* magazine printed an autobiographical essay entitled "Fat Is a Black Woman's Issue." Author Retha Powers was herself appropriating the title of Susie Orbach's path-breaking book *Fat Is a Feminist Issue.* Orbach had helped to pioneer second-wave feminism's exploration of dieting and food obsession as normative female behaviors, but hers was a polemic which largely ignored women of color.

Taking issue with such exclusions, Powers writes about her obsession with the "dirty, sinful act" of eating and details her struggles to stop the (literally) self-destructive cycle of dieting, bingeing, purging, and laxative abuse. (p. 78) She censures, furthermore, persons who told her over the years that her large size was "acceptable in the Black community. . . ." (p. 78) Whereas Chernin and Orbach see pressure on middle-class white women to be thin as a form of cultural gynophobia, Powers views the *lack* of this pressure on her—as an African-American woman—as a sign of racism. In some of the recent essays collected in *Unbearable Weight,* Susan Bordo has begun to develop a systematic assessment of the racial and class inscriptions of the consuming female body. Extrapolating from her subtle and innovative work on bourgeois white women and eating disorders, Bordo suggests that the hegemony of Western culture and upward class mobility have re-sulted in increased pressure on African-American women—such as Powers—to become slender bodies. In other words, they are expected to emulate the controlled bodily boundaries idealized for middle-class white women.[17] While I would not want to downplay the role of the mass media or of class positioning in the demographics of eating disorders, it does, however, seem to me that in the process of linking upward class mobility to compulsory starvation for African-American women, Bordo inadvertently naturalizes lower-class black female appetite.[18]

In this respect, perhaps the most persuasive work being done on African-American women and food is that of sociologist Becky Thompson, who has recently been researching what she calls "eating problems" among women of color. Thompson argues that women across the spectrum of race, ethnicity, class, and sexual orientation display symptoms of a troubled relationship to food. Many eat to suppress emotions, particularly the posttraumatic stress of incest and sexual assault, as well as the strain of living in a white-supremacist, heterosexist, capitalist patriarchy. Clearly one might critique all this work, Thompson's included, for its tendency to naturalize *male* appetites, but my aim here is not to engage in the debate over whether eating disorders are normative or pathological, or to stake out the most purely constructivist position for myself.[19] Rather, I want to stress several different points.

While for the purposes of this essay I have found it useful to assimilate starving, bingeing, and bingeing and purging under one rubric, appetite, it is surely even more important for us to make distinctions among the discourses, practices, and spectacles of anorexia, bulimia, and obesity. One reason I particularly mention Powers's essay is that she not only denaturalizes but also foregrounds the conflation of African-American women's bodies and *fat.* For if black women have been absences in the discourses of eating disorders, they most certainly have been highly visible in the specularization of corpulence in American culture. Donald Bogle recounts in *Toms, Coons, Mulattoes, Mammies, and Bucks,* for instance, the gastronomic lengths to which actress Louise Beavers was forced in order to replicate the stereotypical bodily boundaries of "mammy." Perhaps best known currently for her portrayal of Delilah in John Stahl's film version of *Imitation of Life* (1934), Beavers regularly went on "force-feed diets, compelling herself to eat beyond her normal appetite. Generally, she weighed close to two hundred pounds, but it was a steady battle for her to stay overweight. During filming . . . she often lost weight and then had to be padded to look more like a full-bosomed domestic who was capable of carrying the world on her shoulders." (p. 63) Beavers's ordeal would tend to suggest, then, that the widespread conflation of black female bodies and fat is inseparable from the phantasmatic desires (and cultural representations) of the hegemonic white imaginary.[20]

In *Feminism without Women,* cultural theorist Tania Modleski has explicated these desires by analyzing in detail contemporary culture's "horror of the body" and the "special role played by the woman of color as receptacle" of these fears. (p. 130) She argues, for example, that in the film *Crossing Delancey* (1988) the "function of the fat, sexually voracious black woman . . . is to enable the white Jewish subculture, through its heterosexual love story, to represent itself in a highly sentimentalized, romanticized, and sublimated light, while disavowing the desires and discontents underlying the civilization it is promoting." (p. 130) It is imperative, Modleski continues, that we "consider the ways in which ethnic and racial groups are played off against—and play themselves off against—one another." (p. 130) In light of her comments it is surely significant that both Orbach and Chernin explicitly refer to how their identities as Jewish women have shaped their attitudes toward food and body size. "I was a Jewish beatnik," Orbach recalls, "and I would be *zaftig.*" (p. xv)[21]

Even while acknowledging that fat has functioned as a site of (and psychic resolution for) interracial and interethnic conflict, we should not overlook the fact that many African-American women have appropriated the spectacle of the large black female body as a form of political protest. Here one thinks of a tradition stretching from actresses such as Hattie McDaniel to contemporary rappers such as Queen Latifah and Salt 'N' Pepa.[22] In her "Ladies First" video, for example, Queen Latifah flaunts her refusal to conform to American culture's pervasive imagery of female slimness while also positioning herself, according to historian Tricia Rose, "as part of a rich legacy of black women's activism, racial commitment, and cultural pride." (p. 164) The members of Salt 'N' Pepa, by contrast, often foreground butts in their videos; Rose claims that in so doing they appropriate "a complex history of white scrutiny of black female bodies, from the repulsion and fascination with and naked exhibition of Sara Bartmann as 'The Hottentot Venus' in the early 1800s to the perverse and exoticized pleasure many Europeans received from Josephine Baker's aggressively behind-centered dances." (p. 167–8)[23]

In short, African-American women have always been "presences" in eating disorders, particularly in specular form as the naturalized fat body. Consequently, it is important to recognize that what a good many African-American women have been appropriating in recent years is not so much the practices of disorderly eating as the discourses themselves. For by appropriating a set of discourses in which the individual has an "unnatural" relationship to her appetite, African-American women are contesting normative black female subject positions and insisting upon their psychological complexity as human beings. They are refusing to be the constitutive absence, the "natural," in the binary through which American appetites have historically been constructed.

To talk about eating disorders as a discourse which can be appropriated as a tactic of resistance is surely problematic, however, since it threatens to trivialize the health hazards for African-American women of symptoms such as excess weight, bingeing and purging, and laxative abuse. As writers in *The Black Women's Health Book* point out, women of color have less access to nutritional food and quality health care than do economically privileged whites, and, consequently, they are more prone to preventable health problems such as hypertension and "sugar" diabetes. Supporting their claims, the *New York Times* reported in January 1994 that "[d]octors appear to be less likely to tell black women to quit smoking and drinking during pregnancy than they are to tell white women . . . ." ("Study," p. A16) Given such demographic inconsistencies in American medical care, one might well greet with pleasure the news that the health of African-American women is both under investigation and of interest to the editors of the newspaper of record. Yet I have an ulterior motive in referring to this particular article from the *Times*. I repeat: "Doctors appear to be less likely to tell black women to quit smoking and drinking *during pregnancy* than they are to tell white women. . . ." (emphasis added)

It would, after all, surely be inaccurate to say that there have been no discourses in recent years of black female appetite. For if the desires of middle-class adolescent white women have been constructed since the late 1960s largely via eating disorders, so the desires of young black women have been constructed in terms of motherhood and matriarchy. Young white women purportedly want nothing more than to be thin; young black women, nothing more than to be pregnant.[24] The discussions of "crack babies" and "fetal alcohol syndrome" which proliferated during the 1980s were, moreover, far more concerned with black female appetites than with black fetuses. Indeed, while doctors have been careful to warn pregnant white women to quit smoking and drinking, they have reported analogous practices of black women to the police. In the next section of this essay, I hope better to understand not just this conflation of the pregnant black body with the "dangerous" body, but also the reasons underlying this discursive slippage between the appetites of black women and the health of black fetuses.[25]

II. "THE MOST PERILOUS ENVIRONMENT"

Midway through a 1990 article on the emergence of "fetal rights," *Nation* contributor Katha Pollitt pondered: "How have we come to see women as the major threat to the health of their newborns, and the womb as the most dangerous place a child will ever inhabit?" (p. 410) Pollitt was responding to a trend which has been gaining force in conjunction with the movement to recriminalize abortion, a trend epitomized by Gerald Leach's comment in his 1970 book *The Biocrats:* "Quite simply, the womb has become the most perilous environment in which humans have to live." (p. 137) A quarter of a century later, an evolutionary biologist at Harvard, David Haig, has brought Leach's claim to fruition by using Darwinian theory to interpret human pregnancy. Because sexual reproduction results in a child's sharing "only half of its genes with the mother," Haig claims that many "difficulties in pregnancy probably come about because there are genetic conflicts between what is best for the mother's genes and what is best for fetal genes." (in Lipsitch, p. C3) But since under most circumstances the fetus cannot survive if the woman carrying it dies, Haig concludes that pregnancy is "a conflict of interest within a basically peaceful society" (in Lipsitch, p. C3). In *The Mother Machine* (1985), Gena Corea stresses that such utero-phobia "is not a modern idea." (p. 251) This contemporary flowering of concerns about fetal endangerment is, she and such others as Pollitt contend, at least in part a backlash against second-wave feminism and the Supreme Court's 1973 decision granting women (limited) rights to abortion.

Courtesy of modern technologies such as sonograms, the fetus has indeed emerged as a miniature "person" in its own right.[26] It is granted a status theoretically equal to and in practice above that of the woman who carries it by doctors who now officially specialize in the field of Maternal–Fetal Medicine rather than Ob–Gyn. The fetus is even the subject of advertisements by the General Motors Corporation, whose researchers have been developing "the first 'pregnant' crash dummy" because, in their words, "Not all passengers can be seen. But they all need protection." (General Motors, p. A16) "Protection from whom?" one might well ask. In her provocative 1992 essay, "The Abortion Question and the Death of Man," Mary Poovey explains how feminist use of both privacy and equality arguments in advocating for abortion has inadvertently contributed to this sacralization of the fetus as a justification for curtailing women's rights. Certainly feminist arguments for abortion have, she points out, been readily appropriated by persons who oppose that right. Thus the slogan "equal rights for women" becomes the bumper sticker, "Equal Rights for Unborn Women." In the rhetoric of antiabortionists, Poovey writes, terms such as " 'choice,' 'privacy,' and 'rights' invert effortlessly into their opposites, precisely because, regardless of who uses them, these terms belong to a single set of metaphysical assumptions." (p. 249)

Such appropriations are enabled, in other words, by the fact that the "rights" discourses invoked by many feminists rely on the prior figuration of a body—what Poovey calls a "metaphysics of substance"—which is normatively rational, bourgeois, white, heterosexual, and male. (p. 241) In this metaphysics the mark of female difference is the womb, which means that, unlike the male body, the female body is always presumptively pregnable.[27] Poovey's response to this dilemma is to insist that advocates for women's reproductive rights not downplay differences among women, differences such as class, race, sexuality, ethnicity, and nationality which determine any given woman's access to "rights." She insists, more-

over, that we need to develop a politics which foregrounds the contingency of the "body" and which recognizes that rights are only constituted in a matrix of relationships. It would be difficult to find fault with Poovey's efforts to formulate an approach to reproductive freedom which is less easily appropriated by opponents of feminism and which does not privilege heterosexual middle-class white women as the norm. Yet her analysis (like that of Pollitt) falls short in one important respect. Neither fully takes into account the fact that fetal rights have not emerged solely as a backlash against white feminists, a backlash which is simply played out on the bodies of lower-class women of color because they are more vulnerable to social control than are wealthy whites. Rather, women of color have been a primary target of fetal rights activists because fear of the black womb—and by extension, I would argue, fear of the black female appetite—has provided a primary model from which contemporary fears of white wombs have been derived.

Such fears often operate in fascistically friendly ways. Hence my initially optimistic response to the *New York Times* article about the failure of doctors to warn pregnant African-American women about the dangers of smoking and drinking during pregnancy. Yet the punitive underpinnings of such concern for black women's health is amply illustrated by another article which the *New York Times* published the following day, coincidentally, under the heading "Hospital Is Accused of Illegal Experiments." It seems that the Medical University of South Carolina had instituted a drug-testing program "intended to force drug-addicted women who are pregnant to stop using drugs by threatening them with jail if they fail to cooperate with the hospital's regimen of prenatal visits and to attend a drug-treatment program." (Hilts, p. A12) Virtually all the women targeted by this program were African Americans. Nationwide, as legal scholar Dorothy Roberts has demonstrated in "Punishing Drug Addicts Who Have Babies: Women of Color,

Equality, and the Right of Privacy," virtually all the women jailed for taking drugs while pregnant, forced to undergo unwanted caesareans, or otherwise subjected to forms of maternal "prior restraint" have been lower-class women of color.

This obsession with "perilous" black wombs has precedent in the late 1960s and 1970s—precisely the period when the discourses of eating disorders began taking on their current configurations. In addition to the obvious example of the Moynihan report, much Black Power and Black Arts rhetoric shared the era's fascination with black matriarchy, racial genocide, the pill, and abortion. Such African-American political activists as Nation of Islam leader Elijah Muhammad and comic-turned-nutritionist Dick Gregory not only developed extended critiques of black dietary practices (namely of soul food, which they viewed as "filthy" and "unhealthy"), but they also focused their critiques particularly on pregnant and nursing black women.

In the second volume of his dietary manual *How to Eat to Live,* for example, Muhammad advised African-American women to

> EAT GOOD FOOD so that you will be able to give your baby good, pure milk.
>
> You can drink cows' milk; your own milk glands will put it into the right stage for your child. Be careful as to what kind of drugs you take while nursing your baby. And do not take fasts while you are breast-feeding an infant or even while you are pregnant. If you like, you may eat once a day while pregnant or breast-feeding your baby, but you are not forced to do so. You should not go for two or three days without eating. (p. 90)

The fact that from a contemporary vantage point these strictures seem quite mild surely suggests the extent to which we have increasingly become accustomed to treating the bodies of pregnant women as having value only in relation, and in subordination, to the body of the zygote, embryo, or fetus they carry. Muhammad's directive to "eat good food so that you will be able to

give your baby good, pure milk" calls to mind a telling question legal theorist Patricia Williams has posed about a Washington, D.C., case in which a judge imprisoned a pregnant African-American woman, "ostensibly in order to *protect* her fetus" (p. 184). "Why," Williams muses, "is there no state interest in not simply providing for but improving the circumstances of the woman, whether pregnant or not?" (p. 184) Why, I ask, did the study cited in the *New York Times* not ask whether doctors advised black women to quit smoking and drinking, whether pregnant or not?

Indeed, Muhammad's strictures presage the contemporary resurgence of efforts to place the blame for so-called social "pathology" on the behavior of pregnant women—particularly impoverished, unmarried women of color—rather than on structural forces of discrimination such as regressive tax policies, declining wages and benefits, cuts in social spending, and concentration of toxic waste dumps in areas with large minority and poor populations.[28] In the first volume of *How to Eat to Live,* Muhammad begins by chastising black women for their failure to breast-feed but rapidly escalates his rhetoric:

> The baby eats poisonous animals, fowls, and vegetables and drinks milk that is not his milk—it belongs to the cow's baby, goat's baby, and horse's baby. Here the child is reared on animals and cattle's food.
>
> This is why we have such a great percentage of delinquency among minors. The child is not fed from his [sic] mother's breast—she is too proud of her form. . . .
>
> When the baby reaches the age of 10, and if it is a male, most of them begin to indulge in drinking alcoholic beverages and using tobacco in one form or another.
>
> Alcohol and tobacco, with their poisonous effect upon the male, cut his life down, as far as his reproductive organs are concerned. He is unable to produce his own kind. (pp. 88–9)

The selfish vanity of the black woman in refusing to breast-feed her son [sic] leads inexorably to his "delinquency," his alcohol and drug addiction, and then to his impotence or sterility. Yet if such comments are perhaps to be expected from an avowed advocate of black patriarchy, I was somewhat surprised to encounter similar sentiments coming from the more progressive, women's rights sympathizer Dick Gregory. In his *Dick Gregory's Political Primer,* for example, the then-fasting fruitarian claims that "more boy babies die at birth or shortly thereafter than girl babies, because they are unable to survive the mucus in the mother's system." (p. 260) In Gregory's dietary schema, mucus is a form of what structural anthropologists refer to as ritual "pollution."[29] Such pollution results, Gregory contends, from the consumption of an "unhealthy" diet of soul food and dairy products.

Roberts insists that efforts to understand the motivating force behind this fixation on fetal contamination absolutely must begin with reference to the class, race, and sexuality of the women most likely to be punished for violating fetal endangerment laws. The discussions of crack babies which proliferated during the 1980s stemmed, she suggests, far more from a cultural imperative to control impoverished women of color than to ensure the health and safety of their children:

> If prosecutors had instead chosen to prosecute affluent women addicted to alcohol or prescription medication, the policy of criminalizing prenatal conduct very likely would have suffered a hasty demise. Society is much more willing to condone the punishment of poor women of color who fail to meet the middle-class ideal of motherhood. (p. 1436)

Roberts claims, moreover, that the "government's choice of a punitive response" to prenatal drug use "perpetuates the historical devaluation of Black women as mothers." (p. 1423) Whereas Hortense Spillers has explained the hegemony of American belief in the myth of black matriarchy as a legacy of slavery's erasure of the Name and Law of the Black Father,

Roberts construes the current fixation on lower-class black maternity as, in part, a legacy of black women's abuse as "breeders" during slavery (see Spillers, "Mama's"). Thus slaveowners would whip pregnant slaves by forcing them "to lie face down in a depression in the ground while they were whipped. This procedure allowed the masters to protect the fetus while abusing the mother." (Roberts, p. 1438) Such brutality serves, Roberts observes, "as a powerful metaphor for the evils of a fetal protection policy that denies the humanity of the mother." (p. 1438)

In fact, it seems to me that we are witnessing more than a cultural imperative to control women of color; we are witnessing a cultural imperative to control the *appetites* of women of color so as to control the *ontological status* of America. Hence my appropriation of Brillat-Savarin as the speculative thesis of this essay. Given the current level of fixation on national purity, it is, consequently, surely a risky undertaking for African-American women to foreground the individual body and appetite as a strategy of empowerment: as Poovey's analysis of the rhetoric of "rights" would suggest, such discourses can readily be redeployed to legitimate ideologies in which black women are a source of pollution. I envision here the shift from "Fat Is a Feminist Issue" to "Fat Is a Black Woman's Issue" to "Fat Is a Black Fetal Issue"—and indeed studies on whether a "fatty" maternal diet causes childhood cancer have already been conducted (see Raloff). What I wonder is if in constructing the discourse in this fashion, we reinforce American fears of the black feminine as what Julia Kristeva terms the "abject"—as that which calls into question the boundaries between food and not-food, self and not-self, as that which, because of its overdetermined historical conflation with food, reminds us that our bodily boundaries are not impermeable.[30]

Many of the contributors to *The Black Women's Health Book* acknowledge this double bind. To remain silent about black female health problems and appetites is to be complicit in a larger cultural erasure of the lives and needs of women of color. At the same time, it is a tricky business for African-American women to appropriate discourses which originated via the inscription of their oppression. Can there exist an "anorexic" or "bulimic" black woman? Can there exist a Caucasian crack baby? Or is the former inevitably defined as a wanna-be-white and the latter, an honorary black? In the epilogue to his study of male sexuality and social discourse in late nineteenth-century England, *Talk on the Wilde Side,* Ed Cohen writes that we need to "imagine how we can historically problematize the ways the 'oppositional' terms of dominance come to be embedded within the categories of resistance." (p. 213) Cohen is referring here specifically to the widespread use of the term "queer" among activists for lesbian and gay rights, but his general point is surely applicable here as well. (p. 5) In order to develop an agenda for bettering black women's health, scholars and activists must work to develop a vocabulary in which black women are not already inscribed as (1) natural (and therefore never in need of social benefits, such as medical care); or (2) unnatural (and therefore always in need of social regulation).

In a 1987 address entitled "Sick and Tired of Being Sick and Tired: The Politics of Black Women's Health," Angela Davis negotiated these contradictory obstacles by insisting on the "urgency of contextualizing Black women's health in relation to the prevailing political conditions. While our health is undeniably assaulted by natural forces frequently beyond our control, all too often the enemies of our physical and emotional well-being are social and political." (p. 19) Davis proceeded to discuss Department of Defense spending, CIA operations in Angola, Reagan's nomination of Robert Bork to the Supreme Court, apartheid in South Africa, and continuing Congressional support for the Nicaraguan contras—all of which she construed as integral to the politics of black women's health. "We must," she concluded, "learn consistently to place our battle for universally accessible health care in its larger social and political context." (p. 25) In her refusal to distinguish between bodily and social boundaries, in her insistence (along with Audre Lorde) that "[b]attling racism and battling heterosexism and battling apartheid share the same urgency inside me as battling cancer," Davis offers a template for the sort of political praxis Mary Poovey has in mind. (Davis, p. 26)[31] It is a template for a political praxis which, at the very least, attempts to be less than amenable to reappropriation by the reactionary right. The efficacy of such "politics unbound" is yet to be determined, but it seems to me that Davis's lead is, as ever, a wise one to follow.

NOTES

1. I received the two-page release ("Aunt Jemima Trademark Design to Be Updated") from Quaker Oats, along with a publicity pamphlet, *The Quaker Q and How It Grew,* in response to my (repeated) inquiries for information about the trademark.

2. For a concise history of the "mammy" stereotype, see Phil Patton's "Mammy: Her Life and Times."

3. And, of course, "good taste" would be the attribute of the consumer who chooses to buy Aunt Jemima products. Judith Williamson's discussion of such semantic shifts in *Decoding Advertisements* has been very helpful to my thinking about the Aunt Jemima trademark. The title of a 1989 *Newsweek* article by Marcus Mabry, "A Long Way from 'Aunt Jemima' "—which focused on advertisers' efforts to reach an expanding black consumer market in the 1980s— would suggest that the trademark image has been antithetical to the recognition of black consumer appetites.

4. Agnew's description is slightly inaccurate. The kerchief was removed during the 1968 makeover and replaced with a headband.

5. My analysis here draws on an early essay by Julia Kristeva. In "From Symbol to Sign"— excerpted from her thesis *La Révolution du language poétique*—Kristeva argues that the "sec-

ond half of the Middle Ages (thirteenth to fifteenth centuries) was a period of transition for European culture: thought based on the sign replaced that based on the symbol." (p. 64) The mode of the symbol "is a cosmogonic semiotic practice where the elements (symbols) refer back to one or more unknowable and unrepresentable universal transcendence(s). . . . [W]ithin its vertical function, the sign refers back to entities of lesser dimensions that are more *concretized* than the symbol. . . . Within their horizontal function, the units of the sign's semiotic practice are articulated as a *metonymic chain of deflections* [écarts] that signifies a *progressive creation of metaphors.*" (pp. 64–70) In other words, Agnew begins neither with the Quaker Oats press release telling us that the new image preserves the abstract symbolic meaning of the old one, nor with me in treating it as a sign which has "vertical" reference to "entities of lesser dimensions that are more *concretized* than the symbol" (that is, a middle-class consumer). Instead he interprets the trademark via what Kristeva calls its "horizontal" reference, embarking upon a "*metonymic chain of deflections* [écarts] that signifies a *progressive creation of metaphors.*" (p. 70)

6. The *TV Guide* scandal was fodder for tabloids, comedians, and others during the fall of 1989. Joshua Gamson discusses briefly the significance of the *TV Guide* misrepresentation in *Claims to Fame: Celebrity in Contemporary America.* (p. 100) The vicissitudes of Winfrey's weight and the minutiae of her dietary habits are documented by Nellie Bly in *Oprah! Up Close and Down Home.* Her most recent weight loss has also provided the occasion for "the fastest-selling cookbook in history," Rosie Daley's *In the Kitchen with Rosie: Oprah's Favorite Recipes.* (Sanz and Fisher, p. 85) Daley is Winfrey's personal chef.

7. I discuss the history of the trademark in the prologue to my dissertation.

8. See, for example, discussions of the ideology and/or portrayal of black womanhood in Davis's "The Legacy of Slavery: Standards for a New Womanhood"; Christian's "Images of Black Women in Afro-American Literature: From Stereotype to Character"; hooks's *Ain't I a*

Woman; D. White's *Ar'n't I a Woman?;* Spillers's "Mama's Baby, Papa's Maybe: An American Grammar Book"; McDowell's Introduction to Nella Larsen's *Quicksand and Passing,* Collins's *Black Feminist Thought;* and Jewell's *From Mammy to Miss America and Beyond.* Jewell also has a chapter specifically on Aunt Jemima in her dissertation, "An Analysis of the Visual Development of a Stereotype: The Media's Portrayal of Mammy and Aunt Jemima as Symbols of Black Womanhood."

9. This is the fourth aphorism listed in the preamble to *The Physiology of Taste.* (p. 3)

10. Two exceptions include James J. Gray, Kathryn Ford, and Lily M. Kelly, "The Prevalence of Bulimia in a Black College Population," and George L. K. Hsu, "Are the Eating Disorders Becoming More Common in Blacks?"

11. Their comments, I should mention, were unsolicited on my part. The issue arose when each student was explaining excessive class absences and her failure to turn in work on time. Perhaps I was merely adjudged likely to sympathize with such an excuse, but I have no reason to doubt the sincerity of either student.

12. See, for example, the prologue. (pp. 1–3)

13. The text of what is widely known as the "Moynihan Report" is reprinted in *The Moynihan Report and the Politics of Controversy: A Transaction Social Science and Public Policy Report.* (1967)

14. She does so, I stress, just as the neoconservative and new right backlash came to fruition with the ascendancy of Ronald Reagan (and his demonization of "Cadillac-driving welfare queens") to the U.S. presidency.

15. One thinks, for example, of Walker's *Meridian.* Eponymous heroine Meridian Hill displays symptoms of anorexia which might be interpreted using Caroline Bynum's analysis of medieval women saints in *Holy Feast and Holy Fast,* as well as Chernin's psychoanalytic analysis of contemporary anorexia nervosa. In Naylor's *Linden Hills,* aspiring buppie Roxanne Tilson frequently indulges in late-night binges, and one of the Nedeed wives from the book's fictive past has cooked, purged, and starved, until, we are told, she literally "eat[s] herself to death." (p. 190) Honey, the narrator of Ferrell's

"Eating Confessions," is by contrast an over-weight African-American woman who socializes with her friend Rose at the "Monday Night Determination Diet Meeting." (p. 453) Their food-structured relationship is disrupted, however, when Rose meets a man and loses weight, and Honey uses food in an unsuccessful attempt to lure her away from him.

16. See, for example, Georgiana Arnold's "Coming Home: One Black Woman's Journey to Health and Fitness."

17. Thus in *Unbearable Weight* Bordo writes: "Arguably, a case could once be made for a contrast between (middle-class, heterosexual) white women's obsessive relations with food and a more accepting attitude toward women's appetites within African-American communities. But in the nineties, features on diet, exercise, and body image problems have grown increasingly prominent in magazines aimed at African-American readers, reflecting the cultural reality that for most women today—whatever their racial or ethnic identity, and increasingly across class and sexual-orientation differences as well—free and easy relations with food are at best a relic of the past." (p. 103)

18. As she acknowledges, moreover, there have long been regulatory practices of black femininity—hair straightening, skin bleaching, etc.—and any discussion of black women and eating disorders needs to be situated as part of a whole range of practices through which African-American women have, in Judith Butler's term, historically "performed their identities."

19. I am grateful to Valerie Sayers and Kevin Kopelson for questioning my omission of male appetite, and I hope to offer a more detailed response in the near future.

20. In *Imitation of Life,* the book on which subsequent movies were based, Fannie Hurst describes Delilah as "a buxom negro woman who, with the best intentions in the world, swelled the food budget so considerably." (p. 100) Shortly thereafter Hurst writes that "[t]here was no suppressing the enormity that was Delilah, nor was there desire to suppress it." (p. 103)

Curiously, however, notwithstanding the attention recently paid to *Imitation of Life* in the academy, to my knowledge no one has pointed out that two years after *Imitation of Life* appeared, Hurst published a brief autobiographical narrative entitled *No Food with My Meals.* There she describes her obsession with the slimming craze, which she says began to overcome her around 1931—just as she was writing *Imitation of Life.* "Some women are born frail," Hurst announces, with characteristic aplomb. "Some have frailty thrust upon them. Still others achieve it, and at what price glory!" (p. 2) Hurst concludes *No Food with My Meals* with a list of "acknowledgments" (p. 55), including one "To the books written during this period which abound perhaps unduly in foods coveted by their author." (p. 56) Though Hurst never directly mentions *Imitation of Life,* she might be admitting that her own desire for and fear of food (and fat) resulted in her having projected onto the character Delilah a psychology untouched by the slimming fad. Delilah, in other words, represents a dual mode of novelistic wish fulfillment: she is both the object of Hurst's derision, that which Hurst loathes in herself, and she is what Hurst wishes she could be—able to experience and satisfy her appetite "naturally."

21. Brumberg points out that she is "not a recovered anorectic nor . . . the mother of an anorexic daughter" but otherwise does not dwell on possible personal investments she might have in her scholarly work on anorexia. (p. 1) I would like to thank Gloria-Jean Masciarotte for pointing out to me that one can only talk about anorexic, bulimic, or fat bodies via reference to the ethnicity of the body under consideration. There are, in other words, distinctions to be made among Caucasian, Jewish, Italian, Chinese, Chicana, and other ethnic bodily "norms." I hope to respond in greater detail to Mascariotte's comments in future essays.

22. When criticized for playing stereotypical "mammy" characters, McDaniel was known to have responded, "Why should I complain about making seven thousand dollars a week playing a maid? If I didn't, I'd be making seven dollars a week actually being one!" (in Bogle, p. 82)

23. Roxanne Brown's *Ebony* article, "Full-Figured Women Fight Back," offers a less explicitly politicized example of how African-American women have appropriated the large female body as a mode of cultural resistance. My thanks to the audience member at the University of Iowa who questioned my failure to mention "black bottoms" in an earlier draft of this essay.

24. This despite the fact that from 1970 to 1980, according to Mimi Abramovitz, "the unmarried black birth rate . . . fell by 13 percent, while that of whites rose by 27 percent." (p. 354) In *Regulating the Lives of Women,* Abramovitz further points out that the "dramatic increase in the percentage of births to unmarried black women reflects a drop in the overall fertility and birth rates of *married* black women relative to *unmarried* black women, and not an increase in child-bearing by the latter." (p. 354)

25. One reader suggested that I ought perhaps be explicit in stating that because black women are, in the Moynihanian view, always pregnant, "the fat body is interchangeable with the pregnant body." In the process of writing an affirmation of this comment, I realized that I am not at all sure that my analysis actually demonstrates it—at least not in sweeping semiotic terms rather than local historicized ones. In addition, one would need to take into account variations in the representation of the fat body: sometimes breasts are emphasized, sometimes stomachs, sometimes butts. Sometimes the boundaries are (as Susan Bordo would doubtless point out) "wiggly" and at other times, controlled. (see pp. 191–2)

26. Rosalind Petchesky discusses the significance of technologies enabling fetal visualization in her *Abortion and Woman's Choice* (pp. 335–45). See also Robyn Rowland's discussion of fetal personhood in *Living Laboratories.* (pp. 118–55)

27. In *The Female Body and the Law,* feminist political theorist Zillah Eisenstein also explores the ramifications of the legal presumption that the womb is the sign of female difference.

28. I use quotation marks around "pathology" to emphasize my disagreement with the racist, homophobic, patriarchal assumptions embedded in "culture of pathology" arguments about inner cities, for instance, the assumption that male-headed nuclear households should be normative.

29. Ritual pollution, according to Mary Douglas, stems from a violation of socially constructed boundaries such as those of gender. See her *Purity and Danger.*

30. Kristeva develops her theory of abjection in *Powers of Horror.*

31. Davis is quoting here from Audre Lorde's *A Burst of Light.* (pp. 116–27)

REFERENCES

Abramovitz, Mimi. *Regulating the Lives of Women: Social Welfare Policy from Colonial Times to the Present.* Boston: South End, 1988.

Agnew, Jean-Christophe. "Shop Till You Drop: How the West Was Sold." Rev. of *Satisfaction Guaranteed: The Making of the American Mass Market,* by Susan Strasser. *Voice Literary Supplement,* December 1989, pp. 29–30.

Arnold, Georgiana. "Coming Home: One Black Woman's Journey to Health and Fitness." *The Black Women's Health Book: Speaking for Ourselves,* ed. Evelyn C. White. Seattle: Seal, 1990, pp. 269–79.

"Aunt Jemima Trademark Design to Be Updated." News Release. Chicago: Quaker Oat Co., April 27, 1989.

Bly, Nellie. *Oprah! Up Close and Down Home.* New York: Zebra-Kensington, 1993.

Bogle, Donald. *Toms, Coons, Mulattoes, Mammies, and Bucks: An Interpretive History of Blacks in American Fitness.* New York: Continuum, 1991 (orig. 1973).

Bordo, Susan. *Unbearable Weight: Feminism, Western Culture, and the Body.* Berkeley: University of California Press, 1993.

Brillat-Savarin, Jean Anthelme. *The Physiology of Taste.* Trans. M. F. K. Fisher. San Francisco: North Point, 1986 (orig. 1825).

Brown, Roxanne. "Full-Figured Women Fight Back." *Ebony,* March 1990, pp. 27–31.

Brumberg, Joan Jacobs. *Fasting Girls: The History of Anorexia Nervosa.* New York: Plume-Penguin, 1989.

Bynum, Caroline Walker. *Holy Feast and Holy Fast: The Religious Significance of Food to Medieval Women.* Berkeley: University of California Press, 1987.

Chernin, Kim. *The Obsession: Reflections on the Tyranny of Slenderness.* New York: Perennial-Harper, 1981.

Christian, Barbara. "Images of Black Women in Afro-American Literature: From Stereotype to Character." *Black Feminist Criticism: Perspectives on Black Women Writers.* New York: Pergamon, 1985 (orig. 1975), pp. 1–30.

Cohen, Ed. *Talk on the Wilde Side: Toward a Genealogy of a Discourse on Male Sexualities.* New York: Routledge, 1993.

Collins, Patricia Hill. *Black Feminist Thought: Knowledge, Consciousness, and the Politics of Empowerment.* New York: Routledge, 1991.

Corea, Gena. *The Mother Machine: Reproductive Technologies from Artificial Insemination to Artificial Wombs.* New York: Harper, 1985.

Daley, Rosie. *In the Kitchen with Rosie: Oprah's Favorite Recipes.* New York: Knopf, 1994.

Davis, Angela. "The Legacy of Slavery: Standards for a New Womanhood." *Women, Race and Class.* New York: Vintage-Random, 1981, pp. 3–29.

———. "Sick and Tired of Being Sick and Tired: The Politics of Black Women's Health." *The Black Women's Health Book: Speaking for Ourselves,* ed. Evelyn C. White. Seattle: Seal, 1990, pp. 18–26.

Douglas, Mary. *Purity and Danger: An Analysis of the Concepts of Pollution and Taboo.* London: Ark-Routledge, 1966.

Eisenstein, Zillah. *The Female Body and the Law.* Berkeley: University of California Press, 1988.

Ferrell, Carolyn. "Eating Confessions." *Callaloo* 12, no. 3 (1989), pp. 453–64.

Gamson, Joshua. *Claims to Fame: Celebrity in Contemporary America.* Berkeley: University of California Press, 1994.

General Motors. Advertisement. *Washington Post,* May 16, 1994, p. A16.

Gray, James J., Kathryn Ford, and Lily M. Kelly. "The Prevalence of Bulimia in a Black College Population." *International Journal of Eating Disorders* 6, no. 6 (1987), pp. 733–40.

Gregory, Dick. *Dick Gregory's Political Primer,* ed. James R. McGraw. New York: Perennial-Harper, 1972.

Hilts, Philip J. "Hospital Is Accused of Illegal Experiments." *New York Times,* January 21, 1994, p. A12.

hooks, bell. *Ain't I a Woman: Black Women and Feminism.* Boston: South End, 1981.

———. *Sisters of the Yam: Black Women and Self-Recovery.* Boston: South End, 1993.

Hsu, L. K. George. "Are the Eating Disorders Becoming More Common in Blacks?" *International Journal of Eating Disorders* 6, no. 1 (1987), pp. 113–24.

Hurst, Fannie. *Imitation of Life.* 1933. New York: Pyramid, 1974.

———. *No Food with My Meals.* New York: Harper, 1935.

Jewell, Karen Sue Warren. "An Analysis of the Visual Development of a Stereotype: The Media's Portrayal of Mammy and Aunt Jemima as Symbols of Black Womanhood." Dissertation, Ohio State University, 1976.

———. *From Mammy to Miss America and Beyond: Cultural Images and the Shaping of U.S. Social Policy.* New York: Routledge, 1993.

Jordan, June. *Passion: New Poems, 1977–1980.* Boston: Beacon, 1980.

Key, Janet. "At Age 100, a New Aunt Jemima." *Chicago Tribune,* April 28, 1989, sec. 3, pp. 1, 6.

Kristeva, Julia. "From Symbol to Sign." In *The Kristeva Reader,* ed. Toril Moi. Trans. Seán Hand. New York: Columbia University Press, 1986 (orig. 1970), pp. 62–73.

———. *Powers of Horror: An Essay on Abjection.* Trans. Leon S. Roudiez. New York: Columbia University Press, 1982 (orig. 1980)

Leach, Gerald. *The Biocrats.* New York: McGraw-Hill, 1970.

Lipsitch, Marc. "Genetic Tug-of-War May Explain Many of the Troubles of Pregnancy." *New York Times,* July 20, 1993, p. C3.

Lorde, Audre. *A Burst of Light.* Ithaca, NY: Firebrand, 1988.

Mabry, Marcus, with Rhonda Adams. "A Long Way from 'Aunt Jemima': As Black Consumers' Spending Grows, Marketers Target Them with Hipper and More 'Authentic' Ads." *Newsweek,* August 14, 1989, pp. 34–5.

McDowell, Deborah. "Introduction." In *Quicksand and Passing* by Nella Larsen, ed. Deborah McDowell. American Women Writers Series. New Brunswick, NJ: Rutgers University Press, 1987, pp. ix–xxxvii.

Modleski, Tania. *Feminism without Women: Culture and Criticism in a "Postfeminist" Age.* New York: Routledge, 1991.

Morrison, Toni. *The Bluest Eye.* New York: Holt, Rinehart and Winston, 1970.

Moynihan, Daniel P. *The Negro Family: The Case for National Action* ["The Moynihan Report"]. Washington, DC: US Dept. of Labor, 1965.

Muhammad, Elijah. *How to Eat to Live.* Chicago: Muhammad Mosque of Islam No. 2, 1967.

———. *How to Eat to Live.* Book No. 2. Chicago: Muhammad Mosque of Islam No. 2, 1972.

Naylor, Gloria. *Linden Hills.* Viking Penguin, 1985.

Newcomb, Peter, and Lisa Gubernick. "The Top 40." *Forbes,* September 27, 1993, pp. 97–104.

Orbach, Susie. *Fat Is a Feminist Issue: A Self-Help Guide for Compulsive Eaters.* New York: Berkley-Paddington, 1978.

Patton, Phil. "Mammy: Her Life and Times." *American Heritage,* September 1993, pp. 78–87.

Petchesky, Rosalind Pollack. *Abortion and Woman's Choice: The State, Sexuality, and Reproductive Freedom.* Boston: Northeastern University Press, 1990 (orig. 1984).

Pollitt, Katha. "'Fetal Rights': A New Assault on Feminism." *Nation* 26 (March 1990), pp. 409–18.

Poovey, Mary. "The Abortion Question and the Death of Man." In *Feminists Theorize the Political,* ed. Judith Butler and Joan Scott. New York: Routledge, 1992, pp. 239–56.

Powers, Retha. "Fat Is a Black Woman's Issue." *Essence,* October 1989, pp. 75–8ff.

"The Quaker Q and How It Grew." Pamphlet. Chicago: Quaker Oats Co., 1979.

Raloff, Janet. "Mom's Fatty Diet May Induce Child's Cancer." *Science News,* January 6, 1990, p. 5.

Rainwater, Lee, and William L. Yancey, eds. *The Moynihan Report and the Politics of Controversy: A Trans-action Social Science and Public Policy Report.* Cambridge, MA: MIT Press, 1967.

Roberts, Dorothy. "Punishing Drug Addicts Who Have Babies: Women of Color, Equality, and the Right of Privacy." *Harvard Law Review* 104 (May 1991), pp. 1419–82.

Rose, Tricia. *Black Noise: Rap Music and Black Culture in Contemporary America.* Hanover, NH: Wesleyan University Press, 1994.

Rowland, Robyn. *Living Laboratories: Women and Reproductive Technologies.* Bloomington: Indiana University Press, 1992.

Sanz, Cynthia, and Luchina Fisher. "Cookin' for Oprah." *People,* May 16, 1994, pp. 84–8.

Spillers, Hortense J. "Mama's Baby, Papa's Maybe: An American Grammar Book." *Diacritics* 17, no. 2 (1987), pp. 65–81.

"Study Finds Racial Disparity in Warnings to the Pregnant." *New York Times,* January 20, 1994, p. A16.

Thompson, Becky Wangsgaard. "'A Way Outa No Way': Eating Problems among African-American, Latina, and White Women." *Gender & Society* 6, no. 4 (1992), pp. 546–61.

Walker, Alice. "Giving the Party: Aunt Jemima, Mammy, and the Goddess Within." *Ms.,* May/June 1994, pp. 22–5.

———. *Meridian.* New York: Pocket-Simon, 1976.

Weinraub, Judith. "Model with That Something Extra." *Washington Post,* February 4, 1993, pp. C1, 4.

White, Deborah Gray. *Ar'n't I a Woman? Female Slaves in the Plantation South.* New York: Norton, 1985.

White, Evelyn C., ed. *The Black Women's Health Book: Speaking for Ourselves.* Seattle: Seal, 1990.

Williams, Patricia. *The Alchemy of Race and Rights: Diary of a Law Professor.* Cambridge, MA: Harvard University Press, 1991.

Williamson, Judith. *Decoding Advertisements.* London: Boyars, 1978.

READING 24

Jane Fonda, Barbara Bush, and Other Aging Bodies: Femininity and the Limits of Resistance

Myra Dinnerstein and Rose Weitz

Although separated by only half a generation, Jane Fonda and Barbara Bush present us with almost diametrically opposed images of how women can age. Fonda, born in 1937, boasts a "relentlessly improved" body—muscular and nearly fat-free, with dyed hair and surgically enhanced face and breasts. In contrast, Bush, born in 1925, exhibits a "resolutely natural" look, with her matronly figure, white hair, and wrinkled countenance.[1]

The striking contrast between the appearances of these two highly visible women led us to select them for a study of how women manage their aging bodies. Their dissimilar appearances seemed to reflect two different approaches to aging and to the prevailing cultural disclosure which equates femininity with a youthful appearance. (Sontag 1972; Freedman 1986, p. 200; Seid 1989; Woodward 1991, p. 161) Moreover, both describe their behavior and appearance as forms of resistance to these cultural pressures. As we will show, however, their lives testify more to the limits of individual resistance than to its possibilities.

As public figures, with sufficient financial resources to employ all that the beauty and fashion industries can offer, Fonda and Bush differ in important ways from most women. In addition, as white heterosexuals, issues of beauty and aging might have different cultural meanings for them than for many lesbians and minority women. Nevertheless, the narratives of their aging reveal a dilemma that most American women confront as they age: how to handle an aging body in a culture in which aging challenges acceptable notions of femininity.

Changes in the body, of course, represent only one aspect of aging, for aging is as much about wisdom, character, and experience as it is about bodily changes. In other cultures, these other aspects of aging receive considerably more weight in establishing women's social worth. An exploration of a number of societies including the !Kung of South Africa, the Tamarongo of New Guinea, and the Maori of New Zealand indicates that the authority and status of aging women increase as they assume new responsibilities over areas such as spiritual life and are less constrained by social regulations imposed on younger women. (Kerns and Brown 1992) Western women, however, cannot ignore the central role the body plays in the cultural construction of selfhood and, especially, womanhood. (Goffman 1963, pp. 100–1; Turner 1984, pp. 1–7; Conrad 1987) Because of this centrality of the body, Bartky argues, a "woman's sense of herself as a female" depends on having "a body felt to be 'feminine.' " (1988, p. 78) Although scholars now recognize the problematic, arbitrary, and socially constructed nature of the division of the sexes into male and female, cultural demands continue to make "maleness" or "femaleness" salient in the construction of individual identity.

AGENCY, SOCIAL CONTROL, AND THE FEMALE BODY

Part of the problem women face in resisting cultural definitions of femininity is that these definitions influence us in ways that we do not fully recognize. While many women are aware of the barrage of messages from the media about appropriate feminine appearance, few realize how insidiously these notions have entered our individual psyches or think to question their legitimacy. Newspaper articles might report on studies showing that a high proportion of ten-year-old girls diet and that an epidemic of anorexia and bulimia has swept the country, but few women respond to this evidence of the dire consequences of preoccupation with body size by changing their own attitudes and behaviors.

To illuminate the covert and powerful ways that cultural ideas about femininity shape women's conscious and unconscious attitudes toward their bodies, some feminist scholars have drawn on the work of Michel Foucault. (1979, p. 136) Foucault describes the body in some of his writings as an "object and target of power," a field on which the hierarchies of power are displayed and inscribed, and has shown how various institutions such as the army and the school deploy their power by controlling their members' time, space, and movement. Feminists have elaborated his argument, describing how definitions of femininity act, in Foucault's terms, as a "discipline" regulating women's bodies. (Foucault 1979, pp. 136–9; Bartky 1988, pp. 63–4; Bordo 1989, pp. 13–4) As army regulations control a soldier's gestures, walk, and posture, cultural definitions of femininity control female bodies by setting standards that specify what is considered appropriate and "normal." (Foucault 1979, pp. 136–8, 150–3; Bartky 1988, pp. 61–3, 75) These feminist scholars have suggested that women have so internalized the rewards and dictates of femininity that they appear to conform willingly. (Bartky 1988, pp. 81–2) Foucault uses Bentham's design of the Panopticon as a metaphor to describe how such self-surveillance develops. In the Panopticon, a guard in the central tower can observe the behavior of each inmate in a prison building but the inmates cannot see the guard. Unable to ascertain when the guard is on duty, the inmates behave as though the guard is always present. (Foucault 1979, pp. 200–4) In the same way, Bartky (1988) observes, the internalized standards for femininity serve to control women. Bartky metaphorically describes this self-surveillance as a "male connoisseur" firmly planted inside each woman's consciousness, observing, demanding, and criticizing.

In contrast, other feminist scholars contend that this argument overstates the power of cultural norms to discipline women. Critics such as McNay (1991) argue that Foucault and his followers see women only as "docile bodies," ignoring the many ways that women historically have resisted societal prescriptions. Even Bartky concedes that there are "pockets of resistance" and "oppositional discourses" to normative femininity, such as among radical lesbians and female bodybuilders. (Bartky 1988, p. 82)

Our analysis of Fonda and Bush joins this discussion by highlighting the interplay between agency and social control in the reactions of heterosexual white women to their aging appearance, demonstrating how Fonda and Bush simultaneously have attempted to resist the dominant discourse on aging and have been constrained by it. Their experiences delineate the difficulties of resistance and underscore the struggle required to establish oppositional discourses.

For this article, we draw on all articles written about Bush and Fonda in women's magazines (including fashion magazines) indexed in the *Reader's Guide to Periodical Literature* beginning in 1977, when Fonda turned forty.[2] Expectations about women's aging bodies are well-articulated in these magazines, making them a useful source of data.

Although it remains a subject of considerable debate, substantial evidence indicates that the media not only can reflect cultural expectations but also can reinforce the validity of those expectations, suggesting that rewards will accrue to those who conform.[3] More specifically, the media can teach appropriate sex-role behavior, including norms of appearance. (e.g., Busby 1975; Tuchman 1978; Winship 1978; Modleski 1982; Ferguson 1983; Ballaster et al. 1991)

As recent scholarship has shown, however, audiences do not passively consume media messages. (Radway 1984; Rosengren, Wenner, and Palmgreen 1985; Carey 1989; McLeod, Kosicki, and Pan 1991, pp. 249–53; Simonds 1992) Rather, the media present "encoded" messages about cultural values which individuals must then "decode," interpreting these messages in ways that make sense in the context of their lives. (Hall 1980; Gledhill 1988) It may therefore make more sense, as Van Zoonen (1991, p. 43) notes, to view media messages as "sites of struggle over meaning (e.g., of gender [and, we would add, of aging]) rather than as transparent cultural prescriptions." As she further notes (1991, p. 47), however, each encoded text has only a limited number of possible decodings, and "most texts do have a 'preferred reading' which, given the economic and ideological location of most media, will tend to reconstruct dominant values of a society." For example, women's magazines' instruction in the daily rituals of femininity and in how to maintain "femininity" as one ages make these activities seem necessary parts of women's lives. (Weedon 1987, pp. 101–6; Bartky 1988, pp. 69–70)

Because of the nature of our data, our findings refer only to white, heterosexual, economically privileged women. As others have noted, previous research provides relatively little information about the attitudes of working-class women, lesbians, or women of color toward their bodies. (Thomas 1989; Thomas and James 1988, p. 524; Smith, Burlew, and Lundgren 1991, p. 269; Rothblum in press) We would add that previous research provides even less information about their views toward the *aging* body.

Moreover, the available information is contradictory. Some writers have argued that mainstream cultural expectations about appearance have relatively little impact on lesbians and women of color. For example, Hsu (1987) and Brown (1987) attribute the small numbers of identified cases of eating disorders among African Americans and lesbians, respectively, to the lack of pressure within those cultures to be thin. Other writers, however, argue that all American women are subject to similar cultural pressures. (Striegel-Moore, Tucker, and Hsu 1990, p. 497; Dworkin 1989, pp. 32–3; Schwartz 1986; Brand, Rothblum and Solomon 1992, p. 258) Moreover, even if the particular standards for female beauty differ for other groups such as lesbians or working class women, the existence of difficult to achieve and socially controlling standards seems to hold across all social groups.

The limited and contradictory data on attitudes toward the body among working class women, lesbians, and women of color make it difficult to reach any conclusions on this topic. Other problems, such as the use of small and self-selected samples and differential access to diagnosis and treatment of eating disorders, also make them difficult to interpret. As a result, we cannot say to what extent our findings might apply to these women.

AGING FEMALE BODIES: A BRIEF HISTORY

What constitutes a culturally appropriate appearance for aging women has changed considerably over time. (Banner 1983; Schwartz 1986; Seid 1989) Until the mid-twentieth century, American society expected older women to have what was termed a "mature figure" and to wear "mature" fashions. Beginning in the 1950s, however, this demarcation between youthful and aging appearances began to break down. The emphasis on youth accelerated in the 1960s and early 1970s, as both medical and fashion experts, bolstered by the highly visible youth culture, declared the youthful, slim body the standard for all. (Seid 1989, pp. 116–23, 175–6) By the late 1970s, as the baby boomers who had fostered the youth culture aged, the struggle to maintain a youthful appearance had fostered a nationwide fitness craze.

The admonition to become slim and fit, which intensified in the 1980s, ignored the biological realities of aging—the typically unavoidable weight gain, increased ratio of fat to muscle, and, for

women, thickening waists and sagging breasts. (Seid 1989, p. 265) Instead, both medical and popular experts redefined "mature figures" as symbols of self-indulgence and irresponsibility. Failure to take up the new ethic of fitness became a sign of social or even moral failure, with the unfit deemed the secular equivalent of sinners and the fit promised youth and health. (Zola 1972; Crawford 1979; Waitzkin 1981; Stein 1982, pp. 168–9, 174; Turner 1984, p. 202; Tesh 1988)

This new ethic has had greater repercussions for women than for men, for appearance always has formed a more central aspect of how women evaluate themselves and are evaluated by others. (Chernin 1981, pp. 145–61; Bartky 1988, p. 65) Attractiveness often translates not only into feelings of self-esteem but into success in obtaining heterosexual affiliation and professional jobs. (Freedman 1986, pp. 98–9; Morgan 1991, p. 35)

The increased cultural focus since the 1970s on controlling women's bodies has led several critics to label it a "backlash" to the rising power and visibility of women. These commentators suggest that keeping women involved with controlling their bodies diverts their energies from striving to achieve more control in the public arena. (Bordo 1989, p. 14; Bordo 1990, p. 105; Faludi 1991, pp. 203–4; Wolf 1991, pp. 9–12) An analysis of Jane Fonda, who both rode the wave of the new fitness craze and helped to create it and who promotes women's control of the body as a form of "liberation," illuminates the contradictions of preoccupation with the body.

MANAGING THE AGING BODY

Jane Fonda: Relentlessly Improved

Jane Fonda has undergone many metamorphoses in her lifetime, summarized by one magazine writer as "a sex kitten in the 50s, antiwar radical in the late 60s, feminist in the 70s, successful entrepreneur in the 80s," and someone who focused on "personal fulfillment" in the 90s. (Ball 1992, p. 96) Throughout, however, Fonda has worked diligently to maintain a shapely body.

Ever since she turned forty, Fonda has garnered particular attention and admiration as a woman who has aged yet retained her beauty. With each successive year, the women's magazines have marked Jane Fonda's chronological aging by announcing her age and marveling at how well and, specifically, how young she looks. (e.g., Davis 1990, p. 165; Andersen 1989, p. 112) Fonda fascinates aging women, one journalist suggests, "because she has a great body, an over-40 body that offers hope and promise. Along with each book and tape comes convincing evidence that it's possible . . . to remain beautiful and sexy in midlife." (Levin 1987, p. 27)

Ironically, for those who recall her 1968 film role as the sex machine "Barbarella" and her pleasure-filled lifestyle as the wife of French film director Roger Vadim, by the 1970s, Fonda had begun describing herself as a feminist role model. (e.g., Robbins 1977) Fonda began this new phase of her life—as not only a feminist but also an anti-Vietnam war activist—at about the time that her marriage to Vadim was ending and shortly before meeting and marrying political activist Tom Hayden. (Andersen 1990, pp. 214–65) Looking back on her early years from a feminist perspective, Fonda described to interviewers how she had come to reject the cultural stereotypes that formerly oppressed her. In a 1976 magazine story, for example, Fonda bemoaned how she had spent her twenties wearing falsies and declared herself now free from such constraints. She sat before the interviewer "clutching her breasts to make sure the offensive things weren't still around." (*Lear* 1976, p. 145)

In the same article, she described how her feminist awareness had grown when Hayden showed her pictures of Vietnamese women who had plastic surgery to make their eyes round and enlarge their breasts. Fonda was "stunned and I thought my God that same phony *Playboy* image that made me wear falsies for ten years, that made billions of American women dissatisfied with their own bodies, has been transported thousands of miles to another culture and made these women too hate their bodies, made them willing to mutilate themselves." (*Lear* 1976, p. 15)

Fonda and Hayden's political involvement provided the spur for Fonda's emergence as a fitness entrepreneur. To finance their political activities, Fonda in 1979 established her first Workout Studio and in 1982 published her best-selling *Workout Book* and videotape. (Anderson 1990, pp. 302–3)

In the 1980s, as Fonda emerged as an exercise guru, she at first extolled the virtues of intervening only minimally in the aging process. At age 47, writing about aging skin and cosmetic surgery in *Women Coming of Age* (1984, p. 71), her book on midlife, she advised, "The course I prefer: making peace with the growing numbers of fine (and some not so fine) lines you see on your face. . . . Wrinkles are part of who we are, of where we've been. Not to have wrinkles means never having laughed or cried or expressed passion, never having squinted into the sun or felt the bite of winter's wind—never having fully lived!" Similarly, she told an interviewer, "I have a few more wrinkles, a few more gray hairs, and that's okay. I don't obsess about my looks the way I used to." (Kaplan 1985, p. 374)

Despite this rhetoric, however, most of Fonda's pronouncements even during these years centered on changing and controlling rather than accepting the body. Yet in these statements as well, Fonda used feminist rhetoric such as "freedom" and "liberation" to frame this bodily control as a form of resistance to traditional expectations of female emotional and physical weakness. Bodily control, she has argued, "gives me a sense of freedom" (Kaplan 1987, p. 417), for "discipline is freedom" (*Mademoiselle* 1980, p. 38). Similarly, she has described herself as "liberated" from the cultural pressures that led her to engage in binge/purge eating until age 35.

Magazine writers, too, have described Fonda's life in feminist terms. One reporter, for example, comments that "There is a sense she's on the right side, making a political statement in warm-ups and running shoes. On one level, her tapes are about women taking control of their bodies, gaining physical confidence in front of their VCRs, then striding out of their homes to flex their new power." (Kaplan 1987, p. 417)

As she began to promote her fitness methods, Fonda also argued that working to develop bodily control empowers women by improving their health. Although Fonda acknowledges that "exercise isn't a panacea for everything," she nevertheless argues that "much of what ails us can be lessened by making the heart and lungs really work, getting the blood oxygenated and circulating, and limbering up the body." (*Harper's Bazaar* 1980, p. 82) Similarly, Fonda sees exercise as a means toward mental health: "Exercise does a tremendous amount for emotional and mental stability. . . . That is what satisfies me most . . . , the people who come up after a week or two of classes and say, 'Hey, I'm not depressed anymore.'" (*Harper's Bazaar* 1980, p. 82)

Given the prevailing discourse on femininity and on aging, it is not surprising that Fonda and her admirers have characterized her as feminist. In a culture which characterizes women as weak, Fonda's goal of strengthening the body offers an alternative to fragile womanhood. It also disputes the idea that the aging body is a run-down machine. (Martin 1987, pp. 40–6) Fonda demonstrates vigorously that her body— and thus potentially all aging, female bodies— can work. Moreover, the exercise that Fonda advocates challenges the restricted space to which women are constrained in everyday life. Bodies, arms, legs move and extend this space, allowing women to experience a freer use of the body, which many experience as liberating.

The benefits of a reasonable exercise program as a way to enhance emotional and physical health, maintain a healthy body weight, and protect against osteoporosis and heart disease have been well established and should not be minimized.[4] What Fonda and her admirers have overlooked, however, in their litany of the benefits of exercise, is the contrast between the obsessive and punitive self-control and self-surveillance

implicit in the exercise and beauty regimens she advocates and the liberation she claims to derive from them. In the same quote in which she encourages women to accept wrinkles, for example, she also urges "doing your best through nutrition, exercise, proper cleansing, moisturizing, sleep, and healthy living habits to avoid aggravated and premature wrinkles." (Fonda 1984, p. 71) This lengthy list of tasks suggests the level of work needed to age "properly" and not "prematurely."

Similarly, since her twenties, Fonda has controlled her shape through daily exercise. Only recently has she allowed herself to skip exercise for even a few days. (Ball 1992, pp. 97, 143) In one interviewer's words, Fonda is "an exercise addict, like few others." (Levin 1987, p. 28) Her language of war, struggle, and labor indicates the amount of effort and self-surveillance she devotes to bodily control: "I have a constant weight problem. . . . It's just a constant struggle" (*Mademoiselle* 1980, p. 40). Similarly: "I constantly fight against weight, and I don't necessarily have a good figure. I have to work for it, and I do work for it." (Harrison 1978, p. 40)

Moreover, in the same way that she compulsively exercises, she continues to watch her food intake. At luncheon with a reporter, "there's one tense moment when the waiter places a pat of butter on her [Jane's] bread dish. 'No, no, take it away, she demands, flustered.'" (Levin 1987, pp. 25–6)

It seems, then, that Fonda's desire for a culturally appropriate body has tyrannized rather than liberated her. Fonda's life demonstrates that maintaining an "acceptable" body requires constant vigilance. As feminist critics have pointed out, such constant demands for self-surveillance keep women in line. (Faludi 1991; Wolf 1991)

At the same time, Fonda's insistence on the importance of bodily self-control can lead to denigrating those who appear to lack control. In Fonda's worldview, care of the body is not only a personal responsibility but also a moral one. Bodily control signifies self-control, and hence moral superiority. This belief, which permeates the health and fitness movement, has been labeled a "new asceticism" or "new Puritanism." (Turner 1984; Kilwein 1989, pp. 9–10) If in the past individuals disciplined the body to control their passions and submit to God, nowadays individuals discipline the body to extend their lives and increase their pleasures. (Turner 1984, pp. 156, 161–3, 172) Yet the value on self-discipline continues to resonate with its religious origins, for a fit body still announces a good character.

In Fonda's secularized world, personal "salvation" (of the character and body, if not the soul) is possible through self-abnegation—denying oneself food and exercising even to the point of pain (cf., Bordo 1990, p. 83). She has waxed lyrical about the physical benefits of denying herself food: "Going to bed on an empty stomach and waking up hungry is the greatest thing you can do for yourself. If you go to bed hungry and wake up hungry, you've got unbelievable energy." (*Mademoiselle* 1980, p. 40) She speaks in similarly positive tones about the benefits of fasting. (*Mademoiselle* 1980, pp. 38–40) In both her exercise and eating regimens, then, the body becomes a locus of work, something to be subdued.

Fonda explicitly rejects the notion that the ability to control one's body might depend upon such factors as genetics, leisure time, or financial resources. When, for example, a reporter suggested in 1980 that Fonda might have inherited her father's slimness, Fonda bristled and replied, "I don't have my father's body at all. He has absolutely no ass. I like to think a lot of my body is my own doing and my own blood and guts. It's my responsibility." (*Mademoiselle* 1980, p. 40)

By extension, those who do not take responsibility for their bodies have only themselves to blame for their problems. In pressing this philosophy, Fonda both reflects and contributes to the prevailing discourse of the health and fitness movement, which stresses individual accountability for healthy behavior and harshly condemns those who do not take responsibility for their bodies. (Crawford 1979; Tesh 1988;

Nichter and Nichter 1991, p. 253) Despite Fonda's rhetoric of empowerment, therefore, her emphasis on self-control disheartens and disempowers more women than it empowers.

A similar disempowerment results from Fonda's stance on sexuality. Fonda appears to be rescuing aging women from their usual portrayal as asexual by arguing that is possible for aging women to remain active, sexual beings. "I think," she says, "that when you're healthy, no matter what age you are, you have more sexual stamina and desire and flexibility and the things that go into an active sex life." (Orth 1984, p. 416) In Fonda's worldview, however, a woman can retain sexuality only by retaining a youthful body. No alternative vision of aging sexuality is presented or considered. All that remains is the impossible goal of remaining young.

An emphasis on youth is not the only drawback to Fonda's ideal of femininity. Despite her emphasis on fitness, Fonda has not created a new and liberating model of femininity so much as she has adopted a model that unrealistically combines stereotyping masculine and feminine elements. Fonda began her fitness quest by arguing for the virtues of a muscled and virtually fat-free body. When asked why she added body-building exercises, Fonda remarked "I didn't have any muscles. I like to see muscles, I like to see sinews, and after taking this class, I could see definition in my arms, shoulders and back. There's no fat anywhere, not anywhere." (*Mademoiselle* 1980, p. 38) This near-fatless ideal corresponds to an archetypical male body. More recently, as her relationship with Hayden faded, Fonda additionally has strived to achieve the archetypical female hallmark—large breasts—by submitting to cosmetic surgery. (Anderson 1990, pp. 327–8; Ball 1992, p. 97) Since her marriage to cable television owner Ted Turner in 1991, she is now, one magazine writer notes, "playing the part of the glamorous wife—blond, bejeweled, and dressed to kill." (Messina 1993, p. 65)

Fonda's body thus has come to symbolize the duality of current femininity: tight muscles but with large breasts.[5] The desire for a more masculine body, Bordo argues, appeals to some women because it symbolizes power in the public arena and a revolt against maternity and restrictive definitions of femininity. (Bordo 1990, p. 105) Simultaneously, the inflated breasts serve as a reminder that a woman's body is there for male desires. Mainstream American culture idealizes women who are both supermen (in their muscles) and superwomen (in their breasts). These women, their bodies suggest, won't be dependent but will continue to seek the "male gaze" to affirm themselves. Fonda's enthusiastic embrace of this dual-function body represents not resistance but submission to the demands of femininity.

Fonda's use of cosmetic surgery (which did not end with her breast implants) suggests that the value she places on having a culturally acceptable body overrides any philosophical commitment to achieving a fit body through hard work. As one magazine asked rhetorically, "Doesn't cosmetic surgery contradict everything she advocates?" (Messina 1993, p. 65) As Fonda now argues, "If you're trying to buy yourself a new dress, especially if you're in the business of looks the way an actress is, then why not? . . . What the hell is the big deal, as long it's done carefully and with thought?" (Ball 1992, p. 97) In making these decisions, Fonda turns her body into a commodity that can be used, in her words, to "buy" her a few years.

The image of Fonda passively lying on a table while receiving breast implants appears to contradict her active and aggressive advocacy of exercise as a means of achieving self-improvement. Yet all her efforts are really of one piece, aimed at maintaining a youthful and culturally acceptable appearance.

Fonda's struggles to control her inevitably aging body find resonance in many women's lives as they face a culture that rejects the aging female. As one writer said sympathetically about Fonda's "fanatical" physical fitness, "Wasn't it really just the panic of an aging actress with a terror of growing old? Children of Hollywood probably know more than the rest of us what extra wrinkles and pounds mean—and the rest of us know plenty." (Davis 1990, p. 165)

Fonda's marriage to Turner and use of cosmetic surgery seemed to signify still another shift in her persona. Despite this shift, however, the persistent thread in Fonda's life—her devotion to maintaining a youthful, fit body—remains. In the nineties, Fonda has developed a new exercise video, *Jane Fonda's Lower Body Solution,* and remains "her own best advertisement." (Ball 1992, p. 26) But Fonda seemed to be backing off from being a role model for other women. (Davis 1993, p. 55) One interviewer, commenting on her new, luxurious lifestyle with Turner, observed to Fonda that those who had thought of her as a feminist symbol might now be dismayed. Fonda, retreating from her earlier stance, replied, "I never asked to be a role model. . . . I'm not Eleanor Roosevelt." In the end, Fonda admitted, "I don't pretend to be different from any other woman. I'm subject to the same foibles and pressures and ups and downs." (Ball 1992, pp. 97, 145)

Over the years, Fonda has expressed the desire to construct a new image for aging women, saying "You can be big and still be in proportion and well-toned" (Bachrach 1989, p. 82) and that the point is to be the best you can be. (Messina 1993, p. 65) Ultimately, however, she has not done so. Her fit and muscled body and her unwrinkled face offer a standard that few women can attain, suggesting that only by remaining young and fit can women be sexual, strong, and good. As one writer observed, Fonda "at every age . . . has managed to sell her youth. And, most important, we have bought it." (Bachrach 1989)

Not surprisingly, as purveyors of the prevailing discourse on femininity, women's magazines uphold Fonda's body as a standard to which women should aspire. Many of the writers demonstrate both the wish to imitate her and their despair of ever doing so by their barely disguised envy—"her enviable long legs" (Farr 1980, p. 39), "her enviable body" (Glasser and Decatur 1982, p. 22), a body that is "frighteningly firm." (Jong 1984, p. 35) As one writer acknowledged, "most of us would be pleased to look at 34 the way she looks at 54, especially in Lycra" (Ball 1992, p. 96). By continuing to run layouts featuring her exercises (e.g., *Redbook* 1990; Messina 1993) the magazines offer hope to their readers that they too can look like her. There is little acknowledgment that Fonda's body represents an unrealistic goal for most aging women.

Barbara Bush: Resolutely "Natural"

In contrast to Jane Fonda, Barbara Bush at least appears to resist and reject the cultural ideal of femininity that valorizes youthfulness. Bush's white hair and wrinkles seem to challenge the prevailing feminine ideal and signal her rejection of technological "fixes" for aging. (Morgan 1991, p. 28)

Even more than Fonda, Bush frames her appearance as resistance to cultural strictures about women's bodies. In Bush's worldview, her unwillingness to change her appearance beyond dressing well, using light makeup, and exercising regularly and moderately underscores her interest in focusing on what she considers important rather than frivolous and narcissistic concerns. She thus draws on a spiritual tradition that disregards the body and looks to the state of the soul for moral value. (Turner 1984, p. 164)

To emphasize this philosophy, Bush often and not very subtly contrasts herself with Nancy Reagan, her ultra-stylish predecessor. Bush told one interviewer that while she "admires" Reagan's "perfectionism," she herself is "more interested in people than in perfection." (Cook 1990, p. 229) At the same time, her press secretary let writers know that "Mrs. Bush never, but never, borrows designer gowns"; the comparison to Nancy Reagan is obvious. Similarly, Bush distinguished herself from those who dye their hair by saying that "people who worry about their hair all the time are boring." (Avery 1989, p. 192) She, on the other hand, has other priorities, presumably of a superior nature—"I can exercise,

play tennis. I don't have to say to George, 'I can't do that, I just got my hair done.'" (Avery 1989, p. 192) Thus Bush appears not only to present aging positively but also to scorn and mock those who seem more concerned about their looks.

Bush appears to counterpose the value of "naturalness" against the contrivances of anti-aging technology. "What you see is what you get" (*Vogue* 1988, p. 442) is one of her favorite self-descriptions, implying that her relative lack of artifice in appearance means that she stands revealed for who she is without the "disguises" of cosmetics, plastic surgery, or even a diet-improved shape. One writer quotes her remark that all she owes to the public is "to look nice and have a clean mind and a clean head of hair." (Adams 1988, p. 151)

Bush's discourse reflects an older view of aging that made allowances for the weight gain and other changes that can accompany aging and that excused women above a certain age from the burdens of maintaining sexual attractiveness. (Banner 1983; Schwartz 1986; Seid 1989) Despite Bush's rhetoric, however, a close reading of her interviews reveals the great efforts she makes to meet standards of feminine attractiveness and to show herself as reasonably concerned about her appearance. In doing so she reveals her exquisite awareness of the demands of femininity and of her need at least partially to comply. She wears contact lenses and her well-known three strands of false pearls because, she says, she's "too vain" to wear glasses and needs to cover her "sagging neck." (Avery 1989, p. 191) Moreover, although she does not engage in the kind of obsessive exercising Fonda prefers, Bush regularly walks and rides a stationary bicycle to maintain her weight. (Avery 1989, p. 192)

Bush also pays attention to her wardrobe, wearing fashionable designer clothes. As Judith Viorst astutely noted, "though Barbara Bush seems to define herself publicly as a slightly schlumpy Everywoman, she is considerably more than that. . . . Her grooming, from well-coiffed white hair to well-shod toe, is what anyone would call 'impeccable'" (Viorst 1991, p. 40), an observation repeated by other magazine writers. (*Vogue* 1988, p. 444; Cook 1990, p. 230) As one points out, "Her hairdresser attends her regularly, sometimes as often as three times a day." (McClellan 1992, p. 191)

Bush's use of self-deprecating humor further indicates her felt need to explain her deviation from cultural expectations. Self-deprecating humor, in which individuals mock themselves for not meeting social expectations, allows individuals both to demonstrate their commitment to those expectations and to frame their deviations as humorous rather than serious flaws. (Coser 1960; Goffman 1963, pp. 100–1; Ungar 1984; Haig 1988; Koller 1988; Walker 1988) As a result, such humor, which is most common among relatively powerless groups, "is ingratiating rather than aggressive; it acknowledges the opinion of the dominant culture—[and] even appears to confirm it."[6]

Despite her high status, it is this form of humor which Barbara Bush seems to rely upon most often. For example, after photos appeared showing her in a matronly swimsuit, one interviewer reported that Bush "jokingly pleaded with photographers not to take any more: 'My children are complaining.'" (Avery 1989, p. 294) She often explains why she does not dye her hair (e.g., Adams 1988, p. 150), by joking about the time the heat caused her hair dye to run all over her during a campaign trip, and she frequently comments that "fat ladies everywhere" love her. (e.g., Reed 1989, p. 314) Or, speaking of her wardrobe, she comments: "One of the myths is that I don't dress well. I dress very well—I just don't look so good." (Cook 1990, p. 230)

It seems, then, that Bush, like many women, uses self-deprecating humor to try to turn her departures from appearance norms into an unimportant, humorous matter.[7] At least one reporter has recognized this, describing her humor as "a preemptive strike" (Cook 1990, p. 230), in which Bush makes comments about her appearance before interviewers can. Thus, Bush is not,

despite her protests, rejecting femininity standards, but is acknowledging their power and her failure to meet them.

Bush's statements about her sexuality also reveal the limits of her resistance. In her self-descriptions, she often desexualizes herself, referring to herself not merely as a grandmother but as "everybody's grandmother." She uses this exceptional status to place herself outside the bounds of femininity. "I mean," she says, "kissing me is like kissing your grandmother." (Reed 1989, p. 314)

Bush's depiction of herself as outside the definition of normative femininity does not help to construct a positive, alternative model of female aging. Rather, she has escaped the bounds of cultural standards only by forfeiting claims to sexuality— a high price to pay. Thus her model is a bleak one, which denies the sensual possibilities of the aging female body.

Bush's treatment by women's magazines demonstrates the reaction women can expect when, like Bush, their aging appearance seems not to conform to cultural dictates on normative femininity. When Bush first appeared on the scene in the late 1980s, the magazines, whose pages are filled with articles devoted to personal improvement and whose income derives largely from advertisements for fashions, diet aids, and cosmetics, were at a loss. How could they deal with a woman who seemed to transgress ideas about what was acceptably feminine and whose stance seemed to challenge the economic structure which supports and defends their version of femininity, particularly when their readers seemed to like and admire her? Bush's appearance was something that the magazines felt had to be explained.[8]

To "normalize" Bush's appearance, the magazines, like Bush, have stressed her grandmotherly qualities, labeling her "every American's favorite grandmother" (Mower 1992) and an honorific grandmother of us all. They have focused on her work with children and her role as the matriarch of the large Bush clan. (Reed 1989, p. 314) In this role as super-grandmother, the magazines allow Bush to remain outside the normal discipline of femininity, a disembodied maternal archetype.

The magazines also deal with Bush's appearance, as she does herself, by highlighting and praising her apparent "naturalness." For example, in an article entitled "The Natural," the headline notes that "Barbara Bush Remains Doggedly Herself" (Reed 1989, p. 312), while another article proclaims "Barbara Bush Is Real." (*Vogue* 1988, p. 218) Like Bush, the magazines assume that such an entity as a "natural body" exists and disregard the considerable role that culture plays in the construction of this "naturalness." Focusing on her "naturalness" as indicative of a praiseworthy inner self allows the magazines to downplay her body, while underscoring for readers how very noteworthy and thus "unnatural" it is.

Despite these efforts to normalize Bush's appearance, the magazines continue to demonstrate considerable ambivalence toward her looks. For example, in an article published in *Ladies Home Journal* (Avery 1989), the author praises Bush for her apparent acceptance of aging but suggests that other women should hesitate before adopting Bush as a role model, citing the numerous studies that show that attractive women do better in the job market. The writer concludes with the admonition that even "exceptional women" like Bush need to recognize the benefits of attractiveness, and predicts that "perhaps after she's had a year or two squarely in the public eye, we'll begin to notice subtle changes—a wrinkle smoothed here, a pound or two dieted off there." Bush, in other words, will see the light and conform to cultural standards of femininity.

The author and magazine reveal their real attitudes in two full-length pictures of Bush which dominate the article's first two pages. (Avery 1989, pp. 120–1) On the first page is the actual Barbara Bush. Attached to various parts of her in balloon-like fashion are boxes advising her how to deal with her wrinkles, her clothes, and her shape. On the opposite page stands a re-touched Bush with all the suggestions put into practice: slimmer, with fluffed-out hair, wrinkles surgically removed, wearing cosmetics and fashionable clothes. It is the ultimate makeover! This desire to change Bush so that she fits in with prevailing notions of femininity is a frequent theme in women's magazines.

WOMEN'S POWER AND WOMEN'S BODIES

The treatment of Jane Fonda and Barbara Bush by women's magazines explicates the discourse on femininity and illustrates the difficulties women face in resisting cultural dictates regarding their aging bodies. Women's magazines praise Fonda only because she conforms to cultural ideals. The magazines' more ambivalent attitude toward Bush reflects their consternation and ultimate disapproval of those who do not appear to comply with appearance norms, even when such individuals in various ways acknowledge their deviance.

Women do not have to be film stars or political wives to feel the pressures imposed by cultural definitions of femininity. Those pressures are everywhere, and it is the rare woman who can evade them. Although the research is not clear-cut, evidence suggests that even those groups we have looked to for alternative visions of body size and aging cannot effectively resist—let alone change—the pressures of femininity standards. While, for example, we may respect those lesbian communities where appearance is downplayed and celebrate the success of large-sized, middle-aged African-American blues singers who exude a down-to-earth sexuality, these alternatives to the prevailing fashion in aging bodies have not affected the broader society. Nor do these alternative visions seem likely to survive even within these communities. For example, as African-Americans rise on the social–economic scale, they appear to adopt the same body goals as white women (Schwartz 1986), and at least some lesbians have become involved in what one writer has termed "style wars," rejecting the casual and unisexed appearance standards of the past. (Stein 1992) Fat lesbians, meanwhile, describe the same difficulties in attracting sexual partners as do fat heterosexual women. (e.g., Schoenfielder and Wieser 1983)

The pressures to conform to cultural standards of femininity disempower women in insidious ways—insidious because we have internalized them in ways we are hardly aware of and at costs we have not calculated. Cultural standards encourage women's sense of inadequacy and promote frantic use of expensive, time-consuming and sometimes dangerous technologies in a futile effort to check aging and increase one's "femininity." Furthermore, such a focus on the body as a privatistic concern turns people away from focusing on social issues. (Stein 1982, pp. 176–7) This is particularly relevant during this current period of backlash to the feminist movement in which many women now find it easier to focus on their individual selves than to continue struggling for the social betterment of women. As Fonda herself admits about exercising, "in a world that is increasingly out of control, it's something you can control." (Ball 1992, p. 143) Thus an emphasis on the self diverts women from resisting current power relations.

Moreover, as women get older and attempt to move into senior ranks in business, government, and the professions, their employers, clients, and colleagues expect them to maintain norms of femininity. These norms create barriers to advancement for aging women. While on men, gray hair, wrinkles, even a widening waist signify experience, wisdom, maturity, and sometimes sexiness (as in the cases of Clint Eastwood and Sean Connery, for example), on women they denote decline and asexuality. Women's power is diminished, therefore, at the very moment when they might otherwise begin to move into more powerful positions.[9]

Given the difficulties of contesting the discourse on women's bodies, many of which are explicated in the experiences of Fonda and Bush, can we still conclude that effective resistance is possible? We would argue, perhaps op-

timistically, that it is, but only if women become more aware of the insidious, internalized ways that the discipline of femininity disempowers women and join together to fight it.

The successes of the feminist movement have depended on the movement's ability to question received "wisdom" about women and to expose both the cultural construction and harmfulness of that "wisdom." Feminists have challenged pay inequities, inadequate child care arrangements, restrictions on reproductive freedom, and a host of other problems. But the issue of obsessiveness about body size and appearance is a virtually untouched arena for concerted feminist political action, despite the pioneering work of such individuals and groups as Orbach (1982), Wolf (1991), Bordo (1989, 1990, 1991), Faludi (1991), and the fat acceptance and anti-diet movements. (Millman 1980; Kano 1989; Hirschmann and Munter 1988) Their efforts to help women accept their bodies and abandon perpetual dieting have failed to affect large numbers of women, despite the increasing medical evidence that body shape stems largely from genetic factors and that frequent dieting is unhealthy and does not necessarily result in a leaner body[10] and despite increasing coverage of this evidence in popular magazines. (e.g., Brownell 1988; *Good Housekeeping* 1993; Kaufman 1992; Seligmann 1992)

Changing cultural standards of femininity will not be easy, and we concur with Bordo that it would be a mistake to minimize the power that the discourse on femininity has to regulate women's lives. To do so is to underestimate the amount of struggle that is required for change and to minimize the difficulty women experience when they try to accomplish change. (Bordo 1989, p. 13) Yet, as the history of women has shown, it would also be a mistake to dismiss the possibility of resistance. The experiences of Barbara Bush and Jane Fonda demonstrate how difficult it is for any woman, struggling alone, no matter how visible, respected, and in some ways powerful, to fight against entrenched cultural notions. The history of women has taught us that, even in the face of seemingly implacable hegemonic discourses, women can make change when they join together. Perhaps now, with the graying of the feminist movement, feminists will begin to devote more energy to challenging the cultural construction of women's aging bodies. At the same time, the increasing if slow movement of women in their forties and above into positions of power may help a new cultural construction to evolve.

Making changes in our attitudes toward our bodies will not be easy, but it will surely be an important step in empowering women. In such a world, Jane Fonda might be able to moderate her painful and obsessive regimens and Barbara Bush would not have to be so defensive about her appearance.

NOTES

1. We have borrowed the terms "resolutely natural" and "relentlessly improved" from an article by Avery (1989) on Barbara Bush. Bush is referred to as "resolutely natural" while, in this article, it is Cher and not Jane Fonda who is referred to as "relentlessly improved."
2. Bush does not appear to any extent in the magazines until the late 1980s when her husband begins his presidential campaign.
3. Although the presentations of Fonda and Bush offer examples of how the media construct femininity for aging women, we do not in this paper attempt to analyze the impact of this construction on women's attitudes toward aging. Instead, our primary goal is to examine the seemingly disparate ways of negotiating the aging process that these two women appear to have adopted.
4. See, for example, Carlucci, Goldfine, Harvey, Ward, Taylor, Rippe 1991; O'Brien and Vertinsky 1992; Doress and Siegel 1987; and Shangold 1990.
5. We are grateful to Susan Bordo for this suggestion.
6. In contrast, other forms of humor typically serve as demonstrations of aggression and of power (e.g., Coser 1960; Fine 1983; Zillman 1983; Ungar 1984; Haig 1988; Koller 1988; Walker 1988).
7. Bush's self-deprecating humor cannot be dismissed simply as "ice-breakers," designed to put reporters at their ease, for self-deprecating humor is rarely used in this way. Moreover, Bush uses self-deprecating humor not at the beginning of interviews, but scattered throughout whenever the subject of her body appears.
8. Similarly, Bush's 1989 biography, *Simply Barbara* (Radcliffe 1989), written with her cooperation, found it necessary to devote much of its first chapter (entitled "Wrinkles and All") to describing and explaining her appearance— surely a startling introduction to the life story of someone whose fame is unrelated to her looks.
9. We do not mean to suggest, however, that it is morally or politically wrong for women to pay attention to their bodies. Maintaining a reasonable weight and exercising and eating moderately offer substantial health benefits. In addition, it would be foolish to ignore the rewards given to those who conform to cultural values, such as the significantly better chances of obtaining work in many fields. (Wolf 1991, pp. 27–57) And, too, women enjoy looking good, for there is a pay-off in embodying culture. Women can gain not just emotional rewards but power from being attractive, including the power that comes from heterosexual affiliation with higher-status men. What is sad, and ultimately destructive for women, however, is to be caught in an obsessive ritual of body monitoring where the scale determines moral worth, where foods are "good" and "bad," and where we are judged—and judge ourselves—by our body size.
10. See, for example, Brownell (1991, pp. 307–8), Brownell and Wadden (1992, pp. 507–8), Dulloo and Girardier (1990, pp. 418–9), Rodin, Radke-Sharpe, Rebuffe-Scrive, and Greenwood (1990, p. 307), and Wadden, Bartlett, Letizia, Foster, Stundkard, and Conill (1992, p. 206s).

REFERENCES

Adams, Cindy. "Talking with the New First Lady." *Ladies Home Journal,* October 1988.

Andersen, Christopher. *Citizen Jane.* New York: Henry Holt, 1990.

————. "Jane Fonda: I'm Stronger Than Ever." *Ladies Home Journal,* October 1989.

Avery, Caryl S. "How Good Should You Look?" *Ladies Home Journal,* June 1989.

Bachrach, Judy. "Feel the Burn." *Savvy Woman,* October 1989.

Ball, Aimee Lee. "How Does Jane Do It?" *McCall's,* March 1992.

Ballaster, Ros, Margaret Beetham, Elizabeth Frazer, and Sandra Hebron. *Women's Worlds: Ideology, Femininity and the Woman's Magazine.* London: Macmillan, 1991.

Banner, Lois W. *American Beauty.* New York: Alfred A. Knopf, 1983.

Bartky, Sandra Lee. "Foucault, Femininity, and the Modernization of Patriarchal Power." In *Feminism and Foucault,* ed. Irene Diamond and Lee Quinby. Boston: Northeastern University Press, 1988, pp. 61–86.

Bordo, Susan. "The Body and the Reproduction of Femininity: A Feminist Appropriation of Foucault." In *Gender/Body/Knowledge,* ed. Alison M. Jaggar and Susan R. Bordo. New Brunswick, NJ: Rutgers University Press, 1989, pp. 13–33.

————. "Reading the Slender Body." In *Body/Politics: Women and the Discourses of Science,* ed. Mary Jacobus, Evelyn Fox Keller, and Sally Shuttleworth. New York: Routledge, 1990, pp. 83–112.

————. " 'Material Girl': The Effacements of Postmodern Culture." In *The Female Body,* ed. Laurence Goldstein. Ann Arbor: The University of Michigan Press, 1991, pp. 653–77.

Brand, Pamela A., Esther D. Rothblum, and Laura J. Solomon. "A Comparison of Lesbians, Gay Men, and Heterosexuals on Weight and Restrained Eating." *International Journal of Eating Disorders* 11, no. 3 (1992), pp. 253–9.

Brown, Laura S. "Lesbians, Weight, and Eating: New Analyses and Perspectives." In *Lesbian Psychologies: Explorations and Challenges,* eds. Boston Lesbian Psychologies Collective. Urbana, IL: University of Illinois Press, 1987, pp. 294–310.

Brownell, Kelly D., "Yo-Yo Dieting." *Psychology Today* 22 (January 1988), pp. 20–3.

————. "Personal Responsibility and Control Over Our Bodies." *Health Psychology* 10, no. 5 (1991), pp. 303–10.

Brownell, Kelly D. and Thomas A. Wadden. "Etiology and Treatment of Obesity: Understanding a Serious, Prevalent, and Refractory Disorder." *Journal of Consulting and Clinical Psychology* 60, no. 4 (1992), pp. 505–17.

Busby, Linda. "Sex-Role Research on the Mass Media." *Journal of Communication* 25, no. 4 (1992), pp. 107–31.

Carey, James W. *Communication as Culture: Essays on Media and Society.* Boston: Unwin Hyman, 1989.

Carlucci, Daniel, Harvey Goldfine, Ann Ward, Pamela Taylor, and James Rippe. "Exercise: Not Just for the Healthy." *The Physician and Sports Medicine* 19, no. 7 (1991), pp. 46–56.

Chernin, Kim. *The Obsession: Reflections on the Tyranny of Slenderness.* New York: Harper & Row, 1981.

Conrad, Peter. "The Experience of Illness: Recent and New Directions." *Research in the Sociology of Health Care* 6 (1987), pp. 1–31.

Cook, Alison. "At Home with Barbara Bush." *Ladies Home Journal,* March 1990.

Coser, Rose Loeb. "Laughter among Colleagues." *Psychiatry* 23 (1960), pp. 81–95.

Crawford, Robert. "Individual Responsibility and Health Politics." In *Health Care in America: Essays in Social History,* ed. Susan Reverby and David Rosner. Philadelphia: Temple University Press, 1979, pp. 247–68.

Davis, Sally Ogle. "Hollywood Marriages: The Good, The Bad and The Disasters." *Ladies Home Journal,* March 1993.

————. "Jane Fonda Bounces Back." *Cosmopolitan,* January 1990.

Doress, Paula Brown, and Diana Laskin Siegel. *Ourselves, Growing Older.* New York: Simon and Schuster, 1987.

Dulloo, Abdul G., and Lucien Girardier. "Adaptive Changes in Energy Expenditure during Refeeding Following Low-Calorie Intake: Evidence for a Specific Metabolic Component Favoring Fat Storage." *American Journal of Clinical Nutrition* 52 (1990), pp. 415–20.

Dworkin, Sari H. "Not in Man's Image: Lesbians and the Cultural Oppression of Body Image." *Women and Therapy* 8, no. 1–2 (1989), pp. 27–39.

Farr, Louise. "Jane Fonda." *Ladies Home Journal,* April 1980.

Faludi, Susan. *Backlash: The Undeclared War against American Women.* New York: Crown, 1991.

Ferguson, Marjorie. *Forever Feminine: Women's Magazines and the Cult of Femininity.* London: Heinemann, 1983.

Fine, Gary Alan. "Sociological Approaches to the Study of Humor." In *Handbook of Humor Research,* Vol. 1, ed. Paul E. McGhee and Jeffrey H. Goldstein. New York: Springer-Verlag, 1983, pp. 138–57.

Fonda, Jane. *Women Coming of Age.* New York: Simon and Schuster, 1984.

———. *Jane Fonda's Workout Book.* New York: Simon and Schuster, 1986.

Foucault, Michel. *Discipline and Punish.* New York: Vintage Books, 1979.

Freedman, Rita. *Beauty Bound.* New York: D. C. Heath and Co., 1986.

Glasser, Dorothy Ann, and Stephen Decatur. "Jane Fonda." *Ladies Home Journal,* February 1982.

Gledhill, Christine. "Pleasurable Negotiations." In *Female Spectators: Looking at Film and Television,* ed. E. Deidre Pribram. London: Verso, 1988, pp. 64–79.

Goffman, Erving. *Stigma: Notes on the Management of Spoiled Identity.* Englewood Cliffs, NJ: Prentice-Hall, 1963.

Good Housekeeping. "I Was a Yo-Yo Dieter." February 1993.

Haig, Robin A. *Anatomy of Humor.* Springfield, IL: Charles C. Thomas, 1988.

Hall, Stuart. "Encoding/Decoding." In *Culture, Media, Language,* ed. Stuart Hall and the Centre for Contemporary Cultural Studies. London: Hutchinson, 1980, pp. 128–38.

Harper's Bazaar. "The California Workout." January 1980.

Harrison, Barbara Grizzuti. "Jane Fonda: Trying to Be Everywoman." *Ladies Home Journal,* April 1978.

Hirschmann, Jane R., and Carol H. Munter. *Overcoming Overeating.* New York: Ballantine, 1988.

Hsu, George. "Are Eating Disorders Becoming More Common in Blacks?" *International Journal of Eating Disorders* 6 (January 1987), pp. 113–24.

Jong, Erica. "Jane Fonda." *Ladies Home Journal,* April 1984.

Kano, Susan. *Making Peace with Food.* New York: Harper & Row, 1989.

Kaplan, Janice. "Fonda On: Fit after Forty." *Vogue,* February 1985.

———. "The Fitness Queen." *Vogue,* November 1987.

Kaufman, Pamela. "Rethinking Diets." *Vogue,* March 1992.

Kerns, Virginia, and Judith K. Brown (eds). *In Her Prime: New Views of Middle-Aged Women.* 2nd ed. Urbana, IL: University of Illinois Press, 1992.

Kilwein, John H. "No Pain, No Gain: A Puritan Legacy." *Health Education Quarterly* 16 (Spring 1989), pp. 9–12.

Koller, Marvin R. *Humor and Society: Explorations in the Sociology of Humor.* Houston, TX: Cap and Gown Press, 1988.

Lear, Martha Weinman. "Jane Fonda: A Long Way from Yesterday." *Redbook,* June 1976.

Levin, Susanna. "Jane Fonda: From Barbarella to Barbells." *Women's Sports and Fitness,* December 1987.

Mademoiselle. "Fitness." March 1980.

Martin, Emily. *The Woman in the Body.* Boston: Beacon Press, 1987.

McClellan, Diana. "Barbara Bush: The Final Battle." *Ladies Home Journal,* October 1992.

McLeod, Jack M., Gerald M. Kosicki, and Zhongdang Pan. "On Understanding and Misunderstanding Media Effects." In *Mass Media and Society,* ed. James Curran and Michael Gurevitch. London: Edward Arnold, 1991, pp. 235–66.

McNay, Lois. "The Foucauldian Body and The Exclusion of Experience." *Hypatia: A Journal of Feminist Philosophy* 6, no. 3 (1991), pp. 125–39.

Millman, Marcia. *Such a Pretty Face.* New York: Norton, 1980.

Messina, Andrea. "Fonda's Workouts that Work." *Family Circle,* January 12, 1993.

Modleski, Tania. *Loving with a Vengeance: Mass Produced Fantasies for Women.* London: Methuen, 1982.

Morgan, Kathryn Pauly. "Women and the Knife: Cosmetic Surgery and the Colonization of Women's Bodies." *Hypatia* 6, no. 3 (1991), pp. 25–53.

Mower, Joan. "What Kind of First Lady Do We Really Want?" *McCall's,* September 1992.

Nichter, Mark, and Mimi Nichter. "Hype and Weight." *Medical Anthropology* 13, no. 3 (1991), pp. 249–84.

O'Brien, Sandra J., and Patricia A. Vertinsky. *The Gerontologist* 31 (June 1991), pp. 347–57.

Orbach, Susie. *Fat Is a Feminist Issue.* New York: Berkley, 1982.

Orth, Maureen. "Fonda: Driving Passions." *Vogue,* February 1984.

Radcliffe, Donnie. *Simply Barbara Bush.* New York: Warner Books, 1989.

Radway, Janice. *Reading the Romance: Women, Patriarchy and Popular Literature.* Chapel Hill: University of North Carolina Press, 1984.

Redbook. "Relax with Jane Fonda." March 1990.

Reed, Julia. "The Natural." *Vogue,* August 1989.

Robbins, Fred. "Jane Fonda, the Woman." *Vogue,* November 1977.

Rodin, Judith, Norean Radke-Sharpe, Marielle Rebuffe-Scrive, and M. R. C. Greenwood. "Weight Cycling and Fat Distribution." *International Journal of Obesity* 14 (1990), pp. 303–10.

Rosengren, Karl E., Lawrence A. Wenner, and Philip Palmgreen, eds. *Media Gratifications Research: Current Perspectives.* Beverly Hills, CA: Sage, 1985.

Rothblum, Esther D. "Lesbians and Physical Appearance: Which Model Applies?" *Contemporary Perspectives in Lesbian and Gay Psychology,* In press.

Schoenfielder, Lisa, and Barb Wieser, eds. *Shadow on a Tightrope: Writings by Women on Fat Oppression.* San Francisco: Spinsters/Aunt Lute, 1983.

Schwartz, Hillel. *Never Satisfied: A Cultural History of Diets, Fantasies and Fat.* New York: The Free Press, 1986.

Seid, Roberta Pollack. *Never Too Thin.* New York: Prentice Hall, 1989.

Seligmann, Jean. "Let Them Eat Cake." *Newsweek,* August 1992.

Shangold, Mona M. "Exercise in the Menopausal Woman." *Obstetrics and Gynecology* 75, no. 4 (1990), Supplement, pp. 53s–8s.

Simonds, Wendy. *Women and Self-Help Culture: Reading between the Lines.* New Brunswick, NJ: Rutgers University Press, 1992.

Smith, Lori R., Ann Kathleen Burlew, and David C. Lundgren. "Black Consciousness, Self-Esteem, and Satisfaction with Physical Appearance among African-American Female College Students." *Journal of Black Studies* 22, no. 2 (1991), pp. 269–83.

Sontag, Susan. "The Double Standard of Aging." *Saturday Review,* October 1972.

Stein, Arlene. "All Dressed Up, but No Place to Go? Style Wars and the New Lesbianism." In *The Persistent Desire: A Femme–Butch Reader,* ed. Joan Nestle. Boston: Alyson Publicants, 1992, pp. 431–9.

Stein, Howard F. "Neo-Darwinism and Survival through Fitness in Reagan's America." *The Journal of Psychohistory* 10, no. 2 (1982), pp. 163–87.

Striegel-Moore, Ruth H., Naomi Tucker, and Jeanette Hsu. "Body Image Dissatisfaction and Disordered Eating in Lesbian College Students." *International Journal of Eating Disorders* 9, no. 5 (1990), pp. 493–500.

Tesh, Sylvia. *Hidden Arguments: Political Ideology and Disease Prevention Policy.* New Brunswick, NJ: Rutgers University Press, 1988.

Thomas, Veronica G., "Body-Image Satisfaction among Black Women." *The Journal of Social Psychology* 129, no. 1 (1989), pp. 107–12.

Thomas, Veronica G. and Michelle D. James. "Body Image, Dieting Tendencies, and Sex Role Traits in Urban Black Women." *Sex Roles* 18, no. 9/10 (1988), pp. 523–29.

Tuchman, Gaye. *Hearth and Home: Images of Women and the Media.* New York: Oxford University Press, 1978.

Turner, Bryan S. *The Body and Society: Explorations in Social Theory.* New York: Basil Blackwell, 1984.

Ungar, Sheldon. "Self-Mockery: An Alternative Form of Self-Presentation." *Symbolic Interaction* 7, no. 1 (1984), pp. 121–33.

Van Zoonen, Liesbet. "Feminist Perspectives on the Media." In *Mass Media and Society,* eds. James Curran and Michael Gurevitch. London: Edward Arnold, 1991, pp. 35–54.

Viorst, Judith. "It's Time to Bring Back the Family." *Redbook,* May 1991.

Vogue. "First Ladies, First Impressions." October 1988.

———. "Winning Style: Kitty Dukakis and Barbara Bush on First Lady Dressing." November 1988.

Wadden, T. A., S. Bartlett, K. A. Letizia, G. D. Foster, A. J. Stunkard, and A. Conill. "Relationship of Dieting History to Resting Metabolic Rate, Body Composition, Eating Behavior, and Subsequent Weight Loss." *American Journal of Clinical Nutrition* 56, no. 1 (1992), Supplement, pp. 203–8s.

Waitzkin, Howard. "The Social Origins of Illness: A Neglected History." *International Journal of Health Services* 11 (1981), pp. 77–103.

Walker, Nancy A. *A Very Serious Thing: Women's Humor and American Culture.* Minneapolis: University of Minnesota, 1988.

Weedon, Chris. *Feminist Practice and Poststructuralist Theory.* London: Basil Blackwell, 1987.

Winship, Janice. *Inside Women's Magazines.* London: Pandora, 1978.

Wolf, Naomi. *The Beauty Myth.* New York: William Morrow, 1991.

Woodward, Kathleen. *Aging and Its Discontents.* Bloomington, IN: Indiana University Press, 1991.

Zillman, Dolf. "Disparagement Humor." In *Handbook of Humor Research,* vol. 1, eds. Paul E. McGhee and Jeffrey H. Goldstein. New York: Springer-Verlag, 1983, pp. 85–108.

Zola, Irving K. "Medicine as an Institution of Social Control." *Sociological Review* 20, no. 4 (1972), pp. 487–504.

PART FOUR

TRANSFORMATION, BORDER CROSSING, AND FEMINIST THEORY

CHAPTER 11

Social Change and Cultural Transformation

The very idea of feminism implies the projects of changing social structure and transforming culture. Feminists want a different world, though they differ a good deal in how much and what kinds of change they favor. Some advocate overhauling our institutions and culture so that gender virtually disappears as a basis for dividing labor and a peg for establishing people's identities. Others favor tinkering with them without changing their fundamental shapes. In the next chapter we will look at the various schools of thought where feminists congregate. In the meantime, this chapter explores the themes of change and transformation lending continuity to various strands of feminist theory and praxis.

EQUALITY, DIFFERENCE, AND SISTERHOOD

Equality has long been associated with feminist movements insofar as they problematize gender and challenge male privilege. Equal rights, equal opportunities, and equal payoffs are principles unifying a great deal of feminist discourse. These principles are rooted in the political history of subjugated groups struggling for the same constitutional and statutory recognition taken for granted by property-owning white males. Social movements, such as those women have forged over the past 150 years, dramatize not only the struggle for but also the problematics of "equality."

Modernist conceptions of equality—those historically linked with democratic states—are stubbornly universalist. They presuppose a human being we have met up with before: highly individuated, consistently self-interested, and habitually calculating. This being's needs revolve around "freedom," conceived not only as the relatively unfettered capacity to act but also as the continual negotiation of one's obligations to other individuals. Overall, freedom *from* took practical priority over freedom *to* in modernist thinking about humanness. That priority shows up in modernist approaches to equality, which center on freedom from various forms of discrimination rather than freedom to develop one's full self.

In the modernist scheme, then, equality implies equivalence or fundamental sameness. It presupposes that people have equal opportunities if they are demonstrably treated like the universal human being articulated in law and social policy. As we have seen, though, that creature central to the relations of ruling is no more universal than the systems that create him. Instead, he is an expression of "false universalism" that masks "a type of *particularity.*"[1] As we saw in Chapter 2, the particularity obscured by "human being" is masculine, white, straight, able-bodied, and higher class. In practical terms, then, modernist notions of equality boil down to being treated like higher-class, able-bodied male members of the racial and sexual majorities. If such treatment results in some groups being disproportionately left on the lower rungs of social hierarchies, so be it, according to modernist liberals.

This posture found expression in culture-of-poverty arguments during the 1960s and is now regaining momentum in the welfare-reform and anti-affirmative action rhetoric of the 1990s. It revolves around untenable notions about how cultures work. To wit, those with modernist conceptions of equality who blame the victims of inequality like to assume that those victims' culture is somehow deficient or misbegotten. In the 1960s, the alleged fatalism of the poor and their inability to defer gratification made their culture a supposed precursor to their destitution. In the 1990s, teenage pregnancies and single-parent households signal a deficient culture, which promotes welfare dependence and other social evils.

Such arguments naively assume that culture precedes social circumstances and thus creates them. In actuality, groups build up their cultures in response to social circumstances. Where marriage to the father of one's child is prohibited by law, where pregnancy results from rape by one's "owner," where one's social status is that of breeder, where family has to be whatever sheer ingenuity and stubborn will can make it, there will arise a culture forgiving of unwed motherhood, conducive to othermothers, and nonjudgmental about the conditions whereby people claim their children and do their damnedest by them even though it may look like woefully little through more privileged eyes.

Its culture, then, offers no ready explanation for a group's outcomes. Put differently, a group's departures from the mandates of universalist humanness offer few clues about how that group fares in the hierarchical scheme of things. Instead, its culture is likelier to reflect how group members get treated *unequally* in the process of being treated *equivalently.* I am arguing that being treated the same as a male with the aforementioned characteristics is for most women as well as for most men of color a denial of their circumstances. Treating female students and male students of color in a professional or graduate program the same as their white male counterparts may, for example, mean setting them up for lesser achievement. Without some *system* for mentoring them and making them feel welcome, they may remain disadvantaged by subtle and not so subtle signals that they are interlopers, upstarts, or affirmative-action opportunists.

Some years ago, for instance, I mentioned to one of my colleagues that a female student entering his department's doctoral program could benefit from his reaching out to her. His response was that he would wait for her to take some initiative. He would, in a word, wait for her to act like a man of privilege. Such "equal" treatment ignores the lived inequalities shaping people's sense of themselves as well as their sense of what they can rightfully expect of other people, especially members of dominant groups.

In any event, second-wave feminism in American society got its bearings by focusing on equality with men. In *Le Temps des Femmes* Julia Kristeva characterizes this first phase as liberal feminism resting on identification with masculinist values and pursuits. This phase emphasized sisterhood up against an entrenched brotherhood. It thus deemphasized differences among women in favor of interests women supposedly have in common with one another. At the same time it deemphasized the privileged positionings of those (relatively few) women who could expect, given equivalent treatment, to compete effectively with men of privilege. The first phase of second-wave feminism thus downplayed some women's privilege by exaggerating their kindredness with all other women while dramatizing their subordination to those men of privilege with whom they actually had a lot in common. This phase also minimized or even denied substantial differences between women and men (and thus any substantial grounds for treating them differently).

Feminists of color and white lesbian feminists, in particular, challenged this "sisterly" feminism. They underscored their own erasure from the calculus of interests wherein "equal opportunity" had a white, heterosexist cast and middle-class underpinnings. Theorists like Angela Davis[2] saw that in the hands of some influential feminists, equality often amounted to a quest for the same unfair advantages enjoyed by their white, middle-class fathers, brothers, husbands, friends, and colleagues. With other feminists of color and white lesbian feminists, theorists like her threw sisterhood into serious question and put "differences" squarely at the forefront of feminist theorizing.

Although I favor a less romantic conception of sisterhood—one closer to the knots and bows of real-life sisterhood—I agree that "sisterhood" did a disservice to countless women whose experiences and priorities never really counted in its rhetoric. Gradually, this metaphor got deflated as a rhetoric of differences gained force. In its most dramatic forms this later rhetoric defined a second phase where radical feminism took hold with its logic of disidentification, emphasizing rejection of patriarchal values and separation from patriarchal institutions.

As Kristeva saw, these first two phases of second-wave feminism thus pitted "equality" and "difference" against one another as the only choices, with "the implicit masculine standard of reference going unchallenged." Kristeva held out the prospect of a third phase focused on "dismantling the very terms of the opposition altogether, of stepping over the threshold to postmodernity, where sexual beings are no longer polarized."[3]

Kristeva thus pointed to the need for a third feminist phase where equality gets reworked as a goal and differences find expression without censure. Her prognostications found their way into print in 1979. By now, they have proven accurate. Feminist theorists have substantially complicated the idea of equality and have taken positive hold of the differences among women. They have stirred the theoretical pot enough to create some distinctively feminist insights into the ideal of equality and the reality of differences. Although they have not uniformly rejected universalism, they have documented "the need for a new type of articulation between the universal and the particular."[4] At the same time they have laid the theoretical groundwork for a revitalized feminist politics, as we will see in the last section.

Elizabeth Minnich's work illustrates these theoretical advances. Arguing against equality as sameness, she says that "equality protects our right to be different." It "challenge[s] us to make distinctions that are relevant and appropriate to a particular situation or set of considerations or principles." Thus, equality entails neither consistently dismissing nor consistently considering the differences among us. Instead, it makes differences a matter of variable, context-bound significance. Minnich observes that "all that marks us as the same or different *can* be held irrelevant for some purpose, with regard to some provision or standard or act or protection or intellectual inquiry." (emphasis added) Whether any social marker or identity *should* be treated as irrelevant, though, is a matter for ongoing, careful attention. Minnich says,

> To establish equality, and to protect it, we need to locate very carefully which distinctions must be recognized in order to be neutralized, which can be ruled entirely out of order, which may need (if only temporarily) to be privileged to allow all to start on an even footing.[5]

Francoise Collin echoes those ideas. She insists that equal rights in no way necessitate a common identity. Equality differs from making everyone into "equivalent and interchangeable examples of humanity." It allows for people's idiosyncrasies and "falls apart as soon as the many are dissolved into a single voice which is the voice of no one at all."[6]

These theorists and others conceptualize equality so that it allows for, even promotes, diversity. Their conceptualizations entail postmodernist notions of identity as a performative process. In tandem with such notions, theorists like Minnich and Collin reject the essentialism postulating significant sameness within a grouping such as women. At least implicitly, their work emphasizes the historically contingent, culturally conditioned identities available to individuals variously situated in the matrix of domination. Such insights lead to understanding that women cannot possibly develop the "same" identity. Women's diverse social positionings and unequal cultural resources guarantee divergent identities among them. To that extent, any social movement aiming to bring them together has got to grapple with intragroup as well as intergroup differences.

Doing so is frequently painful and counterproductive, but social *movement* demands no less. As Flora Davis puts it, "a social movement is a messy, volatile conglomeration of groups and individuals, all inspired by similar ideas and bent on making changes."[7] Within such messy enterprises feminist conceptualizations of equality, serving as a huge tent over differences rather than an eraser of them, can prove enormously helpful. At the very least such notions keep participants honest about the extent of their commitment to women as a diverse grouping with divergent as well as convergent goals and interests.

Yet grappling with differences is difficult, especially for those whose overall positioning is privileged and comfortable. Coming to terms with women's differences from one another requires nothing less than overcoming societal stereotypes about who is *really* and *fully* a woman. It means saying, "You are no less a woman than I" and meaning it, even when "you" belongs to one of the many groupings of women widely deemed unfeminine or unwomanly. It means, more often than not, letting go of the class privilege that lets some women believe that they know more than other women, that their male-approved credentials entitle them to greater respect as well as greater credibility, and that their well-developed voices represent greater wisdom and insight than the voices of their more frequently silenced sisters.

Theoretically, too, coming to terms with differences is no easy task. For the most part, we all like to talk more about how we are dominated than how we are dominating, more about how we are disprivileged rather than privileged. But I have gotten to the point where I believe that those of us theorizing about social injustices and inequalities need, *if we are going to talk about our own social positionings at all,* to describe the terms of our privileging more than those of our disprivileging. Almost all of us theorists are richly and diversely privileged. Let the few among us whose multiple oppressions outweigh their multiple privileges focus on those oppressions in describing the place where they stand to look at the world. For the sake of egalitarian, pathbreaking theory the rest of us should, I think, come clean about how our multiple privileges define as well as limit that place.

Yet this matter of how to inscribe oneself explicitly in one's theoretical work is more complex than it might initially seem. To say, for instance, "I am white" is to say very little indeed about who *I* am and how *I* behave, even though it says a great deal about the privileges I can expect or even take for granted. To say "I am black" is also to say very little, even though it does say a lot about the oppressive experiences I can expect and may even take for granted if I have bought into the mainstream's definition of me. "White" or "black" says what people in racist society see and how they are likely to respond, but neither identifier says whether *I* am radical or moderate, activist or apolitical, resistant or compliant, identified more with what might be or more with what is.

Those reciting a litany of their social characteristics, then, do no more than point to the crude contours of the matrix of domination. I myself find such litanies offensive, both intellectually and politically. On the first front they assume that I am unable to sniff out a renegade white person or a white-identified black person; on the second front, they invite me to infer people's politics and lifeways on uncertain, if not silly, grounds. That said, let us return to the challenge of grappling theoretically with women's differences from one another.

As Trinh T. Minh-ha notes, "difference" means "division" to many people.[8] Perhaps that circumstance is both cause and effect of liberal democracy's variable but decided tendency to "deny difference."[9] In any event, as Hester Eisenstein has observed, in the United States second-wave feminists started out denying or at least downplaying the differences between women and men.[10] Perhaps aligned with that strategy was a parallel one of ignoring or downplaying the differences among women. Particularly in a multicultural society such a stance is tempting, for embracing differences can seem overwhelming or just plain impractical.

In the final analysis, whether differences get embraced or not, they have to be acknowledged. Such acknowledgment may be extensive enough to result in a focus on heterogeneity or limited enough to allow for a "unitary standpoint," as Patricia Hill Collins implies. At least in her authorship of *Black Feminist Thought,* Hill decided to acknowledge differences among African American women in limited fashion. Her fear is that

> The use of difference taken to its logical conclusion leaves us with a group of politically unorganized, unique "individuals" and firmly entrenches us in liberal democratic politics that allegedly protects the "individual's" right to be "free."[11]

For different but related reasons, Susan Bordo also expresses reservations about a wholesale embracing of "differences." Theoretically attuned to "the totalitarian nature of generalization" and the "rush to protect difference from its homogenizing abuses," Bordo nevertheless argues,

> Too relentless a focus on historical heterogeneity . . . can obscure the transhistorical hierarchical patterns of white, male privilege that have informed the creation of the Western intellectual tradition.[12]

Similarly, Martha Albertson Fineman deems it "an error for women to proceed as though [their] differences were *always* relevant."[13]

Theoretically and practically, then, the challenge would seem to be balancing the claims of commonality against those of difference. Such balance cannot be achieved once and for all, not even for the time being. Those engaged in theorizing and those active in movements must continually negotiate a course that brings common concerns to the fore while seeing that differences never get buried or overridden in the process. The image of a trapeze artist comes to mind, and that image invites its opposite—perhaps the ticket taker at the gate who sees not people coming to the circus but only the potential stubs in their hands. Such an image is central to identity politics, a form of social movement that is losing ground in the wake of calls to acknowledge diversity.

IDENTITY POLITICS

What has come to be called *identity politics* is a form of seeking social change and cultural transformation by mobilizing people around a social identity such as woman, lesbian, gay man, senior citizen, or person of color. Unlike earlier social movements based primarily on social class, new social movements based on social identities emphasize, however implicitly, the homogeneity among their participants. New social movements thus tend to reify identity by treating it as a fixed, thinglike phenomenon expressive of a person's core being. In the process such movements lean toward essentialist understandings.

In 1989, Shane Phelan's *Identity Politics* made all these points and more. Subtitled *Lesbian Feminism and the Limits of Community,* Phelan's study had as much to say about the limits of identity politics as the limits of anything else. Her opening sentence comes as no surprise: "Lesbian feminism began with and has fueled itself by the rejection of liberalism." The first chapter then dissects the political shortcomings of liberalism. Yet Phelan goes on to show that the identity politics built up around lesbian feminism is also deeply problematic. She observed, for instance, "Most lesbian feminists did not learn the lesson that global theories are dangerous; they learned that other global theories were defective."[14] Specifically,

> The issue is not simply how lesbians are portrayed, but that they are being portrayed as some homogeneous group about which lesbian feminists can speak. . . . The community that is defined by this valuation is indeed a home, but it is not the home of free, adult human beings. . . . The legitimate drive for community degenerates into unmediated unity, a unity that carries as its twin an excessive fear of difference. (p. 57)

This fear of difference is endemic to identity politics. It is the fear that led Betty Friedan to call lesbians in the women's movement, particularly in the National Organization for Women (which was still getting on its feet), the "lavender menace"; it is the fear that leads some lesbians and gay men to shudder at their more flamboyant counterparts marching in lesbigay parades; it is the fear that leads some feminists to make derisive assumptions about Patricia Ireland's being both a wife and the lover of a woman; it is the fear that makes a *single* way of being female or lesbian or a woman of color or an aging woman the *right* way, at least for movement-related purposes. Within new social movements revolving around identity politics, the fear of difference boils down to the fear that a movement will be held back if its participants reveal the full extent of their diversity. This, then, is a fear that subordinates freedom of expression to a group's need for a politically viable identity.

Phelan finds such tendencies in "the totalizing nature of radical lesbian feminist thought," which "traps its practitioners by commanding that every facet of life be measured by one yardstick that, in turn, is seemingly clear and authentic." (p. 138) Phelan urges that individuals "resist the impulse for total separatism and for purity in our allies in favor of workable coalitions and porous but meaningful communities." She concludes,

> If we are to be free, we must learn to embrace paradox and confusion; in short, we must embrace politics. Identity politics must be based not only on identity but on an appreciation for politics as the art of living together. Politics that ignores our identities . . . is useless; but nonnegotiable identities will enslave us whether they are imposed from within or without. (p. 170)

More and more feminist theorists are landing where Phelan did in 1989. Julia Penelope, for example, argues that for lesbians the only given is "being deviant," that is, "one definition of Lesbian will never be satisfactory or comprehensive."[15] Judith Butler articulates resonant insights: "The feminist 'we' is always and only a phantasmatic construction. . . ." Identity politics falters on its assumption "that an identity must first be in place in order for political interests to be elaborated and, subsequently, political action to be taken." Butler goes on to address more differentiated terms of identification:

> The theories of feminist identity that elaborate predicates of color, sexuality, ethnicity, class, and able-bodiedness invariably close with an embarrassed "etc." at the end of the list. Through this horizontal trajectory of adjectives, these positions strive to encompass a situated subject but invariably fail to be complete.[16]

Like Phelan and Penelope, then, Butler implies the need to overhaul, if not abandon, identity politics to make space for people's lived identities. These theorists extend Elizabeth Spelman's earlier insights about how "the notion of a generic 'woman' functions in feminist thought much the way the notion of generic 'man' has functioned in Western philosophy." Deeming "the phrase 'as a woman' . . . the Trojan horse of feminist ethnocentrism," Spelman insists that people's identities "are much more complicated than what might be suggested by the simple and straightforward use of terms like 'Black,' 'white,' 'woman,' 'man.' "[17]

By now, then, feminist theorists have indeed complicated "equality" and "identity" and the politics that brings these two phenomena together. By now, they have begun carving out that theoretical space Nancie E.

Caraway alludes to when she observes that "a critical identity politics cautions us not to become too comfortable too long in *that spot* with *that identity,* lest we forget and stifle the ways in which we change, contradict, and grow in history."[18] By now, in sum, feminist theory provides for the practical balance and theoretical acumen Collin achieves in the closing paragraph of her "Plurality, Difference, Identity":

> I claim the right, says a woman, to be a human being without having to pretend I am not a woman. I claim the right, says a woman, . . . both to my being as a woman and to my freedom. I am neither a specimen of the human race nor a specimen of the female gender, but someone who, endowed with the gift of speech, says "I" coming and going through the "we" of open borders. I am a woman, but "I" is not a woman.[19]

Such an "I" forswears identity politics for a politics both more modest and more effective.

THE POLITICS OF PARTIALITY

Five years after the publication of *Identity Politics,* Phelan published another work on the politics of social change and cultural transformation. As its subtitle suggests, *Getting Specific: Postmodern Lesbian Politics* draws on postmodernist thinking to theorize a politics that avoids the pitfalls of an essentialist identity politics while advancing its central aims. In her preface Phelan paints the broad contours of such a politics by juxtaposing it against what has not worked:

> one of the problems . . . in early lesbian feminism was the construction of a "lesbian" who was different from all nonlesbians but not significantly different from any other "lesbian." This was not a politics of alliance or coalition but of identity as homogeneity. Such a politics will always be brittle and nondemocratic, even as its participants try to treat one another well.[20]

Phelan's theoretical effort builds up around the intent to resist the "bait of identity." (p. 96) At the same time it reorients conventional thinking about community and commonality. Phelan conceptualizes community as something developed "only by negotiating about what we will have in common, what we will share and how we will share it." (p. 95) Another key theoretical move she makes is to shift away from the idea of liberation to that of power, including rights as "a form of power" that "authorize people to perform certain actions, largely by forbidding others to restrain them." (pp. 114, 125)

On these conceptual grounds Phelan makes her way to this conclusion: "Our politics must be informed by affinity rather than identity, not simply because we are not all alike but because we each embody multiple, often conflicting, identities and locations." (p. 140) To be sure, such a politics is hard to practice. In Phelan's judgment, anti-essentialist, social-constructionist perspectives enable that practice. She says,

Once we see that social formations and memberships are not naturally given but are invented or imagined, we can see the bonds between us. These bonds are not ones of mutual affection or concern, not ones of nature, but are the creation of systems of discursive power and hegemony that tell us who we are and where we fit. (p. 144)

The coalitional politics Phelan advocates thus shifts questions away from identities toward "shared commitments," away from identities toward "sympathy and affinity." (p. 155) Such a politics revolves around questions not about which people "are 'really' allies but how to *make* them allies." This politics takes shape around the question of "whether we can *decide* to be allies and whether we have the strength to follow through on that decision." (p. 156) This politics thus has a distinctly multicultural cast. It is a border-crossing politics, a bridge-building politics, a derring-do politics that refuses the easy exclusions, whether intentional or not, associated with identity politics.

At the same time, this politics refuses heavy emphasis on differences. It builds up around a sense that giving too much weight to differences is as hazardous as giving too little (that is, denying or ignoring differences). This politics refuses to let attention to differences get to the point of "disguis[ing] shared interests and undermin[ing] the possibility of friendship, alliances, and working relations."[21] This, then, is a "politics of provisional identities," as Martha A. Ackelsberg puts it. It embeds identity in dynamic communities where "diverse voices" resound without being drawn into a univocal chorus. As Ackelsberg also indicates, what is being theorized is "a kind of 'localist' politics."[22]

Among other theorists whose work points to such a politics, one of the most important is Gloria Anzaldúa. Central to her framework are "borderlands" and "*mestiza* consciousness." Anzaldúa conceptualizes *borderlands* (or margins) as "place[s] of contradictions" where "keeping intact one's shifting and multiple identity and integrity is like trying to swim in a new element, an 'alien' element."[23] For example,

The U.S.–Mexican border *es una herida abierta* where the Third World grates against the first and bleeds. And before a scab forms it hemorrhages again, the lifeblood of two worlds merging to form a third country—a border culture. . . . A borderland is a vague and undetermined place created by the emotional residue of an unnatural boundary. It is in a constant state of transition. (p. 3)

An "alien" consciousness—"a new *mestiza* consciousness"—takes shape in the face of all these contradictions, hemorrhages, and transitions: "It is a consciousness of the Borderlands." (p. 77) Its hallmark is "a tolerance for ambiguity." The new *mestiza* "learns to juggle cultures. She has a plural personality, she operates in a pluralistic mode—nothing is thrust out, . . . nothing rejected, nothing abandoned." (p. 79) Anzaldúa says,

The new mestiza [*sic*] is grounded in her own home ethnic culture but has been exposed to these other worlds and is open to working, living, doing coalition, and building alliances with people who recognize each other's home ethnic cultures.[24]

A third theorist laying grounds for alternatives to identity politics is Chantal Mouffe, who asks that "we discard the view of the subject as an agent both rational and transparent to itself and discard as well the supposed unity and homogeneity of the ensemble of its positions. . . ." In its stead we put a "multiple and contradictory subject."[25] For women's movements toward social change and cultural transformation, this means that "woman" need no longer preoccupy us definitionally. Instead,

> The central issues become: How is "woman" constructed as a category within different discourses? How is sexual difference made a pertinent distinction in social relations? And how are relations of subordination constructed through such a distinction? The whole false dilemma of equality-versus-difference is exploded since we no longer have a homogeneous category "woman" facing another homogeneous category "man," but a multiplicity of social relations in which sexual difference is always constructed in very diverse ways and where the struggle against subordination has to be visualized in specific and differential forms. To ask whether women should become identical to men in order to be recognized as equal, or whether they should assert their difference at the cost of equality, appears meaningless once essential identities are put into question. (p. 78)

Mouffe theorizes against the grain of the liberal and civic republican traditions. Her radical democratic perspective emphasizes that diverse

> situations of domination . . . must be challenged if the principles of liberty and equality are to apply. It indicates the common recognition by the different groups struggling for an extension and radicalization of democracy that they have a common concern. . . . The aim is to construct a "we" as radical democratic citizens, a collective political identity articulated through the principle of democratic *equivalence*. It must be stressed that such a relation of *equivalence* does not eliminate *difference*. . . . It is only in so far as democratic differences are opposed to forces or discourses which negate all of them that these differences can be substituted for each other. (p. 84)

Mouffe's radical democratic "we" emerges only amidst diversity and contestation (p. 84) and thus points to the impossibility of ever finally establishing democracy—or equality, for that matter. Citizenship becomes a multifaceted, collective process in a political arena big enough to encompass not only the "public" but also the "private" sphere. Identity gets constituted through projects associated with citizenship, not vice versa.

In Mouffe's theoretical framework, feminism remains a struggle for women's equality. As such, though, it

> should not be understood as a struggle to realize the equality of a definable empirical group with a common essence and identity—that is, women—but rather as a struggle against the multiple forms in which the category "woman" is constructed in subordination. (p. 88)

For Mouffe, then, feminist struggle is always tied to specific social and cultural forms that inferiorize and subordinate "women." Like Ackelberg's and Anzaldúa's, Mouffe's is a multicultural politics in the theoretical making.

Mouffe's theorizing resonates with the "localist" politics mentioned earlier. Ien Ang calls this a *politics of partiality,* which entails "consciously construct[ing] the *limits* of its own field of political intervention."[26] This politics involves "becom[ing] more specific," as Zillah R. Eisenstein puts it, when she announces that she will be meaning "women of color" when she refers to "individuals" in her analysis of democracy. This, she observes, actually "encompass[es] more of humanity" than meaning "white men" when one talks about "individuals."[27] Minnich describes such a move this way:

> We need to learn to particularize whatever and whomever we study, and then to contextualize, to historicize—to hold whatever abstractions we draw from the material of our study close to that material for as long as is necessary to keep us from thinking that apparently parallel [men/women, Black/white] but actually hierarchical categories are reversible.[28]

Theorizing the "privilege of partial perspective," Donna Haraway says it this way: "The only way to find a larger vision is to be somewhere in particular."[29]

All these ideas bring us back to Phelan, who emphasizes specificity not only as a political strategy but also "as a methodological precept for social theory."[30] Resonating with Eisenstein, Phelan observes that "women of color in the United States have been a major source of 'specific theory.' " (p. 24) Phelan's call for "more modest theory" (p. 3) parallels her call for a more modest but more effective politics. On both fronts she insists that

> without decency and love, bringing us toward one another without requiring sameness, our rhetorical and heartfelt commitments to others will continually be frustrated in the face of ineluctable difference. (p. 158)

In the end, then, Phelan's theorizing has a lot in common with bell hooks's in Reading 25. Exploring feminism as "a transformational politic," hooks says we need to confront the differences among us as expressions of "interlocking systems of domination" that we ourselves "reinforce and perpetuate." Thereby we establish solidarity and lay "the foundation of feminist movement." At the same time we come to recognize our feminist work as a "gesture of love."

Such learning finds acknowledgment in Reading 26, where Sara Ruddick explores the transformational possibilities of "maternal thinking." Like the other theorists at hand, Ruddick emphasizes solidarity, not sisterhood. Also like them, she places great weight on what she calls the political potency of "imaginative collectives" driven less by a shared identity and more by shared commitments and daring creativity.

Overall, social change and cultural transformation demand a heady and creative politics-not-as-usual. As the chapters and readings in *Contemporary Feminist Theory* have illustrated, such a politics demands more of the law, the workplace, schools, and other institutions than does the status-quo, mainstream politics of interest groups, lobbyists, opinion polls, and nonstop campaigning in one form or other. Such a transformational politics also demands more of culture—of mass-circulated magazines and megabucks movies, popular music and talk shows, the fine and performing arts, and the knowledge systems that are part and parcel of the relations of ruling.

Such politics demands more, finally, of individuals like (and unlike) you and me. It demands that we take responsibility for the shape and texture of our world; that we care enough about ourselves and others to resist systems of domination and telltale signs of elitism; that we grow by coming to grips with the boundless diversity that ensures each of us a unique individuality while making "us" a continual problematic of (post)modern life. Phelan says that "feminist theory always returns to the challenge of social change."[31] So does everyday life for those who believe enough in the possibility of a decent world to labor toward that end.

NOTES

1. Jean Grimshaw, "Philosophy, Feminism and Universalism," *Radical Philosophy* 76 (March/April 1996), p. 19.
2. Angela Y. Davis, *Women, Race & Class* (New York: Vintage Books, 1983 (orig. 1981)). Davis's focus is first-wave feminism, but her points apply to a lot of second-wave theory and practice.
3. Jill Marsden, "Strange Alliances: Feminism, Poststructuralism and the Possibility of Affirmation," *Women: A Cultural Review* 4, no. 2 (Autumn 1993), p. 195.
4. Chantal Mouffe, *The Return of the Political* (London: Verso, 1993), p. 97.
5. Elizabeth Kamarck Minnich, *Transforming Knowledge* (Philadelphia: Temple University Press, 1990), pp. 70, 107, 108.
6. Francoise Collin, "Plurality, Difference, Identity," *Women: A Cultural Review* 5, no. 1 (Spring 1994), pp. 18, 15.
7. Flora Davis, *Moving the Mountain: The Women's Movement in America since 1960* (New York: Simon & Schuster, 1991), p. 10.
8. Trinh T. Minh-ha, *Woman, Native, Other: Writing Postcoloniality and Feminism* (Bloomington: Indiana University Press, 1989), p. 82.
9. Julia Edwards, *Local Government Women's Committees: A Feminist Political Practice* (Aldershot, England: Avebury Ashgate Publishing Co., 1995), p. 172.
10. Hester Eisenstein, *Inside Agitators: Australian Femocrats and the State* (Philadelphia: Temple University Press, 1996), p. 82.
11. Patricia Hill Collins, "Reply," *Gender & Society* 6 (September 1992), p. 518.
12. Susan Bordo, *Unbearable Weight: Feminism, Western Culture, and the Body* (Berkeley: University of California Press, 1993), p. 260; "Feminism, Postmodernism, and Gender-Scepticism" in Linda J. Nicholson (ed.), *Feminism/Postmodernism* (New York: Routledge, 1990), p. 149.
13. Martha Albertson Fineman, "Feminist Theory in Law: The Difference It Makes," *Columbia Journal of Gender and Law* 2, no. 1 (1992), p. 21.
14. Shane Phelan, *Identity Politics: Lesbian Feminism and the Limits of Community* (Philadelphia: Temple University Press, 1989), p. 56.

15. Julia Penelope, *Call Me Lesbian: Lesbian Lives, Lesbian Theory* (Freedom, CA: The Crossing Press, 1992), pp. xi, 36.

16. Judith Butler, *Gender Trouble: Feminism and the Subversion of Identity* (New York: Routledge, 1990), pp. 142, 143.

17. Elizabeth V. Spelman, *Inessential Woman: Problems of Exclusion in Feminist Thought* (Boston: Beacon Press, 1988), pp. ix, x, 135.

18. Nancie E. Caraway, "The Riddle of Consciousness: Racism and Identity in Feminist Theory" in Lois Lovelace Duke (ed.), *Women in Politics: Outsiders or Insiders?* (Upper Saddle River, NJ: Prentice-Hall, 1996), p. 27.

19. Collin, "Plurality, Difference, Identity," p. 24.

20. Shane Phelan, *Getting Specific: Postmodern Lesbian Politics* (Minneapolis: University of Minnesota Press, 1994), p. x.

21. Jan Pettman, *Living in the Margins: Racism, Sexism and Feminism in Australia* (St. Leonards, Australia: Allen & Unwin, 1992), p. 77.

22. Martha A. Ackelsberg, "Identity Politics, Political Identities: Thoughts toward a Multicultural Politics," *Frontiers* XVI, no. 1 (1996), pp. 87–100.

23. Gloria Anzaldúa, *Borderlands/La Frontera: The New Mestiza* (San Francisco: Aunt Lute Books, 1987), Preface.

24. Eileen Hernandez, "Re-Thinking Margins and Borders: An Interview with Gloria Anzaldúa," *Discourse* 18, no. 1/2 (Fall/Winter 1995–1996), p. 10.

25. Chantal Mouffe, *The Return of the Political,* p. 77.

26. Ien Ang, "I'm a Feminist but . . . 'Other' Women and Postnational Feminism" in Barbara Caine and Rosemary Pringle (eds.), *Transitions: New Australian Feminisms* (New York: St. Martin's Press, 1995), p. 73.

27. Zillah R. Eisenstein, *The Color of Gender: Reimaging Democracy* (Berkeley: University of California Press, 1994), p. 4.

28. Minnich, *Transforming Knowledge,* p. 71.

29. Donna Haraway, "Situated Knowledges: The Science Question in Feminism and the Privilege of Partial Perspective," *Feminist Studies* 14, no. 3 (1988), p. 590.

30. Phelan, *Getting Specific,* p. 11.

31. *Ibid.,* p. 31.

READING 25

Feminism: A Transformational Politic

bell hooks

We live in a world of crisis—a world governed by politics of domination, one in which the belief in a notion of superior and inferior, and its concomitant ideology—that the superior should rule over the inferior—affects the lives of all people everywhere, whether poor or privileged, literate or illiterate. Systematic dehumanization, worldwide famine, ecological devastation, industrial contamination, and the possibility of nuclear destruction are realities which remind us daily that we are in crisis. Contemporary feminist thinkers often cite sexual politics as the origin of this crisis. They point to the insistence on difference as that factor which becomes the occasion for separation and domination and suggest that differentiation of status between females and males globally is an indication that patriarchal domination of the planet is the root of the problem. Such an assumption has fostered the notion that elimination of sexist oppression would necessarily lead to the eradication of all forms of domination. It is an argument that has led influential Western white women to feel that feminist movement should be *the* central political agenda for females globally. Ideologically, thinking in this direction enables Western women, especially privileged white women, to suggest that racism and class exploitation are merely the offspring of the parent system: patriarchy. Within feminist movement in the West, this has led to the assumption that resisting patriarchal domination is a more legitimate feminist action than resisting racism and other forms of domination. Such thinking prevails despite radical cri-

tiques made by black women and other women of color who question this proposition. To speculate that an oppositional division between men and women existed in early human communities is to impose on the past, on these nonwhite groups, a worldview that fits all too nearly within contemporary feminist paradigms that name man as the enemy and woman as the victim.

Clearly, differentiation between strong and weak, powerful and powerless, has been a central defining aspect of gender globally, carrying with it the assumption that men should have greater authority than women, and should rule over them. As significant and important as this fact is, it should not obscure the reality that women can and do participate in politics of domination, as perpetrators as well as victims—that we dominate, that we are dominated. If focus on patriarchal domination masks this reality or becomes the means by which women deflect attention from the real conditions and circumstances of our lives, then women cooperate in suppressing and promoting false consciousness, inhibiting our capacity to assume responsibility for transforming ourselves and society.

Thinking speculatively about early human arrangement, about women and men struggling to survive in small communities, it is likely that the parent–child relationship with its very real imposed survival structure of dependency, of strong and weak, of powerful and powerless, was a site for the construction of a paradigm of domination. While this circumstance of dependency is not necessarily one that leads to domination, it lends itself to the enactment of a social drama wherein domination could easily occur as a means of exercising and maintaining control. This speculation does not place women outside the practice of domination, in the exclusive role of victim. It centrally names women as agents of domination, as potential theoreticians and creators of a paradigm for social relationships wherein those groups of individuals designated as "strong" exercise power both benevolently and coercively over those designated as "weak."

Emphasizing paradigms of domination that call attention to woman's capacity to dominate is one way to deconstruct and challenge the simplistic notion that man is the enemy, woman the victim; the notion that men have always been the oppressors. Such thinking enables us to examine our role as women in the perpetuation and maintenance of systems of domination. To understand domination, we must understand that our capacity as women and men to be either dominated or dominating is a point of connection, or commonality. Even though I speak from the particular experience of living as a black woman in the United States, a white-supremacist, capitalist, patriarchal society, where small numbers of white men (and honorary "white men") constitute ruling groups, I understand that in many places in the world oppressed and oppressor share the same color. I understand that right here in this room, oppressed and oppressor share the same gender. Right now as I speak, a man who is himself victimized, wounded, hurt by racism and class exploitation is actively dominating a woman in his life—that even as I speak, women who are ourselves exploited, victimized, are dominating children. It is necessary for us to remember, as we think critically about domination, that we all have the capacity to act in ways that oppress, dominate, wound (whether or not the power is institutionalized). It is necessary to remember that it is first the potential oppressor within that we must resist—the potential victim within that we must rescue—otherwise we cannot hope for an end to domination, for liberation.

This knowledge seems especially important at this historical moment when black women and other women of color have worked to create awareness of the ways in which racism empowers white women to act as exploiters and oppressors. Increasingly this fact is considered a reason we should not support feminist struggle even though sexism and sexist oppression is a real issue in our lives as black women (see, for example, Vivian Gordon's *Black Women, Feminism, Black Liberation: Which Way?*). It be-

comes necessary for us to speak continually about the convictions that inform our continued advocacy of feminist struggle. By calling attention to interlocking systems of domination—sex, race, and class—black women and many other groups of women acknowledge the diversity and complexity of female experience, of our relationship to power and domination. The intent is not to dissuade people of color from becoming engaged in feminist movement. Feminist struggle to end patriarchal domination should be of primary importance to women and men globally not because it is the foundation of all other oppressive structures but because it is that form of domination we are most likely to encounter in an ongoing way in everyday life.

Unlike other forms of domination, sexism directly shapes and determines relations of power in our private lives, in familiar social spaces, in that most intimate context—home—and in that most intimate sphere of relations—family. Usually, it is within the family that we witness coercive domination and learn to accept it, whether it be domination of parent over child, or male over female. Even though family relations may be, and most often are, informed by acceptance of a politic of domination, they are simultaneously relations of care and connection. It is this convergence of two contradictory impulses—the urge to promote growth and the urge to inhibit growth—that provides a practical setting for feminist critique, resistance, and transformation.

Growing up in a black, working-class, father-dominated household, I experienced coercive adult male authority as more immediately threatening, as more likely to cause immediate pain than racist oppression or class exploitation. It was equally clear that experiencing exploitation and oppression in the home made one feel all the more powerless when encountering forces outside the home. This is true for many people. If we are unable to resist and end domination in relations where there is care, it seems totally unimaginable that we can resist and end it in other institutionalized relations of power. If we cannot convince the mothers and/or fathers who care not to humiliate and degrade us, how can we imagine convincing or resisting an employer, a lover, a stranger who systematically humiliates and degrades?

Feminist effort to end patriarchal domination should be of primary concern precisely because it insists on the eradication of exploitation and oppression in the family context and in all other intimate relationships. It is that political movement which most radically addresses the person—the personal—citing the need for transformation of self, of relationships, so that we might be better able to act in a revolutionary manner, challenging and resisting domination, transforming the world outside the self. Strategically, feminist movement should be a central component of all other liberation struggles because it challenges each of us to alter our person, our personal engagement (either as victims or perpetrators or both) in a system of domination.

Feminism, as liberation struggle, must exist apart from and as a part of the larger struggle to eradicate domination in all its forms. We must understand that patriarchal domination shares an ideological foundation with racism and other forms of group oppression, that there is no hope that it can be eradicated while these systems remain intact. This knowledge should consistently inform the direction of feminist theory and practice. Unfortunately, racism and class elitism among women has frequently led to the suppression and distortion of this connection so that it is now necessary for feminist thinkers to critique and revise much feminist theory and the direction of feminist movement. This effort at revision is perhaps most evident in the current widespread acknowledgment that sexism, racism, and class exploitation constitute interlocking systems of domination—that sex, race, and class, and not sex alone, determine the nature of any female's identity, status, and circumstance, the degree to which she will or will not be dominated, the extent to which she will have the power to dominate.

While acknowledgment of the complex nature of woman's status (which has been most impressed upon everyone's consciousness by radical women of color) is a significant corrective, it is only a starting point. It provides a frame of reference which must serve as the basis for thoroughly altering and revising feminist theory and practice. It challenges and calls us to re-think popular assumptions about the nature of feminism that have had the deepest impact on a large majority of women, on mass consciousness. It radically calls into question the notion of a fundamentally common female experience which has been seen as the prerequisite for our coming together, for political unity. Recognition of the inter-connectedness of sex, race, and class highlights the diversity of experience, compelling redefinition of the terms for unity. If women do not share "common oppression," what then can serve as a basis for our coming together?

Unlike many feminist comrades, I believe women and men must share a common understanding—a basic knowledge of what feminism is—if it is ever to be a powerful mass-based political movement. In *Feminist Theory: from margin to center,* I suggest that defining feminism broadly as "a movement to end sexism and sexist oppression" would enable us to have a common political goal. We would then have a basis on which to build solidarity. Multiple and contradictory definitions of feminism create confusion and undermine the effort to construct feminist movements so that it addresses everyone. Sharing a common goal does not imply that women and men will not have radically divergent perspectives on how that goal might be reached. Because each individual starts the process of engagement in feminist struggle at a unique level of awareness, very real differences in experience, perspective, and knowledge make developing varied strategies for participation and transformation a necessary agenda.

Feminist thinkers engaged in radically revisioning central tenets of feminist thought must continually emphasize the importance of sex, race, and class as factors which *together* determine the social construction of femaleness, as it has been so deeply ingrained in the consciousness of many women active in feminist movement that gender is the sole factor determining destiny. However, the work of education for critical consciousness (usually called consciousness-raising) cannot end there. Much feminist consciousness-raising has in the past focused on identifying the particular ways men oppress and exploit women. Using the paradigm of sex, race, and class means that the focus does not begin with men and what they do to women, but rather with women working to identify both individually and collectively the specific character of our social identity.

Imagine a group of women from diverse backgrounds coming together to talk about feminism. First they concentrate on working out their status in terms of sex, race, and class, using this as the standpoint from which they begin discussing patriarchy or their particular relations with individual men. Within the old frame of reference, a discussion might consist solely of talk about their experiences as victims in relationship to male oppressors. Two women—one poor, the other quite wealthy—might describe the process by which they have suffered physical abuse by male partners and find certain commonalities which might serve as a basis for bonding. Yet if these same two women engaged in a discussion of class, not only would the social construction and expression of femaleness differ, so too would their ideas about how to confront and change their circumstances. Broadening the discussion to include an analysis of race and class would expose many additional differences even as commonalities emerged.

Clearly the process of bonding would be more complex, yet this broader discussion might enable the sharing of perspectives and strategies for change that would enrich rather than diminish our understanding of gender. While feminists have increasingly given "lip service" to the idea of diversity, we have not developed strategies of communication and inclusion that allow for the successful enactment of this feminist vision.

Small groups are no longer the central place for feminist consciousness-raising. Much feminist education for critical consciousness takes place in Women's Studies classes or at conferences which focus on gender. Books are a primary source of education, which means that already masses of people who do not read have no access. The separation of grassroots ways of sharing feminist thinking across kitchen tables from the spheres where much of that thinking is generated, the academy, undermines feminist movement. It would further feminist movement if new feminist thinking could be once again shared in small group contexts, integrating critical analysis with discussion of personal experience. It would be useful to promote anew the small group setting as an arena for education for critical consciousness, so that women and men might come together in neighborhoods and communities to discuss feminist concerns.

Small groups remain an important place for education for critical consciousness for several reasons. An especially important aspect of the small group setting is the emphasis on communicating feminist thinking, feminist theory, in a manner that can be easily understood. In small groups, individuals do not need to be equally literate or literate at all because the information is primarily shared through conversation, in dialogue which is necessarily a liberatory expression. (Literacy should be a goal for feminists even as we ensure that it not become a requirement for participation in feminist education.) Reforming small groups would subvert the appropriation of feminist thinking by a select group of academic women and men, usually white, usually from privileged class backgrounds.

Small groups of people coming together to engage in feminist discussion, in dialectical struggle make a space where the "personal is political" as a starting point for education for critical consciousness can be extended to include politicization of the self that focuses on creating understanding of the ways sex, race, and class together determine our individual lot and our collective experience. It would further feminist movement if many well known feminist thinkers would participate in small groups, critically re-examining ways their works might be changed by incorporating broader perspectives. All efforts at self-transformation challenge us to engage in ongoing, critical self-examination and reflection about feminist practice, about how we live in the world. This individual commitment, when coupled with engagement in collective discussion, provides a space for critical feedback which strengthens our efforts to change and make ourselves new. It is in this commitment to feminist principles in our words and deeds that the hope of feminist revolution lies.

Working collectively to confront difference, to expand our awareness of sex, race, and class as interlocking systems of domination, of the ways we reinforce and perpetuate these structures, is the context in which we learn the true meaning of solidarity. It is this work that must be the foundation of feminist movement. Without it, we cannot effectively resist patriarchal dominations; without it, we remain estranged and alienated from one another. Fear of painful confrontation often leads women and men active in feminist movement to avoid rigorous critical encounter, yet if we cannot engage dialectically in a committed, rigorous, humanizing manner, we cannot hope to change the world. True politicization—coming to critical consciousness—is a difficult, "trying" process, one that demands that we give up set ways of thinking and being, that we shift our paradigms, that we open ourselves to the unknown, the unfamiliar. Undergoing this process, we learn what it means to struggle and in this effort we experience the dignity and integrity of being that comes with revolutionary change. If we do not change our consciousness, we cannot change our actions or demand change from others.

Our renewed commitment to a rigorous process of education for critical consciousness will determine the shape and direction of future feminist movement. Until new perspectives are created, we cannot be living symbols of the power of feminist thinking. Given the privileged lot of many leading feminist thinkers, both in terms of status, class, and race, it is harder these days to convince women of the primacy of this process of politicization. More and more, we seem to form select interest groups composed of individuals who share similar perspectives. This limits our capacity to engage in critical discussion. It is difficult to involve women in new processes of feminist politicization because so many of us think that identifying men as the enemy, resisting male domination, gaining equal access to power and privilege is the end of feminist movement. Not only is it not the end, it is not even the place we want revitalized feminist movement to begin. We want to begin as women seriously addressing ourselves, not solely in relation to men, but in relation to an entire structure of domination of which patriarchy is one part. While the struggle to eradicate sexism and sexist oppression is and should be the primary thrust of feminist movement, to prepare ourselves politically for this effort we must first learn how to be in solidarity, how to struggle with one another.

Only when we confront the realities of sex, race, and class, the ways they divide us, make us different, stand us in opposition, and work to reconcile and resolve these issues will we be able to participate in the making of feminist revolution, in the transformation of the world. Feminism, as Charlotte Bunch emphasizes again and again in *Passionate Politics,* is a transformational politics, a struggle against domination wherein the effort is to change ourselves as well as structures. Speaking about the struggle to confront difference, Bunch asserts:

A crucial point of the process is understanding that reality does not look the same from different people's perspective. It is not surprising that one way feminists have come to understand about differences has been through the love of a person from another culture or race. It takes persistence and motivation—which love often engenders—to get beyond one's ethnocentric assumptions and really learn about other perspectives. In this process and while seeking to eliminate oppression, we also discover new possibilities and insights that come from the experience and survival of other peoples.

Embedded in the commitment to feminist revolution is the challenge to love. Love can be and is an important source of empowerment when we struggle to confront issues of sex, race, and class. Working together to identify and face our differences—to face the ways we dominate and are dominated—to change our actions, we need a mediating force that can sustain us so that we are not broken in this process, so that we do not despair.

Not enough feminist work has focused on documenting and sharing ways individuals confront differences constructively and successfully. Women and men need to know what is on the other side of the pain experienced in politicization. We need detailed accounts of the ways our lives are fuller and richer as we change and grow politically, as we learn to live each moment as committed feminists, as comrades working to end domination. In reconceptualizing and reformulating strategies for future feminist movement, we need to concentrate on the politicization of love, not just in the context of talking about victimization in intimate relationships, but in a critical discussion where love can be understood as a powerful force that challenges and resists domination. As we work to be loving, to create a culture that celebrates life, that makes love possible, we move against dehumanization, against domination. In *Pedagogy of the Oppressed,* Paulo Freire evokes this power of love, declaring:

> I am more and more convinced that true revolutionaries must perceive the revolution, because of its creative and liberating nature, as an act of love. For me, the revolution, which is not possible without a

theory of revolution—and therefore science—is not irreconcilable with love. . . . The distortion imposed on the word "love" by the capitalist world cannot prevent the revolution from being essentially loving in character, nor can it prevent the revolutionaries from affirming their love of life.

That aspect of feminist revolution that calls women to love womanness, that calls men to resist dehumanizing concepts of masculinity, is an essential part of our struggle. It is the process by which we move from seeing ourselves as objects to acting as subjects. When women and men understand that working to eradicate patriarchal domination is a struggle rooted in the longing to make a world where everyone can live fully and freely, then we know our work to be a gesture of love. Let us draw upon that love to heighten our awareness, deepen our compassion, intensify our courage, and strengthen our commitment.

READING 26

Notes toward a Feminist Maternal Peace Politics

Sara Ruddick

. . . There is no litmus test for identifying a "feminist." Internationally and in the United States, feminism is a multifaceted social movement in the process of change and self-creation. When I speak of feminism I refer, minimally, to a politics that is dedicated to transforming those social and domestic arrangements that deliberately or unwittingly penalize women because of their sex. Second, whatever their other politics

From *Maternal Thinking* by Sara Ruddick © 1989, 1995 by Sara Ruddick. Reprinted by permission of Beacon Press, Boston.

and interests, feminists focus seriously on the ways that gender—the social construction of masculinity and femininity—organizes political, personal, and intellectual life. The feminist assumption is that gender divisions of work, pleasure, power, and sensibility are socially created, detrimental to women and, to a lesser degree, to men, and therefore can and should be changed. Most important, though perhaps controversially, feminists are partisans of women, fighting on their side, sometimes against, often with, men.[1] As women, or in solidarity with them, feminists struggle against any social, racial, economic, or physical abuse that threatens women's capacity to work and to love.

This is a general and elastic definition that leaves open virtually every specific disagreement among feminists about policy or theory. It is a definition that in no way commits feminists to antimilitarism. In many parts of the world, feminist women organize to procure arms in defense of themselves and their people and in despair of getting powerful, violent men to disarm. Some feminists support military recruitment in less desperate circumstances, arguing that women benefit from the wages, work, travel, and education military life offers; moreover, they insist, if allowed to prepare for and participate in combat, women could acquire the courage and skills fostered by battle.

More politically, many feminists believe that it is a part of citizenship in a democratic society to assume the privileges and burdens a military state imposes on its citizens. In the United States, individual men have bought and begged their way out of combat; Black Americans and other men of "minority" races have had to fight to be included in combat and command; "minority" and poor men are selectively conscripted for unpopular wars. Nonetheless, despite these violations, many North American feminists endorse an ideal of civic virtue according to which no class of people, whether marked by race, sex, or ethnicity, should be excluded or exempted from military combat and command.

Whether they are sober liberals or struggling liberationists, feminists can take heart from a developing feminist *women's* militarist politics. The feminist soldier heroine may be most perfectly represented by a young woman with a baby in her arms and a gun over her shoulder, although an armed girl dressed as and sometimes passing for a comely man is a close second. The many distinctly feminine, and often distinctly sexy, soldier heroines of exemplary spirit simultaneously domesticate violence, expand women's imaginative aggressiveness, and rewrite, in a manner titillating and scary, the sexual scripts of battle.

Whether or not feminists are militarist, feminist politics transforms maternal militarism. Like a women's politics of resistance, feminism shifts the balance within maternal practice from denial to lucid knowledge, from parochialism to awareness of others' suffering, and from compliance to stubborn, decisive capacities to act. This transformation begins, paradoxically, in a tense relationship between feminists and women who are mothers. Mothers and feminists cannot leave each other alone. Almost every feminist had a mother; many are mothers; few think coolly about the institutions and passions of mothering that shaped their mothers' and often their own lives. For their part, many mothers, even those who are feminists, fear that feminism offers heartless or oversimple solutions to the social and personal dilemmas of mothering.

Nonetheless, the actual confrontation of mothers and feminists—whether practical or psychological—is deeply beneficial to mothering. Although some feminists have indeed been guilty of contempt for mothers, no other movement has taken so seriously or worked so effectively to ensure women's economic and psychological ability to engage in mothering without undue sacrifice of physical health and nonmaterial projects. Organizing women workers, fighting for day-care centers, adequate health care, and maternal and parental leave, demanding birthgivers' right to participate in mothering as and when they choose—in these and many other struggles feminists have proved many times over that, as partisans of women, they are sturdy allies of mothers. In this practical support of mothers in their daily work the feminist transformation of maternal militarism is rooted.

Either because of their own experience of sexual prejudice and abuse or because they are heartened by particular feminist policies and fights on their behalf, many previously skeptical mothers become feminists. That is, with varying degrees of conviction, they tend to become partisans of women, able to focus on the impact of gender on their lives and to set themselves to change the sexual and domestic arrangements that oppress them. In becoming feminists, mothers acquire a "feminist consciousness," a confusing, often painful, but irresistible recognition that the stories they have told themselves bout "being a woman" are self-deceptive and do not serve their interests. With this new knowledge comes an unsettling conviction that certain realities of their lives are intolerable and must be changed.

Sandra Bartky's early account of feminist consciousness—suggestive of the later standpoint theory—is especially useful:

> Coming to have a feminist consciousness is the experience of coming to know the truth about oneself and one's society. . . . The very *meaning* of what the feminist apprehends is illuminated by the light of what ought to be. . . . The feminist apprehends certain features of reality *as* intolerable, as to be rejected in behalf of a transforming project for the future. . . . Social reality is revealed as deceptive. . . . What is really happening is quite different from what appears to be happening.[2]

For a mother, "coming to know the truth" includes looking at the real feelings and conflicts of mothering. It is a feminist project to describe realistically the angers and ambivalences of maternal love. A feminist consciousness also requires mothers to look undefensively at women's social status and the political relations between men and women, which exact from mothers— even those who are men—unnecessary and unacceptable sacrifices of power and pleasures.

A feminist mother's growing ability to name and resist the forces ranged within and against her undermines many varieties of self-denial to which maternal thinking is susceptible. This does not mean that cheery denial, inauthenticity, or self-loss in attentive love—to take only three examples—can be "cured" by feminism. These are temptations endemic to maternal work. But a clear-sighted rather than mystifying apprehension of "oneself and one's society," combined with real increases in women's opportunities and self-respect, shifts the balance away from illusion and passivity toward active responsibility and engagement. A mother acquiring feminist consciousness ferrets out the meaning of dominant values, asking whose interests they serve and how they affect her children. To be a feminist mother is to recognize that many dominant values—including, but not limited to, the subordination of women—are unacceptable and need not be accepted.

These feminist habits of lucidity strengthen maternal nonviolence in distinctive ways. Although mothers are committed to resisting violence directed against their children, children themselves often remember being betrayed by mothers, who blamed them for "provoking" the violence they suffered or who asked them to "understand" the violator. Nearly as frightening are memories of protective mothers unable to protect themselves from physical abuse or from silencing and contempt that border on violence. Feminists name the many kinds of violence women suffer—from lovers, employers, husbands, and strangers—and recognize women's tendencies to "submit" or take the blame for men's violence, or, worse, get their children to do so.

Although feminists may be appalled when mothers abuse or neglect their children, and although feminist voices are prominent in protesting the poverty and desperation that often lie behind abuse and neglect, it is sometimes harder for feminists to see violence clearly and condemn it unequivocally when it is committed by women. Nonetheless, in scholarly works, fiction, and letters to the editors, feminists have insisted on looking at maternal violence in order to understand and take action against it. It is a feminist task to identify the violence involved when mothers take nature as an enemy, breaking the wills and sometimes the bodies of children. More generally, when feminists analyze the effects of repressive sexuality or a maternal rage for order born of fear and deprivation, they also write about and against maternal violence. Feminists do all this as partisans of women, not only analyzing but also creating policies and spaces that give women the economic possibility and physical safety to take care of themselves and those they care for—to start again.

In sum, a feminist mother becomes increasingly clear-sighted about the violences she has suffered or inflicted and increasingly able to resist them. As she develops a critical stance toward violences that she previously accepted, she is also likely to become suspicious of the fantasies and theories that dominate organized, public violence. Myths of beastly males, alluring warriors, omniscient defense intellectuals, conspiracies, emergencies, and nuclear protection are all vulnerable to the lucid, knowing gaze. When conjoined with the commitment to protect, lucid, suspicious knowledge may in itself be sufficient to inspire a mother's resistance to militarist plans and "strategic defense initiatives" that threaten her children.

But lucid knowledge cannot in itself inspire a mother's resistance to violence that threatens "other" children, not even when it is violence funded and perpetrated by her own government. For extended maternal antimilitarism, the best knowledge must be motivated and tested by a sympathetic apprehension of *others'* suffering as "intolerable, to be rejected in behalf of a transforming project for the future." I [have] suggested [elsewhere] that there is a basis in maternal practice for extending the range of domestic nonviolence through maternal identification with other mothers' particular commitments

to protect and cherish lives. I have just celebrated the extension of sympathy in Argentinian and Chilean women's politics of resistance. Feminist politics too makes a distinctive contribution to transnational and transcultural solidarity among mothers.

Unlike maternal thinking, which is rooted in particular passions and loyalties, feminism explicitly proclaims an ideal of solidarity and loudly rues its failures to implement the ideal. The ideal of solidarity is a successor to an earlier ideal of "sisterhood," which some feminists espoused as recently as a decade ago.[3] The sisterhood of women was based on allegedly shared oppression and shared responsibility for caring labor. The romantic hope of sisterhood did not survive class and racial division, the marked disparity between the kind and degree of women's oppression, and the myriad cultural and individual varieties of women's participation in caring labor. Along with the ideal of sisterhood the idea that men were other and enemy briefly held sway. This militarist construction belied the alliances of women with men of their race and class and the affectionate camaraderie that often flourishes among women and men who are colleagues and friends. Nor could a feminism that identified men as enemies enlist the allegiance of countless women who, whatever their sexuality, loved men—brothers, fathers, sons, other kin, friends, and sometimes lovers.

The feminist ideal of identifying with women's struggles quite different from one's own survived romantic and militarized sisterhood. While feminists no longer claimed that all women shared a common oppression or common experiences of mothering and tending, they did develop an alternative ideal based on solidarity with women who suffered from and resisted sexual, racial, intellectual, economic, or other abuse. The ideal of solidarity does not reflect an attitude feminists have to any or all women. Most obviously, the subjects of feminist solidarity are women who suffer abuse from individual men or from sexist and heterosexist institutions. Second, whatever their individual experiences, feminists tend to ally themselves politically with women who are abused—out of whatever combination of class, race, and sexual oppression—as birthgivers, mothers, or female kin. Solidarity extends indefinitely with different emphases depending on the feminist. But it does not extend to "women" in general, but rather to women in particular situations of struggle.

A mother who is a woman acquiring feminist consciousness will likely encounter the ideal of solidarity among women, especially if she finds herself in the company of other feminists. Whether they meet in a shelter, reading group, health center, union, or peace action, feminists proclaim ideals of solidarity in explicit ideological statements, often through bitter recriminations and acknowledgments of failure that attest to the force of the ideal. To the extent that a mother herself acquires the ideal of solidarity, the purview of her lucid knowledge will extend to "other" women, including often mothers who are targets of her own government's violence. Solidarity with women in struggle tends to undercut military loyalty to states. It eschews abstract labels of cause or party—"communist," "fascist," "democrat"—in favor of a closer look at what women actually suffer and how they act. Military loyalties require women and men to kill—or at least to pay for and train killers—in the name of abstract enmity. Feminist solidarity searches among these abstract enemies and allies to identify with women's culturally specific struggles to work, care, and enjoy, to think and speak freely, and to resist abuse.

As feminism transforms the denial and parochialism that encourage maternal militarism, mothers are likely to act first against particular policies and forces of violence that threaten them and their children, then against those that are deployed by their own government against others, and finally on behalf of children anywhere who suffer violence. Mothers are not especially altruistic; nonetheless they are capable of responsibility and solidarity. Mothers engage in various kinds of action, from writing letters to blockading a military base, usually in concert with women and men who are not mothers, sometimes in groups that are specifically maternal or feminist. Insofar as they become publicly visible *as mothers* who are resisting violence and inventing peace, they transform the meaning of "motherhood."

It is also true that when mothers become publicly visible as peace activists, feminists may prove reluctant to support them. As many feminists have pointed out, women can act individually or collectively as women without making for themselves or for women generally typical feminist claims such as for the right to equal pay, promotion, and management, self-respecting sexual pleasure, control of the conditions of giving birth, or autonomy within marriage and the option of fair divorce. Any politics that does not make explicit claims about injustice to women will be seen by many feminists as diverting women's energies from feminist demands. Many feminists will be especially skeptical of a maternal antimilitarist politics that turns on women's identities as mothers, caretakers, kin workers, and shelterers. In drawing strength from women's work, this politics seems to ignore the exploitation of the workers and to reinforce a conception of women's responsibilities that has boded ill for women themselves. Unlike a women's politics of resistance that proudly draws on traditional identities even as it transforms them, a feminist politics subjects all traditional womanly roles to critical reflection.

Nonetheless, despite these inevitable tensions I believe that feminists strengthen mothers' power to act whether as individuals, in mixed groups, or in a women's politics of resistance. Feminists themselves point out that whenever women act publicly or in conjunction with other women they tend to acquire the self-respect and skills that feminists wish for all women. Feminist literature and art celebrate these strengths and consequently legitimate them for the women themselves and often in the eyes of their culture, whatever the cause in which they are developed. Less happily, it is also true that women acting militantly, once they are at all effective, are invariably subject to misogynist insult from strangers and political opponents and often from the men they live among. Despite local variations in vocabulary and emphasis, there is a depressing redundancy in the vocabulary of abuse: women's judgment is impugned as "crazy," "hysterical," naive, and sentimental; their "castrating" anger arises from sexual envy or deprivation; they are witches, whores, and lesbians. It is feminists who have deconstructed these terms of abuse, revealing the ways in which psychiatric insult, sexual superstition, and homophobia have been tools of intimidation that separate women from each other and deny them confidence in their minds, angers, and desires. In a feminist culture, even without explicit feminist support, contempt that would otherwise be dispiriting can issue in appropriate anger and pride.

In sum, mothers who acquire a feminist consciousness and engage in feminist politics are likely to become more effectively nonviolent and antimilitarist. By increasing mothers' powers to know, care, and act, feminism actualizes the peacefulness latent in maternal practice. Feminism has these transformative powers whether or not feminists are antimilitarist. As I have insisted, in any generous understanding of feminism, it is possible to applaud organized violence without violating feminist commitments.

It does not, however, follow that feminism and peace politics are opposed. Indeed, it is my belief that feminism is already conjoined with a peace politics that is marked by its double origins in women's traditional work and feminist resistance to abuse against women. It should be obvious that insofar as feminist mothers are antimilitarist, so too is that part of the feminist movement made up of mothers and mother-identified men and women. Quite aside from its maternal membership, there are inherently antimilitarist features of feminism. In revealing connections between making "masculine" men and making war, feminists cut beneath the abstractions of just-war theory to the sexual fantasies

and fears that sustain the allure of violence. Often feminists take violence against women both as emblematic of military and ecological violence and as causally responsible for them; to resist the one is to resist the other. Feminism is a global movement committed to a solidarity that respects differences despite anger and bitterness. Even in their efforts to support one another effectively, feminists have to invent the techniques of "peace."

It is not surprising that a distinctly *feminist* peace politics is one of the most vital parts of the international peace movement. If feminism at its most militarist challenges maternal militarism, is it unreasonable to hope that an antimilitarist feminism can effectively transform a latent maternal peacefulness into an instrument of peace? Feminist peace activists offer peacemaking mothers resources, theoretical insights, psychological support, and solidarity in action. The direction is not only one way. Mothers strengthen even as they are strengthened by feminism, bringing to a collective peace politics distinctive habits of mind and principles of nonviolence honed by daily use.

I do not want to suggest that feminism assimilates either to mothering or to peace politics. Many feminists are appalled by the conditions of mothering and by the women who submit to them; many feminist women are engaged in organized violence as part of their resistance to the unrelenting economic and racial violence they suffer. Nonetheless, there is truth—and hope—in the poster slogan "A feminist world is a peaceful world." A feminist consciousness can be both antimilitarist and maternal; the standpoint achieved in the feminist transformation of mothering is also a distinct and powerful antimilitarist vision. To paraphrase Sandra Bartky's account of coming to feminist consciousness that I cited earlier:

Coming to have an antimilitarist and feminist maternal consciousness is the experience of coming to know the truth about the social uses of organized violence and one's own excited or timid responses to them. Social reality, the reality of organized violence is deceptive. . . . What is really happening is quite different from what appears to be happening. . . . Coming to have a maternal feminist and antimilitarist consciousness is the experience of coming to know what violence does to one's children and to oneself, as victim or perpetrator, and then casting one's lot in solidarity with women who resist violence. . . . The very *meaning* of what the maternal feminist antimilitarist apprehends, the brutality and costliness of violence, is illuminated by the light of the peace that ought to be, by the promise of birth that violence destroys. The maternal antimilitarist apprehends certain features of reality as intolerable, as to be rejected in behalf of a transforming project for the future.

EPILOGUE

A feminist maternal politics of peace: peacemakers create a communal suspicion of violence, a climate in which peace is desired, a way of living in which it is possible to learn and to practice nonviolent resistance and strategies of reconciliation. This description of peacemaking is a description of mothering. Mothers take their work seriously and create a women's politics of resistance. Feminists sustain that politics, devising strategies, celebrating strength, resisting violence and contempt. Together mothers, feminists, and women in resistance are members of an "imaginative collective."[4] As a collective, the group draws strength from the act and symbol of birth and from the passionate labor of women who, throughout most of history, have assumed the responsibilities of protection and care. Yet because it is feminist, this imaginative collective subverts the mythical division between men and women, private care and public defense, that hobbles both maternal and peacemaking endeavors. As men become mothers and mothers invent public resistances to violence, mothering and peacemaking become a single, womanly–manly work—a feminist, maternal politics of peace.

The "imaginative collective" of mothers, feminists, and women in resistance is an odd political entity. It is made up of a practice and two political movements, each element often at odds with the other two. Either political movement would, on its own, transform maternal practice; together they work on the imaginations of mothers and anyone who identifies with preservative love. Actual coalitions of mothers, feminists, and women in resistance is rare. Yet the imaginative conjunction inspires a new political identity: the feminist, maternal peacemaker who draws upon the history and traditions of women to create a human-respecting politics of peace. The forms and ideologies of a feminist maternal peace politics are various and still being invented out of different combinations of maternal, feminist, and resistant women's commitments. Individuals participate in ways that their economic situation, political loyalty, temperament, and skill suggest. Yet even in its inchoate forms, this politics already contributes distinctively to the many-faceted, polymorphous inventions of "peace."

. . .

NOTES

1. The phrase "partisans of women" is Terry Winant's in "The Feminist Standpoint: A Matter of Language," *Hypatia: A Journal of Feminist Philosophy* 2 no. 1 (Winter 1987).
2. Sandra Lee Bartky, "Toward a Phenomenology of Feminist Consciousness" in *Feminism and Philosophy,* ed. Mary Vetterlin-Braggin, Frederick A. Elliston, and Jane English (Totowa, NJ: Littlefield Adams, 1977), pp. 22–34.
3. My discussion here is directly indebted to bell hooks's discussion of solidarity in *Feminist Theory: From the Margin to the Center* (Boston: South End Press, 1984).
4. I take the idea of an "imaginative collective," which I have found valuable in several contexts, from a conversation with Helen Longino following reading an article by Valerie Miner where Miner used the term: "Rumors from the Cauldron: Competition among Feminist Writers," in *Competition: A Feminist Taboo?* ed. Valerie Miner and Helen Longino (New York: Feminist Press, 1987), pp. 183–94.

CHAPTER 12

Feminist Theorizing

We have traveled a long road along the major sites where feminist theorists work. Along the way you have probably discerned some commonalities that justify grouping certain theorists together as this or that *type*. This chapter explores various groupings that make some theoretical sense and are generally acknowledged among feminist theorists. Before embarking on such typological efforts, though, we can gain a strong foothold by looking at a theorist whose ideas have substantially widened our road. Having launched this effort with her thinking and having revisited it along the way, I find it fruitful as well as fitting to come full circle by taking one more look at bell hooks's theorizing.

THEORETICAL PLURALISM

None of us gains by identifying ourselves as this or that type of feminist theorist, social theorist, or literary theorist. In practical terms, naming ourselves in greater detail often means narrowing the theoretical riches we turn to for inspiration and insight while limiting how our theoretical work is likely to be received. Besides, we cannot do justice to the topics that concern feminist theorists by relying on a single theoretical perspective. How, for instance, to theorize heterosexuality or selfhood or ways of knowing? How to conceptualize work, oppression, feminist consciousness, or the welfare state? Such dense realities invite an ambitious eclecticism, what is sometimes called theoretical pluralism.

Among contemporary feminist theorists, Sandra Lee Bartky, Patricia J. Williams, Susan Bordo, Gloria Anzaldúa, and many others do work that is insistently eclectic or pluralistic. Anzaldúa, for example, is formally eclectic.

469

She says, "I code switch, use a lot of Spanish and switch genres—I go from poetry to journalism, to myth, to history, to folk story, to lived experience, to theory."[1] Bell hooks also illustrates eclectic theorizing.

To get a handle on such eclecticism, let us look at the misbegotten but understandable notion that theory is a pie-in-the-sky enterprise. Too often its creators work at a level of abstraction far removed from people's lived experiences, if only because they get rewarded more for the technical polish of their work than for its human promise. Students' tendency to fear or scorn theory reflects that state of affairs. They seek (not unreasonably) concepts and ideas applicable to their lives. Also reasonably, they dislike needing their professors as translators of highly abstract theory.

At its best, feminist theory short-circuits such problems. As Elizabeth E. Wheatley sees it, a feminist imagination entails a "flexibility of mind" leading to "*feminist eclecticism*—the aims, claims, and intentions we articulate often depend upon the particular audiences who read and respond to our positions or who are affected by our political agendas."[2] To a considerable extent, then, theoretical eclecticism among feminist theorists grows out of their responsiveness to various audiences coming to their works with diverse needs and purposes. Centering our attention on hooks's work, let us now look at the specifics such eclecticism typically exhibits.

Hooks's work steers past undue abstraction. Rooted in the experiences of its creator and addressing timely issues mostly in the vernacular, hooks's theorizing is consistently accessible. Hooks talks about Spike Lee's films, violence against women (including herself), therapy and self-help, black churches, homophobia, Basquiat, and her grandmother's quilting alongside feminist consciousness and systems of domination. Her theorizing spans an unusual range of lived experiences, popular culture, and social-justice issues. Respecting rather than manipulating language, partnering theory with practice, and tackling matters of widespread interest, hooks turns out accessible work.

Her theorizing builds on insights like this: "As with any other 'hot' marketable topic, feminism . . . can be pimped opportunistically by feminists and nonfeminists alike."[3] A volume like the one in your hands can involve such pimping. It can take shape around market considerations as much as theoretical issues; it can mean more to its author/editor as a career boost than as a contribution to feminist theorizing and feminist education; it can focus on trendy topics rather than pressing problems. By pointing to the possibilities of careerism or even out-and-out hucksterism among respectable folks like scholars and academicians, hooks situates theory in the real-life circumstances where its practitioners work. She does not, in other words, let us think of it as something formulated Nowhere by a disembodied Nobody-in-Particular.

To the extent that it is accessible, then, theory is in touch with what is embodied, concrete, and sensory. Hooks writes, for example, that for the oppressed, the exploited, the dominated, domination is not just a subject for radical discourse, for books. It is about pain—the pain of hunger, the pain of overwork, the pain of degradation and dehumanization, the pain of loneliness, the pain of loss, the pain of isolation, the pain of exile—spiritual and physical.[4]

These sorts of pain inform all her writing, including her memoir *Bone Black* (1996). More generally, bodily experiences, concrete places and objects, and specific faces and gestures anchor her theorizing in the world of actual experiences, where the sensory is inescapable. Probably the most concrete theorist among the authors of our readings is Patricia J. Williams (Reading 13) whose analyses return again and again to experiences like those hooks describes as corporeal signals of oppression.

A third feature of hooks's, Williams's, and other pluralist theorists' writing is that technical language (or jargon) plays second fiddle to everyday language. These theorists write as if they are talking with us; theirs is the language of conversations rather than treatises, diatribes, or highfalutin monographs. Listen to hooks: "Oppressed people resist by identifying themselves as subjects, by defining their reality, shaping their new identity, naming their history, telling their story."[5]

Where hooks could have talked about resistance in terms of transgressive performativity or destabilizing deviations from hegemonic heteronormativity or other linguistically inflated usages, she points instead to activities all of us can more or less identify with and imagine. To identify oneself as a subject, for instance, conjures up images of saying to oneself, "I'm Somebody" or "I am entitled to better treatment than this" or "I can do something about this shitty situation." Although "hegemony" and other academic buzzwords do show up in her work, hooks largely abjures such usages. In their stead she favors the tried-and-true vocabulary of lived experiences, the lexicon of everyday life.

Much to her credit, hooks also abjures the narrative paraphernalia associated with academic prose. She rarely uses footnotes or parenthetical citations. Instead, she offers her incisive analyses in sturdy essays disrespectful of such conventions. Hooks says that she "actually spent a great deal of time deliberating on whether or not to use footnotes." Finding that many nonacademic readers take them as signs that a book is not for them, hooks made her decision "informed by questions of class, access, and literacy levels rather than a simple devaluation of footnotes. . . ."[6] Yet hooks's analyses do rest on grounds beyond her own thinking, on ideas from other theorists, themes from novels and poems, insights from popular culture. Hooks acknowledges such sources in much the way we acknowledge them in our everyday talk—by *mentioning* them, as when she observes that "the introduction to [Zora Neale Hurston's] *Mules and Men* can be seen as testimony, bearing witness to the 'fictive' scholar/ anthropologist [she] created for the sake of her work and the sake of her narrative." Similarly, hooks points out that "in *The Art of Sexual Ecstasy,*

Margo Anand reminds us that self-love enables us to experience pleasure, a sense of the ecstatic. . . . " On the same page hooks also cites
Toni Morrison's *Beloved,* specifically the passage where "Baby Suggs
preaches a prophetic sermon in the midst of nature, in the woods, calling
on black folks to love our flesh. . . ."[7]

Hooks's departures from the conventional forms of academic prose not
only bolster her work's accessibility but also show that theory involves no
radical break from the thinking and accounting that pervade everyday life.
Instead, theorists take greater than usual linguistic care with those activities while pursuing them with a self-consciousness unsustainable in
everyday life, if only because our daily projects typically require a consciousness freed for action by lots of taken for grantedness.

A fifth feature of hooks's theorizing is that it keeps struggle, exploitation, oppression, domination, and closely related experiences at the forefront. Rarely, if ever, does hooks stray into the decidedly esoteric, unduly
intellectualized arena where human suffering and struggle disappear as
language gets manipulated for ambiguous ends. Time and again, she underscores the lived experiences of indignity and the lived commitment to
resist it. She says, for instance,

> Colonization made of us the colonized—participants in daily rituals of power
> where we . . . find pleasure in ways of being and thinking, ways of looking at
> the world that reinforce and maintain our positions as the dominated.

Yet such pleasures can be forsworn. One can, especially in concert with
others, find "that space of refusal, where one can say no to the colonizer
. . . "; that space "is located in the margins." Hooks goes on to describe
"that marginality one chooses as site of resistance—as location of radical
openness and possibility. This site is continually formed in that segregated
culture of opposition that is our critical response to domination."[8]

A final feature of hooks's theorizing, its recurrent attention to praxis,
is tightly interwoven with her focus on domination and other forms of
robbing people of their full agency. Hooks never engages in "pure" theory disconnected from practice. The practices she advocates can be as
broad as seeing "love as the effort we make to create a context of growth
. . . " or as specific as seeing that "a repudiation of the ethic of materialism is central to transformation of our society. . . . "[9] Typically, hooks's
concern with praxis occupies a middle ground between generality and
specificity.

Hooks's theorizing speaks to the parts of one's consciousness that are
attuned to real-life, real-world challenges. Her concern with accessibility
and praxis, coupled with her respect for everyday language and lived realities in their full fleshiness, joins her with other eclectic feminist theorists.
Hers is a way of theorizing that is finding favor among feminists insistent
that theory serve urgent human purposes.

VARIETIES OF FEMINIST THEORY

Now the time has come to look at the various groupings feminist theorists constitute by virtue of commonalities across and differences among their theoretical projects. Any typology is ultimately arbitrary. Its measure is not, therefore, "truth" but usefulness. What, specifically, does such a typology help us see? Whose interests does it serve? These sorts of questions govern the construction and evaluation of typologies like the ones on our horizon.

Let us begin with two analytical issues generically dividing social theorists. The first concerns level of analysis, either primarily micro or macro level; the second concerns the locus of control, either primarily human agents or social structures and cultures. As Joan Alway implies, feminist theorists typically carve out a strong middle ground along both dimensions of theorizing about social worlds and their inhabitants.[10] Although some do focus more on micro-level phenomena such as the division of household labor or on macro-level phenomena such as the welfare state, they incline toward linking such phenomena to the larger and smaller structures, respectively, that help to constitute them. Thus, theorists of the gendered division of domestic labor commonly pay some attention to the gendered division of paid labor and the gendered distribution of rewards and opportunities in society at large. Similarly, theorists of the welfare state commonly tie their considerations to such realities as the patriarchal family, whose structure makes patriarchal welfare programs like Aid to Families with Dependent Children seem reasonable to more than resentful taxpayers.

More and more over the past two decades, feminist theorists have also been attuning their frameworks to individuals' agency alongside social structure and culture. Unwilling to reinforce views of women as passive or helpless victims, they have woven notions of resistance, transgression, and subversion into their portrayals of how social structure and culture bear down on and disadvantage women variously situated in the matrix of domination. In such theoretical frameworks female agents remain constrained, but their fields of effective action get enlarged and their prospects for achieving more than mere survival get recognized. Patricia Hill Collins's treatment of the power of self-definition (Reading 22) is illustrative.

Feminist theorists thus steer past some of the one-sidedness of other varieties of theory. Yet they do diverge in consequential ways. The most theoretically instructive divergences among them derive from how they address unavoidable issues in feminist theorizing. One issue is how much influence women's bodies and their material circumstances have on their experiences and prospects. Some theoretical divergence takes shape, then, along the materialist/idealist axis broadly separating those who emphasize the weight of material circumstances from those who emphasize the weight of consciousness and ideas. Those like Nancy Hartsock (Reading 15), who focus on women's bodies and the physical character of their work, diverge from those like Carol Gilligan (Reading 19), who focus more on how women think and the structure of their consciousness. This axis, like the others considered here, is a continuum whose endpoints are seldom, if ever, reached. Instead, theorists lean more or less strongly toward one or the other pole. Thus, Hartsock does attend to women's consciousness, just as Gilligan acknowledges their embodiment. Nevertheless, their frameworks tilt away from each other.

Among materialist theorists another divergence is evident. Some, such as Johanna Brenner (Reading 12), are socialist feminists working from a Marxian or neo-Marxian base. These theorists assign great weight to people's work and their access to and control over material resources. In their frameworks, paid work, its material conditions, and social class weigh heavily. Other materialist theorists are more attuned to embodiment than to its circumstances. Often influenced by Michel Foucault and French feminist theorists like Luce Irigaray, these theorists advance a somatic materialism that sometimes includes essentialist principles. Eclectic as her work is, Susan Bordo (Reading 14) sometimes illustrates such theorizing along anti-essentialist lines.

Another unavoidable issue among feminist theorists concerns criticism of the status quo. Since feminists are dissatisfied seekers of change, their theorizing necessarily criticizes current arrangements. Some criticism is lodged in frameworks that point toward dismantling the status quo, while other criticism presupposes its fundamental viability. Thus, some theorists come across as radical (or revolutionary, at least in the sociocultural sense), while others are liberal (or reformist).

Among the authors of our readings, bell hooks (Reading 25) leans toward the radical pole, where the very existence of the class structure and white-skin privilege gets called into serious question. Other theorists imply that such realities call for serious, extensive reforms but not extreme transformations, let alone upheavals, of the current culture and institutional structure. Carol Robb (Reading 16), for instance, believes some theologies offer grounds for making capitalist economies decidedly less unfair to women (woman-friendly, in fact), an outcome radical theorists see as impossible.

A third unavoidable issue among feminist theorists concerns those observable differences between women and men that extend beyond their reproductive systems and secondary sex characteristics. Constructionists emphasize that those differences overwhelmingly, if not entirely, derive from social conditioning and social positioning, while essentialists emphasize that they substantially, if not overwhelmingly, derive from physiology and anatomy.

English-language feminist theorists strongly lean toward constructionist perspectives like Judith Lorber's (Reading 2) and Myra Dinnerstein and Rose Weitz's (Reading 24). Some do, though, leave room for a measure of essentialism. Sara Ruddick (Reading 26) is illustrative. The largest well-known grouping of feminist theorists inclined toward essentialist assumptions, however, comprises Irigaray and some other prominent French feminist theorists, especially Julia Kristeva and Helene Cixous. To a large extent that inclination derives from the neopsychoanalytic perspective these theorists sometimes adopt.

Paradoxically, the same perspective that alienates some North American feminist theorists is the one that often lends great force to these and other theorists' work (for example, Nancy Chodorow). After all, as Lynne Segal reminds us, this perspective shows how "individual psychic realities consistently [fail] to reflect the consciously learned norms of social realities, exposing the[ir] inevitable incommensurability."[11]

A fourth issue that contemporary feminist theorists cannot avoid has to do with modernism and postmodernism. Broadly at issue is whether or not the circumstances of people's lives in postindustrial societies have undergone a dramatic enough transformation in the recent past to mark a transition out of modern conditions into postmodern ones. Modernist theorists such as Arlie Russell Hochschild presuppose a world with a decidedly stable structure whose meanings are substantially institutionalized and thus widely shared and whose members have identities that do hold despite their dynamism.

Postmodernist theorists such as Judith Butler (Reading 21) offer a different spin on the world. Their work revolves around notions of a world in flux, where meanings are continuously negotiated and contested, knowledges are substantially localized and thus not widely shared, and members' identities are destabilized and fluid. By now, a rapprochement of sorts is emerging along this axis. Barbara E. Marshall, for one, theorizes a "critical modernism" that is

> post-positivist, critical of the hegemony of Western "reason," listens to "local stories," rethinks the notion of a coherent pre-existing "subject" and rejects the universalizing impulse of "grand narratives" . . . without severing all ties to [modernism's] emancipatory aspirations.[12]

Marshall's critical modernism thus draws from postmodernist characterizations of society and culture while keeping firm hold of modernist values such as liberation and social justice. Similarly, Pauline Johnson wants to salvage some humanist values and projects without rejecting postmodernism. She emphasizes "freedom and life as universals without . . . attempting to underpin these claims to universality by any recourse to traditional natural rights theory or philosophical anthropology." Johnson thus favors a postmodern feminism that "understands itself as beneficiary and advocate of an emancipatory practical reason."[13]

In my judgment, the remaining bases for grouping feminist theorists are less theoretically important than the preceding ones. Among these secondary bases are social identity, disciplinary bent, and geocultural location.

Various social identities are sometimes invoked to illustrate the diversity and divergences among feminist theorists. The most common identities cited are sexual and racial. Often "lesbian feminist theorists" are presented as a distinctive grouping. Oddly (and predictably) enough, however, "heterosexual feminist theorists" or other sexually identified theorists are rarely cited as such.

True enough, lesbian theorists Julia Penelope, Sarah Lucia Hoagland, Claudia Card, Jeffner Allen, Joyce Trebilcot, Teresa de Lauretis, Judith Butler, Gloria Anzaldúa, and many others have made contributions about sexual identity, particularly as enacted in the lives of lesbians. Yet a great deal of the work some of these theorists do has only indirectly or implicitly (if at all) to do with their lesbian identities. Hoagland's contributions to feminist ethics, for instance, extend way beyond lesbian-specific principles; de Lauretis has shaped feminist film theory, not just lesbian-feminist film theory; Butler has theorized identity in general as rigorously as she has lesbian identities in particular.

To describe these theorists as lesbian feminist theorists is often, then, unduly limiting. I suspect that only those theorists who explicitly identify their work with that label are best named that way. In any case, such naming makes little theoretical sense if related labels such as "bisexual feminist theorist" are not also put into play.

Racial identity has also served to distinguish among feminist theorists. Like sexual identity, it is often invoked by the theorist herself as a way of identifying her priorities and commitments. Many, if not most, black feminist theorists identify themselves that way. Some prefer Alice Walker's "womanist" instead of "black feminist." Of interest here is hooks's observation that

> For me, the term womanist is not sufficiently linked to a tradition of radical political commitment to struggle and change. . . . I believe women should think less in terms of feminism as an identity and more in terms of "advocating feminism"; to move from emphasis on personal lifestyle issues toward creating political paradigms and radical models of social change that emphasize collective as well as individual change.[14]

In any event, the meaningfulness of grouping theorists by their racial identities raises the same sorts of issues as grouping us by our sexual identities. On the one hand, such groupings seem meaningful as theoretical markers indicating who has forged ahead in theorizing neglected matters such as lesbian motherhood, the experiences of paid domestic workers, or family making that goes against the grain of the white mainstream. On the other hand, such groupings seem misleading insofar as they are often taken to mean that lesbians and black women theorize only those respective subject positions, which is a far cry from the empirical "truth."

Similar ambiguities arise when one looks at disciplinary grounds for grouping feminist theorists, as Judith Stacey powerfully points out in Reading 28. Some emerge as feminist sociologists or anthropologists or psychologists who do theory; others, as feminist philosophers or feminist literary theorists; still others, as feminist film critics or feminist culture critics. As with social identities, disciplinary affiliations make for meaningful identifications in some respects. They alert us to the broad influences on a theorist's work and the scholarly traditions she is resisting and reorienting, if not rejecting.

But such labels suggest that a theorist's work is mostly for those in her discipline when, in fact, we stand to learn a lot about women's experiences and prospects from *all* women-centered theorizing. Besides, like most other theorists, feminist theorists commonly jump the fences marking off their disciplines. As Stacey suggests, they wander about the theoretical terrain in search of concepts, ideas, and perspectives that will advance their thinking and sharpen their insights, not for what will further secure their disciplinary affiliations.

Another basis for grouping theorists that strikes me as more consistently consequential but still problematic is geocultural location. Here one finds "French feminists" or "Australian femocratic theorists" or "Scandinavian feminist theorists." These labels, of course, describe the positioning of theorists in distinctive linguistic, geopolitical, and cultural communities likely to affect the texture and tenor of their work. Such labels do point to important connections between planetary social locations and theoretical products. Yet sometimes the singular contributions of specific individuals get lost in these groupings.

Let me cite one example, Christine Delphy. Trained in sociology, Delphy is an activist as well as a feminist theorist who works mostly from a materialist perspective. Her 1984 book *Close to Home: A Materialist Analysis of Women's Oppression* is a collection of her papers on unpaid domestic work, marriage, family, antifeminism, knowledge, feminist consciousness, and much else. Delphy argues, for example, that "marriage is the institution by which unpaid work is extorted from a particular category of the population, women-wives" and that "feminist consciousness is not acquired once and for all, it is a long and never-ending process."[15]

Trained as an undergraduate in sociology at the Sorbonne and later in graduate sociology programs at the University of Chicago and the University of California at Berkeley, Delphy is much less well known than her sister French feminist theorists Irigaray, Kristeva, and Cixous. Yet labeling her a "French feminist" is misleading because of how that phrase has gotten associated with the French triumvirate's work. To say a feminist theorist is Australian or Zimbabwean or Peruvian, then, is to say something significant but preliminary about her work. To that extent such labels seem hazardous except in the context of cross-cultural comparisons of theorists' work.

In sum, feminist theorists work from a variety of perspectives. The perspectives most in use are materialist and nonmaterialist, radical and liberal, essentialist and constructionist, and modernist and postmodernist.

Beyond those broad groupings much else can be said, as we have seen. Whether or not more needs to be said, however, depends on one's analytical purposes. All the while, such labeling of theorists can be hazardous, as Zillah R. Eisenstein further illustrates in Reading 27. She also provides a rich survey of theorists we have read as well as some we have not. Discussing the problems with theorizing feminism alongside our need for feminism, Eisenstein offers a virtual retrospective on some of the issues addressed in *Contemporary Feminist Theory.* She implies the theoretical pluralism stamping the work of many, if not most, feminist theorists.

In the last of our readings, Judith Stacey also offers us a virtual retrospective. Her first-person narrative in Reading 28 traces the intersections of her personal ("private") and professional ("public") lives. Her discussion of the disciplinary transgressions associated with feminist theory at its most daring touches upon many of the topics we have considered. Stacey returns us, above all, to the politics of knowledge, where her experiences with socialist-feminist and postmodernist perspectives inform her standpoint. Stacey also devotes attention to family, parenting, selfhood and identity, community, education, culture (and cultural studies), and unpaid as well as paid work. Hers is a border-crossing narrative in more senses than one.

POSTCOLONIAL FEMINIST THEORY AND BORDER CROSSING

Let me leave you with an extended introduction to another border-crossing theorist whose eclecticism is stunning and whose work, therefore, fits no clear-cut niche. Nevertheless she is often cited as a "postcolonial" theorist, thus illustrating anew the hazards of naming. Gayatri Chakravorty Spivak first got academic attention as a translator of Jacques Derrida's work. Thus, she was early seen as a deconstructionist, a portrayal she continually quibbles with and clarifies. Spivak grew up in India and earned her doctoral degree at Cornell University. By her own accounting, which situates her among other postcolonial theorists, she is "bicultural, but my biculturality is that I'm not at home in either of the places."[16] In general, "postcolonial" concerns theoretical work "that positions cultural production in the fields of transnational economic relations and diasporic identity constructions."[17] It thus concerns "hybridity," which Spivak likens to "androgyny" in early feminist theory.[18]

Spivak's feminism is far-reaching. Attuned to both privilege and history, she observes that "all of us who can make public the question of feminist practice . . . have been enabled by a long history to be in that position, however personally disadvantaged we might be." (p. 9) More specifically,

> the women who can . . . engage in this particular "winning back" of the position of the questioning subject are in very privileged positions in the geopolis today. So, from that point of view, I would not say that as a woman that my particular enemy is the male establishment of the most privileged Western tradition.

They are my enemy in the house where I give interviews, where I teach, and so on, but the house of the world is much bigger than that little house. (p. 42)

Spivak's feminism is geocosmic in its reach as well as profoundly aware of its privilege:

if I think in terms of the much larger female constituency in the world for whom I am an infinitely privileged person, . . . what I really want to learn about is what I have called the unlearning of one's privilege. So that not only does one become able to listen to that other constituency but one learns to speak in such a way that one will be taken seriously by that other constituency. (p. 42)

Moreover, Spivak sees that broad, diverse constituency as her "judges." (p. 70) To the women of the world, literally, she looks for validation of her work and certification of its meaningfulness. Understandably, then, Spivak has little patience with "high feminism," whereby women of considerable privilege look "in the mirror and define 'woman' . . . in terms of the reflection that they see there." Similarly, she is impatient with good-manners feminism—linguistic proprieties such as s/he, for instance—whereby "the phallocrats can be like real feminists." (pp. 119, 148)

This feminist theorist finds in novels like Virginia Woolf's *To the Lighthouse* grounds for "a thematic of womb-envy." Not unlike Irigaray, she "speculate[s] that the womb has always been defined as a lack *by* men in order to cover over a lack *in* man, the lack, precisely, of a tangible place of production."[19] That said, Spivak concludes that having "a tangible place of production in the womb situates the woman as an agent in any theory of production." Such a theory would center attention on the "woman in the traditional social situation produc[ing] more than she is getting in terms of her subsistence and therefore [being] a continual source of the production of surpluses." (p. 79)

Spivak surpasses not only her own attention to the womb but also Irigaray's to women's two pairs of lips (and two mouths) when she turns attention to the clitoris. Spivak sees that organ of pleasure as "a shorthand for women's excess in all areas of production and practice, an excess that must be brought under control to keep business going as usual." She thus proposes a "discourse of the clitoris" that might revolve around how its repression bolsters patriarchy and family. (pp. 82, 153) Such a discourse, one assumes, would counteract what Spivak calls "nuclear-familial hysterocentrism." (p. 83)

Although some of her thinking illustrates second-wave somatic materialism, Spivak is no essentialist. She does recognize, though, the essentialism that creeps willy-nilly into her own and others' work. Spivak sees it as a "trap" while also seeing that she is "an essentialist from time to time."[20] She aligns herself with those who "pick up the universal that will give you the power to fight against the other side," thus "throwing away . . . your theoretical purity." The alternative, as she sees it, is to join the motley crew of "the great custodians of the anti-universal" who "keep themselves clean by not committing themselves to anything."[21]

Thus does a sort of theoretical realism stamp Spivak's feminist thinking. So too does a fierce opposition to the binaries infiltrating most knowledge systems. Spivak sees feminist activity as a challenge to the public/private dualism. On that score she joins hands with many other feminist theorists, as we have seen. Spivak, though, stands out for drawing critical attention to another institutionalized dualism, namely, the "binary opposition between the economic and the cultural."[22]

As you may have already inferred from Spivak's concern with production and privilege, hers is a feminism drawn substantially from Marxian frameworks. In her judgment feminist theory must remain in touch with class, work, exploitation, and alienation, while Marxist theory must remain in touch with the gendered processes and structures of class inequality. Above all, Spivak illustrates that feminist discourse can be no "special-interest glamorization of mainstream discourse" (p. 130); the two discourses are discontinuous with one another from her standpoint.

That standpoint is distinctly postcolonial. Theorizing from what Mary E. John calls the "discrepant dislocations" of "immigrant feminists," Spivak uses a multilingual voice to interrupt the provincial standpoint whereby First World women theorize about their own situations as if their oppressive character were patently, even dramatically, obvious. Spivak bursts that bubble of relative privilege by situating her ideas within sweeping critiques of international capitalism. She observes, for example,

> No one can deny the dynamism and civilizing power of socialized capital. The irreducible search for greater production of surplus-value (dissimulated, simply, as "productivity") through technological advancement; the corresponding necessity to train a consumer who will need what is produced and thus help realize surplus-value as profit; the tax breaks associated with supporting humanist ideology through "corporate philanthropy"; all conspire to "civilize." (p. 90)

Such efforts to civilize often pass as "economic development," a benign phrase given that global

> economic restructuring is affecting all states, but the fragile economies of the developing states are getting more brutally "liberalized"—that's how economic restructuring is described. The possibility of social redistribution is being whittled away. All of these developing states are being redefined in terms of very small consumerist classes.[23]

In these "civilizing" and "liberalizing" processes Spivak situates the disenfranchised woman, whom she calls the "gendered subaltern." (pp. 102–3) Spivak says,

> I like the word "subaltern" for one reason. It is truly situational. "Subaltern" began as a description of a certain rank in the military. . . . [Antonio] Gramsci . . . call[ed] the proletarian "subaltern." That word . . . has been transformed into the description of everything that doesn't fall under a strict class analysis. (p. 141)

Left out of such analysis are imperialistic stances such as "Do not question Third World mores"; also left out is the "immense heterogeneity" of Third World women, who often get lumped together under that swift, simple phrase. (pp. 90, 136)

An antidote to such exclusions, Spivak's postcolonial work offers many multicultural riches. Class and race, in particular, stand alongside gender in her theorizing, which disrespects national boundaries except as markers of imperialism, neocolonialism, and other travesties perpetuating exploitation. Given the reach of Spivak's thinking, it comes as no surprise that she challenges—or at least complicates—yet one more dualism. Unlike the economic/cultural or public/private ones, however, this one positively informs a lot of feminist theorizing. In fact, hooks invokes it in the subtitle of her first book *Feminist Theory: From Margin to Center.*

Spivak problematizes the margin/center dualism by observing that in some sense nothing is central: "The center is always constituted in terms of its own marginality."[24] Thus, the "relationship between margin and center is intricate and interanimating."[25] So too is the relationship between voice and silence. In *The Post-Colonial Critic* Spivak says that she finds "the question 'Who should speak?' . . . less crucial than 'Who will listen?'" Aware that there are "card-carrying listeners, the hegemonic people, the dominant people," Spivak is also aware that "when you are perceived as a token, you are also silenced in a certain way." (pp. 59, 60, 61) Linked with that awareness is Spivak's insistence that "all political work is for human beings."[26]

Out of such thoughts comes a commentary on "theory" that is much in the spirit of hooks's theorizing. Spivak favors theory that "wants the other actually to be able to answer back" and that gets interrupted and informed by practice and vice versa. (pp. 42, 44) She characterizes her work as shaped by feminism, Marxism, psychoanalysis, and deconstruction. In that vein she identifies herself as "a very eclectic person" who "use[s] what comes to hand."[27] Resonant with that characterization, perhaps, are Spivak's thoughts about one's embodied positioning: "I think it's important for people not to feel rooted in one place. So wherever I am, I feel I'm on the run in some way."[28]

Perhaps that thought is a fitting one for drawing toward the end of this theoretical journey. As Kay Leigh Hagan puts it,

> feminism is at its best on the run, in motion. Its ideas become real in the daily lives of women inventing freedom as we go. Feminism is created constantly by women questioning everything, from a society that deems us inferior to men . . . to the feminist movement itself.[29]

Put differently, we can never achieve "a comprehensive or completely representative feminism."[30] Instead, we face the exhilarating pleasure and exhausting challenge of shaping feminism and feminist theory in the folds of our actual lives—in the interactions and actions we undertake each day, in the work (unpaid as well as paid) we do, in our growing sense of entitlement to a full, rich life for ourselves and other women, both like and unlike ourselves. For me, feminism is a lot like intimacy, as Hagan describes it: It is "a dynamic of awareness, assertion, and courage."[31]

NOTES

1. Eileen Hernandez, "Re-Thinking Margins and Borders: An Interview with Gloria Anzaldúa," *Discourses* 18, no. 1/2 (Fall/Winter 1995–1996), p. 13.

2. Elizabeth E. Wheatley, "How Can We Engender Ethnography with a Feminist Imagination? A Rejoinder to Judith Stacey," *Women's Studies International Forum* 17, no. 4 (1994), p. 412.

3. bell hooks, *Outlaw Culture: Resisting Representations* (New York: Routledge, 1994), p. 92.

4. bell hooks, *Talking Back: Thinking Feminist, Thinking Black* (Boston: South End Press, 1989), pp. 3–4.

5. *Ibid.,* p. 43.

6. bell hooks and Cornel West, *Breaking Bread: Insurgent Black Intellectual Life* (Boston: South End Press, 1991), p. 72.

7. bell hooks, *Yearning: Race, Gender, and Cultural Politics* (Boston: South End Press, 1990, p. 137); bell hooks, *Sisters of the Yam: Black Women and Self-Recovery* (Boston: South End Press, 1993), p. 121.

8. *Yearning,* pp. 155, 150, 153.

9. bell hooks, *Killing Rage: Ending Racism* (New York: Henry Holt and Co., 1995), pp. 16, 173.

10. Joan Alway, "The Trouble with Gender: Tales of the Still-Missing Feminist Revolution in Sociological Theory," *Sociological Theory* 13, no. 3 (November 1995), p. 221.

11. Lynne Segal, "Gender Uncertainties and the Limits of Psychology," *Women: A Cultural Review* 6, no. 2 (Autumn 1995), p. 216.

12. Barbara E. Marshall, *Engendering Modernity: Feminism, Social Theory and Social Change* (Boston: Northeastern University Press, 1994), p. 159.

13. Pauline Johnson, "Does Postmodern Feminism Have a Future?" *Australian Feminist Studies* 22 (Summer 1995), pp. 121, 133, 136.

14. bell hooks, *Talking Back,* p. 182.

15. Christine Delphy, *Close to Home: A Materialist Analysis of Women's Oppression* (Amherst: University of Massachusetts Press, 1984), trans. and ed. Diana Leonard, pp. 98, 118. For a fine survey of Delphy's work, see Stevi Jackson, *Christine Delphy* (London: Sage, 1996).

16. Gayatri Chakravorty Spivak, *The Post-Colonial Critic: Interviews, Strategies, Dialogues* (New York: Routledge, 1990), ed. Sarah Harasym, p. 83.

17. Inderpal Grewal and Caren Kaplan, "Introduction: Transnational Feminist Practices and Questions of Postmodernity" in Inderpal Grewal and Caren Kaplan (eds.), *Scattered Hegemonies: Postmodernity and Transnational Feminist Practices* (Minneapolis: University of Minnesota Press, 1994), p. 15; see also the special issue of *Signs: Journal of Women in Culture and Society* on "Postcolonial, Emergent, and Indigenous Feminisms," 20, no. 4 (Summer 1995). For criticisms of postcolonial work, see Djelal Kadir, "The Posts of Coloniality," *Canadian Review of Comparative Literature* 22, no. 3/4 (September/December 1995), pp. 431–42; Anne McClintock, "The Angel of Progress: Pitfalls of the Term 'Post-Colonialism,'" *Social Text* 31/32, pp. 84–98.

18. Gayatri Chakravorty Spivak, *Outside in the Teaching Machine* (New York: Routledge, 1993), p. 243; see also Ella Shohat, "Notes on the 'Post-Colonial,'" *Social Text* 31/32, pp. 108–9.

19. Gayatri Chakravorty Spivak, *In Other Worlds: Essays in Cultural Politics* (New York: Methuen, 1987), p. 45. Irigaray says "being deprived of a womb [may be] the most intolerable deprivation of man . . . "; Luce Irigaray, *Speculum of the Other Woman* (Ithaca, NY: Cornell University Press, 1985 (orig. 1974)), trans. Gillian C. Gill, p. 23.

20. Spivak, *In Other Worlds,* p. 89; *The Post-Colonial Critic,* p. 11.

21. *Ibid.,* p. 12.

22. Spivak, *In Other Worlds,* pp. 103, 166.

23. Spivak in " 'What Is It For?'—Gayatri Chakravorty Spivak on the Functions of the Postcolonial Critic: An Interview with Gayatri Chakravorty Spivak and Gloria-Jean Masciarotti," *Nineteenth-Century Contexts* 18, no. 1 (1994), p. 71.

24. Spivak, *The Post-Colonial Critic,* p. 40.

25. Spivak, *In Other Worlds,* p. 109.

26. "Gayatri Spivak on the Politics of the Subaltern: Interview by Howard Winant," *Socialist Review* 20, no. 3 (July/September 1990), p. 91.

27. Spivak, *In Other Worlds,* p. 77; *The Post-Colonial Critic,* p. 55. On how post-colonial feminists can use psychoanalysis, see Kalpana Seshadri-Crooks, "The Primitive as Analyst: Postcolonial Feminism's Access to Psychoanalysis," *Cultural Critique* 28 (Fall 1994), pp. 175–218.

28. *Ibid.,* p. 37.

29. Kay Leigh Hagan, *Fugitive Information: Essays from a Feminist Hothead* (San Francisco: Pandora Books, 1993), p. 2.

30. Diane Elam and Robyn Wiegman, "Contingencies" in Diane Elam and Robyn Wiegman (eds.), *Feminism beside Itself* (New York: Routledge, 1995), p. 7.

31. Hagan, *Fugitive Information,* p. 47.

READING 27

Imagining Feminism

Zillah R. Eisenstein

. . .

THE PROBLEM OF THEORIZING FEMINISM

I need theory because it pushes me to find connections outside myself. In the realm of theory, I generalize from what I know and stretch to think about what I do not directly experience. In the realm of theory, I am allowed to imagine other ways of being.

Theorizing pushes me to find the similarities that exist across and within the specificities that make me different from others. As an individual, I am both uniquely particular and similar to other people. The similarity constitutes what defines me as human; we are enough alike that we are not *completely* different. Without thinking about and theorizing these connections, we only have disparate moments; we are discrete, disconnected individuals, with no possibility of imagining a common politics.

Black feminist bell hooks writes of theory: "I came to theory because I was hurting. The pain within me was so intense that I could not go on living. I came to theory desperate, wanting to comprehend—to grasp what was happening around and within me. . . . I saw in theory then a location for healing."[1]

Feminist theory involves moving beyond the self, when the starting point is the self. It re-

From Zillah R. Eisenstein, "Imagining Feminism." Pp. 207–214 and 266–268 In: *The Color of Gender: Reimaging Democracy.* Berkeley: University of California Press, 1994. Reprinted by permission of the Regents of the University of California and the University of California Press. Copyright © 1994 by the Regents of the University of California. All rights reserved.

quires a notion of a collective "we," of the collectivities of women. There is a shared sense of other women who are like you, although not identical to you.

Feminists of color have rightly charged white feminists with not imagining far enough beyond themselves. White feminists, of varying political stripes, have tended to equate the experience of white middle-class women with that of all women. Feminists of color, such as bell hooks, Barbara Smith, and Chandra Mohanty, demand that feminism be rethreaded through the imaginings of racial diversity and the problems of racism. Recognizing differences, particularly the racial and economic differences between women, can assist in uncovering the way power is distributed among and between women. It allows an understanding of power and oppression, discrimination, inequality, and domination among women themselves.

There is a partial conundrum here. Feminist theories must be written from the self, from the position of one's life—the personal articulates the political. Yet such theories have to move beyond the self to the conception of a collective woman, which requires recognizing the diversity of women and the contexts of oppression. Some women are skeptical that such theory can be constructed.

Hazel Carby writes that there is no lost sisterhood to be found; that there are definite "boundaries" to the possibility of sisterhood.[2] White feminist Adrienne Rich has described the phrase "all women" as a faceless, raceless, classless category.[3] Black feminist Evelyn Brooks-Higginbotham says it is impossible to generalize womanhood's common oppression.[4]

Black feminist Barbara Christian believes that theory—particularly the feminist theory of the academy, which is dominated by poststructuralism—is exclusive and elitist. She is troubled that the overtly political literature of African American women and of the women of South America and Africa is being preempted by a postmodern view that assumes that "reality does not exist" and that "everything is relative and partial."[5] Thus, recent insights by women of color are dismissed as only partial, rather than as a needed corrective to existing views. Black activist and feminist June Jordan unequivocally argues that post-structuralism and deconstruction reflect the "worshipping of European fathers at their worst." They express the "tyrannies of language that are antidemocratic and proud of it."[6]

The critiques offered by Christian and Jordan help clarify an important difference between the postmodern focus on diversity and the political focus offered by black feminists since the mid- to late seventies. Most women of color focus on difference in order to understand problems of oppression: how difference is used to discriminate against people. They struggle to theorize a feminism that is diverse at its core, rather than to theorize difference as an end in itself. This differs from poststructural theorizing that inadvertently silences politics, because the connections of similarity are lost. Feminism is then often rejected, along with any recognition of women's collectivity.[7]

The excesses of postmodernism reject any focus on universalism or continuity in a transhistorical sense as essentialist. From this vantage point, specificity is set up in opposition to likeness or similarity. You must have one or the other. We are left with positions like Judith Butler's statement that gender coherence is a fiction.[8]

I do not mean to position feminism in opposition to postmodernism. Rather, I think that much of black feminist theory pre-dates and informs the developments of postmodern thought. Postmodernism has recently pushed feminism to defend itself as political argument, while feminists of color specify the different meanings of feminism.

Wendy Brown claims that feminists fear the disorientation and depoliticization of postmodern intellectual maneuvers. She sees feminists as too protective of their fixed and circumscribed categories.[9] She obviously is not thinking of black feminists like hooks, Smith, and

Williams, who have demanded a rethinking of the concept of sex class. Nor is she thinking, for example, of black feminist Angela Harris, who critiques essentialism and invites readers to subvert her own generalizations.[10]

Black feminist Bernice Reagon recognizes the problems with white feminist categorizations of women. She recognizes the multiple identities of women of color and the problems they pose for women's collectivity. "It does not matter at all that biologically we have being women in common. We have been organized to have our primary cultural signals come from some other factors than that we are women." She says we are not acculturated to be "women people," "capable of crossing our first people boundaries—Black, White, Indian, etc." Yet Reagon argues that political coalitions are necessary and possible. They allow for connection through conflict. Coalition work can create a commonness of experience between women because it recognizes, rather than denies, diversity.[11]

Susan Bordo, a white feminist critical of the abuses of the new poststructural pluralism, argues against the neutralizing of difference. If everyone is simply different, then it is no longer problematic; the problem of discrimination is removed. One needs a way to orient the context in order to distinguish between the differences: to compare and assess them in order to find patterns and similarity.[12] Significantly, Bordo asks: "Could we now speak of the differences that inflect *gender* if gender had not first been shown to make a difference?"[13] When we pluralize our understanding of power, we should not erase the continuities of power, but rather clarify the specific contexts in which continuity exists, in its various forms. The possibility of politics depends on theorizing—on recognizing connections.

Hooks argues that we need to be careful about how we think of theory and about the place of abstraction in theory and politics. She writes of the multiple ways blacks abstract and theorize in their everyday language. She is unwilling to accept the idea that theory is what white Westerners do.[14] It is important not to equate a particular kind of theory—abstracted, overgeneralized, and homogenized—with the very notion of theory. Various kinds of theory already exist within the personal narratives or daily life descriptions of women of color. We must recognize the way women of color express their feminist and antiracist politics in order to find moments of connection.

Audre Lorde argued that a major problem of the white feminist movement was its insufficient response to issues of difference: the refusal to recognize difference in the first place; the mis-naming of differences; and the disconnecting of the relations that tie difference together.[15] To say the least, such blindness distorts our differences of race, age, and sexual preference and makes them more problematic. Difference itself is not the problem.

How do we rethread the recognition of "power differences" into a notion of gender and racial equality which could redirect the assault against democracy for women of color and, with them, white women? We must rethink the political once again, as politics shift and are redefined through new locations of gender and racial privilege. The intersections of racialized patriarchy are key for defining feminist activity. By locating the particular relationships of racialized sexual domination, we can better understand the shifting nature of politics and the possibilities of an antiracist feminism.[16]

ON NEEDING FEMINISM

White women and women of color both need feminism, because women need a politics that names the problems of women through the structures of oppression across and through racism. Language is not helpful here. The phrases "women of color" and "white women" wrongly homogenize each and therefore distort the relationship within and between the two. Each group appears monolithic instead of formed of the particulars which define individual women's lives.

White feminist Catherine MacKinnon asks, "What is a white woman anyway?" She argues that the category "white woman" is often used to trivialize white women's subordination. It is used to delegitimize the idea of oppression as a woman—as though white skin insulates white women from the brutality and misogyny of men. Although there is some truth to this point, MacKinnon does not make enough of the complicated dilemma. The category "white woman" is used to divide women from themselves. Yet white women do have privileges as white, compared with women of color. The racialized aspects of patriarchy can be used to subvert the idea of feminism, but it is also the case that white skin privilege necessitates specifying the category "as a woman."[17]

The problem is that women as a homogeneous group do not exist, whereas feminism must posit that women do exist in some sense as a group.[18] Feminists need to distinguish between the false homogeneity constructed by silent exclusions (or silent equations)—such as assuming that white middle-class women represent women per se—and a real, viable collectivity of women rich in diversity.[19] There is nothing inherent in feminism or in the discourse of rights that denies the latter.

The fact that women's experiences are not homogeneous, as they have been falsely depicted as being, does not negate the existence of real similarities. White feminists have solipsistically assumed a stance of homogeneity which denies a truly democratic feminism.[20] Feminists of color have reacted to this stance by radically pluralizing and nurturing new feminist ways of writing and speaking. Susan Willis has called this method a process of "specifying."[21] The pluralism of the term "feminism" to "feminisms" was instigated predominantly by women of color.[22]

Feminist of color bell hooks has been at the forefront of the criticism of white feminism. She has suggested ways to open up and pluralize the relationship between feminism and black women. She distinguishes between advocating feminism and identifying as a feminist, in order to challenge the univocal stance of many white feminists.[23] She thinks of feminism less as a personal identity than as a politics. She fears that politics become reduced to the personal. Therefore, hooks moves from the "I" to the collective "we."[24] The move requires the dislocation of the singular individual to the complex plural. Also, hooks speaks of "women's movement" rather than of "*the*" women's movement" in an attempt to use language to refigure our perception of feminism as a process which is open rather than something performed and exclusive.

For hooks, feminism is not simply a struggle to end male chauvinism, but rather a struggle to eradicate the very ideology of domination.[25] Domination is a large and more plural category that encompasses the specific system of male privilege. Although hooks criticizes white women and "the" white women's movement for its racial and economic class bias, she has also struggled with black women to "separate feminism as a political agenda from white women" in order to "focus on the issue of sexism as it affects black communities."[26]

Barbara Smith, another significant early voice of black feminism, has argued that the simultaneity of the oppressions of race, gender, sexual preference, and economic class make it impossible to choose only one identity. The systems are integrated and interlocking, not simply added on to each other. The relations of power implicate each other. The layers cannot be simply taken apart because they are marbled.[27] Smith struggles against racism and sexism as a black lesbian feminist; she argues that black women experience racism not as "blacks" but as black women.[28] From a slightly different angle, June Jordan writes: "Overall, Black men dominate Black America."[29]

Chandra Mohanty, as an Indian woman of color, also writes with a critical eye about white women and the white women's movement, but her skepticism does not require her to reject the import of feminism as a language or a politics.

Mohanty argues that to disembrace the term "feminism" might be a retreat from the debate where women are central. Although there are keen differences of color, which oppress women both inside and outside the women's movement, Mohanty wants to imagine "potential alliances," which are not essentialist, but based in politics.[30] Cheryl Johnson-Odim similarly argues that we should not lose sight of the "fair amount of universality in women's oppression." Problems exist, but they can be addressed by allowing the "potential" bond of gender to underline feminist politics. This potential bond exists despite the fact that "women participate in the oppression of other women all over the world."[31] Conflict exists, but it does not have to be immobilizing. Feminist politics remain possible.

Alice Walker, black feminist and writer, has searched for a language which would embody the richness of feminism without this racist history. The term she chooses to use is *womanist*. It refers to a black feminist or feminist of color; it refers to outrageous and willful behavior; it refers to someone committed to the survival and wholeness of an entire people, male and female. "Womanist is to feminist as purple is to lavender."[32] It is a matter of shading. I wonder what has been gained with this subtle switch. What is lost is clearer: a language that identifies the continuity in the politics and history of feminism, however troublesome it has been.

Gloria Anzaldúa, a Chicana/Mexicana feminist, is wary of the "totalizing identity" called forth by feminist politics. She is eager to create *teorías* (theories) that enable us to interpret what happens in the world in specific ways "that will reflect what goes on between inner, outer, and peripheral 'I's of our ethnic communities." Anzaldúa wants to encompass the overlapping of many worlds, while recognizing that she is always partially inside and partially outside these Western frames.[33]

To create a feminist theory of women of color requires straddling a multiplicity of contexts. Often it requires rejecting the culture that oppresses women to affirm a once-colonized culture:[34] The various contexts do not merely parallel each other; they conflict and demand choices. Because there is no smooth layering that allows for easy separation, one's choice may even feel artificial and unsatisfactory.

Gayatri Spivak explores the further complexities of this point when she argues that one must try simultaneously to affirm feminism and to undo sexism. She writes: "I emphasize discontinuity, heterogeneity, and typology as I speak of such a sex analysis." Spivak does not want to obliterate race or economic class. Instead, she would like to chart "a sense of our common yet history-specific lot." One cannot simply make women's liberation identical with reproductive liberation or allow the problem of oppression to define one's liberation. One has to try to stand outside. In the end, the best one can come up with is provisional generalizations, rather than universals.[35]

Susan Willis's method of "specifying . . . represents a form of narrative integrity" which takes feminists to new sites in order to expand their imagination.[36] Important imaginings are to be found in music, daily conversations, everyday behavior, and actual political organizing.[37] When we explore such places, we hear the voices that explain why 85 percent of black women say they see a need for a strong women's movement (compared with 64 percent of white women).[38] When we visit the homes of strong and hard-working women in the African American community, we see some of the roots of feminism.[39] Feminism is not foreign to black women, even if the white feminist movement has been so.

Feminists of color embrace difference because they must; they focus on complexity and intersection because their lives demand it. So they struggle to find moments of connection and similarity, while recognizing the barriers of racism and economic class privilege. Feminisms of color push to radicalize a more inclusive and cohesive feminism by "specifying." This process moves toward a more inclusive democratic theory that continually reinvents universal claims by particularizing their meaning. It is a part of the continual process of democratizing feminism. As Trinh T. Minh-ha puts it, "The story never stops beginning or ending. It appears headless and bottomless for it is built on differences."[40]

NOTES

1. See bell hooks, "Theory as Liberatory Practice," *Yale Journal of Law and Feminism* 4 (Fall 1991), p. 1.

2. Hazel V. Carby, *Reconstructing Womanhood: The Emergence of the Afro-American Woman Novelist* (New York: Oxford University Press, 1987), pp. 6, 19.

3. Adrienne Rich, "Notes toward a Politics of Location (1984)," in her *Blood, Bread, and Poetry: Selected Prose 1979–1986* (New York: Norton, 1986), p. 219.

4. Evelyn Brooks-Higginbotham, "The Problem of Race in Women's History," in Elizabeth Weed, *Coming to Terms: Feminism, Theory, Politics.* New York: Routledge, 1989, p. 125.

5. Barbara Christian, "The Race for Theory," *Feminist Studies* 14, no. 1 (Spring 1988), pp. 74, 73. For a different understanding of postmodernism and the problem of racism, see Howard Winant, "Postmodern Racial Politics: Difference and Inequality," *Socialist Review* 10, no. 1 (January/March 1990), pp. 121–50.

6. June Jordan, as stated in an interview, "Voices of Change: The State of the Art," *Women's Review of Books* 7, no. 5 (February 1991), p. 24.

7. See, e.g., several of the articles in Weed, *Coming to Terms.* See also Kathleen Barry, "Deconstructing Deconstructionism (Or, Whatever Happened to Feminist Studies?)," *Ms.* 1, no. 4 (January/February 1991), pp. 83–5, for a highly critical discussion of postmodern feminism.

8. Judith Butler, "Gender Trouble, Feminist Theory, and Psychoanalytic Discourse," in *Feminism/Postmodernism,* ed. Linda Nicholson (New York: Routledge, 1990), pp. 324–40; and Judith Butler, *Gender Trouble: Feminism and the Subversion of Identity* (New York: Routledge, 1990).

9. Wendy Brown, "Feminist Hesitations, Postmodern Exposures," *differences* 3, no. 1 (Spring 1991), pp. 68, 73.

10. Angela Harris, "Race and Essentialism in Feminist Legal Theory," *Stanford Law Review* 42 (February 1990), p. 585.

11. Bernice Johnson Reagon, "Coalition Politics: Turning the Century," in *Home Girls: A Black Feminist Anthology,* ed. Barbara Smith (New York: Kitchen Table Women of Color Press, 1983), pp. 361, 363.

12. Susan Bordo, " 'Material' Girl: The Effacements of Postmodern Culture," *Michigan Quarterly Review* 29, no. 4 (Fall 1990), pp. 662, 664.

13. Susan Bordo, "Feminism, Postmodernism, and Gender-Scepticism," in Nicholson, *Feminism/Postmodernism,* p. 141.

14. See especially bell hooks, *Talking Back: Thinking Feminist, Thinking Black* (Boston: South End Press, 1989). See also bell hooks, *Black Looks, Race and Representation* (Boston: South End Press, 1992); and bell hooks and Cornel West, *Breaking Bread, Insurgent Black Intellectual Life* (Boston: South End Press, 1991).

15. Audre Lorde, "Age, Race, Class, and Sex: Women Redefining Difference," in *Out There: Marginalization and Contemporary Cultures,* ed. Russell Ferguson, Martha Gever, Trinh T. Minh-ha, Cornel West (Cambridge, MA: MIT Press, 1990), p. 285. For interesting and related discussions of the concept difference, see Carol Lee Bacchi, *Same Difference: Feminism and Sexual Difference* (Boston: Allen & Unwin, 1990); Zillah Eisenstein, *The Female Body and the Law;* and Iris Marion Young, *Justice and the Politics of Difference* (Princeton, NJ: Princeton University Press, 1990).

16. Gloria I. Joseph and Jill Lewis, *Common Differences: Conflicts in Black and White Feminist Perspectives* (Boston: South End Press, 1981; New York: Doubleday, 1986).

17. Catherine MacKinnon, "From Practice to Theory, or What Is a White Woman Anyway?" *Yale Journal of Law and Feminism* 4 (Fall 1991), p. 20.

18. Denise Riley, *Am I That Name? Feminism and the Category of 'Women' in History* (Minneapolis: University of Minnesota, 1988), pp. 1, 112. See also Johnnetta B. Cole, ed., *All American Women: Lines That Divide, Ties That Bind* (New York: The Free Press, 1986).

19. A few representative white feminists who address the issue of racism are Marilyn Frye, *The Politics of Reality* (Trumansburg, NY: Crossing Press, 1983); Ann Ferguson, *Sexual Democracy: Women, Oppression, and Revolution* (Boulder, CO: Westview Press, 1991); Minnie Bruce Pratt, "Identity: Skin Blood Heart," in Elly Bulkin, Minnie Bruce Pratt, and Barbara Smith, *Yours in Struggle: Three Feminist Perspectives on Anti-Semitism and Racism* (Brooklyn, NY: Long Haul Press, 1984); Adrienne Rich, "Disloyal to Civilization: Feminism, Racism and Gynephobia," in her *Lies, Secrets, and Silence* (New York: Norton, 1979); and Elizabeth V. Spelman, *Inessential Woman: Problems of Exclusion in Feminist Thought* (Boston: Beacon Press, 1988).

20. For a discussion of white solipsism, see Rich, "Disloyal to Civilization."

21. Susan Willis, *Specifying: Black Women Writing the American Experience* (Madison: University of Wisconsin Press, 1987).

22. Marianne Hirsch and Evelyn Fox Keller, in *Conflicts in Feminism* (New York: Routledge, 1990), p. 2, choose to reject the term *feminisms* as no improvement over the term *feminism.* It merely multiplies the problems contained in its original form.

23. See bell hooks, *Feminist Theory: From Margin to Center* (Boston: South End Press, 1984), p. 30.

24. Hooks, *Talking Back,* pp. 182, 105, 105.

25. See bell hooks, *Ain't I A Woman: Black Women and Feminism* (Boston: South End Press, 1981), p. 194.

26. Hooks, *Talking Back,* p. 180.

27. Barbara Smith, Introduction to *Home Girls,* p. xxiii. See also Combahee River Collective, "The Combahee River Collective Statement," *Home Girls,* pp. 272–82 [Reading 1 of this collection]; and Gloria T. Hull, Patricia Bell Scott, and Barbara Smith, eds., *All the Women Are White, All the Blacks Are Men, but Some of Us Are Brave* (New York: Feminist Press, 1982).

28. Barbara Smith, "Toward a Black Feminist Criticism," in Hull, Scott, and Smith, eds., *All the Women Are White,* p. 162.

29. June Jordan, *On Call: Political Essays* (Boston: South End Press, 1985), p. 38.

30. Chandra Talpade Mohanty, "Introduction: Cartographies of Struggle: Third World Women and the Politics of Feminism," in *Third World Women and the Politics of Feminism,* ed. Chandra Talpade Mohanty, Ann Russo, and Lourdes Torres (Bloomington: Indiana University Press, 1991), p. 4. Also see Chandra Talpade Mohanty, "Under Western Eyes: Feminist Scholarship and Colonial Discourses," also in Mohanty, Russo, and Torres, eds., *Third World Women.* For an interesting discussion of the complicated meanings of essentialism, see Diana Fuss, *Essentially Speaking: Feminism, Nature and Difference* (New York: Routledge, 1989).

31. Cheryl Johnson-Odim, "Common Themes, Different Contexts: Third World Women and Feminism," in Mohanty, Russo, and Torres, eds., *Third World Women,* pp. 316, 325.

32. Alice Walker, *In Search of Our Mothers' Gardens* (New York: Harcourt Brace Jovanovich, 1983), p. xi.

33. Gloria Anzaldúa, "An Introduction: Haciendo caras, una entrada," in *Making Face, Making Soul: Creative and Critical Perspectives by Women of Color,* ed. Gloria Anzaldúa (San Francisco: Aunt Lute, 1990), pp. xxi, xxv, xxvi. See also Cherrie Moraga and Gloria Anzaldúa, eds., *This Bridge Called My Back* (Watertown, MA: Persephone Press, 1981).

34. Uma Narayan, "The Project of Feminist Epistemology: Perspectives from a Non-Western Feminist," in *Gender/Body/Knowledge: Feminist Reconstructions of Being and Knowing,* ed. Alison M. Jaggar and Susan R. Bordo (New Brunswick, NJ: Rutgers University Press, 1989), p. 259.

35. Gayatri Chakravorty Spivak, *In Other Worlds: Essays in Cultural Politics* (New York: Routledge, 1988), pp. 151, 152, 208.

36. Susan Willis, *Specifying,* p. 16.

37. Patricia Hill Collins, *Black Feminist Thought: Knowledge, Consciousness, and the Politics of Empowerment* (Boston: Unwin Hyman, 1990), p. 202.

38. See Lisa Belkin, "Bars to Equality of Sexes Seen as Eroding Slowly," *New York Times,* August 20, 1989, p. A26.

39. An interesting study of teenage girls by Carol Gilligan raises the question of whether the impact of strong black women on black teenage girls may explain why black teenage girls appear often to have higher self-esteem than white teenage girls. See Suzanne Daley, "Little Girls Lose Their Self-Esteem on Way to Adolescence, Study Finds," *New York Times,* January 9, 1991, p. B6.

40. Trinh T. Minh-ha, *Woman, Native, Other* (Bloomington: Indiana University Press, 1989), p. 2. For a more particular historical discussion of the process of specifying feminism, see Aihwa Ong, *Spirits of Resistance and Capitalist Discipline: Factory Women in Malaysia* (Albany: State University of New York Press, 1987).

READING 28

Disloyal to the Disciplines: A Feminist Trajectory in the Borderlands

Judith Stacey

It is nearly a decade now since Barrie Thorne and I commenced a set of public discussions about the impact of feminism on sociology that we summarized in an essay with the somewhat reproachful title "The Missing Feminist Revolution in Sociology." (Stacey and Thorne 1985) The initial impetus for that project was my participation in a session at a National Women's Studies Association conference in 1982 that had the more politically specific, and, for its period, unremarkable title, "Socialist-Feminist Perspectives on the Disciplines." Few feminist conferences or lecture series would be likely to adopt such a title today, nor would I be likely, if one did so, to be invited,

From Judith Stacey, "Disloyal to the Disciplines: A Feminist Trajectory in the Borderlands." Pp. 311–329 in Domna C. Stanton and Abigail J. Stewart, (Eds.) *Feminisms in the Academy.* University of Michigan Press, 1995. Reprinted by permission of the University of Michigan Press. Copyright © 1995 by the University of Michigan Press. All rights reserved.

or to agree, to assess sociology under such an aegis. I remain committed to the ideals of economic and gender justice and to those of political and cultural democracy that once undergirded my earlier socialist-feminist identity, but too much has happened in global geopolitics and in feminist theoretical developments to sustain my earlier comfort with the first political term or with the dual structure of such an identity.

Moreover, I can no longer imagine undertaking an essay that presumed that sociology, or any of the existing disciplines, was the appropriate terrain to excavate for a feminist revolution in knowledge. To anticipate discrete revolutions in discrete scholarly disciplines is to betray a decidedly unrevolutionary conception of the disciplinary constructions of knowledge. Had such a feminist "revolution" occurred in sociology, should it not have challenged the discipline's recognizable borders or "essence?"

Shifts in feminist labeling fashions and in my own disciplinary self-conception index a significant set of transformations within feminist political discourse as well as in feminist relations to the disciplines. I discuss these transformations autobiographically by "reading" the trajectory of my own work as a feminist sociologist as emblematic, perhaps some will think it symptomatic, of shifts that have taken place in theoretical and disciplinary fashions in women's studies and social theory more generally. To take this tack is to enact my current "disciplinary" location as an ambivalently postmodernist, reflexive ethnographer. Or, for those unsympathetic with what some have called "the postmodernist turn in anthropology" (Mascia-Lees, Sharpe, and Cohen 1989), it may confirm the judgment of a hostile reviewer of my ethnography *Brave New Families* (Stacey 1990), who labeled its first-person narrative approach "self-indulgent."

Certainly, my trajectory is unique—indeed, in certain aspects, idiosyncratic—and I do not presume that the evolution of my own theoretical and substantive interests typifies that of feminist sociologists. The core of American sociol-ogy, if such a decentered discipline can be said to have a core, remains deeply positivist, while its diverse qualitative, interpretive, and theoretical schools have, in varying degrees, accommodated themselves to feminist inquiry without much evidence of conceptual turmoil. Thus, a great many—perhaps a statistical majority—of feminist sociologists continue to conduct valuable empirical research, often with significant policy implications, unaffected and unfazed by shifts in theoretical climates that I have found so compelling and unsettling.[1]

In fact, I believe that it is the idiosyncratic character of my feminist trajectory that might help to illuminate certain notable recent developments in feminist scholarship. My scholarship has always been centered not in sociology but, rather, on the disciplinary borderlands that have nurtured the intellectual audacity feminists have needed to think our ways radically through the disciplines. But in this regard I have begun to find myself increasingly out of step. A great deal of feminist scholarship today seems more entrenched in and bound by academic disciplinary identities than it did when Barrie Thorne and I recorded our reflections on feminist knowledge transformations.

The increased strength of disciplinarity observable in contemporary feminist scholarship can be read, of course, as a cheering index of our astonishing successes. In most humanities and social science disciplines today feminist inquiry has achieved undisputable legitimacy—in some, a level of acceptability approaching normalcy—and the demographic trends seem irreversible. The Sex and Gender section of the American Sociological Association, for example, has displaced the far-better funded research subspecialty of Medical Sociology as the largest "subfield" represented in the organization. In my own sociology department four-fifths of the entering graduate students in the last few years have identified feminism, gender, or women as one of their central areas of interest, and nationally as well as locally, sociology, like other social sciences and humanities disciplines, is a feminizing field.[2]

Yet I am worried, as well as cheered, by these achievements, for this success also breeds new intellectual and political dangers. Because so many feminists can now enjoy sympathetic collegiality and legitimacy within our disciplinary enclaves, there is less compelling impulse for extradisciplinary migrations. As it becomes increasingly possible for feminists to achieve (what was once unthinkable) a fully respectable and rewarded academic career within a conventional discipline, there is less incentive or demand for feminists to acquire counterdisciplinary language and research questions or to participate in the more transgressive forms of knowledge renovation, which I still consider to be crucial. I worry that this may blunt the critical edge as well as the public intelligibility of our once visionary project. Perhaps this anxiety signals my personal anomalous experience. For, precisely during this period of feminization and of feminist incorporation in my official discipline, I have been experiencing my own work and identity as increasingly marginal to "actually existing sociology." Is it this traveler or her disciplinary itinerary that has provoked this anomaly?

Sketched schematically my trajectory through my discipline travels from socialist-feminist historical sociology to feminist and "postsocialist," ethnographic sociology. I have spent most of my research time since my first year as a graduate sociology student at Brandeis University in 1973 studying family revolutions and always by transgressing disciplinary boundaries. The two major research projects I completed since then were preoccupied with a common set of substantive issues—gender, family, and rapid processes of broad-scale social change. They differ greatly, however, in their geopolitical settings, research methods, and textual products. The first, about peasant families and revolution in modern China, trafficked in historical sociology. The book that resulted was a theoretical analysis of secondary literature, organized chronologically and written in a conventional third-person narrative format.

(Stacey 1983) My second long-term research focused on family change among white, working people living in postindustrial "Silicon Valley," California. After three years of commuter fieldwork, I wrote an ethnography in a first-person, reflexive mode, which incorporated dialogic elements, organized the book somewhat novelistically, and dusted it with *post*-words. (Stacey 1990) In my current research, a collaborative study, with feminist literary critic Judith Newton, of male cultural critics, I am no longer studying family revolutions, but I am still gathering life histories to illuminate and intervene in broader political and intellectual transformations.

What little unity is discernible in my work lies in Left feminist political and theoretical domains rather than in research topic, methodology, or epistemology. For better and worse, I work as a disciplinary dilettante. If the undisciplined character of my academic affiliations is somewhat unusual, it has historical roots in the social movement that generated feminist scholarship. It seems crucial to note that, when I entered the doctoral program in sociology at Brandeis University in 1973, I did so as a feminist who had already participated in establishing a women's studies program elsewhere.[3] Indeed, it was my "conversion" to feminism, my commitment to emergent women's studies, and my desire to study and build feminist theory that led me to abandon a doctoral degree in education that I had been pursuing and to enter a social science discipline instead. Feminism was (and remains) my primary—and sociology a secondary, and, indeed, somewhat of an arbitrary—disciplinary affiliation. In fact, when in the early 1970s I looked for a disciplinary context in which to pursue my/our then new interest in feminist theory, I applied for admission to doctoral programs in anthropology as well as in sociology. Looking back, it seems less surprising to me that I should have migrated from the historical to the anthropological borders of my nominal discipline than that it has taken me so long to do so.

My un-disciplined proclivities met few constraints in the Brandeis sociology department, a decidedly maverick program that foregrounded and enacted the decentered character of the discipline that was depicted in one of the first influential books I read about my new field, Alvin Gouldner's *The Coming Crisis in Western Sociology.* (1970) Profoundly affected by the radical pedagogy and self-actualization ideals promoted by political and countercultural movements during the 1960s, the Brandeis faculty had eliminated a shared curriculum, or set of degree requirements. Even more unusual for an American sociology department was its pervasive hostility to positivism. Interpretive sociology and theory were privileged at Brandeis, and the privileged body of theory for my cohort of New Left veterans then was Marxism and its Frankfurt School elaborations. My sister graduate students and I quickly identified as socialist-feminists and steeped ourselves in the emergent Marxist-feminist "discourse," a word we had not yet heard of.

We were trailblazing here. Although there were a couple of feminists on the Brandeis faculty, they were no more advanced in this then nascent endeavor than we. Consequently, my principal graduate school experience involved a form of collective self-education. With and without faculty participation, feminist graduate students formed study groups in which we made up a decidedly transdisciplinary approach to feminist sociology as we went along. I also benefited from an exhilarating extracurricular graduate education. By participating in one of the Northeast coast Marxist-feminist groups that emerged in the early 1970s, by teaching (while learning) "Marxism for Women" at a local grassroots Women's School, and later, and most significantly, by serving for more than a decade on the editorial collective of the interdisciplinary journal *Feminist Studies,* I "interned" in feminist theory and developed my un-disciplined approach to feminist sociology. The startling overrepresentation of Brandeis degree holders among feminist sociologists who have published widely recognized work suggests the creative potential of a highly permissive approach to disciplinary training.[4]

This was the intellectual milieu that enabled the audacity of selecting for my dissertation topic a subject about which I had received no formal schooling: patriarchy and socialist revolution in China. Of course, the political milieu that fostered that decision was equally heady and is hard to recapture. Highly romanticized images of Cultural Revolution in China and wildly inflated (or grossly understated) reports that "Women Hold Up Half the Sky" were being deposited on overly receptive anti-Vietnam War shores by waves swelling in the wake of Nixon's historic thaw with China; these inspired enormous curiosity and enthusiasm among American socialist-feminists. Although twenty-five years had passed since the Chinese revolution, the Chinese Communists did not seem to have followed the disappointing precedent set by the Russian Bolsheviks in their earlier postrevolutionary backlash against family and gender policy in the Soviet Union.[5] I was eager to explore the sources and effects of the seemingly more resilient Maoist family revolution.

"Dual-systems" theory, the dominant socialist-feminist framework of the period, which presumed that gender and social class represent two distinct and interrelated systems of domination, influenced my original conceptualization of my study. Because dual-systems theory asserted the relative autonomy and equal significance of gender, it seemed then to be the most promising strategy for liberating feminism from the subordinate position in its "unhappy marriage" to Marxism.[6] Examining the history of the Chinese revolution through the lens of gender and family dynamics, my analysis pushed feminist claims for the fundamental significance and the relative autonomy of gender about as far as they could go. So far, in fact, that they upturned the dual-systems premise with which I had begun my research. The prerevolutionary agrarian crisis, I argued, was also inseparably a patriarchal peasant family crisis, and the resolution of that crisis through policies that built patriarchal socialism was a central vehicle for the victory of the Chinese Communists. Thus, I concluded, gender and class dynamics were inextricably intertwined in the Chinese revolution, and a fully feminist historical materialism rather than a dual-systems model was needed to comprehend this.

By the time I completed my study of the Chinese family revolution I was dissatisfied not only with dual-systems theory but also with the abstract and secondary character of this research and book and their remoteness from the agency of women to which I was committed theoretically. This fed my determination that my next project would involve the sort of primary, "hands-on," qualitative research, that I, like many feminists by the early 1980s, had come to presume was the privileged method for feminist research.[7] Coinciding with my newly expanded personal family commitments—the birth of my son in 1981—this conviction conspired to place geographic restrictions on my possible research fields. The demands and delights of delaying mothering, also characteristic of my generation of feminists, confined my field research options to locations accessible to my San Francisco Bay Area residence. In fact, it seems plausible to me that the emergence of what anthropologists George Marcus and Michael Fischer (1986) approvingly call "repatriated anthropology" in the United States may have been propelled by changes in the gender and demographic composition of their discipline as much as by a principled response to the politically troubled conditions of postcolonial ethnography. The influx into anthropology of women whose family commitments were less portable or expendable than those typical of their male counterparts would in itself have fostered interest in formulating geographically accessible ethnographic questions.[8] Certainly, my own ethnographic impulses were about to be "disciplined" in this manner.

It was during this personal period of research transition that Barrie Thorne and I wrote "The Missing Feminist Revolution in Sociology" (Stacey and Thorne 1985), in which, in a passing comment, we lamented the dearth of feminist sociologists who had chosen to work within the discipline's own rich, ethnographic tradition of community studies. This aside unwittingly foreshadowed the project I was soon to engage—my accidental ethnography of the families of white, working people in California's Silicon Valley. Once again I began with a vintage socialist-feminist subject—working-class gender relationships under postindustrial conditions. Again, too, I began with a historical sociological orientation. In fact, in the project's initial stages I was collaborating with a historian. Our plan was to integrate a historical overview of occupational and demographic shifts in the region and the nation with my untrained conception of a conventional sociological qualitative research design involving numerous semistructured interviews. The political impetus for this research, however, contrasted sharply with the optimistic and innocent motivations for my China study. It was my mounting concern with the antifeminist "profamily" backlash movement in the United States that had been "credited" by many as the grass roots kindling for the 1980s "Reagan revolution."

Given my geographic constraints, it is fortuitous that I lived within commuter reach of an ideal research site for my project. The Silicon Valley was not only a vanguard region of postindustrialization but also one in which the demographic indices of family change were stark and in which feminist ideology once had been articulate and politically consequential. While I selected this research site for its vanguard features, I chose to study a population that I erroneously presumed to manifest the opposite tendencies. Like most white, middle-class feminists, I regarded white and Latino working-class people as the most "traditional" in their family convictions and behaviors, and thus the primary appreciative audience for the remarkably successful "profamily" performance of the quite untraditional (and unsuccessful) Reagan family.

My formal research design, to interview a large sample of "Anglo" and Latino people working in and around the electronics industry, unraveled rapidly. As my book describes, two interviews that I conducted immediately after Reagan's landslide reelection in November 1984 profoundly challenged my own class and gender prejudices and provoked my surrender to the lures of an open-ended ethnographic quest. First, "Pam," a woman I had known for four months and thought to be a feminist, revealed to me her recent conversion to evangelical Christianity and her participation in Christian marriage counseling. One week later "Dotty," a survivor of an often abusive, thirty-year-long marriage, surprised me with her feminist convictions. Abandoning my research plans, I spent the next three years conducting intermittent fieldwork among these women and their kin.

This accidental—but, I later came to believe, overdetermined—turn to ethnographic methods shifted my disciplinary cross-dressing impulses to anthropology (the discipline that Barrie Thorne and I had earlier rated comparatively high in our feminist transformation assessments), just when that discipline was turning reflexive about the power/knowledge nexus of field research and textuality.[9] This was also a period when postcolonial consciousness, in addition to demographic changes, had encouraged increasing numbers of anthropologists to cross-dress as sociologists studying "others" at home.[10] Here, however, I enjoyed an advantage as a sociologist. Most practitioners of "repatriated anthropology" in the United States were still struggling for full legitimacy in their discipline, in part because foreign fieldwork has long been one of that discipline's best-equipped border guards patrolling the research terrain it shares with sociology.

Doing urban anthropology (or a postcommunity study) as a Jewish, secular feminist among born-again Christians and hard-living, crisis-riddled people more than sated my craving for engaged research. It also propelled me spontaneously to struggle with numerous ethical, political, and textual questions about representation and to engage with some postmodern feminist debates that, by the late 1980s, were beginning to migrate from literary criticism and the humanities into anthropology, and to a lesser extent into history, but not yet noticeably into sociology. I lost my feminist ethnographic innocence in the field, as I explain in an essay written in the midst of this upheaval, "Can There Be a Feminist Ethnography?" (Stacey 1988) Only a "partially" feminist one is possible, I concluded, intending both senses of the term and placing myself thereby in the camp of those who reject as utopian the claim that there is such a thing as a specifically feminist research methodology or even the view that any one method is specifically suitable for feminist research.[11]

The partially feminist ethnography I wrote about Pam and Dotty (and me) bears the traces of these disciplinary and political transitions. I structured the book as two documentary novellas and wrote it, against resistance from my male editor, in a reflexive, first-person, and occasionally dialogic narrative style. The novellas, however, are sandwiched inside a more conventionally authoritative, third-person, interpretive sociological account of the history of family revolutions in the United States. Thus, in its structure and style this book enacts my ambivalent relationship to the postmodernist turn in feminist anthropology and exhibits an un-disciplined feminist research and rhetorical stance.

The same tension besets the book's two central arguments. One is avowedly postmodernist, the other an empirically grounded revision of conventional sociological understandings of family and social transformations. I argued first that "the postmodern family" is a useful conceptual category for analyzing the transformation of gender and kinship that has accompanied and helped to shape postindustrial society. Literary critics in a Humanities Institute seminar in which I participated while struggling for an interpretive vocabulary for my ethnography prodded me to develop a theoretical understanding of the elusive concept of "postmodern." Not surprisingly, therefore, I turned to humanists to explicate what I meant when I used "the postmodern family" to signal the collapse of a hegemonic family system. I found that I could readily apply art historian Clive Dilnot's answers to his own rhetorical question, "What is the post-modern?" in an essay on postmodern culture, to current family conditions in the United States. The postmodern, Dilnot maintains, "is first, an uncertainty, an insecurity, a doubt." Most of the *post*-words provoke uneasiness, because they imply, simultaneously, "both the end, or at least the radical transformation of, a familiar pattern of activity or group of ideas," and the emergence of "new fields of cultural activity whose contours are still unclear and whose meanings and implications . . . cannot yet be fathomed." (Dilnot 1986, p. 245) The postmodern, moreover, is "characterized by the process of the linking up of areas and the crossing of the boundaries of what are conventionally considered to be disparate realms of practice." (p. 249) Similarly, I argued that contemporary U.S. family arrangements are diverse, fluid, and unresolved and that *the* postmodern family is not a new model of family life equivalent to that of the modern family, not the next stage in an orderly progression of family history but, rather, the stage in that history when the belief in a logical progression of stages breaks down. Donning unmistakable postmodernist drag, I wrote: "Rupturing the teleology of modernization narratives that depict an evolutionary history of the family and incorporating both experimental and nostalgic elements, 'the' postmodern family lurches forward and backward into an uncertain future."

The book's second major argument, however, remained a plainclothes' historical sociological one about family revolutions and vanguard classes. A major shift, I argued, has taken place in the class direction of U.S. family change. Most historians agree that the white middle classes were in the vanguard of the "modern" family revolution, that is, the transformation from a premodern, corporate, patriarchal family economy to the male breadwinner "companionate" family that transpired between the late eighteenth and the early twentieth centuries. Although the modern family pattern achieved cultural and statistical dominance, most working-class people attained the male family wage, their economic passport to its practice, very late, if at all. I interpreted this to suggest that by the time, the 1960s, that white working-class people got there, another family revolution was already well under way. Once again middle-class, white families appeared to be in the vanguard; frustrated middle-class homemakers and their more militant daughters subjected modern domesticity to a sustained critique, at times with little sensitivity to the effects our antimodern family ideology might have on women, for whom full-time domesticity had rarely been feasible. Thus, feminist family reform came to be regarded widely as a white, middle-class agenda and white, working-class families its most resistant adversaries. These, after all, had been the presumptions that led me to focus my study of postindustrial family change on white, working-class people in the first place.

But this time appearances were deceptive. Field research convinced me that white, middle-class families have been less the innovators than the propagandists and principal beneficiaries of contemporary family change. Instead, I argued that postindustrial conditions have reversed the trickle-down trajectory of family change once predicted by modernization theorists. By studying a family revolution ethnographically, I upturned many of my preconceptions about gender, class, and even about born-again Christianity more profoundly than would have been possible using only the more distant research methods of historical sociology. I discovered on the ground, for example, that evangelical Christians are not monolithically antifeminist, nor are their family relationships uniformly "traditional" or patriarchal. And I observed firsthand some of the ways in which many evangelical women and even antifeminist women have been reinventing family forms as creatively as have many feminists. Feminists have received far too much credit and blame for instigating postmodern contests over the meaning of "the family," perhaps because we have done so much to challenge the "essentialist" connotations of the term.

Ethnographic research also brought "home" for me the grounds for pervasive ambivalence about postmodern family and social crises. Observing the everyday traumas and tragedies caused by the irrationality and injustice of contemporary occupational and social conditions reinforced my feminist and still democratic socialist beliefs that equitable, humane, and democratic gender and family policies could go a long way to alleviate "surplus" family oppression that most women and many men suffer. But I no longer fantasize (as I did when I concluded my book on China with the claim that the People's Republic of China [PRC] had achieved a family revolution but not a feminist family revolution) that even a feminist family revolution could put an end to family distress. There are human costs to the fruition of a fully voluntary sexual and kinship system that no social policy can fully eradicate. No nostalgic efforts to restore the traditional modern family system, however, can offer a more effective, let alone democratic, resolution to family upheaval. For better or worse, the postmodern family revolution is here to stay.

The last chapter of *Brave New Families* ends on that note—indeed, with that sentence. It acknowledges just cause for widespread ambivalence about postmodern family and social conditions but offers no parallel reflections on my own ambivalence about my current relationship to feminist sociology and postmodernist theo-

ries. The book itself does not end there, however. Displaying, perhaps allaying, some of my unresolved ethical–textual–political anxieties, I chose to end the book instead with an epilogue in which Pamela appears to have the provocative last word on my reading of her life: "You could never capture me." This somewhat disingenuous democratic gesture, which masks my asymmetrical control over the dialogic and textual conditions of its production, also signals the straddle position I currently occupy within and among contemporary debates about feminism and ethnography.

While my ethnographic rhetorical strategies in *Brave New Families* were somewhat reflexive, dialogic, and decentered, they produced a book that remained incurably humanist in the same sense that feminism and socialism have been humanist projects, committed to the emancipation of subjects who are comfortable naming themselves in gender and class terms. My humanist feminism sympathizes with the critique made by Francis Mascia-Lees, Patricia Sharpe, and Colleen Cohen (1989) of the premature forfeit of a female subject and of the frequent excesses of textual experimentation for its own sake sometimes found in "the postmodernist turn in anthropology." Nonetheless, I am not willing to polarize feminism and postmodernism in this way, for I believe that feminism has been one of the enabling conditions for, as well as a generative force in, the development of theoretical developments often designated loosely as "postmodern." Gender crises embedded in the kinds of family revolutions I have studied through both historical sociology and ethnography have been among the important sources of the crisis of representation, the critiques of unified subjectivity, and the preoccupation with questions of difference, identity, failure, and authority that galvanize postmodern theories.

Consequently, I have recently turned from the study of family revolutions to a project designed to explore the relationships between feminism and postmodernist cultural criticism by men. Migrating even further "afield" from most sociological projects, and adopting the surprising new feminist fashion here of studying men, I am collaborating with feminist literary critic Judith Newton on a project that combines ethnographic and literary critical approaches to contemporary fashions in cultural critique. I suspect that both my choice of collaborator and the linguistic shift evident in our defining this project as *cultural* rather than *social* criticism reflect and reinforce recent shifts in the primary locus of feminist and other radical theories. First, the historic collapse of "actually existing socialist societies" has deepened a crisis in Marxist social thought. At the same time, and perhaps as a result, a right-wing intellectual backlash in the United States has directed much of its energies to an assault on feminist and multicultural challenges to the classic Western canon. Perhaps this explains why the gravitational center of critical theory seems to have swung from the social sciences to literary criticism and the humanities.[12] I worry about and want to understand this tendency even as I find myself participating in it. Thus, beginning with the "new historicism" in literary studies and with what some have termed "the new ethnography" in anthropology, Judith Newton and I began to study and rewrite the stories of the genesis of these discourses in ways that write feminisms into the narrative of these postmodern "turns," even if primarily as a displaced "other." (Newton and Stacey 1993)[13]

As we navigate our routes through the turbulent waters of postmodern feminist debates on men "in" or "and" feminism,[14] we are pursuing a middle course that we began charting while team-teaching a graduate seminar on feminist theory. With most of our students we found many insights developed by feminist and other postmodern theorists persuasive and useful. Striving for ethnographic and textual reflexivity about the nexus of power and knowledge in cultural research and representation seems crucial to us, as do efforts to historicize the conceptual

vocabulary feminists employ in our work. Feminists of color, along with other postcolonial as well as postmodern critics, have taught us to mistrust dominant conceptual categories that falsely universalize the experiences and conditions of dominant subjects.[15] And, like other feminists influenced by Foucault, we understand power to be productive as well as repressive.

At the same time, however, we retain conceptions that some poststructuralist theorists eschew, still finding fruitful notions of agency, experience, resistance, and social referentiality, even if the social world that agents construct, experience, and resist is one in which images dominate and, to a significant extent, constitute social reality. Thus, while I can no longer sustain the socialist-feminist confidence with which I once represented the narrative of family revolution in China, and I now find all metanarratives to be inevitably provisional, I nonetheless find them indispensable vehicles for representing relationships of power and injustice, such as those distributed along old-fashioned axes of gender, class, race, and sexuality. For this reason (and others) I am willing to employ, as Gayatri Spivak advocates, a "strategic" use of essentialism. (Spivak 1990, p. 10) Indeed, I confess that, reminded during the Gulf War of the ubiquity of male associations with militarism and physical violence, I found myself entertaining more than strategic ideas about essentialism. I even dared publicly to interrogate monolithic refusals by most feminists, like myself, to consider the possibility that biology might provide more than a semiotic resource for the more lethal aspects of masculinity.[16]

As my trajectory picks its un-disciplined and anxious way through feminist and other bodies of postmodern social theory, my feminist colleagues in literary criticism report a mounting feminist backlash in their discipline against the hegemony of poststructuralist theories, while some feminist critics of postmodern anthropology appear to be moving beyond critique to creative appropriations.[17] Meanwhile, ironically enough, my home discipline, sociology, is exhibiting increasing symptoms of postmodern courtship: sessions on postmodern selfhood and society have begun to infuse the annual meetings of the American Sociological Association; a late 1990 issue of *Social Problems,* the official journal of the Society for the Study of Social Problems (SSSP), an organization and publication heretofore more noted for its liberal and Marxist sensibilities, featured "Three Papers on Postmodernity and Panic" (one by the 1991–92 president of the organization), followed by "Two Papers on Feminism, Language and Postmodern" (*Social Problems* [November 1990]); and the theme of the 1992 meeting of the SSSP was explicitly "Postmodernity as a Social Problem: Race, Class, Gender and the *New World Order.*"

Interestingly, perhaps perversely, just as the postmodern theory industry has begun to outsource some of its knowledge production sites from a humanities "core" to an anthropological "semiperiphery" to heretofore peripheral sociology, "cultural studies" has migrated from Birmingham, England, to displace postmodern theory, as well as feminist theory, as the favored sign and institutional site for left-wing inter-, trans-, and counterdisciplinary intellectual work in the United States. The rise of cultural studies over the past few years has been meteoric, with new centers, institutes, conferences, journals, graduate programs, and even undergraduate majors proliferating, despite the severe, often devastating, impact of the economic crisis on higher education. Moreover, this displacement of postmodern theory by cultural studies seems to be coinciding with a notable transfer of intellectual energies from gender and class—the foundational cross-bars of socialist feminism—to race and sexuality as the privileged sites of radical theorizing. What is more, this shift from gender and class to race and sexuality is evident not only in the U.S. version of cultural studies, broadly defined, but even within women's studies and feminist theory. So fully has feminist attention to differences among women and to conceptions of multiple subjectivities displaced unitary formulations of gender differences between women and men that it has become challenging to decide whether one still can identify an intellectual terrain that remains a specifically *feminist* project.

Indeed, what many feminists of color came to label "white feminist theory" has been so successfully "mainstreamed" into most of the humanities and a few of the social sciences that queer theory and multiculturalism are displacing feminism as the primary targets of conservative backlash. New Leftist-turned-neoconservative intellectual entrepreneur David Horowitz makes the vanguard role of queer theory explicit in "Queer Revolution: The Last Stage of Radicalism," a rather loathsome diatribe he presented at a self-consciously backlash session of the 1992 meetings of the American Studies Association. Parodying *The Communist Manifesto,* Horowitz begins: "A specter is haunting the American academy, the last refuge of the political left. It is the specter of queer theory."[18] He proceeds to portray queer theory as the final assault by radical theories of social construction on nature, normalcy, and civilization, thereby transferring to queer revolution the privileged status of pariah once "enjoyed" by feminism. Similarly, the widespread political backlash against affirmative action, both on and off U.S. campuses, seems to be directed more vocally against compensatory remedies for racial than gender imbalances.

The rhetoric and outcomes of the 1992 electoral campaign reflected these shifts, as homophobia and racism proved far more potent than sexism in galvanizing backlash voters. Tangible feminist gains in the "Year of the Woman" coincided with antigay rights victories in Colorado and in Tampa, Florida, and a frighteningly close call for a draconian antigay proposition in Oregon, whose language about perversity and abnormality is echoed in the David Horowitz pamphlet. Likewise, Year of the Woman hoopla helped to mask the Democratic Party's active suppression of its traditional racial equality and antipoverty discourses in favor of universalist appeals to a "forgotten" middle class, not so subtly coded as white.

I have indulged these meditations on recent shifts in politics and theory trends at some length, because they are impinging on my own current work as well. Judith Newton and I initially formulated our project as feminist scrutiny of straight, white, male cultural critics, whose attraction to postmodernist and cultural studies projects we first read as efforts to recenter white male theory by displacing both women's studies and ethnic studies. Gradually, however, our project began to evolve into an exploration of biographical, historical, and institutional conditions that foster in intellectuals the development of multiple "traitorous identities,"[19] that is, identification across axes of privilege—with feminism on the part of men, antiracism on the part of whites, antihomophobia on the part of heterosexuals, and with the poor on the part of the well-heeled. Thus, we have begun to expand our "sample" in multicultural, multisexual, and, though this is more difficult, even in limited multiclass directions. At the same time, in conducting oral histories with male cultural critics, we have found ourselves shifting our political posture from one of rectitude, too frequently indulged in identity politics, to a less self-righteous, more collegial, collaborative mode. Although we worry a bit about the risk of fostering our own "traitorous" gender identities in the process, we believe that more would be lost were we to miss this opportunity to help construct a fully feminist multicultural studies as well as to contribute feminist genealogies about its emergence, through active engagement and critical alliance with men.

From a sociological standpoint it is interesting to note that the standard, and generally male-authored, genealogies of cultural studies locate its roots in the 1970s Birmingham Centre for Cultural Studies, an interdisciplinary project in which sociology, particularly of a critical Marxist cast, played an integral part.

Yet sociology failed to survive the late 1980s transatlantic crossing of this intellectual vessel, which disembarked primarily in humanities settlements, perhaps, partly because many of the indigenous roots of cultural studies in the United States can be found in feminism, ethnic studies, and American studies, projects in which literature and humanities scholars increasingly dominate. From this perspective it was oddly comforting to observe anthropologists at their 1992 meetings organizing plenary sessions to express, and to analyze the sources of, their own widespread feelings of marginalization from the vortex of multicultural and cultural studies discourses, intellectual territory in which many anthropologists presumed proprietary disciplinary interests.[20]

These disciplinary disjunctures provide "disloyal" feminists like myself paradoxical new constraints against and opportunities for interdisciplinary work. On the one hand, the increased disciplinarity, specialization, and sheer magnitude of feminist scholarship make cross-disciplinary feminist discourse ever more difficult. On the other hand, feminism has become a significant presence in cultural studies, a key site of interdisciplinary theory and politics but one in which sociology is even more marginal than anthropology. Consequently, I find myself engaged in an ethnographic project that self-consciously seeks to intervene in the construction of the very "fields"—of cultural studies, feminism, ethnic studies, and queer studies—that we are trying to map.

I conclude these reflections on my travels in feminist disciplinary borderlands with thoughts provoked by Avery Gordon, a decidedly post-modernist, feminist, disloyal sociologist, in her discussion of disciplinary impediments to writing ethnography and literary fictions as sociology:

> Perhaps the key methodological question is not: what method have you adopted for this research? but what paths have been disavowed, left behind, covered over and remain unseen. In what fields does field work occur? (Gordon 1990)

Looking back over my travels to and from the study of family revolutions, I have no desire to disavow my un-disciplined migrant labors in cross-fertilized feminist fields, least of all those which challenge arbitrary and increasingly atavistic disciplinary divisions of knowledge. Indeed, I worry rather less about the consequences of my personal disloyalty to the disciplines than about the costs to feminism of what strike me as increasingly conducive conditions for disciplinary loyalty now evident in the social sciences and humanities. Certainly, I broach my current work on male theorists and feminism confident that attentiveness to what Gordon labels "structures of exclusion" will prove indispensable. After more than two decades laboring in feminist fields, however, I am equally confident that my current project, like all others, will inevitably commit and conspire to conceal its own exclusions and illusions. Yet I find comfort as well as concern in my conviction that it will thereby provide a fertile "field day" for an emerging generation of feminist cultural studies theorists who must confront the challenge of keeping success from spoiling academic feminism.

NOTES

1. Even the most cursory, arbitrary list suggests the continued vitality and value of contributions by feminist sociologists whose work thus far displays little interest in postmodern theory disputes, for example: Arlene Kaplan Daniels, Evelyn Nakano Glenn, Rosanna Hertz, Arlie Hochschild, Carole Joffe, Kristin Luker, Ruth Milkman, Marcia Millman, Barbara Reskin, Judith Rollins, Barbara Katz Rothman, Lillian Rubin, Diana Russell, Lenore Weitzman, Candace West, and Maxine Baca Zinn. The *American Sociological Review*—the major, and primarily positivist, journal published by the American Sociological Association—routinely publishes feminist articles on such issues as female employment, fertility, family behaviors, status attainment, political behaviors, deviance, and gender attitudes. Feminist work permeates *Social Problems,* the more qualitative and critical journal published by the less mainstream Society for the Study of Social Problems, and Sociologists for Women in Society publishes its own journal of feminist sociology, *Gender & Society.*

2. The proportion of sociology PhD degrees awarded to females increased from 33 percent in 1977 to 51 percent in 1989 (National Science Foundation, "Science and Engineering Degrees: 1966–1989, A Source Book," NSF 91–314 [Washington, DC: USGPO, 1991], table 54). Compare this 50 percent increase and achievement of female numerical dominance with the 20 percent increase of PhD degrees awarded to females in all fields: in 1980, 30 percent of all PhD degrees in the United States were awarded to females, and in 1990 the proportion had risen to 36 percent (National Research Council, "Summary Report 1990: Doctorate Recipients from United States Universities" [Washington, DC: National Academy Press, 1991]). These figures for completed doctoral degrees likely understate the feminization trends evident among currently enrolled graduate students in sociology and other fields.

3. In 1971 I joined female faculty and students at what was then called Richmond College of the City University of New York in implementing a women's studies program. As I was an instructor in education, I developed a course on "Women in Education," which inspired my first feminist publication, an anthology I coedited with Susan Bereaud and Joan Daniels (1974).

4. To name just an arbitrary sample of feminists who received degrees from the Brandeis sociology department: Natalie Allon, Wini Breines, Nancy Chodorow, Patricia Hill Collins, Marjorie Davies, Elizabeth Higginbotham, Lynda Holmstrom, Elizabeth Long, Fatima Mernissi, Marcia Millman, Shulamit Reinharz, Judith Rollins, Nancy Shaw, Barrie Thorne, Gaye Tuchman, and Lise Vogel. Barrie Thorne provides a longer list and an insightful analysis of the conditions at Brandeis that fostered this feminist renaissance in "Feminist Sociology: The Brandeis Connection," a presentation she gave at a symposium in April 1984 honoring the twenty-fifth anniversary of the department's graduate program.

5. Because early Bolshevik efforts to undermine patriarchal sexual and family practices were rescinded after the Soviet regime consolidated its power, most social scientists theorized that revolutionary gender policies were strictly instrumental and short-lived. Reactionary gender and family policies would inevitably follow the consolidation of state power by a formerly revolutionary regime. See, for example, Coser and Coser 1977.

6. Heidi A. Hartmann (1981) wrote the essay that galvanized attention to theoretical relations between feminism and Marxism. An important early anthology of "dual-systems" theory was Zillah Eisenstein's. (1979)

7. I discuss some of the feminist literature extolling the virtues of interactive field research in "Can There Be a Feminist Ethnography?" (Stacey 1988)

8. I am grateful to Abby Stewart for initiating a provocative dialogue on this issue with me and others.

9. The collection that canonized the reflexive, experimental turn in anthropology was Clifford and Marcus 1986. It was foreshadowed, however, by numerous earlier essays and ethnographies, most of which are surveyed in Marcus and Fischer 1986. Of course, as Barrie Thorne has properly reminded me, my turn to ethnography in itself need not have propelled me outside sociology, where there is also a rich, honorable tradition of ethnographic work starting with the early-twentieth-century urban studies of the Chicago school and continuing in the community studies tradition to which our earlier essays pointed. Once again the primacy of my feminist, antidisciplinary grounding proved decisive.

10. In addition to the works discussed by Marcus and Fischer, see Moffatt 1989; Ginsburg 1989; Zavella 1987; di Leonardo 1984; and Myerhoff 1978. A recent fine collection of feminist anthropological studies of the United States is Ginsberg and Tsing 1990.

11. For other analyses of the quest for a feminist research methodology, see Bowles and Duelli Klein 1980; Harding 1987; Gross 1987; Stanley and Wise 1983.

12. Thus, humanists rather than social scientists have taken the initiative in organizing Teachers for a Democratic *Culture* (my emphasis), an organization to defend multicultural and feminist curricular reforms against the pernicious antipolitical correctness campaign of the National Association of Scholars and other reactionary groups; the organizational meeting of TDC was held at the December 1991 meetings of the Modern Language Association. George Marcus offers a helpful comparison of the significance of texts, and hence textual politics, in diverse disciplines and sheds light on the stakes of literary critics in "worlding" their texts, in "A Broad(er) Side to the Canon," an unpublished conference paper he is expanding for book-length publication.

13. I find it gratifying that other feminists are challenging genealogies of postmodernist theory and cultural studies that marginalize feminist contributions. See, for example, Morris 1988; . . . Long 1989; and Schwichtenberg 1989.

14. Much of the academic debate about the proper preposition, conjunction, and character of the two terms was initiated by Jardine and Smith (1987). See also Boone and Cadden 1990.

15. The critical literature on this theme is vast. See, for example, Baca Zinn et al. 1986; Mohanty et al. 1991; hooks 1984; and Anzaldúa 1990.

16. I raised this issue while serving as a commentator at the "Unraveling Masculinities" conference at the University of California, Davis, in February 1991. These have been revised for publication. (Stacey 1993)

17. Four particularly articulate critiques of the critical excesses of the antiessentialist "club" are Christian 1987; Modleski 1991; . . . and Fuss 1989. At the November 1990 meeting of the American Anthropological Association, Frances Mascia-Lees, Patricia Sharpe, and Colleen Cohen, the authors of a widely discussed feminist critique of postmodern anthropology, gave, or rather performed, a paper that was decidedly reflexive about its textual as well as political dimensions. They did so, moreover, at a session on feminism and postmodernism organized by Mascia-Lees.

18. Horowitz 1992.

19. We have borrowed this term from Sandra Harding's essay "Reinventing Ourselves as Others," in Harding 1991.

20. This was the basic premise of an entire panel on "Multiculturalism and the Concept of Culture" and other panels. See, for example, Ortner 1992.

REFERENCES

Anzaldúa, Gloria, ed. *Making Face, Making Soul: Haciendo Caras.* San Francisco: Aunt Lute Foundation, 1990.

Baca Zinn, Maxine, Lynn Weber Cannon, Elizabeth Higginbotham, and Bonnie Thornton Dill. "The Costs of Exclusionary Practices in Women's Studies." *Signs: Journal of Women in Culture and Society* 11, no. 2 (1986), pp. 290–303.

Boone, Joseph A., and Michael Cadden, eds. *Engendering Men: The Question of Male Feminist Criticism.* New York: Routledge, 1990.

Bordo, Susan. "Feminism, Postmodernism and Gender Skepticism." In *Feminism/Postmodernism,* ed. Linda J. Nicholson. New York: Routledge, 1990.

Bowles, Gloria, and Renate Duelli Klein. *Theories of Women's Studies.* London: Routledge and Kegan Paul, 1983.

Christian, Barbara. "The Race for Theory." *Cultural Critique* 6 (1987), pp. 51–63.

Clifford, James, and George Marcus, eds. *Writing Culture: The Poetics and Politics of Ethnography.* Berkeley: University of California Press, 1986.

Coser, Rose L., and Lewis A. Coser. "The Principles of Legitimacy and Its Patterned Infringement in Social Revolutions." In *Cross-National Family Research,* ed. Marvin B. Sussman and Betty E. Cogswell. Leiden: E. J. Brill, 1972.

di Leonardo, Micaela. *The Varieties of Ethnic Experience: Kinship, Class, and Gender among California Italian-Americans.* Ithaca, NY: Cornell University Press, 1984.

Dilnot, Clive. "What Is the Post-Modern?" *Art History* 9, no. 2 (June 1986), 245–63.

Eisenstein, Zillah R., ed. *Capitalist Patriarchy and the Case for Socialist-Feminism.* New York: Monthly Review Press, 1979.

Fuss, Diane. *Essentially Speaking: Feminism, Nature, Difference.* New York: Routledge, 1989.

Ginsburg, Faye. *Contested Lives: The Abortion Debate in an American Community.* Berkeley: University of California Press, 1989.

Ginsburg, Faye, and Anna Tsing, eds. *Uncertain Terms: Negotiating Gender in American Culture.* Boston: Beacon Press, 1990.

Gordon, Avery. "Feminism, Writing and Ghosts." *Social Problems* 37, no. 4 (November 1990), pp. 485–500.

Gouldner, Alvin. *The Coming Crisis in Western Sociology.* New York: Basic Books, 1970.

Gross, Elizabeth. "Conclusion: What Is Feminist Theory?" In *Feminist Challenges: Social and Political Theory,* ed. Carole Pateman and Elizabeth Gross. Boston: Northeastern University Press, 1987.

Harding, Sandra. *Whose Science? Whose Knowledge? Thinking from Women's Lives.* Ithaca, NY: Cornell University Press, 1991.

———., ed. *Feminism and Methodology.* Bloomington: Indiana University Press, 1987.

Hartmann, Heidi. "The Unhappy Marriage of Marxism and Feminism: Towards a More Progressive Union." In *Women and Revolution,* ed. Lydia Sargent. Boston: South End Press, 1981.

hooks, bell. *Feminist Theory: From Margin to Center.* Boston: South End Press, 1984.

Horowitz, David. "Queer Revolution: The Last Stage of Radicalism." Pamphlet, Studio City, CA: Center for the Study of Popular Culture, 1992.

Jardine, Alice, and Paul Smith, eds. *Men in Feminism.* New York: Methuen, 1987.

Long, Elizabeth. "Feminism and Cultural Studies." *Critical Studies in Mass Communications* 6, no. 2 (1989), pp. 427–35.

Marcus, George E., and Michael M. J. Fischer. *Anthropology as Cultural Critique.* Chicago: University of Chicago Press, 1986.

Mascia-Lees, Frances E., Patricia Sharpe, and Colleen Ballerino Cohen. "The Postmodernist Turn in Anthropology: Cautions from a Feminist Perspective. *Signs* 15, no. 1 (Autumn 1989), pp. 7–33.

Modleski, Tania. *Feminism without Women: Culture and Criticism in a "Postfeminist" Age.* New York: Routledge, 1991.

Moffatt, Michael. *Coming of Age in New Jersey: College and American Culture.* New Brunswick, NJ: Rutgers University Press, 1989.

Mohanty, Chandra, Ann Russo, and Lourdes Torres, eds. *Third World Women and the Politics of Feminism.* Bloomington: Indiana University Press, 1991.

Morris, Meaghan. *The Pirate's Fiance: Feminism, Reading, Postmodernism.* London: Verso, 1988.

Myerhoff, Barbara. *Number Our Days.* New York: Simon and Schuster, 1978.

Newton, Judith, and Judith Stacey. "Learning Not to Curse, or, Feminist Predicaments in Cultural Criticism by Men: Our Movie Date with James

Clifford and Stephen Greenblatt." *Cultural Critique,* no. 23 (Winter 1992–93), pp. 51–82.

Ortner, Sherry. "Anthropology's War of Position: Changing the Face of the Field." Paper presented at American Anthropological Association meeting, San Francisco, December 1992.

Schwichtenberg, Cathy. "Feminist Cultural Studies." *Critical Studies in Mass Communication* 6, no. 2 (1989), pp. 202–9.

Spivak, Gayatri. *The Postcolonial Critic: Interviews, Strategies, Dialogue.* New York: Routledge, 1990.

Stacey, Judith. *Patriarchy and Socialist Revolution in China.* Berkeley: University of California Press, 1983.

———. "Can There Be a Feminist Ethnography?" *Women's Studies International Quarterly* 11, no. 1 (1988), pp. 21–7.

———. *Brave New Families: Stories of Domestic Upheaval in Late Twentieth Century America.* New York: Basic Books, 1990.

———. "Toward Kindler, Gentler Uses for Testosterone: Reflections on Bob Connell's Views on Western Masculinities." *Theory and Society* 27 (1993), pp. 711–21.

Stacey, Judith, Susan Bereaud, and Joan Daniels, eds. *And Jill Came Tumbling After: Sexism in American Education.* New York: Dell, 1974.

Stacey, Judith, and Barrie Thorne. "The Missing Feminist Revolution in Sociology." *Social Problems* 32, no. 4 (April 1985), pp. 301–16.

Stanley, Liz, and Sue Wise. *Breaking Out: Feminist Consciousness and Feminist Research.* London: Routledge and Kegan Paul, 1983.

Thorne, Barrie. "Feminist Sociology: The Brandeis Connection." Paper presented at the Twenty-fifth Reunion Symposium of Sociology Department, Brandeis University, April 1984.

Zavella, Patricia. *Women's Work and Chicano Families.* Ithaca, NY: Cornell University Press, 1984.